Advanced Graphics on VGA and XGA Cards Using Borland C++

Advanced Graphics on VGA and XGA Cards Using Borland C++

Ian O. Angell and
Dimitrios Tsoubelis

Department of Information Systems
London School of Economics
University of London
Houghton Street, London WC2A 2AE

Halsted Press: an Imprint of
JOHN WILEY & SONS, INC.

NEW YORK TORONTO

First published 1992 by
THE MACMILLAN PRESS LTD
London and Basingstoke
ISBN 0-333-56765-X (Macmillan)

Published in the United States and Canada by
Halsted Press, an Imprint of John Wiley & Sons, Inc., New York

Library of Congress Cataloging-in-Publication Data
Angell, Ian O.
Advanced graphics on VGA and XGA cards using Borland C++ / Ian O. Angell and Dimitrios Tsoubelis.
p. cm
Includes bibliographical references and index.
ISBN 0-470-21833-9 (Halsted Press)
1. Computer graphics. 2. C++ (Computer program language)
3. Borland C++. 4. Expansion boards (Microcomputers)
I. Tsoubelis, Dimitrios. II. Title
T385.A517 1992
006.6′765—dc20 92-10223
CIP

A 3.5 in. MS-DOS disk containing all the program listings, plus VGA communication with the XGA driver, and other utilities, is available at the price of £25.00 or $40.00 (inc. postage/packing – airmail overseas).
Please send your personal check to: Globe Book Services Ltd, Houndmills, Basingstoke, Hampshire, RG21 2XS, UK.
Access/Visa/American Express/Diners Club accepted. Please quote number and expiry date.
Please quote ISBN 0-333-56766-8 (disk) when ordering.

Printed in Hong Kong

dedicated to

Florence and Αγγελική

Contents

Preface

This book will enable you to produce top quality three-dimensional computer graphics images, using only a VGA or XGA graphics adapter; images of a quality that would normally need very expensive computer graphics terminals and software. Now, in this book you will find *all* the program listings required to create highly sophisticated three-dimensional graphics. Apart from the cards all you need buy is a copy of the Borland C++ compiler, and this book of course!

There are many excellent books available on computer graphics; however, very few give actual program listings, and even those that do are aimed at expensive installations. We give listings that run on IBM PS/2 compatible machines, and include the polygonal mesh, quad-tree, oct-tree and ray-tracing display methods. We cover such topics as modelling and transformation of objects, hidden surface removal, smooth shading, shadows, transparency and reflections. A full explanation of all these concepts, including the underlying mathematics and data structures, is given alongside the listings.

With this book, advanced computer graphics is no longer restricted to a few well-funded institutions and research groups. The real benefit is that any college, polytechnic or university, that probably already own microcomputers with standard VGA (or with the more advanced XGA) screens can now offer an advanced practical course in computer graphics without incurring any further expenditure; they no longer need costly graphics terminals.

This book is the culmination of fifteen years experience of research in computer graphics and of teaching the subject at undergraduate and postgraduate level at three colleges of the University of London. The text contains all of the program listings for the course; the Borland C++ programming environment was chosen because of its growing popularity and ease of use. The Borland Project mechanism is a highly effective means of bringing together all the listings in the book and building it into a comprehensive graphics package. (See chapter 2 for a full description of structure of programs using the Project mechanism.) This package is intended to be the basis from which students can experiment in advanced graphics. All the listings in the book are available on a 3.5 inch flexible disk. No copyright restrictions are placed on academic use of the programs, although the permission of the authors is needed for any commercial application.

Prior to this book, one of the authors, Ian Angell has published four highly successful books (using Pascal and C, and two using Fortran) based on his very practical approach to teaching computer graphics. Universities and polytechnics from all around the world have based their courses on the text and programs in these earlier books. Researchers too, in subjects as diverse as archaeology, architecture, agriculture, chemistry, geography, geology, marine biology and physics, to name but a few, have found the programs invaluable in their work.

For the present book, Ian Angell has been joined by Dimitrios Tsoubelis and together they have produced a major rewrite of the course. All the programs were completely redesigned to make the fullest use of the object oriented nature of C++. A totally new section (theory and listings) on analytic methods has been added. All of the colour plates and most of the line drawings are new; to be true to their pedagogical approach, all the three-dimensional images have been drawn using the programs given in this book, using the VGA and XGA cards, and not on more sophisticated (and expensive) graphics equipment.

The course starts with an introduction to the VGA (or XGA) graphics cards. Then, using some small, yet quite sophisticated graphics programs, we show how to 'drive' either card from within C++ programs running on IBM PS/2 compatible machines to draw pictures. We then introduce the idea of a window in continuous two-dimensional space, which is designed so that points, lines or areas defined in the window can be drawn on the screen; again some very interesting images illustrate these ideas.

Then we start in earnest. Data structures necessary for graphics are described in the third chapter, and useful concepts from two-dimensional co-ordinate geometry are introducd in chapter 4. Then follows a discussion of manipulating points, lines and polygonal facets in the window. But before we can draw 'solid' objects, in chapter 6 we introduce three-dimensional co-ordinate geometry. Then we can introduce a database for descriptions of three-dimensional scenes, and explain how matrices are used to transform those scenes (chapter 7). Here we introduce the polygonal-mesh approach in which we approximate to the surfaces of objects in a three-dimensional scene with a mesh of polygonal facets. Then the idea of an observer is introduced, so that we can project three-dimensional space onto a two-dimensional window, from which we can draw the scene on the graphics screen. In chapter 9 we consider how to generate complex models.

In chapter 10 we show how parts of the surfaces of objects, obscured from view by the bulk of objects in the scene (so-called hidden surfaces), can be eliminated from the drawing. In chapter 11 we make these pictures look more realistic by introducing a light source, and by shading the surfaces of objects. Then in chapter 12 we consider shadows, transparency and reflection.

At that stage we have come close to the limits of the polygonal mesh approach, and in the last four chapters we introduce a totally different way of modelling objects: the analytic approach. From the basis of this new type of mathematical modelling, we give three ways of drawing such objects: with a quad-tree algorithm, an oct-tree algorithm, and we finish with ray-tracing.

C++ is a joy to use when writing graphics programs. By its very nature it gives the programmer a great variety of predefined data types, but what is more important it gives the freedom to create new data types that can be manipulated with the same efficiency as the standard ones. Another important feature of all object oriented languages is the ability to partition a huge application program into smaller, more manageable chunks. This lets the programmer break projects into a set of distinct concepts, and to program each of them separately. This is a very efficient way of implementing large projects, since each logical concept can be programmed and tested independently. Additionally, processes common to more than one logical concept need be programmed once only, and reused. This programming approach, emphasising the reduction of the initial problem into sub-problems, lends itself directly to the theoretical way we organized this graphics course, so the book consists of building up files (see chapter 2).

It comes as no surprise therefore that the literature on object oriented programming contains so many examples from computer graphics applications. However, we do not adopt the very common practice of choosing the point on the screen (the pixel) or the point in space as the basic object (*class*) out of which everyting else *inherits*. We place our emphasis on the great variety of complex processes involved in a typical computer graphics application, rather than on the set of pixels composing the final image. Our primary focus is on the analysis and understanding of the algorithms used in computer graphics. As a result, our design approach will split a typical computer graphics application in entities (classes) like the **Viewport**, the **Palette**, the graphics **Window**, the *object database* **Cluster**, and so on. Moreover, a toolbox of useful data structures like **Matrix**, **Stack**, **Mesh** and **Tree** are also defined and used extensively. Another advantage of our approach is that it has been designed to cope with the segmentation of the DOS system, even when dealing with large data sets.

So read on. We hope that you find our programs, examples, exercises and projects interesting and useful, and that they inspire you to go on to experiment with computer graphics and to discover much more about this enjoyable subject. For computer graphics really is fun. So take this book straight back to your microcomputer and start enjoying yourself!

Ian Angell and Dimitrios Tsoubelis

1 Familiarization with graphics adapters and C++ programs

In this book we will be concentrating on the techniques of *modelling* and *rendering* (that is, drawing, colouring, shading, etc.) mainly three-dimensional objects. We will give a software package and application programs, constructed in the Borland C++ environment, that can run on IBM AT and PS/2 machines (and compatibles), with graphics interfaces driven by the most popular graphics adapters, the VGA and XGA 'cards'.

The graphics device driver

Each of these cards switches the computer monitor from text mode into a graphics mode, and then manipulates the screen according to a sequence of graphics commands received along a predefined input/output channel. Each graphics command is a *command code*, possibly followed by a list of characters and integers referring to pixels, colours and/or text. These graphics commands will be issued from a DOS *device driver*. We recommend you create a directory named **\A&T\driver** on drive **c:** of your computer, and store the VGA driver as **"vgadrive.sys"**, and the XGA driver as **"xgaaidos.sys"**. Listings and other information about these drivers can be found in the Appendix of this book. A particular device driver (VGA for example) can then be installed by rebooting your machine, thus loading a **"config.sys"** file that includes the statement

device=c:\A&T\driver\vgadrive.sys

But beware, the XGA card is known to cause problems with certain 'mouse drivers' – so read your manual carefully should you want to use a 'mouse'.

Viewport and Palette classes

We wish to make the programs given in this book as straightforward as possible and readily portable between the two cards mentioned (and others), and between computers, possibly even to other implementations of C++. To achieve this we limit the communication between our programs and any given device driver (and hence the graphics adapter) via two C++ classes named **Viewport** and **Palette**, which we will call our general *device model*. Following the object-oriented terminology, **Viewport** is the *base* class, which **Palette** *inherits*. The underlying structure of these classes for manipulating the VGA card via our model is given in listings 1.1 and 1.2 respectively. The versions for the XGA graphics card can be found in the Appendix. The user will interact with the model via the basic functions (*methods*) of these classes, and these methods will in turn compose and transfer command sequences to the VGA (or XGA) card so that coloured shapes are drawn on the graphics screen. You must take the two two-part listings (or the version corresponding to the card you have installed), and store the class header declarations as files **"viewport.h"** (1.1a) and **"palette.h"** (1.2a), and the code as files **"viewport.cpp"** (1.1b) and **"palette.cpp"** (1.2b) as indicated by our in-line comments; the former two files may then be **#included** into later C++ programs.

File **"viewport.h"** contains the design of the **Viewport** class, that is, its *declaration*. This is a 'header file' that has to be included at the beginning of file **"viewport.cpp"**, where the code implementing the **Viewport**'s methods is held. The most important method of the **Viewport** class is its *constructor*. It is easily recognized as the function that has exactly the same name as the class. This function is implicitly invoked when an *object* (an *instantiation* of the class) of type **Viewport** is declared. The constructor contains the necessary code for the proper initialization of the declared object. In our implementation (in file **"viewport.cpp"**) there are two constructors of the **Viewport** class. This is achieved by *overloading* the function name **Viewport**. Overloading is a C++ mechanism that enables us to use, without conflict, more than one C++ function with the same name but with different argument lists, and therefore with different *signatures* in the C++ compiler. The first constructor, **Viewport()**, the one without any arguments, is used to assign the details of the default '*text mode 3*' for both our adapters. The second constructor, **Viewport(Viewport *v)**, initializes a **Viewport** object, that is our graphics screen, with the details that are supplied to it through its argument list. When a method of a class consists of a trivial piece of code (such as a **return** statement only), it is treated as an *in-line function*. Such functions are usually defined with their declaration, and therefore will be found in their corresponding header file (in this case **"viewport.h"**).

In order to use the **Viewport** class, an application program has to declare at least one such object of this class (an instantiation), for example **my_viewport**. This is achieved by the insertion of the following line of C++ code in the declaration part of an application program:

```
Viewport my_viewport;
```

The definition of **Viewport**, both the declaration and the implementation parts **"viewport.h"** and **"viewport.cpp"**, needs to be accessible by any application program and also it needs to be known to the compiler. The obvious solution of **#includ(e)ing** both files in the application program can prove inconvenient for

Listing 1.1a

```
// This code to be saved as "viewport.h"
// This header file is valid for both VGA and XGA cards

#include <iostream.h>
#include <fstream.h>
#include <math.h>

const int maxpoly = 32 ;
enum {FALSE,TRUE} ;

typedef struct {int x, y ; } pixelvector ;
typedef pixelvector pixelarray[maxpoly] ;

//--------------//
  class Viewport
//--------------//
 {protected :
   int colour_resolution ;
   int currcol ;
   int maximum_colours ;
   int graphics_mode ;
   int nxpix ;
   int nypix ;
   ofstream fout ;
   ofstream *VGA_fout ;   // XGA card uses interrupts and not files
   float aspect ;
   pixelvector lastpixel ;

  public:
   int Get_col(void) { return (colour_resolution) ; }
   int Get_currcol(void) { return (currcol) ; }
   int Get_mxc(void) { return (maximum_colours) ; }
   int Get_mode(void) { return (graphics_mode) ; }
   int Get_nxpix(void) { return (nxpix) ; }
   int Get_nypix(void) { return (nypix) ; }
   ofstream * Get_fout(void) { return (VGA_fout) ; }
   float Get_rat(void) { return (aspect) ; }
   pixelvector Get_last(void) { return (lastpixel) ; }
   Viewport() ;
   Viewport(Viewport *v) ;
   void setpix(pixelvector pixel) ;
   void movepix(pixelvector pixel) ;
   void linepix(pixelvector pixel) ;
   void polypix(int n, pixelarray q) ;
   void setcol(int i) ;
   void finish(void) ;
   void close(void) ;
   void erase(int i) ;
   void prepit(int modenumber) ;
   void setype(int op) ;
  } ;  // End of class Viewport
```

Listing 1.1b

```
// This code to be saved as "viewport.cpp"

// This code is specific to the VGA card
// The XGA version is found in the Appendix

#include "viewport.h"
#include <conio.h>        // Needed for a call to function kbhit
#include <stdlib.h>       // Needed for a call to function exit
```

```
//--------------------//
  Viewport::Viewport()
//--------------------//
 { graphics_mode = 3 ;
   nxpix = 0 ;  nypix = 0 ;
   maximum_colours = 2 ;  colour_resolution = 1 ;
   lastpixel.x =0 ;  lastpixel.y =0 ;
   VGA_fout = &fout ;
 }  // End of Viewport

//-------------------------------//
  Viewport::Viewport(Viewport *v)
//-------------------------------//
 { graphics_mode = (*v).graphics_mode ;
   nxpix = (*v).nxpix ;   nypix = (*v).nypix ;
   aspect = (*v).aspect ;
   maximum_colours = (*v).maximum_colours ;
   colour_resolution = (*v).colour_resolution ;
   currcol = (*v).currcol ;
   lastpixel = (*v).lastpixel ;
   VGA_fout = (*v).VGA_fout ;
 }  // End of Viewport

//----------------------------//
  void Viewport::setcol(int i)
//----------------------------//
 { i = i % maximum_colours ;   currcol = i ;
   *VGA_fout << "3," << i << ";" ;
 }  // End of setcol

//---------------------------//
  void Viewport::finish(void)
//---------------------------//
 { // wait until Return is hit, using Borland C++ function kbhit
   VGA_fout->flush() ;
   while (!kbhit() ) ;
   *VGA_fout << "2;" ;
   VGA_fout->flush() ;   // Now the screen is back to text mode
 }  // End of finish

//--------------------------//
  void Viewport::close(void)
//--------------------------//
 { *VGA_fout << "2;" ;   VGA_fout->close() ;
 }  // End of close

//----------------------------//
  void Viewport::erase(int i)
//----------------------------//
 { setcol(i) ;   *VGA_fout << "4;" ;
 }  // End of erase

//-----------------------------------------//
  void Viewport::setpix(pixelvector pixel)
//-----------------------------------------//
 { *VGA_fout << "5," << pixel.x << "," << pixel.y << ";"  ;
 }  // End of setpix

//------------------------------------------//
  void Viewport::movepix(pixelvector pixel)
//------------------------------------------//
 { *VGA_fout << "6," << pixel.x << "," << pixel.y << ";"  ;
 }  // End of movepix

//------------------------------------------//
  void Viewport::linepix(pixelvector pixel)
//------------------------------------------//
 { *VGA_fout << "7," << pixel.x << "," << pixel.y << ";"  ;
 }  // End of linepix
```

```
//-----------------------------------//
  void Viewport::prepit(int modenumber)
//-----------------------------------//
 { int error = FALSE ;
   switch ( modenumber)
   { case 18 :  nxpix = 640 ;  nypix = 480 ;     aspect = 1.0 ;
                colour_resolution = 3 ;  maximum_colours = 16 ;     break ;
     case 19 :  nxpix = 320 ;  nypix = 200 ;   aspect = 0.833333 ;
                colour_resolution = 63 ; maximum_colours = 256 ;   break ;
     default :  error = TRUE ; break ;
   }
   if (error)
     { cerr << "\n Error, mode "<< modenumber <<" not supported" ; exit(1); }
   graphics_mode = modenumber ;   VGA_fout->open("VGA_") ;
   (*VGA_fout) << "=2;1," << graphics_mode << ";" ;  VGA_fout->flush() ;
   setcol(15) ;
 }  // End of prepit

//----------------------------//
  void Viewport::setype(int op)
//----------------------------//
 { *VGA_fout << "8,"<< op <<";" ;
 }  // End of setype

//------------------------------------------//
  void Viewport::polypix(int n, pixelarray q)
//------------------------------------------//
 { int iv,ix,iy,nv,xmin,xmax,ymin,ymax ;
   pixelvector pix1,pix2 ;
   float factor ;
   ymax=q[0].y ; ymin=ymax ;
   for (iv=1 ; iv<n ; iv++)
   { if (q[iv].y > ymax) ymax=q[iv].y ; if (q[iv].y < ymin) ymin=q[iv].y ; }
   if (ymax >= nypix)  ymax=nypix-1 ;
   if (ymin < 0)  ymin=0 ;
   for (iy=ymin ; iy<=ymax ; iy++)
   { xmin=nxpix ; xmax=-1 ; iv=n-1 ;
     for (nv=0 ; nv<n ; nv++)
     { if (((q[iv].y >= iy) || (q[nv].y >= iy)) &&
         ((q[iv].y <= iy) || (q[nv].y <= iy)) &&  (q[iv].y != q[nv].y) )
       { factor=(float)(q[nv].x-q[iv].x)/(q[nv].y-q[iv].y) ;
         ix=(int) (q[iv].x+ (iy-q[iv].y)*factor +0.5) ;
         if (ix < xmin) xmin=ix ;      if (ix > xmax) xmax=ix ;
       } ;
       iv=nv ;
     } ;
     if (xmax >= nxpix) xmax=nxpix-1 ; if (xmin < 0.0) xmin=0 ;
     if (xmin <= xmax)
       { pix1.x=xmin ; pix1.y=iy ;
         pix2.x=xmax ; pix2.y=iy ;
         movepix(pix1) ; linepix(pix2) ;
       } ;
   }
 } // End of polypix
```

two main reasons. First, the **Viewport** class definition is very rarely changed, therefore, re-compiling it in every application program is a waste of resources. Second, certain implementations of C++, especially in small PC configurations, restrict the size of the data and code segments of RAM to 64K each (this is the maximum configuration of the Borland HUGE model), and consequently, that part of the segment unoccupied by the **Viewport** class definition would be unavailable for the application's data or code, or anything else for that matter.

Listing 1.2a

```
// This code to be saved as file "palette.h"
// This header file is valid for both VGA and XGA cards

#define Max_Pal_entries 256
#define maxmaterl 15

//-------------------------------//
  class Palette : public Viewport
//-------------------------------//
 { int  tabnum ;  // Maximum number of palette colours
   int  lutsize ; // Current size of Look-Up Table; lutsize < tabnum
   int  colptr[Max_Pal_entries] ;
   float red[Max_Pal_entries] ;
   float green[Max_Pal_entries] ;
   float blue[Max_Pal_entries] ;
   int  matlist[maxmaterl] ;
   int  newcolour ;

  public:
   Palette() ;
   void init(Viewport *scr) ;
   void rgblog(int i, int r, int g, int b ) ;
   void rgblog(int i, float r, float g, float b ) ;
   void Get_lut(int i,float *r, float *g, float *b) ;
   int Get_lutsize(void) { return ( lutsize ) ; }
   void colourtable(void) ;
   int findlogicalcolour(int abscol,float intensity) ;
   int findlogicalcolour(float r, float g, float b, int i) ;
 } ;  // End of class Palette
```

Listing 1.2b

```
// This code to be saved as file "palette.cpp"
// This code is specific to the VGA card
// The XGA version is found in the Appendix

#include "viewport.cpp"
#include "palette.h"

//  Subsequent to listing 11.2, un-comment the following two lines.
//  #include "material.h"
//  extern Material mrl ;

//---------------------------------//
  Palette::Palette() : Viewport()
//---------------------------------//
 { int n = maximum_colours ;
   if ( (n<1) || (n>Max_Pal_entries)) n = Max_Pal_entries ;
   tabnum = n ;   lutsize = 0 ;
 }  // End of Palette

//----------------------------------//
  void Palette::init(Viewport *scr)
//----------------------------------//
 { maximum_colours = scr->Get_mxc() ; tabnum = maximum_colours ;
   if ( (tabnum<1)||(tabnum>Max_Pal_entries)) tabnum = Max_Pal_entries ;
   lutsize = 0 ; colour_resolution = scr->Get_col() ;
   graphics_mode = scr->Get_mode() ;
   currcol= scr->Get_currcol() ;  lastpixel = scr->Get_last() ;
   nxpix = scr->Get_nxpix() ;     nypix = scr->Get_nypix() ;
   VGA_fout = scr->Get_fout() ;
   aspect = scr->Get_rat() ;
   colourtable() ;
 }  // End of init
```

```
//-----------------------------------------------//
  void Palette::rgblog(int i, int r, int g, int b)
//-----------------------------------------------//
 { int c = 256/(colour_resolution+1) ;
   i = i % tabnum ;  if (lutsize <= i) lutsize = i+1 ;
   red[i] = r / 255.0 ;   green[i] = g / 255.0 ;   blue[i] = b / 255.0 ;
   *VGA_fout << "9," << i << "," << r/c << "," << g/c << "," << b/c << ";" ;
 }  // End of rgblog

//-----------------------------------------------------//
  void Palette::rgblog(int i, float r, float g, float b)
//-----------------------------------------------------//
// We overload previous rgblog function, now using floats rather than ints
 { int rr, gg, bb ;
   i = i % tabnum ;
   if (lutsize <= i) lutsize = i+1 ;
   red[i] = r ;  green[i] = g ; blue[i] = b ;
   rr = (int) (r * (float)colour_resolution) ;
   gg = (int) (g * (float)colour_resolution) ;
   bb = (int) (b * (float)colour_resolution) ;
   *VGA_fout << "9," << i << "," << rr << "," << gg << "," << bb << ";" ;
 }  // End of rgblog

//---------------------------------------------------------//
  void Palette::Get_lut(int i,float *r, float *g, float *b)
//---------------------------------------------------------//
 { if ( (i >= tabnum) || (i<0) ) i=0 ;
   *r = red[i] ;  *g = green[i] ; *b = blue[i] ;
 }  // End of Get_lut

//-------------------------------//
  void Palette::colourtable(void)
//-------------------------------//
// Create the default colour table.
 { float z = 0.0,  m = 0.67, f = 1.0 ;     // zero, mid and full intensities
   rgblog(0,z,z,z) ;  rgblog(1,z,z,m) ;  rgblog(2,z,m,z) ;  rgblog(3,z,m,m) ;
   rgblog(4,m,z,z) ;  rgblog(5,m,z,m) ;  rgblog(6,m,m,z) ;  rgblog(7,m,m,m) ;
   m = 0.33 ;
   rgblog(8,m,m,m) ;  rgblog(9,z,z,f) ;  rgblog(10,z,f,z) ; rgblog(11,z,f,f) ;
   rgblog(12,f,z,z) ; rgblog(13,f,z,f) ; rgblog(14,f,f,z) ; rgblog(15,f,f,f) ;
 }  // End of colourtable
```

Apart from a few very exceptional cases, all the programs that we give in this book will use these two classes, **Viewport** and **Palette**, to drive your chosen graphics adapter. Even the most complex of our programs will interface with your particular card, through a machine-dependent implementation of these two classes. Our programs will ultimately build up into a graphics package that is readily portable to any other graphics card. Note that we are deliberately using only a small fraction of the functionality of the VGA and XGA cards, to form a 'lowest common denominator' of functions. Then, to run our package on a card different from these two, it is a relatively easy job to write your own card-specific **Viewport** and **Palette** classes by creating your own version of the two **".cpp"** files (the **".h"** files need not be changed): our versions for the VGA and XGA cards should guide you in this task. You should also note that the mathematical functions **<math.h>** of C++, the standard input/output functions **<iostream.h>**, and the file input/output functions **<fstream.h>** are implicitly **#include**d into our application programs from within these classes.

The model graphics device

We assume that each graphics adapter drives a graphics screen composed of a rectangular array of points (or *pixels* – picture elements). The screen contains a *viewport* (or *frame*), in our case we will instantiate our model made up of an object **vpt** of class **Viewport** and an object **plt** of class **Palette**, that is designed to correspond to the whole screen. This matrix of points measures **nxpix** pixels horizontally by **nypix** pixels vertically, counting from the top left corner of the viewport. The values of **nxpix** and **nypix** are initialized in the class **Viewport**, along with constant **maxpoly**, the maximum size allowed for a polygon with pixel vertices. The data type **pixelvector** is declared, as well as the current **pixelvector** position **lastpixel** (initially set to the pixel origin (0,0)).

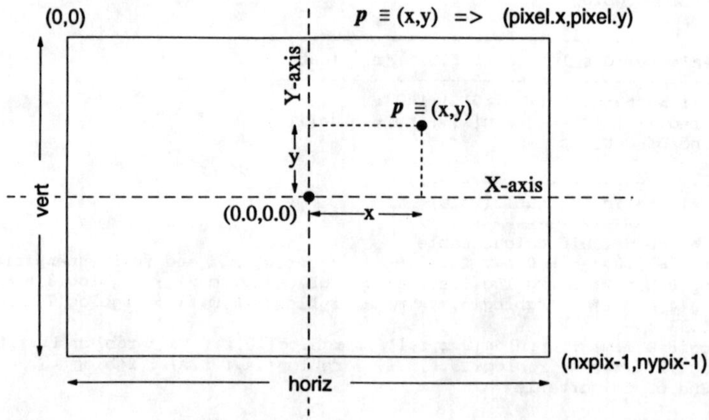

Figure 1.1

An individual pixel in the viewport can be accessed by referring to its *pixel co-ordinates*, a pair of integers stored as structure type **pixelvector**, which gives the position of the pixel relative to the *top left-hand corner* of the viewport. The current **pixelvector** position, **pixel** (say), is the co-ordinate pair **(pixel.x, pixel.y)** which is **pixel.x** pixels horizontally and **pixel.y** pixels vertically from the top left-hand corner (which naturally has pixel co-ordinates (0,0)). Note that for all pixels, 0 ≤ **pixel.x** < **nxpix** and 0 ≤ **pixel.y** < **nypix**, and the bottom right corner is **(nxpix–1, nypix–1)**. See figure 1.1. Some commercial graphics systems count pixels starting from the bottom left corner as (0,0), but this can be compensated for in the functions in the class **Viewport**, and will not require a major rewrite of the larger programs.

Colouring in pixels

RGB *colour monitors* work on the principle of any colour being a mixture of red, green and blue components. Each pixel is made up of three tiny dots, one each for shades of red, green and blue; different colours are produced by varying the relative brightness of the dots. Red is given by a bright red dot with no green or blue; yellow is produced by bright red and green dots with no blue, and so on. For this reason most graphics devices define colours in terms of RGB (red, green, blue) components. We assume that the display on the model graphics device is based upon a *bit-map*; that is, it can be thought of as a special memory holding integer values, and each memory location is associated with a single pixel on the screen. Each integer value (called a *logical colour*) corresponds to a combination of red, green and blue components (of an *actual colour*). In our model device, colour will be dealt with in a class **Palette**, which is declared in file **"palette.h"** with methods listed in file **"palette.cpp"**. Since **Palette** inherits from **Viewport**, file **"viewport.cpp"** is **#include**d in it. We assume that our graphics device has a *colour look-up table* (or *palette*), which contains the definitions (the relationship between the logical and actual colours) of **tabnum** colours, stored in arrays **red**, **green** and **blue**, each accessed by an integer logical colour value between 0 and **tabnum**–l. Only one colour can be used at a time – this is called the current logical colour, which is identified by an integer variable **currcol**. The entries in the look-up table may be redefined by the user (see example 2.4), but initially we assume the entries take on the 16 *default values* described in the next section.

We then imagine a *cursor* that can move about the viewport; the co-ordinates of this cursor at any time, **pixel**, is called its *current position*. Shapes are drawn by moving the cursor around the viewport and then setting the value in the bit-map for the current position to the required logical colour.

The methods that manipulate the Viewport bit-map and Palette

Before a particular viewport object, **vpt** say, can be used for graphical display it must be prepared by making the method (function) call

```
vpt.prepit(modenumber) ;
```

Integer **modenumber** indicates which graphics mode is to be entered. The particular mode define the number of pixels on the screen (the *resolution*) and the number of available colours **tabnum**. For example on the VGA card and its emulation on other cards, mode 18 offers a resolution 640 by 480 and 16 colours from a choice of 64, while mode 19 offers resolution 320 by 200 and 256 colours from a choice of 2^{18}. On the XGA card we will use mode 255, which gives a resolution of 640 by 480 and 256 colours from a choice of 256K, or 1024 by

768, and 2, 4, 8, 16 or 256 colours depending on the capability of the monitor that you are using and the video memory available.

We have not explicitly mentioned, nor will we mention how to mix text with graphics as such a description can be quite time consuming, and the required code would take up many pages of this book. We leave it to readers to write their own functions for mixing text and graphics, should they require it. Instead we take the easy way out and assume that in all the programs that follow, all the text communication with programs is completed before the graphics screen is initialized by a call to the method

vpt.prepit(modenumber) ;

After pictures have been drawn, some 'housekeeping' is needed to finish the frame: such as waiting for the 'Return' key to be pressed before returning to text mode 3, and more importantly *flushing the buffers*; for efficiency, data is buffered (grouped together), and only when the buffer is full is the data sent to the device driver – at the end of a program a partially full buffer must be 'flushed' out to the driver in order to complete the image. This is done by the method call

vpt.finish( ) ;

Only one logical colour can be used at a time. In order to change the *current colour* **currcol**, which is a variable *private* to the **Viewport** class, to logical colour **col**, $0 \leq$ **col** $<$ **plt.tabnum**, we use the call

vpt.setcol(col) ;

We erase all the pixels in the viewport **vpt** in (background) colour **col** by

vpt.erase(col) ;

We can set the current pixel to **pixel**, of structure type **pixelvector**, and colour it in the current colour by

vpt.setpix(pixel) ;

The graphics cursor can be moved about the viewport to its current position **pixel** without changing the colour by the method call

vpt.movepix(pixel) ;

Or we can draw a line in the current colour from the current position to a new position **pixel**, which then becomes the current position, with the call

vpt.linepix(pixel) ;

Using the current colour, we can fill in a polygon, whose vertices are defined by **n pixelvectors poly[i]**, where $0 \leq$ **i** $<$ **n** $\leq$ **maxpoly** taken in order, by the call

vpt.polypix(n,poly) ;

Some cards, such as the XGA, have area fill available in the hardware, and so we can implement the **polypix** method using this function (see the Appendix). However, with the VGA card this method has to be constructed from basics by drawing neighbouring *scan lines* of pixels that lie inside the polygon, and for this we use the function described in chapter 5.

Note that the C++ language counts the elements in an array starting at 0 (and not 1), hence the last in a list of **n** elements has index **n–1**! We have already seen this in our definition of the colour look-up table, and we shall use this counting logic throughout this book. But please **BE VERY CAREFUL.** The change in logic of counting from 0 to **n**–1, rather than from 1 to **n**, can introduce some very peculiar errors, as the latter method is so subtly ingrained in our thinking, and there is no range checking of arrays in C++.

Finally, we need a method which defines the actual colours in the colour look-up table for our particular **Palette, plt**. Method **init** must be called to associate the palette with the viewport. There are several methods for dealing with such definitions (Foley, van Dam, Feiner and Hughes, 1990), but we assume that the table entry, referred to by logical colour **i**, is made up of **r**(red), **g**(green) and **b**(blue) components (either given by floating point numbers between 0 and 1, or by integers between 0 and 255), which may be set by

```
plt.rgblog(i,r,g,b) ;
```

The intensity of each component lies between zero and one (or between zero and 255): zero means no component of that colour is present, one (or 255) means full colour intensity. Thus, black has RGB **float** components 0 , 0 , 0; white has 1 , 1 , 1; the components of red are 1 , 0 , 0; while cyan is 0 , 1 , 1. These colours can be 'darkened' by reducing the intensities from one to a fractional value. **Palette** method **colourtable** sets the default **red, green** and **blue** arrays for VGA and XGA cards, with values chosen to be the sixteen VGA default actual colours, comprising black (logical colour 0), blue (1), green (2), cyan (3), red (4), magenta (5), brown (6), light grey (7), dark grey (8), light blue (9), light green (10), light cyan (11), light red (12), light magenta (13), yellow (14), white (15). Treating these values as four-bit binary numbers, the high bit represents light (1) or dark (0), and the remaining three bits of the numbers give the presence (1) or absence (0) of the three component colours. Our default brown is a dirty yellow; if you prefer you can change our default logical colour 6 to RGB components (0.56,0.28,0.0). The default background and foreground logical colours set at be 0 (black) and 15 (white) respectively, but for the purpose of producing line diagrams for this book we used a white background and a black foreground for obvious reasons. You can of course use each card's own default colours; if you are using the XGA or any other card for that matter, check your manual for these default colours. Later in the book, when we come to *smooth shading* three-dimensional scenes we will introduce an alternative version of **colourtable.**

The above methods (functions) are by no means the last word, quite the contrary. We give them simply because they are the smallest set of methods that can support all the sophisticated programs given in this book. Users of special-purpose graphics devices, or those who want to stretch their use of their graphics card to the limit, should extend our list of methods in order to make full use of the potential of their particular adapter. For example, many cards allow different styles of line drawing; thus a line need not simply be drawn in a given (numerical) colour, each pixel along the line may be coloured by a bit-wise Boolean binary operation (such as exclusive OR) on the value of the present colour of that pixel and the current drawing colour. A line could be dashed! To demonstrate this we have already introduced a new method in listing 1.1 above for setting up different *line styles*, although we will never use it except for a simple illustration. This is because in this book we will concentrate on geometric modelling; and so we do not consider line types or the whole area of computer graphics relating to the construction and manipulating of two-dimensional objects which are defined as rectangular blocks of pixels (*user-defined characters, icons, sprites etc.). You could introduce your own methods for the **Viewport** class which can manipulate these objects should your particular graphics application need them. In fact you will have noticed that we have not even explained all our methods (**Get_nxpix** for example) given in listing 1.1, but we feel that they are fairly self-explanatory, and so we leave it to the reader to understand them.

Linking files into a C++ Project

We now have to link our graphics model into applications programs. We could of course use the **#include** facility of C++; however, as our programs get larger we find that the amount of RAM space available to store both functions and data on objects, becomes very restricted. So we will start in the way we intend to continue for the whole book. C++ offers the option of compiling smaller files independently, and then linking them together into a complete executable file. The book-keeping of the files that need to be linked together, in order to produce an executable file, is very much simplified in Borland C++ with the use of a Project. A Project, a term used by C and C++ vendors, is a mechanism that ensures that all the necessary files, or *modules*, are compiled and are up to date, so that their linkage will produce an executable application. When we refer to a C++ 'Project' we will always write it with an upper case 'P' so as to distinguish it from 'project', the verb meaning to transform images of objects in three-dimensional space onto a flat two-dimensional screen.

Listing 1.3

```
// A simple application program to demonstrate communication with cards

#include "viewport.h"
#include "palette.h"

Viewport vpt ;
Palette plt ;

//-----------//
  void main()
//-----------//
 { pixelvector pt0,pt1,pt2,pt3,centre ;
   pixelvector poly[3] ;
// Prepare graphics viewport
   vpt.prepit(18) ;        // 18 for VGA mode, use 255 for XGA
   plt.init(&vpt) ;        // Associate palette 'plt' with the 'vpt' viewport
// Define logical colour 8 to be grey and current colour
   plt.rgblog(8,(float)0.4,0.4,0.4) ; vpt.setcol(8) ;
// Define the vertices of a triangle
   poly[0].x=0 ; poly[0].y=0 ;
   poly[1].x=vpt.Get_nxpix()-1 ; poly[1].y=0 ;
   poly[2].x=0 ; poly[2].y=vpt.Get_nypix()-1 ;
// Fill in this triangle in current colour
   vpt.polypix(3,poly) ;
// Define the vertices of a square centred in the viewport
// First the bottom left-hand corner
   pt0.x=vpt.Get_nxpix()*0.25 ; pt0.y=vpt.Get_nypix()*0.25 ;
// Then the top right-hand corner
   pt2.x=vpt.Get_nxpix()*0.75 ; pt2.y=vpt.Get_nypix()*0.75 ;
// Then the other two corners
   pt1.x=pt0.x ; pt1.y=pt2.y ;
   pt3.x=pt2.x ; pt3.y=pt0.y ;
// Set current colour to red
   vpt.setcol(4) ;
// Draw the outline of the square
   vpt.movepix(pt0) ;
   vpt.linepix(pt1) ; vpt.linepix(pt2) ;
   vpt.linepix(pt3) ; vpt.linepix(pt0) ;
// Draw red dot in the centre of the viewport
   centre.x=vpt.Get_nxpix()*0.5 ; centre.y=vpt.Get_nypix()*0.5 ;
   vpt.setpix(centre) ;
// Call the end of frame procedure
   vpt.finish() ;
 }  // End of main
```

With the Project mechanism, since each file is compiled independently, it is allocated the maximum data and code memory space depending on the model of compilation (we shall be using the HUGE model). Additionally, it avoids re-compiling files that have not changed since a previous compilation. Consequently, this book will use the Project mechanism; however, if this mechanism is not available in your particular environment, it is up to you to ensure that all files are up to date and linked together. Then, file **"viewport.cpp"** will be compiled independently to produce the corresponding **"viewport.obj"** file. When an application needs to use the **Viewport** class it will have to be compiled separately, but linked together with the **"viewport.obj"** and possibly other **".obj"** files. For the remainder of this book we will use the term 'link' very loosely, to mean the association of **".cpp"** files into a C++ Project, which will implicitly *link* the corresponding **".obj"** files. Remember that the compiler's directives (that is, memory model, segment alignment, length of pointers etc.) should be identical for all the files being linked together. Also, remember that in order to reference the **Viewport** class within another file, that class must be known and so its declaration, **"viewport.h"**, will have to be **#included**. In order to demonstrate the use of our model device of the two classes **Viewport** and **Palette**, the remainder of this chapter will consist of a number of program examples that highlight various features of the model device.

Example 1.1
Consider the **main** function (listing 1.3), that must be stored in a file; suppose we name it **"one3.cpp"**. Linked to our two classes, it completes a rather contrived program for drawing a trivial pattern of dots, lines and polygonal areas. The program uses many of the methods mentioned above – **erase** is implicit in **prepit**. Notice how files **"viewport.h"** and **"palette.h"** are **#included** in the listing to complete the program. The final picture is created by forming a Project of this listing, file **"one3.cpp"**, and **"palette.cpp"** – note there is no need to place file **"viewport.cpp"** explicitly in the Project, it is already **#included** by **"palette.cpp"**.

Exercise 1.1
Implement the **Viewport** and **Palette** classes on the Borland Graphics Interface. You will notice that this is basically equivalent to the VGA mode 18.

Restricting ourselves to a world made up of pixel vectors can be very limiting, although we can nonetheless achieve some very sophisticated images, as the following four 'fractal' examples (see Mandelbrot, 1977) will demonstrate.

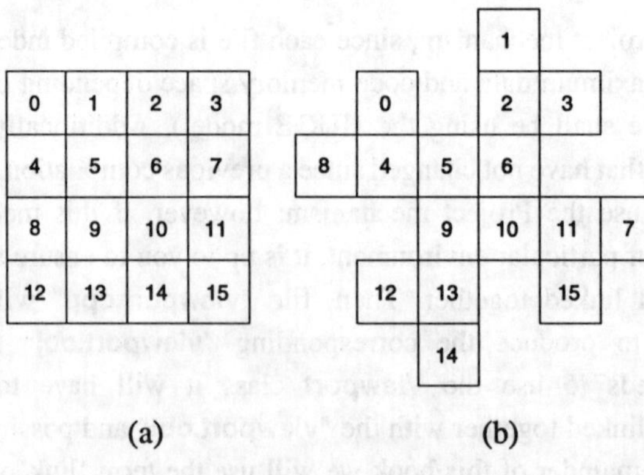

Figure 1.2

Example 1.2

To draw the simple fractal shown in figure 1.3 we proceed as follows. Consider a square of side 4^n. This may be divided into 16 smaller squares, each with sides of length 4^{n-1}; the smaller squares are numbered from 0 to 15 in accordance with the pattern of figure 1.2a. Four of these smaller squares, numbers 1, 7, 8 and 14, are rearranged to produce figure 1.2b.

Listing 1.4

```
#include "viewport.h"
Viewport vpt ;

int a[16], b[16], i ;
pixelvector firstoffset ;

//---------------------------------------------//
  void fractal(pixelvector offset, int sqsize)    // Koch snowflake
//---------------------------------------------//
 { pixelvector newoffset ;
   int i ;
   for (i=0 ; i<16 ; i++)
   { newoffset.x=offset.x+a[i]*sqsize ; newoffset.y=offset.y+b[i]*sqsize ;
     if (sqsize==1) vpt.setpix(newoffset) ;
     else fractal(newoffset,sqsize/4) ;
   }
 }  // End of fractal

//-----------//
  void main()
//-----------//
 { ifstream indata ;
   int levels = 64 ;   // Should be a power of 4
// "fractal.dat" contains offset coordinates of fractal squares
   vpt.prepit(18) ;    // Use 255 for XGA
   indata.open("fractal.dat") ;
   for (i=0 ; i<16 ; i++) indata >> a[i] >> b[i] ;
   firstoffset.x = vpt.Get_nxpix() / 2 - 2*levels ;
   firstoffset.y = vpt.Get_nypix() / 2 - 2*levels ;
   vpt.erase(1) ; vpt.setcol(2) ; fractal(firstoffset,levels) ;
   vpt.finish() ;
 }  // End of main

/* File "fractal.dat"
 0 0            2 0    3 0
 0 1     1 1    2 1
         1 2    2 2    3 2
 0 3     1 3           3 3
 2 -1    4 2   -1 1    1 4        */
```

In the same way, each of the squares in the rearranged pattern is now split up into 16 even smaller squares, of side length 4^{n-2}, and these are similarly rearranged. This *self-similar* process is repeated until finally the squares are of side length 1. These squares can now be identified with individual pixels – knowing the graphics mode, and hence the number of pixels in the viewport, we find the maximum value of n so that the completed pattern makes the best use of the viewport size. Listing 1.4 gives the **main** function, which when linked to file **"palette.cpp"** in a C++ Project, completes the program to draw figure 1.3.

Figure 1.3

In our listings thus far, input is from the keyboard by the operator >> ('get from' the standard input stream **cin**), and text-screen output by the operator << ('send to' the standard output stream **cout**). Note also that operator >> is valid for objects from the file input class **ifstream,** as is << for objects from output class **ofstream.** Respective functions **open** and **close** will be needed, and they are implemented in the I/O classes (see **<iostream.h>** and **<fstream.h>**). Also >> and << will be overloaded for the input and output of our own data types.

Figure 1.4

Example 1.3

Consider the Sierpinski triangle in figure 1.4, produced from listing 1.5. We fix three pixel points **fixed[3]**, at the top centre and two bottom corners of the viewport. Then, starting at the top left pixel (0 , 0), a variable pixel **p** is repeatedly calculated to be half-way between the present value of **p** and one of the fixed pixels chosen at random. After the process has settled down, the pixel is coloured in to give this surprising result.

Listing 1.5

```
// Application program to draw Sierpinski gasket

#include "viewport.h"

Viewport vpt ;

#include <stdlib.h>  // Needed for a call to functions randomize, random
#include <conio.h>   // Needed for a call to function kbhit

//-----------//
  void main()
//-----------//
 { pixelvector fixed[3], p ;
   int i, j ;
   vpt.prepit(18) ;  vpt.setcol(12) ;
   fixed[0].x = vpt.Get_nxpix() / 2 ; fixed[0].y = 1 ;
   fixed[1].x = 1 ; fixed[1].y = vpt.Get_nypix() -1 ;
   fixed[2].x = vpt.Get_nxpix() -1 ; fixed[2].y = vpt.Get_nypix() -1 ;
   for (i=0 ; i<3 ; i++) vpt.setpix(fixed[i]) ;
   p.x = 0 ; p.y = 0 ;
   randomize() ;
   for (i=0 ; i<30 ; i++)    // Leave some time to settle
   { j = random(3) ;
     p.x = (p.x + fixed[j].x) / 2 ;
     p.y = (p.y + fixed[j].y) / 2 ;
   }
// continue generating fractal points until key is pressed
   while (!kbhit())
   { j = random(3) ;
     p.x = (int) ( (float)(p.x + fixed[j].x) / 2.0 + 0.5) ;
     p.y = (int) ( (float)(p.y + fixed[j].y) / 2.0 + 0.5) ;
     vpt.setpix(p) ;
   }
   vpt.finish() ;
 }  // End of main
```

Example 1.4

We can use the concept of self-similarity to produce some quite realistic-looking maps. Consider the square in figure 1.5, with top left co-ordinates (0 , 0) and bottom right $(2^n , 2^n)$, with values *a*, *b*, *c* and *d* allocated to the corners. Suppose the square is now divided into four squares of side 2^{n-1}, and values allocated by interpolation to the five new corners: *0.5*(a+b)*, *0.5*(a+c)*, *0.25*(a+b+c+d)*, *0.5*(b+d)* and *0.5*(c+d)*. Each of these new squares can be divided further into four squares of side 2^{n-2}, and so on, until we ultimately end with a rectangular grid of $(2^n+1)^2$ points (i , j), where $0 \le i \le 2^n$ and $0 \le j \le 2^n$. Each point is allocated a value calculated by repeated interpolation, and we can think of these values as vertical heights above a horizontal grid. By relating ranges of values with a set of colours, and then identifying the points with screen pixels, we can produce some reasonable, if somewhat smooth, contour maps.

But real contours are not that smooth! Luckily, we can introduce ruggedness by adding in a random value with each interpolation. This sounds simple, but there are two problems that have to be overcome. If we think of each interpolated value as the average height between two end points, and the random variation as a slight movement up or down to this height, then the maximum range of vertical movement for a particular interpolation should be related in some way to the horizontal distance between the two end points. This can be achieved by ensuring that the value added to the interpolated average is proportional to this distance and multiplied by a random variate that is uniformly distributed between –0.5 and 0.5. Setting the constant of proportionality (**scaleup** in listing 1.6) to zero gives the original smoothly interpolated image. Increasing this constant will increase the effect of the random variation of the contours, until eventually the constant of proportionality gets so large that the picture breaks up and no contours are apparent in the random noise.

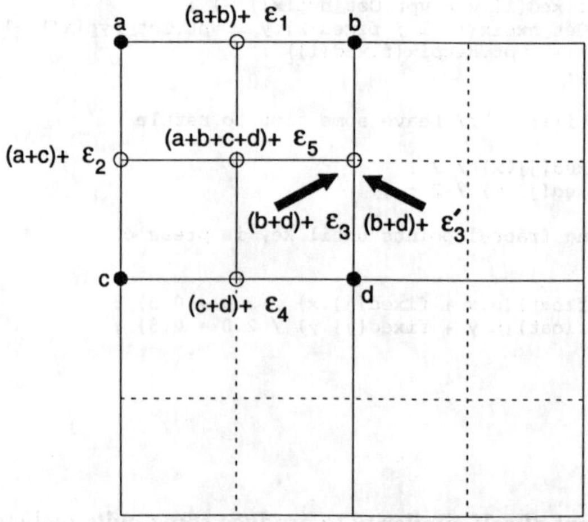

Figure 1.5

There is another far greater problem, however, but one that we can avoid by cheating! The problem, which occurs at all points except for the first nine, can be seen clearly when we consider the point $(2^{n-1}, 2^{n-2})$ indicated by the arrows in figure 1.5. The interpolated value associated with this point will be calculated twice, once from within the top left square and once from within the top right. If we are using a typical random number generator, then the two random values (ε_3 and ε_3') which are added to the separate interpolations are going to be different. This means that the point will be given two different heights on the two separate occasions that it is calculated. So which height do we choose, or do we guarantee that the 'random value' for any given point is the same no matter from which sequence of outer squares it is calculated during the above recursive procedure? The trick is to use the integer co-ordinates of each point as parameters for a pseudo-random number generator! Then the values generated are not random, yet appear to be! And, what is more, they are unique to that point no matter from what direction it is approached.

Referring to figure 1.5, notice that only the original four corners of the outer square are predictable. In order to get a realistic looking map, and to keep it under some form of control, we need to impose a number of predefined heights at so-called 'reference points'. Instead of fixing just four heights, we define the height values for $(m+1)^2$ points placed in an m by m grid of side 2^n. By treating each of these grid squares in the above way (we have the four values at its corners) we can generate values for $(m\times 2^n + 1)^2$ points (i, j), where $0 \leq i \leq m\times 2^n$ and $0 \leq j \leq m\times 2^n$. But what values of m and n do we choose, and why? The value of m is arbitrary, depending on how we use reference points to constrain the map.

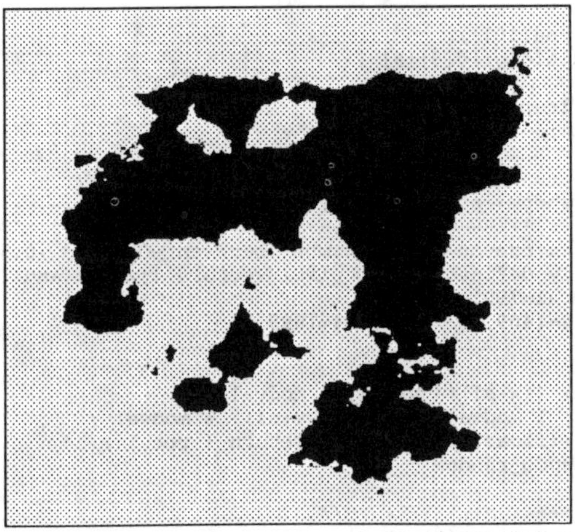

Figure 1.6

We should, however, give some thought to the value of n. Let us take the case when m is 1, a single original square, but now assume that the edge length is 2^{n+1}. Its area has now quadrupled, and the interpolated values of the original square will form the top left quarter of the new square. Ideally, we would have preferred the new map to be the same as the old, but at a higher resolution. This too can easily be achieved; we start with a large value for n (11 say) and, as we recursively break it into quarters, we stop before reaching unit squares, say at 2^k, and identify pixels in the viewport with points $(i\times 2^k, j\times 2^k)$, where $0 \leq i \leq 2^{(n-k)}$ and $0 \leq j \leq 2^{(n-k)}$. Decreasing k by 1 doubles the resolution of the map in each of the two directions, and a single point in the old map is transformed into a two by two square of neighbouring pixels in the new; the value associated with the old point is now given to the top left of the new. These ideas are incorporated in listing 1.6, file **"one6.cpp"**, which when used with a 7 by 7 set of reference data taken from file **"map.dat"**, and linked to file **"palette.cpp"** in a C++ Project, generates the map shown in figure 1.6, by drawing all points with an interpolated value less than 0.5 in the background colour, and the other points in foreground. Note that we will use this idea in chapter 10 to create realistic images of three-dimensional terrain.

Listing 1.6

```
// Application program to draw a fractal map

#include "viewport.h"
Viewport vpt ;

const int elementsperpixel = 32 ;
const int elementsperblock = 2048 ;

typedef float wtype[10] ;
typedef float initialgrid[8][8] ;

float factor,scaleup ;
pixelvector offs ;

//----------------------------------------------------//
  float pseudo_random(int jx, int jy, int kx, int ky)
//----------------------------------------------------//
// Generation of a pseudo-random number between -0.5 and +0.5
// Number uniquely defined by two pixel vectors (jx,jy) and (kx,ky)
 { const int modval=7901 ;
   int s1=997, s2=1409, s3=1597, s4=1999 ;
   float ret ;
   long int t ;
   t= ((long int) (jx+s1)*(jy+s2)) % modval ;
   t= (t*(kx+s3)) % modval ; t= (t*(ky+s4)) % modval ;
   ret= (float)t/(float)modval-0.5 ; return ( ret ) ;
 }  // End of pseudo_random

//---------------------------------//
  void choosecolour_given(float z)
//---------------------------------//
// Sea in blue (z<0.5), land in green (z>=0.5)
{ if (z<0.5) vpt.setcol(9) ;     else vpt.setcol(10) ;
 }  // End of choosecolour_given

//--------------------------------------------------------------------------//
  void drawpixel(int jx, int jy, float v1, float v3, float v7, float v9)
//--------------------------------------------------------------------------//
// Find the height of pixel (jx,jy) and colour it appropriately
{ float height ;
   pixelvector pix ;
   height=(v1+v3+v7+v9)*0.25*scaleup ;
   pix.x=offs.x+jx ; pix.y=offs.y+jy ;
   choosecolour_given(height) ; vpt.setpix(pix) ;
 }  // End of drawpixel

//---------------------------------------------------------------------------//
 void map_rec(int kx,int ky,int size,float v1,float v3,float v7,float v9)
//---------------------------------------------------------------------------//
// Recursively draw a square of pixels with opposite corners (kx,ky) and
// (kx+size,ky+size). Values associated with four corners are v1,v3,v7,v9.
 { wtype w ;
   float r,r2,scale ;
// Recursion has reached pixel level, so draw the pixel
   if (size == elementsperpixel)
     { drawpixel((kx/size),(ky/size),v1,v3,v7,v9) ; }
```

```
   else
// Random perturbation is made proportional to the size of the grid
// Constant of proportionality has been input
     { scale=factor*(float)size/(float)elementsperblock ;
// Imagine 9 points in a three by three square grid
// we are given the corner values w[1], w[3], w[7] and w[9].
       w[1]=v1 ; w[3]=v3 ; w[7]=v7 ; w[9]=v9 ;
// Find edge mid-points w[2], w[4], w[6] and w[8],
// average appropriate corner values and add random perturbation
       r=pseudo_random(kx,ky,kx+size,ky) ;
       w[2]=(w[1]+w[3])*0.5+r*scale ;
       r=pseudo_random(kx,ky,kx,ky+size) ;
       w[4]=(w[1]+w[7])*0.5+r*scale ;
       r=pseudo_random(kx+size,ky,kx+size,ky+size) ;
       w[6]=(w[3]+w[9])*0.5+r*scale ;
       r=pseudo_random(kx,ky+size,kx+size,ky+size) ;
       w[8]=(w[7]+w[9])*0.5+r*scale ;
// Find centre-point w[5], average four corners and add random perturbation
       r=pseudo_random(kx,ky,kx+size,ky+size) ;
       r2=pseudo_random(kx+size,ky,kx,ky+size) ; r=(r+r2)*0.5 ;
       w[5]=(w[1]+w[3]+w[7]+w[9])*0.25+r*scale ;
// Divide map into four and recursively look at each quarter
       size=size / 2 ;
       map_rec(kx,ky,size,w[1],w[2],w[4],w[5]) ;
       map_rec(kx+size,ky,size,w[2],w[3],w[5],w[6]) ;
       map_rec(kx,ky+size,size,w[4],w[5],w[7],w[8]) ;
       map_rec(kx+size,ky+size,size,w[5],w[6],w[8],w[9]) ;
     }
 }  // End of map_rec

//-----------//
  void main()
//-----------//
// World consists of '7' by '7' blocks, 'elementsperblock' square
// Each block is displayed as a 'pixelperblock' square of pixels
 { int jx,jy,p1,p2,size,pixacross,pixelsperblock ;
   pixelvector pix ;
   ifstream indata ;
   initialgrid v ;
   size = elementsperblock ;
   pixelsperblock = elementsperblock / elementsperpixel ;
// Read in '7 by 7' data points that will define map
   indata.open("map.dat") ;
   for (jx=1 ; jx<8 ; jx++)
       for (jy=1 ; jy<8 ; jy++)  indata >> v[jx][jy] ;
   indata.close() ;
   cout <<"\n Type random perturbation scaling and scale up factors " ;
   cin >> factor >> scaleup ;     // 2, 2 is a good choice
// Prepare graphics device
   vpt.prepit(18) ;
// Move map to the viewport's centre; first place boundary lines around map
   vpt.setcol(7) ; pixacross= 6*pixelsperblock ;
   offs.x = (vpt.Get_nxpix() - pixacross) / 2 ;
   offs.y = (vpt.Get_nypix() - pixacross) / 2 ;
   pix.x=offs.x-1           ; pix.y=offs.y-1           ; vpt.movepix(pix) ;
   pix.x=offs.x+pixacross ; pix.y=offs.y-1           ; vpt.linepix(pix) ;
   pix.x=offs.x+pixacross ; pix.y=offs.y+pixacross ; vpt.linepix(pix) ;
   pix.x=offs.x-1           ; pix.y=offs.y+pixacross ; vpt.linepix(pix) ;
   pix.x=offs.x-1           ; pix.y=offs.y-1           ; vpt.linepix(pix) ;
// Map is made up of 36 squares, each recursively subdivided
   for (jx=1 ; jx<7 ; jx++)
   { p1=(jx-1)*size ;
     for (jy=1 ; jy<7 ; jy++)
     { p2=(jy-1)*size ;
       map_rec(p1,p2,size,v[jx][jy],v[jx+1][jy],v[jx][jy+1],v[jx+1][jy+1]) ;
     }
   }
   vpt.finish() ;
 }  // End of main
```

```
/*  Sample file "map.dat"
  -1    -1     -1     -1     -1     -1     -1
  -1    -0.1   0.4    0.8    0.1    -0.1   -1
  -1     0.6   0.5    -0.5   -0.1    0.0   -1
  -1     0.3   1      -0.1    0.4   -0.3   -1
  -1     1     1.1     0.8    0.3    0.5   -1
  -1     1.1   0.8    -0.1   -0.5    0.4   -1
  -1    -1     -1     -1     -1     -1     -1
*/
```

Listing 1.7

```
// Application program to produce Mandelbrot pattern

#include "viewport.h"
Viewport vpt ;

const int resolution=255 ;

//----------------------//
  void mandelbrot(void)
//----------------------//
// Mandelbrot pattern between points (startx,starty) to (endx,endy), is
// scaled to fit the monitor: No account is taken of the aspect-ratio.
 { int xpix,ypix,repeatcount ;
   float cx,cy,endx,endy,newx,startx,starty,stepx,stepy,x,y ;
   pixelvector p ;
   startx = -0.1705 ; endx = -0.163 ;
   stepx = (endx-startx)/(float)vpt.Get_nxpix() ;
   starty = 1.0375 ;  endy = 1.043125 ;
   stepy = (endy-starty)/(float)vpt.Get_nypix() ;
   cy=starty-stepy ;
   for (ypix=0 ; ypix<vpt.Get_nypix() ; ypix++)
   { cy += stepy ; cx = startx-stepx ; p.y = ypix ;
     for (xpix=0 ; xpix<vpt.Get_nxpix() ; xpix++)
     { x = 0.0 ; y = 0.0 ;
       cx += stepx ; repeatcount = -1 ;
       while ( (repeatcount++ < resolution) && ((x*x+y*y) < 4.0) )
       { newx = x*x-y*y + cx ; y = 2*x*y + cy ; x = newx ; }
       p.x = xpix ; vpt.setcol(repeatcount) ; vpt.setpix(p) ;
     }
   }
 } // End of mandelbrot

//-----------//
  void main()
//-----------//
 { vpt.prepit(19) ;
   mandelbrot() ;
   vpt.finish() ;
 } // End of main
```

Example 1.5

There are very few real graphics applications where shapes are defined using discrete pairs of integers. The patterns shown so far look very attractive, but in order to make full use of computer graphics we have to stop thinking in terms of pixels as discrete dots on a graphics screen, and instead consider them as representative of small areas in continuous two-dimensional space. We have to look no further than the popular fractal pattern, the Mandelbrot set, shown in Plate IIIa for an example of this approach. The seemingly complex Plate is very easy to produce, as a look at listing 1.7, linked of course to **"palette.cpp"**, will demonstrate. Take complex numbers ***c*** (a constant) and ***z*** (a variable initially set to zero) which is repeatedly recalculated to be z^2+c. Note that a complex number ***z*** is in fact just a two-dimensional vector, (*zx* , *zy*) say, and its square z^2 is then ($zx \times zx - zy \times zy$, $2 \times zx \times zy$). The value of ***z*** then jumps about two-dimensional space, and we count the number of iterations, ***n***, it takes for ***z*** to lie outside a circle of radius 2. If we think of the viewport corresponding to a rectangular area defined by corners with co-ordinates (**startx** , **starty**) and (**endx** , **endy**), each pixel can be used to define a value for ***c***, which in turn is used to calculate a sequence of values for ***z***, which in turn gives us a value for ***n***. We then colour that pixel in logical colour ***n***, and eventually we have the required pattern.

Line types

Before considering 'real' space, we first leave single pixels behind to consider drawing lines of pixels, and in particular different types of lines. In order to do this it is important to realize how a line is represented on our pixel-based viewport model. The line is obviously constructed as a discrete set of pixels joining the pixel end-points of the line. A number of algorithms for deciding which pixels go into this set, and how they are coloured, are available (Newman and Sproull, 1973; or Foley, van Dam, Feiner and Hughes, 1990): we assume that this is achieved either by the hardware or in the 'drivers' – for example, we have implemented Bresenham's algorithm in our VGA driver. These algorithms colour in each component pixel on the line in a logical colour which is calculated from the line colour and the original colour of the pixel.

Table 1.1

Original colour	0	1	2	3	4	5	6	7
Binary bits	000	001	010	011	100	101	110	111
OR with 6(110)	110	111	110	111	110	111	110	111
AND with 6	000	000	010	010	100	100	110	110
XOR with 6	110	111	100	101	010	011	000	001

In the book thus far we have used the default line type – that is, a *solid line* of pixels in the given fixed line colour and intensity that obliterates the original colour of every pixel it covers. The variety of graphics devices available to us allows for many different line types. A solid line type ignores the original colour of the pixels obliterated by the line. Instead, Boolean operators AND, OR, XOR (exclusive OR) can operate *bit-wise* on the binary value of these two logical colours. Suppose that we have a line of logical colour 6 (binary 110) running through pixels coloured 0 through 7 (binary 000 through 111). Table 1.1 above gives the resulting 3-bit pixel colours for the above three operators.

We have such facilities on the VGA and XGA cards, and so in listing 1.1 (and in the Appendix) where we give the code for the **Viewport** class, you will find a method **setype(op)**, where **op** is an integer, which enables normal plotting (REPLACE), OR, AND (if available on the card) or XOR, corresponding to **op** values 0, 1, 2 or 3 respectively.

Example 1.6

Figure 1.7, produced by listing 1.8 linked in a C++ Project to **"palette.cpp"**, gives an example of XOR plotting. Each pixel on the topmost row and leftmost column is joined to the pixels diametrically opposite on the bottommost row and rightmost column respectively to give a *Moiré pattern.* Each pixel is finally coloured in the foreground colour if, in total, an odd number of lines pass through it, and in the background colour if an even number of lines do so.

Listing 1.8

```
// Application program to draw a Moire pattern

#include "viewport.h"

Viewport vpt ;

//------------//
  void main()
//------------//
 { int i, nxpix, nypix, xstep, ystep ;
   pixelvector p0, p1 ;
   vpt.prepit(18) ; vpt.setype(3) ; vpt.setcol(15) ;
   nxpix = vpt.Get_nxpix() ; nypix = vpt.Get_nypix() ;
   xstep = 1 ; ystep = 1 ;
// Join points on top line to those diametrically opposite on bottom line
   for (i=0 ; i<nxpix ; i += xstep )
   { p0.x = i ; p0.y = 0 ;
     p1.x = nxpix - i -1 ; p1.y = nypix-1 ;
     vpt.movepix(p0) ; vpt.linepix(p1) ;
   }
// Join points on left edge to those diametrically opposite on right
   for (i=0 ; i<nypix ; i += ystep )
   { p0.x = 0 ;  p0.y = nypix - i -1 ;
     p1.x = nxpix-1 ;  p1.y = i ;
     vpt.movepix(p0) ; vpt.linepix(p1) ;
   }
   vpt.finish() ;
 }  // End of main
```

Exercise 1.2

The last line type we consider is an *anti-aliased* line (see Foley, van Dam, Feiner and Hughes, 1990). Lines of fixed colour and intensity drawn on raster devices tend to look jagged (aliased), since they are simply groups of squares (the pixels) that approximate to the line, and so naturally they display this staircase effect. Lines are considered to have a thickness, and the pixels that are intersected by this line are not given a fixed colour; instead they are given a mix of the background colour and line colour proportional to just how much of the pixel is covered by the thick line. The same ideas are used to construct solid text characters so that they do not display the irritating jagged edge effect. If you have hardware anti-aliasing then incorporate it in new line-drawing methods.

Figure 1.7

Exercise 1.3

Line drawing is often used in conjunction with a peripheral device called a *mouse* that is held in the hand and moved over a rectangular *graphics tablet* or *digitizing tablet*. The position of the mouse on this tablet corresponds to the position of the *cursor* in the viewport, and its position is communicated when one of a number of buttons on the mouse is 'clicked'. In order for our programs to gain access to the pixel information that is indicated by such a peripheral device, you should add another method, **mouse(pixelvector *q)**, to the **Viewport** class; this method should return an integer value which is set to 1 when a button is clicked, and 0 otherwise. The pixel co-ordinates of **q** are changed to the current pixel position indicated by the mouse.

Example 1.7

We assume that you do not have a mouse, so instead, in listing 1.9, we emulate this function on the keyboard by using the cursor keys to indicate movement of the mouse, and the 'space bar' for the button 'click'.

It is important to note here that when two identical XOR lines are drawn, one directly over the other, then the colour of the pixel components of the line will return to their original colours before the first line was drawn. This type of Boolean plotting is available on many microcomputers for drawing blocks of pixels (sprites), and it is the basis of many video games. Great care must be taken when using XOR in complicated scenes; it is very easy to change, inadvertently, parts of objects other than those you intend.

We use XOR lines in a very useful operation known as *rubber-banding*. To illustrate we give a very simple example in which we draw a line from a fixed **pixelvector p1** on the viewport to another, but we are not sure where that pixel **p** is to be positioned. The idea is that a mouse moves around the tablet, and with each new position the corresponding cursor indicates a pixel, and hence a new line. Naturally, the old line has to be deleted and a new line drawn for each new pixel position; the process is programmed in listing 1.9 as function **rubber.** Note how XOR is used repeatedly inside a loop to achieve this. This function terminates if the **status** value is reset to 0 (by releasing the button on the mouse) and the final value of **p** is used. If needed, add the function **mouse** and **rubber** to the **Viewport** class in files **"viewport.h"** and **"viewport.cpp"**.

Listing 1.9

```
// Application program of rubber banding emulation

#include "viewport.h"
#include <bios.h>          // Needed for a call to function bioskey

#define SPACE 32
#define UPKEY 328
#define DOWNKEY 336
#define LEFTKEY 331
#define RIGHTKEY 333

Viewport vpt ;

//-----------------//
  int getkey(void)   // Uses the BIOS to read the next keyboard character
//-----------------//
 { int key, lo, hi ;
   key = bioskey(0) ;
   lo = key & 0X00FF ;  hi = (key & 0XFF00) >> 8 ;
   return((lo == 0) ? hi + 256 : lo);
 }  // End of getkey

//--------------------------------//
  void show_cursor(pixelvector p)     // Draw a cursor cross
//--------------------------------//
 { pixelvector p0, p1 ;
   int size = 5 ;
   p0.x = p.x - size ; p0.y = p.y ;
   p1.x = p.x + size ; p1.y = p.y ;
   vpt.movepix(p0) ; vpt.linepix(p1) ;
   p0.x = p.x ; p0.y = p.y - size ;
   p1.x = p.x ; p1.y = p.y + size ;
   vpt.movepix(p0) ; vpt.linepix(p1) ;
 }  // End of show_cursor
```

```
//-------------------------//
  int mouse(pixelvector *q)      // Emulate mouse on the keyboard
//-------------------------//
 { int stepx = 4, stepy = 4 ;
   static int status = 1 ;
   pixelvector p ;
   vpt.setcol(15) ; vpt.setype(3) ;
   p = *q ;  show_cursor(p) ;
   if (bioskey(1) != 0)  // Mouse has moved
   { switch ( getkey() )
     { case SPACE     : status = 1 - status ; break ;
       case UPKEY     : (q->y)-=stepy ; break ;
       case DOWNKEY   : (q->y)+=stepy ; break ;
       case LEFTKEY   : (q->x)-=stepx ; break ;
       case RIGHTKEY  : (q->x)+=stepx ; break ;
     }
   }
   show_cursor(p) ; vpt.setcol(14) ;
   return ( status ) ;
 }  // End of mouse

//--------------------------------------------//
  void rubber(pixelvector p1, pixelvector *p2)
//--------------------------------------------//
// Routine using rubber banding to define a line from fixed
// pixel point '*p1' to a moveable pixel point '*p2'
 { pixelvector *p ;
   int status = 0 ;
   p2->x =p1.x ; p2->y =p1.y ;
   vpt.setcol(14) ; // Assume colour 14 for the line, 15 for the cursor
   status = mouse(&p1) ;
// Draw the first line //
   vpt.setype(0) ; vpt.movepix(p1) ; vpt.linepix(*p2) ;
// Hold button down while moving mouse, release button when
// required end of line achieved
// Store old end of line and use mouse for new '*p2'
   do { p->x=p2->x ; p->y=p2->y ; status = mouse(p2) ;
// XOR away the old line
       vpt.setype(3) ; vpt.movepix(p1) ; vpt.linepix(*p) ;
// REPLACE it with new line from '*p1' to '*p2'
       vpt.setype(0) ; vpt.movepix(p1) ; vpt.linepix(*p2) ;
     }
   while (status != 0) ;
// exit procedure when button is released
 }  // End of rubber

//-----------//
  void main()
//-----------//
 { pixelvector p1, p2 ;
   vpt.prepit(19) ;
   p1.x = 100 ; p1.y = 100 ; rubber(p1,&p2) ;
   vpt.finish() ;
   cout << "\n Final pixel: " << p2.x << " , "<< p2.y ;
 }  // End of main
```

Exercise 1.4

Use rubber-banding in a program that modifies a polygon on the viewport. A mouse is used first to indicate a vertex of the polygon, and then it must indicate movement of the chosen vertex about the viewport (the two polygon edges that enter that vertex must also move). Note that if XOR plotting is not available, then you have to clear the viewport and totally redraw every edge of the polygon for each new position of the mouse, and not just the two relevant edges.

Exercise 1.5

It is very difficult to point at a particular pixel using a mouse; you are lucky to keep your hand steady to within one or two pixels of the target. One of the most common ways to avoid this problem is to insist that only a subset of the screen pixels, set up as a *rectangular grid*, can be accessed. Then whenever a pixel is indicated by a shaking hand, the computer 'snaps' to the grid pixel nearest to the mouse position. One very useful process in computer graphics that uses this approach is the *menu*: a displayed list of possible options (as text or perhaps *icons*: idealized symbols, stored as blocks of pixels, representing a concept) is drawn on the viewport and the mouse is used to indicate which you require. Having written menu options on the viewport, we now have to ensure that the correct icon is indicated by the mouse. To do this we relate the position of the screen images with the discrete rectangular grid of pixels, by storing, or by calculating in real time, a list of grid points nearest to each displayed option. Then, when the mouse indicates a pixel, the program 'snaps' to the nearest grid pixel, and hence it has found the intended menu item.

Include this idea in a simple program that draws three rectangles, each 256 pixels wide and 16 pixels deep, one under the other, which will hold various shades of red, green and blue respectively. Each of these rectangles will be composed of 32 squares, each 16 pixels by 16 pixels, containing 32 shades of the colours red, green and blue, starting with black on the left through to the full intensity colour on the right. Set up a 32 by 3 grid near the centres of these squares. Use the mouse to indicate a choice of a red, a green and a blue shade, which should then be combined by using them as parameters in a call to **rgblog** to define logical colour 254. Then use this colour to draw a large square at the bottom of the screen, so that you can see the actual colour that you have chosen.

2 A window on two-dimensional space

The WINDOW system

Example 1.5 ought to convince us that we should consider plotting views on the graphics display where the objects drawn are defined not in terms of pixels, but in real *continuous* units, whether these be millimetres or miles. Therefore, we have to put the relationship between the viewport and continuous space onto a formal footing. Since our **Viewport** methods draw using pixels, we now have to consider a file of constants, structure types, variables and functions which relate *real space* with the pixels of our viewport. In listing 2.1 we create a class named **Window**; the declarations (2.1a) should be stored in file **"window.h"**, and the methods (2.1b) in **"window.cpp"**. However, before explaining these listings, we must first discuss ways of representing two-dimensional Euclidean space by means of Cartesian co-ordinate geometry.

We may imagine two-dimensional space as the plane of the page holding figure 1.1, but extending to infinity in all directions. In order to specify the position of points uniquely, we have to impose a Cartesian co-ordinate system on the plane. We start by arbitrarily choosing a fixed point in this space, which is called the *co-ordinate origin*, or *origin* for short. A line that extends to infinity in both directions is drawn through the origin – this is the *x-axis*. The normal convention, which we follow, is to imagine that we are looking at the page so that the *x*-axis appears from left to right on the page (the horizontal). Another two-way infinite axis, the *y-axis*, is drawn through the origin perpendicular to the *x*-axis; hence conventionally this is placed from the top to the bottom of the page (the vertical). We now draw a scale along each axis; unit distances need not be the same on both axes or even linearly distributed along the axes, but this is normally the case. We assume that values on the *x*-axis are positive to the right of the origin and negative to the left: values on the *y*-axis are positive above the origin and negative below.

We can now uniquely fix the position of point $\boldsymbol{p}$ in space with reference to this co-ordinate system by specifying its *co-ordinates*. The *x co-ordinate*, x say, is that distance along the *x*-axis (positive on the right-hand half-axis, and negative on the left) at which the line perpendicular to the *x*-axis, that passes through $\boldsymbol{p}$, cuts the axis. The *y co-ordinate*, y say, is correspondingly defined by using the *y*-axis. These two values, called a *co-ordinate pair* or *two-dimensional point vector*, are normally written in brackets thus: (x, y), the x co-ordinate coming before the *y* co-ordinate. We shall usually refer to the pair as a vector – the dimension (in this case dimension two) will be understood from the context in which we use the term. A vector, as well as defining a point (x, y) in two-dimensional space, may also be used to specify a direction, namely the direction that is parallel to the line joining the origin to the point (x, y) – but more of this (and other objects such as lines, curves and polygons) later.

It must be realized that the co-ordinate values of a point in space are totally dependent on the choice of co-ordinate system. During our analysis of computer graphics algorithms we will be using a number of different co-ordinate systems to represent the same objects in space, and so a single point in space may have a number of different vector co-ordinate representations. For example, if we have two co-ordinate systems with parallel axes but different origins – say separated by a distance 1 in the *x* direction, and 2 in the *y* direction – then the point (0 , 0) in one system (its origin) could be (1 , 2) in the other: the same point in space but different vector co-ordinates. In order to clarify the relationships between different systems we introduce an arbitrary but fixed co-ordinate system, called the WINDOW system, and ensure that all other systems can be defined in relation to it. This WINDOW system, although chosen arbitrarily, remains fixed throughout our discussion of two- and three-dimensional space. (Some authors call this the *World Co-ordinate System* of two-dimensional space.) Normally we will define the position and shape of objects in relation to this system.

Having imposed this fixed origin and axes on two-dimensional space, we now isolate a finite rectangular area (or *window*) of size **horiz** by **vert** units, within the WINDOW system. This window is to be identified with the graphics viewport, so that we can draw views of two-dimensional scenes on the model graphics device, by simply relating the real co-ordinates of points in the window with their corresponding pixels in the screen viewport.

Functions that map a window onto the Viewport

We continue the development of our graphics package by introducing a new class, **Window**, that also *inherits* from the *base* **Viewport** class. The **Window** class is declared in **"window.h"**, and implemented in **"window.cpp"** (listing 2.1). Here again, the **"palette.cpp"** class definition is **#included**, as is **"viewport.cpp"** by implication. Note that in file **"window.cpp"**, we declare three standard objects that will be used throughout this book: **vpt**, an object of the **Viewport** class; **plt**, an object of the **Palette** class; and **win** an object of the new **Window** class. Now, application programs that need to refer to methods of the **Window** class will not need to declare a new object, but simply use **win** defined in **"window.cpp"**. Hence the following C++ commands should be entered in applications:

```
#include "viewport.h"
#include "palette.h"
#include "window.h"
extern Viewport vpt ; extern Palette plt ; extern Window win ;
```

If some of the objects are not needed, their corresponding **extern**al declaration may by omitted. But the inclusion of all three header (**".h"**) files is essential.

We give methods (functions) that operate on points in the form of floating point co-ordinates in the WINDOW system, convert them to the corresponding pixels in the viewport, and finally operate on these pixels with the viewport methods mentioned earlier. These functions will then be *adapter-independent*, and to transport the package between different computers and graphics cards all that is needed is a C++ compiler and the small number of *adapter specific* methods in the **Viewport** and **Palette** classes. Programs dealing with the display of three-dimensional scenes should rarely directly call the **Viewport** methods: all communication with these *primitive* methods should be done indirectly using the **Window** functions below, which treat objects in terms of their floating point (rather than pixel) co-ordinates (listing 2.1).

We assume that the window is **horiz** units horizontally, hence the vertical side of the window (**vert**) is **(horiz*(float)nypix)/(aspect*(float)nxpix)** units, and we identify the centre of the window with the WINDOW co-ordinate origin (see figure 1.1). Note that the vertical scaling may have to be adjusted because the pixels on some cards, or in some graphics modes, are not square; that is the *aspect-ratio* is not unity. In VGA mode 19 the **aspect**-ratio is 5/6, whereas in VGA mode 18 and in XGA mode 255 it is unity: the particular mode chosen is stored in **graph_mode**. In order to identify the viewport with this window we must be able to find the pixel co-ordinates corresponding to any point within the window. The horizontal (and vertical) scaling factor relating window to viewport is called **xyscale=(float)nxpix/horiz**, and since the WINDOW origin is in the centre of the window, we note that a point vector in space with WINDOW co-ordinates (**x** , **y**) will be mapped into a pixel in the viewport with horizontal component given by the expression **(int)(x*xyscale+(float)nxpix*0.5–0.5)** and vertical component **(int)(–y*xyscale*aspect+(float)nypix*0.5–0.5)**. The **y** value is made negative because, when moving down the screen, the *y*-pixel co-ordinate gets more positive whereas the WINDOW *y* co-ordinate becomes more negative. Here the C++ integer cast **(int)** is used to *truncate* floating point numbers. The final **–0.5** in both expressions is needed in order to guarantee that the four corner points (**±horiz/2,±vert/2**) are all mapped onto pixel vectors that lie within the boundaries of the viewport. These two definitions of the horizontal and vertical scaling components are coded as functions **fx** and **fy** respectively, and they are included as class methods in **"window.cpp"**.

Listing 2.1a

```
// Save as file "window.h"
// This code remains the same for both VGA and XGA cards

const double pi = 3.1415926535 ;
const double epsilon = 0.000001 ;

// typedef declares synonyms and not new types.
typedef struct {float x, y ; }    vector2 ;
typedef struct {float x, y, z ; } vector3 ;
typedef vector2 polygon[maxpoly] ;

//------------------------------//
  class Window : public Viewport
//------------------------------//
 { float xyscale ;
   float vert ;
   float horiz ;
   float nxp2 ;
   float nyp2 ;
   vector2 lastvector ;
   float halfhoriz ;
   float halfvert ;

  public:
   Window() ;
   void init(Viewport *scr) ;
   int fx(float x) ;
   int fy(float y) ;
   void moveto(vector2 pt) ;
   void lineto(vector2 pt) ;
   void polyfill(int n, polygon p) ;
   void start(void) ;
   float Get_horiz(void) { return ( horiz ) ; } ;
   float Get_vert(void) { return ( vert ) ; } ;
   float Get_xyscale(void) { return ( xyscale ) ; } ;
   void Set_parameters(void) ;

// The following methods are not defined in listing 2.1B
// They will be given later in the listings that are indicated

   void hatch(int m,vector2 *p, vector2 b, vector2 d, float dist) ;  //5.2
  private :
   int trisect(float z, float screendimension) ;                     //5.1
   void clip(vector2 p1, vector2 p2) ;                               //5.1
  } ;  // End of class Window

//  Utilities defined in "window.cpp"

#define max(a,b) ((a) > (b) ? (a) : (b))
#define min(a,b) ((a) < (b) ? (a) : (b))
vector3 operator + (vector3 a, vector3 b) ;
vector3 operator * (float mu, vector3 a) ;
vector3 operator - (vector3 a, vector3 b) ;
vector3 operator - (vector3 a) ;
ostream& operator << (ostream &a, vector3 v) ;
istream& operator >> (istream &a, vector3 &v) ;
float angle(float x, float y) ;
float random(void) ;

// Utilities defined in other listings

void draw_a_picture(void) ;
int ill2(vector2 v1,vector2 v2,vector2 v3,vector2 v4,vector2 *v) ;    //4.1
int sign(float r) ;                                                  //5.4
int orient2(vector2 p0, vector2 p1, vector2 p2) ;                    //5.4
```

```
float dot3(vector3 p1, vector3 p2) ;                                    //6.1
int ilpl(vector3 b,vector3 d,vector3 n,float k,vector3 *p,float *mu) ; //6.2
vector3 refpp(vector3 p, vector3 n, float k) ;                          //6.3
int ill3(vector3 b1, vector3 d1, vector3 b2, vector3 d2, vector3 *p) ; //6.4
vector3 vectorproduct(vector3 p, vector3 q) ;                           //6.5
float mindist(vector3 a, vector3 c, vector3 b, vector3 d) ;             //6.6
float plane(vector3 p1, vector3 p2, vector3 p3, vector3 *n) ;           //6.7
int invert(double A[4][4], double AINV[4][4]) ;                         //6.8
int i3pl(vector3 n1,float k1,vector3 n2,float k2,vector3 n3,
                                        float k3,vector3 *v) ;          //6.9
int commonline(vector3 n1, float k1, vector3 n2, float k2,
                                       vector3 *b, vector3 *d) ;        //6.10
int orient3(vector3 p1, vector3 p2, vector3 p3, vector3 e) ;            //6.11
```

Listing 2.1b

```
// Save code as file "window.cpp"
// Use the following two lines to increase the size of the system's stack

#include <dos.h>                   // To adjust the length of DOS's stack
extern unsigned _stklen = 32000U ;

#include "palette.cpp"
#include "window.h"

Viewport vpt ;
Palette  plt ;
Window   win ;
static int   graph_mode ;
static float horizontal ;

//------------------------------//
  Window::Window() : Viewport()
//------------------------------//
 { xyscale = 1.0 ; vert = 1.0 ; horiz = 1.0 ;
   nxp2 = 0.0 ; nyp2 = 0.0 ;
 }  // End of Window

//----------------------------------//
  void Window::init(Viewport *scr)
//----------------------------------//
 { colour_resolution = scr->Get_col() ;
   maximum_colours = scr->Get_mxc() ;   currcol = scr->Get_currcol() ;
   graphics_mode = scr->Get_mode() ;    aspect = scr->Get_rat() ;
   lastpixel = scr->Get_last() ;
   nxpix = scr->Get_nxpix() ;    nypix = scr->Get_nypix() ;
   VGA_fout = scr->Get_fout() ;  horiz = horizontal ;
   vert = horiz * (float)nypix / (aspect * (float)nxpix) ;
   xyscale = (float)nxpix / horiz ;
   nxp2 = (float)nxpix * 0.5 - 0.5 ;   nyp2 = (float)nypix * 0.5 - 0.5 ;
   halfhoriz = 0.5 * horiz ;   halfvert = 0.5 * vert ;
 }  // End of init

//------------------------------------//
  void Window::Set_parameters(void)
//------------------------------------//
 { vpt.prepit(graph_mode) ;  aspect = vpt.Get_rat() ;
   nxpix = vpt.Get_nxpix() ;  nypix = vpt.Get_nypix() ;
   horiz = horizontal ; vert = horiz * (float)nypix/(aspect * (float)nxpix) ;
   xyscale = (float)nxpix / horiz ;
   halfhoriz = 0.5 * horiz ;  halfvert = 0.5 * vert ;
   vpt.close() ;
 }  // End of Set_parameters

//-----------------------//
  int Window::fx(float x) { return ((int)(x*xyscale + nxp2)); }
//-----------------------//
```

```
//-----------------------//
  int Window::fy(float y) { return ((int)(-y*xyscale* aspect + nyp2)); }
//-----------------------//

//-------------------------------//
  void Window::moveto(vector2 pt)
//-------------------------------//
 { pixelvector pixel ;
   pixel.x = fx(pt.x) ;   pixel.y = fy(pt.y) ;
   movepix(pixel) ;
 }  // End of moveto

//-------------------------------//
  void Window::lineto(vector2 pt)
//-------------------------------//
 { pixelvector pixel ;
   pixel.x = fx(pt.x) ;   pixel.y = fy(pt.y) ;
   linepix(pixel) ;
 }  // End of lineto

//-----------------------------------------//
  void Window::polyfill(int n, polygon p)
//-----------------------------------------//
// Function to fill CONVEX polygon;  Maximum polygon size is maxpoly=32
 { pixelvector q[maxpoly] ;
   int i ;
   for (i=0 ; i<n ; i++)
       { q[i].x=fx(p[i].x) ; q[i].y=fy(p[i].y) ; }
   polypix(n,q) ;
 }  // End of polyfill

//-------------------------//
  void Window::start(void)
//-------------------------//
 { vpt.prepit(graph_mode) ;
   plt.init(&vpt) ;   win.init(&vpt) ;
 }  // End of start

//-----------//
  void main()
//-----------//
 { cout << "\n Type in the graphics mode \n" ;
   cin >> graph_mode ;
   cout << "\n Type in horizontal size of window \n" ;
   cin >> horizontal ;
   win.Set_parameters() ;
   draw_a_picture() ; vpt.finish() ;
 }  // End of main

//===================U T I L I T I E S=======================================

//-------------------------------------------//
  ostream& operator << (ostream &a, vector3 v)
//-------------------------------------------//
 { return a << v.x << "  " << v.y << "  " << v.z ;
 }  // End of <<

//--------------------------------------------//
  istream& operator >> (istream &a, vector3 &v)
//--------------------------------------------//
 { a >> v.x >> v.y >> v.z ;  return a ;
 }  // End of >>

//-----------------------------------------//
  vector3 operator + (vector3 a, vector3 b)
//-----------------------------------------//
 { vector3 v ;
   v.x = a.x + b.x ; v.y = a.y + b.y ; v.z = a.z + b.z ;  return ( v ) ;
 }  // End of +
```

```
//----------------------------------------//
  vector3 operator * (float mu, vector3 a)
//----------------------------------------//
 { vector3 v ;
   v.x = mu * a.x ;  v.y = mu * a.y ;  v.z = mu * a.z ;  return ( v ) ;
 }  // End of *

//-----------------------------------------//
  vector3 operator - (vector3 a, vector3 b)
//-----------------------------------------//
 { vector3 v ;
   v.x = a.x - b.x ;  v.y = a.y - b.y ;  v.z = a.z - b.z ;  return ( v ) ;
 }  // End of -

//------------------------------//
  vector3 operator - (vector3 a)
//------------------------------//
 { vector3 v ;
   v.x = - a.x ;  v.y = - a.y ;  v.z = - a.z ;  return ( v ) ;
 }  // End of -

//-----------------------------//
  float angle(float x, float y)
//-----------------------------//
// Returns the 'angle' whose tangent is 'y/x'
// All anomalies such as 'x=0' are also checked
 { if (fabs(x) < epsilon)
     if (fabs(y) < epsilon)  return(0.0) ;
     else if (y > 0.0) return(pi*0.5) ;
          else return(pi*1.5) ;
   else if (x < 0.0)  return(atan(y/x)+pi) ;
        else return(atan(y/x)) ;
 }  // End of angle

//------------------//
  float random(void)
//------------------//
// Overloads the "int random(int)" function declared in <stdlib.h>
 { return ( (float) ( (float) rand() / (float) RAND_MAX ) ) ;
 }  // End of random
```

All classes, methods, constants, structure data types and variable information regarding the dimensions of the window are declared in listing 2.1. From now on all graphics programs given in this book (that is, all but those in chapter 3), will use floating point co-ordinate systems via file **"window.cpp"**. This file contains the **main** function (needed in all C++ programs), and **#include**s file **"palette.cpp"** (and hence **"viewport.cpp"**), and so from now on there is no need to include explicitly either a **main** function or the **Viewport** or **Palette** methods. The structure data type **vector2** is declared here to hold the floating point x, y co-ordinates of two-dimensional vectors. For convenience we also declare data type **vector3** to hold floating point x, y, z co-ordinates of three-dimensional vectors.

struct vector2 {float x,y ;} ;
struct vector3 {float x,y,z ;} ;

We declare an array structure type named **polygon** that can hold up to **maxpoly vector2** vertices. We also **#define pi** (π), **epsilon** the smallest acceptable positive floating point number, and the two Boolean constants **TRUE** and **FALSE**.

Listing 2.1 also contains the constructor method **Window**, invoked by **main**, which defines a window with horizontal side length **horiz**. For later convenience the values of **halfhoriz** and **halfvert** are calculated here. The cleared viewport is identified with the window, and the value **xyscale** that maps the window onto the viewport is calculated. We clear the window (=viewport) in a black background (logical colour 0), and the current colour is set to white (logical 15). These default colours can, of course, be changed, at the beginning in **prepit**, or at any other time using **setcol** and/or **erase** methods.

In our **Viewport** methods we have functions which move between pixels or join them in pairs with a line (**movepix** or **linepix**), and we naturally require functions which do the same for points defined in our floating point WINDOW co-ordinate system. Functions **moveto** and **lineto** (listing 2.1) do this by changing a floating point co-ordinate pair to its equivalent pixel and then calling either **movepix** or **linepix**. We also have **polyfill** for area-filling a **polygon** in the current colour. Note that from now on users of our programs need not write a **main** function, it is already given in listing 2.1, from where it reads in the graphics mode and the value of **horiz**. The chosen graphics mode is entered where the viewing parameters are determined, before returning to text mode for further communication with the user. (A subsequent call to **start** will re-enter the chosen graphics mode.) Function **main** then calls function **draw_a_picture**, which precipitates the drawing of all graphics images in the viewport.

Listing 2.2

```
// Application program to draw simple square

#include "viewport.h"
#include "palette.h"
#include "window.h"
extern Window win ;

//---------------------------//
  void draw_a_picture(void)
//---------------------------//
{ vector2 pt1={-1,-1},pt2={1,-1},pt3={1,1},pt4={-1,1} ;
   win.start()    ;   win.moveto(pt1) ;
   win.lineto(pt2) ;                    //  **  interchange  **
   win.lineto(pt3) ;                    //  ** these two lines **
   win.lineto(pt4) ;  win.lineto(pt1) ;
} // End of draw_a_picture
```

Example 2.1

To demonstrate this, a window of horizontal size **horiz** is created (4 is a suitable choice), and a square of side 2 units is drawn inside. (See **draw_a_picture** of listing 2.2 and figure 2.1). Note that the order in which the lines are drawn is critical: if the two marked lines in the listing had been interchanged, then the incorrect figure 2.1b would be produced.

By running a C++ Project that links listing 2.2 (stored as **"two2.cpp"**) with **"window.cpp"** we have the complete program for drawing figure 2.1a.

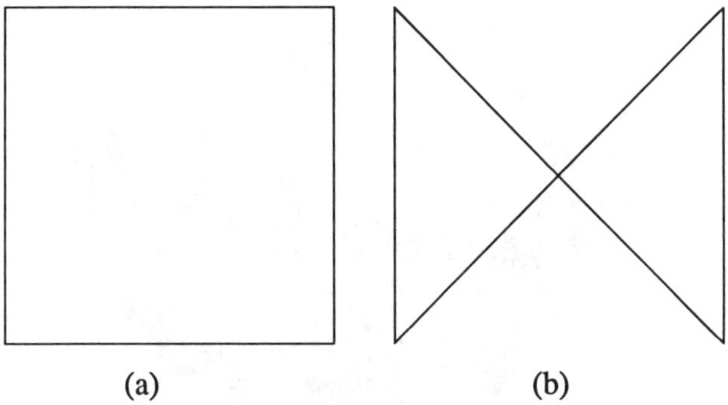

Figure 2.1

Exercise 2.1

Draw separate line pictures of equilateral triangles, pentagons and hexagons; use only calls to **moveto** and **lineto** in code similar to listing 2.2 above. Perhaps you can use a mouse to position the centre of each shape, and to indicate its radius and one of its vertices. Also use **polyfill** to draw a picture with all of these figures in the same window, but with each polygon drawn in a different colour, and at a different centre and orientation.

Example 2.2

All the co-ordinate points constructed in example 2.1 are given explicitly in the program. This is a relatively rare event; usually points are implicitly calculated as the program progresses, as in the next example. Here we produce a general program that places n points ($n \leq$ **maxpoly**) equally spaced at the vertices of a regular n-sided polygon (an *n-gon*), and joins each of these points to every other.

Figure 2.2 shows the pattern produced by **"window.cpp"** linked to the code in listing 2.3, with $n = 21$. The n points are required over and over again in the program, and so it is sensible to calculate them once only, store them in an array, and recall them when necessary. The points are

$$\textbf{pt}[i] = (x_i, y_i) = ((\cos(2\pi i/n), \sin(2\pi i/n)) \quad \text{where } i = 0, 1, ..., n-1.$$

Also note that if the values of i and j are such that $j \leq i$ then the ith point is not joined to the jth point at this stage, since the line will have already been drawn in the opposite direction.

Figure 2.2

Listing 2.3

```
// Application program to draw simple 'point to point' plot
#include "viewport.h"
#include "window.h"
extern Window win ;

//---------------------------//
  void draw_a_picture(void)
//---------------------------//
 { polygon pt ;
   int i,j,n ;
   float theta,thinc ;
// Read in 'n', the number of points (not more than 'maxpoly')
   cout <<  "Type in number of points\n" ; cin >> n ;
// Calculate 'n' points on a unit circle
   theta=0.0 ; thinc=2*pi/n ;
   for (i=0 ; i<n ; i++)
   { pt[i].x=cos(theta) ; pt[i].y=sin(theta) ; theta+=thinc ; } ;
   win.start() ;
// Join point 'i' to point 'j' for all '0 <= i < j < n'
   for (i=0 ; i<n-1 ; i++)
   { for (j=i+1 ; j<n ; j++)
     { win.moveto(pt[i]) ; win.lineto(pt[j]) ; }
   }
 }  // End of draw_a_picture
```

Example 2.3

We draw a circle, centred in the window, with radius value read by the program. We do not assume the availability of a machine-dependent circle function, and use only **moveto** and **lineto**. If your device has a circle-drawing function then also write an alternative circle-drawing function that makes use of this utility.

Obviously it is impossible to draw a smoothly rounded curve with the currently defined **moveto** and **lineto** methods; we can only draw straight lines!

However, we are rescued from this dilemma by the inadequacy of the human optical equipment – the failure of our eyes to resolve very small lines. Notice that in figure 2.2, the boundary of the figure approximates to a circle. If a continuous sequence of small lines is drawn, and this approximates to the curve, then provided that the lines are small enough and the resolution of the viewport large enough, our eyes convince our brain that a proper curve has been drawn. Obviously this process can only produce a picture up to the quality of the resolution of the graphics device you are using. Low-resolution and medium-resolution devices will display circles (and lines) with jagged edges – the *jaggies* or more formally *aliasing*. Some highly sophisticated (and therefore expensive) graphics cards have hardware *anti-aliasing* to minimize this problem.

Therefore, the problem of drawing a circle reduces to one of specifying which lines approximate to that circle. An arbitrary point on a circle of radius r and centre (0.0 , 0.0) may be represented by a vector ($r\cos\theta$, $r\sin\theta$), where θ is the angle that the radius through the point makes with the *positive x-axis*. Hence by incrementing θ between 0 and 2π radians in n equal steps of $2\pi/n$ radians, n+1 points are produced (the first and last are identical), and these, if joined in the order that they are calculated, define an equilateral n-gon with n=**numsides**. If n is large enough then it approximates to a circle. **"window.cpp"** linked into a C++ Project with **"two4.cpp"** (listing 2.4, which incidentally is almost the solution to exercise 2.1), draws a circle (a 100-gon) of given **radius**, centred in the window. Note that in this listing we also draw a *disc* – a coloured-in circle.

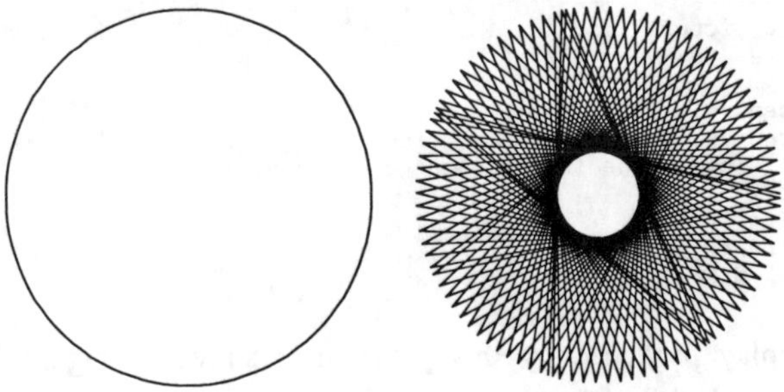

(a) (b)

Figure 2.3

Listing 2.4

```
// Application program to draw a circle and a disc

#include "viewport.h"
#include "window.h"

extern Window win ;
```

```
//--------------------//
  void circle(float r)
//--------------------//
// Draw a circle radius r, centred on the origin
 { float theta = 0.0,thinc = 2.0*pi/100.0 ;
   int i ;
   vector2 pt ;
// Move to first point
   pt.x=r ; pt.y=0.0 ; win.moveto(pt) ;
// Draw edges of 100-gon
   for (i=0 ; i<100 ; i++)
   { theta+=thinc ;
     pt.x=r*cos(theta) ; pt.y=r*sin(theta) ;  win.lineto(pt) ;
   }
 }  // End of circle

//-----------------------------------//
  void disc(vector2 centre, float r)
//-----------------------------------//
// Draw a disc radius r, centred at vector 'centre'
 { float theta,thinc ;
   int i ;
   polygon pt ;
   theta=0.0 ; thinc=2.0*pi/100.0 ;
// Calculate first point
   pt[0].x=centre.x ; pt[0].y=centre.y ;
// Move around 100-gon drawing triangles: origin and 2 neighbouring points
   pt[1].x=centre.x+r ; pt[1].y=centre.y ;
   for (i=0 ; i<100 ; i++)
   { theta+=thinc ;
     pt[2].x=centre.x+r*cos(theta) ; pt[2].y=centre.y+r*sin(theta) ;
// Draw triangle then edge line
     win.setcol(2) ; win.polyfill(3,pt) ;
     win.setcol(4) ; win.moveto(pt[1]) ; win.lineto(pt[2]) ;
     pt[1]=pt[2] ;
   }
 } // End of disc

//-------------------------//
  void draw_a_picture(void)
//-------------------------//
 { float r ;
   vector2 centre = {1,1} ;
// Read in radius; draw circle and disc
   cout << " Please type in radius\n" ;   cin >> r ;
   win.start() ;
   circle(r) ;
   disc(centre,r) ;
 }  // End of draw_a_picture
```

The display produced by this program is shown in figure 2.3a and, as previously stated, the 100 points are not stored but calculated, used and then discarded as the program progresses. This listing also demonstrates that in a C++ program it is essential to give all angular measurement in radians and *not* degrees. If angles are given in degrees – that is **thinc** = 3.6 (=360/100) – then the disastrous figure 2.3b is drawn.

Exercise 2.2

Draw an ellipse with a major axis of 6 units and a minor axis of 4 units centred on the window. Choose the **horiz** value so that the ellipse fits inside the window.

Note that a typical point on this ellipse may be represented as a point vector $(6\cos\theta, 4\sin\theta)$, where $0 \leq \theta < 2\pi$, but it must be remembered that this angle θ is *not* the angle made by the radius through that point with the positive x-axis; it is simply a descriptive parameter. Extend the program so that it draws a super-ellipse $(a \times \cos^r\theta, b \times \sin^r\theta)$, where r is a floating point number. Try the special cases where $r = 3.0$ (an *astroid*) and $r = 0.8$.

Exercise 2.3

Draw a spiral centred on the origin with six turns, and which has an outer radius of six units. A typical point on a spiral of n turns centred on the origin is again of the form $(r\cos\theta, r\sin\theta)$, where now $0 < \theta < 2n\pi$, and the radius r depends on θ – it equals the outer radius multiplied by $\theta/2n\pi$. Give a general function which centres the spiral of outer radius **radius** and **n** turns at any **vector2** point **centre**. Also generalize your function so that the value of θ now varies between a given angle **phi** and **phi+2nπ**.

It is now time to consider some more attractive examples to illustrate how, even with only a beginner's knowledge of computer graphics, it is still possible to draw aesthetically pleasing patterns. Drawing such patterns is an excellent way of familiarizing yourself with your graphics device, before going on to the more complex three-dimensional displays.

Figure 2.4

Example 2.4

The following two examples will also involve the sine (**sin**) and cosine (**cos**) functions. Consider figure 2.4, composed of a sequence of **numtriang** equilateral triangles, with radii diminishing from **outer_radius** in equal steps down to almost zero, placed on top of one another. Each triangle is rotated by a constant angle from its predecessor, so that the angle between first and last triangles is **total_rotation** radians. The colours of neighbouring triangles cycle through logical colours 1 to 7. This is programmed in listing 2.5.

Listing 2.5

```
// Application program to draw a spiral of triangles; then rotate palette
#include "viewport.h"
#include "palette.h"
#include "window.h"

extern Palette plt ;
extern Window  win ;
//------------------------------------------------------------------------//
 void triangles(int numtriang, float outer_radius, float total_rotation)
//------------------------------------------------------------------------//
 { int i ;
   float r,rdif,theta,thinc ;
   polygon pt ;
// Draw numtriang triangles; outer triangle has radius numlevel
// Reduce each new triangle by rdif, and rotate it by angle thinc
   r=outer_radius ;  rdif=outer_radius/numtriang ;
   theta=0.0 ;  thinc=total_rotation/(numtriang-1) ;
   for (i=0 ; i<numtriang ; i++)
   { pt[0].x=r*cos(theta)         ; pt[0].y=r*sin(theta)         ;
     pt[1].x=r*cos(theta+2*pi/3) ; pt[1].y=r*sin(theta+2*pi/3) ;
     pt[2].x=r*cos(theta+4*pi/3) ; pt[2].y=r*sin(theta+4*pi/3) ;
// Run through the colours modulo 7
     win.setcol(1+(i % 7)) ; win.polyfill(3,pt) ;
     theta+=thinc ; r-=rdif;
   }
 }  // End of triangles

//-------------------------//
 void draw_a_picture(void)
//-------------------------//
 { int numtriang,i,cycle,index ;
   float outer_radius,total_rotation ;
   float red[8], green[8], blue[8] ;
// Create spiral of triangles
   cout << "Type number of triangles, outer radius and total rotation " ;
   cin >> numtriang >> outer_radius >> total_rotation ;
   win.start() ;
   triangles(numtriang,outer_radius,total_rotation) ;
// Store RGB components of logical colours 1 to 7
   for (i=1 ; i<8 ; i++)
   { red[i]   = (float) ((i / 4) % 2) ;
     green[i] = (float) ((i / 2) % 2) ;
     blue[i]  = (float) (i % 2) ;
     plt.rgblog(i, red[i], green[i], blue[i]) ;
   }
// cycle through the logical colours
   for (cycle=0 ; cycle <100 ; cycle++)
   { index = cycle ;
     for (i=1 ; i<8 ; i++)
     { index = index % 7 + 1 ;
       plt.rgblog(i,red[index],green[index],blue[index]) ;
     }
   }
 }  // End of draw_a_picture
```

Also notice how, after the figure is complete, these logical colours are redefined cyclically using **Palette** method **rgblog.** On some cards, particularly the VGA, you will notice that the time for cycling through the colours is irregular – this is the effect of the finite time needed to fill the communication buffer.

Example 2.5

The last program in this chapter can be used to produce shapes like that in figure 2.5. These images are reminiscent of the art of Vasarely. The idea is to consider points inside a square of side two, and to distort those that lie inside a unit circle (the sums of squares of the x and y co-ordinates are not greater than unity). This distortion takes two forms. Firstly, each point inside the unit circle is put into the form ($\mathbf{r}\cos\theta$, $\mathbf{r}\sin\theta$), where θ is the angle made by that point with the positive x-axis, and **r** (≤ 1) is its distance from the centre. It is then moved to position ($\mathbf{r}^{\mathbf{p}}\cos\theta$, $\mathbf{r}^{\mathbf{p}}\sin\theta$) for some value of **p.** Secondly, the point is rotated by a further angle **(1–r) * rotation.** Obviously we cannot draw the infinity of points inside the square, and this raises the question of exactly what do we draw? What we actually do is to consider the square divided into a 21 by 21 grid lines, with each grid line defined as a sequence of 201 points. It is these points on the grid lines that are distorted, and then joined in their original sequence order.

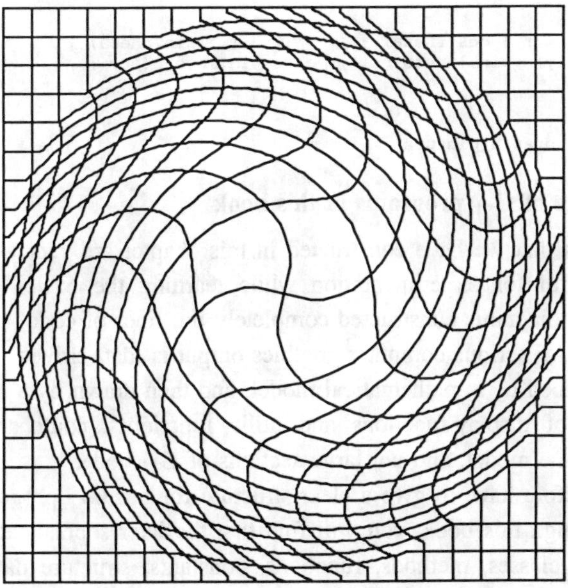

Figure 2.5

Listing 2.6

```
// Application program to draw Vasarely figure

#include "viewport.h"
#include "palette.h"
#include "window.h"

extern Window win ;

//--------------------------//
  void draw_a_picture(void)
//--------------------------//
 { int ix,iy,inhorizontal ;
   float r,p,rotation, theta,x,y,xyswap ;
   vector2 pt ;
   cout << "\nType in power factor for distortion and rotation value : " ;
   cin >> p >> rotation ;              // Try with 0.5 and 2.0
   win.start() ;
   win.setcol(14) ;
   for (inhorizontal = 0 ; inhorizontal <= 1 ; inhorizontal++ )
   { for (ix = 0 ; ix <=20 ; ix++)
     { for (iy = 0 ; iy <= 200 ; iy++ )
       { x = ix * 0.1 - 1.0 ;
         y = iy * 0.01 - 1.0 ;
         if (inhorizontal)
           { xyswap = x ; x = y ; y = xyswap ; }
         r = sqrt(x*x+y*y) ;
         theta = angle(x,y) ;
         if( r < 1.0 )
           { if ( r > 0.0 )
               { r=exp(log(r)*p) ;
                 theta += (1.0-r)*rotation ;
               } ;
           } ;
         pt.x = r * cos(theta) ;    pt.y = r * sin(theta) ;
         if (iy)  win.lineto(pt) ;  else win.moveto(pt) ;
       }
     }
   }
 }  // End of draw_a_picture
```

The structure of C++ programs in this book

The diagrams that we have constructed in this chapter are very attractive, and they are useful for experimentation while learning the basics of computer graphics. But diagrams constructed completely by 'lines of code' can only ever be 'one off'. All serious computer graphics output is 'data-driven' – each scene will be described by a mathematical model, and then drawn by a sophisticated, yet fixed, set of 'display functions' and 'utility functions'. You change the scene by changing the model, and not large sections of C++ code.

We therefore have to give a clear structure for our C++ programs. As you progress through this book, you will find that the later sophisticated programs build on the classes, methods, functions, constants, structure data types and variables defined earlier. The C++ language, and particularly the Borland implementation, has ideal mechanisms (classes, **#include, extern** and Project) to enable this requirement. These language constructs can be defined and stored in named **".cpp"** files, and their header declarations, **".h"** files, can be **#include**d into larger programs. The **".h"** form of classes **Viewport, Palette** and **Window** will be **#include**d, either directly or indirectly, into *every* graphics program given in this book.

In the many listings that follow, each function is intended to solve a specific problem, and there may be a number of different versions of each one: see the Index of Functions at the end of the book for the complete list. Groups of functions dealing with a specific problem domain will be added to an include-library file. For example, the function **seefacet** is used to prepare the display of a polygonal facet on the surface of a three-dimensional object. There are a number of versions of this function, one which prepares to fill the facet in a fixed colour, and others which use smooth shading. The particular version of **seefacet** that you will need for a particular choice of shading, along with the other functions dealing with the display of objects, will be added to a file we call **"display.cpp"**.

In fact our package will consist of a series of pairs files, with names like **"display"**, **"material"**, **"matrix"**, **"mesh"**, **"model"**, **"stack"**: we have already seen **"viewport"**, **"palette"** and **"window"**. Those files containing the code for functions will have a **".cpp"** extension, while the corresponding header files will have a **".h"** extension. Every listing we give, other than final applications, will contain the code that should be added to one such file: a comment at the beginning of each listing will indicate the file name and its extension. Some listings will give an initial version of a particular **".cpp"** file, while later listings give further functions to extend files, or to replace functions within such a file. To make things simpler, when it comes to creating a new file, if at all possible, the corresponding **".h"** file will be given in its final and complete form. It will include all the definitions necessary for every version of the corresponding **".cpp"** file that we may generate as we progress through the book. When we give a **".cpp"** and **".h"** pair, the listing numbers will be extended by an 'a' and a 'b' respectively, such as listings 2.1a and 2.1b.

As we mentioned above, if a named function from a particular listing is to be used either to extend a file, or to replace a function with the same name in that file, then the name of the file will be indicated by a comment at the beginning of the code listing. Listings without such a comment are the application programs (such as **build_it**) that are to be expanded into a complete program by means of **#includ(e)**ing the **".h"** library files indicated in that listing, and linking the corresponding **".cpp"** files into a C++ Project.

As you delve deeper into this book, culminating with the display of complex three-dimensional scenes, you will find that you have already been given most of the files you will need. Note that the unique **main** function for all our remaining graphics programs has already been defined in the file that contains the **Window** class (listing 2.1b). In turn, **main** calls **draw_a_picture**; we will give a few simple examples of its use in the next few chapters. But when it comes to drawing three-dimensional images, **draw_a_picture** will be stored in file **"model.cpp"**, that in turn will call functions to control the modelling of mathematically defined scenes (a function that will be called **build_it**), to set the position of the observer and light sources, and to display the model. In fact you will only need to write a few functions for modelling space, to be called from your own particular version of **build_it**. With most of our three-dimensional programs that follow, it is the **build_it** function that initiates the sequence of **#include**d functions, which culminates in complete programs. You will be given a number of examples showing you how to create your own **build_it** functions, each of which will link into the book's package of files and classes using the Project mechanism of Borland C++.

To be in a position to create these files and three-dimensional models, it is first necessary to understand some basic data structures and elementary mathematical techniques. Therefore the next few chapters, which lead on to the drawing of three-dimensional scenes, will, for the most part, leave the graphics temporarily behind in order to concentrate on these theoretical prerequisites, and on the setting up of files essential for later programs.

Project 2.1

Construct a database suitable for drawing various views of a spherical globe, storing point data in the form of Mercator projection: a point on a rectangular plane is identified by two angular parameters θ (latitude) and ϕ (longitude). The values of these two parameters lie in the ranges $-\pi \le \theta \le \pi$ and $-\pi/2 \le \phi \le \pi/2$. Line and polygon data are defined as pairs and lists of points respectively. A Mercator point (θ,ϕ) can be projected onto a three-dimensional vector (x, y, z) on a unit sphere by the formulae:

$$x = \sin\theta \times \cos\phi \; ; \quad y = \sin\phi \; ; \quad z = \cos\theta \times \cos\phi$$

Unfortunately lines (and of course the edges of polygons) are projected into curves on the globe. But if we move in small steps between Mercator end points of such lines, and projecting each small line segment onto the sphere, then we create a sequence of lines on the globe that approximate to the required curve. These lines can be drawn by ignoring the z-values of the end points, treating them as simple x/y coordinates. However, care must be taken because these curves may move round the edge of the globe onto the 'dark side', when they should then disappear: you must find the point where the curve crosses the edge of the globe, and only draw line segments up to and including that point.

3 Data structures

In the previous chapter we saw examples of subscripted variables, otherwise known as arrays. Here we are going to discuss the general use in computer graphics of this and other *abstract data structures*. In particular, we consider the implementation in C++ of those structures that are necessary for the complex graphics algorithms we describe later. In this chapter we limit our discussion to only those data structures that will be of value in this book; for readers who wish to find out more about this subject we recommend books by Knuth (1973), Aho, Hopcroft and Ullman (1983), and Horowitz and Sahni (1990).

Arrays and subscripted variables

We assume that readers are well aware of the concept of *subscripts* – that is, the grouping together of data of the same type under one name (or *identifier*), and the accessing of individuals within the grouping (or *array*) by use of subscripts. Counting with subscripts can start at either 0 or 1. In FORTRAN 77 and other computer languages, and in most mathematical texts, counting starts at 1. For example, the first five prime numbers can be given the name $\boldsymbol{p}$ – that is $\boldsymbol{p}$ represents all the numbers 2, 3, 5, 7, 11. $\boldsymbol{p}$ is an array of five elements, and an individual from within that grouping is indicated by a subscript; thus $\boldsymbol{p}_5$ indicates the fifth and final member of the array (the prime number 11). In C++, however, subscript counts always start at 0 – we have already seen this in chapter 1. So in the above example, the five prime numbers would be $\boldsymbol{p}_0$, $\boldsymbol{p}_1$, $\boldsymbol{p}_2$, $\boldsymbol{p}_3$ and $\boldsymbol{p}_4$, where the prime 11 is now final member $\boldsymbol{p}_4$ of the array, and there is NO member $\boldsymbol{p}_5$! The first method of counting subscripts (starting at 1) is deeply ingrained in our mathematical culture, as well as in our thought processes, so a change to the C++ way of counting, which is also the computer science way, can cause subtle problems (the peculiar idea that the second member of a group is $\boldsymbol{p}_1$!). On the surface, it would appear wise to be consistent and choose just one method of counting; and that obviously has to be the C++ method since we are programming in the C++ language. But it is just as obvious to use the mathematical method, since so much of computer graphics relies heavily on the standard mathematical texts and the notation of matrix algebra! One compromise, that is often adopted by applications programmers when using C++, is to declare an array with one element more than is actually needed (6 in our prime number example), and then to ignore totally (and waste) the element with subscript 0, thus emulating the mathematical methods, and restoring p_5 in the prime example above! There are many situations in the computer science domain, however, where it is sensible to start the count at 0! For example, most graphics devices based on the concept of 8 *bit-planes*, that is those with a 256 colour display such as VGA mode 19, use one 8-bit word to hold the index to the colour table, and so the indices of the colour subscripts are naturally 0 to 255! Because of this impasse, our book will compromise, mostly using the C++ method of counting, except in situations where it is more convenient to use the mathematical approach. But you must always be aware of which method is being used, or you can easily lose elements from the front or back of arrays! Remember there is no range checking in C++, and errors in array indices can be disastrous.

Naturally, in C++ all statements occur on a line, not above or below the line, and so no subscripts (or superscripts for that matter) are possible – instead each one (or more) subscript is placed inside pairs of square bracket[s]. In listing 1.3 for example, the three elements of array **poly** are the triangle of pixel vectors **poly[0]**, **poly[1]** and **poly[2]**.

Often the subscript is identified by a *variable name*; therefore p_i is the element i (in whatever counting method we are using) of the array, where i must be in the range of possible subscripts (allowing for the counting method). In the text that follows, double dots (..) will be used to specify a *range* or *subrange* of index values; for example, **p[3..k]** indicates the array values **p[3]**, **p[4]**, ..., **p[k]**.

It is possible for an array to have multiple subscripts; for example, in an m by n array (a double subscripted array – an array of arrays) identified with the name a, the individual element in *row* i and *column* j ($0 \le i < m$ and $0 \le j < n$) is indicated by a_{ij}. In a C++ program, this array would be declared as **a[m][n]**, and the individual element would be **a[i][j]**, but remember, because of index counting, elements **a[i][n]** and **a[m][j]** do not exist for any values of **i** and **j**. This is a major problem when dealing with *matrices*, and so in this book we have decided always to differentiate between an **m** by **n** array and an **m** by **n** matrix. Mathematical texts always vary the matrix indices from 1 to **m** and from 1 to **n**, yet the array **a** above, declared in C++, has indices varying from 0 to **m**−1 and from 0 to **n**−1. Therefore, in order to conform with mathematical notation, in this book an **m** by **n** matrix will always be declared as an (**m**+1) by (**n**+1) array. (In order to highlight this further, the array will always be given an identifier written in upper case letters (**A** say).) Then by using the subranges **A[1..m][1..n]**, it is possible to implement the mathematical interpretations of matrices.

We shall see the importance and power of matrices and arrays when we deal with the concept of vertex co-ordinates and facets in the chapters on three-dimensional space. (A *facet* is a closed convex polygon which is normally defined by the co-planar vertices that form the corners of the polygon.) For example, a set of three-dimensional vertices can be grouped together, and the *x*, *y* and *z* co-ordinates can be stored as an array of the structure type **vector3**, **v** (say), where the vertex **i** is **v[i]**. Hence the vertex **i** from the set will have Cartesian co-ordinates **(v[i].x , v[i].y , v[i].z)**.

However, the use of arrays has drawbacks in certain situations, as in the case where the grouping of data in a double subscripted array is *sparse*. For example, we could have a *static array* of **m** *sets* of integer data which we call a *mesh*, where the largest set contains **n** values, but on average the sets contain **n/4** values (say). If we store the mesh as an **m** by **n** array, then only about a quarter of the array locations **(m*n/4)** would be used. This is exactly the situation we find when creating models of geometrical objects in three-dimensional space.

A polygonal mesh

When creating such models we approximate to the surface of each geometrical object with a mesh of polygonal facets, just as in chapter 2 we approximated a curve (a circle) with a sequence of small line segments. So our *mesh data structure* will be an array of facets. This still leaves us with the problem of how to represent each facet! The simplest way is the one mentioned above, that is an array of arrays. But suppose in a given polygonal approximation we have a total of **nof** facets, that could be either triangles or dodecagons (say). Each individual facet can be defined by an array holding the vertices on its perimeter, taken in order. If most of the polygons are triangles, it is obviously inefficient to use a **nof** by 12 array (an array of **nof** elements, each element an array of 12 values) to store the vertices in the scene.

Instead we will use a mesh data structure that is set up in a special class, as an array of *pointers*, each pointer indicating another data structure that represents an individual facet. The mesh therefore may be implemented as an array of C++ pointers. Many programming languages (including C++) have pointers built into the language; however, there are some cases where it is more efficient to implement pointers explicitly using arrays of integers. Below we will give both explicit and implicit methods for solving this problem, which is fundamental to our manipulation of three-dimensional space. Surprisingly, the explicit integer array method (listing 3.1) uses less storage space than the implicit method (listing 3.3), and so it is the former method that will be used in the rest of this book.

We describe the explicit method first. Suppose each of **nof** polygonal facets, **nof ≤ maxf**, is identified by an integer value **i** between **0** and **nof–1**. An integer index, **firstoffacet[i]**, sometimes called a *cursor* (that is, a pointer), is used to indicate the beginning of the data about facet **i**. The data on each facet is placed within a large array, **listofverts**, to store the indices of the vertices of each facet, so that all the data of facet **i** (except facet 0) comes immediately after those of facet **i–1**. Given that facet **i** has the indices of **size[i]** vertices stored in locations of array **listofverts**, these indices of the vertices of this facet are to be found in the **size[i]** consecutive locations:

listofverts[firstoffacet[i]], ... , listofverts[firstoffacet[i]+size[i]–1]

Note that in our implementation, the index of the final vertex of facet **i** is not **firstoffacet[i]+size[i]** but **firstoffacet[i]+size[i]–1**. Also we introduce a variable **firstfree** which points to the first available unused location in the **listofverts** array, which makes it easier to add a new facet to the mesh. The declarations of this data structure are stored in file **"mesh.h"**, with methods in **"mesh.cpp"**; see listings 3.1a and 3.1b respectively. Note that in listings 7.3a and 7.3b we will be introducing a brand new version of the **Mesh** class, with new functions that must replace the present versions of files **"mesh.h"** and **"mesh.cpp"**.

When we expand file **"mesh.cpp"** later in the book, the real value of this data structure will become apparent. But in order to demonstrate the use of the mesh data structure here, we give a rather artificial example in listing 3.2, which will **#include** the two files of the **Mesh** class. This allows the user to create a set of up to 800 facets by inputting, for each of **nof** facets, a list of the vertex indices that make up that facet. Afterwards, by typing in the number of any facet, the program prints out the list of vertex indices for that facet.

In the study of data structures it is often useful to draw diagrams that represent them. One-dimensional arrays are normally represented as a row (or column) of boxes holding the array values; if necessary integer indices are placed outside the relevant boxes. If an integer value is used as a pointer then it is sometimes drawn in the diagram as an arrow; one end indicates where the integer is stored and the other which location is being pointed at. A pointer which points nowhere (!), the *null pointer* (see figure 3.2), as in the case where the size of a facet is zero, is usually represented by a diagonal line.

Example 3.1

Figure 3.1 shows a data structure diagram that represents the outcome of the program given in listing 3.2, which **#include**s the **Mesh**.

Exercise 3.1

There is strictly no need to include the **size** array in the **Mesh** class, after all **size[i]** is equal to **firstoffacet[i+1]–firstoffacet[i]**. We only used the **size** array explicitly to aid our explanation in the text. You can change our programs to avoid using the **size** locations if you wish; try it with listing 3.1b, but note that you will now need a value for **firstoffacet[nof]**.

Listing 3.1a

```
// Store as file "mesh.h"
#define maxf       800        // Maximum number of facets allowed
#define maxlist   3000        // Maximum size of the heap
//----------//
  class Mesh
//----------//
 { int firstoffacet[maxf] ;
   int size[maxf] ;
   int listofverts[maxlist] ;
   int firstfree ;
   int nof ;
  public:
   Mesh() ;
   void add(int flength, int *verts) ;
   void printfacet(int facetid) ;
   int Get_nof(void) { return ( nof ) ; } ;
 } ;  // End of class Mesh
```

Listing 3.1b

```
// Store as file "mesh.cpp"

//------------//
  Mesh::Mesh()
//------------//
 { int i ;
   firstfree = 0 ;  nof = 0 ;
   for (i=0 ; i<maxf ; i++)
      { firstoffacet[i] = 0 ;  size[i] = 0 ;
      }
 }  // End of Mesh

//----------------------------------------//
  void Mesh::add(int flength, int *verts)
//----------------------------------------//
 { int j ;
   if (flength != 0)
   { size[nof] = flength ;
     firstoffacet[nof] = firstfree ;
     if (firstfree > maxlist)
       { cerr << "\n Error, size of list array exceeded" ;
         return ;
       }
     firstfree = firstoffacet[nof]+flength ;
     for (j=0 ; j<flength ; j++)
       { listofverts[firstoffacet[nof]+j] = verts[j] ;
       }
     nof++ ;
   }
 }  // End of add

//----------------------------------//
  void Mesh::printfacet(int facetid)
//----------------------------------//
 { int j ;
   if ((facetid >= 0) & (facetid < nof))
   { if (size[facetid] == 0) cout << "Empty facet \n" ;
     else
       { for (j=0 ; j<size[facetid] ; j++)
           cout << "  " << listofverts[firstoffacet[facetid]+j] ;
         cout << "\n" ;
       } ;
   } ;
 }  // End of printfacet
```

Listing 3.2

```
// Trivial application program to demonstrate the use of the Mesh

#include <iostream.h>
#define maxpoly 32

#include "mesh.h"
#include "mesh.cpp"

//-----------//
  void main()
//-----------//
 { int i, j, nof, whichfacet, length ;
   int a_facet[maxpoly] ;
   Mesh msh ;
// Create sets and place in array 'listofsets'
   do { cout << " How many facets in mesh ?\n" ;  cin >> nof ; }
   while ((nof <= 0) || (nof >maxf)) ;
// Read in members of i'th set
   for (i=0 ; i<nof ; i++)
   { cout << " How many vertices in facet " <<  i << "\n" ;
     cin >> length ;
     if (length!= 0)
     { cout << " Type in " << length << " integers\n" ;
       for (j=0 ; j<length ; j++)   cin >> a_facet[j] ;
     } ;
     msh.add(length,a_facet) ;
   } ;
// Output any facet
   do { cout << " Which facet do you wish output\n" ;
        cin >> whichfacet ;
        if ((whichfacet >= 0) & (whichfacet < msh.Get_nof()))
        msh.printfacet(whichfacet) ;
      }
   while (whichfacet < msh.Get_nof() ) ;
// Finish by entering facet number greater than nof
 }  // End of main
```

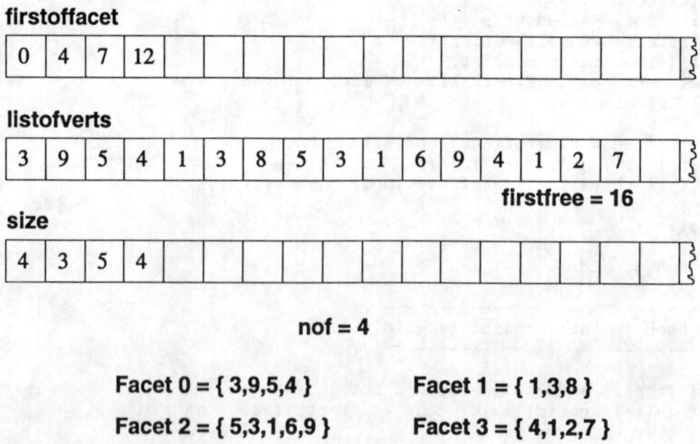

Figure 3.1

Linked lists

Not all information is static. There are so-called *dynamic* data structures where information can be added and/or discarded from the grouping. When using arrays to represent such structures, we have to allow space for the maximum size of the grouping. But worse, discarded information will leave holes in the array, which often requires resequencing of the array entries – a very time-consuming process. One such dynamic data structure which avoids these problems, and which will be used many times throughout this book, is the *linked list* or *linear list.*

Like an array, a linked list is a means of grouping together elements of the same type, but, unlike an array, the information in such a structure is not accessed by an index, but instead by a movable pointer. A linked list is made up of separate cells, and each cell consists of two parts: the *information part* which contains a value of the type being grouped together, and the *pointer part* which links the cell to the next in the chain. This implies the existence of

(a) a pointer to the front cell of a list
(b) a *null pointer* which indicates an empty list or the end of a list, and
(c) a facility whereby a variable pointer will enable us to move along the list, accessing individual cells one at a time.

The manipulation of such a structure can be quite complex. We could

(1) add new cells to the front, back or at a specified position within a list
(2) read/print/delete cells from the front, back or specified position in a list
(3) make copies of a list
(4) reverse a list
(5) impose an *ordering* on how new elements are stored in a list.

Since most implementations of the C++ language incorporate the identifier **NULL** to represent the null pointer, and this value is usually set to zero, we will use the same convention. If **NULL** is not implicitly part of your system then you must **#define** it as zero.

To illustrate these ideas we give in listings 3.3a and 3.3b, a second version of the **Mesh** class that uses pointers, and can be used to replace listings 3.1a and 3.1b respectively. **#included** into listing 3.2, they give a program equivalent to that of example 3.1. Note the similarities and the differences in these two forms of **Mesh**. The second pair of listings show how to set up dynamic data structures in C++, by defining the type of a list element, **facetnode**, one of whose members will be a pointer, **ptr**, to (or address of) another element of the same type.

Note how again we have an array **firstoffacet** with **maxf** locations, although now each location is a pointer to a structure type **facetnode**. Initially empty, when the mesh is complete each location will point to a linear list representing a single facet. The information part of each cell will contain the index of one vertex on the facet, and the sequence of vertices in each list is in the order they occur on the facet by moving from the first vertex through its neighbours in turn. Figure 3.2 shows a diagram involving pointers, that is equivalent to figure 3.1.

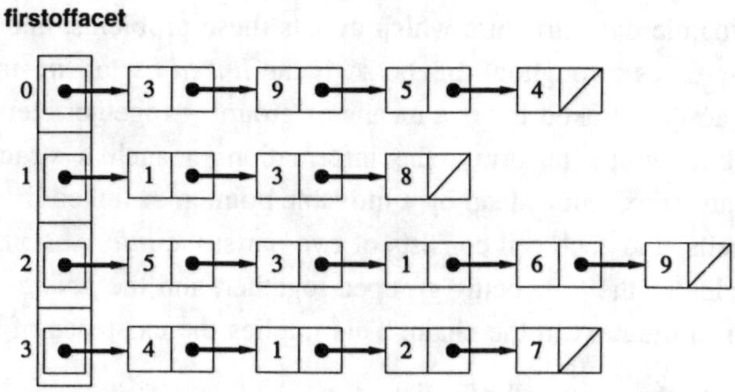

Figure 3.2

Listing 3.3a

```
// Store as file "mesh.h"; basis of Mesh, extra methods added in chapter 7
#include <iostream.h>
#define maxf        800                     // Maximum number of facets allowed
struct facetnode { int vertex ; facetnode * ptr ; } ;

//----------//
  class Mesh
//----------//
 { facetnode * firstoffacet[maxf] ;
   int size[maxf] ;
   int nof ;
  public:
   Mesh() ;
   void add(int flength, int *verts) ;
   void printfacet(int facetid) ;
   int Get_nof(void) { return ( nof ) ; } ;
 } ;   // End of class Mesh
```

Listing 3.3b

```
// Store as file "mesh.cpp"; extra methods added in chapter 7

//------------//
  Mesh::Mesh()
//------------//
 { int i ;
   nof = 0 ;
   for (i=0 ; i<maxf ; i++)
   { firstoffacet[i] = NULL ;  size[i] = 0 ;
   }
 }  // End of Mesh
```

```
//---------------------------------------//
  void Mesh::add(int flength, int *verts)
//---------------------------------------//
 { int i ;
   facetnode *p, *q ;
   p = NULL ;
   if (flength != 0)
   { size[nof] = flength ;
     for (i=flength-1 ; i>=0 ; i--)
     { q = new (facetnode) ;
       if (q==NULL) { cerr << "\n Error, out of memory" ; return ; }
       q->vertex = verts[i] ;
       q->ptr = p ;
       p = q ;
     }
   }
   firstoffacet[nof++] = p ;
 }  // End of add

//----------------------------------//
  void Mesh::printfacet(int facetid)
//----------------------------------//
 { facetnode *p ;
   if ((facetid >= 0) & (facetid < nof))
   { p = firstoffacet[facetid] ;
     if (p == NULL) cout << "Facet is empty\n" ;
     else
       { while (p != NULL)
         { cout << p->vertex << "  " ;
           p = p->ptr ;
         }
         cout << "\n" ;
       } ;
   } ;
 }  // End of printfacet
```

Stacks

There are many, many more possibilities and variations of the list data structure and the use of pointers. The linked list is a very powerful tool, and has a wide range of applications in computer science. For the needs of this book, however, we will concentrate on a restricted form of a list, known as a *stack*, where cells can only be added to, and deleted from, the front of the list: the so-called *push* and *pop* functions respectively. In order to make our implementation of a stack as general as possible, the information part of elements in the list will be a general record structure, **stackinfo**, to be read in from a file **"stackinf.cpp"**.

We use C++ pointers in implementing a class **Stack**, with the details stored as two files **"stack.h"** and **"stack.cpp"**, in listings 3.4a and 3.4b respectively. We will use this class extensively; some more complex versions of **Stack** can be seen in the chapters on analytical modelling to be found at the end of the book. In our version there are six methods for manipulating the **Stack**, namely the constructor, destructor, **push, pop, Get_stack** (which puts all the information stored in the stack into an array), and **empty** which returns **TRUE** (1) or **FALSE** (0) depending on whether the stack is empty or not. When needed a new stack is instantiated as an object of the class **Stack** and is initialised by its declaration.

Listing 3.4a

```
// Store this code as file "stack.h"
#include <iostream.h>
#include "stackinf.cpp"
struct stackcell { stackinfo info ; stackcell *ptr ; } ;

//-----------//
  class Stack
//-----------//
 { stackcell *top ;

  public:
   Stack() ;
   ~Stack() ;
   void push(stackinfo value) ;
   stackinfo pop(void) ;
   int Get_stack(stackinfo *l) ;
   int empty(void) { return ( top == NULL ) ; }
 } ;  // End of class Stack
```

Listing 3.4b

```
// Store this code as file "stack.cpp"

//--------------//
  Stack::Stack()   { top = NULL ; }  // End of Stack
//--------------//

//---------------//
  Stack::~Stack()
//---------------//
 { stackcell *p ;
   while (top != NULL) { p=top->ptr ; delete top ; top=p ; }
   delete top ;
 }  // End of ~Stack

//----------------------------------//
  void Stack::push(stackinfo value)
//----------------------------------//
 { stackcell *p ;
   p = new stackcell ;
   if (p == NULL) { cerr << "\n Error, stack out of memory" ; return ; }
   p->info=value ;   p->ptr=top ;   top=p ;
 }  // End of push

//---------------------------//
  stackinfo Stack::pop(void)
//---------------------------//
 { stackinfo value ;
   stackcell *p ;
   value=top->info ;  p=top->ptr ; delete (top) ;  top=p ;
   return(value) ;
 }  // End of pop

//------------------------------------//
  int Stack::Get_stack(stackinfo *l)
//------------------------------------//
 { int count = 0 ;
   stackcell *p ;
   p=top ;
   while (p != NULL)  { l[count++] = p->info ;  p=p->ptr ; }
   return ( count ) ;
 }  // End of Get_stack
```

Example 3.2
We demonstrate this with a contrived program, listing 3.5, which **#include**s the files **"stack.h"** and **"stack.cpp"**, and instantiates and manipulates two simple stack objects, **stack1** and **stack2**, each holding a **stackinfo** structure consisting of a single integer. The necessary file **"stackinf.cpp"** is given in listing 3.4c.

Listing 3.4c

```
// Store this line as file "stackinf.cpp"
 struct stackinfo { int i ; } ;
```

The program in listing 3.5 manipulates two lists **stack1** and **stack2** – note the authors' preference for the mathematical counting method and their avoidance of a **stack0**! The *box and pointer diagram* of the resulting data structure is given in figure 3.3, where boxes now show the individual cells in the linear list, and the arrows indicate connections between the cells. These data structure diagrams are typical examples of those found in most data structure textbooks.

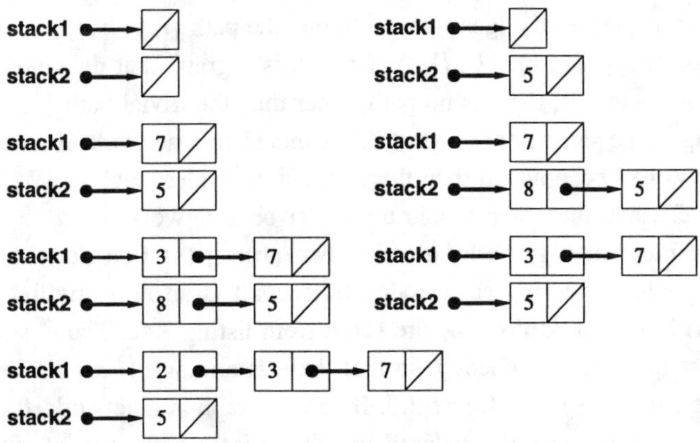

Figure 3.3

Listing 3.5

```
// Application program to demonstrate 'push' and 'pop' Stack methods

#include "stack.h"
#include "stack.cpp"

ostream& operator << (ostream &a, stackinfo v) { return a << v.i ; }

//----------------------------//
  void printstack(Stack *stk)
//----------------------------//
 { while ( ! stk->empty() ) cout << "  " << stk->pop() ;
 }  //End of printstack
```

```
//-----------//
  void main()
//-----------//
// Create two stacks : 'stack1' and 'stack2'
 { Stack stack1, stack2 ;
   stackinfo s ;
   s.i = 5 ;  stack1.push(s) ; s.i = 7 ;  stack1.push(s) ;  // Sample 'push'es
   s.i = 8 ;  stack2.push(s) ; s.i = 3 ;  stack2.push(s) ;
   cout << "\nPopping " << stack2.pop() << " from stack2" ; // A sample 'pop'
// Another 'push'
   s.i = 2 ;  stack1.push(s) ;
// write out the two stacks
   cout << "\n stack1: " ; printstack(&stack1) ;
   cout << "\n stack2: " ; printstack(&stack2) ;
// In Borland C++ type ALT F5 to view screen output
 }  // End of main
```

Directed graphs and networks

Another very important data structure in computer graphics is the *directed graph*, or more specifically the restricted form of graph called a *directed network*. A directed graph is a set of *nodes* and *directed edges*: see figure 3.4. For simplicity we label the n nodes of a graph with the integers 0, ..., n–1. A directed edge, say from node i to node j, is denoted by $\{i , j\}$. A *path* in a directed graph is a consecutive sequence of edges – for example, the path $\{i , j , k , l\}$ consists of the three edges $\{i , j\}$, $\{j , k\}$, $\{k , l\}$. A network is a graph that does not contain a *cycle* or *loop* – that is, there is no path, other than the trivial path $\{i , i\}$, starting and ending at the same node. Figure 3.4 is therefore a network: if an extra edge $\{5 , 2\}$ (say) had been added then there would be cycles, such as $\{2 , 5 , 2\}$ and $\{2 , 3 , 5 , 2\}$, and the graph would no longer be a network.

We implement a graph by creating two arrays; the first **edgein** holds the number of edges entering each node, the second is an array **netlist** of **Stack** objects, with the **stackinfo** structure taken from listing 3.4c. The ith stack object holds a list of all node indices j, so that there is an edge $\{i , j\}$ in the network from node i to node j. See figure 3.5. If such a graph is a network, then we say that the n nodes are *partially ordered*, and that it is possible to print out the node labels in a *topological order*. A topological order of a network is a permutation of the integers 0, ..., n–1,

$$[I_0 , I_1 , \dots , I_{n-1}]$$

such that there are no values i and j, $0 \le i < j < n$, for which there is a path in the network leading backwards in the order from node I_j to node I_i. Note that a topological order for a network need not be unique. For example, in figure 3.4 the permutations [0 , 1 , 2 , 3 , 4 , 5 , 6] and [0 , 2 , 1 , 3 , 5 , 4 , 6] are both valid topological orders.

A function to find a topological order for a network is given in listing 3.6. It **#includes** the **"stack.h"** and **"stack.cpp"** files, the former **#includes** the file

"stackinf.cpp", to deal with all stack manipulation needed by the algorithm. This algorithm also keeps another stack of integers, **entrystack**, which holds a list of all the nodes in the network with no edges entering them. Each time **entrystack** is popped, we delete that node and any edges leaving that node, from the network. Traversing the list in **netlist** for the deleted node allows us to delete edges from the network and decrement the corresponding values in the **edgein** array. This throws up further nodes with no edges entering them, and these are also pushed onto **entrystack**. After *n* pops, we have a topological ordering: if the stack becomes empty before this point, then the graph has a cycle, and is therefore not a network.

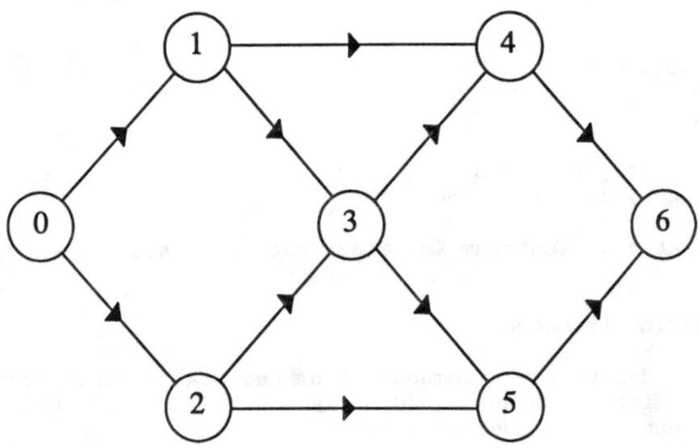

Figure 3.4

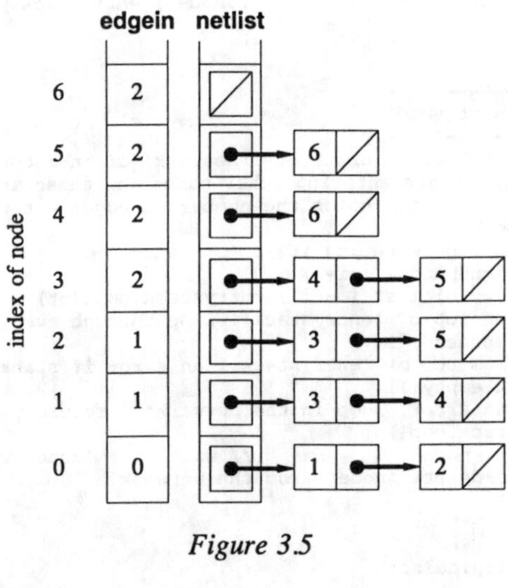

Figure 3.5

This method is fundamental to the hidden surface algorithm of chapter 10, where the nodes represent polygonal facets, and the edges denote overlapping relationships between facets. For example, if, on viewing, facet I is behind facet J, then there will be an edge from node I to node J in the network representing the scene. If the facets do not overlap then there is no edge between them in the network. The topological ordering of such a network gives a (non-unique) order of facets in the scene, starting from the back and moving forward, and hence furnishes us with a straightforward algorithm for hidden surface elimination.

Listing 3.6

```
// Application program to demonstrate topological sorting

#include "stack.h"
#include "stack.cpp"

#define maxnet 100

int edgein[maxnet], numnodes ;
Stack entrystack, netlist[maxnet] ;

ostream& operator << (ostream &a, stackinfo v) { return a << v.i ; }

//--------------------------//
  void denode(int fromnode)
//--------------------------//
// Function to delete the 'fromnode' from network. It must scan
// the linear list of nodes joined by an edge 'fromnode' 'tonode'
// and decrement their 'edgein' value by 1.
{ int tonode ;
  stackinfo st ;
  while ( ! netlist[fromnode].empty() )
  { st=netlist[fromnode].pop() ;
    tonode = st.i ;    (edgein[tonode]) -- ;
// If this 'tonode' now has no edges entering it then it can
// be pushed onto the stack ready for writing.
    if (edgein[tonode] == 0)  { st.i = tonode ; entrystack.push(st) ; }
  }
 }  // End of denode

//---------------------------//
  void topologicalsort(void)
//---------------------------//
// Calculate the topological order of a'network' of 'numnodes' nodes
// The 'i'th node has edges entering other nodes and these are stored in a list
// 'netlist[i]'. 'edgein[j]' holds the number of edges entering node 'j'
 { stackinfo st, node ;
// Any node with no edge entering it is 'stack'ed
   for (int i=0 ; i<numnodes ; i++)
     if (edgein[i] == 0) { st.i = i ; entrystack.push(st) ; }
// Deal with node on top of 'entrystack'. Loop through every node.
   for (i=0 ; i<numnodes ; i++)
// Remove 'node' from top of 'entrystack'; an error if stack is empty
   { if (entrystack.empty())
       { cerr << "\n Error, loop in the network" ; return ; }
     node = entrystack.pop() ;
     cout << "   " << node ;                // write out 'node' value
// Call 'denode' to delete 'node' from the network.
     denode(node.i) ;
   }
   cout << "\n" ;
 }  // End of topologicalsort
```

```
//-----------//
  void main()      // network example
//-----------//
// To demonstrate a simple network and topological sort. The network is
// represented by a 'netlist' of up to 'maxnet' stacks. The 'netlist[i]' stack
// holds the indices of all nodes 'j', such that there is an edge from 'i' to
// 'j'. 'edgein[j]' holds the number of edges entering node 'j'
 { int i,j ;
   stackinfo st ;
// Set up the network data structure
   cout << " type in number of nodes\n" ;
   cin >> numnodes ;
   for (i=0 ; i<numnodes ; i++)  edgein[i]=0 ;
// Read in edge information : node 'i' to node 'j'. Process ends when 'i=j'
   cout << " type in edges\n" ;   cin >> i >> j ;
   while (i != j)
   { (edgein[j])++ ;  st.i = j ;  netlist[i].push(st) ;  cin >>i >>j ; }
   cout << "Topological order of network is\n" ;
   topologicalsort() ;
 }  // End of main network example
```

N-way trees

The last structure to be considered in this chapter is the *n-way tree* holding data of a particular type. Such a tree is a special form of network in which there is a unique node called the *root* with no edges entering it. All other nodes have just one edge entering, and at most n edges leaving. A node with no edges leaving is called a *leaf*. Each node in the tree will hold an information part (data of the required type), and n pointers (possibly null) referring to n *subtrees*. Each non-null subtree is itself an n-way tree.

Initially we consider the very special case of the *binary tree* ($n = 2$) of integers. Each node has two edges (possibly null) leaving it, one to the left, and one to the right of the node. The integer values stored on the nodes can be used to introduce a *left-right ordering*, by insisting that all the node values in the left subtree are less than the value on the node, and all values in the right subtree are greater than that on the node. See figure 3.6, of the tree created from the file **"tree.dat"** given in listing 3.7.

There are a number of different ways of implementing trees in C++. Which way you choose really depends on the complexity of the tree manipulation you require. See Knuth (1973) and for an explicit C++ pointer implementation of trees see Stroustrup (1987). We will cover some simple manipulations to introduce the concept, some of which will be needed by the algorithms given later in this book.

We assume initially that the binary tree will be ordered, and is created by the overloaded method **extend** (listing 3.7) from an input stream of integer data. Each new node is added to a tree as a leaf, and each time a new node is created, its required position is found using the left-right ordering. A variable pointer moves left or right through the edges of the tree until it finds a null pointer: this null pointer is replaced by a pointer to the new leaf node. This listing also contains three overloaded output functions **inorder, preorder** and **postorder** to print out the tree information recursively in infix, prefix and postfix notation respectively. Note that the use of brackets is needed within the infix notation if we are to reconstruct the tree unambiguously from the output data, whereas, given the left-right ordering, the latter two outputs (sometimes called Forward and Reverse Polish notation) will enable us to reconstruct the tree uniquely. We also include a **main** function which reads in data from a file **"tree.dat"** in order to create a binary tree, which is then printed out in all three notations.

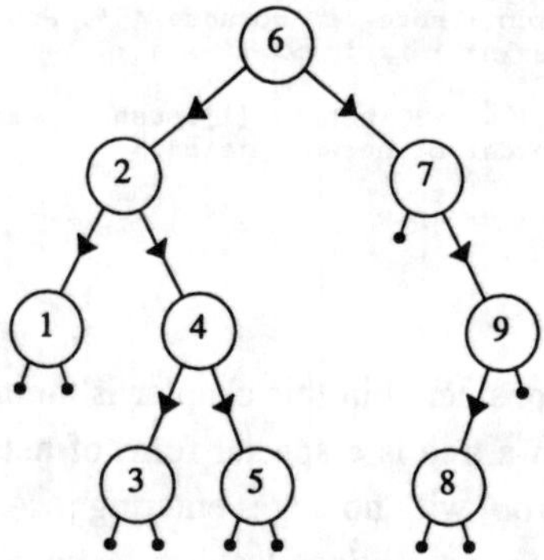

Figure 3.6

Listing 3.7

```
// Application program to demonstrate the input/output of trees
#include <fstream.h>
struct treecell { int info ;  treecell *tl, *tr ; } ;
//-----------//
  class Tree
//-----------//
{ treecell *root ;
  public:
   Tree() ;
   ~Tree() ;
   void del_subtree(treecell *tp) ;
   void extend(int v) ;
   void extend(int v,treecell **subtree) ;
   void preorder(void) ;
   void preorder(treecell *subtree) ;
   void inorder(void) ;
   void inorder(treecell *subtree) ;
   void postorder(void) ;
   void postorder(treecell *subtree) ;
 } ;  // End of class Tree

//-------------//
  Tree::Tree()   { root = NULL ; }
//-------------//

//--------------//
  Tree::~Tree()
//--------------//
{ if (root!=NULL) del_subtree(root) ;  }
```

```
//----------------------------------//
  void Tree::del_subtree(treecell *tp)
//----------------------------------//
 { treecell *left, *rigt ;
   left = tp->tl ; if (left != NULL)  del_subtree(left) ;
   rigt = tp->tr ; if (rigt != NULL)  del_subtree(rigt) ;
   delete tp ;
 }  // End of del_subtree

//----------------------//
  void Tree::extend(int v) { extend(v,&root) ; }
//----------------------//

//----------------------------------------//
 void Tree::extend(int v, treecell **subtree)
//----------------------------------------//
 { if (*subtree==NULL)
     { *subtree = new treecell ;
       if (*subtree==NULL)
          { cerr << "\nError : not enough memory"; return; }
       (*subtree)->info = v ; (*subtree)->tl = NULL ; (*subtree)->tr = NULL ;
     }
   else
     { if (v < (*subtree)->info) extend(v,&((*subtree)->tl)) ;
       else extend(v,&((*subtree)->tr)) ;
     } ;
 }  // End of extend

//-----------------------//
  void Tree::preorder(void)  { preorder(root) ; cout << "\n" ; }
//-----------------------//

//-----------------------------------//
  void Tree::preorder(treecell *subtree)
//-----------------------------------//
 { if (subtree!=NULL)
     { cout << " " << subtree->info ;
       preorder(subtree->tl) ;    preorder(subtree->tr) ;
     }
 }  // End of preorder

//------------------------//
  void Tree::postorder(void)   { postorder(root) ; cout << "\n" ; }
//------------------------//

//------------------------------------//
  void Tree::postorder(treecell *subtree)
//------------------------------------//
 { if (subtree!=NULL)
     { postorder(subtree->tl) ;   postorder(subtree->tr) ;
       cout << " " << subtree->info ;
     }
 }  // End of postorder

//----------------------//
  void Tree::inorder(void)  { inorder(root) ; cout << "\n" ; }
//----------------------//

//----------------------------------//
  void Tree::inorder(treecell *subtree)
//----------------------------------//
 { if (subtree!=NULL)
     { cout << "(" ;
       inorder(subtree->tl) ;
       cout << "" << subtree->info ;
       inorder(subtree->tr) ;
       cout << ")" ;
     }
 }  // End of inorder
```

```
//-----------//
  void main()
//-----------//
 { ifstream datafile ;
   int i ;
   Tree tree ;
   datafile.open("tree.dat") ;  datafile >> i ;
   while (! datafile.eof() ) { tree.extend(i) ; datafile >> i ; }
   tree.preorder() ;  tree.inorder() ;  tree.postorder() ;
 }  // End of main

/* Sample file "tree.dat"
   6  2  7  9  4  1  3  5  8
*/
```

Exercise 3.2

There are many ways of operating on trees. Write functions to do the following:

(i) add a node to an existing ordered tree
(ii) delete a node
(iii) copy a tree
(iv) 'balance' a tree

Example 3.3

Trees are inherently recursive. The output functions we give in listing 3.7 uses the recursion mechanisms of the C++ language. Such mechanisms implicitly use stacks generated by the C++ compiler. We now give a non-recursive function in order to implement these ideas, as it is very informative to see an output function for a tree that explicitly uses the **Stack** class described earlier in this chapter. Listing 3.8 gives such a version of the **preorder** function; this should replace the previous version given in listing 3.7, and the program should be run again.

Listing 3.8

```
// Delete both preorder functions and replace with the following code
// File "stackinfo.cpp" should be replaced with that shown below

#include "stack.h" ;
#include "stack.cpp" ;

//-------------------------//
  void Tree::preorder(void)
//-------------------------//
 { Stack stack ;
   stackinfo v ;
   treecell *subtree ;
   if (root != NULL)
   { v.ptrcell = root ;  stack.push(v) ;
     while (!stack.empty())
     { v = stack.pop() ; subtree = v.ptrcell ; cout << " " << subtree->info ;
       if (subtree->tr != NULL) { v.ptrcell=subtree->tr ; stack.push(v) ; }
       if (subtree->tl != NULL) { v.ptrcell=subtree->tl ; stack.push(v) ; }
     }
   }
   cout << "\n" ;
 }  // End of preorder
```

```
/* File "stackinfo.cpp"

   struct stackinfo { treecell *ptrcell ; } ;
*/
```

The CSG tree

The uniqueness of the prefix and postfix representations of a binary tree can prove very useful, when we consider oct-trees (*8-way trees*) in chapter 15. In that chapter the 8-way tree is used to subdivide space, but we will also be using a binary tree to implement a constructive solid geometry representation of a scene as a combination of objects using geometrical operators intersection ($\cap$), union ($\cup$) and complement (–); these operators can be compared to the Boolean operators AND, OR and NOT respectively. Each leaf in this binary *constructive solid geometry tree*, or *CSG tree* will indicate the index of an object, whose surface is represented by a series of mathematical functions. The absolute value of the integer is a label of a unique object; if it is positive then it represents all space 'inside' the object, if negative the space 'outside', that is the complement (–) of, the object. The values stored on the non-leaf nodes represent the binary operators ($\cap$ and $\cup$) – we will store these as integers (11,111 stands for intersection, and 22,222 for union).

This tree structure, which we name as class **CSGtree**, will be declared in file **"CSGtree.h"** (listing 3.9a) and methods given in **"CSGtree.cpp"** (listing 3.9b). A particular instantiation of a tree will be generated by method **Set_tree** to create it from a postfix representation of that tree. The class is used in algorithms that check, for a given object, whether or not a given sphere lies INSIDE (which is interpreted as the Boolean constant TRUE), OUTSIDE (which is interpreted as FALSE), or possibly we are UNSURE of whether it crosses the boundary of that object. With this data we can check which parts of the tree representing the scene can be ignored in our processing, and which must be processed further. We will be only interested in the boundaries, and we will want to *reduce* the tree: that is delete all nodes with INSIDE (TRUE) or OUTSIDE (FALSE) values from the tree; see chapter 15 for more details. That is we operate on the tree as follows:

node $\cup$; left/right subtree INSIDE: replace node by leaf node INSIDE
node $\cup$; left/right subtree OUTSIDE: replace node by right/left subtree
node $\cap$; left/right subtree INSIDE: replace node by right/left subtree
node $\cap$; left/right subtree OUTSIDE: replace node by leaf node OUTSIDE

These are equivalent to normal Boolean operations of OR, AND on the constants TRUE and FALSE; the complement NOT inverts the Boolean constant. This procedure (implemented as method **reduce**, and supported by secondary private methods) will be repeatedly applied until no node with an INSIDE or OUTSIDE status remains in the tree. The sequence of operations is as follows. Method **tree_to_list** stores the postfix representation of the tree presently under consideration as an array list. **objects_in_tree** then makes a list of the indices of all the objects remaining in the tree. **evaluate_objects** then checks on the status of these objects: INSIDE, OUTSIDE or UNSURE (in our simple demonstration program these values are input). **mark_status** then runs through the tree marking the status of all nodes (leaves and operator nodes) using the above logical operators. **prune_list** then uses this information to prune out unnecessary parts of the tree. Then finally method **list_to_tree** reconstructs the reduced tree from this postfix list.

*Listing 3.9*a

```
// Save code as file "csgtree.h"
#include <alloc.h>
#include <conio.h>
#define UNION  22222
#define INTERS 11111
#define maxtreelist 1250
enum { INSIDE, OUTSIDE, UNSURE } ;
struct csgtreecell { int info, status ; csgtreecell *tl, *tr ; } ;

//-------------//
  class CSGtree
//-------------//
 { csgtreecell *root ;

 public:
  CSGtree() ;
  ~CSGtree() ;
  CSGtree(CSGtree& mtree) ;              // Tree initialisation
  void operator = (CSGtree& mtree) ;     // Tree assignment =
  void list_to_tree(int c, int *list) ;
  int tree_to_list(int *list) ;
  void reduce(CSGtree *trtr) ;
  int objects_in_tree(int *objectlist) ;

 private:
  void del_leaves(csgtreecell *tp) ;
  void append(int *list, csgtreecell **tp, int il, int ir) ;
  void traverse(int *c, int *list, csgtreecell *tp) ;
  void mark_status(csgtreecell *tp) ;
  void prune_list(int *c, int *list, csgtreecell *tp) ;
  void objects_in_subtree(int *c, int *objectlist, csgtreecell *tp) ;
 } ;  // End of class CSGtree
```

Listing 3.9b

```
// Save code as file "csgtree.cpp"

// Truth tables for UNION and INTERSection
int FUNION[3][3] = { INSIDE,  INSIDE,  INSIDE,
                     INSIDE,  OUTSIDE, UNSURE,
                     INSIDE,  UNSURE,  UNSURE } ;

int FINTERS[3][3] = { INSIDE,  OUTSIDE, UNSURE,
                      OUTSIDE, OUTSIDE, OUTSIDE,
                      UNSURE,  OUTSIDE, UNSURE } ;
```

```
//-------------------//
  CSGtree::CSGtree()    { root = NULL ; }
//-------------------//

//-------------------//
  CSGtree::~CSGtree()   { if (root!=NULL) del_leaves(root) ; }
//-------------------//

//----------------------------------------//
  void CSGtree::del_leaves(csgtreecell *tp)
//----------------------------------------//
 { if ( tp->tl != NULL)  del_leaves(tp->tl) ;
   if ( tp->tr != NULL)  del_leaves(tp->tr) ;
   delete tp ;
 }  // End of del_leaves

//----------------------------------------//
  void CSGtree::operator = (CSGtree& mtree)
//----------------------------------------//
 { int c, postorderlist[maxtreelist] ;
   if (this == &mtree) return ;
   if (root!=NULL) del_leaves(root) ;
   root = NULL ;
   c = mtree.tree_to_list(postorderlist) ;
   list_to_tree(c,postorderlist) ;
 }  // End of =

//--------------------------------//
  CSGtree::CSGtree(CSGtree& mtree)
//--------------------------------//
 { int c, postorderlist[maxtreelist] ;
   root = NULL ;
   c = mtree.tree_to_list(postorderlist) ;
   list_to_tree(c,postorderlist) ;
 }  // End of assignment+initialization

//-----------------------------------//
  int CSGtree::tree_to_list(int *list)
//-----------------------------------//
 { int c = 0 ;
   traverse(&c,list,root) ;
   return ( c ) ;
 }  // End of tree_to_list

//--------------------------------------------------------//
  void CSGtree::traverse(int *c, int *list, csgtreecell *tp)
//--------------------------------------------------------//
 { if (tp != NULL)
     { traverse(c,list,tp->tl) ;    traverse(c,list,tp->tr) ;
       list[(*c)++] = tp->info ;
     }
 }  // End of traverse

//-----------------------------------------------------------------//
  void CSGtree::append(int *list, csgtreecell **tp, int il, int ir)
//-----------------------------------------------------------------//
 { int operands = 0, operators = 0, i ;
   (*tp) = new csgtreecell ;
   if ( (*tp) == NULL ) { cerr << "\n ERROR: OUT OF MEM" ; return ; }
   (*tp)->info = list[ir-1] ;  (*tp)->status = UNSURE ;
   (*tp)->tl = NULL ;  (*tp)->tr = NULL ;
   if ( (ir-il)>1 )
     { i = ir-1 ;             // Separate left from right subtree
       while( (operands-operators) != 1)
       { i-- ; if (list[i] > 9999) operators++ ; else operands++ ; }
       if (i>0) append(list,&((*tp)->tl),il,i) ;
       if ((ir-i)>0) append(list,&((*tp)->tr),i,ir-1) ;
     } ;
 }  // End of append
```

```
//---------------------------------------------//
  void CSGtree::list_to_tree(int c, int *list)
//---------------------------------------------//
 { if (root!=NULL) del_leaves(root) ;
   if (c>0) append(list,&root,0,c) ;
   else root = NULL ;
 }  // End of list_to_tree

//------------------------------------------//
  void CSGtree::mark_status(csgtreecell *tp)
//------------------------------------------//
 { csgtreecell *left, *rigt ;
   int c ;
   left = tp->tl ; if (left != NULL) mark_status(left) ;
   rigt = tp->tr ; if (rigt != NULL) mark_status(rigt) ;
   c = tp->info ;
   if (c<9999)  // It is not an operator
     { if (c>0) tp->status = ival[c] ;
       else   // Invert INSIDE with OUTSIDE
         { if (ival[-c] == INSIDE) tp->status = OUTSIDE ;
           else if (ival[-c] == OUTSIDE) tp->status = INSIDE ;
           else tp->status = UNSURE ;
         } ;
     }
   else           // The corresponding operator has to apply
     switch (c)
    { case UNION : tp->status = FUNION[left->status][rigt->status] ; break ;
      case INTERS: tp->status = FINTERS[left->status][rigt->status] ; break ;
      default    : cerr << "\nERROR: Unknown operator" ; break ;
    }
 }  // End of mark_status

//-------------------------------------------------------------------//
  void CSGtree::prune_list(int *c, int *prunedlist, csgtreecell *tp)
//-------------------------------------------------------------------//
 { csgtreecell *left, *rigt ;
   if (tp->status == UNSURE)
   { left = tp->tl ;    rigt = tp->tr ;
     if (left != NULL)        // Node is not a leaf
     { if ( (left->status == UNSURE) && (rigt->status == UNSURE))
       { prune_list(c,prunedlist,left) ;  prune_list(c,prunedlist,rigt) ;
         prunedlist[(*c)++] = tp->info ;
       }
       else            // Replace with subtree
       { if (left->status == UNSURE) prune_list(c,prunedlist,left) ;
         if (rigt->status == UNSURE) prune_list(c,prunedlist,rigt) ;
//  Do not advance (*c) since it is subtree replacement
       } ;
     }
     else prunedlist[(*c)++] = tp->info ;
   } ;
 }  // End of prune_list

//------------------------------------//
  void CSGtree::reduce(CSGtree *trtr)
//------------------------------------//
 { int c = 0, newlist[maxtreelist] ;
   if (root!=NULL)
     { mark_status(root) ;  prune_list(&c,newlist,root) ; };
   trtr->list_to_tree(c,newlist) ;
 }  // End of reduce

//-----------------------------------------------//
  int CSGtree::objects_in_tree(int *objectlist)
//-----------------------------------------------//
 { int c = 0 ;
   if (root!=NULL) objects_in_subtree(&c,objectlist,root) ;
   return (c) ;
 }  // End of object_in_tree
```

```
//----------------------------------------------------------------------//
  void CSGtree::objects_in_subtree(int *c,int *objlist,csgtreecell *tp)
//----------------------------------------------------------------------//
 { int i, found ;
   if (tp->tl != NULL) objects_in_subtree(c,objlist,tp->tl) ;
   if (tp->tr != NULL) objects_in_subtree(c,objlist,tp->tr) ;
   found = FALSE ;
   if ( (tp->info) < 9999 )
     { for (i=0 ; i<*c ; i++)
       { if (abs(tp->info) == objlist[i]) { found=TRUE ; i=*c+1 ; }; }
       if (!found)  { objlist[*c] = abs(tp->info) ;  (*c)++ ; } ;
     } ;
 }  // End of objects_in_subtree
```

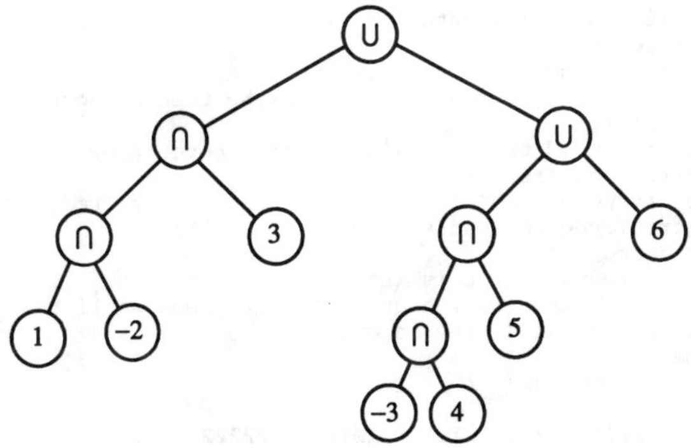

Figure 3.7

Example 3.4

Listing 3.10 gives a **main** function that reads in a tree given in postfix notation. For each object indicated by an integer label, the program then reads in whether the status of that object is INSIDE, OUTSIDE or UNSURE. The program reduces the tree according to the above rules, and prints out the resulting tree in postfix notation. Figure 3.7 shows the example tree given in file **"csgtree.dat"**

Listing 3.10

```
// Application program to demonstrate CSGtree reduction

#include <fstream.h>
#include <math.h>

#define FALSE 0
#define TRUE  1
#define maxobjects 100

#include "csgtree.h"
int ival[maxobjects] ;              // 'ival' has to be defined before the
#include "csgtree.cpp"              // compilation of the 'Csgtree' class
ifstream datafile ;
```

```
//---------------------------//
 void evaluate_objects(void)
//---------------------------//
// Set 'ival' for 6 objects: INSIDE (=0), OUTSIDE (=1) or, UNSURE (=2)
 { ival[1] = 2 ;  ival[2] = 1 ;  ival[3] = 1 ;
   ival[4] = 2 ;  ival[5] = 0 ;  ival[6] = 2 ;
 }  // End of evaluate_objects

//---------------//
 void main(void)
//---------------//
 { int lista[maxtreelist],reduced_list[maxtreelist],length,i, n ;
   CSGtree tree, reduced_tree ;
   datafile.open("CSGtree.dat") ;
// Read the length of the postorder list of the tree representation
   datafile >> length ;
// Read the list representation of the tree
   for (i=0 ; i<length ; i++) datafile >> lista[i] ; datafile.close() ;
// Create a Csgtree from the list
   tree.list_to_tree(length,&(lista[0])) ;
// Assume there are six different objects in the tree structure
   evaluate_objects() ;
// Determine the 'reduced_tree' version of the above 'tree'.
   tree.reduce(&reduced_tree) ;
// Retrieve the 'reduced_tree' in the form of postorder 'reduced_list'
   n = reduced_tree.tree_to_list(&(reduced_list[0])) ;
// Print the 'reduced_list'
   cout << "\n The reduced list is \n" ;
   if (n)  for (i=0 ; i<n ; i++) cout << "  " << reduced_list[i] ;
   else cout <<" The reduced tree is empty" ;
 }  // End of main
/* Sample file "CSGtree.dat"
   13
   1 -2 11111  3 11111  -3 4 11111 5 11111 6 22222  22222
*/
```

Generation/traversal of n-way trees

Another form of tree structure, the 8-way tree, is also used in the oct-tree program; and a similar implementation is used in the quad-tree (4-way) and ray-tracing (2-way) programs. In all three of these programs you will see that the trees are being generated at the same time as they are being traversed. In these cases, data from the root of the tree is initially placed on a stack. Then, when a node of any subtree is 'visited' by popping it off the stack, the data on that node is used to create further data for the root nodes of up to two further subtrees in the case of ray-tracing, for up to four extra subtrees in quad-tree encoding, and for up to eight extra subtrees in oct-tree encoding. The data on these extra nodes are pushed onto the stack; the potentially explosive nature of this algorithm is counteracted by the fact that a visit to a leaf does not generate new nodes. The program terminates when the stack becomes empty.

In this chapter we have given you only the very basic data structure types and operations that are needed to understand the graphics algorithms in this book. We recommend that readers study the advanced text books on the topic; it will certainly pay dividends in the long run.

4 An introduction to two-dimensional co-ordinate geometry

The underlying mathematical theory is important in any branch of computer programming, but particularly so in graphics. The majority of techniques presented in this book rely entirely upon a solid background of co-ordinate and vector geometry, and it is imperative that the reader gains some grounding in the methods involved before progressing to the later applications.

We work with the *x-y* rectangular Cartesian co-ordinate system that was introduced in the second chapter; the positive *x*-axis is horizontal and to the right of the co-ordinate origin, and the positive *y*-axis is vertical and above the origin. A typical point $\boldsymbol{p}$ in this system is represented by the *co-ordinate pair* (x, y). The two values x and y are the perpendicular projections of the point onto the respective axes. This co-ordinate pair is also sometimes called a *vector pair*, or *point vector*, and may be written in vector notation $\boldsymbol{p} \equiv (x, y)$. Note that the symbol $\equiv$ means 'equivalent to'.

Of course a straight line or, more specifically, a typical point (x, y) on a line, may be represented in the familiar form of a linear equation

$$y = mx + c$$

which is better expressed as

$$ay = bx + c$$

where b/a is the tangent of the angle that the line makes with the positive *x*-axis (called the *gradient*, or *slope* of the line), and c/a (if finite) is the intercept of the line with the *y*-axis (see figure 4.1). The former formulation of the line cannot represent the situation when $a = 0$, that is, c/a is infinite, when the line is parallel to the *y*-axis and so has infinite slope.

There is another (and as we shall see more useful in computer graphics) way of representing a line. But first we must define two operations on vectors, *scalar multiple* and *vector addition*, as well as explaining what we mean by the *magnitude* or *modulus* of a vector. Suppose we have two vectors $\boldsymbol{p_1} \equiv (x_1, y_1)$ and $\boldsymbol{p_2} \equiv (x_2, y_2)$. Multiplying the individual components of the vector $\boldsymbol{p_1}$ by a scalar real (floating point) value k gives the *scalar multiple*

$$k\boldsymbol{p_1} \equiv (k \times x_1, k \times y_1)$$

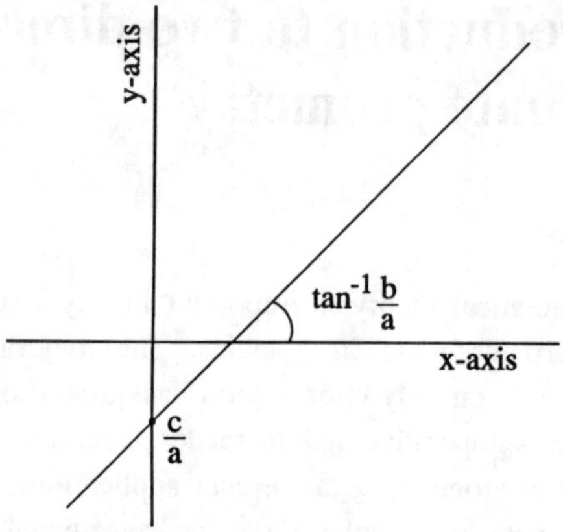

Figure 4.1

while adding the *x* components together and the *y* components together by *vector addition* gives the vector

$$p_1 + p_2 \equiv (x_1 + x_2 \, , \, y_1 + y_2)$$

The *modulus* of a vector p_1 is defined as the distance of the point $(x_1 \, , y_1)$ from the origin, denoted by $|p_1|$

$$|p_1| = \sqrt{(x_1^2 + y_1^2)}$$

To define a line in the new way we mentioned, we choose any two fixed points on the line, which we again call $p_1 \equiv (x_1 \, , y_1)$ and $p_2 \equiv (x_2 \, , y_2)$. The typical point on the line, $p(\mu) \equiv (x \, , y)$, is given by the vector combination

$$(1-\mu)p_1 + \mu p_2$$

for some real number μ. This is the vector pair

$$((1-\mu)x_1 + \mu x_2 \, , \, (1-\mu)y_1 + \mu y_2)$$

For the time being we place the μ in brackets after p to show the dependence of the vector on the value of μ. If $0 \le \mu \le 1$ then $p(\mu)$ lies on the line between p_1 and p_2. For any specified point $p(\mu)$, the value of μ is given by the ratio

$$\mu = \frac{\textit{distance of } p(\mu) \textit{ from } p_1}{\textit{distance of } p_2 \textit{ from } p_1}$$

where the measure of distance is positive if $p(\mu)$ is on the same side of p_1 as p_2, and negative if on the other side.

The (positive) distance between any two vector points $\boldsymbol{p_1}$ and $\boldsymbol{p_2}$ is given by

$$|\boldsymbol{p_2} - \boldsymbol{p_1}| \equiv \sqrt{\{(x_2 - x_1)^2 + (y_2 - y_1)^2\}}$$

Figure 4.2 shows a line segment between points (−3 , −1) = $\boldsymbol{p}(0)$ and (3 , 2) = $\boldsymbol{p}(1)$: the point (1 , 1) lies on the line as $\boldsymbol{p}(2/3)$. Note that (3 , 2) is at a distance $3\sqrt{5}$ away from (−3 , −1) whereas (1 , 1) is $2\sqrt{5}$ away. From now on the (μ) is omitted from the point vector representation.

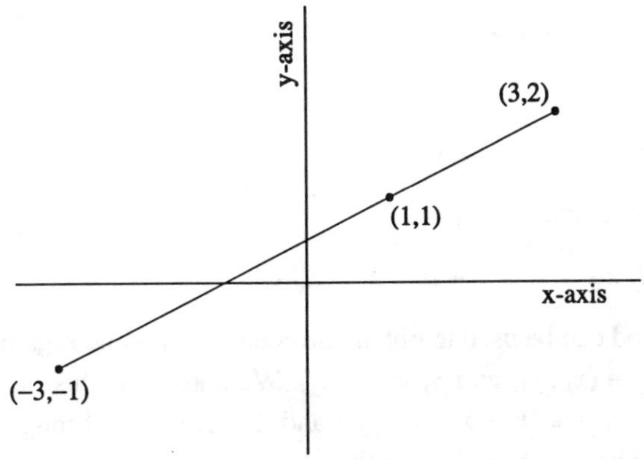

Figure 4.2

Note that the vector form that represents a line can be reorganized.

$$\boldsymbol{p_1} + \mu(\boldsymbol{p_2} - \boldsymbol{p_1})$$

When given in this new representation, the vector $\boldsymbol{p_1}$ may be called a *base vector*, and $(\boldsymbol{p_2} - \boldsymbol{p_1})$ called the *direction vector*. In fact any point on the line can stand as a base vector; it simply acts as a point to anchor a line that is parallel to the direction vector. The concept of a vector acting as a direction needs some further explanation. It has already been noted that a vector pair, (x , y) say, may represent a point; a line joining the co-ordinate origin to this point may be thought of as specifying a direction – any line in space which is parallel to this line is defined to have the same direction vector. A line that goes from the origin $\boldsymbol{O} \equiv (0 , 0)$ towards (x , y) has the so-called *positive sense*; a line from (x , y) towards the origin has *negative sense*.

The linear equation and the vector forms of a line are, of course, related. It was mentioned earlier that the line $ay = bx + c$ had slope b/a. This means that the line has direction vector (a , b). Thus, given any point on the line, (x_1 , y_1) towards the origin say, we may derive its vector representation

$$(x_1 , y_1) + \mu(a , b)$$

Conversely, a line given in base and direction vector form $\boldsymbol{b} + \mu\boldsymbol{d}$ (where base vector $\boldsymbol{b} \equiv (b_x , b_y)$ and direction vector $\boldsymbol{d} \equiv (d_x , d_y)$) has slope d_y / d_x, will have a linear equation of the form

$$d_x \times y = d_y \times x + c'$$

The value of c' can be determined by inserting the co-ordinates of any point on the line into the above equation; in particular we may use (b_x , b_y)

$$d_x \times b_y = d_y \times b_x + c'$$

and so

$$c' = d_x \times b_y - d_y \times b_x$$

and this gives the equation

$$d_x \times y = d_y \times x + d_x \times b_y - d_y \times b_x$$

This method can be used to obtain the equation of a line segment joining two given points $\boldsymbol{p_1} \equiv (x_1 , y_1)$ and $\boldsymbol{p_2} \equiv (x_2 , y_2)$. We know that this line has direction vector $\boldsymbol{d} = (\boldsymbol{p_2} - \boldsymbol{p_1}) \equiv (x_2 - x_1 , y_2 - y_1)$ and that it passes through $\boldsymbol{p_1}$ (which we take as base vector $\boldsymbol{b}$). Substituting these values into the above equation we get

$$(x_2 - x_1) \times y = (y_2 - y_1) \times x + (x_2 - x_1) \times y_1 - (y_2 - y_1) \times x_1$$

which, when reorganized, gives

$$(x_2 - x_1) \times (y - y_1) - (y_2 - y_1) \times (x - x_1) = 0$$

Exercise 4.1
Use the above theory to write a function **dash(n, p1, p2)** which draws a line consisting of **n** dashes between the two **vector2** points **p1** and **p2** in the window. Note that the dashes must start and end on these points. So given the distance between the two end-points is **d**, and that the size of dashes equals the size of the gap between dashes, then the size of the dash must be **d/(2n – 1)**. But what if you require the dashes to be twice the size of the gaps? What if, instead, you wanted to make each dash a given size, and the gaps only approximately equal to the solid line segments?

The intersection of two lines

The base and direction representation is also a very convenient way of calculating the point of intersection of two given lines, a problem that frequently crops up in two-dimensional graphics. Suppose we are given two lines $\boldsymbol{p} + \mu\boldsymbol{q}$ and $\boldsymbol{r} + \lambda\boldsymbol{s}$, where $\boldsymbol{p} \equiv (x_1 , y_1)$, $\boldsymbol{q} \equiv (x_2 , y_2)$, $\boldsymbol{r} \equiv (x_3 , y_3)$ and $\boldsymbol{s} \equiv (x_4 , y_4)$ and $-\infty < \mu, \lambda < \infty$.

These lines will intersect at an infinity of points if they are identical. However if they are parallel and non-identical there will be no point of intersection. In the general case there will be a unique point of intersection, defined by values of μ and λ satisfying the vector equation

$$\boldsymbol{p} + \mu\boldsymbol{q} = \boldsymbol{r} + \lambda\boldsymbol{s}$$

that is, it is a point that lies on lines. This vector equation can be written as two separate co-ordinate equations

$$x_1 + \mu \times x_2 = x_3 + \lambda \times x_4 \tag{4.1}$$

$$y_1 + \mu \times y_2 = y_3 + \lambda \times y_4 \tag{4.2}$$

Rewriting these two equations

$$\mu \times x_2 - \lambda \times x_4 = x_3 - x_1 \tag{4.3}$$

$$\mu \times y_2 - \lambda \times y_4 = y_3 - y_1 \tag{4.4}$$

Then multiplying (4.3) by y_4, (4.4) by x_4, and subtracting

$$\mu \times (x_2 \times y_4 - y_2 \times x_4) = (x_3 - x_1) \times y_4 - (y_3 - y_1) \times x_4$$

If the calculated value of $(x_2 \times y_4 - y_2 \times x_4)$ is zero, then we cannot divide it into the right hand side of the equation to find μ. This happens when the lines are parallel and there can be no unique point of intersection, otherwise

$$\mu = \frac{(x_3 - x_1) \times y_4 - (y_3 - y_1) \times x_4}{(x_2 \times y_4 - y_2 \times x_4)} \tag{4.5}$$

and similarly

$$\lambda = \frac{(x_3 - x_1) \times y_2 - (y_3 - y_1) \times x_2}{(x_2 \times y_4 - y_2 \times x_4)} \tag{4.6}$$

Naturally the solution becomes even simpler if one of the lines is parallel to a co-ordinate axis. Suppose that this line is $x = d$, then we can set $\boldsymbol{r} = (d, 0)$ and $\boldsymbol{s} = (0, 1)$, which we can substitute into equation (4.5) to give

$$\mu = (d - x_1)/x_2$$

and similarly if the line is $y = d$

$$\mu = (d - y_1)/y_2$$

Substituting the value of μ (or λ) thus found, into $\boldsymbol{p} + \mu\boldsymbol{q}$ (or $\boldsymbol{r} + \lambda\boldsymbol{s}$), yields the point of intersection.

Example 4.1
Find the point of intersection of the two infinite lines:
(a) joining (1 , −1) to (−1 , −3) and (b) joining (1 , 2) to (3 , −2).

The lines may be written:

$$(1-\mu)(1\,,-1) + \mu(-1\,,-3) \qquad -\infty < \mu < \infty \tag{4.7}$$

$$(1-\lambda)(1\,,2) + \lambda(3\,,-2) \qquad -\infty < \lambda < \infty \tag{4.8}$$

or when placed in the base/direction vector form

$$(1\,,-1) + \mu(-2\,,-2) \tag{4.9}$$

$$(1\,,2) + \lambda(2\,,-4) \tag{4.10}$$

Substituting these values in equation (4.5) gives

$$\mu = \frac{(1-1)\times -4 \;-\; (2+1)\times 2}{(-2\times -4 \;-\; (-2)\times 2)} = -0.5$$

whence the point of intersection is

$$(1\,,-1) - 0.5(-2\,,-2) = (2\,,0)$$

The general case is solved by the function **ill2** given in listing 4.1 and should be used to extend our file **"window.cpp"**; note that the declaration of this function was given earlier in **"window.h"** in listing 2.1a.

Listing 4.1

```
// Extend file "window.cpp" with this function

//-------------------------------------------------------------------//
  int ill2(vector2 v1,vector2 v2,vector2 v3,vector2 v4,vector2 *v)
//-------------------------------------------------------------------//
{ float mu,delta ;
  int intersect ;
// Finds the point vector of intersection, 'v', of two lines
//    'v1 + mu.v2'  and 'v3 + lambda.v4'
// 'intersect' is set to TRUE if intersection exists, else FALSE
// 'intersect' is returned as the value of the function
  delta=v2.x*v4.y-v2.y*v4.x ;
// If 'delta' is zero then the lines are parallel : no intersection
  if ( fabs(delta) < epsilon )  intersect=FALSE ;
  else
    { intersect=TRUE ;
// Find 'mu' value for (v.x,v.y) on first line
      mu=((v3.x-v1.x)*v4.y-(v3.y-v1.y)*v4.x)/delta ;
// Calculate x and y co-ordinates of 'v'
      v->x=v1.x+mu*v2.x ;
      v->y=v1.y+mu*v2.y ;
    } ;
  return ( intersect ) ;
}  // End of ill2
```

Exercise 4.2
Repeat the calculations of example 4.1 using your own vector values. Write a small program that inputs the values $\boldsymbol{p}$, $\boldsymbol{q}$, $\boldsymbol{r}$ and $\boldsymbol{s}$, and calls **ill2** to find the point of intersection of $\boldsymbol{p} + \mu\boldsymbol{q}$ and $\boldsymbol{r} + \lambda\boldsymbol{s}$. Use your program to check your results.

Direction vectors

A vector ($\boldsymbol{d} \equiv (x , y) \neq (0 , 0)$, say) can represent a direction. Any positive scalar multiple $k\boldsymbol{d}$, for $k > 0$, represents the same direction and sense as $\boldsymbol{d}$; and if k is negative then the direction has its sense inverted. In particular, setting $k = 1/|\boldsymbol{d}|$ produces a vector $(x/\sqrt{(x^2+y^2)}, y/\sqrt{(x^2+y^2)})$ which has unit modulus.

A typical point on a line, $\boldsymbol{p}+\mu\boldsymbol{d}$, is a distance $|\mu\boldsymbol{d}|$ from the base point $\boldsymbol{p}$, and if $|\boldsymbol{d}|=1$ ($\boldsymbol{d}$ is a *unit vector*) then the point is a distance $|\mu|$ from $\boldsymbol{p}$.

Now consider the angles made by direction vectors with various fixed directions. Suppose that θ is the angle between the positive x-axis and the line joining $\boldsymbol{O}$ (the origin) to $\boldsymbol{d} = (x , y)$, the angle being measured anti-clockwise from the positive x-axis. Then $x = |\boldsymbol{d}| \times \cos\theta$ and $y = |\boldsymbol{d}| \times \sin\theta$ – see figure 4.3.

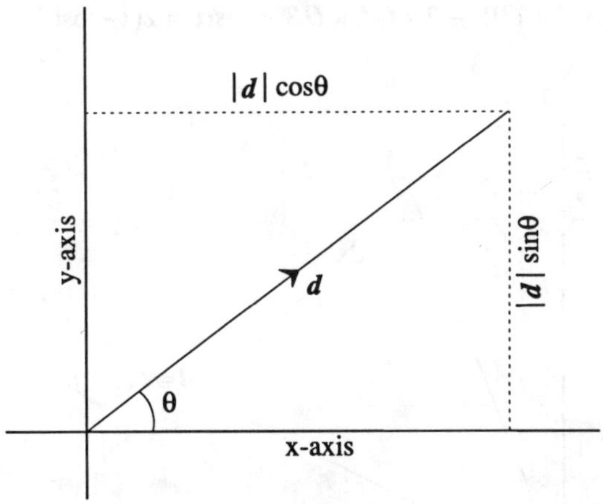

Figure 4.3

If $\boldsymbol{d}$ is a unit vector (that is $|\boldsymbol{d}|=1$) then $\boldsymbol{d} \equiv (\cos\theta , \sin\theta)$. Note that for all values of θ, $\sin\theta = \cos(\theta-\pi/2)$. Thus direction $\boldsymbol{d}$ may be rewritten as the vector $(\cos\theta , \cos(\theta-\pi/2))$. But $\theta-\pi/2$ is the angle that the vector makes with the positive y-axis. Hence the co-ordinates of a unit direction vector are called its *direction cosines*, since they are the cosines of the angles that the vector makes with the corresponding positive co-ordinate axes.

Before continuing, we should take a brief look at the limitations of the trigonometric functions available in C++. The two **<math.h>** functions **sin** and

cos return respectively the sine and cosine of an angle (in radians) provided as a parameter. The values of **sin** and **cos** lie, of course, between −1 and 1. C++ also includes the inverse of the tangent function, **atan**, which returns an angle whose tangent is equal to the given floating point parameter. The angle returned lies within a principal range between $-\pi/2$ and $\pi/2$.

However, there is a common requirement in graphics algorithms for finding the angle that a typical direction $\boldsymbol{d} = (x, y)$ makes with the positive x-axis, and this angle must not be restricted to a principal range but must be able to take any value between 0 and 2π. This problem is solved by the function **angle** which will be used extensively in the chapters dealing with three dimensions, and has already been placed in file **"window.cpp"** in chapter 2 (see listing 2.1).

Now suppose there are two direction vectors $\boldsymbol{A} \equiv (x_1, y_1)$ and $\boldsymbol{B} \equiv (x_2, y_2)$: for simplicity both are assumed to be unit vectors and to pass through the origin (see figure 4.4). The acute angle, α, between these lines is required. From the figure it is seen that $\boldsymbol{OA}=\surd(x_1^2+y_1^2)=1$ and $\boldsymbol{OB}=\surd(x_2^2+y_2^2)=1$.

So by the Cosine Rule

$$\boldsymbol{AB}^2 = \boldsymbol{OA}^2 + \boldsymbol{OB}^2 - 2 \times \boldsymbol{OA} \times \boldsymbol{OB} \times \cos\alpha = 2(1-\cos\alpha)$$

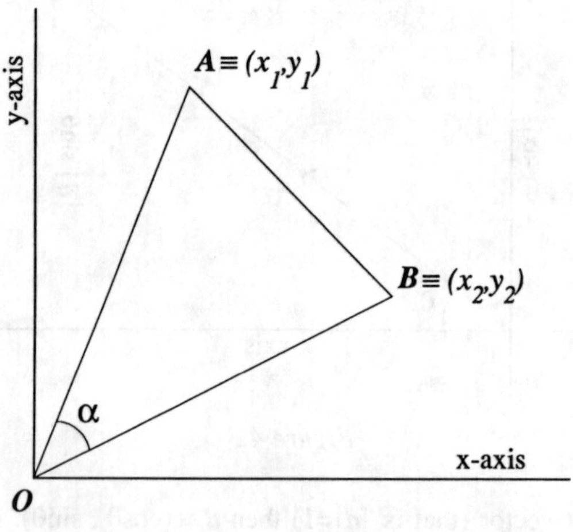

Figure 4.4

But also, by Pythagoras' theorem

$$\begin{aligned}\boldsymbol{AB}^2 &= (x_1 - x_2)^2 + (y_1 - y_2)^2 \\ &= (x_1 + y_1)^2 + (x_2 + y_2)^2 - 2(x_1 \times x_2 + y_1 \times y_2) \\ &= 2 - 2(x_1 \times x_2 + y_1 \times y_2)\end{aligned}$$

Thus $(x_1 \times x_2 + y_1 \times y_2) = \cos\alpha$. It is possible that the value of $(x_1 \times x_2 + y_1 \times y_2)$ is negative, in which case $\cos^{-1}(x_1 \times x_2 + y_1 \times y_2)$ is obtuse and the required acute angle is $\pi - \alpha$. Since $\cos(\pi - \alpha) = -\cos\alpha$, then the acute angle is given immediately by $\cos^{-1}(|x_1 \times x_2 + y_1 \times y_2|)$.

Suppose, for example, that we are given two lines with direction cosines $(\sqrt{3}/2\ ,\ 1/2)$ and $(-1/2\ ,\ -\sqrt{3}/2)$, then $(x_1 \times x_2 + y_1 \times y_2) = -\sqrt{3}/2$, and thus $\alpha = \cos^{-1}(\sqrt{3}/2) = \pi/6$.

This simple example was given in order to introduce the *scalar product* (or *dot product*, denoted by •) of two vectors: $(a\ ,\ b) \bullet (c\ ,\ d) = a \times c + b \times d$. Scalar product is extendable into higher-dimensional space (see chapter 6 for a three-dimensional example), and it always has the property that it gives the cosine of the angle between any pair of lines that have directions defined by the two unit vectors.

Now suppose that we have a direction vector $\boldsymbol{d} \equiv (d_x\ ,\ d_y)$. We know that any line parallel to $\boldsymbol{d}$ can be described by direction vector $\lambda\boldsymbol{d}$ for some $\lambda \neq 0$, but we may also determine the direction vector of any line perpendicular to $\boldsymbol{d}$.

Using the scalar product defined above, we know that any vector $\boldsymbol{s} \equiv (s_x\ ,\ s_y)$, perpendicular to $\boldsymbol{d}$, must satisfy $\boldsymbol{s} \bullet \boldsymbol{d} = 0$, since the cosine of the angle between the two vectors is zero. That is

$$(s_x\ ,\ s_y) \bullet (d_x\ ,\ d_y) = 0 \qquad \text{and so}$$

$$s_x \times d_x + s_y \times d_y = 0$$

which gives

$$-s_x\ /\ d_y = s_y\ /\ d_x = \mu \text{ (say)}$$

Thus

$$s_x = -\mu d_y \quad \text{and} \quad s_y = \mu d_x$$

and so $\quad \boldsymbol{s} \equiv \mu(-d_y\ ,\ d_x)$

But since $\mu\boldsymbol{s}$ is parallel to $\boldsymbol{s}$ for all μ, we may take $\boldsymbol{s} \equiv (-d_y\ ,\ d_x)$ to be the direction vector of any line perpendicular to $\boldsymbol{d}$. Furthermore, if $(d_x\ ,\ d_y)$ is a unit vector then the perpendicular $(-d_y\ ,\ d_x)$ is also a unit vector.

This method may also be used to find a perpendicular to a line given in linear equation form. Since the line $ay = bx + c$ has direction vector $(a\ ,\ b)$, a perpendicular line has direction vector $(-b\ ,\ a)$ and an equation

$$-by = ax + c'$$

The value of c' does not affect the direction of the line, and so every value of c' gives a line perpendicular to $ay = bx + c$.

Curves: analytic representation and parametric forms

A curve in two-dimensional space can be considered as a relationship between x and y co-ordinate values – the *analytic form*, or alternatively the co-ordinates can be individually specified in terms of other variables or parameters – the *parametric form.*

It has already been seen that a line may be expressed as $ay = bx + c$. If the equation is rearranged so that one side is zero – that is, $ay - bx - c = 0$, then the algebraic expression on the left-hand side of the equation, which relates the x and y values, is called an *analytic representation* of the line, and may be written as a function definition

$$f(x,y) \equiv ay - bx - c$$

All, and only those points with the property $f(x,y) = 0$ lie on the straight line (which is a special form of curve). This representation gives a *point membership classification* which divides all two-dimensional point vectors into three sets: the *zero set*, with $f(x,y) = 0$; the *positive set*, with $f(x,y) > 0$; and the *negative set*, with $f(x,y) < 0$. This is true for all curves with given analytic representation $f(x,y)$. If the function divides space into the curve and two other *connected areas* only (that is, any two points in a connected area may be joined by a finite curvilinear line which does not cross the curve), then these areas may be identified with the positive and negative sets defined by f. However, be wary, there are many functions (such as $g(x,y) \equiv \cos(y) - \sin(x)$), which define not one but a series of curves, and hence divide space into possibly an infinite number of connected areas (note $g(x,y) = g(x{+}2m\pi\ , y{+}2n\pi)$ for all integers m and n), so it is possible that two disconnected areas can both belong to the positive (or negative) set.

It is important to note that the analytic representation need not be unique. For example, the typical line can be put in an equivalent form

$$f(x,y) \equiv bx + c - ay$$

for which the positive set is now the negative set of the original, and vice versa.

The case where the curve does divide space into two connected areas is very useful in computer graphics, as will be seen in the study of three-dimensional graphics algorithms. Take the straight line for example

$$f(x,y) \equiv ay - bx - c$$

A point (x_1 , y_1) is on the same side of the line as (x_2 , y_2) if and only if $f(x_1 , y_1)$ has the same non-zero sign as $f(x_2 , y_2)$. The analytic representation tells more about a point (x_1 , y_1) than just on which side of a line it lies – it also enables the distance of the point from the line to be calculated.

Consider the line defined above. Its direction vector is $(a\ ,\ b)$; and a line perpendicular to it will have direction vector $(-b\ ,\ a)$. So the point $\boldsymbol{q}$ on the line closest to the point $\boldsymbol{p} \equiv (x_1\ ,\ y_1)$ is of the form

$$\boldsymbol{q} = (x_1\ ,\ y_1) + \mu(-b\ ,\ a)$$

that is, a new line joining $\boldsymbol{p}$ and $\boldsymbol{q}$ is perpendicular to the original line. Since $\boldsymbol{q}$ lies on this original line

$$f(\boldsymbol{q}) = f((x_1\ ,\ y_1) + \mu(-b\ ,\ a)) = 0$$

that is

$$f(x_1 - \mu b\ ,\ y_1 + \mu a) = a\times(y_1 + \mu a) - b\times(x_1 - \mu b) - c$$

$$= f(x_1\ ,\ y_1) + \mu(a^2 + b^2) = 0$$

Hence $\mu = -f(x_1\ ,\ y_1)/(a^2 + b^2)$

The point $\boldsymbol{q}$ is a distance $|\mu(-b\ ,\ a)| = |\mu|\surd(a^2 + b^2)$ from $(x_1\ ,\ y_1)$, which naturally means that the distance of point $(x_1\ ,\ y_1)$ from the chosen line is given by $|-f(x_1\ ,\ y_1)/\surd(a^2+b^2)|$. The sign of the value of $-f(x_1\ ,\ y_1)$ denotes the side of the line on which the point lies. If $a^2 + b^2 = 1$ then $|f(x_1\ ,\ y_1)|$ gives the distance of the point $(x_1\ ,\ y_1)$ from the line.

Inside and outside

We may use these ideas in the consideration of *convex* areas (an area is convex if it totally contains a straight line segment joining any two points lying inside it). More specifically, we consider only *convex polygons*, but any convex area may be approximated by a polygon, provided that the polygon has enough sides.

Consider the convex polygon with n vertices $\{\boldsymbol{p}_i \equiv (x_i\ ,\ y_i) \mid i=0,1,2,\ldots, n-1\}$ taken in order around the polygon (either clockwise or anti-clockwise). Such a description of a convex polygon is called an *oriented convex set of vertices*. The problem of finding whether such a set is presented in clockwise or anti-clockwise order is considered in the next chapter. The n boundary edges of the polygon are segments of the lines

$$f_i(x\ ,\ y) \equiv (x_{i+1} - x_i) \times (y - y_i) - (y_{i+1} - y_i) \times (x - x_i)$$

where $i = 0,\ldots, n-1$, and the addition in the subscripts is modulo n (that is $j \equiv n+j$ for $0 \le j < n$).

The analytic representation of a given line segment, say the one joining $\boldsymbol{p}_i$ to $\boldsymbol{p}_{i+1}$ for some i, is calculated in the above way in order to take advantage of an interesting property of this formulation. If you imagine yourself astride the line looking from $\boldsymbol{p_i}$ towards $\boldsymbol{p_{i+1}}$ then the positive side of the line is to the left and the negative side to the right.

If the vertices of a convex polygon are oriented anti-clockwise, then the *inside* of the polygon is classified by the set

$$\{(x , y) \mid f_i (x , y) > 0 \text{ for all } i, \ 0 \le i < n\}$$

A point *on the boundary* is given by

$$\{(x , y) \mid f_i (x , y) \ge 0 \text{ for all } i, \ 0 \le i < n \text{ and there is at least one } i \text{ such that } f_i (x , y) = 0 \}$$

The *outside* of the polygon is defined by

$$\{(x , y) \mid f_i (x , y) < 0 \text{ for at least one } i, \ 0 \le i < n\}$$

This technique of 'inside and outside' is fundamental to the calculation of the intersection of two polygons in chapter 5, and a hidden surface algorithm of chapter 10.

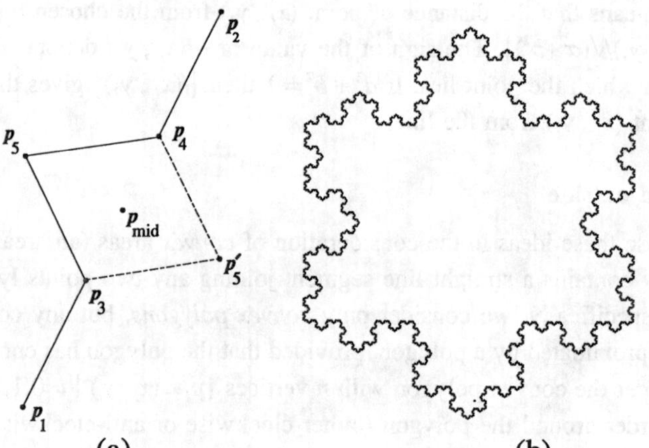

Figure 4.5

Example 4.2

We will now use the ratio of the distance between vectors, the perpendicular to a given direction, and the positive and negative sides of a line, to produce another fractal diagram – the Koch snowflake of figure 4.5b. First consider figure 4.5a, of a line $\boldsymbol{p}(\mu) \equiv (1-\mu)\boldsymbol{p_1} + \mu\boldsymbol{p_2}$, joining two vectors $\boldsymbol{p_1} \equiv (x_1 , y_1)$ and $\boldsymbol{p_2} \equiv (x_2 , y_2)$, which is divided into three equal segments at points $\boldsymbol{p_3} \equiv \boldsymbol{p}(1/3)$ and $\boldsymbol{p_4} \equiv \boldsymbol{p}(2/3)$. The perpendicular line through $\boldsymbol{p_{mid}} \equiv \boldsymbol{p}(1/2)$, the mid-point of the line segment, is of the form $\boldsymbol{p_{mid}} + \lambda\boldsymbol{d}$, with direction vector $\boldsymbol{d} \equiv (-(y_2-y_1) , (x_2-x_1))$. The point

p_5 that forms an equilateral triangle with p_3 and p_4 is a distance $\sqrt{3}/2$ of the triangle edge length (that is $|p_2 - p_1|/(2\sqrt{3})$) from the original line. All that remains is to choose λ as $-1/(2\sqrt{3})$, rather than $+1/(2\sqrt{3})$ – the former value gives p_5, the latter p_5', since the positive value for λ gives a point on the left of the line when viewed from p_1 and p_2.

Using this method to run anti-clockwise around an equilateral triangle, each of the three edges of the triangle will be divided into four lines, and each of those can be divided into four, and so on. We repeat the process until we reach the limits of the resolution of the screen, so as to produce figure 4.5b, generated by function **draw_a_picture** of listing 4.2, when it is stored as **"four2.cpp"** and linked in a C++ Project with **"window.cpp"**.

Listing 4.2

```
// Application program to draw the Koch snowflake

#include "viewport.h"
#include "palette.h"
#include "window.h"

extern Window win ;

const float over_root3 = 1.0 / sqrt(3.0) ;

//-------------------------------------------//
  void fractal(int l, vector2 p1, vector2 p2)
//-------------------------------------------//
 { vector2 pmid, p3, p4, p5, d ;
// draw line at zero level, else recursively subdivide that line
   if (l==0) { win.moveto(p1) ; win.lineto(p2) ; }
   else
     { p3.x = p1.x *2.0/3.0 + p2.x /3.0 ;
       p3.y = p1.y *2.0/3.0 + p2.y /3.0 ;
       p4.x = p1.x /3.0 + p2.x *2.0/3.0 ;
       p4.y = p1.y /3.0 + p2.y *2.0/3.0 ;
       pmid.x = (p1.x + p2.x) * 0.5 ;
       pmid.y = (p1.y + p2.y) * 0.5 ;
       d.x = -(p2.y - p1.y) ;      d.y = p2.x - p1.x ;
       p5.x = pmid.x - d.x * over_root3 * 0.5 ;
       p5.y = pmid.y - d.y * over_root3 * 0.5 ;
       fractal(l-1,p1,p3) ;   fractal(l-1,p3,p5) ;
       fractal(l-1,p5,p4) ;   fractal(l-1,p4,p2) ;
     }
 }  // End of fractal

//-------------------------//
  void draw_a_picture(void)
//-------------------------//
 { vector2 triangle[3] =
           { 0.0, 2/3.0, -over_root3, -1/3.0, over_root3, -1/3.0 } ;
   int level ;
   cout << "Type in the level of recursion\n" ;
   cin >> level ;
// level 5 is about right for VGA mode 18
   win.start() ;
   fractal(level,triangle[0],triangle[1]) ;
   fractal(level,triangle[1],triangle[2]) ;
   fractal(level,triangle[2],triangle[0]) ;
 }  // End of draw_a _picture
```

Example 4.3

Consider the convex polygon with vertices (1 , 0), (5 , 2), (4 , 4) and (–2 , 1): see figure 4.6. In this order the vertices obviously have an anti-clockwise orientation. Are the points (3 , 2), (1 , 4), (3 , 1) inside, outside or on the boundary of the polygon? What is the distance of (4 , 4) from the first line?

$$f_0(x , y) \equiv (5 - 1) \times (y - 0) - (2 - 0) \times (x - 1) \equiv 4y - 2x + 2$$

$$f_1(x , y) \equiv (4 - 5) \times (y - 2) - (4 - 2) \times (x - 5) \equiv -y - 2x + 12$$

$$f_2(x , y) \equiv (-2 - 4) \times (y - 4) - (1 - 4) \times (x - 4) \equiv -6y + 3x + 12$$

$$f_3(x , y) \equiv (1 + 2) \times (y - 1) - (0 - 1) \times (x + 2) \equiv 3y + x - 1$$

Hence point (3 , 2) is inside the body because $f_0(3 , 2)=4$, $f_1(3 , 2)=4$, $f_2(3 , 2)=9$ and $f_3(3 , 2)=8$: all have positive signs.

Point (1 , 4) is outside the body because $f_2(1 , 4)=-9$ (negative).

Point (3 , 1) is one the boundary because $f_0(3 , 1)=0$, and the values $f_1(3 , 1)=5$, $f_2(3 , 1)=15$ and $f_3(3 , 1)=5$ are all positive.

Point (4 , 4) is at a distance $f_0(4 , 4)/\sqrt{(4^2+2^2)}(=10/\sqrt{20}=\sqrt{5})$ from the first line.

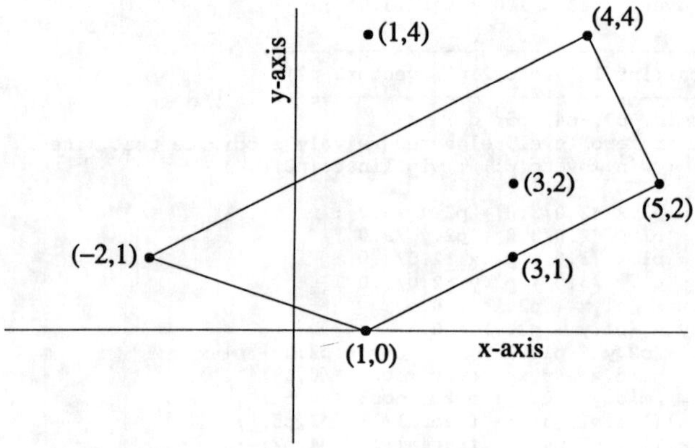

Figure 4.6

Exercise 4.3

Write a small program that reads in the corners of a convex *n*-gon, and then when further vector points are input, prints out whether these points lie inside, outside or on the boundary of the polygon.

Having dealt with the analytic representation of a line, what about the parametric form? It was noted above that this form is one where the *x* and *y* co-ordinates of a typical point on the curve are given in terms of parameter(s) (which could be the x or y values themselves), together with a range for the parameter(s). A parametric form of a line has already been considered. It is simply the base and direction representation

$$\boldsymbol{b} + \mu\boldsymbol{d} \equiv (x_1, y_1) + \mu(x_2, y_2)$$

$$\equiv (x_1 + \mu \times x_2, y_1 + \mu \times y_2) \quad \text{where } -\infty < \mu < \infty$$

μ is the parameter, and $x_1 + \mu \times x_2$ and $y_1 + \mu \times y_2$ are the respective x and y values which depend only on parameter μ.

Analytic representations and parametric forms can be produced for most well-behaved curves. For example, a sine curve is given by $f(x,y) \equiv y - \sin(x)$ in analytic representation, and by $(x, \sin(x))$ with $-\infty < x < \infty$ in its parametric form. The general conic section (ellipse, parabola and hyperbola) is represented by the typical function

$$f(x,y) \equiv a \times x^2 + b \times y^2 + h \times x \times y + f \times x + g \times y + c$$

Coefficients a, b, c, f, g, h uniquely identify a curve. A circle centred at the origin of a radius r has $a = b = -1, f = g = h = 0$ and $c = r^2$, whence the analytic form $f(x,y) \equiv r^2 - x^2 - y^2$. All the points (x,y) on the circle are such that $f(x,y)=0$, the inside of the circle has $f(x,y) > 0$, and the outside of the circle $f(x,y) < 0$. The parametric form of this circle is $(r\cos\alpha, r\sin\alpha)$, where $0 \leq \alpha < 2\pi$. (The parametric forms of a circle, ellipse and spiral were met in chapter 2.)

These concepts are very useful in the study of graphics and experimenting with them now will prove to be of great value later. There will be many occasions when such ideas will be used in the solution of problems including, of course, the generation of co-ordinate data for the modelling of scenes.

5 Points, lines and polygonal facets

The programs introduced so far enable us to create and draw specific simple two-dimensional diagrams. In this chapter we shall consider a number of more sophisticated techniques that use the ideas of two-dimensional co-ordinate geometry from chapter 4, not only to draw more complex two-dimensional pictures, but also to develop algorithms that will have general utility in displaying three-dimensional scenes.

Clipping points and lines to fit on the window/viewport

The diagrams drawn in earlier chapters, using the **Window** methods **moveto** and **lineto** (but as we shall see, not **polyfill**), assumed that the width of the window, **horiz**, was chosen so that all points and lines fitted neatly inside the viewport. Obviously, by making **horiz** ridiculously small we can always falsify this assumption. Try it out, with the Vasarely figure from listing 2.6 with **horiz** set at 0.1, and observe what happens – you will see that our drivers throw up an error message and the diagrams are ruined. This has to be corrected, so that whenever part of the shape, be it point or line (or polygon), lies completely or partly outside the window, then we must be able to identify the parts of the shape that lie inside the window, and these parts only should be drawn. Our approach will be used to replace the methods **moveto** and **lineto** in the **Window** class, so that all our other previous programs will remain totally unchanged, and yet they can now be executed without exhibiting the above problems.

The positioning of single points provides no problem, since we can adjust the **moveto** function so that it only moves to points that lie inside the **horiz** by **vert** window – see listing 5.1. Also note that we store the **lastvector** referenced, as this will be needed for dealing next with **lineto**. The problem of polygons lying wholly, or partly, outside the window area is considered later in this chapter.

Different graphics devices deal with line segments that are external to the viewport/window in a variety of ways in hardware or in system software; some *clip* lines correctly, but some reflect lines back into view causing great confusion, and some leave such lines undrawn. We need to implement correct clipping of line segments that are partly or totally external to the window, such as those illustrated in figure 5.1 – figure 5.1a should be clipped to give figure 5.1b.

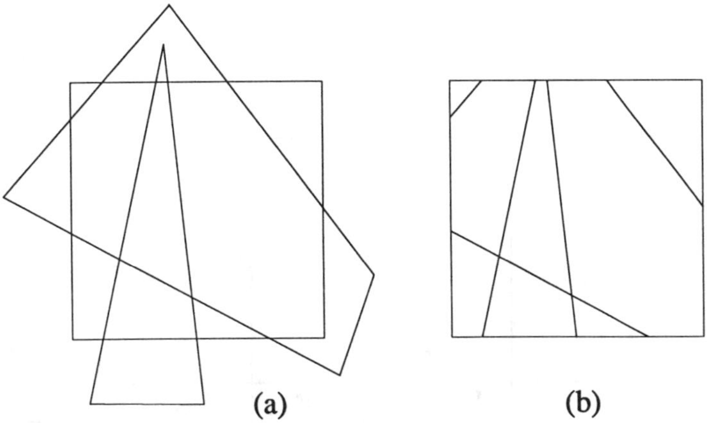

(a) (b)

Figure 5.1

In practice we will clip each line just before it is drawn by **lineto**, so the problem reduces to calculating which part (if any) of a line segment joining point (x_1, y_1) to point (x_2, y_2) lies within the window. The following algorithm, due to Cohen and Sutherland, achieves this. The window is a rectangular area with the co-ordinate origin at its centre and has length **horiz** and depth **vert**; so that the corners have vertices **(±horiz/2 , ±vert/2)**, or as we will rename them for efficiency **(±halfhoriz , ±halfvert)**.

We start by extending the sides of the rectangular window, in effect dividing the whole of two-dimensional space into nine sectors, see figure 5.2. A number of different line segments have been drawn in this figure in order to aid the explanation of the algorithm. Each point in space may now be classified by two parameters **ix** and **iy**, where

(1) **ix** = −1, 0 or +l, depending on whether the x co-ordinate value of the point lies to the left, within the x bounds, or to the right of the clipping rectangle (the window/viewport).

(2) **iy** = −1, 0 or +l, depending on whether the y co-ordinate value of the point lies below, within the y bounds, or above the clipping rectangle.

These values are calculated by function **trisect** that is stored in the file **"window.cpp"**, along with the primary clipping function **clip** and the replacement methods **lineto** and **moveto** of listing 5.1. Remember that in chapter 2 we scaled the window/viewport so that points **(±horiz/2 , ±vert/2)** and all points on the boundary of the viewing window are considered to be on the screen.

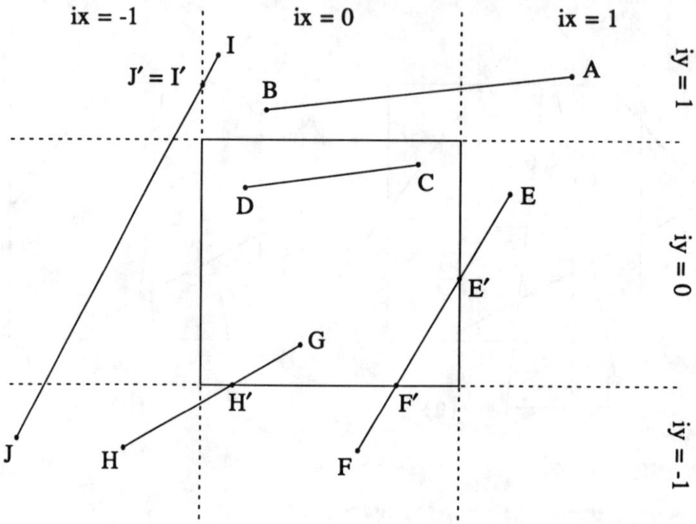

Figure 5.2

Listing 5.1

```
// Place private methods 'trisect' and 'clip' in file "window.cpp"
//-------------------------------------------------------//
 int Window::trisect(float z, float screendimension)
//-------------------------------------------------------//
// Returns -1 if 'z < -screendimension',
// 0 if '-screendimension <= z <= screendimension'
// and  1 if 'screendimension < z'
 {if (z < -screendimension) return(-1) ;
  else  if (screendimension < z) return(1) ;
        else  return(0) ;
 }  // End of trisect

//-----------------------------------------//
  void Window::clip(vector2 p1, vector2 p2)
//-----------------------------------------//
// Routine to find that segment of the line from vector 'p1'
// to vector 'p2' which lies within the clipping rectangle
// The required segment will be between vectors 'p1d' and 'p2d'
 { vector2 p1d,p2d ;
   int ix1,iy1,ix2,iy2 ;
   float xx,yy ;
   pixelvector pix1, pix2 ;
// Initially identify 'p1d' with 'p1' and 'p2d' with 'p2'
   p1d = p1 ; p2d = p2 ;
// Find frame trisect values of 'p1' and 'p2'
   ix1=trisect(p1d.x,halfhoriz) ; iy1=trisect(p1d.y,halfvert) ;
   ix2=trisect(p2d.x,halfhoriz) ; iy2=trisect(p2d.y,halfvert) ;
// ignore points that are in same sector outside clipping rectangle
   if ((ix1*ix2 != 1) && (iy1*iy2 != 1))
     { if (iy1 != 0)
// If first point is outside the y bounds of the clipping rectangle
// then move it to the nearest y edge
```

```
        { yy=halfvert*iy1 ;
          p1d.x=p1d.x+(p2d.x-p1d.x)*(yy-p1d.y)/(p2d.y-p1d.y) ;
          p1d.y=yy ; ix1=trisect(p1d.x,halfhoriz) ;
        } ;
       if (ix1 != 0)
// If first point is outside the x bounds of the clipping rectangle
// then move it to the nearest x edge
        { xx=halfhoriz*ix1 ;
          p1d.y=p1d.y+(p2d.y-p1d.y)*(xx-p1d.x)/(p2d.x-p1d.x) ;
          p1d.x=xx ;
        } ;
       if (iy2 != 0)
// If second point is outside the y bounds of the clipping rectangle
// then move it to the nearest y edge
        { yy=halfvert*iy2 ;
          p2d.x=p1d.x+(p2d.x-p1d.x)*(yy-p1d.y)/(p2d.y-p1d.y) ;
          p2d.y=yy ; ix2=trisect(p2d.x,halfhoriz) ;
        } ;
       if (ix2 != 0)
// If second point is outside the x bounds of the clipping rectangle
// then move it to the nearest x edge
        { xx=halfhoriz*ix2 ;
          p2d.y=p1d.y+(p2d.y-p1d.y)*(xx-p1d.x)/(p2d.x-p1d.x) ;
          p2d.x=xx ;
        } ;
// Plot line between new points if they are not coincident
       if ((fabs(p1d.x-p2d.x) > epsilon) || (fabs(p1d.y-p2d.y) > epsilon))
        { pix1.x = fx(p1d.x) ;  pix1.y = fy(p1d.y) ;  movepix(pix1) ;
          pix2.x = fx(p2d.x) ;  pix2.y = fy(p2d.y) ;  linepix(pix2) ;
        } ;
     } ;
 }  // End of clip

//============================================================================//
// Replace existing moveto and lineto methods in  "window.cpp" (listing 2.1b)
// with the following functions

//--------------------------------//
  void Window::moveto(vector2 pt)
//--------------------------------//
 { pixelvector pixel ;
   pixel.x = fx(pt.x) ;  pixel.y = fy(pt.y) ;
   lastvector = pt ;
   if ((pixel.x>=0) && (pixel.x <nxpix) && (pixel.y>=0) && (pixel.y<nypix))
        movepix(pixel) ;
 }  // End of moveto

//--------------------------------//
  void Window::lineto(vector2 pt)
//--------------------------------//
 { clip(lastvector,pt) ; lastvector = pt ;
 }  // End of lineto
```

The clipping algorithm needs the two end-points of the line segment, **vector2** points **p1** and **p2** – remember **lineto** has only one **vector2** parameter, and this is why we have to store the **lastvector** created by **moveto** and **lineto**. Suppose the points **p1** and **p2** have parameters **ix1** and **iy1**, and **ix2** and **iy2** respectively, then there are a number of possibilities to consider.

(i) If **ix1** = **ix2** $\neq 0$ or **iy1** = **iy2** $\neq 0$, then the whole line segment is outside the rectangle, and hence may be safely ignored – for example, line **AB** in figure 5.2.

(ii) If **ix1** = **iy2** = **ix2** = **iy2** = 0, then the whole line segment lies in the rectangle, and so the complete line must be drawn – for example, line **CD**.

(iii) The remaining case must be considered in detail. If the values of **ix1** ≠ 0 and/or **iy1** ≠ 0, then the **vector2** point **p1** ≡ (x_1, y_1) lies outside the window, and so new values of x_1 and y_1 must be found – to avoid confusion these are called x_1' and y_1'. We need to calculate **p1d** ≡ (x_1', y_1'), the **vector2** point on the line segment where it cuts the clipping rectangle nearer to **p1**. The formula for this calculation was considered in chapter 4 – that is, the intersection of a given line with another line that is parallel to a co-ordinate axis. If the given line misses the clipping rectangle, then **p1d** is defined to be that point where the line cuts one of the extended vertical edges. If the values of **ix1** = **iy1** = 0 then **p1d** = **p1**.

The **vector2** point **p2d** ≡ (x_2', y_2') is calculated in a similar manner. The required clipped line segment is that joining **p1d** to **p2d**. If the original line misses the rectangle, then the algorithm ensures that **p1d** = **p2d** and the new line segment degenerates to a point and is ignored. In figure 5.2, for example, **EF** is clipped to **E′F′**, **GH** is clipped to **GH′(G=G′)** and **IJ** degenerates to a point **I′** = **J′**.

The function **clip** takes the two end-points of the line, **p1** and **p2**, and discovers which of the above three possibilities is relevant, dealing with it thus

(i) exit the function immediately or
(ii) join the two points with a line segment, or
(iii) calculate the ‘dashed’ points and join them with a line segment.

Since our drawing of lines is achieved by a combination of calls to the functions **moveto** and **lineto**, replacing the original versions of these two functions in **"window.cpp"** and adding the functions **clip** and **trisect**, we have achieved the algorithm that solves clipping around the **horiz** by **vert** window centred on the origin of the WINDOW system, which of course is sufficient to ensure that no drawing is attempted outside the viewport.

Exercise 5.1

All references to the clipping rectangle in the description of this algorithm should be understood to apply, not only to the entire window/viewport, but equally to any smaller rectangle within it. The algorithm given above may be adjusted to clip lines outside a rectangle of any size, but care should be taken to ensure that any such *clipping rectangle* actually lies totally within the viewport, otherwise the problem of external line segments will remain. Rewrite the program in listing 5.1 to give a general clipping function – but you will have to think very carefully before arbitrarily changing **moveto** and **lineto**. Also, consider clipping lines to lie within a rectangle which is neither centred on the origin of WINDOW space, nor with edges parallel to the co-ordinate axes.

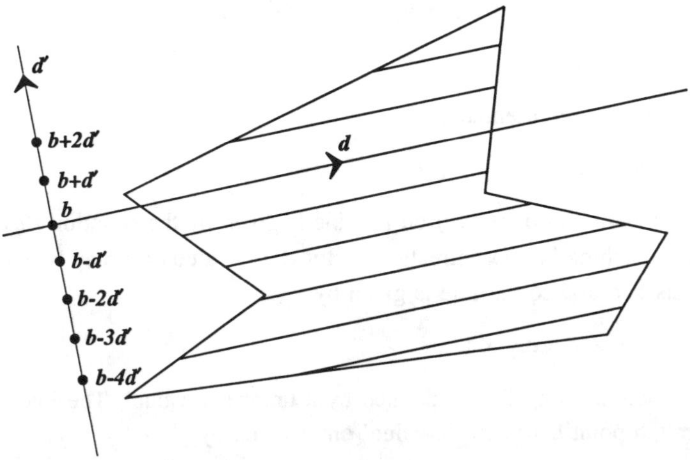

Figure 5.3

Hatching polygons

Before proceeding to the clipping of polygonal areas within the window, we first consider a generalization of clipping, in fact one of the most useful functions in any line-graphics package – the hatching of a polygonal area using equi-spaced parallel lines (see figure 5.3). This facility is built into many graphics systems, but for the benefit of readers not having access to these systems, and also for a useful demonstration of an application of the geometry introduced so far, we will discuss the theory behind such a function. The polygon is assumed to have m vertices $\{p_i \equiv (x_i, y_i) \mid i=0, ..., m-1\}$ taken in order and implemented as a **vector2** array **p** (with less than **maxpoly** vertices). It may be convex or concave, and its boundary may even cross itself. Without loss of generality it may be assumed that there is only one set of parallel hatching lines. For combinations of sets of hatching lines, the following theory is repeated for each set in turn.

The algorithm we give uses both the analytic and parametric forms of a line. Suppose the direction of the parallel lines is given by **vector2 d ≡ (d.x , d.y)**, and the distance between neighbouring hatching lines is defined to be **dist**. This still leaves an infinite number of possible sets of parallel lines! To define one set uniquely, it is still necessary to specify a **vector2** base point, **b ≡ (b.x , b.y)** , on any one of the lines from the set.

Note that a line with direction **d** which passes through **b** has the typical vector form in the base/direction vector notation

$$\mathbf{b} + \mu\mathbf{d} \quad \text{where} \quad -\infty < \mu < \infty$$

As we have seen, a straight line may also be defined in the form

$$a \times y = b \times x + c$$

which has analytic representation

$$f(x, y) \equiv a \times y - b \times x - c$$

whence a typical point $q \equiv (x, y)$ on the line is given by the equation $f(q) = 0$.

Since a hatching line has direction vector **d**, the value of a may be taken as **d.x** and b as **d.y**, and so the line is given by

$$\mathbf{d.x} \times y = \mathbf{d.y} \times x + c$$

Therefore, each hatching line is defined by a unique 'c-value'. The line which passes through point **b** has the 'c-value' **cmid** given by:

$$\mathbf{cmid} = \mathbf{d.x} \times \mathbf{b.y} - \mathbf{d.y} \times \mathbf{b.x}$$

We can now calculate all the 'c-values' for the m lines with direction **d** which pass through each of the m vertices of the polygon (note that these do not necessarily belong to the set of hatching lines), and then find the extreme values **cmax** and **cmin** thus

$$\mathbf{cmax} = \max_{0 \le i < m} \{ \mathbf{d.x} \times y_i - \mathbf{d.y} \times x_i \}$$

$$\mathbf{cmin} = \min_{0 \le i < m} \{ \mathbf{d.x} \times y_i - \mathbf{d.y} \times x_i \}$$

This means that the polygon lies totally between the two lines

$$\mathbf{d.x} \times y = \mathbf{d.y} \times x + \mathbf{cmin} \quad \text{and} \quad \mathbf{d.x} \times y = \mathbf{d.y} \times x + \mathbf{cmax}$$

In order to hatch the given polygon with lines parallel to **d**, naturally only lines with 'c-values' that fall between these extremes need be considered from the set. It should be noted that even though vector **b** is used to *anchor* the set of parallel lines with inter-line distance **dist**, there is no need for the line which passes through **b** to intersect the polygon. For ease of calculation it is now sensible to resort to the vector notation for lines. Note that the hatching lines are all in the form

$$\mathbf{q} + \mu\mathbf{d} \quad \text{where} \quad -\infty < \mu < \infty$$

Here $\mathbf{q}$ represents a base point on a typical hatching line. So it is necessary to find a vector $\mathbf{q}$ for each of the hatching lines that cuts the polygon. The $\mathbf{q}$ values are defined to be the points of intersection of this set of hatching lines with the line through $\mathbf{b}$ with direction $\mathbf{d'}$ (which is perpendicular to the hatching lines – that is to $\mathbf{d}$). Note that $\mathbf{d'}$ may be represented by the vector (–**d.y** , **d.x**).

Hence the base points $\mathbf{q}$ are all of the form

$$\mathbf{q} = \mathbf{b} + \lambda\mathbf{d'} \quad \text{where} \quad -\infty < \lambda < \infty$$

This formulation naturally represents every point on the new line perpendicular to the hatching lines, but only its points of intersection with the hatching lines are required. Note that any non-zero scalar multiple of $\mathbf{d'}$ may also represent the direction of the new line, and choose $\mathbf{s} = (\mathbf{dist}/|\mathbf{d'}|)\,\mathbf{d'}$ which means that vector $\mathbf{s}$ has length (or modulus) **dist**. Now note that $\mathbf{q}$ can be considered

$$\mathbf{q} = \mathbf{b} + \mathbf{n} \times \mathbf{s} = \mathbf{b} + \mathbf{n} \times (\mathbf{dist}/|\mathbf{d'}|)\,\mathbf{d'} \quad \text{for some } \mathbf{n}$$

If **n** is an integer, this vector combination gives all, but only, the points of intersection of the new line with a set of parallel lines of direction **d** in which neighbouring lines are a distance **dist** apart. Since **b** is one of these intersections (**n**=0), then this formulation contains the base vectors for the required set of hatching lines. However, lines still have to be restricted to those with '*c*-values' that lie between **cmin** and **cmax**. This is achieved by insisting that the '**n**-values' of the base points of the hatching lines lie between **nmin** and **nmax**, where

$$\mathbf{nmin} = \lceil(\mathbf{cmin} - \mathbf{cmid})/(\mathbf{dist}/|\mathbf{d'}|)\rceil$$

and

$$\mathbf{nmax} = \lfloor(\mathbf{cmax} - \mathbf{cmid})/(\mathbf{dist}/|\mathbf{d'}|)\rfloor$$

Here $\lceil r \rceil$ gives the smallest integer not less than r, and $\lfloor r \rfloor$ gives the largest integer not greater than r. Note that 0, the '**n**-value' corresponding to **b**, need not lie in this range.

Given any integer **n**, the corresponding vector **q** which then identifies a particular hatching line can be calculated. This line is then intersected with the edges of the polygon defined by vertices p_0 ,..., p_{m-1}. Suppose there is an intersection between points p_i and p_{i+1}, then note that the intersection on this edge may be given in the form

$$p_i + \alpha(p_{i+1} - p_i) \quad \text{where} \quad 0 \le \alpha \le 1,$$

as well as by $\mathbf{q} + \mu\mathbf{d}$ on the hatching line. The hatching line only cuts the polygon at this edge if the α value lies between 0 and 1. The μ value for each valid intersection must be stored.

As i varies through all the edges of the polygon (when $i = m-1$, then p_{i+1} is identified with p_0), all the μ values of proper intersections are calculated and then placed in increasing numerical order. Care must be taken with rounding errors and coincident points! There is always an even number of these μ values. Having found points on the hatching line corresponding to the μ values, the first is joined to the second, the third to the fourth etc., and this gives the correct hatching on one line. Varying **n** between **nmin** and **nmax** gives the complete hatching for the polygon. The process is implemented as function **hatch** in listing 5.2, which is used to extend the code of file **"window.cpp"** (listing 2.1b). The declarations have already been given in file **"window.h"** of listing 2.1a. Listing 5.3 gives a demonstration **draw_a_picture** function that uses **hatch**.

Listing 5.2

```
// Place function in file "window.cpp"

//----------------------------------------------------------------------//
  void Window::hatch(int m,vector2 *p, vector2 b, vector2 d, float dist)
//----------------------------------------------------------------------//
// Hatches an 'm-gon' with vertices 'p[0],...,p[m-1]' using equi-spaced
// parallel lines. Distance between neighbouring lines is 'dist' and each
// line has direction vector 'd'. One hatching line anchored by 'b'.
 { int i,isec,j,lasti,n,nmin,nmax,nint,nnp,npoint[maxpoly] ;
   float  alpha,c,cmax,cmid,cmin,dmod,mu[maxpoly],mu1,mu2 ;
   vector2 e,inter,p1,p2,q,s ;
// Find 'cmid', 'cmin' and 'cmax'
   cmid=d.x*b.y-d.y*b.x ;
   cmin=d.x*p[0].y-d.y*p[0].x ;
   cmax=cmin ;
   for (i=1 ; i<m ; i++)
   { c=d.x*p[i].y-d.y*p[i].x ;
     if (c < cmin)  cmin=c ;
     else  if (c > cmax)  cmax=c ;
   }
// Construct vector 's'
   dmod=sqrt(d.x*d.x+d.y*d.y) ;
   s.x=-dist/dmod*d.y ; s.y=dist/dmod*d.x ;
// Calculate 'nmin' and 'nmax'
   nmin=(int)((cmin-cmid)/(dist*dmod)+0.9999) ;
   nmax=(int)((cmax-cmid)/(dist*dmod)) ;
// Hatch the polygon
   for (n=nmin ; n<=nmax ; n++)
// Find 'q' the base vector of the hatching line
   { q.x=b.x+n*s.x ; q.y=b.y+n*s.y ;
// Find 'nint' intersections of hatching line with edges of polygon
     nint=0 ; lasti=m-1 ;
     for (i=0 ; i<m ; i++)
     { e.x=p[i].x-p[lasti].x ;  e.y=p[i].y-p[lasti].y ;
       isec = ill2(p[lasti],e,q,d,&inter) ;
       if (isec == 1)
         { alpha=(inter.x-p[lasti].x)/e.x ;
           if ((alpha >= 0) && (alpha <= 1))
             { nint++ ;
               npoint[nint]=nint ;
               mu[nint]=(inter.x-q.x)/d.x ;
             } ;
         } ;
       lasti=i ;
     } ;
```

```
// Sort 'mu' values into order
     for (i=1 ; i<nint; i++)
     { for (j=i+1 ; j<=nint ; j++)
       { if (mu[npoint[i]] < mu[npoint[j]])
           { nnp=npoint[i] ;  npoint[i]=npoint[j] ; npoint[j]=nnp ;
           } ;
       }
     }
// Join corresponding pairs of intersections
     i=1 ;
     while (i < nint)
     { mu1=mu[npoint[i]] ;
       p1.x=q.x+mu1*d.x ;  p1.y=q.y+mu1*d.y ;
       mu2=mu[npoint[i+1]] ;
       p2.x=q.x+mu2*d.x ;  p2.y=q.y+mu2*d.y ;
       win.moveto(p1) ;  win.lineto(p2) ;
       i+=2 ;
     }
   }
 }  // End of hatch
```

Listing 5.3

```
// Application program to demonstrate hatching; set horiz = 16

#include "viewport.h"
#include "palette.h"
#include "window.h"

extern Window win ;

//-------------------------//
  void draw_a_picture(void)
//-------------------------//
 { int i ;
// Setup test values of polygon, base and direction vectors
   static vector2 b={2,1}, d={3,2} ;
   static vector2 pt[9]         \
        = {5,1, -3,-1, 2,4, -1,-4, -5,5, 3,-3, 1,2, -4,6, 3,1 } ;
   win.start() ;
// Hatch polygon in red
   win.setcol(12) ; win.hatch(9,pt,b,d,0.2) ;
// Draw outline of polygon in white
   win.setcol(15) ; win.moveto(pt[8]) ;
   for (i=0 ; i<9 ; i++) win.lineto(pt[i]) ;
 }  // End of draw_a_picture
```

Exercise 5.2

If the polygon is composed of a large number of vertices then there is no need to waste time calculating all the intersections, only to discover that most of the α values do not lie between 0 and 1 and are, therefore, irrelevant. A trick to save time is to put the hatching line in analytic form

$$f(\boldsymbol{v}) \equiv f(x, y) \equiv a \times y - b \times x - c$$

Now if consecutive point vectors $\boldsymbol{p}_i$ and $\boldsymbol{p}_{i+1}$ are such that $f(\boldsymbol{p}_i)$ and $f(\boldsymbol{p}_{i+1})$ have the same sign – that is, either they are both positive or both negative – then there cannot be a useable point of intersection between them. Incorporate this idea into the function above.

Listing 5.4

```
// Replace function 'polyfill' in file "window.cpp" with the following

//---------------------------------------//
  void Window::polyfill(int n, polygon p)
//---------------------------------------//
 { int iv,ix,iy,nv,xmin,xmax,ymin,ymax ;
   pixelvector pix1,pix2 ;
   float factor, winx, winy ;
   pixelarray q ;
   for(iv=0 ; iv<n ; iv++)
   { q[iv].x = fx(p[iv].x) ;    q[iv].y = fy(p[iv].y) ;    }
   ymax=q[0].y ; ymin=ymax ;
   for (iv=1 ; iv<n ; iv++)
   { if (q[iv].y > ymax) ymax=q[iv].y ;
     if (q[iv].y < ymin) ymin=q[iv].y ;
   }
   if (ymax >= nypix)  ymax=nypix-1 ;
   if (ymin < 0)  ymin=0 ;
   for (iy=ymin ; iy<=ymax ; iy++)
   { xmin=nxpix ; xmax=-1 ; iv=n-1 ;
     winy = -(float)iy/xyscale/aspect + halfvert ;
     for (nv=0 ; nv<n ; nv++)
     { if (((q[iv].y >= iy) || (q[nv].y >= iy)) &&
           ((q[iv].y <= iy) || (q[nv].y <= iy)) &&
            (q[iv].y != q[nv].y) )
         { factor = (winy - p[iv].y) / (p[nv].y-p[iv].y) ;
           if (factor <0.0) factor = 0.0 ;
           else if (factor > 1.0) factor = 1.0 ;
           winx = p[iv].x + (p[nv].x - p[iv].x) * factor ;
           ix = fx(winx) ;
           if (ix < xmin) xmin=ix ;
           if (ix > xmax) xmax=ix ;
         } ;
       iv=nv ;
     } ;
     if (xmax >= nxpix) xmax=nxpix-1 ;
     if (xmin < 0.0) xmin=0 ;
     if (xmin <= xmax)
       { pix1.x=xmin ; pix1.y=iy ;
         pix2.x=xmax ; pix2.y=iy ;
         movepix(pix1) ; linepix(pix2) ;
       } ;
   } ;
 }  // End of polyfill
```

Convex polygonal area filling

A function which fills in a convex polygon with a given colour is a simple example of the general hatching problem, where the hatching lines are taken as horizontal and the distance between them is chosen so that they correspond to neighbouring rows of pixels (or *scan line*). The simplest form of this approach has already been coded in listings 1.1a and 1.1b, as function **polypix** in the files **"viewport.h"** and **"viewport.cpp"**. The algorithm is given a polygon with corners defined by at most **maxpoly pixelvectors**; it then finds the indices **ymin** and **ymax** of the two rows of pixels ($0 \leq$ **ymin** $\leq$ **ymax** $<$ **nypix**) that bound the polygon from above and below respectively. It then calculates the pixel columns where each scan line between these limits cuts the polygon; there will be two intersections which are joined by a line of the required colour. Note that the XGA card has its own hardware fill, which we used in the XGA version of **polypix** given in the Appendix.

Notice that, by limiting the scan line range to between 0 and **nypix**-1, and if we also limit the range of pixels along each scan line to be between 0 and **nxpix**-1, we have correctly clipped the polygon to fit inside the viewport.

In order to fill in a **polygon** defined by **vector2** corners in a **Window** object, we give method **polyfill** in **"window.cpp"**. This function simply maps the **polygon** corners into **pixelvectors** and calls **polypix**. However, there can be problems with this simple form of **polyfill**. There are occasions when drawing two **polygons** that abut at a common edge, that 'pixel holes' appear along that edge. This is caused by the fact that we are approximating twice in this process: the first time changing the **vector2 polygon** into one of **pixelvectors**, and again when we intersect each scan line with (aliased) lines of pixels that approximate to the edges of the **polygon**. In listing 5.4 we give an alternative **polyfill** method that should replace the old version in listing 2.1b. In this method, each scan line is mapped back into a horizontal **vector2** line, which is intersected with the **polygon** to give two accurate points of intersection. These can then be mapped onto the viewport, and joined as a sequence of pixels along a scan line.

Exercise 5.3
Write a function which hatches a polygon using both vertical and horizontal hatching lines. Again this is an easier problem than the typical case. Incorporate this function in a program which produces hatched histograms or bar-charts, types of diagrams that are essential in packages for so-called business graphics.

Exercise 5.4
Write a function which hatches a segment of a circle for use in pie-charts. This problem is more complicated because checks must also be made for intersections of the hatching lines with the circular arc bounding each pie.

The orientation of a convex polygon

In the last chapter we defined a convex polygon with n sides in terms of an ordered list of its vertices $\{p_i \equiv (x_i , y_i) \mid i = 0,..., n-1\}$. These vertices were ordered, either as they occur in a clockwise orientation around the boundary of the polygon, or in an anti-clockwise direction. As we discovered then, it is very important that we know in what orientation the polygon is defined – clockwise or anti-clockwise. We shall now consider how to determine this information from the list of vertices.

Since the polygon is convex, then given the relative orientation of any two consecutive edges, we may deduce the orientation of the whole. Thus we need consider only the first three vertices and the two lines joining them. Consider the line from $\boldsymbol{p_0}$ to $\boldsymbol{p_1}$. The analytic representation of this line may be written

$$f_0(x, y) \equiv a \times y - b \times x - c$$

where $a = (x_1 - x_0)$, $b = (y_1 - y_0)$ and $c = a \times y_1 - b \times x_1$.

In chapter 4 it was shown that when looking from $\boldsymbol{p_0}$ to $\boldsymbol{p_1}$, a point (x, y) with $f_0(x, y) > 0$ lies to the left of the line $\boldsymbol{p_0}$ to $\boldsymbol{p_1}$, and if $f_0(x, y) < 0$ then it lies to the right.

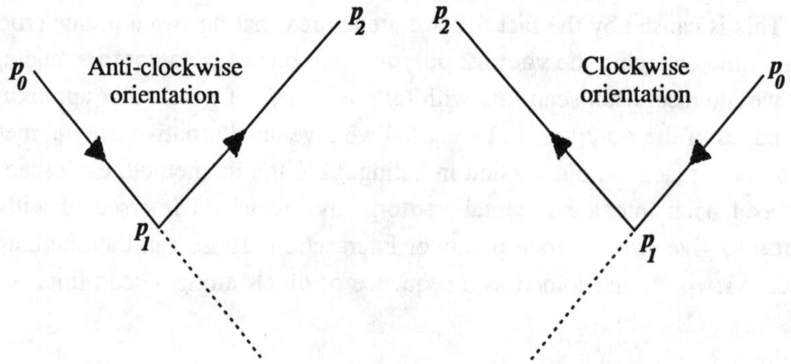

Figure 5.4

From figure 5.4 it may be seen that in order for the polygon to be in anti-clockwise orientation, $\boldsymbol{p_2}$ should lie to the left of the line from $\boldsymbol{p_0}$ to $\boldsymbol{p_1}$, and for clockwise orientation it should lie to the right. Therefore, in order to determine the orientation of a polygon defined in the above analytic representation, we need simply calculate $f_0(x_2, y_2)$

$$\begin{aligned} f_0(x_2, y_2) &\equiv a \times y_2 - b \times x_2 - c \\ &\equiv (x_1 - x_0) \times y_2 - (y_1 - y_0) \times x_2 - (x_1 - x_0) \times y_1 + (y_1 - y_0) \times x_1 \\ &\equiv (x_1 - x_0) \times (y_2 - y_1) - (y_1 - y_0) \times (x_2 - x_1) \end{aligned}$$

If this is positive then the polygon is oriented anti-clockwise, and if negative then the orientation is clockwise. If $f_0(x, y)$ is zero then the three vertices $\boldsymbol{p_0}$, $\boldsymbol{p_1}$ and $\boldsymbol{p_2}$ are collinear, and thus the orientation of the polygon cannot be determined. The inclusion of three consecutive collinear vertices in the boundary of a polygon is never necessary and should be avoided, since it may cause problems. The integer function **orient2** (listing 5.5) determines the orientation of a polygon. The value 1 is returned if the polygon is in anti-clockwise orientation, and –1 if it is clockwise. If the polygon is degenerate (that is, if the three points are collinear or even coincident) then the value 0 is returned. **orient2** calls another function **sign** (also given in listing 5.5) which returns the sign (+ 1, 0 or −1) of a floating point number; **sign** will be used many times in the three-dimensional functions that follow. The code for these functions, **sign** and **orient2**, should be used to extend the **"window.cpp"** file of listing 2.1b; their declarations have already been made in file **"window.h"** of listing 2.1a.

Listing 5.5

```
// Place functions in file "window.cpp"

//-----------------//
  int sign(float r)
//-----------------//
// Returns   1 if r>0,  0 if r=0   or   -1 if r<0
 { if (r > epsilon)  return(1) ;
   else if (r < -epsilon) return(-1) ;
        else return(0) ;
 }  // End of sign

//---------------------------------------------//
  int orient2(vector2 p0, vector2 p1, vector2 p2)
//---------------------------------------------//
// Returns the orientation of the polygon with consecutive
// vertices p0, p1 and p2 |  -1 : clockwise orientation
//                           +1 : anti-clockwise orientation
//                            0 : degenerate - line or point
 { vector2 d1,d2 ;
   d1.x=p1.x-p0.x ; d1.y=p1.y-p0.y ;
   d2.x=p2.x-p1.x ; d2.y=p2.y-p1.y ;
   return(sign(d1.x*d2.y-d1.y*d2.x)) ;
 }  // End of orient2
```

Example 5.1

What is the orientation of the polygon defined by the five vertices: (2 , 1), (5 , 4), (4 , 7), (1 , 8) and (−1 , 5)?

The three points we use are (2 , 1), (5 , 4) and (4 , 7). Inserting these values into the formula above we get

$$f_0(4\ ,7) = (5-2)\times(7-4) - (4-5)\times(4-2) = 9 + 3 = 12$$

which is positive, and so the given polygon is in an anti-clockwise orientation. This fact may be checked easily, by plotting the points in order given. Note that it does not matter which three vertices you choose to determine orientation, however, they must be used in the same order relative to one another, as given above. Try it with any three consecutive vertices, or the first, third and last. You should get a positive result every time. However, if you take any of these choices of three vertices, but consider them in the opposite order, then naturally the calculation will now return a negative value.

The intersection of two convex polygons

Imagine two convex polygons **A** and **B**. Their area of intersection is either null or a convex polygon (possibly **A** or **B** if one totally includes the other). The following method for finding the polygon of intersection of two convex polygons has far-reaching applications in the three-dimensional work later in this book and should consequently be studied very carefully. Because the 'inside and outside' method of chapter 4 will be used, it is necessary that both polygons are given in the same orientation – we assume anti-clockwise. This may be checked using the method given in listing 5.5 above.

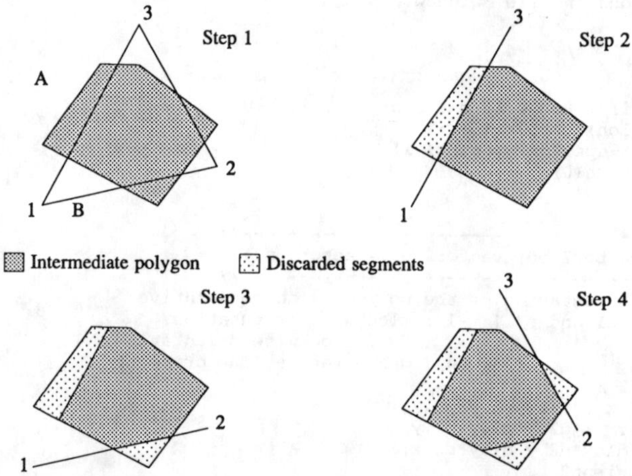

Figure 5.5

Suppose polygon **A** has **numa** vertices and polygon **B** has **numb** vertices, the co-ordinates of which are stored in the arrays **apoly[numa]** and **bpoly[numb]**. The area of intersection is that part of polygon **A** which is also part of polygon **B**. The method employed to find this area is to take each of the boundary lines of polygon **B** in turn, and repeatedly 'slice off' the area of polygon **A** which lies on the negative side of the extended line.

In order to describe the process, we introduce the term *intermediate polygon* to mean the polygon which contains precisely the sections of polygon **A** which have not been proved to lie outside polygon **B**. The various stages of construction of this intermediate polygon are stored in the **vector2** array **ip[2][n]**; the process also needs switch variables **l1**, initially of value 0, and **l2**, initially 1. As we have mentioned previously, the array structure is not very flexible. The value **n** must be specified precisely, so a value greater than the maximum possible index must be chosen. See chapter 3 for a description of the use of arrays.

Initially, of course, the whole of polygon **A** may lie within polygon **B**, so the intermediate polygon is **A**, and the co-ordinates of **A**, that is **apoly[0..numa–1]**, should be copied into array **ip[l1][0..numa–1]**. At each stage of the slicing process we begin by taking a slicing line from the boundary of polygon **B** and finding its intersection with an intermediate polygon **C**, the **numc** vertices of which have been stored in array **ip[l1][0..numc–1]**. Those parts of this area lying on the negative side of the slicing line will be discarded leaving a new intermediate polygon **C′**, that has **numcdash** vertices, and entered into **ip[l2][0..numcdash–1]**. The values of **l1** and **l2** are then switched, and the value of **numc** replaced with that of **numcdash**; then the process is repeated with the next boundary line from polygon **B**. If, at any stage during the slicing, the intermediate polygon has fewer than 3 vertices then it may be considered empty (since a triangle is the polygon with fewest vertices), and so the process may stop as no further slicing could revive it. After each of the **numb** boundary lines of **B** has been used to slice the intermediate polygon, the vertices of the true polygon of intersection are left in the array **ip[l2][0..numc–1]**. These vertex indices may be copied into new array **cpoly[0..numc–1]** for return. If the area of intersection is empty then the function **overlap** (listing 5.6), which implements this algorithm, returns **numc** as zero.

The only question remaining is how to execute the slicing. This is where we use the 'inside and outside' technique. We must discard the part of the area of possible intersection which lies to the negative side of the slicing line, **bpoly[*i*]** to **bpoly[*j*]**, with $j = i + 1$ modulo **numb**.

The analytic representation of this line is

$$f_i(x , y) \equiv a \times y - b \times x - c$$

where $a =$ **bpoly[*j*].x** $-$ **bpoly[*i*].x** ; $b =$ **bpoly[*j*].y** $-$ **bpoly[*i*].y** ;
$c = a \times$ **bpoly[*i*].y** $- b \times$ **bpoly[*i*].x** ;

It can easily be determined whether or not the vertices of the intermediate polygon lie on the negative side of a given line by finding the value of $f_i(x , y)$ for each vertex (x , y). The problem is to find the co-ordinates of the points where the slicing line actually cuts the boundary of the intermediate polygon. We do this by considering this boundary one line segment at a time. Consider line segment from $\boldsymbol{v}_k \equiv$ **ip[l1][*k*]** to $\boldsymbol{v}_l \equiv$ **ip[l1][*l*]**, where $l = k + 1$ modulo **numc**. If the value of $f_i(\boldsymbol{v}_k) \geq 0$, then $\boldsymbol{v}_k$ is copied to the array containing the new intermediate polygon, but if the value of $f_i(\boldsymbol{v}_k) < 0$ the point is not copied. If the points $\boldsymbol{v}_k$ and $\boldsymbol{v}_l$ lie on strictly opposite sides of the slicing line, then find the point of intersection of the line from $\boldsymbol{v}_k$ to $\boldsymbol{v}_l$ with the slicing line and store this vector in the next position in **ip[l2][]**.

This process will, in fact, suffice as the solution of our problem when we let the value of *k* vary from 0 to **numc**–1 independently of the value of *i* varying from 0 to **numb**–1. The process may be better understood through figure 5.5. If you discover that you have need of this **overlap** function then you should declare it in file **"window.h"** and place the code of the function in file **"window.cpp"**.

Listing 5.6

```
// Application program demonstrating calculation of overlapping polygons

#include "viewport.h"
#include "palette.h"
#include "window.h"

extern Window win ;

//-------------------------------------------------------------------//
  void overlap(int numa, vector2 *apoly, int numb, vector2 *bpoly,
               int *numc, vector2 *cpoly, int *inters, int orien)
//-------------------------------------------------------------------//
// Finds the area of intersection between the two polygons 'apoly' and
// 'bpoly' with given 'orientation's (1 means anti-clockwise,-1 clockwise
// The area of intersection is returned with 'numc' vertices stored in
// the 'cpoly' array. If no intersection exists then 'inters' is 0 else 1
 { int i,j,index1,index2,l1,l2,numcdash ;
   vector2 ip[2][maxpoly],end1,end2,v1,v2 ;
   float ca,cb,cc,fv1,fv2,absfv1,absfv2,delta ;
// Copy the details of polygon 'apoly' into the first 'ip' store
   l1=0 ; *numc=numa ;
   for (i=0 ; i<*numc ; i++) ip[l1][i]=apoly[i] ;
// Slice intermediate polygon (in arrays 'ip[1][1..numc]' with each edge of
// 'bpoly'. The end points of the slicing edge are 'end1' and 'end2'
   end1=bpoly[numb-1] ;
   for (i=0 ; i<numb ; i++)
// Sliced area will be stored in the second storage area 'ip[l2][1..newc]'
   { l2=1-l1 ; end2=bpoly[i] ;
// Calculate the functional representation of the line 'end1' to 'end2'
//             ' f(X,Y)=ca*Y+cb*X+cc '
     ca=end2.x-end1.x ; cb=end1.y-end2.y ; cc=-end1.x*cb-end1.y*ca ;
// Consider the intermediate polygon one edge at a time.
// The edge under consideration is from 'v1' to 'v2'
     v1=ip[l1][*numc-1] ;
// Calculate 'f(v1)' and determine whether it lies on,
// to the inside of or to the outside of the slicing edge.
     fv1=ca*v1.y+cb*v1.x+cc ; absfv1=fabs(fv1) ;
     index1=sign(fv1)*orien ;
     numcdash=0 ;
     for (j=0 ; j<*numc ; j++)
     { v2=ip[l1][j] ;
// Calculate whether 'v2' lies on, to the inside of
// or to the outside of the slicing edge.
       fv2=ca*v2.y+cb*v2.x+cc ; absfv2=fabs(fv2) ;
       index2=sign(fv2)*orien ;
// If 'v1' lies on or to the inside of the slicing edge
// edge then include it in the new intermediate polygon.
       if (index1 >= 0)  ip[l2][numcdash++]=v1 ;
// If 'v1' and 'v2' lie on strictly opposite sides of the slicing edge
// then include the point of intersection in the new intermediate polygon
       if ((index1!=0) && (index1!=index2) && (index2!=0))
         { delta=absfv1+absfv2 ;
           ip[l2][numcdash].x=(absfv2*v1.x+absfv1*v2.x)/delta ;
           ip[l2][numcdash].y=(absfv2*v1.y+absfv1*v2.y)/delta ;
           numcdash++ ;
         } ;
```

```
// The second point of this edge will be the first of the next edge
        fv1=fv2 ; absfv1=absfv2 ;
        index1=index2 ; v1=v2 ;
      } ;
// If the intermediate polygon degenerates then no overlap exists
      if (numcdash < 3) { *inters=0 ; *numc=0 ; return ;  }
// The new intermediate polygon becomes the next polygon to be sliced
      *numc=numcdash ; l1=l2 ; endl=end2 ;
// Move on to the next edge of bpoly
   } ;
// Reach here when all slicing is complete. Copy the remaining
// intermediate polygon to the array 'cpoly' for return.
   *inters=1 ;
   for (i=0 ; i<*numc ; i++)
   { cpoly[i]=ip[l1][i] ; }
 }  // End of overlap

//-------------------------//
  void draw_a_picture(void)      //  overlap demonstration, Set horiz = 20
//-------------------------//
 { int i, nc, inters ;
// Setup test values of polygon, base and direction vectors
   vector2 apoly[4] = { -1, -5, 6, -1, -2, 4, -7, 0 } ;
   vector2 bpoly[5] = { 2, 5, -4.5, 2, -4, -2.5, 4, -4, 6, -1 } ;
   vector2 cpoly[maxpoly] ;
   win.start() ;
// Hatch polygon in red
   win.setcol(12) ;
   overlap(4,apoly,5,bpoly,&nc,&(cpoly[0]),&inters,1) ;
   if (inters) win.polyfill(nc,cpoly) ;
// Draw outline of polygons in white
   win.setcol(15) ;
   win.moveto(apoly[3]) ;
   for (i=0 ; i<4 ; i++) win.lineto(apoly[i]) ;
   win.moveto(bpoly[4]) ;
   for (i=0 ; i<5 ; i++) win.lineto(bpoly[i]) ;
 }  // End of draw_a_picture
```

Exercise 5.5

The use of this algorithm is particularly useful in the three-dimensional hidden surface removal algorithm that is introduced in chapter 10, but it may also be used to solve a problem already mentioned – the clipping of polygonal areas in two dimensions.

When using the area-fill function **polypix** (listing 1.1b) you will have noted that clipping within the window rectangle is automatic. Many graphics cards have their own hardware area-filling function, such as on the XGA card, and you could rewrite **polypix** using this function. However it is by no means certain that the areas drawn will be clipped to the viewport. In order to draw only the part of a polygon which lies within the window area, and thus the viewport, we must draw the area of intersection between the polygon and the **horiz** by **vert** window rectangle. This can be achieved by adjusting the **overlap** function (listing 5.6), using polygon **B** as the four vertices of the window given in anti-clockwise order.

6 Three-dimensional co-ordinate geometry

Before we lead on to a study of the graphical display of objects in three-dimensional space, we first have to come to terms with the three-dimensional Cartesian co-ordinate geometry and introduce some useful procedures for manipulating objects in three-dimensional space. (For further reading we recommend books by Cohn (1961) and McCrae (1953).) As with two-dimensional space, we arbitrarily fix a point in the space, named the *co-ordinate origin* (origin for short). We then imagine three mutually perpendicular lines through this point, each line extending to infinity in both directions. These are the *x-axis*, *y-axis* and *z-axis*. Each axis is thought to have a positive and negative half, both starting at the origin – that is, distances measured from the origin along the axis are positive on one side and negative on the other.

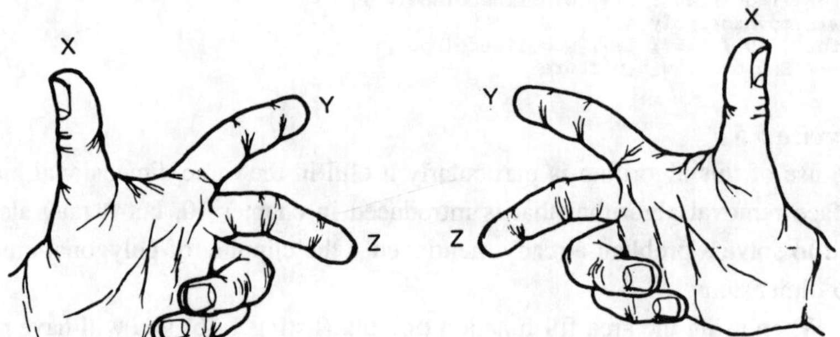

Figure 6.1

We may think of the *x*- and *y*-axes in a way similar to two-dimensional space, both lying on the page of this book say, the positive *x*-axis horizontal and to the right of the origin, and the positive *y*-axis vertical and above the origin. This just leaves the position of the *z*-axis: it has to be perpendicular to the page (since it is perpendicular to both *x*- and *y*-axes). The positive *z*-axis can be into the page (the so-called *left-handed triad* of axes) or out of the page (the *right-handed triad*). You can realise this difference on your own hands. On either hand, hold the thumb, index finger and middle finger at right angles to one another with the middle finger perpendicular to the palm of your hand: the thumb may be taken as the positive x-axis, the index finger as the positive y-axis and the middle finger the positive z-axis. See figure 6.1.

There are advantages and disadvantages with both systems; however, the graphics community has standardized on the right-handed triad, and so this is the axial system that we will use throughout this book. What we say in the remainder of the book, using right-handed axes, has its equivalent in the left-handed system – it does not matter which notation you finally decide to use so long as you are consistent, and are aware of the implications of your choice.

We specify a typical point $\boldsymbol{v}$ in three-dimensional space by means of a *vector* or *co-ordinate triple* (x , y , z), where the individual co-ordinate values are the perpendicular projections of the point on to the respective x-, y- and z- axes. By projection we mean the unique point on the specified axis, such that a line from that point to $\boldsymbol{v}$ is perpendicular to the axis.

In order to deal with three-dimensional modelling and display, we need the constant, structure data type, variable and function declarations of classes **Window, Palette** and **Viewport**. We will also need the very useful functions given in this and future chapters. All the functions from this chapter will be used to extend the file **"window.cpp"**; these functions will have already been declared in file **"window.h"** of listing 2.1a, along with the **vector3** structure type.

Initially there are two vector operators that we need to consider for three-dimensional vectors. Suppose we are given two point vectors $\boldsymbol{p_1} \equiv (x_1 , y_1 , z_1)$ and $\boldsymbol{p_2} \equiv (x_2 , y_2 , z_2)$. Then a *scalar multiple* of $\boldsymbol{p_1}$, $k\boldsymbol{p_1}$, is obtained by multiplying the three individual co-ordinate values of $\boldsymbol{p_1}$ by a scalar number k

$$k\boldsymbol{p_1} \equiv (k \times x_1 , k \times y_1 , k \times z_1)$$

and the *vector sum* of the two vectors, $\boldsymbol{p_1} + \boldsymbol{p_2}$, is calculated by adding their x co-ordinates together, their y co-ordinates together and their z co-ordinates together to give a new vector

$$\boldsymbol{p_1} + \boldsymbol{p_2} \equiv (x_1 + x_2 , y_1 + y_2 , z_1 + z_2)$$

Should you have a frequent need for these functions you can always overload the + and * operators.

Definition of a straight line

A straight line in three-dimensional space passing through two such vector points $\boldsymbol{p_1} \equiv (x_1 , y_1 , z_1)$ and $\boldsymbol{p_2} \equiv (x_2 , y_2 , z_2)$ may be defined by describing the co-ordinates of a typical point $\boldsymbol{v} \equiv (x , y , z)$ on the line with three equations

$$(x - x_1) \times (y_2 - y_1) = (y - y_1) \times (x_2 - x_1)$$
$$(y - y_1) \times (z_2 - z_1) = (z - z_1) \times (y_2 - y_1)$$
$$(z - z_1) \times (x_2 - x_1) = (x - x_1) \times (z_2 - z_1)$$

Although these are three equations in three unknowns, we will find that they are *linearly dependent* (interrelated), and so there is no unique solution (naturally, since we are generating a general form for points on the line, and not just one point). These equations enable us to calculate two of the co-ordinates in terms of a third (see example 6.1)

As in the two-dimensional case, this is not the only way of representing a straight line. We may also use a direct extension of the vector representation introduced in chapter 4. The typical point on the line is represented as a vector combination of $\boldsymbol{p}_1$ and $\boldsymbol{p}_2$, dependent upon the real (floating point) number μ

$$\boldsymbol{v}(\mu) \equiv (1-\mu)\boldsymbol{p}_1 + \mu\boldsymbol{p}_2 \qquad \text{where} \quad -\infty < \mu < \infty$$

that is

$$\boldsymbol{v}(\mu) \equiv ((1-\mu)x_1 + \mu x_2 \, , \, (1-\mu)y_1 + \mu y_2 \, , \, (1-\mu)z_1 + \mu z_2)$$

The μ may be interpreted in a manner exactly analogous to the two-dimensional case and is again placed in brackets after $\boldsymbol{v}$, in order to demonstrate the dependence of $\boldsymbol{v}$ on this value. However, when this concept has been fully investigated then (μ) will be omitted. Note that when $\mu = 0$ the equation returns point $\boldsymbol{p}_1$, and when $\mu = 1$ it gives $\boldsymbol{p}_2$.

We may rewrite this vector expression

$$\boldsymbol{v}(\mu) \equiv \boldsymbol{p}_1 + \mu(\boldsymbol{p}_2 - \boldsymbol{p}_1)$$

and like its counterpart in two-dimensions, $\boldsymbol{p}_1$ is called a *base vector* and $(\boldsymbol{p}_2 - \boldsymbol{p}_1)$ a *direction vector*. We normally write this as $\boldsymbol{b} + \mu\boldsymbol{d}$. This once again reveals the dual interpretation of a vector. A vector may be used to specify a unique point in three-dimensional space, or it may be considered as a general direction, namely any line parallel to that line which joins the origin to the point that the vector represents. We can move along a line in one of two directions, so we say that the direction from the origin to the point has *positive sense*, and from the point to the origin *negative sense*. Hence the two direction vectors $\boldsymbol{d} \equiv (x, y, z)$ and $-\boldsymbol{d} \equiv (-x, -y, -z)$ represent the same directions in space but they are of opposite senses. We define the *length* of a vector $\boldsymbol{d} \equiv (x, y, z)$ (sometimes called its *modulus*, and its *absolute value* $|\boldsymbol{d}|$), to be the distance of the point vector from the co-ordinate origin

$$|\boldsymbol{d}| \equiv \surd(x^2 + y^2 + z^2)$$

and a vector having unit length is called a *unit vector*.

So any point on the line $\boldsymbol{b} + \mu\boldsymbol{d}$ is found by moving to the point $\boldsymbol{b}$ and then travelling along a line which is parallel to the direction $\boldsymbol{d}$, a distance $|\mu\boldsymbol{d}|$ in the positive sense of $\boldsymbol{d}$ if μ is positive, and in the negative sense if negative. Note that any point on the line can act as a base vector $\boldsymbol{b}$, and the direction vector $\boldsymbol{d}$ may be replaced by any non-zero scalar multiple of itself (a negative scalar multiple will reverse the sense of the line).

If the direction vector $\boldsymbol{d} \equiv (x , y , z)$ with positive sense makes angles θ_x, θ_y and θ_z with the respective positive x-, y- and z-axial directions, then we have the ratio equation

$$x : y : z = \cos\theta_x : \cos\theta_y : \cos\theta_z$$

which means that

$$\boldsymbol{d} \equiv (\lambda\times\cos\theta_x , \lambda\times\cos\theta_y , \lambda\times\cos\theta_z) \quad \text{for some } \lambda > 0$$

We know from the properties of three-dimensional geometry that

$$\cos^2\theta_x + \cos^2\theta_y + \cos^2\theta_z = 1$$

Hence $\lambda = |\boldsymbol{d}|$, and if the direction vector is a unit vector (that is, the modulus of the vector $= \lambda = 1$), then the co-ordinates of this point vector must be given by the triple $(\cos\theta_x , \cos\theta_y , \cos\theta_z)$. The co-ordinates of a direction vector given in this way are called the *direction cosines* of the set of lines generated by the vector. In general, if the direction vector is $\boldsymbol{d} \equiv (x , y , z)$, then the direction cosines are

$$\left(\frac{x}{|\boldsymbol{d}|} , \frac{y}{|\boldsymbol{d}|} , \frac{z}{|\boldsymbol{d}|}\right)$$

Example 6.1
Describe the line joining (1 , 2 , 3) to (−1 , 0 , 2), using the methods shown so far.

The typical point (x , y , z) on the line satisfies the equations

$$(x - 1) \times (0 - 2) = (y - 2) \times (-1 - 1)$$
$$(y - 2) \times (2 - 3) = (z - 3) \times (0 - 2)$$

and

$$(z - 3) \times (-1 - 1) = (x - 1) \times (2 - 3)$$

That is

$$-2x + 2y = 2 \quad (6.1)$$
$$-y + 2z = 4 \quad (6.2)$$
$$-2z + x = -5 \quad (6.3)$$

Notice that equation (6.1) is −2 times the sum of equations (6.2) and (6.3). Thus we need only consider these latter two equations, to get

$$y = 2z - 4 \quad \text{and} \quad x = 2z - 5$$

whence the typical point on the line depends only on the one variable, in this case z, and it is given by $(2z - 5 , 2z - 4 , z)$. We easily check this result by noting that when $z = 3$ we get $(1 , 2 , 3)$ and when $z = 2$ we get $(-1 , 0 , 2)$, the two original points defining the line.

In vector form, the typical point on the line (depending on μ) is

$$\boldsymbol{v}(\mu) = (1 - \mu)(1 , 2 , 3) + \mu(-1 , 0 , 2) = (1 - 2\mu , 2 - 2\mu , 3 - \mu)$$

These co-ordinate values depend on just one parameter (μ), and in order to check the validity of this representation of a line we note that points $\boldsymbol{v}(0) = (1 , 2 , 3)$ and $\boldsymbol{v}(1) = (-1 , 0 , 2)$.

If we put the line into base/direction vector form we see that

$$\boldsymbol{v}(\mu) = (1 , 2 , 3) + \mu(-2 , -2 , -1)$$

with $(1 , 2 , 3)$ as the base vector, and $(-2 , -2 , -1)$ as the direction vector (which incidently has modulus $\sqrt{(4+4+1)} = \sqrt{9} = 3$). We also note that any point on the line can act as a base vector, and so we can give another form for the typical point on this line, $\boldsymbol{v}'$

$$\boldsymbol{v}'(\mu) = (-1 , 0 , 2) + \mu(-2 , -2 , -1)$$

We can change the direction vector of the line into its equivalent unit vector by dividing by the modulus to give $(-2/3 , -2/3 , -1/3)$, and represent the line in another version of the base/direction form

$$\boldsymbol{v}''(\mu) = (1 , 2 , 3) + \mu(-2/3 , -2/3 , -1/3)$$

Naturally, the same μ value will give different points for different representations of the same line – for example, vectors $\boldsymbol{v}(3) = (-5 , -4 , 0)$, $\boldsymbol{v}'(3) = (-7 , -6 , -1)$ and $\boldsymbol{v}''(3) = (-1 , 0 , 2)$. The direction of this line makes angles $131.81° = \cos^{-1}(-2/3)$, $131.81°$ and $109.47° = \cos^{-1}(-1/3)$ with the positive x, y and z directions respectively.

The angle between two direction vectors

In order to calculate such an angle we need the operator •, the *dot product* or *scalar product* (function **dot3** in listing 6.1 which is added to **"window.cpp"**.) This operates on two vectors and returns a scalar (floating point) result thus

$$\boldsymbol{p} \bullet \boldsymbol{q} = (x_1 , y_1 , z_1) \bullet (x_2 , y_2 , z_2) = x_1 \times x_2 + y_1 \times y_2 + z_1 \times z_2$$

Listing 6.1

```
// Place function in file "window.cpp"

//-----------------------------------//
  float dot3(vector3 p1, vector3 p2)
//-----------------------------------//
// Returns the scalar product of the two vectors p1 and p2
 { return(p1.x*p2.x+p1.y*p2.y+p1.z*p2.z) ;
 }  // End of dot3
```

If $\boldsymbol{p}$ and $\boldsymbol{q}$ are both unit vectors (that is, in direction cosine form), and θ is the angle between the lines, then $\cos\theta = \boldsymbol{p} \bullet \boldsymbol{q}$. The equivalent two-dimensional relationship was mentioned in chapter 4. In general, therefore, the angle between two direction vectors $\boldsymbol{p}$ and $\boldsymbol{q}$, which we can assume meet at the origin, is

$$\cos^{-1}\left(\frac{\boldsymbol{p}}{|\boldsymbol{p}|} \bullet \frac{\boldsymbol{q}}{|\boldsymbol{q}|}\right)$$

Thus $\boldsymbol{p}$ and $\boldsymbol{q}$ are mutually perpendicular directions if and only if $\boldsymbol{p} \bullet \boldsymbol{q} = 0$.

Definition of a plane

We now consider representing a plane in three-dimensional space. The typical point vector $\boldsymbol{v} \equiv (x, y, z)$ on the plane is given by the vector equation

$$\boldsymbol{n} \bullet \boldsymbol{v} = k$$

where the *plane constant* k is scalar, and $\boldsymbol{n}$ is a direction vector which represents the set of lines perpendicular to the plane (see example 6.2). These lines are said to be *normal* to the plane. If $\boldsymbol{a}$ is any point on the plane then naturally $\boldsymbol{n} \bullet \boldsymbol{a} = k$, and so by replacing k in the above equation, we may rewrite it as

$$\boldsymbol{n} \bullet \boldsymbol{v} = \boldsymbol{n} \bullet \boldsymbol{a} \quad \text{or} \quad \boldsymbol{n} \bullet (\boldsymbol{v} - \boldsymbol{a}) = 0$$

This latter equation is self-evident from the property of the dot product, that two mutually perpendicular lines have zero dot product. For any point $\boldsymbol{v} \equiv (x, y, z)$ in the plane, which is not coincident with $\boldsymbol{a}$, we see that $(\boldsymbol{v} - \boldsymbol{a})$ can be taken as the direction of a line in the plane. Since $\boldsymbol{n}$ is plane normal, and consequently perpendicular to every line in the plane, $\boldsymbol{n} \bullet (\boldsymbol{v} - \boldsymbol{a}) = \delta \times \cos(\pi/2) = 0$ (δ is a scalar value $= |\boldsymbol{n}| \times |\boldsymbol{v} - \boldsymbol{a}|$).

Expanding the original equation of the plane with normal $\boldsymbol{n} \equiv (n_1, n_2, n_3)$, we get the usual co-ordinate representation of a plane

$$(n_1, n_2, n_3) \bullet (x, y, z) = n_1 \times x + n_2 \times y + n_3 \times z = k$$

Note that two planes with normals $\boldsymbol{n}$ and $\boldsymbol{m}$ (say) are parallel if and only if one normal is a scalar multiple of the other – that is, $\boldsymbol{n} = \lambda\boldsymbol{m}$ for some $\lambda \neq 0$.

The point of intersection of a line and a plane

Suppose the line is given by $\boldsymbol{b} + \mu\boldsymbol{d}$ and the plane by $\boldsymbol{n} \bullet \boldsymbol{v} = k$. The two either do not intersect at all (if they are parallel), intersect at an infinite number of points (if the line lies in the plane) or have a unique point of intersection which lies on both the line and the plane. We need the unique value of μ (if one exists) for which

$$\boldsymbol{n} \bullet (\boldsymbol{b} + \mu\boldsymbol{d}) = k$$

that is $\quad \mu = (k - \boldsymbol{n} \bullet \boldsymbol{b})/(\boldsymbol{n} \bullet \boldsymbol{d})$ provided $\boldsymbol{n} \bullet \boldsymbol{d} \neq 0$ (6.4)

If $\boldsymbol{n} \bullet \boldsymbol{d} = 0$, the line and plane are parallel, and therefore no unique point of intersection exists.

The distance of a point from a plane

The distance of a point $\boldsymbol{p_1}$ from a plane $\boldsymbol{n} \bullet \boldsymbol{v} = k$ is the distance of $\boldsymbol{p_1}$ from the nearest point $\boldsymbol{p_2}$ on the plane. Hence the normal from the plane at $\boldsymbol{p_2}$ must pass through $\boldsymbol{p_1}$. This normal line can be written $\boldsymbol{p_1} + \mu\boldsymbol{n}$, and from equation (6.4) above, the μ value that defines $\boldsymbol{p_2}$ is such that

$$\mu = (k - \boldsymbol{n} \bullet \boldsymbol{p_1})/(\boldsymbol{n} \bullet \boldsymbol{n})$$

The distance of the point $\boldsymbol{p_2} \equiv \boldsymbol{p_1} + \mu\boldsymbol{n}$ from $\boldsymbol{p_1}$ is

$$\mu|\boldsymbol{n}| = |k - \boldsymbol{n} \bullet \boldsymbol{p_1}|/|\boldsymbol{n}| \tag{6.5}$$

In particular, if $\boldsymbol{p_1}$ is the origin $\boldsymbol{O}$, then the distance of the plane from the origin is $|k|/|\boldsymbol{n}|$. Furthermore, if $\boldsymbol{n}$ is a direction cosine (unit) vector, we see that the distance of the origin from the plane is $|k|$, the absolute value of the scalar plane constant k.

Example 6.2

Find the point of intersection of the line joining (1 , 2 , 3) to (–1 , 0 , 2) with the plane $(0, -2, 1) \bullet \boldsymbol{v} = 5$, and also find the distance of the plane from the origin.

$$\boldsymbol{b} \equiv (1, 2, 3) \qquad \boldsymbol{n} \equiv (0, -2, 1)$$
$$\boldsymbol{d} \equiv (-1, 0, 2) - (1, 2, 3) \equiv (-2, -2, -1)$$
$$\boldsymbol{n} \bullet \boldsymbol{b} = (0 \times 1 + -2 \times 2 + 1 \times 3) = -1$$
$$\boldsymbol{n} \bullet \boldsymbol{d} = (0 \times -2 + -2 \times -2 + 1 \times -1) = 3$$

hence the μ value of the point of intersection is (5–(–1))/3=2, and the vector is

$$(1, 2, 3) + 2(-2, -2, -1) \equiv (-3, -2, 1)$$

and the distance from the origin is $5/|\boldsymbol{n}| = 5/\sqrt{5} = \sqrt{5}$.

The function **ilpl** in listing 6.2 (to be added to **"window.cpp"**) enables us to calculate the point of intersection of a line and a plane. The line has base vector **b** and direction **d**, and the plane has normal **n** and real (floating point) plane constant **k**. The point of intersection is calculated and returned as **p**. Variables **b**, **d**, **n** and **p** are all of structure data type **vector3**.

Listing 6.2

```
// Place function in file "window.cpp"

//-------------------------------------------------------------------//
  int ilpl(vector3 b,vector3 d,vector3 n,float k,vector3 *p,float *mu)
//-------------------------------------------------------------------//
// Calculates the point of intersection, 'p',of a line 'b+mu.d'
// and the plane with equation 'n.v=k'.
// 'insect' is returned as 1 if an intersection exists, 0 if not
 { float dotprod1,dotprod2,mustore ;
   int insect ;
   dotprod1=dot3(d,n) ;
// If the line and plane are parallel then return 'insect=0'
   if (fabs(dotprod1) < epsilon)  insect=0 ;
// Else a point of intersection does exist
   else
     { insect=1 ; dotprod2=dot3(b,n) ;
       mustore=(float)(k-dotprod2)/dotprod1 ;
       *p = b + mustore * d ;  *mu=mustore ;
     } ;
   return ( insect ) ;
 }  // End of ilpl
```

The reflection of a point in a plane

Consider the point $\boldsymbol{p} \equiv (x\,,y\,,z)$ and the infinite plane $\boldsymbol{n} \bullet \boldsymbol{v} = k$. We wish to find the point $\boldsymbol{p}' \equiv (x'\,,y'\,,z')$, the reflection of $\boldsymbol{p}$ in the plane (see figure 6.2).

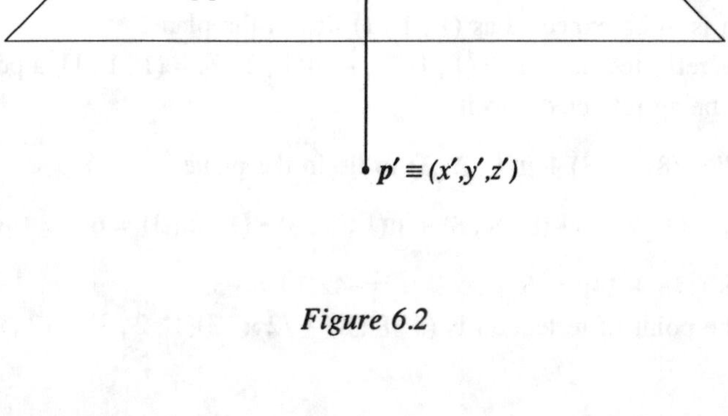

Figure 6.2

The perpendicular distance of the reflection p' from the plane is equal to the perpendicular distance of p from the plane. Furthermore, p and p' lie on the same line perpendicular to the plane but on opposite sides. The vector n is simply a direction common to all lines normal to the plane, so the normal containing p and p' may be represented by $p + \mu n$, $-\infty \leq \mu \leq \infty$.

If we can find a value μ such that $p + \mu n$ lies in the plane $n \bullet v = k$, then the reflected point p' is $p + 2\mu n$. Thus the μ value of the point of intersection of the line $p + \mu n$ with the plane $n \bullet v = k$ must be found using the method above (equation 6.5), and thence the reflected point calculated.

The function **refpp** in listing 6.3 returns **r** the reflection of point **p** in the plane **n** • v = **k**. Vectors **r, p** and **n** are all of structure data type **vector3**. Again the code for this function should be stored in **"window.cpp"**; it has already been declared in file **"window.h"**.

Listing 6.3

```
// Place function in file "window.cpp"

//-----------------------------------------------//
  vector3 refpp(vector3 p, vector3 n, float k)
//-----------------------------------------------//
// Calculates 'r', the reflection of 'p' in the plane 'n.v=k'
 { vector3 dummy, r, zero = {0.0 , 0.0 , 0.0} ;
   float mu ;
   int insect ;
   insect = ilpl(p,n,n,k,&dummy,&mu) ;
   if (insect)  r = p + 2.0 * mu * n ;  else r = zero ;  return ( r ) ;
 } // End of refpp
```

Example 6.3

What are the reflections of the points

(i) (1 , 1 , 1) and (ii) (8 , 8 , 8) in the plane (1 , 2 , 3) • v = 6?

(i) for p' = (1 , 1 , 1) + μ(1 , 2 , 3) to lie in the plane

$$(1, 2, 3) \bullet p' = (1, 2, 3) \bullet (1, 1, 1) + \mu(1, 2, 3) \bullet (1, 2, 3) = 6$$

that is $6 + 14\mu = 6$ and so $\mu = 0$

which is to be expected as (1 , 1 , 1) lies in the plane!

So the reflected point $p' = (1, 1, 1) + 2\mu(1, 2, 3) = (1, 1, 1)$, a point in the plane being reflected into itself.

(ii) for p'' = (8 , 8 , 8) + μ(1 , 2 , 3) to lie in the plane

$$(1, 2, 3) \bullet (8, 8, 8) + \mu(1, 2, 3) \bullet (1, 2, 3) = 6$$

that is $48 + 14\mu = 6$ so $\mu = -42/14 = -3$

and the point of reflection is $(8, 8, 8) + (2 \times -3)(1, 2, 3) = (2, -4, -10)$.

Listing 6.4

```
// Place function in file "window.cpp"

//------------------------------------------------------------------//
  int ill3(vector3 b1, vector3 d1, vector3 b2, vector3 d2, vector3 *p)
//------------------------------------------------------------------//
// Point of intersection of two lines in 3 dimensions
 { float b1a[3],b2a[3],d1a[3],d2a[3] ;
   float delta,value,factor1,factor2,lambda,mu ;
   int i,i0,i1,i2,insect ;
// Assume no independent equations then no intersection
   insect=0 ;
// Store x,y,z co-ordinates in arrays to find two independent equations
   b1a[0]=b1.x ; b2a[0]=b2.x ;
   b1a[1]=b1.y ; b2a[1]=b2.y ;
   b1a[2]=b1.z ; b2a[2]=b2.z ;
   d1a[0]=d1.x ; d2a[0]=d2.x ;
   d1a[1]=d1.y ; d2a[1]=d2.y ;
   d1a[2]=d1.z ; d2a[2]=d2.z ;
   for (i=0 ; i<3 ; i++)
   { i0=i ; i1= (i+1) % 3 ;
     delta=d1a[i0]*d2a[i1]-d1a[i1]*d2a[i0] ;
// Two independent equations , find point of intersection
     if (fabs(delta) > epsilon)
       { factor1=b2a[i0]-b1a[i0] ; factor2=b2a[i1]-b1a[i1] ;
         mu=(d2a[i1]*factor1-d2a[i0]*factor2)/delta ;
         lambda=(d1a[i1]*factor1-d1a[i0]*factor2)/delta ;
         i2=(i1+1) % 3 ;
         value=b1a[i2]+mu*d1a[i2]-b2a[i2]-lambda*d2a[i2] ;
         if (fabs(value) <= epsilon)
           { insect=1 ;
             *p = b1 + mu * d1 ;
             break ;                    // Break the 'for' loop
           } ;
       } ;
   } ;
   return ( insect ) ;
 }  // End of ill3
```

The point of intersection of two lines

Suppose we have two lines $\boldsymbol{b_1} + \mu\boldsymbol{d_1}$ and $\boldsymbol{b_2} + \lambda\boldsymbol{d_2}$. Their point of intersection, if it exists (if the lines are neither co-planar nor parallel, then they will not intersect), is identified by finding unique values for μ and λ which satisfy the vector equation (three separate co-ordinate equations)

$$\boldsymbol{b_1} + \mu\boldsymbol{d_1} = \boldsymbol{b_2} + \lambda\boldsymbol{d_2}$$

Having three equations in two unknowns means that, for the equations to be meaningful, there must be at least one pair of equations which are independent, and the remaining equation must be a combination of these two. Remembering that two lines are parallel if one direction vector is a scalar multiple of the other, we take two independent equations, find the values of μ and λ (we have two equations in two unknowns), and put them into the third equation to see if they are consistent. The following example 6.4 will demonstrate this method, and the function **ill3** in listing 6.4 implements it in C++: add **ill3** to **"window.cpp"**. The first line has base and direction vectors stored as **b1** and **d1** respectively, and the second line as **b2** and **d2**: if it exists (**insect**=1), the calculated point of intersection is returned as **p**, otherwise **insect** is returned as 0. Since floating point values are used, equality may not be exact in the third equation because of rounding errors. We therefore check the difference between the value on the left-hand side and that on the right-hand side to see if it is negligible (< **epsilon**), although not necessarily zero. Note that if the two independent equations are

$$a_{11} \times \mu + a_{12} \times \lambda = k_1$$
$$a_{21} \times \mu + a_{22} \times \lambda = k_2$$

then the *determinant* of this pair of equations, $\Delta = a_{11} \times a_{22} - a_{12} \times a_{21}$, will be non-zero (because the equations are not related), and we have the solutions

$$\mu = (a_{22} \times k_1 + a_{12} \times k_2)/\Delta$$
$$\lambda = (a_{11} \times k_2 + a_{21} \times k_1)/\Delta$$

Example 6.4

Find the point of intersection (if any) of

(i) (1 , 1 , 1) + μ(2 , 1 , 3) with (0 , 0 , 1) + λ(−1 , 1 , 1)

(ii) (2 , 3 , 4) + μ(1 , 1 , 1) with (−2 , −3 , −4) + λ(1 , 2 , 3)

In (i) the three equations are

$$1 + 2\mu = 0 - \lambda \quad (6.6)$$
$$1 + \mu = 0 + \lambda \quad (6.7)$$
$$1 + 3\mu = 1 + \lambda \quad (6.8)$$

From equations (6.6) and (6.7) we get μ = −2/3 and λ = 1/3, which, when substituted in equation (6.8), gives 1 + 3(−2/3) = −1 on the left-hand side and 1 + 1(1/3) = 4/3 on the right-hand side, which are obviously unequal, and so the lines do not intersect.

From (ii) we get the equations

$$2 + \mu = -2 + \lambda \quad (6.9)$$
$$3 + \mu = -3 + 2\lambda \quad (6.10)$$
$$4 + \mu = -4 + 3\lambda \quad (6.11)$$

and from equations (6.9) and (6.10), we get μ = −2 and λ = 2, and these values also satisfy equation (6.11) (left-hand side = right-hand side = 2). So the point of intersection is

$$(2 , 3 , 4) + (-2\,(1 , 1 , 1)) = (-2 , -3 , -4) + 2\,(1 , 2 , 3) = (0 , 1 , 2)$$

We now introduce a new vector operator, × the *vector product* (or *cross product*) which operates on two vectors $\boldsymbol{p} \equiv (p_x , p_y , p_z)$ and $\boldsymbol{q} \equiv (q_x , q_y , q_z)$ (say) giving the *vector* result

$$\begin{aligned}\boldsymbol{p} \times \boldsymbol{q} &\equiv (p_x , p_y , p_z) \times (q_x , q_y , q_z) \\ &\equiv (p_y{\times}q_z - p_z{\times}q_y , p_z{\times}q_x - p_x{\times}q_z , p_x{\times}q_y - p_y{\times}q_x)\end{aligned}$$

If $\boldsymbol{p}$ and $\boldsymbol{q}$ are non-parallel direction vectors, then $\boldsymbol{p} \times \boldsymbol{q}$ is the direction vector perpendicular to both $\boldsymbol{p}$ and $\boldsymbol{q}$. It should also be noted that this operator is *non-commutative*. This means that, in general, $\boldsymbol{p} \times \boldsymbol{q} \neq \boldsymbol{q} \times \boldsymbol{p}$ for given values of $\boldsymbol{p}$ and $\boldsymbol{q}$; these two vector products represent the direction of a single line, but they will have opposite senses. For example, $(1 , 0 , 0) \times (0 , 1 , 0) = (0 , 0 , 1)$ but $(0 , 1 , 0) \times (1 , 0 , 0) = (0 , 0 , -1)$; $(0 , 0 , 1)$ and $(0 , 0 , -1)$ are both parallel to the z-axis (and so perpendicular to the directions $(1 , 0 , 0)$ and $(0 , 1 , 0)$, but they are of opposite senses. This can also be realized by using your hands. Using right or left hand (depending on the axial system you choose) identify the palm of the hand with the plane holding the two direction vectors, with the thumb pointing along the first direction and the index finger along the second direction; the middle finger perpendicular to the palm now points along the direction of the cross product. Note that in order to change the order of the vectors in the cross product, that is, identify the thumb with the second vector and the index finger with the first vector, it is necessary to twist your palm through two right angles. Now the middle finger is pointing along the same line but in an opposite sense. A function, **vectorproduct**, which returns the vector product of two vectors **p** and **q**, returning **v**, is given in listing 6.5 and must be added to **"window.cpp"**.

Listing 6.5

```
// Place function in file "window.cpp"

//--------------------------------------------//
  vector3 vectorproduct(vector3 p, vector3 q)
//--------------------------------------------//
// Calculates 'v', the vector product of two vectors 'p' and 'q'
 { vector3 v ;
   v.x=p.y*q.z-p.z*q.y ;    v.y=p.z*q.x-p.x*q.z ;    v.z=p.x*q.y-p.y*q.x ;
   return ( v ) ;
 }  // End of vectorproduct
```

The minimum distance between two lines

It was mentioned above that if two lines are either parallel or non-coplanar then they do not intersect. Therefore there is a minimum distance between two such lines which is greater than zero. We shall now calculate this distance. The two situations where the lines are parallel or non-parallel are different, and we consider first the non-parallel case.

Suppose the two lines are $\boldsymbol{a} + \mu\boldsymbol{c}$ and $\boldsymbol{b} + \lambda\boldsymbol{d}$. The minimum distance between these two lines must be measured along a line perpendicular to both. This line must, therefore, be parallel to the direction $\boldsymbol{l} \equiv \boldsymbol{c} \times \boldsymbol{d}$.

Now since both $\boldsymbol{a} + \mu\boldsymbol{c}$ and $\boldsymbol{b} + \lambda\boldsymbol{d}$ are perpendicular to $\boldsymbol{l}$, they both lie in planes with $\boldsymbol{l}$ as normal. Also, since we know points on both lines ($\boldsymbol{a}$ and $\boldsymbol{b}$), we may uniquely identify these planes: $\boldsymbol{l} \bullet (\boldsymbol{v} - \boldsymbol{a}) = 0$ and $\boldsymbol{l} \bullet (\boldsymbol{v} - \boldsymbol{b}) = 0$.

These planes are, of course, parallel, and so the required minimum distance is simply the distance from a point on one plane, say $\boldsymbol{b}$, to the other plane. We have already derived a formula (6.4) for this, giving the required answer

$$\frac{|(\boldsymbol{c}\times\boldsymbol{d})\bullet\boldsymbol{a} - (\boldsymbol{c}\times\boldsymbol{d})\bullet\boldsymbol{b}|}{|\boldsymbol{c}\times\boldsymbol{d}|}$$

$$= \frac{|(\boldsymbol{c}\times\boldsymbol{d})\bullet(\boldsymbol{a}-\boldsymbol{b})|}{|\boldsymbol{c}\times\boldsymbol{d}|}$$

If the two lines are co-planar then this expression yields the result zero, since the lines must intersect as they are not parallel.

Now suppose the two lines $\boldsymbol{a} + \mu\boldsymbol{c}$ and $\boldsymbol{b} + \lambda\boldsymbol{d}$ are parallel. In this case direction $\boldsymbol{d} \equiv \phi\boldsymbol{c}$ for some $\phi \neq 0$ and consequently $|\boldsymbol{c} \times \boldsymbol{d}|=0$, making the above expression undefined.

However, both these lines are normal to the same planes. Take the plane containing $\boldsymbol{a}$ with normal $\boldsymbol{c}$ (parallel to $\boldsymbol{d}$)

$$\boldsymbol{c} \bullet (\boldsymbol{v} - \boldsymbol{a}) = 0$$

We simply find the point of intersection, $\boldsymbol{e}$ say, of the line $\boldsymbol{b} + \lambda\boldsymbol{d}$ with this plane and the required distance is $|\boldsymbol{a} - \boldsymbol{e}|$

$$\boldsymbol{e} = \boldsymbol{b} + \lambda\boldsymbol{d}$$

where from equation (6.4)

$$\lambda = \frac{\boldsymbol{c}\bullet(\boldsymbol{a}-\boldsymbol{b})}{\boldsymbol{c}\bullet\boldsymbol{d}}$$

The function **mindist** in listing 6.6 (added to **"window.cpp"**) calculates the minimum distance, **dist**, between two lines using this method.

Example 6.5
Find the minimum distance between
(i) (1 , 0 , 0) + μ(1 , 1 , 1) and (0 , 0 , 0) + λ(1 , 2 , 3)
(ii) (2 , 4 , 0) + μ(1 , 1 , 1) and (−2 , −1 , 0) + λ(2 , 2 , 2)

In (i) $\boldsymbol{a} \equiv (1\,,0\,,0)$ $\quad \boldsymbol{c} \equiv (1\,,1\,,1)$

$\boldsymbol{b} \equiv (0\,,0\,,0)$ $\quad \boldsymbol{d} \equiv (1\,,2\,,3)$

$\boldsymbol{c} \times \boldsymbol{d} \equiv (1\,,-2\,,1)$ $\quad \boldsymbol{a} - \boldsymbol{b} \equiv (1\,,0\,,0)$

So the minimum distance between the lines is

$$\frac{|(1,-2,1)\cdot(1,0,0)|}{|(1,-2,1)|} = \frac{1}{\sqrt{6}}$$

In (ii) $\boldsymbol{a} \equiv (2\,,4\,,0)$ $\quad \boldsymbol{c} \equiv (1\,,1\,,1)$

$\boldsymbol{b} \equiv (-2\,,-1\,,0)$ $\quad \boldsymbol{d} \equiv (2\,,2\,,2)$

$\boldsymbol{c} \times \boldsymbol{d} \equiv (0\,,0\,,0)$ and so the lines are parallel ($\boldsymbol{d} = 2\boldsymbol{c}$)

$\boldsymbol{c} \cdot \boldsymbol{d} \equiv 6$ $\quad \boldsymbol{a} - \boldsymbol{b} \equiv (4\,,5\,,0)$

$$\lambda = \frac{|(1,1,1)\cdot(4,5,0)|}{(1,1,1)\cdot(2,2,2)} = \frac{9}{6} = \frac{3}{2}$$

$$\boldsymbol{e} \equiv (-2\,,-1\,,0) + 3/2(2\,,2\,,2) = (1\,,2\,,3)$$
$$\boldsymbol{a} - \boldsymbol{e} \equiv (2\,,4\,,0) - (1\,,2\,,3) = (1\,,2\,,-3)$$

so the minimum distance between the lines is $\sqrt{14}$.

Listing 6.6

```
// Place function in file "window.cpp"

//-------------------------------------------------------------//
  float mindist(vector3 a, vector3 c, vector3 b, vector3 d)
//-------------------------------------------------------------//
// Finds minimum distance between two lines in 3 dimensions
 { vector3 aminusb,aminuse,p ;
   float lambda,pmod,dist ;
   p = vectorproduct(c,d) ; pmod=sqrt(dot3(p,p)) ; aminusb = a-b ;
   if (pmod > epsilon)  dist=fabs(dot3(p,aminusb))/pmod ;
   else
     { lambda=dot3(c,aminusb)/dot3(c,d) ;
       aminuse = a -b -lambda*d ; dist=sqrt(dot3(aminuse,aminuse)) ;
     } ;
   return ( dist ) ;
 }  // End of mindist
```

The plane through three given non-collinear points

Suppose we are given three non-collinear points $\boldsymbol{p_1}$, $\boldsymbol{p_2}$, and $\boldsymbol{p_3}$. Then the two vectors $\boldsymbol{p_2} - \boldsymbol{p_1}$ and $\boldsymbol{p_3} - \boldsymbol{p_2}$ represent the directions of two lines coincident at $\boldsymbol{p_2}$, both of which lie in the plane containing the three points. We know that the normal to the plane is perpendicular to every line in the plane, and in particular to the two lines mentioned above. Also, because we are given non-collinear points, $\boldsymbol{p_2} - \boldsymbol{p_1}$ is not parallel to $\boldsymbol{p_3} - \boldsymbol{p_2}$, and so the normal to the plane is given by the vector $\boldsymbol{n} \equiv (\boldsymbol{p_2} - \boldsymbol{p_1}) \times (\boldsymbol{p_3} - \boldsymbol{p_2})$. See figure 6.3.

We know that p_1 lies in the plane, so the equation may be written

$$((p_2 - p_1) \times (p_3 - p_2)) \bullet (v - p_1) = 0 \tag{6.12}$$

The three points in the plane define a triangle, which appears from one side of the plane to be in anti-clockwise orientation, but from the other side to be in clockwise orientation. The above equation imposes a consistent sense upon the normal, which implies that the normal direction points towards that side of the plane from which the triangle appears in anti-clockwise orientation. (This is dependent on the use of right-handed axes; in the left-handed system the normal thus found points towards the clockwise side.) The function, **plane**, in listing 6.7 calculates the plane through three non-collinear **vector3** points. Again add this to file **"window.cpp"**.

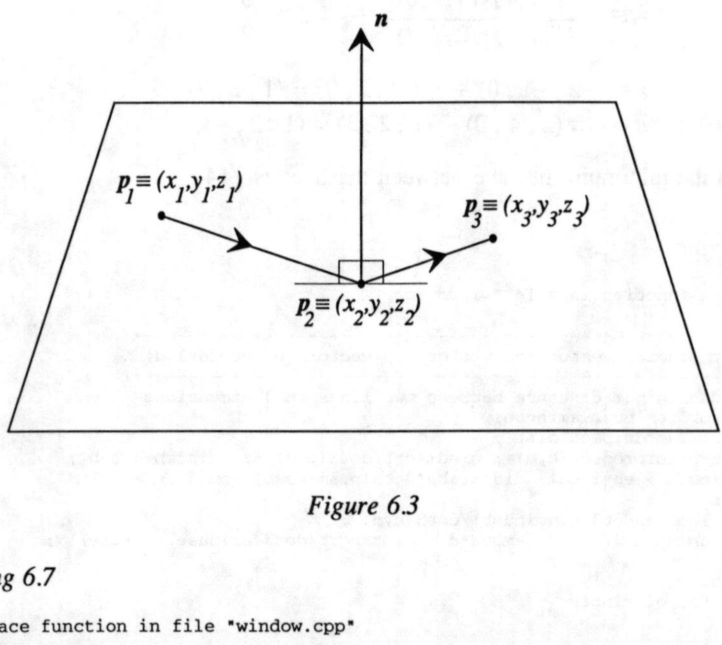

Figure 6.3

Listing 6.7

```
// Place function in file "window.cpp"

//----------------------------------------------------------//
  float plane(vector3 p1, vector3 p2, vector3 p3, vector3 *n)
//---------------------------------------------------------//
// Calculates the vector equation of the plane 'n.v=k' passing through
// the three points 'p1', 'p2' and 'p3'. Return value of k.
 { vector3 d1,d2 ;
   float k ;
// Calculate the direction vectors of two lines in the plane
   d1 = p2 - p1 ;   d2 = p3 - p2 ;
// Calculate the normal to the plane using the vector product of
// these two lines. Calculate 'k' using point 'p1' in the plane
   *n = vectorproduct(d1,d2) ; k=dot3(*n,p1) ;
   return ( k ) ;
 }  // End of plane
```

Example 6.6
Give the co-ordinate equation of the plane through the vector points (0 , 1 , 1), (1 , 2 , 3) and (−2 , 3 , −1).

This is given by the typical point $\boldsymbol{v} \equiv (x , y , z)$ where

$$(((1 , 2 , 3)-(-2 , 3 , -1)) \times ((-2 , 3 , -1)-(1 , 2 , 3))) \bullet ((x , y , z)-(1 , 2 , 3)) = 0$$

that is $\quad ((1 , 1 , 2) \times (-3 , 1 , -4)) \bullet (x , y-1 , z-1) = 0$

so $\quad (-6 , -2 , 4) \bullet (x , y-1 , z-1) = 0$

or $\quad (-6 , -2 , 4) \bullet (x , y , z) = -(-6 , -2 , 4) \bullet (0 , -1 , -1)$

or, equivalently

$$(-6 , -2 , 4) \bullet \boldsymbol{v} = 2$$

In co-ordinate form this equation is $-6x - 2y + 4z - 2 = 0$, or when reorganized $3x + y - 2z = 1$.

The point of intersection of three planes

We assume that the three planes are defined by equations (6.13) to (6.15) below. The point of intersection of these three planes, $\boldsymbol{v} \equiv (x , y , z)$ must lie in all three planes and satisfy

$$\boldsymbol{n_1} \bullet \boldsymbol{v} = k_1 \tag{6.13}$$
$$\boldsymbol{n_2} \bullet \boldsymbol{v} = k_2 \tag{6.14}$$
$$\boldsymbol{n_3} \bullet \boldsymbol{v} = k_3 \tag{6.15}$$

where $\boldsymbol{n_1} \equiv (n_{11} , n_{12} , n_{13})$, $\boldsymbol{n_2} \equiv (n_{21} , n_{22} , n_{23})$ and $\boldsymbol{n_3} \equiv (n_{31} , n_{32} , n_{33})$.

We can rewrite these three equations as one matrix equation

$$\begin{pmatrix} n_{11} & n_{12} & n_{13} \\ n_{21} & n_{22} & n_{23} \\ n_{31} & n_{32} & n_{33} \end{pmatrix} \times \begin{pmatrix} x \\ y \\ z \end{pmatrix} = \begin{pmatrix} k_1 \\ k_2 \\ k_3 \end{pmatrix}$$

and so the solution for $\boldsymbol{v}$ is given by the column vector

$$\begin{pmatrix} x \\ y \\ z \end{pmatrix} = \begin{pmatrix} n_{11} & n_{12} & n_{13} \\ n_{21} & n_{22} & n_{23} \\ n_{31} & n_{32} & n_{33} \end{pmatrix}^{-1} \times \begin{pmatrix} k_1 \\ k_2 \\ k_3 \end{pmatrix}$$

Listing 6.8

```
// Place function in file "window.cpp"

//---------------------------------------------//
  int invert(double A[4][4], double AINV[4][4])
//---------------------------------------------//
// Calculates 'AINV', the inverse of matrix 'A', using the adjoint method
// 'sing' returned as 1 if 'A' is singular and has no inverse, 0 otherwise
 { double determinant,adj ;
   int i,i1,i2,j,j1,j2,sing ;
// Find the determinant of 'A'
   determinant=  A[1][1]*(A[2][2]*A[3][3]-A[2][3]*A[3][2])
                +A[1][2]*(A[2][3]*A[3][1]-A[2][1]*A[3][3])
                +A[1][3]*(A[2][1]*A[3][2]-A[2][2]*A[3][1]) ;
// If 'determinant'=0 then 'A' is singular
   if (fabs(determinant) < epsilon)  sing=1 ;
// Else the inverse is the adjoint matrix divided by determinant
   else
     { sing=0 ;
       for (i=1 ; i<4 ; i++)
       { i1=(i % 3)+1 ;
         i2=(i1 % 3)+1 ;
         for (j=1 ; j<4 ; j++)
         { j1=(j % 3)+1 ;
           j2=(j1 % 3)+1 ;
           adj=(A[i1][j1]*A[i2][j2]-A[i1][j2]*A[i2][j1]) ;
           AINV[j][i]=adj/determinant ;
         } ;
       } ;
     } ;
   return ( sing ) ;
 }  // End of invert
```

Listing 6.9

```
// Place function in file "window.cpp"

//--------------------------------------------------------------------------//
  int i3pl(vector3 n1, float k1, vector3 n2, float k2, vector3 n3, float k3,
                                                                vector3 *v)
//--------------------------------------------------------------------------//
// Calculates the point of intersection, 'v', of the three planes
// 'n1.v=k1'  ,  'n2.v=k2'  ,  'n3.v=k3'
// 'insect' is returned as 1 if such a point exists, 0 otherwise
 { double N[4][4],NINV[4][4] ;
   int sing, insect ;
// Copy the 3 normal vectors into the rows of matrix 'N'
   N[1][1]=n1.x ; N[1][2]=n1.y ; N[1][3]=n1.z ;
   N[2][1]=n2.x ; N[2][2]=n2.y ; N[2][3]=n2.z ;
   N[3][1]=n3.x ; N[3][2]=n3.y ; N[3][3]=n3.z ;
// Calculate the inverse of 'N'
   sing = invert(N,NINV) ;
   if (sing == 1) insect=0 ;
// If 'N' is singular then no intersection
// Otherwise calculate the intersection
   else
     { insect=1 ;
       v->x=NINV[1][1]*k1+NINV[1][2]*k2+NINV[1][3]*k3 ;
       v->y=NINV[2][1]*k1+NINV[2][2]*k2+NINV[2][3]*k3 ;
       v->z=NINV[3][1]*k1+NINV[3][2]*k2+NINV[3][3]*k3 ;
     } ;
   return ( insect ) ;
 }  // End of i3pl
```

Therefore, any calculation that requires the intersection of three planes necessarily involves the inversion of a 3 by 3 matrix. The function, **invert**, in listing 6.8, uses the Adjoint method of finding **AINV**, the inverse of matrix **A**. The value **sing** is also returned, equalling 1 if the matrix **A** is singular (and so has no inverse) and 0 otherwise. Again place the function in **"window.cpp"**.

In the code of **i3pl**, (listing 6.9 to be stored in **"window.cpp"**) the function to find the point of intersection of three planes, the solution (vector $\boldsymbol{v}$ above) of the three equations (6.13, 6.14 and 6.15) is returned as **vector3** value **v**; the three floating point values **k1**, **k2** and **k3** will contain the respective plane constants, and the x, y and z co-ordinates of the normal vectors are given as **vector3** values **n1**, **n2** and **n3** respectively. Obviously, if any two of the planes are parallel, or the three meet in pairs in three parallel lines, then **sing** is returned as 1 and there is no unique point of intersection.

Example 6.7

Find the point of intersection of the three planes represented by the three equations $(0, 1, 1) \bullet \boldsymbol{v} = 2$, $(1, 2, 3) \bullet \boldsymbol{v} = 4$ and $(1, 1, 1) \bullet \boldsymbol{v} = 0$.

In the matrix form we have

$$\begin{pmatrix} 0 & 1 & 1 \\ 1 & 2 & 3 \\ 1 & 1 & 1 \end{pmatrix} \times \begin{pmatrix} x \\ y \\ z \end{pmatrix} = \begin{pmatrix} 2 \\ 4 \\ 0 \end{pmatrix}$$

The inverse of $\begin{pmatrix} 0 & 1 & 1 \\ 1 & 2 & 3 \\ 1 & 1 & 1 \end{pmatrix}$ is $\begin{pmatrix} -1 & 0 & 1 \\ 2 & -1 & 1 \\ -1 & 1 & -1 \end{pmatrix}$

and so $$\begin{pmatrix} x \\ y \\ z \end{pmatrix} = \begin{pmatrix} -1 & 0 & 1 \\ 2 & -1 & 1 \\ -1 & 1 & -1 \end{pmatrix} \times \begin{pmatrix} 2 \\ 4 \\ 0 \end{pmatrix} = \begin{pmatrix} -2 \\ 0 \\ 2 \end{pmatrix}$$

This solution is easily checked

$$(0, 1, 1) \bullet (-2, 0, 2) = 2$$
$$(1, 2, 3) \bullet (-2, 0, 2) = 4 \quad \text{and}$$
$$(1, 1, 1) \bullet (-2, 0, 2) = 0$$

which means that the point $(-2, 0, 2)$ lies on all three planes, and so must be their point of intersection.

The line of intersection of two planes

Let the two planes be $\boldsymbol{p} \bullet \boldsymbol{v} \equiv (p_1, p_2, p_3) \bullet \boldsymbol{v} = k_1$ and

$$\boldsymbol{q} \bullet \boldsymbol{v} \equiv (q_1, q_2, q_3) \bullet \boldsymbol{v} = k_2$$

We assume that the two planes are not parallel, and so $\boldsymbol{p} \neq \lambda \boldsymbol{q}$ for any λ. The line that is common to the two planes must naturally lie in both planes, and so it must be perpendicular to the normals of those two planes ($\boldsymbol{p}$ and $\boldsymbol{q}$). Therefore the direction of this line of intersection must be $\boldsymbol{d} \equiv \boldsymbol{p} \times \boldsymbol{q}$, and so the line can be written in the form $\boldsymbol{b} + \lambda \boldsymbol{d}$, where base vector $\boldsymbol{b}$ can be any point on the line. In order to classify the line completely we have to find just one such $\boldsymbol{b}$. What we actually do is find a point of intersection of the two planes together with a third, which is neither parallel to them nor cuts them in a common line. Choosing a plane with normal $\boldsymbol{p} \times \boldsymbol{q}$ will satisfy these conditions for the third plane (and remember we have already calculated this vector product). We still need a value for k_3, but any will do, so we take $k_3 = 0$, assuming that this third plane goes through the origin. Thus $\boldsymbol{b}$ is given by the column vector

$$\boldsymbol{b} = \begin{pmatrix} p_1 & p_2 & p_3 \\ q_1 & q_2 & q_3 \\ p_2 \times q_3 - p_3 \times q_2 & p_3 \times q_1 - p_1 \times q_3 & p_1 \times q_2 - p_2 \times q_1 \end{pmatrix}^{-1} \times \begin{pmatrix} k_1 \\ k_2 \\ 0 \end{pmatrix}$$

Example 6.8

Find the line common to the planes $(0, 1, 1) \bullet \boldsymbol{v} = 2$ and $(1, 2, 3) \bullet \boldsymbol{v} = 2$.

$$\boldsymbol{p} \equiv (0, 1, 1) \text{ and } \boldsymbol{q} \equiv (1, 2, 3), \text{ and also}$$

$$\begin{aligned} \boldsymbol{p} \times \boldsymbol{q} &= (1 \times 3 - 1 \times 2, 1 \times 1 - 0 \times 3, 0 \times 2 - 1 \times 1) \\ &= (1, 1, -1). \end{aligned}$$

We require the inverse of $\begin{pmatrix} 0 & 1 & 1 \\ 1 & 2 & 3 \\ 1 & 1 & -1 \end{pmatrix}$ which is $\frac{1}{3}\begin{pmatrix} -5 & 2 & 1 \\ 4 & -1 & 1 \\ -1 & 1 & -1 \end{pmatrix}$

and hence the point of intersection of the three planes is

$$\frac{1}{3}\begin{pmatrix} -5 & 2 & 1 \\ 4 & -1 & 1 \\ -1 & 1 & -1 \end{pmatrix} \times \begin{pmatrix} 2 \\ 2 \\ 0 \end{pmatrix} = \frac{1}{3}\begin{pmatrix} -6 \\ 6 \\ 0 \end{pmatrix} = \begin{pmatrix} -2 \\ 2 \\ 0 \end{pmatrix}$$

and the line is $(-2, 2, 0) + \mu(1, 1, -1)$.

It is easy to check this result, because all the points on the line should lie in both planes

$$
\begin{aligned}
& (0\,,1\,,1) \bullet ((-2\,,2\,,0) + \mu(1\,,1\,,-1)) \\
= \quad & (0\,,1\,,1) \bullet (-2\,,2\,,0) + \mu(0\,,1\,,1) \bullet (1\,,1\,,-1)) \\
= \quad & 2 \;\text{ for all } \mu, \;\text{ and}
\end{aligned}
$$

$$
\begin{aligned}
& (1\,,2\,,3) \bullet ((-2\,,2\,,0) + \mu(1\,,1\,,-1)) \\
= \quad & (1\,,2\,,3) \bullet (-2\,,2\,,0) + \mu(1\,,2\,,3) \bullet (1\,,1\,,-1)) \\
= \quad & 2 \;\text{ for all } \mu.
\end{aligned}
$$

The function **commonline**, to solve this problem is given in listing 6.10 and added to **"window.cpp"**. It is very similar to the previous function, but returns the base vector **b** and the direction **d** of the common line.

Listing 6.10

```
// Place function in file "window.cpp"

//------------------------------------------------------------------------//
  int commonline(vector3 n1, float k1, vector3 n2, float k2, vector3 *b,
                                                              vector3 *d)
//------------------------------------------------------------------------//
// Calculates the line common to the two planes 'n1.v=k1' , 'n2.v=k2'
// 'insect' is returned as 1 if such a line exists, 0 otherwise
// The base vector of the line is 'b' and direction vector 'd'
 { double N[4][4],NINV[4][4] ;
   int sing, insect ;
// Copy the 2 normal vectors into first two rows of matrix 'N'
   N[1][1]=n1.x ; N[1][2]=n1.y ; N[1][3]=n1.z ;
   N[2][1]=n2.x ; N[2][2]=n2.y ; N[2][3]=n2.z ;
// Calculate the direction vector of the line
   *d = vectorproduct(n1,n2) ;
// Create third plane 'd.v=0', and copy into matrix 'N'
   N[3][1]=d->x ; N[3][2]=d->y ; N[3][3]=d->z ;
// 'b' is the point of intersection of these three planes
// Calculate the inverse of 'N'
   sing = invert(N,NINV) ;
   if (sing == 1)  insect=0 ;
// If 'N' is singular then no common line, otherwise calculate intersection
   else
     { insect=1 ;
       b->x=NINV[1][1]*k1+NINV[1][2]*k2 ;
       b->y=NINV[2][1]*k1+NINV[2][2]*k2 ;
       b->z=NINV[3][1]*k1+NINV[3][2]*k2 ;
     } ;
   return ( insect ) ;
 }  // End of commonline
```

Analytic representation of a surface

In our study of two-dimensional space in chapter 4 we noted that curves can be represented in an analytic notation. This idea can be extended into three dimensions for the representation of surfaces. The simplest form of surface is an infinite plane with normal $\boldsymbol{n} \equiv (n_1\,, n_2\,, n_3)$, which we have seen may be given as a co-ordinate equation $\boldsymbol{n} \bullet \boldsymbol{v} - k \equiv n_1 \times x + n_2 \times y + n_3 \times z - k = 0$

Rewriting this in analytic form for a typical point $\boldsymbol{v} \equiv (x, y, z)$ on the surface

$$f(\boldsymbol{v}) \equiv f(x, y, z) \equiv n_1 \times x + n_2 \times y + n_3 \times z - k \equiv \boldsymbol{n} \bullet \boldsymbol{v} - k$$

gives a simple expression in $\boldsymbol{v}$ (the variables x, y and z). It enables us to create a *point membership classification* for all points in space: the *zero set* (all $\boldsymbol{v}$ with $f(\boldsymbol{v}) = 0$), the *negative set* ($f(\boldsymbol{v}) < 0$), and the *positive set* ($f(\boldsymbol{v}) > 0$). A point $\boldsymbol{v}$ lies on the surface if and only if it belongs to the zero set. If the surface divides space in half (each half being connected – that is, any two points in a given half can be joined by a curve which does not cut the surface) then these halves may be identified with the positive and negative sets. Again beware, there are many surfaces that divide space into more than two connected volumes, and then it is impossible to relate analytic representation with connected sets – for example, the surface $f(x, y, z) \equiv \cos(y) - \sin(x^2+z^2)$. There are, however, many useful well-behaved surfaces with this property, the sphere of radius r for example

$$f(\boldsymbol{v}) \equiv r^2 - |\boldsymbol{v}|^2$$

that is $$f(x, y, z) \equiv r^2 - x^2 - y^2 - z^2$$

If $f(\boldsymbol{v}) = 0$ then $\boldsymbol{v}$ lies on the sphere, if $f(\boldsymbol{v}) < 0$ then $\boldsymbol{v}$ lies outside the sphere, and if $f(\boldsymbol{v}) > 0$ then $\boldsymbol{v}$ lies inside it.

The analytic representation of a surface is a very useful concept. It can be used to great effect in the quad-tree, oct-tree and ray-tracing algorithms discussed in later chapters, and also in defining sets of equations necessary in calculating the intersections of various objects. Furthermore, we may determine whether or not two points $\boldsymbol{p}$ and $\boldsymbol{q}$ (say) lie on the same side of a surface which divides space in two: information needed for hidden surface elimination. All we need do is compare the signs of $f(\boldsymbol{p})$ and $f(\boldsymbol{q})$. It they are of opposite signs then a line joining $\boldsymbol{p}$ and $\boldsymbol{q}$ must cut the surface. For example

Is a point on the same side of a plane as the origin?

Suppose the plane is defined (as earlier) by three non-collinear points $\boldsymbol{p}_1$, $\boldsymbol{p}_2$ and $\boldsymbol{p}_3$. Then the equation (6.12) of the plane is

$$((\boldsymbol{p}_2 - \boldsymbol{p}_1) \times (\boldsymbol{p}_3 - \boldsymbol{p}_2)) \bullet (\boldsymbol{v} - \boldsymbol{p}_1) = 0$$

We may rewrite this in analytic form

$$f(\boldsymbol{v}) \equiv ((\boldsymbol{p}_2 - \boldsymbol{p}_1) \times (\boldsymbol{p}_3 - \boldsymbol{p}_2)) \bullet (\boldsymbol{v} - \boldsymbol{p}_1)$$

So all we need do for a point $\boldsymbol{e}$ (say) is to compare $f(\boldsymbol{e})$ with $f(\boldsymbol{O})$, where $\boldsymbol{O}$ is the origin. We assume here that neither $\boldsymbol{O}$ nor $\boldsymbol{e}$ lies in the plane.

Example 6.9
Are the origin and point (1 , 1 , 3) on the same side of the plane defined by points (0 , 1 , 1), (1 , 2 , 3) and (–2 , 3 , –1)?

From example 6.6 we saw that the analytic representation of the plane is

$$f(v) \equiv ((-6\ ,-2\ ,4) \bullet (v - (0\ ,1\ ,1))$$

Thus $\quad f(0\ ,0\ ,0) \equiv -(-6\ ,-2\ ,4) \bullet (0\ ,1\ ,1) = -2$

and $\quad f(1\ ,1\ ,3) \equiv -(-6\ ,-2\ ,4) \bullet ((1\ ,1\ ,3) - (0\ ,1\ ,1)) = 2$

Hence (1 , 1 , 3) lies on the side of the plane opposite to the origin, and so a line segment joining these two points will cut the plane at a point represented by the form $(1 - \mu)(0\ ,0\ ,0) + \mu(1\ ,1\ ,3)$ where $0 \leq \mu \leq 1$.

The orientation of a convex polygon in three-dimensional space

In chapter 5 we introduced a method for determining whether the vertices of a convex polygon in two-dimensional space were in a clockwise or anti-clockwise orientation. Again in three dimensions, all we need do is consider the ordered triangle formed by the first three vertices of the polygon p_1, p_2 and p_3. We saw earlier that the infinite plane containing this triangle is given by the analytic form

$$f(v) \equiv ((p_2 - p_1) \times (p_3 - p_2)) \bullet (v - p_1)$$

Obviously the orientation depends on the side of this plane from which you view the triangle. One way will be clockwise, the other anti-clockwise. If the triangle is set up in the way we describe, relative to right-handed axes, and the observation point is e, then you will note that if $f(e)$ is positive then the orientation is anti-clockwise, and if $f(e)$ is negative then the orientation is clockwise. If $f(e)$ is zero then e is on the plane and the question has no meaning.

When you are constructing three-dimensional mesh objects in later chapters you will be expected to set up facets in an anti-clockwise orientation when viewed from the outside, so this technique will prove an invaluable check!

Example 6.10
This idea is realized as **orient3** in listing 6.11, and as usual in this chapter, it is used to extend file **"window.cpp"** (listing 3.1b); note that it has already been declared in **"window.h"** (listing 2.1a). Use the function to find the orientation of the triangle formed by the vertices (1 , 0 , 0), (0 , 1 , 0) and (0 , 0 , 1).

Note that in analytic form this is given by $f(v) \equiv (1\ ,1\ ,1) \bullet (v - (1\ ,0\ ,0))$. Hence when viewed from (1 , 1 , 1), $f(1\ ,1\ ,1) = 2$ so the triangle is anti-clockwise, and from (0 , 0 , 0), $f(0\ ,0\ ,0) = -1$ and thus the triangle is clockwise.

Listing 6.11

```
// Place function in file "window.cpp"

//-----------------------------------------------------------//
  int orient3(vector3 p1, vector3 p2, vector3 p3, vector3 e)
//-----------------------------------------------------------//
// Returns the orientation of the polygon with consecutive vertices
// 'p1', 'p2' and 'p3' as viewed from vector position 'e'
//        -1 : clockwise orientation
//        +1 : anti-clockwise orientation
//         0 : degenerate - line or point
 { vector3 d1,d2,d1xd2,v ;
   d1 = p2 - p1 ;    d2 = p3 - p2 ;
   d1xd2 = vectorproduct(d1,d2) ;
   v = e - p1 ;
   return( sign(dot3(d1xd2,v)) ) ;
 }  // End of orient3
```

The orientation of a convex polygon in two-dimensional space

Again we consider only the first three vertices on the boundary of the polygon, $\boldsymbol{p_0} \equiv (x_0 , y_0)$, $\boldsymbol{p_1} \equiv (x_1 , y_1)$, and $\boldsymbol{p_2} \equiv (x_2 , y_2)$. Although these are two-dimensional co-ordinates, by giving them all a z co-ordinate value of zero, we may assume that the points lie in the x/y plane through the origin of three-dimensional space. We can therefore use the results of the previous section to check on the orientation of this now three-dimensional triangle. Now since the triangle lies in the x/y plane through the origin, the normal to the plane is of the form $(0 , 0 , r)$. The analytic form is thus

$$f(x , y , z) \equiv (0 , 0 , r) \bullet ((x , y , z) - \boldsymbol{p_1})$$
$$= r \times z$$

since our three-dimensional system is chosen to be right-handed, and we have calculated the normal so that it points out of an anti-clockwise triangle. If we assume that $(x , y , z) = (0 , 0 , 1)$ (implying that we are observing from the positive z side of the x/y plane through the origin), then $f(x , y , z) = r$. Hence if r is positive the polygon is defined in anti-clockwise orientation and if negative then clockwise.

Because the vector $(0 , 0 , r)$ is $(\boldsymbol{p_1} - \boldsymbol{p_0}) \times (\boldsymbol{p_2} - \boldsymbol{p_1})$, then the scalar value of r is $(x_1 - x_0) \times (y_2 - y_1) - (y_1 - y_0) \times (x_2 - x_1)$ and this expression is identical to that derived in chapter 5 (see listing 5.4).

Exercise 6.1

Experiment with the methods of this chapter by creating your own exercises. The answers to your exercises may be readily checked using the functions of this chapter. Of course, when checking each solution, you will need to write a body of a **main** function that will call the requisite functions.

7 Matrix transformations for modelling 3-D space

In chapter 2 we defined the origin, axes and scale of the WINDOW co-ordinate system that was identified with the viewport. But in all the two-dimensional pictures we have drawn so far, this WINDOW system has been fixed relative to a continuous two-dimensional space. From now on we will be drawing pictures of three-dimensional scenes by viewing them through the same WINDOW, but now we will want it to move around in space. Ultimately this will be achieved by changing co-ordinate systems, and then by observing the effect of such transformations on the definition of each graphical object in the scene, be it a point, line or facet. But, as we have seen in earlier, the display of any object in computer graphics is achieved by specifying and then drawing groups of points (and areas defined by points). Therefore, all we need do to draw a scene is to consider all the points that define objects in that scene; we will call them a *cluster*. By discovering what happens to the co-ordinate representation of a cluster with a change of co-ordinate system, and relating the transformed cluster to the WINDOW system, we are able to draw the objects on the viewport.

In fact, for the purposes of modelling and displaying three-dimensional scenes there need be only three fundamental forms of change of co-ordinate system, namely change of scale, translation of origin and rotation of axes; all other changes can be formulated as linear combinations of these types. These changes are examples of *affine transformations*. On some graphics devices these operations are available in hardware, however, they are not available on the VGA and XGA cards, and so we give a full description of the techniques involved.

It will often be necessary to transform large clusters of points, and to do this efficiently the transformations are represented by matrices. Before looking at these transformations and their matrix representations, a brief reminder of the properties of matrices and of column vectors is warranted. In fact only square matrices are required for the study of three-dimensional space, and so our attention may be restricted to 4×4 matrices (said 4 by 4). Following on from the explanation of chapter 3, in listing 7.1a we declare the class **Matrix**, in which we manipulate a **float[5][5]** array, used to hold the values for a 4×4 matrix; note that we will be using only locations **[1..4]** and so ignore the **0** index. If the rounding errors implicit in matrix multiplication become critical, then the **double** data type should be used. In the programs given in this book, a matrix identifier is always given in upper-case characters. Such a 4 × 4 matrix (*A* say) is simply a group of real (floating point) numbers placed in a block of 4 rows by 4 columns, while a column vector (*D* say) is a group of real numbers placed in a column of 4 rows thus

$$\begin{pmatrix} A_{11} & A_{12} & A_{13} & A_{14} \\ A_{21} & A_{22} & A_{23} & A_{24} \\ A_{31} & A_{32} & A_{33} & A_{34} \\ A_{41} & A_{42} & A_{43} & A_{44} \end{pmatrix} \quad \text{and} \quad \begin{pmatrix} D_1 \\ D_2 \\ D_3 \\ D_4 \end{pmatrix}$$

A typical entry in the matrix is usually written A_{ij}, the first subscript denotes the ith row, and the second subscript the jth column (for example, A_{23} represents the value in the second row, third column). The column vector entry, D_i, denotes the value in the ith row. Remember, the index counts start at 1 and not 0! All these named entries will be explicitly replaced by numerical values. It is essential to realise that not only are the values of individual entries in a matrix or column vector significant, but also their positions within the structure are important. Naturally C++ programs are written along a line (no subscripts or superscripts) and hence matrices and vectors are implemented as arrays; the subscript values appear inside square brackets following the array identifier. We declare the class **Matrix** and all functions necessary for manipulating these matrices in listing 7.1a, with the code given in listing 7.1b. These listings should be stored in files **"matrix.h"** and **"matrix.cpp"** respectively.

Matrices can be added. Matrix $C = A + B$, the sum of two matrices *A* and *B*, is defined by the typical entry C_{ij} thus

$$C_{ij} = A_{ij} + B_{ij} \qquad 1 \le i, j \le 4$$

Matrix *A* can be multiplied by a scalar *r* to form a new matrix *B*

$$B_{ij} = r \times A_{ij} \qquad 1 \le i, j \le 4$$

Matrix *A* can be multiplied by a column vector *D* to produce another column vector *E* thus

$$E_i = A_{i1} \times D_1 + A_{i2} \times D_2 + A_{i3} \times D_3 + A_{i4} \times D_4 = \Sigma A_{ij} \times D_j \qquad 1 \le i, j \le 4$$

The ith row element of the new column vector is the sum of the products of the corresponding elements of the ith row of the matrix with those in the column vector. This operation, multiplying a matrix by a column vector (actually we use a **vector3** value with the entry 1 in the fourth column implied) is overloaded onto the multiply operator *****.

The product (matrix) $C = A \times B$ of two matrices A and B may be calculated

$$C_{ij} = A_{i1} \times B_{1j} + A_{i2} \times B_{2j} + A_{i3} \times B_{3j} + A_{i4} \times B_{4j} = \Sigma A_{ik} \times B_{kj} \quad 1 \le i, j, k \le 4$$

The $(i, j)^{th}$ element of the product matrix is the sum of each element in the ith row of the first matrix multiplied by the corresponding element in the jth column of the second. This operator too is overloaded onto * in listing 7.1. Note that the product of matrices is not necessarily *commutative* – that is, $A \times B$ need not be the same as $B \times A$. For example

$$\begin{pmatrix} 0 & 1 & 0 & 0 \\ 0 & 0 & 1 & 0 \\ 1 & 0 & 0 & 0 \\ 0 & 0 & 0 & 1 \end{pmatrix} \times \begin{pmatrix} 0 & 0 & 1 & 0 \\ 0 & 1 & 0 & 0 \\ 1 & 0 & 0 & 0 \\ 0 & 0 & 0 & 1 \end{pmatrix} = \begin{pmatrix} 0 & 1 & 0 & 0 \\ 1 & 0 & 0 & 0 \\ 0 & 0 & 1 & 0 \\ 0 & 0 & 0 & 1 \end{pmatrix}$$

but

$$\begin{pmatrix} 0 & 0 & 1 & 0 \\ 0 & 1 & 0 & 0 \\ 1 & 0 & 0 & 0 \\ 0 & 0 & 0 & 1 \end{pmatrix} \times \begin{pmatrix} 0 & 1 & 0 & 0 \\ 0 & 0 & 1 & 0 \\ 1 & 0 & 0 & 0 \\ 0 & 0 & 0 & 1 \end{pmatrix} = \begin{pmatrix} 1 & 0 & 0 & 0 \\ 0 & 0 & 1 & 0 \\ 0 & 1 & 0 & 0 \\ 0 & 0 & 0 & 1 \end{pmatrix}$$

Experiment with these ideas until you have enough confidence to use them in the theory that follows. For those who want more details about the theory of matrices, books by Finkbeiner (1978), and by Stroud (1982) are recommended.

There is a special matrix called the *identity matrix*, I (sometimes called the *unit matrix*): it will be generated by method **unit** in listing 7.1b.

$$I = \begin{pmatrix} 1 & 0 & 0 & 0 \\ 0 & 1 & 0 & 0 \\ 0 & 0 & 1 & 0 \\ 0 & 0 & 0 & 1 \end{pmatrix}$$

Every 4 by 4 square matrix A has a *determinant* det(A)

$$\begin{aligned} \det(A) = A_{11} \times \{ & A_{22} \times (A_{33} \times A_{44} - A_{34} \times A_{43}) - A_{23} \times (A_{34} \times A_{41} - A_{31} \times A_{44}) + \\ & A_{24} \times (A_{31} \times A_{42} - A_{32} \times A_{41}) \} \\ + A_{21} \times \{ & A_{32} \times (A_{43} \times A_{14} - A_{44} \times A_{13}) - A_{33} \times (A_{44} \times A_{11} - A_{41} \times A_{14}) + \\ & A_{34} \times (A_{41} \times A_{12} - A_{42} \times A_{11}) \} \\ + A_{31} \times \{ & A_{42} \times (A_{13} \times A_{24} - A_{14} \times A_{23}) - A_{43} \times (A_{14} \times A_{21} - A_{11} \times A_{24}) + \\ & A_{44} \times (A_{11} \times A_{22} - A_{12} \times A_{21}) \} \\ + A_{41} \times \{ & A_{12} \times (A_{23} \times A_{34} - A_{24} \times A_{33}) - A_{13} \times (A_{24} \times A_{31} - A_{21} \times A_{34}) + \\ & A_{14} \times (A_{21} \times A_{32} - A_{22} \times A_{31}) \} \end{aligned}$$

If the bottom row of the matrix has $A_{41} = A_{42} = A_{43} = 0$, and $A_{44} = 1$, which is usually the case, then this result reduces to the determinant of a 3 by 3 matrix.

$$\det(A) = A_{11} \times (A_{22} \times A_{33} - A_{23} \times A_{32}) + A_{21} \times (A_{32} \times A_{13} - A_{33} \times A_{12}) + A_{31} \times (A_{12} \times A_{23} - A_{13} \times A_{22})$$

Any matrix whose determinant is non-zero is called *non-singular*, and matrices with zero determinant are called *singular*. All non-singular matrices A have an *inverse* A^{-1}, which has the property that $A \times A^{-1} = I$ and $A^{-1} \times A = I$; see Finkbeiner (1978). A listing was given in chapter 6 (listing 6.8) which uses the Adjoint method to find the inverse of a 3 by 3 matrix.

Transformation of axes

Now consider the effects of a transformation of axes. Suppose a point **p** has co-ordinates (x, y, z) relative to an existing axis system, and (x', y', z') relative to a set of axes obtained by a transformation of this system. The transformation is totally described if equations are given which relate the new co-ordinate values x', y' and z' to the values of x, y and z. An *affine* transformation is one which defines the new co-ordinate values in terms of linear combinations of the old – that is, the equations contain only multiples of x, y and z and additional scalar values: it includes neither non-unit powers, products, other functions of x, y and z, nor other variables. Such equations may be written

$$x' = A_{11} \times x + A_{12} \times y + A_{13} \times z + A_{14}$$
$$y' = A_{21} \times x + A_{22} \times y + A_{23} \times z + A_{24}$$
$$z' = A_{31} \times x + A_{32} \times y + A_{33} \times z + A_{34}$$

The A values are called the coefficients of the equations. The result of the transformation is a combination of multiples of x values, y values, z values and unity. Another equation may be added

$$1 = A_{41} \times x + A_{42} \times y + A_{43} \times z + A_{44}$$

For this to be true for all values of x, y and z, it follows that $A_{41} = A_{42} = A_{43} = 0$ and $A_{44} = 1$, as we mentioned in the determinant calculation above. This may seem a rather contrived exercise, but it ensures that matrix A is square, and this will prove very useful later. If each point vector (x, y, z) (alternatively called a *row vector* for obvious reasons) is set in the form of a four-rowed *column vector*

$$\begin{pmatrix} x \\ y \\ z \\ 1 \end{pmatrix}$$

then the above three equations can be written as a matrix equation, with, on the right hand side, the matrix of coefficients *pre-multiplying* the column vector

$$\begin{pmatrix} x' \\ y' \\ z' \\ 1 \end{pmatrix} = \begin{pmatrix} A_{11} & A_{12} & A_{13} & A_{14} \\ A_{21} & A_{22} & A_{23} & A_{24} \\ A_{31} & A_{32} & A_{33} & A_{34} \\ A_{41} & A_{42} & A_{43} & A_{44} \end{pmatrix} \times \begin{pmatrix} x \\ y \\ z \\ 1 \end{pmatrix}$$

So, if the transformation of axes is stored as a matrix, the new co-ordinates of any point vector can be calculated by the simple expedient of considering it as a column vector and pre-multiplying it by the matrix.

Many writers on computer graphics do not use column vectors. Instead they prefer to extend the row vector – for example, (x , y , z) to $(x , y , z , 1)$ – and then post-multiply the row vector by the transformation matrix so that the above equations become in matrix form

$$\begin{pmatrix} x', & y', & z', & 1 \end{pmatrix} = \begin{pmatrix} x, & y, & z, & 1 \end{pmatrix} \times \begin{pmatrix} A_{11} & A_{21} & A_{31} & A_{41} \\ A_{12} & A_{22} & A_{32} & A_{42} \\ A_{13} & A_{23} & A_{33} & A_{43} \\ A_{14} & A_{24} & A_{34} & A_{44} \end{pmatrix}$$

Note that this matrix is the *transpose* of the matrix of coefficients in the equations. This can cause a great deal of confusion among those who are not confident in the use of matrices. It is for this reason that this book keeps to the column vector notation. It really does not matter which method you finally use as long as you are consistent. (Note that the transpose B of a matrix A is given by $B_{ij} = A_{ji}$ where $1 \leq i , j \leq 4$.)

We can now turn our attention to the transformations and assume that the transformation is stored in a matrix **A** that is an instantiation of class **Matrix**. Throughout the following sections, bear in mind that the point itself is not being moved – its co-ordinates are simply specified with respect to a new set of axes.

Change of scale

Now the origin and direction of axes are the same in both systems, but the scale of the axes is different; for example, 1 unit on the old x-axis could become 3 units on the new x-axis, while the scale of the y- and z-axes remains the same. Suppose a unit distance on the original x-axis becomes s_x on the new x-axis, a unit distance on the old y-axis becomes s_y on the new, and a unit distance on the old z-axis becomes s_z on the new. Then a point (x, y, z) in the old system has co-ordinates (x', y', z') relative to the new, where

$$x' = s_x \times x + 0 \times y + 0 \times z - 0$$
$$y' = 0 \times x + s_y \times y + 0 \times z - 0$$
$$z' = 0 \times x + 0 \times y + s_z \times z - 0$$

so the matrix describing this transformation is:

$$\begin{pmatrix} s_x & 0 & 0 & 0 \\ 0 & s_y & 0 & 0 \\ 0 & 0 & s_z & 0 \\ 0 & 0 & 0 & 1 \end{pmatrix}$$

Given the values **sx**, **sy** and **sz** (corresponding to s_x, s_y and s_z), **A** is calculated with method **scale** (listing 7.1b), thus:

```
A.scale(sx,sy,sz) ;
```

Translation of Origin

In this case the co-ordinate axes of the old and new systems are in the same direction and are of the same scale; however, the new origin has become a vector point $\boldsymbol{t} \equiv (t_x, t_y, t_z)$ relative to the old axes. Hence in the new system the old origin has co-ordinates $(-t_x, -t_y, -t_z)$, and the typical point (x, y, z) of the old system is represented in the new as (x', y', z'), where

$$x' = 1 \times x + 0 \times y + 0 \times z - t_x$$
$$y' = 0 \times x + 1 \times y + 0 \times z - t_y$$
$$z' = 0 \times x + 0 \times y + 1 \times z - t_z$$

so the matrix describing this transformation is:

$$\begin{pmatrix} 1 & 0 & 0 & -t_x \\ 0 & 1 & 0 & -t_y \\ 0 & 0 & 1 & -t_z \\ 0 & 0 & 0 & 1 \end{pmatrix}$$

Given the values **tx**, **ty** and **tz** (corresponding to t_x, t_y and t_z), **A** is calculated with method **translate** (listing 7.1b), thus:

```
A.translate(tx,ty,tx) ;
```

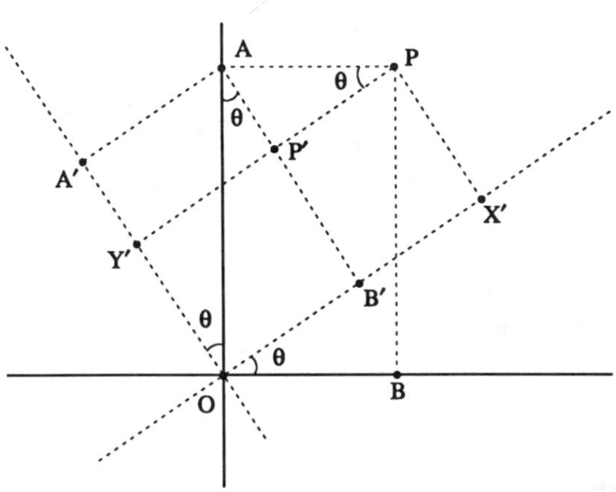

Figure 7.1

Rotation of Axes

Before we can consider rotating axes in three dimensions, we first have to understand the two-dimensional situation. Consider the axial system shown in figure 7.1 with solid lines, and the new system with lines of equi-spaced dashes; the systems have common origin and scale. The new axes are derived by rotating the old ones through an angle θ radians anti-clockwise about the origin. (This is the usual mathematical way of measuring angles.) If the point P in figure 7.1 has co-ordinates (x, y) relative to the old system and (x', y') relative to the new, then we have the relationships

$$\begin{aligned} x' &= \mathrm{OX'} = \mathrm{OB'} + \mathrm{B'X'} = \mathrm{AA'} + \mathrm{P'P} \\ &= \mathrm{OA} \times \sin\theta + \mathrm{AP} \times \cos\theta \quad = \mathrm{OB} \times \cos\theta + \mathrm{OA} \times \sin\theta \\ &= x \times \cos\theta + y \times \sin\theta \end{aligned}$$

$$\begin{aligned} y' &= \mathrm{OY'} = \mathrm{A'O} - \mathrm{A'Y'} = -\mathrm{AP'} + \mathrm{AB'} \\ &= \mathrm{OA} \times \cos\theta - \mathrm{AP} \times \sin\theta \quad = \mathrm{OA} \times \cos\theta - \mathrm{OB} \times \sin\theta \\ &= x \times (-\sin\theta) + y \times \cos\theta \end{aligned}$$

In three-dimensional space, rotation by a given angle implies a torque about a line (called the *axis of rotation*). There are an infinite number of directions which this line may take, and each direction will produce a different form of transformation. We begin, therefore, by considering the simplest cases, where the axis of rotation is coincident with one of the co-ordinate axes. If the positive half of the axis in question goes out of the page, then the other two axes appear to rotate in an anti-clockwise orientation. If a clockwise rotation by an angle θ radians is required, then an anti-clockwise rotation by an angle −θ must be used.

Rotation by an angle θ about the z-axis

Referring to figure 7.2a, the axis of rotation being perpendicular to the page (the positive z-axis is out of the page since we are using right-handed axes), the problem is reduced to a rotation of the x and y axes in two dimensions, the z co-ordinates remaining unchanged. Thus, using the two-dimensional formulae above, we obtain the new co-ordinates, (x', y', z') of the typical point (x, y, z) as follows

$$x' = \cos\theta \times x + \sin\theta \times y$$
$$y' = -\sin\theta \times x + \cos\theta \times y$$
$$z' = z$$

and the matrix:

$$\begin{pmatrix} \cos\theta & \sin\theta & 0 & 0 \\ -\sin\theta & \cos\theta & 0 & 0 \\ 0 & 0 & 1 & 0 \\ 0 & 0 & 0 & 1 \end{pmatrix}$$

Rotation by an angle θ about the y-axis

Referring to figure 7.2b, we now have the positive y-axis out of the page and, since we are using right-handed axes, the positive z-axis is horizontal and to the right of the origin, and the positive x-axis is above the origin. This leads us to the three equations

$$z' = \cos\theta \times z + \sin\theta \times x$$
$$x' = -\sin\theta \times z + \cos\theta \times x$$
$$y' = y$$

and rearranging

$$x' = \cos\theta \times x - \sin\theta \times z$$
$$y' = y$$
$$z' = \sin\theta \times x + \cos\theta \times z$$

which gives the matrix

$$\begin{pmatrix} \cos\theta & 0 & -\sin\theta & 0 \\ 0 & 1 & 0 & 0 \\ \sin\theta & 0 & \cos\theta & 0 \\ 0 & 0 & 0 & 1 \end{pmatrix}$$

Rotation by an angle θ about the x-axis

Referring to figure 7.2c, we find, in a similar manner, that the co-ordinates of the typical point (x, y, z) become (x', y', z') as follows

$$y' = \cos\theta \times y + \sin\theta \times z$$
$$z' = -\sin\theta \times y + \cos\theta \times z$$
$$x' = x$$

which, rearranged, become

$$x' = x$$
$$y' = \cos\theta \times y + \sin\theta \times z$$
$$z' = -\sin\theta \times y + \cos\theta \times z$$

and thus the matrix is

$$\begin{pmatrix} 1 & 0 & 0 & 0 \\ 0 & \cos\theta & \sin\theta & 0 \\ 0 & -\sin\theta & \cos\theta & 0 \\ 0 & 0 & 0 & 1 \end{pmatrix}$$

A method **rotate** to produce **A**, any one of these three matrices, given the angle **theta** (in radians) and the axis number **m** (**m**=1 for x-axis, **m** = 2 for y-axis and **m** = 3 for z-axis) is given in listing 7.1b, and generated by

```
A.rotate(m,theta) ;
```

Exercise 7.1: ***Other transformations***

Obviously these three types of transformation do not exhaust all the possible choices of matrix **A**. There are other types of transformation – *shear*, for example, which will give a matrix in the form of an identity matrix except for one extra off-diagonal non-zero entry:

$$\begin{pmatrix} 1 & a & 0 & 0 \\ 0 & 1 & 0 & 0 \\ 0 & 0 & 1 & 0 \\ 0 & 0 & 0 & 1 \end{pmatrix} \quad \text{or} \quad \begin{pmatrix} 1 & 0 & 0 & 0 \\ 0 & 1 & 0 & 0 \\ 0 & b & 1 & 0 \\ 0 & 0 & 0 & 1 \end{pmatrix}$$

These cause distortions of both space and axes; and so following our policy of keeping things simple we will restrict ourselves to scaling, translation and rotation. You should write functions to construct and experiment with such alternative transformation matrices.

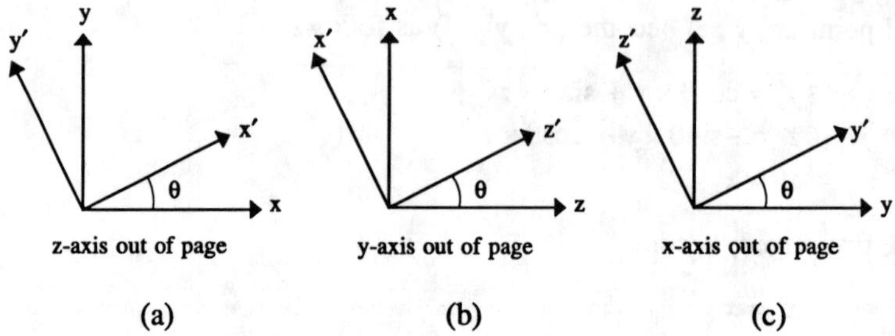

Figure 7.2

Listing 7.1a

```
// Save as file "matrix.h"
//------------//
  class Matrix
//------------//
{ float M[5][5] ;
 public:
  Matrix() ;
  void Set(float m[5][5]) ;
  void translate(float tx, float ty, float tz) ;
  void scale(float sx, float sy, float sz) ;
  void rotate(int m, float theta) ;
  vector3 Get_column(int c) ;
  vector3 dir_transform(vector3 d) ;
  void unit(void) ;
  void print(void) ;
  Matrix genrot(float phi, vector3 b, vector3 d) ;
  friend Matrix operator* (Matrix A, Matrix B) ;
  friend vector3 operator* (Matrix A, vector3 v) ;
 } ;  // End of class Matrix
```

Listing 7.1b

```
// Save as file "matrix.cpp"
//----------------//
  Matrix::Matrix()
//----------------//
 { int i, j ;
   for (i=0 ; i<5 ; i++)
       for (j=0 ; j<5 ; j++) M[i][j] = 0.0 ;
   M[4][4] = 1.0 ;
 }  // End of Matrix
//--------------------------------//
 void Matrix::Set(float m[5][5])
//--------------------------------//
 { int i, j ;
   for (i=1 ; i<5 ; i++)
       for (j=1 ; j<5 ; j++)  M[i][j] = m[i][j] ;
 }  // End of Set
```

```
//---------------------------------------------------------//
  void Matrix::translate(float tx, float ty, float tz)
//---------------------------------------------------------//
// 3-D axes translation matrix; origin translated by vector '(tx,ty,tz)'
 { int i, j ;
   for (i=0 ; i<5 ; i++) for (j=0 ; j<5 ; j++) M[i][j] = 0.0 ;
   for (i=1 ; i<5 ; i++)  M[i][i]= 1.0 ;
   M[1][4]=-tx ; M[2][4]=-ty ; M[3][4]=-tz ;
 }  // End of translate

//-----------------------------------------------------//
  void Matrix::scale(float sx, float sy, float sz)
//-----------------------------------------------------//
// 3-D scaling matrix given scaling vector '(sx,sy,sz)'
// One unit on the x axis becomes 'sx' units, one unit on the y axis
// becomes 'sy' units and one unit on the z axis becomes 'sz' units
 { int  i, j ;
   for (i=0 ; i<5 ; i++) for (j=0 ; j<5 ; j++) M[i][j] = 0.0 ;
   M[1][1]=sx ; M[2][2]=sy ; M[3][3]=sz ; M[4][4]=1.0 ;
 }  // End of scale

//-----------------------------------------//
  void Matrix::rotate(int m, float theta)
//-----------------------------------------//
// 3-D axes rotation matrix. The axes are rotated anti-clockwise through an
// angle 'theta' radians about an axis specified by 'm' :
// m=1 means x axis;  m=2  y axis;  m=3  z axis
 { int i,j,m1,m2 ;
   float c,s ;
   for (i=0 ; i<5 ; i++) for (j=0 ; j<5 ; j++) M[i][j] = 0.0 ;
   M[m][m]=1.0 ; M[4][4]=1.0 ;
   m1=(m % 3)+1 ; m2=(m1 % 3)+1 ; c=cos(theta) ; s=sin(theta) ;
   M[m1][m1]=c ; M[m2][m2]= c ; M[m1][m2]=s ; M[m2][m1]=-s ;
 }  // End of rotate

//-----------------------------------//
  vector3 Matrix::Get_column(int c)
//-----------------------------------//
 { vector3 v ;
   if ( (c < 1) || (c>4) ) c = 4 ;
   v.x = M[1][c] ;  v.y = M[2][c] ;  v.z = M[3][c] ;  return ( v ) ;
 }  // End of Get_column

//-----------------------------------------//
  vector3 Matrix::dir_transform(vector3 d)
//-----------------------------------------//
 { vector3 w ;
   w.x=M[1][1]*d.x + M[1][2]*d.y + M[1][3]*d.z ;
   w.y=M[2][1]*d.x + M[2][2]*d.y + M[2][3]*d.z ;
   w.z=M[3][1]*d.x + M[3][2]*d.y + M[3][3]*d.z ;
   return( w ) ;
 }  // End of direction transformation Matrix * vector3

//-----------------------//
  void Matrix::unit(void)
//-----------------------//
 { int i, j ;
   for (i=0 ; i<5 ; i++) for (j=0 ; j<5 ; j++) M[i][j] = 0.0 ;
   for (i=1 ; i<5 ; i++)  M[i][i]=1.0 ;
 }  // End of unit

//------------------------//
  void Matrix::print(void)
//------------------------//
 { int i,j ;
   for (i=1 ; i<5 ; i++)
   { for (j=1 ; j<5 ; j++) cout << "    " << M[i][j] ;  cout << "\n" ;  }
   cout << "\n" ;
 }  // End of print
```

```
//-----------------------------------------//
  Matrix operator* (Matrix  A, Matrix  B)
//-----------------------------------------//
 { Matrix C ;
   int i, j, k ;
   for (i=1 ; i<5 ; i++)  for (j=1 ; j<5 ; j++)
      { C.M[i][j] = 0.0 ;
        for (k=1 ; k<5 ; k++)  C.M[i][j] += A.M[i][k]* B.M[k][j] ;
      }
   return( C ) ;
 }  // End of *

//-----------------------------------------//
  vector3 operator* (Matrix A, vector3 v)
//-----------------------------------------//
// transform column vector 'v' using matrix 'A' into column vector 'w'
 { vector3 w ;
   w.x=A.M[1][1]*v.x + A.M[1][2]*v.y + A.M[1][3]*v.z + A.M[1][4] ;
   w.y=A.M[2][1]*v.x + A.M[2][2]*v.y + A.M[2][3]*v.z + A.M[2][4] ;
   w.z=A.M[3][1]*v.x + A.M[3][2]*v.y + A.M[3][3]*v.z + A.M[3][4] ;
   return( w ) ;
 }  // End of transformation Matrix * vector3

//------------------------------------------------//
  Matrix genrot(float phi, vector3 b, vector3 d)
//------------------------------------------------//
// Calculates the matrix 'A' representing the rotation of axes through
// an angle 'phi' about a typical line with base 'b' and direction 'd'
 { Matrix F, G, H, W, FI, GI, HI, A ;
   float beta,theta,v ;
   F.translate(b.x,b.y,b.z) ; FI.translate(-b.x,-b.y,-b.z) ;
   theta=angle(d.x,d.y) ;
   G.rotate(3,theta) ; GI.rotate(3,-theta) ;
   v=sqrt(d.x*d.x+d.y*d.y) ; beta=angle(d.z,v) ;
   H.rotate(2,beta) ; HI.rotate(2,-beta) ;
   W.rotate(3,phi) ;
   A = FI * (GI * (HI * (W * (H * (G * F))))) ;
   return ( A ) ;
 }  // End of genrot
```

Combination of transformations

A very useful property of this matrix representation of transformations is that the combination of two transformations, say transformation (or matrix) A followed by transformation B, is represented by their product $C = B \times A$. It is important to note the order in which the matrices are multiplied – the matrix representing the first transformation is pre-multiplied by the second. This is because the final matrix will be used to pre-multiply a column vector representing a point, and so the first transformation must appear on the right of the product and the last on the left. For the mathematical minded, the matrices may be considered as prefix operators on the column vectors. (If the row vector method is used then the matrices act as postfix operators, and the product would appear in the natural(!) order from left to right – this is the price paid for identifying the transformation matrix with the coefficients of the equations.) Also remember that matrix multiplication is non-commutative: $A \times B$ is not necessarily equal to $B \times A$.

We overload the multiplication operator * (listing 7.1), so that it multiplies two 4 by 4 matrices **A** and **B** to return a third 4 by 4 matrix **C** (= **A * B** which is not necessarily equal to **B * A**). Note that because * is inherently a prefix operator, and the way we have described them, transformations are implemented with post-multiplication, then all multiple applications of this operator must be placed in parentheses thus : **C * (B * A)**.

Inverse transformations

We concentrate on the natural transformations of axes, which may be reduced to a combination of the three basic forms of affine transformation: change of scale, translation, and rotation of axes. It should also be noted that all valid applications of these three transformations return *non-singular matrices*, that is those which have an inverse.

Before we can consider the general rotation of axes we must look at these inverse transformations in three-dimensional space. For every one of our three types of basic transformation there is an inverse transformation, which will restore the co-ordinates of a point to their original values. If a transformation is represented by a matrix A, then the inverse transformation is represented by the inverse matrix A^{-1}. The inverse matrices need not be calculated directly, but may instead be obtained by calling the respective transformation matrix creation methods, **scale**, **translate** and **rotate**, with the 'inverse' parameters given below.

(1) A change of scale by **sx**, **sy** and **sz** on the respective x-, y- and z-axes is inverted by changing the scale by **1/sx**, **1/sy** and **1/sz** on the corresponding axes. Naturally **sx**, **sy** and **sz** are non-zero, for otherwise the three-dimensional space would degenerate into a plane, line or point.

(2) A translation of origin to the point **(tx , ty , tz)** is inverted by another translation to the point **(–tx , –ty , –tz)**.

(3) An anti-clockwise rotation of axes by an angle θ is inverted with an opposite rotation by an angle $-\theta$.

(4) If the transformation matrix is a product of a number of scaling, translation and rotation matrices $A \times B \times C \times .... \times L \times M \times N$ (say), then the matrix for the inverse transformation is $N^{-1} \times M^{-1} \times L^{-1} \times .... \times C^{-1} \times B^{-1} \times A^{-1}$.
Note the order of multiplication!

Rotation of axes by an angle ϕ about a general axis $\boldsymbol{b} + \mu\boldsymbol{d}$

Assume $\boldsymbol{b} \equiv (b_x , b_y , b_z)$ and $\boldsymbol{d} \equiv (d_x , d_y , d_z)$. The idea is first to transform the axes so that the line $\boldsymbol{b} + \mu\boldsymbol{d}$ becomes coincident with the z-axis, with the point $\boldsymbol{b}$ moved to the origin and the sense of direction $\boldsymbol{d}$ placed along the positive z-axis. The rotation may then be performed about this new z-axis, and the axis of rotation subsequently transformed back to its original position to complete the general rotation. We break down the task into a number of subtasks

(a) The co-ordinate origin is translated to the point $\boldsymbol{b}$ so that the axis of rotation now passes through the origin. This is achieved by the matrix F

$$F = \begin{pmatrix} 1 & 0 & 0 & -b_x \\ 0 & 1 & 0 & -b_y \\ 0 & 0 & 1 & -b_z \\ 0 & 0 & 0 & 1 \end{pmatrix} \qquad F^{-1} = \begin{pmatrix} 1 & 0 & 0 & b_x \\ 0 & 1 & 0 & b_y \\ 0 & 0 & 1 & b_z \\ 0 & 0 & 0 & 1 \end{pmatrix}$$

The axis of rotation is now of the form $\mu\boldsymbol{d}$. We now require the axis of rotation to be along the *z*-axis. This is achieved by the next two steps.

(b) The axes are rotated about the *z*-axis by an angle $\alpha = \tan^{-1}(d_y/d_x)$. This is represented by the matrix G

$$G = \frac{1}{v}\begin{pmatrix} d_x & d_y & 0 & 0 \\ -d_y & d_x & 0 & 0 \\ 0 & 0 & v & 0 \\ 0 & 0 & 0 & v \end{pmatrix} \qquad G^{-1} = \frac{1}{v}\begin{pmatrix} d_x & -dy & 0 & 0 \\ d_y & d_x & 0 & 0 \\ 0 & 0 & v & 0 \\ 0 & 0 & 0 & v \end{pmatrix}$$

where the positive number v is given by $v^2 = d_x^2 + d_y^2$. The axis of rotation, relative to the resultant co-ordinate axes, is now a line lying in the *x*/*z* plane passing through the point $(v, 0, d_z)$.

(c) The axes are then rotated about the *y*-axis by an angle $\beta = \tan^{-1}(v/d_z)$, a transformation represented by matrix H

$$H = \frac{1}{w}\begin{pmatrix} d_z & 0 & -v & 0 \\ 0 & w & 0 & 0 \\ v & 0 & d_z & 0 \\ 0 & 0 & 0 & w \end{pmatrix} \qquad H^{-1} = \frac{1}{w}\begin{pmatrix} d_z & 0 & v & 0 \\ 0 & w & 0 & 0 \\ -v & 0 & d_z & 0 \\ 0 & 0 & 0 & w \end{pmatrix}$$

where w is the positive number given by

$$w^2 = v^2 + d_z^2 = d_x^2 + d_y^2 + d_z^2$$

So the co-ordinates of the point $(v, 0, d_z)$ are transformed to $(0, 0, w)$, hence the axis of rotation is along the *z*-axis. Thus the matrix combination $H \times G \times F$ identifies the old line $\boldsymbol{b} + \mu\boldsymbol{d}$ with the new *z*-axis, and the old point $\boldsymbol{b}$ with the new origin and old $\boldsymbol{d}$ along the new positive *z*-axis.

(d) The problem of rotating the co-ordinate axes about a typical line has thus been reduced to rotating space about the z-axis, achieved by matrix W, which rotates the triad anti-clockwise through an angle ϕ about the z-axis.

$$W = \begin{pmatrix} \cos\phi & \sin\phi & 0 & 0 \\ -\sin\phi & \cos\phi & 0 & 0 \\ 0 & 0 & 0 & 0 \\ 0 & 0 & 0 & 1 \end{pmatrix}$$

(e) The required rotation, however, is meant to be relative to the original axis positions, so the transformations which were used to transform the axes to a suitable position for the rotation, F, G and H, must be inverted; therefore we pre-multiply by H^{-1}, G^{-1} and finally F^{-1}.

Thus the final transformation matrix P which rotates axes by the angle ϕ about the axis $\boldsymbol{b} + \mu\boldsymbol{d}$ is $P = F^{-1} \times G^{-1} \times H^{-1} \times \mathrm{W} \times H \times G \times F$. Naturally some of these matrices may reduce to the identity matrix in special cases. For example, if the axis rotation goes through the origin then F and F^{-1} are identical to the identity matrix I, and can be safely ignored. The general case of matrix P is created by the function **genrot** given in listing 7.1b and stored in **"matrix.cpp"**.

Example 7.1

Calculate the matrix P that represents the transformation of the axial system by rotating it through $\pi/4$ radians clockwise about an axis $(1 , 0 , 1) + \mu(3 , 4 , 5)$. What are the transformed co-ordinates of the point vectors $(0 , 0 , 0)$, $(1 , 0 , 0)$, $(0 , 1 , 0)$, $(0 , 0 , 1)$ and $(1 , 1 , 1)$ relative to the new co-ordinate axes?

Using the above theory we note that

$$F = \begin{pmatrix} 1 & 0 & 0 & -1 \\ 0 & 1 & 0 & 0 \\ 0 & 0 & 1 & -1 \\ 0 & 0 & 0 & 1 \end{pmatrix} \qquad F^{-1} = \begin{pmatrix} 1 & 0 & 0 & 1 \\ 0 & 1 & 0 & 0 \\ 0 & 0 & 1 & 1 \\ 0 & 0 & 0 & 1 \end{pmatrix}$$

$$G = \frac{1}{5}\begin{pmatrix} 3 & 4 & 0 & 0 \\ -4 & 3 & 0 & 0 \\ 0 & 0 & 5 & 0 \\ 0 & 0 & 0 & 5 \end{pmatrix} \qquad G^{-1} = \frac{1}{5}\begin{pmatrix} 3 & -4 & 0 & 0 \\ 4 & 3 & 0 & 0 \\ 0 & 0 & 5 & 0 \\ 0 & 0 & 0 & 5 \end{pmatrix}$$

$$H = \frac{1}{\sqrt{2}}\begin{pmatrix} 1 & 0 & -1 & 0 \\ 0 & \sqrt{2} & 0 & 0 \\ 1 & 0 & 1 & 0 \\ 0 & 0 & 0 & \sqrt{2} \end{pmatrix} \qquad H^{-1} = \frac{1}{\sqrt{2}}\begin{pmatrix} 1 & 0 & 1 & 0 \\ 0 & \sqrt{2} & 0 & 0 \\ -1 & 0 & 1 & 0 \\ 0 & 0 & 0 & \sqrt{2} \end{pmatrix}$$

and since a clockwise rotation through $\pi/4$ radians is equivalent to an anti-clockwise rotation through $-\pi/4$.

$$W = \frac{1}{\sqrt{2}}\begin{pmatrix} 1 & -1 & 0 & 0 \\ 1 & 1 & 0 & 0 \\ 0 & 0 & \sqrt{2} & 0 \\ 0 & 0 & 0 & \sqrt{2} \end{pmatrix}$$

By multiplying these matrices in the correct order we get

$$P = \frac{1}{50\sqrt{2}}\begin{pmatrix} 41+9\sqrt{2} & -12-13\sqrt{2} & -15+35\sqrt{2} & -26+6\sqrt{2} \\ -12+37\sqrt{2} & 34+16\sqrt{2} & -20+5\sqrt{2} & 32-42\sqrt{2} \\ -15-5\sqrt{2} & -20+35\sqrt{2} & 25+25\sqrt{2} & -10+30\sqrt{2} \\ 0 & 0 & 0 & 50\sqrt{2} \end{pmatrix}$$

where $P = F^{-1} \times G^{-1} \times \mathrm{H}^{-1} \times \mathrm{W} \times H \times G \times F$ is the matrix representation of the required transformation. Pre-multiplying the column vectors equivalent to points (0 , 0 , 0), (1 , 0 , 0), (0 , 1 , 0), (0 , 0 , 1) and (1 , 1 , 1) by P, then changing the resulting column vectors back into row form, and taking out a factor $1/(50\sqrt{2})$, gives the respective co-ordinates

$(-26 + 6\sqrt{2}, 32 - 42\sqrt{2}, -10 + 30\sqrt{2})$, $(15 + 15\sqrt{2}, 20 - 5\sqrt{2}, -25 + 25\sqrt{2})$, $(-38 - 7\sqrt{2}, 66 - 26\sqrt{2}, -30 + 65\sqrt{2})$, $(-41 + 41\sqrt{2}, 12 - 37\sqrt{2}, 15 + 55\sqrt{2})$ and $(-12 + 37\sqrt{2}, 34 + 16\sqrt{2}, -20 + 85\sqrt{2})$.

The placing of an object

When we come to drawing objects in the window, we will need to place them in various positions and at arbitrary orientations. While it may be quite simple to calculate the co-ordinates of the vertices of an object in a simply defined position, about the origin for instance as we did in many of the examples of chapter 2, it may be difficult to do so for peculiar orientations. If, furthermore the same type of object is to be drawn over and over again, but at different positions, then it would be very inefficient to calculate the vertices for every position on 'the back of an envelope' and then to enter them into a program. It is much more preferable to define each type of object as simply as possible, and then to move each occurrence of it to the required position and orientation. But this process conceptually involves transforming the positions of the vertices themselves, rather than transforming the co-ordinate axes. Thankfully, the same three basic axis transformations given above – change of scale, translation and rotation – still suffice; and with a small alteration to the parameters, the functions already written for the transformation of axes may again be used:

Change of scale and reflection

The co-ordinate origin and axes are fixed, and a typical point (x , y , z) is moved to a new position $(x \times s_x , y \times s_y , z \times s_z)$. This transformation is equivalent to changing the scale of the co-ordinate axes so that 1 unit on the x-axis becomes s_x units, 1 unit on the y-axis becomes s_y units, and 1 unit on the z-axis becomes s_z units. The transformation matrix may thus be calculated by

```
A.scale(sx,sy,sz) ;
```

Furthermore, if one of the vertex co-ordinates is multiplied by a negative factor (by s_x, s_y or s_z), then this corresponds to a reflection in the plane containing the other two axes; for example, $s_x = -1$, $s_y = 1$, $s_z = 1$ gives a reflection in the y/z plane through the origin.

Translation

An object is to be moved by a vector $\boldsymbol{t} \equiv (t_x , t_y , t_z)$, thus a vertex (x , y , z) is moved to $(x+t_x , y+t_y , z+t_z)$. This is exactly equivalent to keeping the object fixed and translating the origin of the axes to $(-t_x , -t_y , -t_z)$. Thus the matrix representing this transformation may be calculated by

```
A.translate(-tx,-ty,-tz) ;
```

Rotating an object about the origin

Rotating an object anti-clockwise about the origin by an angle θ (**theta**) is equivalent to keeping the object fixed and rotating the axes by an angle θ clockwise, or alternatively by an angle −θ anti-clockwise. The rotation matrix is therefore returned by

```
A.rotate(m,-theta) ;
```

where **m** is the index of the co-ordinate axis about which the rotation occurs.

As for rotation of vertices about a general axis, this may be achieved in exactly the same way we achieved a rotation of axes earlier. Matrices F, G and H are used to transform the co-ordinate axes into such a position that the axis of rotation is coincident with the *z*-axis. Then space (not axes) is rotated with the matrix W so that the vertices move about this new *z*-axis. Finally H^{-1}, G^{-1} and F^{-1} replace the axes in their original positions. The complete rotation, as before, is achieved by $F^{-1} \times G^{-1} \times H^{-1} \times W \times H \times G \times F$.

Also note that listing 7.1b contains other utility functions for the manipulation of matrices: apart from the constructor, **Set** copies a 4 by 4 array into its matrix form, **Get_column** turns the first three entries in the column of a matrix into a **vector3** value, **dir_transform** uses the matrix to transform a direction vector, **unit** sets up an identity matrix, and **print** prints out the matrix.

SETUP and ACTUAL positions

In order to describe a scene consisting of a set of geometrical objects placed in particular positions and orientations in three-dimensional space, we define an arbitrary but fixed co-ordinate system for three-dimensional space: this we call the *ABSOLUTE system.*

Next the co-ordinates of the vertices of a particular object are defined in some simple way, usually about the origin of the ABSOLUTE system. This we call the *SETUP position* for that object. Polygonal facets within the object are defined by specifying, and giving the order of, the vertices forming their corners.

Each particular object must be moved from its SETUP position to the desired position in space, its *ACTUAL position.* The matrix which relates the SETUP and ACTUAL positions for a given object will be called P throughout this book, and it may be calculated using one, or a combination, of the transformations described above. The object is moved by pre-multiplying the column vector form of each of its defining vertices with the same matrix P. The vertex co-ordinates are still specified with respect to the ABSOLUTE system, whether they are in SETUP or ACTUAL position. Facet relationships, such as co-planarity and the order of vertices, are preserved with the transformed vertices. Naturally, different objects will have unique SETUP to ACTUAL matrices P.

We must reiterate here that the co-ordinates of all vertices in the SETUP and ACTUAL positions are defined with respect to the same set of axes – those of the ABSOLUTE system.

Storing information about scenes

We are now ready to consider the various methods of creating and storing data about a scene. This data always consists of: a cluster of vertices identified by their vector co-ordinates relative to an arbitrary but fixed co-ordinate system, which we called the ABSOLUTE system; a set of lines, each line joining a pair of vertices (although we will not use lines explicitly in our displays of three-dimensional space); and a 'mesh' of polygonal facets, with each facet identified by the ordered vertices at its corners. Most of the pictures we have created so far have been drawn by specific functions, that both create the data (subject to some implicit transformations of the vertex co-ordinates) and draw the scene. In the work that follows, however, the data that represents objects will undergo various manipulations between its creation and the eventual drawing of the scene; and so we need to store it in an easily accessible from within our database.

The construction of a section of the database relevant to a single occurrence of one particular object will be achieved by a call to a *construction function* for that type of object, which will normally have a SETUP to ACTUAL matrix P as a parameter to take a SETUP object and place it in its correct ACTUAL position. The SETUP information can be input from file or calculated inside the function. If the same ACTUAL scene is used repeatedly, then it is possible to create the scene just once, and then store it on file using the **dataout** function (listing 7.4b), so that when needed the ACTUAL positions of all objects in the scene can be read back directly into the database using function **datain** (listing 7.4b). Frequently used construction functions (such as the **cube** of listing 7.5b), and any functions that support construction (such as body of revolution of listing 9.9), will be placed in file **"construc.cpp"**, which is **#included** into our programs. One-off functions are usually declared directly in an application program.

Clusters

Following their introduction in chapter 3, we define three-dimensional objects as a mesh of polygonal facets that approximates to the curved surface of a three-dimensional object – just as a sequence of small lines approximates to a curve in two dimensions (this is how we drew a circle). Our approximation to a surface will be an array of lists of vertices (a mesh): a vertex consists of the three components, the x , y and z co-ordinates, but a facet may have any number of sides and hence any number of vertices around its boundary, as well as peculiar material attributes including colour, reflective and refractive properties etc. Lines may be considered as edges of faces; should we need a line in our models, we describe it as a double-sided triangular facet with one side of zero length.

The surfaces of objects in a three-dimensional scene are approximated with a polygonal mesh, and we initially assume that it consists of **nov** vertices and **nof** facets. We will call the total set of vertices in the scene, the *scene cluster*. During our processing of the scene, the vertices will be related to different axial systems. The scene cluster will appear in various *cluster positions*, that is with co-ordinates given relative to particular axial systems; and in various *cluster projections*. Every time we relate the scene to a different set of axes we create a new cluster position – so far we have only considered the cluster in ACTUAL position; every time we project the cluster, as when we draw vertices on a (necessarily two-dimensional) window/viewport (see chapter 8), we create a new cluster projection. The order of the vertices within each cluster position and projection will be in the same order that they occur in the scene cluster. In order to represent different cluster positions we introduce class **Cluster3d** (with vertices of type **vector3**), and for cluster projections we have **Cluster2d** (with vertices of type **vector2**). The declarations for these classes are in listing 7.2a (**"cluster.h"**) and the code for the methods in listing 7.2b (**"cluster.cpp"**).

Each cluster position (or projection) uses the array **vertices[maxv]** of type **vector3[]** (or **vector2[]**) to hold data on the vertices; **maxv** is arbitrarily set to 1000. Initially there are **nov** vertices in the scene cluster, but after clipping so that the chosen view of the scene fits onto the window, this number will be increased to **extendednov**. The polygonal mesh describes each facet as a linked list of vertex indices, with each index indicating the position of that vertex in the scene cluster. Although each new cluster position will hold different values of the co-ordinate triples (and each new projection will hold different co-ordinate pairs), the ordering of the vertices within each position and projection remains unchanged. This ensures that the topology of the facets is independent of the position of objects, the choice of co-ordinate system, or the projection used.

The programs in this book will eventually need seven different cluster positions and three different cluster projections. In order to allow for as many vertices as possible within the limitations of DOS memory segmentation, we set up nine separate files for these positions and projections: named **"ClusterA.cpp"**, ..., **"ClusterI.cpp"**. You must take listing 7.2c and divide it up into these nine separate files. Then by linking the required files into a Borland C++ Project, this will allow a maximum of 64K storage for each position and projection. If memory size is still a problem then you must merge these **cluster** files together, thereby reducing the space available for each cluster. You can of course trade off memory against execution-time by calculating individual vertex positions and projections directly from their ACTUAL position each time they are needed.

The *x*, *y* and *z* co-ordinates of the cluster of vertices in ACTUAL position are stored in **"ClusterA.cpp"**, and it is instantiated in our programs as a **Cluster3d** object named **act**. The scene cluster is set up in ACTUAL position and it holds **nov** (not more than **maxv**) vertices. Originally **nov** is set to zero, and as the scene is generated (by calls to construction functions from within a function we call **build_it**), vertices, say with co-ordinates **(v.x , v.y , v.z)**, are added one by one to the ACTUAL cluster position by calling, for each **v**

```
act.add(v) ;
```

with the value of **nov** increased by one for each new vertex. Alternatively, a vertex **v** can be inserted into the **k**th position in the cluster by calling function

act.Put_vertex(k,v) ;

and the **k**th vertex may be retrieved from the **act** cluster position as

act.Get_vertex(k) ;

Other methods are available in the **Cluster** classes: to return the value of **nov** (**Get_nov**), and to set and to return the value of **extendednov** (**Set_extendednov** and **Get_extendednov** respectively).

Listing 7.2a

```
// Save as file "cluster.h"

#define maxv  1000

//---------------//
  class Cluster3d
//---------------//
{ int nov ;
  int extendednov ;
  vector3 vertices[maxv] ;
 public:
  Cluster3d() ;
  void add(vector3 v) ;
  void put_vertex(int k, vector3 v) ;
  vector3 Get_vertex(int id) { return ( vertices[id] ) ; }
  int Get_nov(void) { return ( nov ) ; }
  int Get_extendednov(void) { return ( extendednov ) ; }
  void Set_extendednov(int n) { extendednov = n ; }
} ;  // End of class Cluster3d

//---------------//
  class Cluster2d
//---------------//
{ int nov ;
  int extendednov ;
  vector2 vertices[maxv] ;

 public:
  Cluster2d() ;
  void add(vector2 v) ;
  void put_vertex(int k, vector2 v) ;
  vector2 Get_vertex(int id) { return ( vertices[id] ) ; }
  int Get_nov(void) { return ( nov ) ; }
  int Get_extendednov(void) { return ( extendednov ) ; }
  void Set_extendednov(int n) { extendednov = n ; }
} ;  // End of class Cluster2d
```

Listing 7.2b

```
// Save as file "cluster.cpp"

//----------------------//
  Cluster3d::Cluster3d()
//----------------------//
 { nov = 0 ;
   for (int i=0 ; i<maxv ; i++) vertices[i] = zero ;
 }  // End of Cluster3d
```

```
//--------------------------------//
  void Cluster3d::add(vector3 v)
//--------------------------------//
 { if (nov < maxv) vertices[nov++] = v ;
   else cerr << "\n Error, maximum number of vertices exceeded" ;
   extendednov = nov ;
 }  // End of add

//-----------------------------------------------//
  void Cluster3d::put_vertex(int k, vector3 v)
//-----------------------------------------------//
 { if (k < maxv) vertices[k] = v ;
   else cerr << "\n Error, maximum number of vertices exceeded" ;
   if (extendednov <= k) extendednov = k+1 ;
 }  // End of put_vertex

//----------------------//
  Cluster2d::Cluster2d()
//----------------------//
 {  int i ;
    nov = 0 ;
    for ( i=0 ; i<maxv ; i++)
       { vertices[i].x = 0.0 ;
         vertices[i].y = 0.0 ;
       } ;
 }  // End of Cluster2d

//--------------------------------//
  void Cluster2d::add(vector2 v)
//--------------------------------//
 { if (nov < maxv) vertices[nov++] = v ;
   else cerr << "\n Error, maximum number of vertices exceeded" ;
   extendednov = nov ;
 }  // End of add

//-----------------------------------------------//
  void Cluster2d::put_vertex(int k, vector2 v)
//-----------------------------------------------//
 { if (k < maxv) vertices[k] = v ;
   else cerr << "\n Error, maximum number of vertices exceeded" ;
   if (extendednov <= k) extendednov = k+1 ;
 }  // End of put_vertex
```

Listing 7.2c

```
// Save the following two lines of code as file "ClusterA.cpp"
#include "model.h"
Cluster3d act ;

// Save the following two lines of code as file "ClusterB.cpp"
#include "model.h"
Cluster3d obs ;

// Save the following two lines of code as file "ClusterC.cpp"
#include "model.h"
Cluster2d pro ;

// Save the following two lines of code as file "ClusterD.cpp"
#include "model.h"
Cluster3d vna ;

// Save the following two lines of code as file "ClusterE.cpp"
#include "model.h"
Cluster3d vno ;
```

```
// Save the following two lines of code as file "ClusterF.cpp"
#include "model.h"
Cluster3d vl ;

// Save the following two lines of code as file "ClusterG.cpp"
#include "model.h"
Cluster2d prol ;

// Save the following two lines of code as file "ClusterH.cpp"
#include "model.h"
Cluster3d reflect ;

// Save the following two lines of code as file "ClusterI.cpp"
#include "model.h"
Cluster2d proref ;
```

The mesh

The most efficient method of representing a polygonal facet without imposing an unreasonable limit upon the number of vertices around any boundary involves an extension of the **Mesh** class we described in chapter 3. The class contains a large array of integers **listofverts[maxlist]; maxlist** is arbitrarily set to 5000, and each integer value in the array indicates the position of a vertex in the scene cluster, that is within array **vertices**. Each of **nof** facets is defined by two integer indices pointing into this array. These indices are stored in arrays **firstoffacet[maxf]** and **size[maxf]; maxf**, arbitrarily set to 1200, is not less than **nof**, the total number of facets in the scene. **firstoffacet[i]** points to that element of the **listofverts** array which holds the index of the first vertex of facet **i**; thus **firstoffacet[0]**=0. The value **size[i]** contains the number of vertices on the boundary of the facet **i**, and these in turn are stored in sequence in the **listofverts** array as values

listofverts[firstoffacet[i]], ..., **listofverts[firstoffacet[i]+size[i]–1]**.

The only constraint is that the total number of sides of all facets must not exceed **maxlist**, the size of the **listofverts** array. To aid our calculations a special integer variable **firstfree** is used to indicate the location in **listofverts** one place beyond the entry for the final vertex of the last facet added (if any); this is very useful when updating the mesh database within construction functions. In our programs the **Mesh** class for geometrical objects in the scene will be instantiated as **mesh.**

Care must be taken to ensure that all the vertices of every given facet are coplanar. If this is so in their SETUP position, then it is maintained through any combination of affine transformations.

We also introduce the idea of material attributes associated with each facet. Array **material[maxf]** holds integers, one entry per facet, which initially will indicate the logical colour of that facet. Later, when we come to shade in the images, we will introduce a set of **maxmaterl** different material types. Each material will have several *attributes*, including properties to do with reflection and transparency. For all materials, each attribute will be stored in a named array, one entry per material; a particular attribute of material **i** is stored as entry **i** of the corresponding attribute array. Then for each facet the integer value stored in the **material** array will indicate the material composition of that facet, and the corresponding attribute values can be found directly from the attribute arrays.

A further variable is stored: the integer count **extendednof** (corresponding to **extendednov** of the clusters). Neither of these two values are used yet, but later they will represent respectively the total numbers of facets and vertices in the scene, inclusive of any extra which may be created after clipping the scene to fit in the window. When drawing facets, each original facet may have pieces that lie outside the window clipped off, so that the visible portion of each may be represented by a new list of vertices that composes a new facet (hence the need for **extendednov** and **extendednof**). The array **clipfac[]** holds an integer pointer to each new facet, or to the original if there is no clipping, or to -1 if the facet has been clipped away.

A number of methods are given for the **Mesh** class, including those to **Get** values from the mesh; these are not described here as their functionality is self-evident. Listing 7.3a, which is to be stored as file **"mesh.h"**, declares all the methods for the **Mesh** class, and the code for file **"mesh.cpp"** is introduced in listing 7.3b, with further code introduced in later listings as their need arises. Listing 7.3b contains the code for four methods only: the constructor; **add** inserts a new facet at the end of the mesh; **Get_a_sup** returns a facet that is superficial to facet **fid** (see chapter 9); and **printfacet**.

Other arrays related to superficial facets, namely **firstsup** and **superf** (see chapter 9) are also declared here. Also, for dealing with shadows, array **lsh** and methods **displayshadows**, **shadow**, **midpoint** and **orient** are declared in file **"mesh.h"**, but their explanation (and code for the functions) is left for later.

Listing 7.3a

```
// Save as file "mesh.h"

#define maxf       1200   // Maximum number of facets allowed
#define maxlist    5000   // Maximum size of the list of facets
#define maxsuplist 1000   // Maximum no. of facets superficial to single host

//----------//
  class Mesh
//----------//
 { int firstoffacet[maxf] ;
   int size[maxf] ;
   int listofverts[maxlist] ;
   int firstfree ;
   int nof ;
   int extendednof ;
   int material[maxf] ;
   int clipfac[maxf] ;
   int superf[maxf] ;
   Stack firstsup[maxf] ;
// For shadows:
   Stack lsh[maxf] ;
   int inside[maxpoly],kfacet[2][maxpoly] ;
   int ksize ;
```

```
 public:
  Mesh() ;
  void add(int flength, int *verts, int mater, int host) ;
  void printfacet(int facetid) ;
  void clipscene(void) ;
  int Get_nof(void) { return ( nof ) ;  } ;
  int Get_extendednof(void) { return ( extendednof ) ; } ;
  int Get_size(int fid) { return ( size[fid] ) ; } ;
  int Get_material(int fid) { return ( material[fid] ) ; } ;
  int Get_clipfac(int fid) { return ( clipfac[fid] ) ; } ;
  int Get_super(int fid) { return ( superf[fid] ) ; } ;
  int Get_faclist(int f,int v) { return listofverts[firstoffacet[f]+v] ; } ;
  int Get_a_sup(int fid, int *flist) ;
  Stack * Get_firstsup(int fid) { return (& (firstsup[superf[fid]]) ) ; } ;
  void shadow(void) ;
  void displayshadows(int face) ;
  vector3 midpoint(int face) ;
  int orient(int face, Cluster2d *clst) ;

 private:
  int clip(int k) ;
  void locate(int l, int flag, float tth, Cluster3d *oc) ;
  void compare(int i,int j,int *front,int *back,int *nsh,vector3 *shadpol);
} ;  // End of class Mesh
```

Listing 7.3b

```
// Save as file "mesh.cpp"

//------------//
  Mesh::Mesh()
//------------//
 { int i ;
   firstfree = 0 ;  nof = 0 ;
   for (i=0 ; i<maxf ; i++)
   { firstoffacet[i] = 0 ;  size[i] = 0 ;
     clipfac[i] = i ;
     superf[i] = -1 ;
     material[i] = 0 ;
   }
 }  // End of Mesh

//--------------------------------------------------------------//
  void Mesh::add(int flength, int *verts, int mater, int host)
//--------------------------------------------------------------//
 { int j ;
   stackinfo st ;
   if (flength != 0)
     { if (nof >= maxf)
         { cerr <<"\n Error: Maximum number of facets exceeded" ;
           return ;
         }
       size[nof] = flength ;
       firstoffacet[nof] = firstfree ;
       if (firstfree > maxlist)
         cerr << "\nError: Size of list array exceeded" ;
       firstfree = firstoffacet[nof]+flength ;
       for (j=0 ; j<flength ; j++)
         listofverts[firstoffacet[nof]+j] = verts[j] ;
       material[nof] = mater ;
       superf[nof] = host ;
       clipfac[nof]=nof ;
       if (host != -1) { st.i = nof ; firstsup[host].push(st) ; }
       nof++ ;
       extendednof = nof ;
     } ;
 }  // End of add
```

```
//---------------------------------------//
  int Mesh::Get_a_sup(int fid, int *flist)
//---------------------------------------//
 { int i, count ;
   stackinfo st[maxsuplist] ;
   count = firstsup[fid].Get_stack(&st[0]) ;
   if (count >= maxsuplist)
     { cerr << "\nError: List of superficial facets out of range" ;
       return ( 0 ) ;
     }
   else
     { for(i=0 ; i<count ; i++) flist[i] = st[i].i ; return( count ) ;  } ;
 }  // End of Get_a_sup

//----------------------------------//
  void Mesh::printfacet(int facetid)
//----------------------------------//
 { int j ;
   if ((facetid >= 0) && (facetid < nof))
   { if (size[facetid])
       { for (j=0 ; j<size[facetid] ; j++)
           { cout << "  " << listofverts[firstoffacet[facetid]+j] ; }
         cout << "\n" ;
       }
     else cout << "Empty Set \n" ;
   } ;
 }  // End of printfacet
```

The model of a three-dimensional scene

All these ideas must now be put together in a C++ program for modelling and displaying a three-dimensional scene. The model which initially describes the scene is set up as two instantiations: one, **mesh**, of the **Mesh** class and the other, **act**, of the **Cluster3d** class. We can assume that the necessary methods and other functions have all been properly declared and stored in the requisite files – **"viewport.h"**, **"palette.h"**, **"window.h"**, **"matrix.h&.cpp"**, **"mesh.h&.cpp"**, **"cluster.h"** and **"stack.h&.cpp"** (with the **"stackinf.cpp"** of listing 3.4c) – where they may be **#included** together in two files we name **"model.h"** (listing 7.4a) and **"model.cpp"** (listing 7.4b). Note that in listing 7.4b there are three functions, **datain** and **dataout** that input/output data on the model of the scene. But most importantly we give the **draw_a_picture** function which is used to link the model to the window, and hence to the viewport so that the scene can be drawn. **draw_a_picture** divides the process of displaying a three-dimensional scene into three separate and quite distinct stages:

1) function **build_it** constructs the data structure which describes the scene in terms of a **mesh** and a cluster **act**.

2) function **look_at_it** introduces the observer (and later the light source), and prepares a new cluster position, **obs**, relative to the observer, and forms the cluster projection, **pro**, for a given projection plane.

3) function **draw_it** takes the **mesh** and **pro** data and uses it to draw a picture of the scene on the graphics viewport object **vpt**, via window object **win**.

We will give various versions of functions **look_at_it** and **draw_it** later in the book, which should be stored in files **"display.h"** and **"display.cpp"**. However, you will be expected to produce your own **build_it** functions; in fact that is all you will be expected to do! To help you in this task we will give you a number of examples of **build_it** functions which form *application programs* when each is linked to a Borland C++ Project containing files **"construc.cpp"**, **"window.cpp"**, **"model.cpp"**, **"display.cpp"** and **"ClusterA(BCDEFGH&I).cpp"**. In order to introduce the idea of the **build_it** function in this chapter, and so that you can experiment with working application programs before considering **look_at_it** and **draw_it** (but for this chapter only), null versions of these two functions are given in listing 7.4b. When you have read and fully understood this chapter then these functions must be deleted from this file before you go on to chapter 8. To ensure our programs compile we have also commented out some lines that must be un-commented when **"display.h"** is introduced in chapter 8 and **"material.h"** in chapter 11. Also note we declare the **zero** vector here, and the variable **ambient** (set to 0.4) that will be used in later shading models.

Listing 7.4a

```
// Save as file "model.h"
// ATTENTION: The order that files are included is significant

#include "viewport.h"
#include "palette.h"
#include "window.h"
#include "matrix.h"
#include "stack.h"                // Use "stackinf.cpp" from listing 3.4c
#include "cluster.h"
#include "mesh.h"
//#include "material.h"          //  Un-comment for chapter 11 listings

const vector3 zero = { 0.0, 0.0, 0.0 } ;
#define ambient 0.4

void dataout(char *filename) ;
void datain(char *filename) ;
```

Listing 7.4b

```
// Save as file "model.cpp"

#include "model.h"

// #include "display.h"   // Un-comment for listings from next chapter

void build_it(void) ;
void look_at_it(void) ;
void draw_it(void) ;

extern Cluster3d act, obs ;
extern Cluster2d pro ;

Mesh mesh ;
int a_facet[maxpoly] ;

//#include "material.cpp"   // Un-comment two lines for chapter 11 listings
// Material mrl ;
#include "matrix.cpp"
#include "stack.cpp"
#include "mesh.cpp"
#include "cluster.cpp"
```

```
//----------------------------//
  void dataout(char *filename)   // function to output ACTUAL scene to file
//----------------------------//
 { int i,j ;
   vector3 v ;
   ofstream outdata ;
   outdata.open(filename) ;
   outdata << act.Get_nov() << "  " << mesh.Get_nof() << "\n" ;
   for (i=0 ; i<act.Get_nov() ; i++)
   { v = act.Get_vertex(i) ;  outdata << v << "\n" ;  }
   for (i=0 ; i<mesh.Get_nof() ; i++)
   { outdata << mesh.Get_size(i) << "  " << mesh.Get_material(i) ;
     outdata << "  " << mesh.Get_super(i) << "\n" ;
     for (j=0 ; j<mesh.Get_size(i) ; j++)
     { outdata << " " << mesh.Get_faclist(i,j) ; }
     outdata << "\n" ;
   } ;
   outdata.close();
 }  // End of dataout

//---------------------------//
  void datain(char *filename)  // function to input ACTUAL scene from file
//---------------------------//
 { int i,j ;
   int nov, nof, oldnov ;
   int fsize, fmater, fsuper ;
   Stack *stackpointer ;
   stackinfo st ;
   vector3 v ;
   ifstream indata ;
   oldnov = act.Get_nov() ;
   indata.open(filename) ;  indata >> nov >> nof ;
   for (i=0 ; i<nov ; i++)
   { indata >> v ;   act.add(v) ;  }
   for (i=0 ; i<nof ; i++)
   { indata >> fsize >> fmater >> fsuper ;
     fsuper += oldnov ;
     for (j=0 ; j<fsize ; j++)
     { indata >> a_facet[j] ; (a_facet[j]) += oldnov ; }
     mesh.add(fsize,&(a_facet[0]),fmater,fsuper) ;
// Clear lists of superficial facets
// See chapter 9 for explanation of storing superficial facets
// Ensure host facet input before superficial facets
     if (mesh.Get_super(i) != -1)
     { stackpointer = mesh.Get_firstsup(i) ;
       st.i = i ; stackpointer->push(st) ;
     }
   }
   indata.close() ;
 }  // End of datain

// Both these functions will be replaced in the next chapter
void look_at_it(void) { } ;
void draw_it(void)    { } ;

//-------------------------//
  void draw_a_picture(void)
//-------------------------//
 { build_it() ;  look_at_it() ;  draw_it() ;
 }  // End of draw_a_picture
```

Apart from declaring the **act Cluster3d** of **vector3** vertices at this stage, we also introduce here the **obs Cluster3d** position (file **"ClusterB.cpp"**) as well as the **pro Cluster2d** projection (file **"ClusterC.cpp"**), that will be explained in the next chapter when we consider an observer viewing the scene.

Listing 7.5a

```
// Save as file "construc.h"
#include "model.h"

void cube(Matrix P, int col) ;
void pyramid(Matrix P, int col) ;
void checkerboard(float s, float d, int t, int c1, int c2, Matrix P) ;
void hollow(Matrix P1,int col1, int col2) ;
void extrude(Matrix P, float d, int col, int n, vector2 *v) ;
void bodyrev(Matrix P, int col, int nvert, int nhoriz, vector2 *v) ;
```

Listing 7.5b

```
// Save code as file "construc.cpp"

#include "construc.h"

extern Mesh mesh ;
extern Cluster3d act ;

// data for setting up a cube of side 2

vector3 cubevert[8]=
{ 1,1,1, 1,-1, 1, 1,-1,-1, 1,1,-1, -1,1,1, -1,-1,1, -1,-1,-1, -1,1,-1 } ;

int cubefacet[6][4]=
{ 0,1,2,3, 0,3,7,4, 0,4,5,1, 2,6,7,3, 1,5,6,2, 4,7,6,5 } ;
//----------------------------//
  void cube(Matrix P, int col)
//----------------------------//
// Construction routine for a rectangular block. Initially a cube
// the block is distorted by the scaling matrix component of 'P'
// Assume cube has logical colour of col
 { int i, j, facet[4], current_nov ;
// Update facet data base with 6 new facets
   current_nov = act.Get_nov() ;
   for (i=0 ; i<6 ; i++)
   { for (j=0 ; j<4 ; j++)   facet[j] = cubefacet[i][j] + current_nov ;
     mesh.add(4,&(facet[0]),col,-1) ;
   }
// Update vertex data base with 8 new vertices in ACTUAL position
   for (i=0 ; i<8 ; i++)  act.add( (P * cubevert[i]) ) ;
 } // End of cube
```

Construction functions

We now have to consider how to write **build_it** functions. In general, we start the description of a scene with an initially empty database (**nov** and **nof** are zero and all stacks are empty), and then it will be constructed step by step with calls to particular construction functions, each of which adds the data for a particular type of geometrical object to the database that consists of the **mesh** and the cluster position **act**. Among the parameters to such a construction function will be the SETUP to ACTUAL matrix *P*. Each function will create a single object in as simple a position as possible, which we have called its SETUP position, and then matrix *P* moves it to its ACTUAL position in space. Another parameter of such a function is likely to be the integer that indicates the material composition of the object. The most commonly used construction functions will be declared and coded in files we name **"construc.h"** and **"construc.cpp"** respectively. The full declaration for **"construc.h"** needed in this book is given in listing 7.5a. One of the most elementary construction functions, namely to create a **cube**, is given in the initial **"construc.cpp"** of listing 7.5b. This file contains the data for the SETUP cube in arrays **cubevert[8]** and **cubefacet[6][4]**, and a function **cube** which, by transforming the SETUP cube by a matrix P, adds the data for a single ACTUAL cube of a given colour **col** to the **mesh** and **act** cluster database.

By organizing our approach in this modular way, readers will only have to write specific **build_it** functions for their application program and perhaps construction functions for file **"construc.cpp"**. Even these functions will be in a form similar to the examples we give, so this task should not prove too difficult. It is therefore very important that the reader recognizes, from this point, the various stages in construction and drawing.

To illustrate the use of the elementary **cube** construction function, we give two very simple **build_it** application programs in this chapter (listings 7.6 and 7.7) which merely print out data on a scene containing just one cube. In chapter 8 we will go further than just building a scene (via construction functions stored in the **"construc.cpp"** file), and introduce the observer (and later the light source) in function **look_at_it** and finally draw the scene in function **draw_it**.

Example 7.2

In order that the initial explanation of our algorithms is not obscured by too complicated objects, we will start all our descriptions by using a single cube. In the next chapter we will consider observing and displaying, but to begin with we just set up the scene and store its description on file. Only when these ideas are fully understood, will we add complexity into the scenes with other objects. Since the cube is such a useful object, we have already created the special SETUP array **cubevert[8]** for the vertices and array **cubefacet[6][4]** for the facets in **"construc.cpp"**. The construction function **cube** is then used to take the data and add a single example of a cube in a particular ACTUAL position to the database.

The SETUP vertex co-ordinates of the cube are defined to be the 8 vertex triples (1 , 1 , 1); (1 , −1 , 1); (1 , −1 , −1); (1 , 1 , −1); (−1 , 1 , 1); (−1 , −1 , 1); (−1 , −1 , −1) and (−1 , 1 , −1): numbered 0 through 7. The six facets are thus the sets of four vertices 0 , 1 , 2 , 3; 0 , 3 , 7 , 4; 0 , 4 , 5 , 1; 2 , 6 , 7 , 3; 1 , 5 , 6 , 2 and 4 , 7 , 6 , 5; see figure 7.3. The peculiar ordering of the vertex indices in the facet definitions is to ensure that, when viewed from the outside, the vertices are in anti-clockwise orientation – this will be useful later for hidden surface removal. If you are not sure of the orientation of your vertices then you should check using function **orient3** of listing 6.11 in **"window.cpp"**.

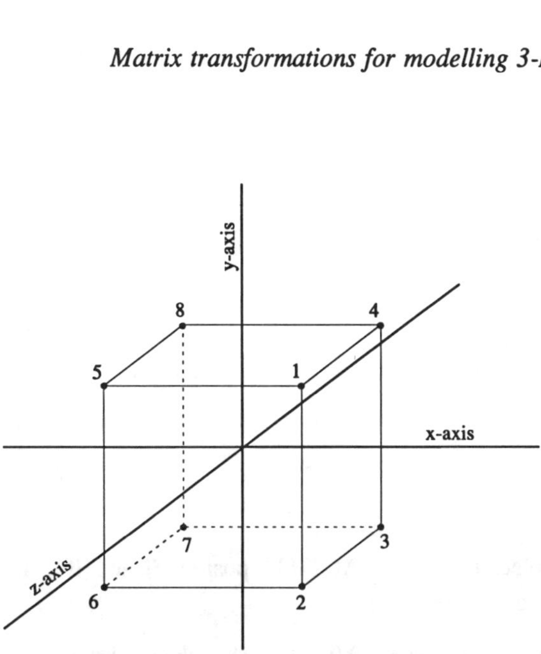

Vertices

1: (+1,+1,+1)
2: (+1,–1,+1)
3: (+1,–1,+1)
4: (+1,+1,–1)
5: (–1,+1,+1)
6: (–1,–1,+1)
7: (–1,–1,–1)
8: (–1,+1,–1)

Facets

1: 1, 2, 3, 4
2: 1, 4, 8, 5
3: 1, 5, 6, 2
4: 3, 7, 8, 4
5: 2, 6, 7, 3
6: 5, 8, 7, 6

Figure 7.3

In this particular example we enter the construction function with an identity matrix, so that the cube is placed in ACTUAL position identical to its SETUP position. Since we are not yet in a position to draw a three-dimensional scene, listing 7.6 includes a **build_it** function which takes the cube and places it in this simple ACTUAL position and then just stores the ACTUAL scene on disk using the **dataout** function. (The inverse function, **datain**, that recreates this ACTUAL scene from disk, in the same format generated by **dataout**, will be used in the example 8.1.) To run this program, store listing 7.6 as the application file **"seven6.cpp"**, and link it in a Borland C++ Project with **"construc.cpp"**, **"window.cpp"**, **"model.cpp"** and **"ClusterA(BCDEFGH&I).cpp"** (but in this case not file **"display.cpp"**, since we are not displaying the scene, and we have not yet created this file). Note that the eight files **"ClusterB(CDEFGH&I).cpp"** are linked to the application program even though we are not using them yet.

Listing 7.6

```
// Application program to construct a scene of one cube
#include "construc.h"
//--------------------//
  void build_it(void)                 // Place one Cube in its SETUP position
//--------------------//
 { Matrix P ;
   P.unit() ; cube(P,4) ;
   dataout("filename.dat") ;
 }  // End of build_it
```

Listing 7.7

```
// Application program to construct a scene of one cube

#include "construc.h"

//--------------------//
  void build_it(void)
//--------------------//
 { Matrix A, B, C, P ;
   float alpha = -0.927295 ;
// Place Cube as per Example 7.3
   A.rotate(3,-alpha) ;  B.translate(1.0,0.0,0.0) ;   C.rotate(2,alpha) ;
   P = C * (B * A) ;
   cube(P,2) ;
// Store the database
   dataout("filename.dat") ;
 }  // End of build_it
```

Example 7.3

In our next example we place the cube in ACTUAL position (**build_it** listing 7.7) with the following three transformations

(1) Rotate the cube by an angle $\alpha = -0.927205218$ radians about the z-axis: matrix A. This example is contrived so that $\cos\alpha=3/5$ and $\sin\alpha=-4/5$, in order that the rotation matrix consists of uncomplicated elements.

(2) Translate it by a vector $(-1, 0, 0)$: matrix B.

(3) Rotate it by an angle $-\alpha$ about the y-axis: matrix C.

Remember that these rotations are anti-clockwise with regard to the right-handed axes. Also note these three transformations are not of axes but of the object itself.

The SETUP to ACTUAL matrix is thus $P = C \times (B \times A)$, where

$$A = \begin{pmatrix} 3/5 & 4/5 & 0 & 0 \\ -4/5 & 3/5 & 0 & 0 \\ 0 & 0 & 1 & 0 \\ 0 & 0 & 0 & 1 \end{pmatrix} \quad B = \begin{pmatrix} 1 & 0 & 0 & -1 \\ 0 & 1 & 0 & 0 \\ 0 & 0 & 1 & 0 \\ 0 & 0 & 0 & 1 \end{pmatrix} \quad C = \begin{pmatrix} 3/5 & 0 & 4/5 & 0 \\ 0 & 1 & 0 & 0 \\ -4/5 & 0 & 3/5 & 0 \\ 0 & 0 & 0 & 1 \end{pmatrix}$$

and P is given by

$$P = \frac{1}{25}\begin{pmatrix} 9 & 12 & 20 & -15 \\ -20 & 15 & 0 & 0 \\ -12 & -16 & 15 & 20 \\ 0 & 0 & 0 & 25 \end{pmatrix}$$

Note that in the listings we force post-multiplication by the use of brackets. The above eight SETUP co-ordinates are transformed to the co-ordinate triples

(26/25 , –5/25 , 7/25); (2/25 , –35/25 , 39/25); (–38/25 , –35/25 , 9/25); (–14/25 , –5/25 , –23/25); (8/25 , 35/25 , 31/25); (–16/25 , 5/25 , 63/25); (–56/25 , 5/25 , 33/25) and (–32/25 , 35/25 , 1/25).

For example, (1 , 1 , 1) is transformed into (26/25 , –5/25 , 7/25) because

$$\frac{1}{25}\begin{pmatrix} 9 & 12 & 20 & -15 \\ -20 & 15 & 0 & 0 \\ -12 & -16 & 15 & 20 \\ 0 & 0 & 0 & 25 \end{pmatrix} \times \begin{pmatrix} 1 \\ 1 \\ 1 \\ 1 \end{pmatrix} = \frac{1}{25}\begin{pmatrix} 26 \\ -5 \\ 7 \\ 25 \end{pmatrix}$$

The values can be checked by printing out the array values by using **dataout**. To run this application program, store listing 7.7 as file **"seven7.cpp"**, and as above, link it in a Borland C++ Project with files **"window.cpp"**, **"construc.cpp"**, **"model.cpp"** and **"ClusterA(BCDEFGH&I).cpp"**.

Exercise 7.2

Use the SETUP information of the cube and a scaling matrix as part of the SETUP to ACTUAL matrix P so that the **cube** construction function places a rectangular block a units long, by b units high by c units deep in its ACTUAL position using a matrix P.

Exercise 7.3

Create construction functions for

1) A tetrahedron: an object with four vertices (labelled 0 to 3): (1 , 1 , 1); (–1 , 1 , –1); (–1 , –1 , 1) and (1 , –1 , –1) and four triangular facets 0 , 1 , 2; 0 , 2 , 3; 0 , 3 , 1 and 3 , 2 , 1.

(2) An icosahedron: $\tau = (1 + \sqrt{5})/2$: with twelve vertices (0 , 1 , –τ); (τ , 0 , –1); (1 , τ , 0); (0 , –1 , –τ); (τ , 0 , 1); (–1 , τ , 0); (0 , 1 , τ); (–τ , 0 , –1); (1 , τ , 0); (0 , –1 , τ); (τ , 0 , 1) and (–1 , –τ , 0).

The twenty triangular facets are 0 , 2 , 1; 0 , 1 , 3; 0 , 3 , 7; 0 , 7 , 5; 0 , 5 , 2; 1 , 2 , 4; 1 , 8 , 3; 3 , 11 , 7; 7 , 10 , 5; 2 , 5 , 6; 1 , 4 , 8; 3 , 8 , 11; 7 , 11 , 10; 5 , 10 , 6; 2 , 6 , 4; 4 , 9 , 8; 8 , 9 , 11; 11 , 9 , 10; 10 , 9 , 6; 6 , 9 , 4.

(3) Find your own data for other Archimedean solids such as the octahedron, rhombic dodecahedron, pentagonal dodecahedron, cuboctahedron etc.

Project 7.1

Construct a class **Matrix2** of three by three matrices, which is a two-dimensional equivalent of the three-dimensional transformation matrices given in this chapter. Include them in a *draw, drag, delete* program. You will need a series of functions that can draw two-dimensional objects (such as plan views of chairs, tables etc.) at mouse-specified positions in the window/viewport. The whole scene (for example, furniture in a room) must then be edited interactively using a mouse. The grid/menu/mouse method described in chapter 1 should be used to indicate your wish to draw a new occurrence of an object, to drag an indicated object around the viewport using XOR plotting, or to delete an object altogether.

Project 7.2

Produce a package that can draw data diagrams in VGA mode 18. It must be able to draw Bar Charts, Histograms, Pie Charts (the hatching function of chapter 5 will be useful), Scatter Graphs, both Discrete and Continuous Graphs, and the many other types of pictorial data display. You must be able to add text to, and delete it from, your diagrams; in particular you must have the facility of drawing labelled axes. The package must also have the facility of picking up identified parts of the diagram and translating, scaling and rotating them in relation to the rest of the diagram, using the system of two-dimensional matrices designed in project 7.1.

Far greater consideration will be given to the creation of data on more complex objects in chapter 9, but for the moment we need worry only about the form of this data, and so the next chapter will discuss the display of three-dimensional scenes on a graphics viewport, using only the simple cube to introduce the ideas.

This may be a good opportunity to return to listings 7.4a&b and un-comment the statement that **#includes** file **"display.h"**, as well as delete the **void** versions of **look_at_it** and **draw_it**, ready for the following chapters. Also remember that when you have introduced materials in chapter 11, you must return to this listing and un-comment the statements that **#include "material.h"** and **"material.cpp"**, and instantiate the **Material** object **mrl**.

8 The observer. Orthographic and perspective projections. Clipping

We now introduce the concept of an observer. Our eventual aim is to represent, in the graphics viewport, a three-dimensional scene as viewed by a person standing at a given position and looking in a given direction; with position and direction specified relative to the ABSOLUTE system. Imagine someone having a graphics screen fixed firmly in front of their face, and as they walk, run, jump, fly, somersault through space, they can only view that space through the screen. It is these images that we will simulate on the graphics viewport, so that the observer sitting comfortably in front of the screen can experience the same sights as our energetic 'space-traveller'.

In chapter 7 we saw how to construct a model of a three-dimensional scene in its ACTUAL position. In this chapter we consider observing the scene and displaying the corresponding view. The display of the scene is co-ordinated by function **draw_it**, which may take a number of different forms, depending on the type of image required (line drawing, colour etc). This function will be called at the end of the **draw_a_picture** function, that is after all the data has been keyed in during the construction of the model in **build_it** and during the positioning of the observer (and later the light source) in **look_at_it**. Only when all text has been input do we enter graphics mode by calling **win.start()** from inside **draw_it**.

We shall assume that the information about the scene (the model, observer and light source) will be stored initially in terms of **vector3** co-ordinates in ACTUAL position relative to the ABSOLUTE co-ordinate system. The eye of the observer (note only one eye!) is placed at a **vector3** position **eye** relative to the ABSOLUTE axes looking in a fixed **vector3** direction that we name **direct**. The head can also be tilted, but more of this later.

Matrix transformations are used to calculate the co-ordinates of the vertices relative to a new triad of axes, called the *OBSERVER system*, which has the eye at the origin and direction of view along the negative z-axis. (It would make more sense to use left-handed axes here, so that the observer looks along the positive z-axis, with distances positive in front of the eye and negative behind. But because of standardization in the graphics community, we remain with the right-handed system!) These new values are called the *OBSERVED position of the cluster* of vertices. The matrix which represents the transformation from

ABSOLUTE to OBSERVER systems, and which transforms the ACTUAL cluster position to OBSERVED cluster position, will be called Q throughout this book. It is calculated from within function **look_at_it**, given in listing 8.1b. We also declare variables **ppd, shadpd**, and **src**, which will be needed later in the book. Listing 8.1b gives the code for the functions needed to manipulate the observer; these should be used to create the file **"display.cpp"** that will be linked into our C++ Projects. The previous declaration and code for **look_at_it** and **draw_it** that were used temporarily in **"model.h"** (listing 7.4b) should now be deleted, and the statement that **#includes "display.h"** should be un-commented. Function **look_at_it** is declared in listing 8.1a, and stored in **"display.h"**.

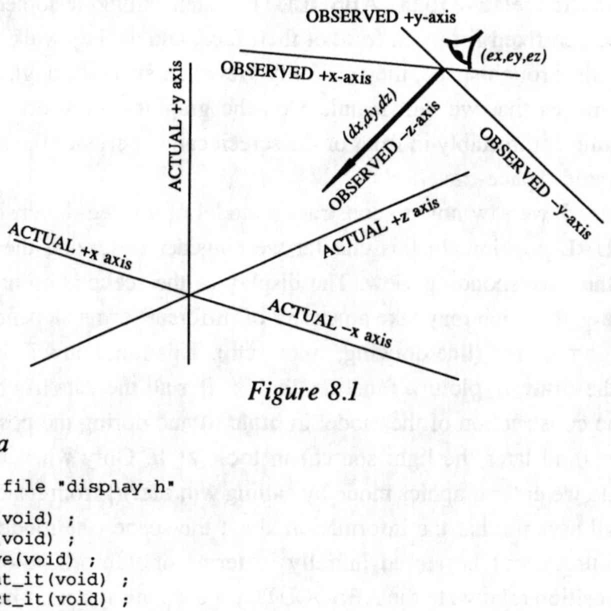

Figure 8.1

Listing 8.1a

```
// Save as file "display.h"
void findQ(void) ;
void look3(void) ;
void observe(void) ;
void look_at_it(void) ;
void project_it(void) ;
void wireframe(void) ;
void draw_it(void) ;
void hidden(void) ;
void facetfill(int face) ;
void seefacet(int face) ;
void cshade(vector3 p, vector3 norm, int ic, float *red, float *green,
                                                          float *blue) ;
vector3 normal(int face, float *k, Cluster3d *clst) ;
void overlap(int m1, int n1, int *front, int *back, int *numv, vector2 *p,
             Cluster2d *v2d, Cluster3d *v3d, float pd, int orientation) ;
int network(int *nob,Stack *list,Cluster2d *p,Cluster3d *v,int orientation) ;
void unstack(int face, int *nob, Stack *list, Stack *netstack) ;
float intensityshade(vector3 p, vector3 norm, int index) ;
void randomcolour(int col, float lambda) ;
void facetfill(int face, float lambda) ;
void facetfill(int face, int index) ;
void lightsystem(void) ;
void prepare_shadows(void) ;
void restore(int face, int nsh, vector3 *shadpol) ;
```

Listing 8.1b

```
// Save as file "display.cpp"

#include "model.h"
#include "display.h"

extern Window win ;
extern Palette plt ;
extern Mesh mesh ;
extern Cluster3d act ;
extern Cluster2d pro ;
extern Cluster3d obs ;
extern Cluster3d vna ;
extern Cluster3d vno ;
extern Cluster3d reflect ;
extern Cluster2d proref ;
extern Cluster3d vl ;
extern Cluster2d prol ;
// extern Material mrl ;       // Un-comment line for chapter 11 listings

Matrix Q,S,SI ;
vector3 direct,eye ;
float ppd ;
vector3 src ;
float shadpd ;

//-----------------//
  void findQ(void)      // Calculate observation matrix 'Q' for given observer
//-----------------//
 { Matrix F, G, H, U ;
   float alpha,beta,gamma,v,w ;
// Calculate translation matrix 'F'
   F.translate(eye.x,eye.y,eye.z) ;
// Calculate rotation matrix 'G'
   alpha=angle(-direct.x,-direct.y) ; G.rotate(3,alpha) ;
// Calculate rotation matrix 'H'
   v=sqrt(direct.x*direct.x+direct.y*direct.y) ;
   beta=angle(-direct.z,v) ; H.rotate(2,beta) ;
// Calculate rotation matrix 'U'
   w=sqrt(v*v+direct.z*direct.z) ;
   gamma=angle(-direct.x*w,direct.y*direct.z) ;
   U.rotate(3,-gamma) ;
// Combine the transformations to find 'Q'
   Q = U * (H * ( G * F ) ) ;
 }  // End of findQ

//-----------------//
  void look3(void)      // Read vector 'eye' looking in direction 'direct'
//-----------------//
// Read in observation data
 { cout << " Type in eye position and direction of view\n" ;
   cin >> eye >> direct ;
 }  // End of look3

//------------------//
  void observe(void)
//------------------//
 { for (int i=0 ; i<act.Get_extendednov() ; i++)
     obs.add( (Q * act.Get_vertex(i)) ) ;
 }  // End of observe

//---------------------//
  void look_at_it(void)
//---------------------//
 { look3() ;
// then calculate the observation matrix 'Q'
   findQ() ; observe() ;
   project_it() ;
 }  // End of look_at_it
```

Construction of the ABSOLUTE to OBSERVER transformation matrix *Q*

Relative to the ABSOLUTE system, the OBSERVER system has origin at point vector **eye**, with the negative *z*-axis parallel to, and with the same sense as, the direction vector **direct**: see figure 8.1. If the observer looks at the ABSOLUTE origin then **direct.x** = **–eye.x**, **direct.y** = **–eye.y** and **direct.z** = **–eye.z**.

Given a point with co-ordinates specified relative to the ABSOLUTE system, we want to determine its co-ordinates relative to the OBSERVER system. These co-ordinates may be found by pre-multiplying a column vector holding the ABSOLUTE co-ordinates of a point by a matrix which represents the series of steps required to transform the ABSOLUTE axes into the OBSERVER axes. The calculation of this matrix is similar to that considered in chapter 7, that is to the matrix that rotates a point about a general line $\boldsymbol{b} + \mu\boldsymbol{d}$. This involved transforming the axial system so that the origin moved to $\boldsymbol{b}$ with the positive *z*-axis in direction $\boldsymbol{d}$. In this case, therefore, we take vectors $\boldsymbol{b} \equiv$ (**eye.x**, **eye.y**, **eye.z**) and $\boldsymbol{d} \equiv$ (**–direct.x**, **–direct.y**, **–direct.z**), and carry out the equivalent steps: note the minus signs in the definition of $\boldsymbol{d}$, since the eye must look along the negative *z*-axis of the OBSERVER system! So we have the following procedure:

(1) The co-ordinate origin is translated to the point $\boldsymbol{b}$ so that the axis of rotation passes through the origin. This achieved by the matrix F

$$F = \begin{pmatrix} 1 & 0 & 0 & -eye.x \\ 0 & 1 & 0 & -eye.y \\ 0 & 0 & 1 & -eye.z \\ 0 & 0 & 0 & 1 \end{pmatrix}$$

The *z*-axis is now in form $\mu\boldsymbol{d} \equiv \mu$(**–direct.x**, **–direct.y**, **–direct.z**) relative to the transformed system. We now require the *z*-axis of the OBSERVER system and that of the transformed ABSOLUTE system to be coincident. This achieved by the next two steps.

(2) Matrix G is calculated, which performs a rotation of the co-ordinate axes about the *z*-axis by an angle $\alpha \equiv \tan^{-1}$(**–direct.y/–direct.x**).

$$G = \frac{1}{v}\begin{pmatrix} -direct.x & -direct.y & 0 & 0 \\ direct.y & -direct.x & 0 & 0 \\ 0 & 0 & v & 0 \\ 0 & 0 & 0 & v \end{pmatrix}$$

where the positive number v is given by v^2 = $\mathbf{direct.x}^2$ + $\mathbf{direct.y}^2$. The OBSERVER *z*-axis, relative to the resultant co-ordinate axes, is a line lying in the *x*/*z* plane passing through the point (v, 0, **–direct.z**).

(3) The axes are then rotated about the y-axis by an angle $\beta \equiv (v/-\textbf{direct.z})$, a transformation represented by matrix H

$$H = \frac{1}{w}\begin{pmatrix} -direct.z & 0 & -v & 0 \\ 0 & w & 0 & 0 \\ v & 0 & -direct.z & 0 \\ 0 & 0 & 0 & w \end{pmatrix}$$

where w is the positive number given by

$$w^2 = v^2 + \textbf{direct.z}^2 = \textbf{direct.x}^2 + \textbf{direct.y}^2 + \textbf{direct.z}^2$$

The combination $H \times G \times F$ transforms the z-axis of the ABSOLUTE system into the z-axis of the OBSERVER system. Although the z-axes of the two systems are coincident, this does not mean that the triads are identical. Nothing has been said about the positions of the x and y axes of the OBSERVER triad. We cannot assume that the ABSOLUTE and OBSERVER x/y axes are parallel – far from it, for the rotation transformations used to relate ABSOLUTE and OBSERVER axes can induce a torque. There is a simple physical demonstration of this phenomenon using three rotations. Place your right arm at your side, palm inwards. Hold the arm stiff and lift it directly in front of you to shoulder level. Now move the arm, keeping at shoulder level, until it is to the right of your body. Then, still with the arm stiff, drop it to your side. The arm has returned to its original direction, but it has twisted through a right angle.

These rotations of the arm were all right angles; arbitrary rotations can introduce quite peculiar torques. We therefore have to standardize in order to avoid spurious torques that are by-products of the rotations used in the method of linking the two systems and which have nothing to do with the observer or the scene. Since the OBSERVER system represents the position and orientation of the viewer's head, we adopt the convention that the y-axis is in the vertical plane and parallel to the y/z plane of the ABSOLUTE system, which means that the OBSERVER is always standing upright. This convention is called *maintaining the vertical* and results in the vertical line through the eye, with general vector point **eye** + $\mu(0, 1, 0)$ relative to the ABSOLUTE system, being transformed to $(0, 0, 0) + \mu\times(0, y', z')$ relative to the OBSERVER system. Pre-multiplication of points on the line in the ABSOLUTE system by matrix $E = H \times G \times F$ gives the new co-ordinates:

$$(\mu\times(v\times w))(\textbf{direct.y} \times \textbf{direct.z}, -w \times \textbf{direct.x}, -v \times \textbf{direct.y}) = (p, q, r) \text{ say.}$$

In order that the vertical be maintained, we must further rotate the system about the z-axis (thus leaving z co-ordinates unchanged), so that the vector (p, q, r) has a new x co-ordinate of zero. This is achieved by rotation of axes about the z-axis through an angle $\tau = -\tan^{-1}$ (−**direct.y** × **direct.z**/w × **direct.x**) = $\tan^{-1}(p/q)$, which is represented by the matrix U.

$$U = \frac{1}{t}\begin{pmatrix} q & -p & 0 & 0 \\ p & q & 0 & 0 \\ 0 & 0 & t & 0 \\ 0 & 0 & 0 & t \end{pmatrix}$$

where $t^2 = p^2 + q^2$, and thus

$$U \times \begin{pmatrix} p \\ q \\ r \\ 1 \end{pmatrix} = \frac{1}{t}\begin{pmatrix} q & -p & 0 & 0 \\ p & q & 0 & 0 \\ 0 & 0 & t & 0 \\ 0 & 0 & 0 & t \end{pmatrix} \times \begin{pmatrix} p \\ q \\ r \\ 1 \end{pmatrix} = \begin{pmatrix} 0 \\ t \\ r \\ 1 \end{pmatrix}$$

Thus the complete transformation from co-ordinates in SETUP position to those in OBSERVED position, while maintaining the vertical, can be achieved by pre-multiplication with the matrix $R = Q \times P$, where P is the matrix for transforming from SETUP to ACTUAL positions, and $Q = U \times H \times G \times F$, the ABSOLUTE to OBSERVER matrix. The OBSERVED cluster position of the vertices in the model will be instantiated as a **Cluster3d** object, **obs**, that should have already been stored in file **"ClusterB.cpp"** (listing 7.2c), ready to be linked into C++ Projects when required. For all i, the co-ordinates of the ith vertex of the OBSERVED cluster position **obs**, will be the co-ordinates of the ith vertex of ACTUAL cluster position **act**, transformed by matrix Q.

The functions **look3** and **findQ**, given the co-ordinate values of **eye** and **direct**, generate the matrix Q. The transformation from the ACTUAL cluster **act** to OBSERVED cluster **obs** is achieved with function **observe**. Listing 8.1b holds **findQ**, **look3** and **observe** as part of file **"display.cpp"**.

Exercise 8.1
If required, you can extend this function to deal with the situation where the head is tilted through an angle ϕ from the vertical. This is achieved by rotating the axes by a further ϕ radians about the z-axis. Thus matrix U should rotate about the z-axis by an angle $\tau + \phi$.

Of course if we are looking down the vertical then this approach would have no meaning, and furthermore if our procedure is part of an animation sequence then maintaining the vertical would also create a discontinuity in the value of Q. Similarly if we are simulating a somersault, or a 'loop-the-loop', then maintaining the vertical is not suitable. We want to feel the world spinning! This can be achieved by first choosing a line (different from the direction of view) that is to be identified with the vertical – the y-axis of the OBSERVER system. Strictly speaking this line should be perpendicular to our direction of view, but by the simple expedient of choosing any line that we can transform into the OBSERVER y/z plane, we have in effect achieved the required result. Alter the **findQ** function to incorporate this new form of vertical adjustment.

Exercise 8.2
Rewrite the **look3** and **findQ** functions so that the position of the observer, the direction of view and tilt of the head are given in spherical polar co-ordinates.

Henceforth, throughout our discussion of projections and unless otherwise stated, all three-dimensional co-ordinate values should be understood to refer to the OBSERVER system. These ideas will be graphically illustrated in example 8.1, however, we first have to describe how to project a three-dimensional scene cluster onto the graphics viewport, which is necessarily two-dimensional.

Projections: the view plane, the window and the viewport

We now come to the drawing of the scene on the graphics viewport, a procedure that is initiated from within function **draw_it**. We wish to represent, in the viewport, the scene as viewed by the observer. The viewport is two dimensional (a plane), and in order to create an image of a three-dimensional scene, a mapping from the three-dimensional space onto this plane is required.

What the eye sees when looking at a three-dimensional scene is a *projection* of the vertices, lines and facets of the objects in the scene onto a *view plane,* which is assumed to be perpendicular to the line of sight. A projection is defined by a set of lines which we call *the lines of projection.* The projection of a point onto a plane is the point of intersection of the plane with the unique line of projection which passes through the point. The projection of a line segment onto a plane is the line segment in the plane which joins the projections of its two end-points. The projection of a facet onto a plane is the polygon formed by the projection of each of its corner vertices joined in the same order. It is important to note that the sequence in which points, lines and facets are drawn may be critical; on raster devices such as the VGA and XGA cards, earlier points, lines and facets can be obscured by later over-drawing.

In the OBSERVER system we have defined the view plane to be of the form $z = -d$ (for some $d \geq 0$) – a plane parallel to the x/y plane and perpendicular to the z-axis. Vertices are projected onto this plane by some method (via a function we will call **project_it**), producing projected points with co-ordinates of the form $(xp , yp , -d)$, where xp and yp depend upon the type of projection and on d, the fixed perpendicular distance of the view plane from the eye. The OBSERVED cluster position, **obs**, will be projected into a cluster projection that is instantiated as object **pro**, stored in **"ClusterC.cpp"** (listing 7.2c). We use class **Cluster2d**, which contains an array **vertices**, to hold up to **maxv** projected vertices of type **vector2**. Thus the ith vertex of the **act** cluster is transformed into the ith vertex of the **obs** cluster, which in turn is projected onto the ith vertex of the **pro** cluster. Thus all the polygonal mesh programs that follow will have to link together **"ClusterA.cpp" (act)**, **"ClusterB.cpp" (obs)** and **"ClusterC.cpp" (pro)**.

We now set up a rectangular area on the view plane (called a *window*, that looks out onto three-dimensional space), and we place on it a two-dimensional co-ordinate system, the WINDOW system, which is centred on the rectangle with axes parallel to its sides. In chapter 2 we saw how such a WINDOW system was defined by a rectangle centred on the origin with edges of length **horiz** parallel to the x-axis and **vert** parallel to the y-axis. We can use the methods described in that chapter (and class **Window**) to identify points in the window with pixels within the viewport using two methods **fx** and **fy**, which transform Cartesian x and y WINDOW co-ordinates to corresponding pixel co-ordinates. Thus for each point, line or polygon in the three-dimensional OBSERVER system, we find the projected point, line and polygon in the two-dimensional WINDOW system, and then finally draw the corresponding pixel point, line or polygon in the viewport.

The obvious WINDOW system to choose has the x- and y- axes parallel to the x- and y-axes (respectively) of the OBSERVER system, with the origin on the OBSERVER z-axis at $z = -d$. Then any point vector on the view plane with OBSERVED co-ordinates $(xp\,, yp\,, -d)$ has WINDOW co-ordinates $(xp\,, yp)$. Of course we still have to calculate the values of xp and yp for every vertex in the **obs** cluster position. The cluster projection, **pro**, is calculated in function **project_it**, which will be called from inside **look_at_it**. As yet we have neither defined the position of the view plane (the value d), nor have we described the type of projection of three-dimensional space onto the plane. These requirements are closely related. In this chapter we will consider two possible projections, first the *orthographic*, sometimes called the *axonometric* or *orthogonal* projection, and then the *perspective* projection.

The orthographic projection

A *parallel projection* is characterised by having parallel lines of projection, and is a projection under which points in three-dimensional space are projected along a fixed direction onto any plane not parallel to those lines. The orthographic projection is a special case whereby the lines of projection are perpendicular to the plane (it is sometimes referred to simply as *the* parallel projection). We can choose the view plane to be *any* plane with normal vector along the line of sight (the line of projection). This means that we can take any plane parallel to the *x/y* plane of the OBSERVER system, and for simplicity we choose the plane through the origin given by the equation $z = 0$. An OBSERVED vertex is thus projected onto the view plane by the simple expedient of setting its *z* co-ordinate to zero, and thus any two different points with OBSERVED co-ordinates (x, y, z) and (x, y, z') say (where $z \neq z'$), are projected onto the same point $(x, y, 0)$ on the view plane, and hence onto the point (x, y) in the WINDOW system. Although we can use the *x* and *y* co-ordinates of the **obs** cluster as the cluster projection in the case of orthographic projection, this will not be so in general. In order to maintain consistency with the later perspective projection, we copy these two values for each vertex into the **pro** cluster projection in function **project_it**. The orthographic **project_it** is given in listing 8.2. Note that the function calculates the projection of all **extendednov** vertices (that is including those created through three-dimensional clipping), and hence **extendednov** must be evaluated before the call to **project_it**. Note that the code for **project_it** must be stored in file **"display.cpp"** for linking into Borland C++ Projects as and when needed.

Listing 8.2

```
// Place this function in file "display.cpp"
//----------------------//
  void project_it(void)       // Orthographic projection of OBSERVED vertices
//----------------------//
 { vector3 v3 ;
   vector2 v2 ;
   for (int i=0 ; i<obs.Get_extendednov() ; i++)
   { v3 = obs.Get_vertex(i) ;
     v2.x = v3.x ;  v2.y = v3.y ;    pro.add(v2) ; }
 }  // End of project_it
```

Drawing a scene

Most of the remainder of this book will be dealing with the drawing of projections of three-dimensional scenes. This will include discussions of three-dimensional clipping, hidden surface removal, shading, shadows etc. You will find that all of these functions are given to you; clipping functions will be stored in **"mesh.cpp"**, while the remainder will be dealt with in **"display.cpp"**. The correct sequence of calls to these functions will be initiated from a controlling function, **draw_it**. Such a function will be employed in a number of different forms throughout the book. In the simplest case (listing 8.3) **draw_it** will call function **wireframe**, which in turn will draw a line diagram of the scene. **draw_it** and **wireframe** are also added to **"display.cpp"**.

You need not worry about initiating these calls, all that you need do is form a Borland C++ Project linking your own application program (usually consisting of a **build_it** function, and perhaps a few construction functions) to our files **"window.cpp"**, **"model.cpp"**, **"display.cpp"**, **"ClusterA(BCDEFGH&I).cpp"** and **"construc.cpp"**. You create the model with **build_it**, which is called from our function **draw_a_picture** (listing 7.4b), and the moment the model is complete control is returned to our programs, which set up the observer (and light source), and then draw the picture from **draw_it.** Remember to **#include** file **"display.h"** in **"model.cpp"**; also erase the null functions **look_at_it** and **draw_it.**

Listing 8.3

```
// Place these functions in file "display.cpp"

//---------------------//
  void wireframe(void)
//---------------------//
// Wire diagram of closed objects + superficial facets
 { int i,j,k,v1,v2, fsize ;
// View each facet 'i' in turn
   for (i=0 ; i<mesh.Get_nof() ; i++)
   { j=mesh.Get_clipfac(i) ;
     if (j != -1 )
       { fsize = mesh.Get_size(j) ;
         win.setcol(mesh.Get_material(j)) ;
         v1 = mesh.Get_faclist(j,fsize-1) ;
// For facet 'i' consider the size[j] lines on its boundary
         for (k=0 ; k< fsize ; k++)
// Typical line joins vertex v1 to vertex v2. Only join vertices if v1<v2 on
// non-superficial facets. If objects are not closed then rewrite the code
// so that lines are drawn in both directions!
         { v2= mesh.Get_faclist(j,k) ;
           if ((v1 < v2) || (mesh.Get_super(i) != -1 ))
             { win.moveto(pro.Get_vertex(v1)) ;
               win.lineto(pro.Get_vertex(v2)) ;
             } ;
           v1=v2 ;
         }
       } ;
   }
 }  // End of wireframe

//------------------//
  void draw_it(void)
//------------------//
// version for wire-frame and simple colour scenes
 { win.start() ;  wireframe() ;
 }  // End of draw_it
```

Example 8.1

We use the above ideas to draw an orthographic projection of the cubes defined in examples 7.2 and 7.3. Line-figures, such as those in figure 8.2, are called *wire diagrams* or *skeletons* (for obvious reasons) and are drawn by the function **wireframe**. The required **build_it** function (listing 8.4) is to be stored as file **"eight4.cpp"**, which when linked into our Borland C++ Project constructs the model by using **datain** to read in the previously constructed scenes from disk, where they were stored by **dataout** (listing 7.4b). They are drawn automatically by **draw_it**, from inside **draw_a_picture**, with no intervention from the user.

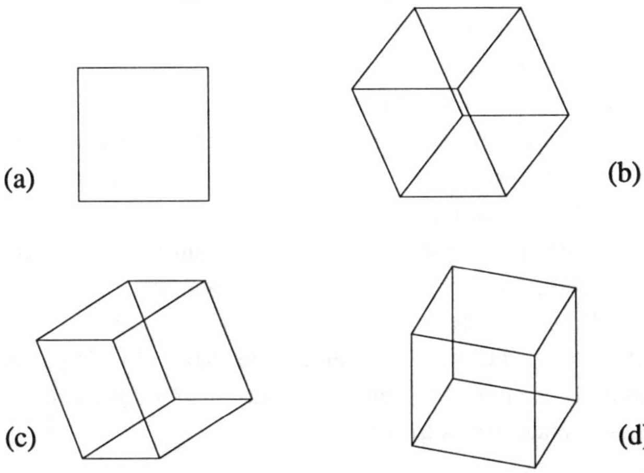

Figure 8.2

Listing 8.4

```
// Application program to read in ACTUAL scene from disk, and draw it

#include "model.h"

//--------------------//
  void build_it(void)
//--------------------//
 { datain("filename.dat") ;
 }  // End of build_it
```

In its SETUP position (relative to the ABSOLUTE co-ordinate system), a cube is defined as consisting of eight vertices (1 , 1 , 1), (1 , −1 , 1), (1 , −1 , −1), (1 , 1 , −1), (−1 , 1 , 1), (−1 , −1 , 1), (−1 , −1 , −1) and (−1 , 1 , −1): labelled numerically 0 to 7. Its twelve lines, each of which is an edge common to two adjacent facets, join vertices 0 to 1, 1 to 2, 2 to 3, 3 to 0; 4 to 5, 5 to 6, 6 to 7, 7 to 0; 0 to 4, 1 to 5, 2 to 6 and 3 to 7. We do not store the line information explicitly, however, if needed it can be derived from the facet data. Since each line occurs twice in the data of a closed convex body, and we have oriented the facets anti-clockwise, then if an edge on one facet joins vertex **i** to vertex **j**, then on an adjacent facet there will be an edge joining **j** to **i**. Therefore, if, as in **wireframe** (listing 8.3), we go round the edges of all the facets in anti-clockwise order (drawing a line between consecutive projected vertices only if the larger vertex index follows the smaller), each line will be drawn once but only once. The line is drawn in the logical colour of the material of the facet concerned. **wireframe** only works with *closed objects*, that is when it is impossible to get inside an object other than by passing through a surface facet. If you wish to draw non-closed objects, then **wireframe** must be rewritten so that each edge line of every facet is drawn, irrespective of the order of the vertex indices!

Figure 8.2a shows the simplest possible example of an orthographic projection of the cube, where both the SETUP to ACTUAL matrix and the ABSOLUTE to OBSERVER matrix are identity matrices (example 7.2) – that is, the cube stays in its SETUP position and the observer is looking along the negative *z*-axis. We get a square. Pairs of parallel lines from the front and back of the cube **project_it** into the same line on the window.

Figure 8.2b shows the cube from example 7.3 drawn in its ACTUAL position but viewed with the observer on the *z*-axis, looking along it in the negative direction (matrix *Q* is then the identity matrix). We calculate the eight ACTUAL co-ordinate triples to be:

(26/25 , –5/25 , 7/25), (2/25 , –35/25 , 39/25), (–38/25 , –35/25 , 9/25), (–14/25 , –5/25 , –23/25), (8/25 , 35/25 , 31/25), (–16/25 , 5/25 , 63/25), (–56/25 , 5/25 , 33/25) and (–32/25 , 35/25 , 1/25).

Since we assume the ABSOLUTE to OBSERVER matrix *Q* to be the identity matrix, the projected WINDOW co-ordinates of the vertices are thus:

(26/25 , –5/25), (2/25 , –35/25), (–38/25 , –35/25), (–14/25 , –5/25), (8/25 , 35/25), (–16/25 , 5/25), (–56/25 , 5/25) and (–32/25 , 35/25).

These WINDOW co-ordinates are identified with pixels in the viewport and the lines defined above are drawn by joining (with straight lines) the projections of the vertices in the correct combinations.

Figure 8.2d shows the image produced of the cube in example 7.2 using these methods with the observer at the ABSOLUTE position (1 , 2 , 3) looking towards the origin in the direction (–1 , –2 , –3), with the vertical maintained. Figure 8.2c shows the image produced by the same process with the maintenance of vertical omitted. Note that this technique works in all cases except where **direct.x** = **direct.z** = 0, the vertical direction, where maintaining the vertical naturally makes no sense. In this case the program would not fail; the final transformation is just an illogical step, producing an arbitrary rotation.

Complicated pictures – the 'building block' method

Pictures containing a number of similar objects can be drawn with a minimum of extra effort. A scene such as figure 8.3 containing two cubes, for example, may be constructed using listing 8.5 by calling **cube** (**"construc.cpp"**, from listing 7.5b) twice within the **build_it** function. Note that, by including

"model.cpp" in our Borland C++ Project, we have access to **"matrix.cpp"**, and for each cube we will generate a different SETUP to ACTUAL matrix *P*. This is what we call the *building block* method. Each call to a construction function creates a block of data relating to one occurrence of that geometrical object type, and this is included in the database that models the scene. Information relating to the observer is introduced, and **look3** and **findQ** calculate the matrix *Q* which is used by function **observe** to calculate the OBSERVED co-ordinates of each vertex. Function **project_it** projects these vertices onto the view plane before finally **draw_it** calls **wireframe** to draw the picture on the window/viewport.

Listing 8.5

```
// Application program to build and draw two cubes

#include "construc.h"

//--------------------//
  void build_it(void)
//--------------------//
 { Matrix A, B, P ;
// First Cube
   P.scale(1.0,1.0,1.0) ;   cube(P,2) ;
// Second cube
   A.scale(1.5,1.5,1.5) ;   B.translate(-4.0,-2.0,-4.0) ;
   P = B * A ;              cube(P,4) ;
 }  // End of build_it
```

Example 8.2
Listing 8.5 is a **build_it** function that, when stored as an application program **"eight5.cpp"**, linked with our files in our Borland C++ Project, and run, creates a scene consisting of two cubes, one of side 2 placed in its SETUP position, and the other with side 3 translated to point (4 , 2 , 4). Note the complete C++ Project uses the construction functions of **"construc.cpp"** (listing 7.5b) to store the data on the model in **"model.cpp"** using cluster files **"ClusterA(BCDEFGH&I).cpp"** (and by implication **#include** matrices (**"matrix.cpp"**), stacks (**"stack.cpp"**) and **"mesh.cpp"**), and uses the **findQ, look3, observe** (listing 8.1), **project_it** (listing 8.2), **draw_it** and **wireframe** (listing 8.3) of **"display.cpp"**, to draw the image on the graphics viewport via functions in **"window.cpp"** (and **"palette.cpp"** and **"viewport.cpp"**).

This modular approach for solving the problem of defining and drawing a picture does greatly clarify the situation for beginners, enabling them to ask the right questions about constructing a required scene. Also when dealing with multiple views (for example, in animation), this approach will minimise problems in scenes where not only are the objects moving relative to one another, but also the observer itself is moving.

In summary, the orthographic projection of wireframe drawings of each object in a three-dimensional scene is produced by the following process

(1) Define objects in the scene in their SETUP position with the co-ordinates of vertices specified in relation to the ABSOLUTE axes. The facets of the scene may also be defined at this stage. Calculate the matrix P which moves the vertices of each object to its ACTUAL position by *pre-multiplication* of its SETUP co-ordinates; note the co-ordinates still relate to the ABSOLUTE system. These co-ordinates are stored in cluster position **act**. If a scene is to be made up of a number of different objects, then this step must be repeated for each object, with the cluster being updated at every pass. (This is achieved in function **build_it**.)

(2) Calculate the matrix Q given the position of the eye relative to the ABSOLUTE system and a direction of view, **vector3** values **eye** and **direct** (functions **look3** and **findQ**). Calculate the OBSERVED co-ordinates of the vertices relative to the OBSERVER axes with eye at the origin and the negative z-axis along the direction **direct**, by pre-multiplying the co-ordinates of the ACTUAL position by Q. These OBSERVED co-ordinates are stored in the cluster **obs** (function **observe**). Find the cluster, **pro**, projected onto the view plane, and thence to the WINDOW system. For the orthographic projection this involved taking their x and y OBSERVED co-ordinates, which are already stored in the array **obs** (function **project_it**). Later a small calculation will be used for the perspective projection. The four functions, and clipping later, are combined together in the function **look_at_it**.

(3) For the moment, in pictures of three-dimensional scenes, we will draw only the facet edges, by joining their projected end-points, and not the facets themselves (function **wireframe** within **draw_it**). Function **wireframe** calls **lineto** and **moveto** to draw WINDOW objects by identifying the projected co-ordinates with the pixel co-ordinate system of the viewport using the real-to-pixel functions **fx** and **fy** and then pixels on the viewport with functions **linepix** and **movepix**. In later chapters we will consider facets when we give other more advanced versions of **draw_it**.

Exercise 8.3

If you require only a single view of a scene, rather than use the intermediate storage of the ACTUAL and OBSERVED positions, it is more efficient (in terms of both speed and memory) to go directly from SETUP position to projected WINDOW co-ordinates. Now each construction function must be called with matrix parameter $R = Q \times P$, and the vertices immediately projected into **pro**. Cannibalise the programs from this chapter in such a way.

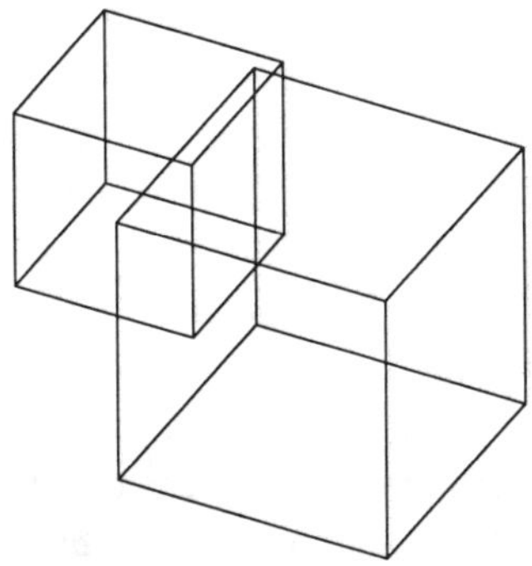

Figure 8.3

The perspective projection

The orthographic projection has the property that parallel lines in three-dimensional space are projected into parallel lines on the view plane. Although they have their uses in certain scientific and architectural applications, such views do look odd! Human comprehension of spatial position is based upon *perspective*. Hence our brains attempt to interpret orthographic figures as if they are perspective views, making the cubes of figure 8.2, for instance, look distorted. Not wanting to linger on such distorted views, and in order to achieve visual realism, we now consider a perspective version of the **project_it** function. It is obviously essential to produce a projection which displays perspective phenomena – that is, parallel lines should meet on the horizon, and an object should appear smaller as it moves away from the observer. The drawing-board methods devised by artists over the centuries are of no value to us, but the three-dimensional co-ordinate geometry introduced in chapter 6 furnishes us with a relatively straightforward technique for achieving this.

What is perspective vision?

To produce a perspective view we introduce a very simple definition of what we mean by vision. We imagine every visible point in space sending out a ray which enters the eye. Naturally the eye cannot see all of space, it is limited to a cone of rays which fall on the retina, the so-called *cone of vision*, which is outlined by the dashed lines of figure 8.4. These rays are the lines of projection. The axis of the cone is called the *direction of vision* (or the *straight-ahead ray*). In what follows, we assume that all co-ordinates relate to the OBSERVER right-handed co-ordinate system, with the eye at the origin and the straight-ahead ray identified with the negative z-axis.

We place the view plane (which we call the *perspective plane* in this special case) perpendicular to the axis of the cone of vision at a distance *d* from the eye (that is, the plane $z = -d$). In order to form the perspective projection we mark the points of intersection of each ray with this plane. Since there is an infinity of such rays, this appears to be an impossible task. Actually the problem is not that great because we need only consider the rays which emanate from the important points in the scene, in particular the corner vertices of polygonal facets. Once the projections of the vertices onto the perspective screen have been determined, the problem is reduced to that of representing the perspective plane (the view plane) on the graphics viewport. The solution to this problem was discussed earlier in this chapter with regard to the orthographic projection and exactly the same process may be followed here – a two-dimensional co-ordinate system, the WINDOW system, is defined on the view plane together with a rectangular window which is identified with the viewport. The image is drawn by joining the pixels corresponding to the end-points of lines or the vertices of facets in exactly the same manner as that used in the simple images of chapter 2.

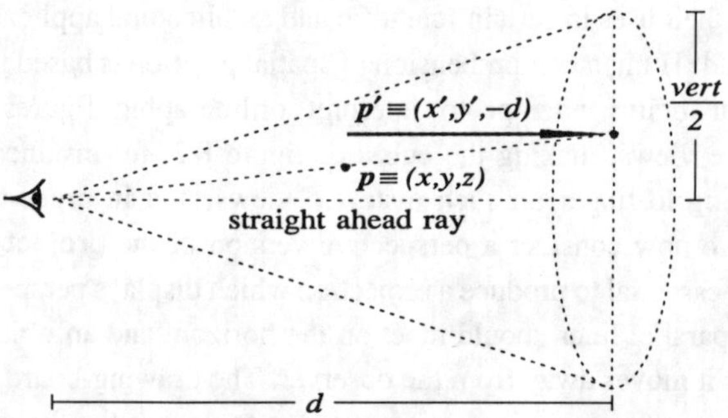

Figure 8.4

Calculation of the perspective projection of a point

We let the perspective plane be a distance *d* from the eye (variable **ppd** declared in listing 8.1b). Consider a point $\boldsymbol{p} \equiv (x\,, y\,, z)$ (with respect to the OBSERVER system) which sends a ray into the eye. We need to calculate the point of intersection, $\boldsymbol{p}' \equiv (x'\,, y'\,, -d)$, where this ray cuts the view plane (the $z = -d$ plane), and thus we determine the corresponding WINDOW co-ordinates $(x'\,, y')$. First consider the value of y' by referring to figure 8.4. By *similar triangles* we see that $y'/d = y/|z|$, that is $y' = -y \times d/z$ (remember that points in front of the eye in the OBSERVER system have negative *z* co-ordinates). Similarly $x' = -x \times d/z$ and hence $\boldsymbol{p}' \equiv (-x \times d/z\ , -y \times d/z\ , -d)$. Thus the WINDOW co-ordinates corresponding to $\boldsymbol{p}$ are $(-x \times d/z\,, -y \times\ d/z)$. The projection makes sense only if the point has negative *z* co-ordinate (that is, it does not lie behind the eye). So until we deal with three-dimensional clipping later in this chapter, we will assume that the eye is positioned in such a way that this is true for all vertices.

Example 8.3

Calculate the perspective projection of a cube with eight vertices, given by the vector sums $(0, 0, -4) + (\pm 1, \pm 1, \pm 1)$, onto the perspective plane $z = -4$, where the eye is at the origin and the direction of vision is along the negative z-axis.

The projected co-ordinates are calculated directly by the method given above since the co-ordinates are already specified relative to the OBSERVER axes (ABSOLUTE system ≡ OBSERVER system). For example corner $(1, 1, -3)$ is projected to $(-1 \times 4/-3, -1 \times 4/-3, -4) = (4/3, 4/3, -4)$ and becomes $(4/3, 4/3)$ in the WINDOW system. So we get the eight projections

$$
\begin{array}{llllll}
(1, 1, -3) & \text{to} & (4/3, 4/3), & (1, -1, -3) & \text{to} & (4/3, -4/3) \\
(-1, 1, -3) & \text{to} & (-4/3, 4/3), & (-1, -1, -3) & \text{to} & (-4/3, -4/3) \\
(1, 1, -5) & \text{to} & (4/5, 4/5), & (1, -1, -5) & \text{to} & (4/5, -4/5) \\
(-1, 1, -5) & \text{to} & (-4/5, 4/5), & (-1, -1, -5) & \text{to} & (-4/5, -4/5)
\end{array}
$$

which are identified with points in the window/viewport, and the resulting diagram is shown in figure 8.5a.

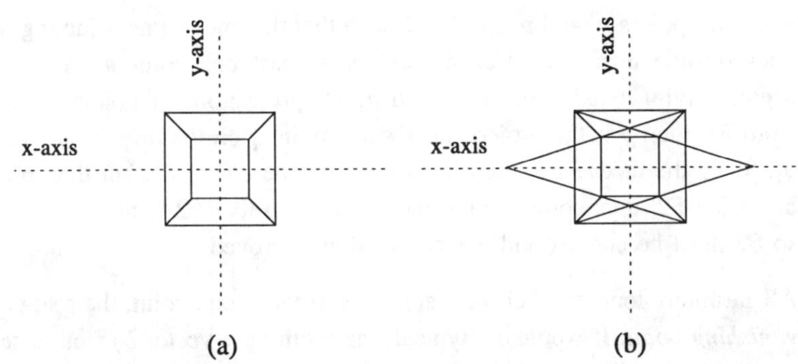

Figure 8.5

Properties of the perspective transformation

(1) The perspective transformation of a three-dimensional straight line (Γ_3 say) is a two-dimensional straight line (Γ_2 say) or a point. This is obvious because the origin (the eye) and the line Γ_3 form a plane (Ω say) in three-dimensional space, and all the rays emanating from points on Γ_3 lie in this plane. (If Γ_3 enters the eye, Ω degenerates into the line Γ_3, which is projected into a single point.) Naturally Ω cuts the perspective plane in a line

Γ_2 (or degenerates to a point) and so the perspective projection of a point on the original line, Γ_3, now lies on the new line Γ_2. It is important to realise that a line does not become curved in this type of perspective projection. Furthermore, we may deduce that the projection of a straight line segment joining two points $\boldsymbol{p_1}$ and $\boldsymbol{p_2}$ is a straight line segment in the perspective plane, which joins the respective perspective projections of $\boldsymbol{p_1}$ and $\boldsymbol{p_2}$.

(2) The perspective transformation of a three-dimensional facet (that is a closed sequence of coplanar line segments) is a two-dimensional facet in the view (perspective) plane. If the facet covers an area bounded by $\boldsymbol{n}$ coplanar line segments then the transformation of this polygonal facet is naturally an area in the $z = -d$ plane bounded by the transformations of the n line segments, since their end-points are the projections of the vertices of the projected facet, each of which is common to two edges. Again note, no curves are introduced in the projection: if they were then the task of producing perspective pictures would be far more complicated.

(3) The projection of a convex facet is also convex. Suppose facet F1 is projected onto facet F2 in the view plane. Since the projection of a closed facet is also closed, and lines are projected into lines, then points inside F1 are projected into points inside F2. Suppose F2 is not convex. Then there exist two points $\boldsymbol{p_1}$ and $\boldsymbol{p_2}$ inside F2 such that the line segment joining them goes outside this facet. Hence there is at least one point $\boldsymbol{p}$ on this line segment lying outside F2. If $\boldsymbol{p_1}$ and $\boldsymbol{p_2}$ are projections of points $\boldsymbol{q_1}$ and $\boldsymbol{q_2}$ from F1, then $\boldsymbol{p}$ is the projection of some point $\boldsymbol{q}$ on the line joining $\boldsymbol{q_1}$ and $\boldsymbol{q_2}$. Since the facet F1 is convex then $\boldsymbol{q}$ must be inside F1, but then $\boldsymbol{p}$ must be inside F2, thus contradicting the assumption that F2 is not convex, and so F2 must be convex and our proposition is proved.

(4) All infinitely long parallel lines appear to meet at one point, their so-called *vanishing point*. If we take a typical line (with base vector $\boldsymbol{b}$) from a set of parallel lines with direction vector $\boldsymbol{h}$ then

$$\boldsymbol{b} + \mu\boldsymbol{h} \equiv (b_x, b_y, b_z) + \mu(h_x, h_y, h_z)$$

where $h_z < 0$, and the perspective transform of a typical point on this line is

$$\left(\frac{-(b_x + \mu h_x) \times d}{(b_z + \mu h_z)}, \frac{-(b_y + \mu h_y) \times d}{(b_z + \mu h_z)} \right)$$

which can be rewritten as

$$\left(\frac{-(h_x + b_x/\mu) \times d}{(h_z + b_z/\mu)}, \frac{-(h_y + b_y/\mu) \times d}{(h_z + b_z/\mu)} \right)$$

As we move along the line towards large negative z co-ordinates, that is as $\mu \to \infty$ (and $1/\mu \to 0$), the line moves towards its vanishing point, which is therefore given by $(-d \times h_x/h_z, -d \times h_y/h_z)$. This vanishing point is independent of $\boldsymbol{b}$, the base point of the line. Hence all lines parallel to the direction $\boldsymbol{h}$ have the same vanishing point. The case $h_z > 0$ is ignored because the line would disappear outside the cone of vision as $\mu \to \infty$.

(5) The vanishing points of all lines in parallel planes are collinear. Suppose that the set of parallel planes have a common normal direction $\boldsymbol{n} \equiv (n_x, n_y, n_z)$. If a typical line in one of these planes has direction $\boldsymbol{h} \equiv (h_x, h_y, h_z)$, then $\boldsymbol{h}$ is perpendicular to $\boldsymbol{n}$ (all lines in these planes are perpendicular to the normal $\boldsymbol{n}$). Thus $\boldsymbol{n} \bullet \boldsymbol{h} = 0$, which in co-ordinate form is

$$n_x \times h_x + n_y \times h_y + n_z \times h_z = 0$$

which, dividing by h_z ($\neq 0$), gives

$$n_x \times h_x/h_z + n_y \times h_y/h_z + n_z = 0$$

and so the vanishing point $(-d \times h_x/h_z, -d \times h_y/h_z)$ lies on the straight line

$$n_x \times x + n_y \times y - n_z \times d = 0$$

and the statement is proved. This concept is very familiar to us – the vanishing points of all lines in horizontal planes lie on the horizon!

Example 8.4
Find the vanishing points of the edges of the cube in example 8.3, and of the diagonals of its top and bottom planes.

We divide the twelve edges of the cube into three sets of four edges, each set being parallel to the x-, y- and z-axis respectively, and so having direction vectors $(1, 0, 0)$, $(0, 1, 0)$ and $(0, 0, -1)$. The first two sets have zero z values, and so their extended edges disappear outside the cone of vision and are ignored, whereas the third direction has vanishing point $(-4 \times 0/-1, -4 \times 0/-1) = (0, 0)$ on the view plane. On both the top and bottom faces the diagonals have direction vectors $(-1, 0, -1)$, the major diagonal, and $(1, 0, -1)$, the minor diagonal. The major diagonal on the top plane is $(1, 1, -3) + \mu(-1, 0, -1)$, and so the vanishing point is $(-4 \times -1/-1, -4 \times 0/-1) = (-4, 0)$. The minor diagonal on the top plane is the line $(-1, 1, -3) + \mu(1, 0, -1)$, and the vanishing point is thus $(-4 \times 1/-1, -4 \times 0/-1) = (4, 0)$. By similar calculations we find the vanishing points of the major and minor diagonals on the lower face are also $(-4, 0)$ and $(4, 0)$ respectively. The relevant edges are extended to their vanishing points in figure 8.5b. Note that all the lines mentioned lie in the two parallel planes (the top and bottom faces of the cube) and so the vanishing points should be collinear: they are, because (–4 , 0), (0 , 0) and (4 , 0) all lie on the *x*-axis. By a similar calculation we would find that the vanishing points of the diagonals of the side faces lie on a vertical line through the origin.

Exercise 8.4

Draw a perspective view of a tetrahedron, assuming the OBSERVED co-ordinates of the figure are (1 , 1 , –5), (1 , –1 , –3), (–1 , 1 , –3) and (–1 , –1 , –5), with perspective plane distance set at unity. Find the vanishing points (inside the cone of vision) of lines which join pairs of mid-points of edges of the tetrahedron.

Programming the perspective transformation

The procedure for drawing a perspective view of a three dimensional scene is the same as that for an orthographic projection outlined above, in all respects other than the calculation of the co-ordinates of the projected vertices. Unlike the orthographic projection, the perspective co-ordinates of a point on the view plane cannot be identified with its OBSERVED *x* and *y* co-ordinates. Instead, we let **i** run through the **obs.Get_extendednov()** vertices of the **obs** cluster (**ClusterB**); each vertex, called **v3**, is projected by function **project_it** (listing 8.6) into **v2**, the vertex **i** of the **pro** cluster (**ClusterC**), provided, of course, that it is in front of the eye (**v3.z** < 0). These values are subsequently identified with points in the WINDOW for use by a display function.

Listing 8.6

```
// Replace function project_it in file "display.cpp"
//----------------------//
  void project_it(void)      // Perspective projection of OBSERVED vertices
//----------------------//
 { vector2 v2 ;  vector3 v3 ;
   ppd=3.0*win.Get_horiz() ;
   for ( int i=0 ; i<obs.Get_extendednov() ; i++)
   { v3 = obs.Get_vertex(i) ;
     if (v3.z < 0.0)
       { v2.x=-v3.x*ppd/v3.z ; v2.y=-v3.y*ppd/v3.z ; pro.put_vertex(i,v2) ; } ;
   }
 } // End of project_it
```

As with the orthographic projection, the cluster projection, **pro**, is calculated in a new version function **project_it** (listing 8.6). Our previous display functions are not specifically orthographic, they simply use **pro** irrespective of how it was calculated. A perspective version of most of our three-dimensional diagrams can be drawn with the simple expedient of replacing the orthographic **project_it** in **"display.cpp"** with the perspective version from listing 8.6 and running the programs in exactly the same way.

The choice of perspective plane

The only value required for the perspective transformation which we have not yet discussed is that of the distance of the perspective plane from the eye (**ppd** in our listings). Different values of **ppd** will necessarily produce pictures of different sizes. This raises the question of which value do we choose? Is there a correct value? Does it make any difference?

Consider the typical situation of an observer sitting in front of the viewport of a graphics device, and where the perspective view plane is identified with the plane of that window/viewport. Normally the observer will be sitting at a distance from the screen which is about three times the width of the graphics monitor. In the scale of our mapping from real-space onto this rectangular window, this will be a distance **3 * horiz**. If we choose a value of **ppd** less than this, we will get a wide-angle effect, while if the value of **ppd** is greater we get a foreshortened effect typical of telephoto images. The identifier **ppd** was declared in file **"display.cpp"** (listing 8.1b), but it is given a value in the replacement **project_it** of listing 8.6. Calculated in this way, it will be seen that perspective pictures are independent of the screen size – and only the ratio of **ppd** to **horiz** matters, not the absolute value of **horiz**. Therefore, for perspective pictures, it is sensible to fix **horiz** to be the constant value 1.0.

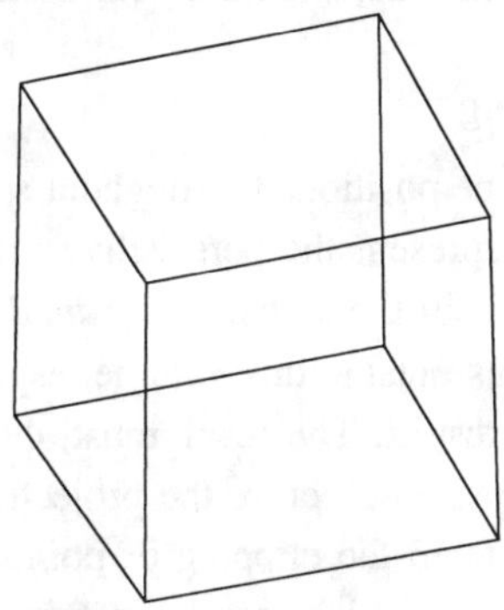

Figure 8.6

Example 8.5

The cube of example 7.4, which was placed in its SETUP position, can now be drawn in perspective by function **draw_it** of listing 8.3, using the new **project_it** given in listing 8.6. Figure 8.6 shows the cube viewed from the observation point (10 , 20 , 30) looking back towards the ABSOLUTE origin with direction vector (–10 , –20 , –30). Remember to ensure at this stage that your views keep *all* of the scene in front of the eye.

On some graphics devices the transformation and projection functions may be incorporated into the hardware. It is, nevertheless, very important that the reader becomes familiar with the idea of axis transformation and projection since it plays a fundamental part in the understanding of many of the more complex techniques covered in this book. Also it should be noted that the polygonal facet approach for the construction of data which we are advancing here is not the only way of tackling the problem. The alternative analytic method, which is discussed later, defines a scene in terms of logical combinations of primitive shapes which are defined by the analytic representations of their surfaces. This method also uses the techniques of transformations using matrices and of projection, which we have discussed in this and the previous chapter.

Exercise 8.5
Construct a dynamic scene. With each new view, the objects will move relative to one another in some well-defined manner. The observer also should move in some simple way; for example, the eye can start at (100 , 100 , 200) looking in direction (−100 , −100 , −200). Some twenty views later the observer is at the point (200 , 100 , 200) looking in direction (−200 , −100 , −200), but with each new view the head is tilted a further 0.1 radians. The values of **eye** and **direct** are no longer read in, but, instead, should be calculated with each new view.

Three-dimensional clipping

Theoretically, objects may be positioned throughout space, even behind the eye. The formulae derived to represent the perspective projection deal successfully only with points that lie within the so-called *pyramid of vision*. Any attempt to apply the formulae to points outside this volume, especially those lying behind the eye, gives nonsensical results. The scene must, therefore, be *clipped* so that all vertices lie within this pyramid before the projection may be applied.

In chapter 5 we considered the clipping of points, lines and facets in two-dimensional space, determining which parts lay within a rectangular window with dimensions **horiz** by **vert**. These methods are also sufficient for dealing with orthographic projections of three-dimensional scenes since the whole space can be projected onto the view plane and clipped in two dimensions. Dealing with perspective projections is rather more complex. Once again we assume that we have a view plane some distance from the eye along the negative z-axis of the right-handed OBSERVER system. A rectangular (**horiz** by **vert**) window on this plane is to be identified with the graphics viewport. In previous chapters we have assumed that the eye is positioned in such a way that each vertex has a strictly negative OBSERVED z co-ordinate. This ensures that every vertex can be

Plate Ia

Plate Ib

Plate Ic

Plate IIa

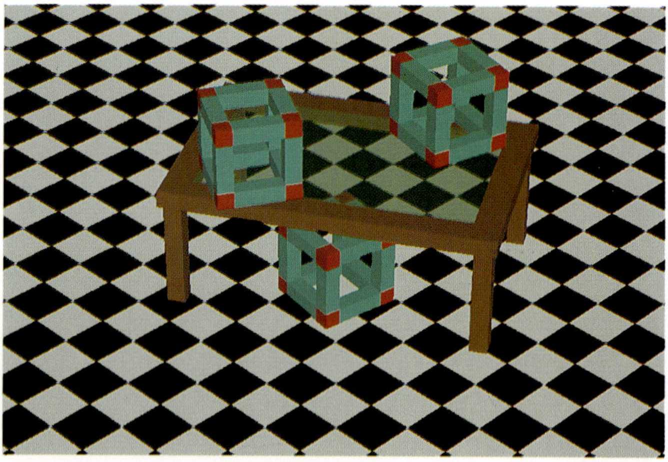

Plate IIb

Plate IIc

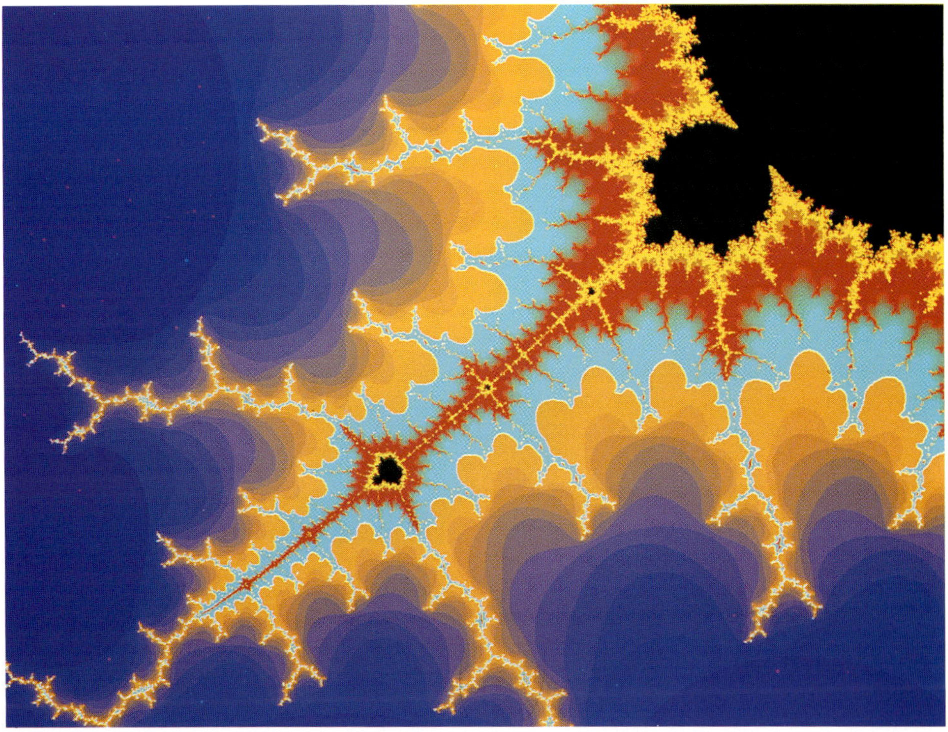

Plate IIIa

Plate IIIb

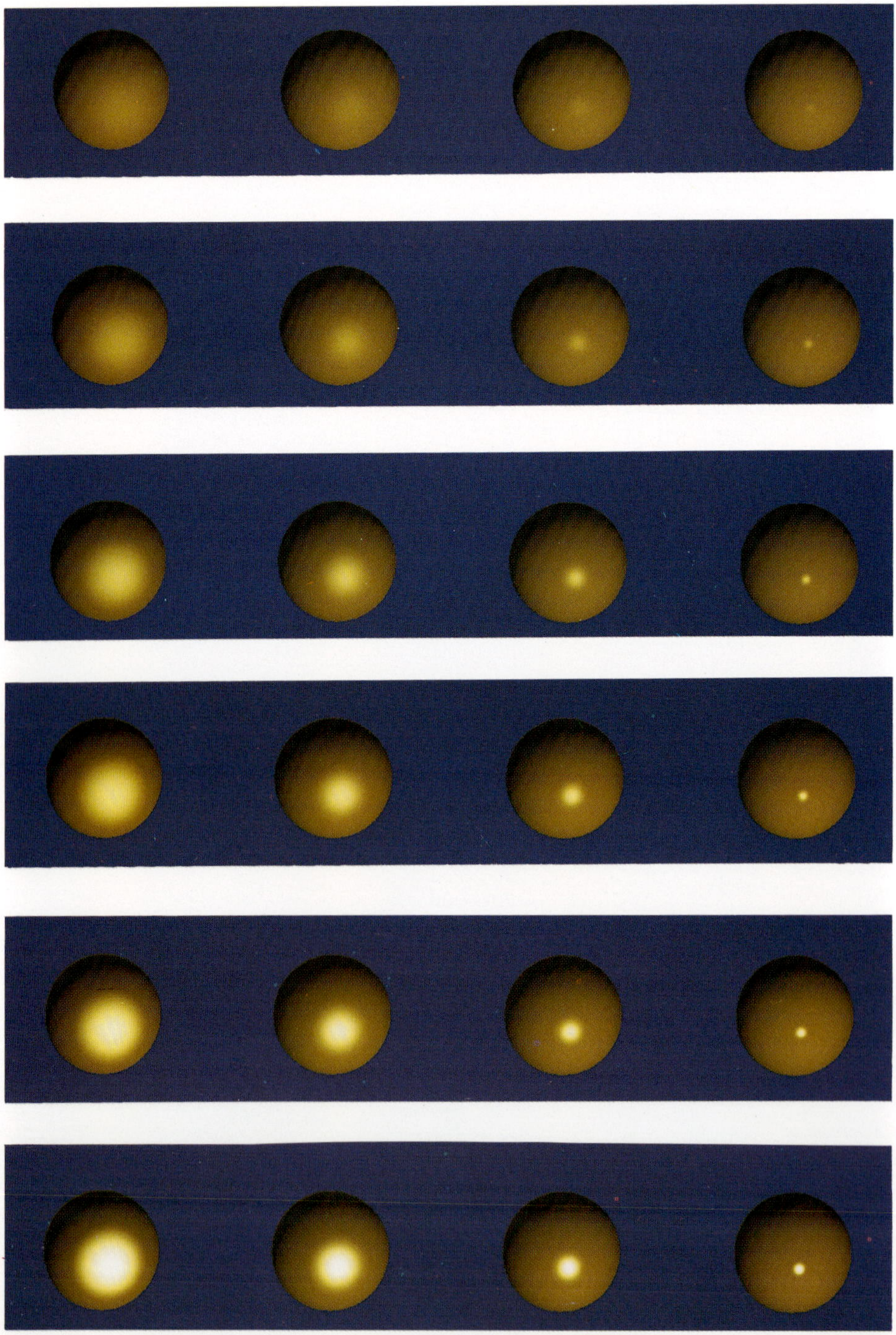

Plate IV

Plate Va

Plate Vb

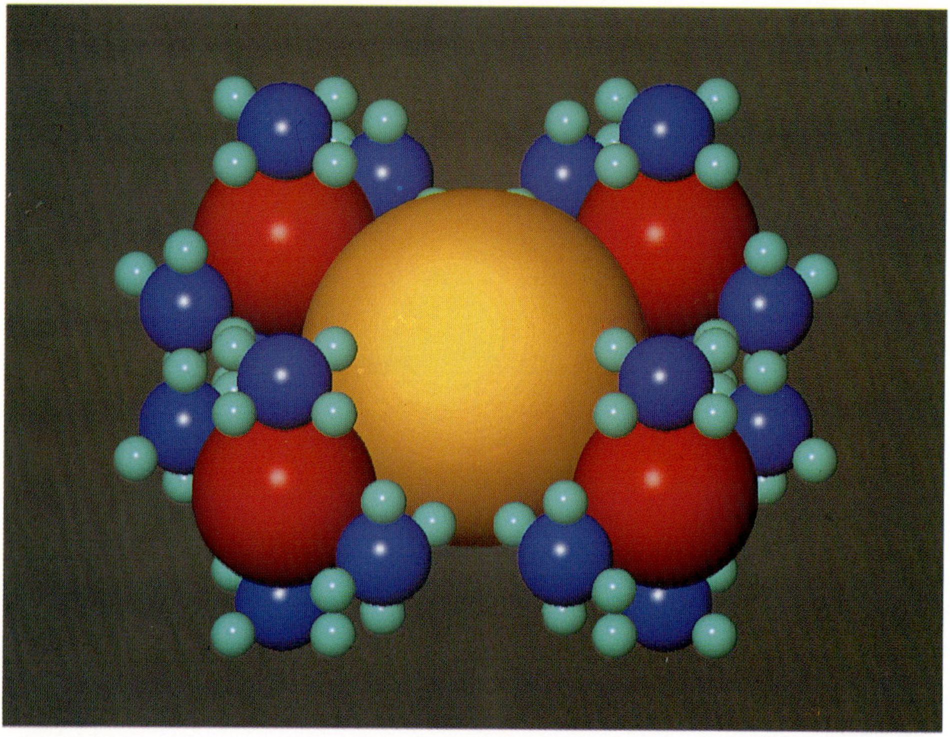

Plate VIa

Plate VIb

Plate VIIa

Plate VIIb

Plate VIIIa

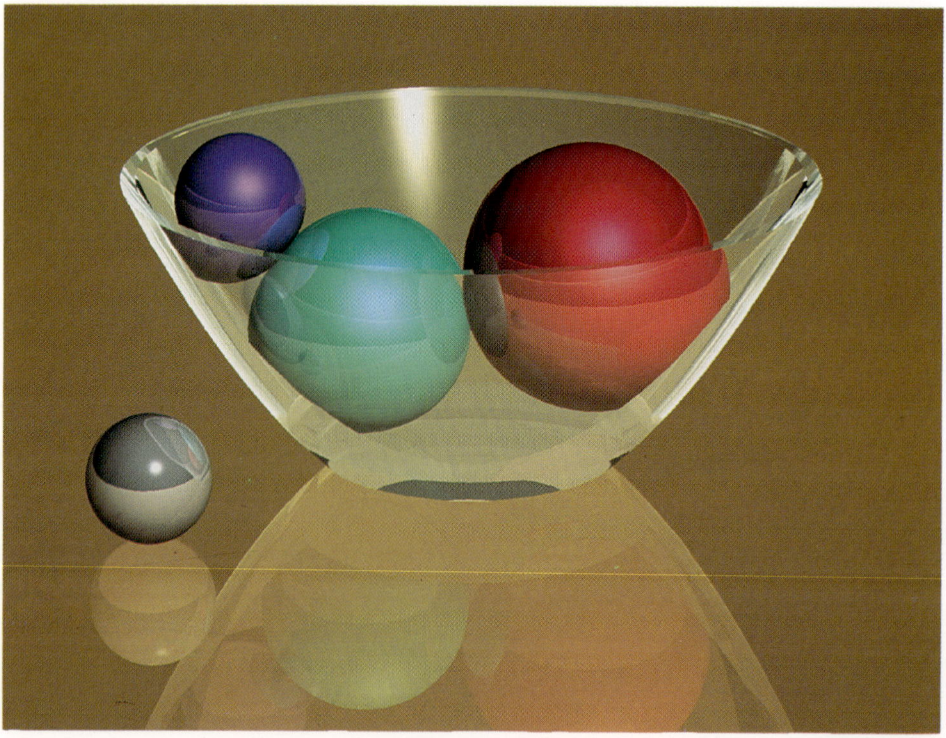

Plate VIIIb

projected onto the view plane by our chosen perspective projection, whence two-dimensional clipping ascertains which parts of the image lie totally within the window. Suppose, however, that we wish to depict a scene as viewed from a position within the model, such as a point lying in a landscape with a large ground plane. Clearly, parts of the model will lie behind the eye and consequently cannot be projected onto the view plane. Such problems cannot be resolved by two-dimensional clipping and so extended methods must be developed. *Three-dimensional clipping* must determine which parts of a line or facet can be projected, and subsequent hidden surface elimination must be executed upon the clipped scene. Hence the information generated by the clipping process must be incorporated into the **Mesh** and **Cluster** data structures.

There are consequently two problems that need to be solved. Firstly, we must determine which part, if any, of a facet lies in the volume of space projected onto the window, and secondly we must incorporate this information into the data structures representing the scene.

The functions required for clipping are entirely self-contained, and are given in listing 8.7. Since they will be manipulating the **Mesh** class they will be added to file **"mesh.cpp"**; they are already declared in **"mesh.h"** (listing 7.3a). Clipping is incorporated into our programs by the simple extension of the **look_at_it** function (listing 8.8), which replaces the present code in **"display.cpp"**.

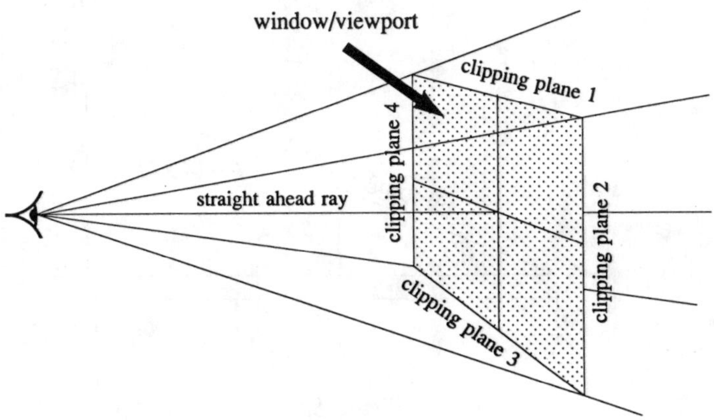

Figure 8.7

The pyramid of vision

The volume of three-dimensional space which is projected onto the window is a rectangular pyramid with axis of infinite length. This pyramid which we call the *pyramid of vision* (a subset of the cone of vision), has its apex at the eye position (the origin of the OBSERVER co-ordinate system) and four infinite edges, each passing through one corner of the window on the view plane. It is thus bounded by four planes (*the clipping planes*), each of which contains the OBSERVER origin and one edge of the rectangular window.

We number the clipping planes as shown in figure 8.7, from 1 to 4 starting from the top plane and moving round clockwise as viewed from the eye position. A point vector, (x, y, z), lying within the pyramid of vision is projected, by perspective projection, onto the point $(-d \times x/z, -d \times y/z)$ in the window (d is the perpendicular distance from the eye to the view plane). Each clipping plane divides space into two halves. The half-space containing the pyramid of vision is said to be the *visible side* of the plane. The four clipping planes must be represented in such a way that we may easily determine whether a point lies on their visible side or not. For example, consider clipping plane 1. This plane passes through the top horizontal edge of the view plane window and it is therefore perpendicular to the y/z plane. The x orthographic projection of this plane is shown in figure 8.8.

If a point (x, y, z) lies in this plane we must have, by similar triangles

$$\frac{y}{-z} = \frac{\mathbf{vert}}{2d} \quad = \tan\theta_v \quad \text{(say)},$$

and so $y = -\tan\theta_v \times z$ (remember z is negative)

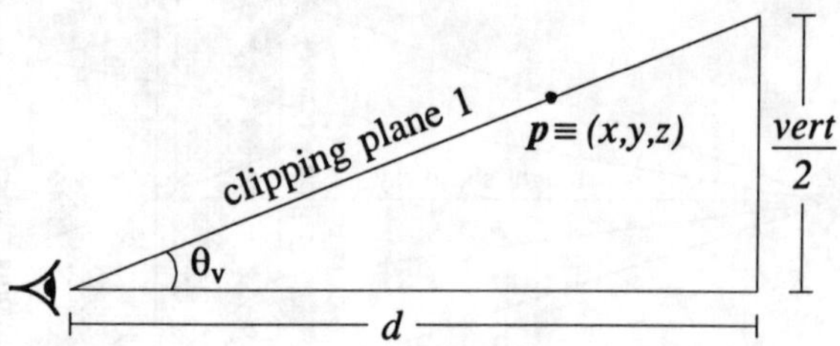

Figure 8.8

and hence for any point lying below the plane, on the visible side

$$y < -\tan\theta_v \times z$$

and for any point above the plane

$$y > -\tan\theta_v \times z$$

Clearly this mathematical description extends directly to the other three clipping planes. Plane number 3 is defined as above with the angle $-\theta_v$ which has tangent $-\tan\theta_v$ and hence we may derive the relationships

On the plane	: $y = \tan\theta_v \times z$
Above the plane (on the visible side)	: $y > \tan\theta_v \times z$
Below the plane (not on the visible side)	: $y < \tan\theta_v \times z$

and the two vertical clipping planes, 2 and 4, may be treated likewise, using the angle θ_h, which has tangent **horiz**/2*d*.

For a point to lie within the pyramid of vision, it must be on the visible side of all four clipping planes. If the *z* co-ordinate of a point is greater than 0 then it is behind the eye and so is not on the visible side of any of the four planes, since if it was on the visible side of one clipping plane, then it must be on the invisible side of the opposite plane. The function **locate** (listing 8.7) determines whether each vertex of a facet lies on the visible side of a given clipping plane, and stores its results in the integer array **inside**. **inside[i]** is set to 1 if the **i**th vertex of the facet lies on the visible side of the clipping plane, 0 if it lies in the plane and −1 if on the invisible side. The position of the **i**th vertex of the facet within the cluster is stored in the array location **kfacet[0][i]**. The meaning of this array will be explained later, but for the moment we just note its declaration.

Any clipping function in three dimensions must involve the calculation of the point of intersection of a given line with a clipping plane. Function **ilpl** has already done this in chapter 6, given two points on the line and the standard vector form for the plane. We must, therefore, determine the vector equations for the clipping planes. Recall that the vector equation of a plane is $\boldsymbol{n} \cdot \boldsymbol{v} = k$, where $\boldsymbol{v}$ is a typical point on the plane, $\boldsymbol{n}$ is the normal to the plane, and $k = \boldsymbol{n} \cdot \boldsymbol{a}$ for any fixed point $\boldsymbol{a}$ lying in the plane. Since all four clipping planes pass through the origin we may take $k = \boldsymbol{n} \cdot \boldsymbol{O} = 0$ for all $\boldsymbol{n}$, and so each plane has the vector form $\boldsymbol{n} \cdot \boldsymbol{v} = 0$. All that now remains, therefore, is to determine the normal vector, $\boldsymbol{n}$, to each plane. Once more we shall consider the top clipping plane first and the results derived from this enable us to find the normals to the other three planes.

Since the top clipping plane is perpendicular to the *y*/*z* plane, its normal is parallel to the *y*/*z* plane and so has zero *x* co-ordinate. The line of intersection of the clipping plane with the *y*/*z* plane has direction $(0 , \tan\theta_v , -1)$, and so the normal vector is perpendicular to this line: $(0 , -1 , -\tan\theta_v)$. (The sense of the normal vector is not important in this instance.)

Accordingly, the normals to the other three planes are

Clipping plane 2: $(-1 , 0 , -\tan\theta_h)$
Clipping plane 3: $(0 , -1 , \tan\theta_v)$
Clipping plane 4: $(-1 , 0 , \tan\theta_h)$

Exercise 8.6

If desired, it is a relatively simple task to constrain the visible part of space further by adding a front and/or back clipping plane. These planes will both be perpendicular to the *z*-axis (which consequently forms the normal to each plane) and have constant *z* co-ordinate z_f and z_b respectively, say. A point is thus on the visible side of the front clipping plane if $z < z_f$, and on the visible side of the back clipping plane if $z > z_b$. The normal to both planes is, as mentioned above, the direction $(n_x , n_y , n_z) \equiv (0 , 0 , 1)$, and the equations have *k* value $n_z \times z_f$ $(= z_f)$ and $n_z \times z_b$ $(= z_b)$, for front and back planes respectively. In our programs we do not use a front or back clipping plane, but it is a useful exercise to incorporate them into the functions, calling them clipping planes 5 and 6.

Polygon clipping in three dimensions

We may now tackle the clipping of a convex polygon in three dimensions in a manner exactly analogous to the **clip** and **overlap** functions for two dimensions described in chapter 5. The facet is sliced in turn by each of the clipping planes (whether four or six), and the resulting polygon either degenerates into a polygon with fewer than three vertices, in which case it lies entirely outside the pyramid of vision, or having been sliced by all clipping planes, it represents the visible portion of the facet, notwithstanding the other facets in the scene.

The information produced by the clipping process must be incorporated into the **Mesh** and **Cluster** data structures representing the scene. At the end of the clipping of a facet there are three possible outcomes .

(i) The facet remains unchanged since it lies entirely within the pyramid of vision.
(ii) The facet degenerates on clipping and is therefore not visible since it lies entirely outside the pyramid of vision.
(iii) We are left with a new facet consisting of that part of the original facet which lies inside the pyramid of vision.

Information regarding clipped facets must not corrupt the original data. Recall that the original model has **nov** vertices and **nof** facets. The total numbers of vertices and facets, inclusive of any which may be created during the clipping of the model, are stored as **extendednov** and **extendednof** respectively. The OBSERVED co-ordinates of the vertices are stored in the **obs** cluster, and pointers to these arrays are stored in the database as the array **listofverts** through which the facets are determined by the arrays **firstoffacet** and **size.** These are the facets of the original model prior to clipping. Each facet also has an associated pointer **clipfac**. We may use this pointer to refer to a new facet created by the clipping process which is stored at the end of the **listofverts** array in the database. Initially **clipfac[i]** is set to **i** for each facet **i**, thus referring to the polygon defined in the original model.

Suppose we are clipping facet **i**. If case (i) occurs we have no problem – the data structure remains unchanged. If case (ii) occurs then the facet should not be drawn, and hence should not be considered in the display algorithms. We indicate this by setting **clipfac[i]** to −1. In subsequent processes we use this fact to indicate that facet **i** lies entirely outside the pyramid of vision – it need neither be drawn nor considered in the hidden surface algorithm; but we shall find later, when dealing with shadows and reflections, that it cannot be ignored entirely! Note that in setting **clipfac[i]** to −1 we do not affect in any way the information in the database which defines facet **i**. Pointers to its vertices are still stored in the **listofverts** array and are accessible via **firstoffacet[i]** and **size[i]**, and in order to restore the structure to its original form we need only reset **clipfac[i]** to **i**.

Now consider case (iii). Suppose that facet **i** lies partially inside the pyramid of vision. A new facet is created which represents that part of facet **i** within the pyramid. We store the data concerning this new facet in the next free portions of the **Mesh** and relevant **Clusters** of the database, also updating the values of **extendednov** and **extendednof. clipfac[i]** refers to this new facet, which is then used instead of facet **i** in both the drawing of the object, and later hidden surface elimination. We must take some care in doing this however, primarily ensuring that the information describing the original, unclipped model is not destroyed, and also we must try to be as undemanding as possible on extra storage space. It would be easy simply to create a brand new set of vertices for the clipped facet and place these *en bloc* at the end of the **obs** cluster in the database, but this could necessitate raising the value of **maxv.** In many cases, however, only one vertex of the original is clipped out, resulting in only two new vertices being created. Therefore, we strive to use as much of the original data as possible.

The first requirement is that vertex co-ordinates are not simply copied into new clusters as they are in the two-dimensional clipping function, but instead we use an array of pointers to the co-ordinate values in the **obs** cluster. We therefore introduce a two-dimensional temporary storage array **kfacet** which shall be used in exactly the same manner as the previously used **ip** array in the **overlap** function (listing 5.5), except that they contain integer indices of vertices rather than raw co-ordinates. We use two variables, **l1** and **l2**, to distinguish the two portions of the **kfacet** array. Initially **l1** is set to 0 and **l2** to 1.

At the start of the process of clipping facet **i**, the contents of the **listofverts** array from **listofverts[firstoffacet[i]]** to **listofverts[firstoffacet[i]+size[i]−1]** are copied to array **kfacet[l1][0..ksize−1]**, the variable **ksize** being set to equal **size[i]**. The polygon described by the **kfacet** array is therefore facet **i**. A new variable **totnov** is also introduced at this stage to record the total number of vertices in the model prior to the clipping of facet **I**. Its value is therefore set to **extendednov**.

The facet is clipped by each of the four clipping planes in turn. The polygon defined by **kfacet[I1][0..ksize−1]** is clipped and indices of the vertices of the resulting polygon are stored as **kfacet[I2][0..n−1]**. Any new vertices created by the clipping are appended to the **obs** cluster and **extendednov** incremented accordingly. The values of **I1** and **I2** are then swapped **ksize** set to equal **n**, and the process is repeated with the next clipping plane.

At the end of the clipping process we have an array of pointers referring to the vertices of a new facet, which may contain a subset of the original vertices together with some new vertices. Once again a number of different cases may arise, each corresponding to one of the three cases outlined above. Firstly, the number of vertices in the reduced polygon may become less than three, indicating that the facet lies completely outside the pyramid of vision. In this case the clipping process may stop – a real gain, particularly if not all of the clipping planes have been used, **clipfac[i]** is set to −1, and any new vertices which may have been created can be ignored (by setting **extendednov** back to **totnov**) and subsequently overwritten. If this does not happen and no new vertices are created (**extendednov** = **totnov**) then the original facet lies completely within the pyramid of vision and no changes need be made to the data structure. The interesting situation, case (iii) above, arises when the final polygon contains at least one new vertex. The new facet must be copied into the database clusters and be referred to by **clipfac[i]**. It is by no means certain, however, that all of the new vertices created during the clipping process will be included in the final polygon – many may themselves be clipped out later. We therefore introduce a form of garbage collection into the function for filtering out those vertices which have been created but not ultimately used (see listing 8.7).

Listing 8.7

```
// Place these functions in "mesh.cpp"

extern float ppd ;
extern Window win ;
//extern Cluster3d vno ;  // Un-comment when using Gouraud and Phong shading

//----------------------------//
  void Mesh::clipscene(void)
//----------------------------//
 { int i,clipindex ;
   for (i=0 ; i<nof ; i++)
   { clipindex = clip(i) ;
     if (clipindex == 3) clipfac[i]=extendednof-1 ;
     else
         { if (clipindex == 2) clipfac[i]=-1 ; }
   }
 } // End of clipscene
```

```
//---------------------//
  int Mesh::clip(int k)
//---------------------//
// Clips facet 'k'
 { int i,j,n,f,s,inter,kfi,l1,l2,totnov,np[maxpoly] ;
   vector3 base,dir,ipt,norm ;
   int vf,vs, clipindex ;
   float rval ;
   vector3 occ, vnovf, vnovs, vnoextendednov ;
   int extendednov ;
   ppd=3.0*win.Get_horiz() ;
// 'totnov' is total number of vertices prior to clipping facet 'k'
   extendednov = obs.Get_extendednov() ;  totnov=extendednov ;
// Copy pointers to facet vertices into first section of 'kfacet' array
   ksize=size[k] ;
   l1=0 ;
   for (i=0 ; i<ksize ; i++)
      kfacet[l1][i]=listofverts[firstoffacet[k]+i] ;
// Loop through clipping planes 1 to 4
   for (i=1 ; i<5 ; i++)
   { n=0 ;
// Find 'norm'al vector of clipping plane and 'in' value of each vertex
     norm.x=-((i-1) % 2) ; norm.y=-(i % 2) ;
     if (fabs(norm.x) < epsilon)
// Horizontal clipping plane
       { norm.z=win.Get_vert()*0.5*(i-2)/ppd ;
         locate(l1,2,-norm.z,&obs) ;
       }
// Vertical clipping plane
     else
       { norm.z=win.Get_horiz()*0.5*(i-3)/ppd ;
         locate(l1,1,-norm.z,&obs) ;
       } ;
     l2=1-l1 ; f=ksize-1 ;
// Slice facet defined by 'kfacet' array with clipping plane 'i'
// Consider facet edge joining vertices 'f'(first) and 's'(second)
     for (j=0 ; j<ksize ; j++)
     { s=j ;
// If vertex 'f' is 'inside' then include in new facet
       if (inside[f] >= 0)
         { kfacet[l2][n]=kfacet[l1][f] ; n++ ; } ;
// If vertices 'f' and 's' are on opposite sides of the plane then
// find the intersection of the edge with the plane and include.
       if (inside[f]*inside[s] == -1)
         { vf=kfacet[l1][f] ;
           vs=kfacet[l1][s] ;
           base= obs.Get_vertex(vf) ;
           occ = obs.Get_vertex(vs) ;
           dir = occ - base ;
           ilpl(base,dir,norm,0.0,&ipt,&rval) ;
// There is always an intersection
           obs.put_vertex(extendednov,ipt) ;
           kfacet[l2][n]=extendednov ;
// When using Gouraud or Phong Shading un-comment the following 4 lines
//           vnovf = vno.Get_vertex(vf) ;
//           vnovs = vno.Get_vertex(vs) ;
//           vnoextendednov = (1-rval) * vnovf + rval * vnovs ;
//           vno.put_vertex(extendednov,vnoextendednov) ;
           n++ ; extendednov++ ;        //consistent with obs.extendednov
         } ;
       f=s ;
     }
// If new facet empty then stop
     if (n <= 2)
       { extendednov = totnov ; obs.Set_extendednov(extendednov) ;
         return(2) ; // Ignore new vertices
       }
     else { ksize=n ; l1=l2 ; } ;
   } ;
```

```
// Reach here if non-empty facet remains. If new vertices have been
// created then sort them and store new facet
    if (extendednov > totnov)
      { clipindex=3 ;
        for (i=0 ; i<ksize ; i++)  np[i]=i ;
        if (extendednof >= maxf)
          { cerr << "\n Error: Maximum number of facets exceeded" ;
            return (2) ;
          } ;
        if (firstfree+ksize > maxlist)
          { cerr << "\n Error: Size of list array exceeded" ;
            return (2) ;
          } ;
        n=totnov ; firstoffacet[extendednof]=firstfree ;
        size[extendednof]=ksize ;
        material[extendednof] = material[k] ;
// Storage of vertices with garbage collection:
// Sort contents of 'kfacet' array into increasing order
        for (i=0 ; i<ksize ; i++)
        { if (i < ksize-1)
            for (j=i+1 ; j<ksize ; j++)
              if (kfacet[l1][np[i]] > kfacet[l1][np[j]])
                { inter=np[i] ; np[i]=np[j] ; np[j]=inter ;  } ;
// If vertex is new (i.e. 'kfi>=totnov') then place in next available
// location, else refer to old location
          kfi=kfacet[l1][np[i]] ;
          if (kfi >= totnov)
            { listofverts[firstoffacet[extendednof]+np[i]]=n ;
              obs.put_vertex(n,obs.Get_vertex(kfi)) ; n++ ;
            }
          else listofverts[firstoffacet[extendednof]+np[i]]=kfi ;
        }
        extendednov=n ; obs.Set_extendednov(extendednov) ;
        firstfree=firstfree+size[extendednof] ; extendednof++ ;
      }
    else clipindex=1 ;
// If no new vertices created then no clipping was needed
    return ( clipindex ) ;
  }  // End of clip

//-----------------------------------------------------------//
  void Mesh::locate(int l, int flag, float tth, Cluster3d *oc)
//-----------------------------------------------------------//
// 'flag' (1 or 2) indicates x or y observed co-ordinates from array oc
// 'tth' is the tangent of relevant angle
// For each vertex 'j', 'inside[j]' is returned as follows:
//       'inside[j] = 1' if 'j' lies on the visible side of clipping plane
//       'inside[j] =-1' if 'j' lies on the invisible side
//       'inside[j] = 0' if 'j' lies in the plane
 { float stth,abstth,coord ;
   int i,j ;
   vector3 occ ;
   stth=sign(tth) ; abstth=fabs(tth) ;
   for (i=0 ; i<ksize ; i++)
   { inside[i]=0 ; j=kfacet[l][i] ;
     occ = oc->Get_vertex(j) ;
     if (flag == 1)  coord=occ.x ;  else coord=occ.y ;
     if (coord*stth < -abstth*occ.z) inside[i]= 1 ;
     if (coord*stth > -abstth*occ.z) inside[i]=-1 ;
   }
 }  // End of locate
```

Also it is essential that you remember to un-comment the relevant lines (five in total) of listing 8.7, that declare and use cluster position **vno**, when you are using Gouraud and Phong shading in chapter 11.

A facet is clipped by the function **clip** in listing 8.7 which is called for each facet of the scene in turn (including superficial facets) by the function **clipscene**. The three different cases which may arise from the clipping function are denoted by a flag **clipindex** which is returned from **clip** with value 1, 2, or 3, and corresponds to cases (i), (ii) and (iii) respectively. **clip** creates a new facet, if necessary, and stores it as facet **extendednof**. The management of the **clipfac** pointers is then carried out by the calling function **clipscene**.

The state of the database

Let us take an overview of the database as it stands after the three-dimensional clipping. The vertex counts **nov** and **extendednov** refer respectively to the number of vertices in the original model clusters and the total number of vertices inclusive of all those created by clipping. Thus **nov ≤ extendednov** throughout. Equivalent definitions apply to the facet counts **nof** and **extendednof**. The pointers in the **clipfac** array refer to the polygon representing the visible portion of a given facet of the model. **clipfac[i]** is no longer necessarily equal to **i** for every facet **i**.

The look_at_it function

We mentioned that the clipping function must be called before any perspective projection onto the view plane can occur, and so we insert the call in the new **look_at_it** function (listing 8.8) immediately before the call to the perspective **project_it** (listing 8.6). Note that, from now on, all perspective views will require this new function **look_at_it** to replace the previous version (listing 8.1b) in our file **"display.cpp"**.

Listing 8.8

```
// Replace function 'look_at_it' in file "display.cpp"

//---------------------//
  void look_at_it(void)
//---------------------//
 { look3() ;
// then calculate the observation matrix 'Q'
   findQ() ;
   observe() ;
   mesh.clipscene() ;
   project_it() ;          // Use perspective projection
 }  // End of look_at_it
```

Figure 8.9 shows a scene of a checkerboard holding two pawns and two kings. It is viewed from a long distance away and so the whole scene fits neatly onto the graphics screen and does not need clipping. Figure 8.10 is a close-up of the same scene, and demonstrates very clearly three-dimensional clipping in action.

Figure 8.9

Figure 8.10

Project 8.1

Extend the three-dimensional polygonal mesh description of objects given in the last two chapters into the fourth dimension (Coxeter, 1973; Banchoff 1978). Produce a class **Matrix4** of five by five matrices that is needed to transform objects in this space. Also extend the **Mesh** and **Cluster** classes to such objects. Now the vertices in a **Cluster4d** class will be a type **vector4**, a structure holding four **float** values. A *polytopal mesh* approximates to objects in four-dimensional space; this consists of *polytopes* (four-dimensional figures), each a list of polyhedra, a polyhedron is a list of facets, a facet is a list of vertices (or of lines, which in turn are defined by a pair of vertices). Write a **project_it** method that projects four-dimensional space onto a two-dimensional screen. The simplest orthographic projection of points ignores two of the four coordinate values (as opposed to ignoring one in three dimensions). Figure 8.11 shows an orthographic projection of a hypercube. Experiment with the many other types of projection.

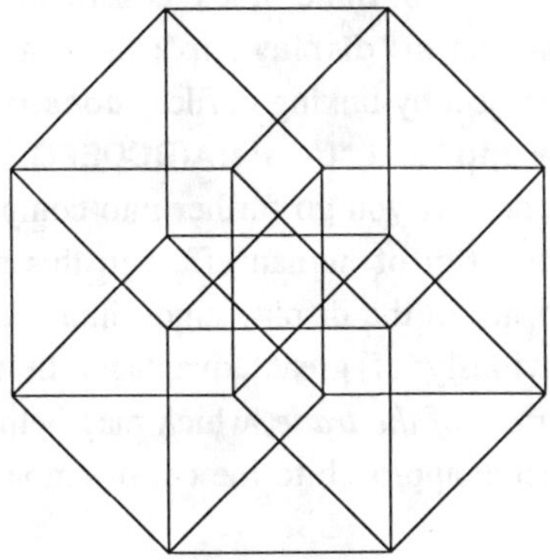

Figure 8.11

Project 8.2

Write a **project_it** function for the *stereoscopic* projection, in which scenes seem to stand out as three-dimensional. This involves drawing two different perspective views simultaneously, one drawn for the left eye and one for the right, taking into account the distance between the two eyes (Angell, 1990). The first view is drawn in shades of red; the second, in shades of green and blue, is added to the first. Viewing the scene through stereoscopic spectacles, a pair of red and cyan filters (one colour for each eye), enables the brain to merge the images together giving the impression of three dimensions. Use this technique for the line drawings given so far, and also adjust it for the 'solid' drawings of later chapters.

9 Generation of model data

The previous chapter introduced our method for constructing and drawing scenes: a function **build_it** is used to construct data about a three-dimensional scene via construction functions, some input from file. Then the vertices are transformed into the OBSERVED position, clipped, projected by **project_it**, and the function **draw_it** is called to display the final scene. In the following chapters we will give a number of different types of **draw_it** and facet display functions, that depend only on the projection and type of picture you require: line drawing, colour with/without shading, shadows etc. All the reader need do is to create the relevant application program consisting of **build_it** and construction functions and set up the required **draw_it** function in **"display.cpp"**; the rest is done for you in our use of the Borland C++ Project by linking in files **"construc.cpp"**, **"model.cpp"**, **"window.cpp"**, **"display.cpp"** and **"ClusterA(BCDEFGH&I).cpp"**.

All the reader need do? As you go further into computer graphics you will discover that the vast majority of human effort in this subject is put into the construction of data and not in the display algorithms. Any technique that will ease this burden is obviously of great advantage. In this chapter we shall introduce you to some *tricks of the trade*, which may help you in specific cases, and lead you into a sensible approach to the construction of data.

Using file input with construction functions

In the previous chapter, using just an elementary construction function and data in SETUP position, we saw how the building block method was used to construct three-dimensional scenes. In this chapter we shall show that this simple idea can give rise to very complicated scenes. We start by considering the use of data files (other than in **datain/dataout** format) holding SETUP information.

Example 9.1

To illustrate this method we give a **build_it** function that forms the application program for drawing figure 9.1a: two peculiarly shaped pyramids on a thin rectangular table-top, which has a checkerboard as one of its faces. A file **"pyramid.dat"** holds the basic data needed to define a pyramid with a square base of side 2 units and height 1 unit. The data on a cube will be used to create the table top. We give two construction functions **pyramid** and **checkerboard** in listing 9.1, and these should be stored in file **"construc.cpp"**. Each function uses a particular SETUP-to-ACTUAL matrix *P* to place in the database the data for each occurrence of an object in its chosen ACTUAL position.

The scale of the SETUP pyramid can be changed by introducing a scaling matrix into the definition of *P*. Note that the ACTUAL positions of each object are individually stated in the definition of the various *P* matrices in the **build_it** application of listing 9.2.

In order to achieve figure 9.1a, file **"display.cpp"** contains the current version of **draw_it** and the **project_it** (perspective) and **wireframe** functions. Figure 9.1b is the same scene drawn with the hidden surfaces removed, that is using the different form of **"display.cpp"** that will be described at the end of chapter 10. You will note there that most functions and files will remain unchanged, which shows the power and ease of use of this modular approach.

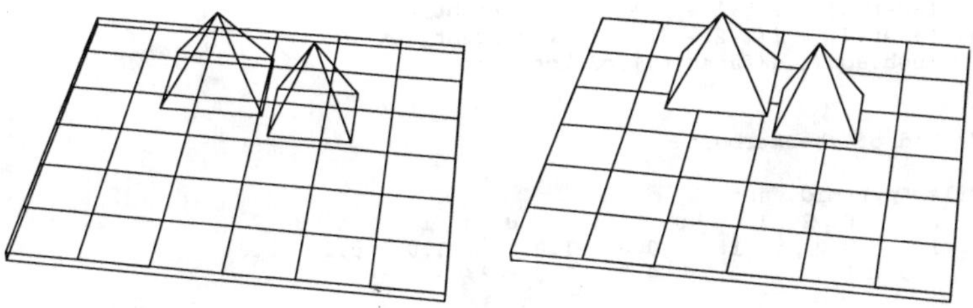

(a) (b)

Figure 9.1

Listing 9.1

```
// Place these functions in file "construc.cpp"
//-------------------------------//
  void pyramid(Matrix P, int col)
//-------------------------------//
// Pyramid construction routine. Initially of unit height and base 2 by 2.
// Block is distorted by scaling matrix P. Logical colour is 'col'
 { int i,j,invalue, facet[4], nov ;
   ifstream indata ;
   vector3 v ;
   indata.open("pyramid.dat") ;
// Update facet data base with 5 new facets. All are triangular
   nov = act.Get_nov() ;
   for (i=0 ; i<5 ; i++)
   { for (j=0 ; j<3 ; j++)
     { indata >> invalue ;  facet[j] = invalue + nov ;   }
     if (i< 4) mesh.add(3,&(facet[0]),col,-1) ;
     else      // Don't forget the 4 vertices on the final facet
       { facet[3] = nov + 1 ; mesh.add(4,&(facet[0]),col,-1) ; }
   }
// Update vertex data base with 5 new vertices in ACTUAL position
   for (i=0 ; i<5 ; i++)  { indata >> v ;  act.add( P * v ) ;  }
   indata.close() ;
 }  // End of pyramid
```

```
//----------------------------------------------------------------------//
  void checkerboard(float s, float d, int t, int c1, int c2, Matrix P)
//----------------------------------------------------------------------//
// Construction routine for a rectangular block. A cubic block is distorted
// by the scaling matrix P. C has logical colour 3
 { int i, j, facet[4], current_nov, host, modj ;
   float step ;
   vector3 v[8] ;
   Matrix A ;
   A.scale(s/2,d/2,s/2) ;   cube(P*A,c1) ;
   if (t<1) return ;
   current_nov = act.Get_nov() ;
   host = mesh.Get_nof() - 5 ;
   step = s / t ;
   for (i=0 ; i<=t ; i++)
     for (j=0 ; j<=t ; j++)
     { v[0].x = -0.5 * s + (float)j * step ;     v[0].y = 0.5 * d ;
       v[0].z = -0.5 * s + (float)i * step ;     act.add(P * v[0]) ;
     }
   for (j=0 ; j<t ; j++)
   { modj = j % 2 ;
     for (i=modj ; i<t ; i+=2)
     { facet[0] = i+1 + (t+1) * j + current_nov ;
       facet[1] = i   + (t+1) * j + current_nov ;
       facet[2] = i+t+1 + (t+1)*j + current_nov ;
       facet[3] = i+t+2 + (t+1)*j + current_nov ;
       mesh.add(4,&(facet[0]),c2,host) ;
     }
   }
 }  // End of checkerboard

/*  File "pyramid.dat"
 0  1  2        0  2  3       0  3  4       0  4  1       4  3  2
 0.0    1.0    0.0      1.0    0.0   -1.0       -1.0    0.0  -1.0
-1.0    0.0    1.0      1.0    0.0    1.0    */
```

Listing 9.2

```
// Application program to draw a scene of two pyramids on a checkerboard

#include "construc.h"

//--------------------//
 void build_it(void)
//--------------------//
 { Matrix A, B, P ;
// First the tabletop
   P.unit() ;    checkerboard(20.0,0.4,6,3,4,P) ;
// Then pyramid 1
   A.scale(2.5,4.0,2.5) ; B.translate(2.0,-2.0,2.0) ;
   P = B * A ;  pyramid(P,11) ;
// Then pyramid 2
   A.scale(2.0,4.0,2.0) ; B.translate(-3.0,-2.0,0.0) ;
   P = B * A ;  pyramid(P,5) ;
 }  // End of build_it
```

Superficial facets

The checkerboard we give is created by using superficial facets. Although superficial facets have an existence in their own right, each must be associated with its relevant host facet. This is achieved by using the array **superf** stored in the database of the **Mesh** class and **#included** in **"model.cpp"**; if facet **i** is superficial to host facet **j**, then **superf[i]** has a value **j**, otherwise **superf[i]** is set to −1. Furthermore each facet **j** is allocated a linked list of indices of all the facets that are superficial to it. This list is stored using a stack such as that described in chapter 3, and given in **"stack.cpp"** (listing 3.4b); **firstsup** is an array of stacks, **firstsup[j]** is the list of facets superficial to facet j. All of the **maxf** stacks are initialised by making their **top** pointer equal to NULL when they are declared in **"mesh.h"**. Construction functions will update these lists by **push**ing the index of every facet superficial to facet **j** onto stack **firstsup[j]**.

Superficial facets are demonstrated in listing 9.2, which is the application program **build_it** which draws two pyramids on a checkerboard, where half of the squares are superficial facets. The listing must be stored as file **"nine2.cpp"** and linked into our standard Borland C++ Project structure.

Exercise 9.1
Use this method to draw arbitrary scenes consisting not only of cubes and pyramids, but also the icosahedron, and other Archimedean solids mentioned in chapter 7.

Graph paper construction

So far we have given little consideration as to the construction of the data that is stored in these data files, either the form of co-ordinates of the vertices or their ordering in the definition of facets. With objects like a cube or pyramid this information is relatively easy to realise, but what if an object like one of the idealised houses in figure 9.3 is required? One popular method for such a construction is to draw rough sketches on squared graph paper of partial orthographic views of the SETUP object from x, y and z directions, as in figure 9.2. In such diagrams, vertices are indicated by their relative index number in the database cluster – each may occur in a number of different projections, and the x, y and z co-ordinates can be read directly from the graph paper. The orientation of the facets can also be taken directly from the graph paper. Note that superficial facets, such as those representing the windows and doors, must be included; and the larger host facets must be clearly understood from the diagram.

Example 9.2
Figure 9.3 shows four such houses defined by data (from file **"house.dat"** given in listing 9.3) containing superficial facets for doors and windows, each house being positioned by the construction function **house** and placed in position by **build_it** (also in listing 9.3). You should draw them using the orthographic **wireframe draw_it** of listing 8.3. However, in order to make the image easier to understand we draw it in perspective (**project_it** of listing 8.6), and with the

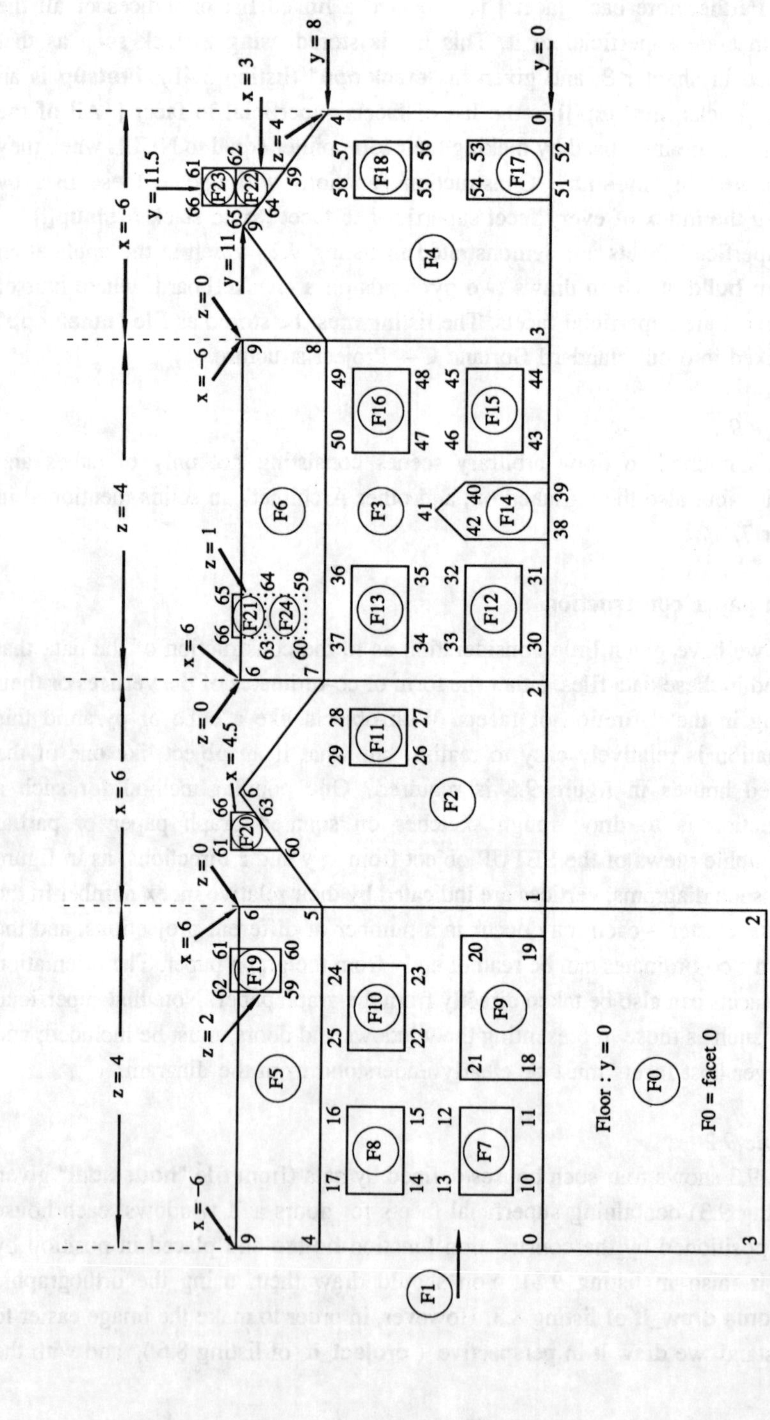

Floor : y = 0
F0 = facet 0
y = 11.5
y = 11
y = 8
y = 0
x = -6
x = 6
x = 4.5
x = 3
z = 4
z = 2
z = 0
z = 1
F0
F1
F2
F3
F4
F5
F6
F7
F8
F9
F10
F11
F12
F13
F14
F15
F16
F17
F18
F19
F20
F21
F22
F23
F24

Figure 9.2

Listing 9.3

```
// Application program to construct and draw idealised house
#include "model.h"

extern Mesh mesh ;
extern Cluster3d act ;

//-------------------//
  void house(Matrix P)
//-------------------//
 { int i,j,host,invalue,nofstore,col,facet[5],nov,fsize,fhost ;
   ifstream indata ;
    vector3 v ;
   indata.open("house.dat") ;
// Update facet data base with 24 new facets
   nov = act.Get_nov() ;  nofstore = mesh.Get_nof() ;
   for (i=0 ; i<25 ; i++)
   { indata >> fsize >> fhost ;
     for (j=0 ; j<fsize ; j++)
     { indata >> invalue ;   facet[j] = invalue + nov ; }
     if (i<7) col = 3 ; else col = 4 ;
     if (i==14) col = 2 ;
     if (i>18) col = 3 ;
     if (fhost != -1) fhost += nofstore ;
     mesh.add(fsize,&(facet[0]),col,fhost) ;
   }
// Update vertex data base with 67 new vertices in ACTUAL position
   for (i=0 ; i<67 ; i++)
   { indata >> v ;   act.add( P * v ) ; }
   indata.close() ;
 }  // End of house

//-------------------//
  void build_it(void)                  // Create ACTUAL scene of 4 houses
//-------------------//
 { float piby2 = 1.5707963268 ;
   Matrix A, B, P ;
   P.translate(0.0,0.0,12.0)                                  ; house(P) ;
   A.rotate(2,-piby2) ; B.translate(12.0,0.0,0.0)  ;  P = B * A ; house(P) ;
   A.rotate(2,pi)     ; B.translate(0.0,0.0,-12.0) ;  P = B*  A ; house(P) ;
   A.rotate(2,piby2)  ; B.translate(-12.0,0.0,0.0) ;  P = B * A ; house(P) ;
 }  // End of build_it

/*  File "house.dat"

4 -1  3  2  1  0    4 -1  0  1  5  4       5 -1  1  2  7  6  5
4 -1  2  3  8  7    5 -1  3  0  4  9  8    4 -1  4  5  6  9
4 -1  7  8  9  6    4  0 10 11 12 13       4  0 14 15 16 17
4  0 18 19 20 21    4  0 22 23 24 25       4  2 26 27 28 29
4  3 30 31 32 33    4  3 34 35 36 37       5  3 38 39 40 41 42
4  3 43 44 45 46    4  3 47 48 49 50       4  5 51 52 53 54
4  5 55 56 57 58    4 -1 59 60 61 62       4 -1 60 63 66 61
4 -1 63 64 65 66    4 -1 64 59 62 65       4 -1 62 61 66 65
4 -1 60 59 64 63
-6   0    4       6   0    4       6   0   -4       -6   0   -4       -6   8    4
 6   8    4       6  11    0       6   8   -4       -6   8   -4       -6  11    0
-4   1    4      -1   1    4      -1   3    4       -4   3    4       -4   5    4
-1   5    4      -1   7    4      -4   7    4        0   0    4        5   0    4
 5   4    4       0   4    4       1   5    4        4   5    4        4   7    4
 1   7    4       6   5   -1       6   5   -3        6   7   -3        6   7   -1
 5   1   -4       2   1   -4       2   3   -4        5   3   -4        5   5   -4
 2   5   -4       2   7   -4       5   7   -4        1   0   -4       -1   0   -4
-1   3   -4       0   4   -4       1   3   -4       -2   1   -4       -5   1   -4
-5   3   -4      -2   3   -4      -2   5   -4       -5   5   -4       -5   7   -4
-2   7   -4      -6   0    1      -6   0    3       -6   3    3       -6   3    1
-6   5    1      -6   5    3      -6   7    3       -6   7    1        3   9.5  2
4.5  9.5  2      4.5 11.5  2       3  11.5  2      4.5 10.25 1        3  10.25 1
 3  11.5  1      4.5 11.5  1    */
```

hidden surface removal **draw_it** (listing 10.1), using the **hidden** of listing 10.8, all of which are stored in file **"display.cpp"**. You must try this when you have read the next chapter. The **hidden** form of file **"display.cpp"** assumes that all objects in the scene are closed: you will have to change the listing slightly if you wish to draw non-closed objects – as in the case when the house has no floor.

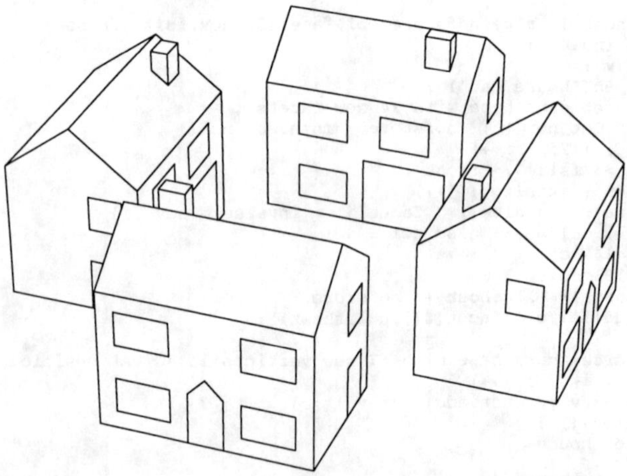

Figure 9.3

Exercise 9.2
Extend the house database so that it includes curtains on the windows, panels on the doors, and other features. Produce a construction function for a second style of house. Add garages. Draw a housing estate of both types of house on a large gridded rectangular area.

Exercise 9.3
Save the data for the houses in example 9.2 on backing store with function **dataout**. Then use the **build_it** function of listing 8.3 to read it back into memory, and draw figure 9.3.

Relative positioning of objects

Thus far, all objects have been considered independent of one another and they are placed in position individually by a **build_it** function. We often need to create complex objects with component parts that are themselves objects with their own construction files.

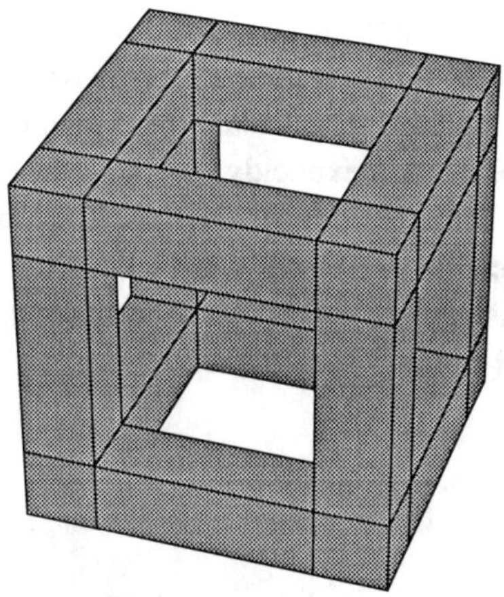

Figure 9.4

Listing 9.4

```
// Place this function in file "construc.cpp"
//--------------------------------------//
  void hollow(Matrix P1,int col1,int col2)
//--------------------------------------//
// Place a hollowed cube in ACTUAL position using matrix P1. Matrix P2 moves
// each component prism into an ACTUAL position which is SETUP for the hollow
// cube. 'P=P1xP2' places component into ACTUAL position for final scene.
 { Matrix A, B, P, P2 ;
   for (int i=0 ; i<8 ; i++)          // Setup the 8 corner cubes
   { P2.translate(4.0*cubevert[i].x,4.0*cubevert[i].y,4.0*cubevert[i].z) ;
     P = P1 * P2 ;  cube(P,col1) ;
   }
   for (i=0 ; i<4 ; i++)            // Setup 12 prisms joining corner cubes
   { A.scale(3.0,1.0,1.0) ;
     B.translate(0.0,4.0*cubevert[i].y,4.0*cubevert[i].z) ;
     P = P1 * (A * B) ; cube(P,col2) ;
     A.scale(1.0,3.0,1.0) ;
     B.translate(4.0*cubevert[i].y,0.0,4.0*cubevert[i].z) ;
     P = P1 * (A * B) ; cube(P,col2) ;
     A.scale(1.0,1.0,3.0) ;
     B.translate(4.0*cubevert[i].z,4.0*cubevert[i].y,0.0) ;
     P = P1 * (A * B) ; cube(P,col2) ;
   }
 }  // End of hollow
```

Example 9.3

Take, for example, the hollow cube shown in figure 9.4. It consists of twenty blocks: twelve rectangular prisms and eight cubes. Each facet has a well-defined position relative to every other. In order to create a SETUP position for this hollow cube, we can imagine each block being moved into an ACTUAL position around the origin by its own unique SETUP-to-ACTUAL matrix. Pre-multiplying each of these twenty matrices by the SETUP-to-ACTUAL matrix of the whole object will enable us to calculate the final ACTUAL position of its component vertices. Also note that in certain geometrically defined objects (such as this hollow cube) it may be possible to calculate these matrices implicitly (within a loop) rather than to type them in explicitly. See how the **cube** data from listing 7.5b is used in **hollow** (listing 9.4) to achieve this. This construction function is stored in file **"construc.cpp"**, so that it can be used by application programs, such as the **build_it** of listing 9.5, which should be stored as file **"nine5.cpp"** and linked into our standard Borland C++ Project.

Listing 9.5

```
// Application program to build a scene of two hollow cubes
#include "construc.h"
//--------------------//
  void build_it(void)
//--------------------//
 { Matrix P ;
   P.translate(0.0,0.0,0.0) ; hollow(P,2,4) ;
   P.translate(4.0,4.0,4.0) ; hollow(P,4,2) ;
 }  // End of build_it
```

Exercise 9.4
Much of the data created in the previous example is redundant. Certain facets occur twice, perhaps in different orientations, being common to two different component blocks; often these lie inside the body anyway, and may be ignored. Also the same absolute vertex may be referred to by different indices; it may have been created separately in different blocks. Write a function which runs through the database and removes such inefficient duplication.

Example 9.4
Example 9.3 is a case when all the vertices come ultimately from transforming vertices given in SETUP position. There are some situations where new vertices can be created within construction functions, with positions given relative to other vertex values. The stellar body shown in figure 9.5 and programmed in listing 9.6 is such an example. Here an icosahedron has pyramids added to each triangular face. Note that twelve new vertices, the points of the star, are added to the database; the original faces of the icosahedron are not included in the final object, since they will be totally obscured by the pyramids, although the original vertices are needed. The orientations of the original faces, however, are used to orientate the star's facets. The application program now consists of this **build_it** and the construction function **icostar**, and is stored as file **"nine6.cpp"**, to be linked into our standard Borland C++ Project.

Listing 9.6

```
// Application program to construct and draw one icosahedral star

#include "model.h"

extern Mesh mesh ;
extern Cluster3d act ;

const float t = (float) (1 + sqrt(5.0)) / 2.0 ;

vector3 icosvert[12]=
{ 0,1,-t,   t,0,-1,   1,t,0,   0,-1,-t,   t,0,1,   -1,t,0,
  0,1,t,   -t,0,-1,   1,-t,0,   0,-1,t,   -t,0,1,   -1,-t,0 } ;

int icosfacet[20][3]=
{ 0,2,1,    0,1,3,    0,3,7,    0,7,5,    0,5,2,    1,2,4,    1,8,3,    3,11,7,
  7,10,5,   2,5,6,    1,4,8,    3,8,11,   7,11,10,  5,10,6,   2,6,4,    4,9,8,
  8,9,11,  11,9,10,  10,9,6,    6,9,4 } ;

//----------------------------------------//
  void icostar(Matrix P, int col, float d)
//----------------------------------------//
// i0, i1, i2 and i3 are the indices of the four vertices of a pyramid
// that will form one point of the star.
 { int i, i0, i1, i2, i3, facet[3], current_nov ;
   vector3 midpoint ;
   current_nov = act.Get_nov() ;
   for (i=0 ; i<12 ; i++)  act.add( (P * icosvert[i]) ) ;
   i3 = 12 ;
   for (i=0 ; i<20 ; i++)
   { i0 = icosfacet[i][0] ;
     i1 = icosfacet[i][1] ;
     i2 = icosfacet[i][2] ;
     midpoint = (d / 3.0) * (icosvert[i0] + icosvert[i1] + icosvert[i2]) ;
     act.add( (P * midpoint) ) ;
     facet[0] = i0 + current_nov ;
     facet[1] = i1 + current_nov ;
     facet[2] = i3 + current_nov ;
     mesh.add(3,&(facet[0]),col,-1) ;
     facet[0] = i1 + current_nov ;
     facet[1] = i2 + current_nov ;
     facet[2] = i3 + current_nov;
     mesh.add(3,&(facet[0]),col,-1) ;
     facet[0] = i2 + current_nov;
     facet[1] = i0 + current_nov ;
     facet[2] = i3 + current_nov ;
     mesh.add(3,&(facet[0]),col,-1) ;
     i3++ ;
   }
 }  // End of icostar

//------------------//
  void build_it(void)
//------------------//
 { Matrix P ;
   P.translate(0.0,0.0,0.0) ;
   icostar(P,14,4.0) ;
 }  // End of build_it
```

Exercise 9.5

Draw stellar bodies based on a tetrahedron, cube, octahedron, dodecahedron etc. Rather than extend the polygonal faces out with a pyramid, why not extrude each face outwards, perhaps adding a slight rotation.

Figure 9.5

Extrusion

We are all used to drawing pictures in two dimensions, but three dimensions is another matter. Therefore any method that will enable us to extend a two-dimensional object into three dimensions will be of enormous value. We will consider two methods here: *extrusion* and *body of revolution*. The first, *extrusion*, takes a two-dimensional polygonal convex facet of, say **n**, ordered vertices that has been stored in a **vector2** array **v** ≡ {(**v[i].x**, **v[i].y**) | **i**=0,..., **n**−1}, and gives it thickness **d**. This will result in a three-dimensional object of **n**+2 facets: the front and back facets (each of **n** sides) and **n** four-sided facets which are created by each of the **n** edges of the original face being extruded in the negative *z* direction of the ABSOLUTE right-handed co-ordinate system. The whole process is programmed in listing 9.7. When viewed from outside the object, each of the final **n**+2 facets in three-dimensional space will have the same orientation as the original two-dimensional polygon. This very commonly used function, which we name **extrude**, is stored in file **"construc.cpp"**.

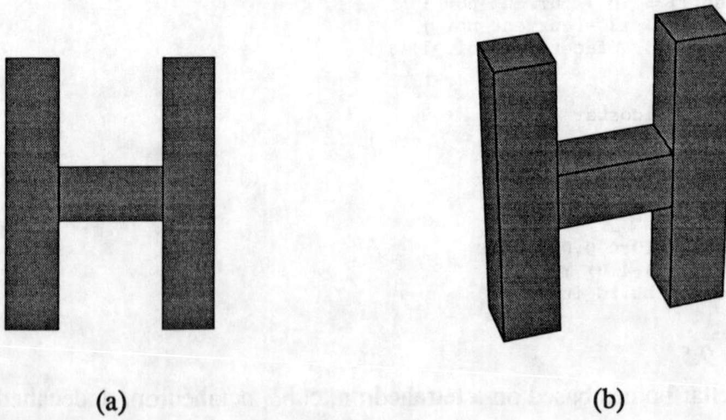

(a) (b)

Figure 9.6

Listing 9.7

```
// Place this function in file "construc.cpp"
//------------------------------------------------------------//
  void extrude(Matrix P, float d, int col, int n, vector2 *v)
//------------------------------------------------------------//
// Extrude in colour 'col', a 2-D polygon defined in a given
// orientation by 'n' vertices   '(v[i].x,v[i].y,0.0) : i=0..n-1'
// The new vertices and facets created by the extruding backwards
// by a distance 'd' are used to extend the ACTUAL data base
 { int i,lasti ;
   vector3 v3 ;
   int nov, facet1[maxpoly], facet2[maxpoly] ;
// First add front and back facets. Front face will contain vertices
// with indices 'nov,..,nov+n-1'. The back vertices 'nov+n,..,nov+2n-1'
// The vertices of the front polygon are in the given orientation
// so the equivalent back polygon will be of opposite orientation
// Hence the orientation of the back face must be reversed
   nov = act.Get_nov() ;
   for (i=0 ; i<n ; i++)
   { facet1[i] = nov + i ;   facet2[i] = nov + 2 * n -i-1 ;   }
   mesh.add(n,&(facet1[0]),col,-1) ;
   mesh.add(n,&(facet2[0]),col,-1) ;
// For each line on the front face there is a quadrilateral side face
// If the line joins vertex 'i-1' to 'i' of the original polygon (given
// orientation), then the side face will have ACTUAL vertices with indices
// 'nov+i,nov+i-1,nov+n+i-1,nov+n+i' (quadrilateral : same orientation)
   lasti=n-1 ;
   for (i=0 ; i<n ; i++)
   { facet1[0] = nov+i ;          facet1[1] = nov +lasti ;
     facet1[2] = nov+n+lasti ;    facet1[3] = nov+n+i ;
     mesh.add(4,&(facet1[0]),col,-1) ;  lasti=i ;
   }
// Front face vertices in ACTUAL position
   for (i=0 ; i<n ; i++)
   { v3.x=v[i].x ;  v3.y=v[i].y ;  v3.z=0.0 ;  act.add(P * v3) ;  }
// Back face vertices
   for (i=0 ; i<n ; i++)
   { v3.x=v[i].x ;  v3.y=v[i].y ;  v3.z=-d ;   act.add(P * v3) ;  }
 }  // End of extrude
```

Listing 9.8

```
// Application program to extrude the letter 'H' in 3-D space
#include "construc.h"
//-------------------//
  void build_it(void)
//-------------------//
 { vector2 letterH[maxpoly] ;
   Matrix P ;
   ifstream indata ;
   indata.open("letterH.dat") ;
   P.unit() ;                          // Place in SETUP position
// Setup three rectangles from the data file 'letterH.dat'
   for (int i=0 ; i< 3 ; i++)
   { for (int j=0 ; j<4 ; j++) indata >> letterH[j].x >> letterH[j].y ;
// Extrude then to a depth 2 in colour 3
       extrude(P,2.0,3,4,letterH) ;
   }
   indata.close() ;
 }  // End of build_it

/* File "letterH.dat"
  4  5     2  5     2 -5     4 -5
  2  1    -2  1    -2 -1     2 -1
 -2  5    -4  5    -4 -5    -2 -5   */
```

Example 9.5

Figure 9.6a shows the letter H drawn by an application program consisting of function **build_it** of listing 9.8. The figure consists of three two-dimensional facets that are extruded into three dimensions. The data for this letter is contained in file **"letterH.dat"** also given in listing 9.8. This application program is stored as **"nine8.cpp"**, and linked as usual to our files **"construc.cpp"**, **"window.cpp"**, **"display.cpp"**, **"ClusterA(BCDEFGH&I).cpp"**, and **"model.cpp"**. Figure 9.6b shows it drawn in perspective and in colour (the colours have been transformed into their grey-scale equivalents) with the hidden surfaces removed using **draw_it** from listing 10.1 and **hidden** of listing 10.8 stored in file **"display.cpp"**.

Exercise 9.6

Try other letters of the alphabet. Run the program with both the **wireframe** and **hidden** surface versions of **"display.cpp"**. Write a **build_it** routine which uses a mouse to input the silhouette data needed for extrusion.

Body of revolution

The second way of turning two-dimensional information into a three-dimensional object is the *body of revolution*. This function, **bodyrev**, is given an ordered sequence of **nvert** two-dimensional vertices stored in the **vector2** array **v**, which, when taken in order, define **nvert**−1 lines. These may be considered to be three-dimensional vertices and lines lying in the *x*/*y* plane through the origin. Each line is now rotated anti-clockwise by angles 2π**i/nhoriz** radians ($1 \le$ **i** $\le$ **nhoriz**) around the vertical *y*-axis into **nhoriz** positions. A line defined by a pair of vertices, neither being on the axis, will define **nhoriz** quadrilateral facets; those with one vertex on the axis will create **nhoriz** triangular facets; and those with both vertices on the axis are degenerate and ignored. The function **bodyrev** in listing 9.9 creates the data for a body of revolution; this will also be stored in file **"construc.cpp"**. The orientation of the original array **v** is defined to be the orientation of the triangle composed of the first, second and last vertex of **v**. Our algorithm imposes the same orientation on the facets of the body of revolution. So, to create facets which are oriented anti-clockwise when viewed from outside, you must ensure that your initial set of vertices **v** is oriented anti-clockwise.

Example 9.6

Figure 9.7 shows an *ellipsoid* created by an application program that consists of the construction function **ellipsoid**, that uses **bodyrev**. All data is created by a program from a semicircle of unit radius (listing 9.10); it is not read from file. The function actually generates a unit *sphere*, but a scaling matrix included in the

SETUP-to-ACTUAL matrix can distort it into an arbitrary-shaped ellipsoid. A **build_it** function is given which should be stored as **"nine10.cpp"** and linked to our standard C++ Project in order to create such a shape.

Listing 9.9

```
// Place this function in file "construc.cpp"
//-----------------------------------------------------------------//
  void bodyrev(Matrix P, int col, int nvert, int nhoriz, vector2 *v)
//-----------------------------------------------------------------//
// Routine to form Body of Revolution by rotating a section of 'nvert'
// points '(v[i].x,v[i].y,0)' around the vertical y axis. Each point in
// the section is rotated into 'nhoriz' points around the axis
// (or degenerates into one point on the axis). The method is to take
// consecutive pairs of vertices from the section, rotate each into
// 'nhoriz'(or 1) positions in a horizontal slice, and then form
// 'nhoriz' facets with each pair of slices. The vertices in the slices
// are first stored in SETUP position. At any one time we have two slices,
// a top and a bottom slice. 'index1' and 'index2' hold the indices of the
// vertices of these two slices. Body is logical colour 'col'. Finally
// ACTUAL vertices are stored. Orientation of the facets the same as in
// the original polygon. Maximum polygon size is 100.
 { float theta=0.0,thetadiff=2*pi/nhoriz ;
   int i,j,newnov ;
   float c[100],s[100] ;
   int index1[101],index2[101] ;
   vector3 setup ;
   int facet[4] ;
// Store the sines and cosines of 'nhoriz' angles around axis
   for (i=0 ; i<nhoriz ; i++)
   { c[i]=cos(theta) ;  s[i]=sin(theta) ;  theta+=thetadiff ;   } ;
// Update ACTUAL data base with new SETUP vertices
   newnov=act.Get_nov() ;
   if (fabs(v[0].x) < epsilon)
// Top slice is degenerate, so only one slice vertex created
     { setup.x=0.0 ; setup.y=v[0].y ; setup.z=0.0 ;
       act.add(P * setup) ;
       for (i=0 ; i<=nhoriz ; i++)  index1[i]=newnov ;
       newnov++ ;
     }
// Create 'nhoriz' vertices for top slice
   else
     { for (i=0 ; i<nhoriz ; i++)
       { setup.x= v[0].x*c[i] ;  setup.y= v[0].y ;  setup.z=-v[0].x*s[i] ;
         act.add( P * setup ) ;  index1[i]=newnov ; newnov++ ;
       }
       index1[nhoriz]=index1[0] ;
     } ;
// Run through 'nvert-1' lines
   for (j=1 ; j<nvert ; j++)
   { if (fabs(v[j].x) < epsilon)
// Bottom slice is degenerate, so only one slice vertex created
       { setup.x=0.0 ; setup.y=v[j].y ; setup.z=0.0 ;
         act.add(P*setup) ;
         for (i=0 ; i<=nhoriz ; i++)  index2[i]=newnov ;
         newnov++ ;
       }
// Create 'nhoriz' vertices for bottom slice
     else
       { for (i=0 ; i<nhoriz ; i++)
         { setup.x= v[j].x*c[i] ; setup.y= v[j].y ;  setup.z=-v[j].x*s[i] ;
           act.add(P* setup) ;   index2[i]=newnov ;  newnov++ ;
         }
         index2[nhoriz]=index2[0] ;
       } ;
```

```
// Create facets
    if (index1[0] != index1[1])
      { if (index2[0] == index2[1])
// bottom slice is degenerate, top isn't
// 'nhoriz' oriented triangles formed by degenerate bottom slice
          { for (i=0 ; i<nhoriz ; i++)
              { facet[0] = index1[i+1] ;
                facet[1] = index2[i] ;
                facet[2] = index1[i] ;
                mesh.add(3,&(facet[0]),col,-1) ;
              }
          }
// neither slice is degenerate
// 'nhoriz' oriented quadrilaterals formed by top and bottom slices
        else
          { for (i=0 ; i<nhoriz ; i++)
              { facet[0] = index1[i+1] ;  facet[1] = index2[i+1] ;
                facet[2] = index2[i]   ;  facet[3] = index1[i] ;
                mesh.add(4,&(facet[0]),col,-1) ;
              }
          } ;
      }
    else
      { if (index2[0] != index2[1])
// top slice is degenerate, bottom is not
// 'nhoriz' oriented triangles formed by degenerate top slice
        { for (i=0 ; i<nhoriz ; i++)
            { facet[0] = index2[i+1] ;
              facet[1] = index2[i] ;
              facet[2] = index1[i] ;
              mesh.add(3,&(facet[0]),col,-1) ;
            }
        } ;
      } ;
// Copy bottom slice into top slice and loop
    for (i=0 ; i<=nhoriz ; i++)  index1[i]=index2[i] ;
  }
 }  // End of bodyrev
```

Listing 9.10

```
// Application program to construct and draw an ellipsoid

#include "construc.h"

//---------------------------------//
  void ellipsoid(Matrix P, int col)
//---------------------------------//
// Construct an ellipsoid. First a semicircle of nvert points. If
// last point is joined to first we get anti-clockwise polygon
 { vector2 v[maxpoly] ;
   int nvert = 21 ;
   float theta=-pi*0.5,thetadiff=pi/(nvert-1);
   int i ;
   for (i=0 ; i<nvert; i++)
   { v[i].x=cos(theta) ; v[i].y=sin(theta) ;  theta+=thetadiff ;  }
// Call Body of Revolution with 30 rotations
   bodyrev(P,col,nvert,30,v) ;
 }  // End of ellipsoid

//-------------------//
  void build_it(void)
//-------------------//
// An ellipsoid with x,y and z axes 3,2,1 respectively
 { Matrix P ;
   P.scale(3.0,2.0,1.0) ; ellipsoid(P,1) ;
 }  // End of build_it
```

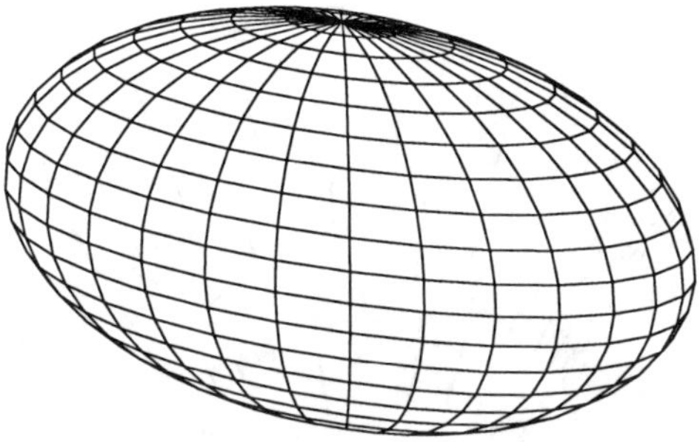

Figure 9.7

Figure 9.8, a goblet, was drawn by the **build_it** and **goblet** functions from listing 9.11 using the same **bodyrev** function from **"construc.cpp"**, naturally **"display.cpp"**, **"model.cpp"**, **"window.cpp"** and **"ClusterA(BCDEFGH&I).cpp"** are also linked. Data is read from file **"goblet.dat"**.

Note that this technique creates data for the surface of the object only. If the two-dimensional vertex sequence is not closed or does not start and end on the *y*-axis, then it will be possible to look inside the object, and this could cause problems with the hidden surface algorithms that follow.

Listing 9.11

```
// Application program to draw a goblet
#include "construc.h"
//------------------------------//
  void goblet(Matrix P, int col)
//------------------------------//
// Construct a goblet in ACTUAL position
 { vector2 gobdat[maxpoly] ;
   int i, nvert ;
   ifstream indata ;
// read in silhouette of goblet into 'goblet.dat'
   indata.open("goblet.dat") ;
   indata >> nvert ;
   for (i=0 ; i<nvert ; i++)  indata >> gobdat[i].x >> gobdat[i].y ;
   indata.close() ;
// Body of Revolution with 20 rotations
   bodyrev(P,col,nvert,20,gobdat) ;
 }  // End of goblet

//-------------------//
  void build_it(void)              // Create a goblet in SETUP position
//-------------------//
 { Matrix P ;
   P.unit() ; goblet(P,12) ;
 }  // End of build_it

/* File "goblet.dat"
  12
  0.0 -16.0      8.0 -16.0      8.0 -15.0      1.0 -15.0
  1.0  -2.0      6.0  -1.0      8.0   2.0     14.0  14.0
 13.0  14.0      7.0   2.0      5.0   0.0      0.0   0.0      */
```

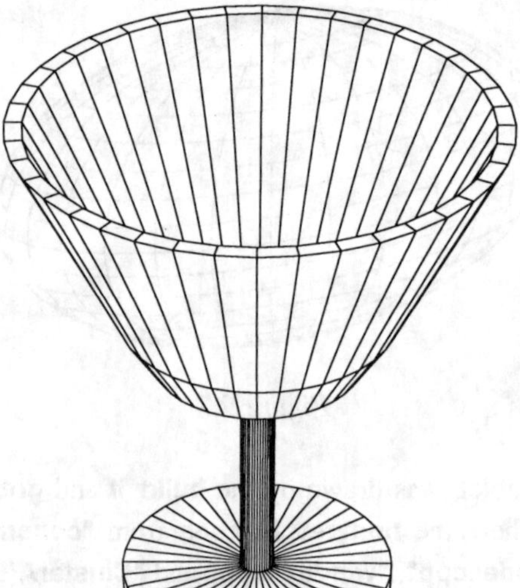

Figure 9.8

Exercise 9.7
Extend the above body of revolution method to create a *body of rotation*. Now the two-dimensional line sequence rotates about the central axis, but with each small rotation, the defining lines will also move a small distance vertically downwards. With this technique you should be able to model a helix such as the one shown in figure 9.9.

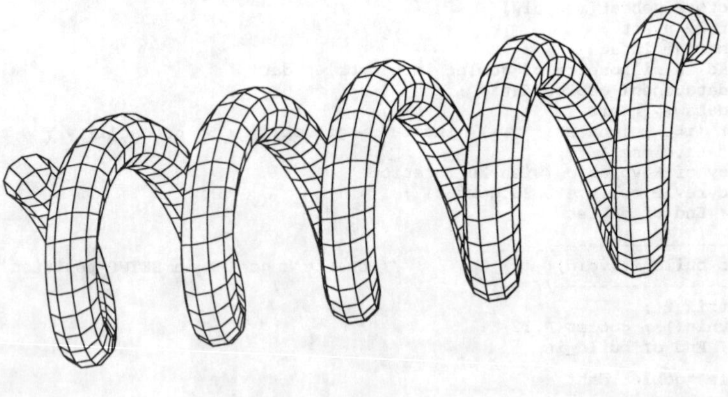

Figure 9.9

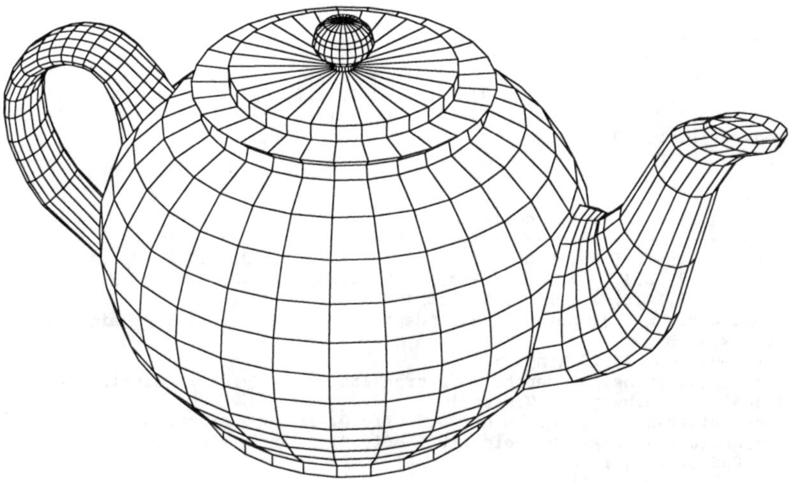

Figure 9.10

Exercise 9.8

Write a function which creates handles and spouts for figures created with the body of revolution method. This function must be given line sequences that form a silhouette, which can be turned into facet data for a handle or spout by imposing a circular or some other such cross-section on the data. In this way you can produce models such as the teapot of figure 9.10. This model was used in Plate I to demonstrate different forms of shading (see chapter 11).

Exercise 9.9

Combine the body of revolution and extrusion techniques to construct the body and fins respectively of a 'space rocket'. Consider the problem of placing superficial characters around the body of the rocket.

Example 9.7

Listing 9.12 gives an application program consisting of a **build_it** function and construction functions for a **pawn** and a **king** drawn on a checkerboard. This model was used to draw figures 8.9 and 8.10, and it was also used for the example of smooth shading and showing reflections in Plate V.

Listing 9.12

```
// Application program to construct and draw various chesspieces

#include "construc.h"

//----------------------------//
  void pawn(Matrix P, int col)
//----------------------------//
 { vector2 pawn[19] = { 0,0, 3,0, 2.8,0.5, 2.2,1, 1.6,1.4, 1,1.5, 2.4,1.5,
          2.4,1.6, 1,1.6, 1,6.9, 2,6.9, 2,7, 0,7, 0.75,7.3, 1.2,7.75,
          1.5,8.5, 1.2,9.25, 0.75,9.7, 0,10 } ;
   bodyrev(P,col,19,20,pawn) ;
 }  // End of pawn

//----------------------------//
  void king(Matrix P, int col)
//----------------------------//
 { vector2 king[20] = { 0,0, 4,0, 4,1, 3.8,1.5, 3.5,2, 3,2.2, 2,2.4, 1,2.5,
          1,3, 2,3.1, 3,3.5, 3.2,4, 2,12, 3,12, 3,12.2, 2,12.2, 3,14.5,
          2.8,14.5, 1.8,13.5, 0,13.5 } ;
   float width = 0.5, height = 2.5, depth = 0.5, offy = 13.5 + height ;
   Matrix A, B ;
   bodyrev(P,col,20,20,king) ;
   A.scale(width,height,depth) ;  B.translate(0,-offy,0) ;  cube(P*B*A,col) ;
   A.scale(width,height*0.2,depth) ;
   B.translate(2.0* width,-height*0.5-offy,0) ;  cube(P*B*A,col) ;
   B.translate(-2.0*width,-height*0.5-offy,0) ;  cube(P*B*A,col) ;
 }  // End of king ;

//-------------------//
  void build_it(void)
//-------------------//
 { Matrix P1, P2, P3 ;
   P1.translate(0.0,6.5,0.0)    ;  checkerboard(72.0,1.0,8,3,4,P1) ;
   P2.translate(4.5,6.0,13.5)   ;  pawn(P2,1) ;
   P3.translate(-4.5,6.0,-4.5) ;  king(P3,2) ;
 }  // End of build_it
```

Project 9.1

All the polygonal mesh objects in this book are assumed to be composed of convex facets. Any concave facet of an object must be split up into convex parts during the SETUP. Write a function which takes a concave polygon, and breaks it into a series of convex polygons (Chazelle and Incerpi, 1984; Fournier and Montuno, 1984), and incorporates them directly into our **Cluster** and **Mesh** database.

Project 9.2

A convex polyhedron can be considered as the body of intersection (the convex hull) of a number of half-spaces, that is all of space to one side of an infinite plane. Given such a set of planes, and assuming that the origin is inside each half-space, then the polyhedron can be calculated by the 'inside and outside' techniques of chapter 6. If you start with a very large cube, and successively cut away any part of the remaining polyhedron that lies outside the half-space, you will eventually be left with the required polyhedron.

Project 9.3
Repeat project 9.2, but this time work in four-dimensional space. Construct polytopes that are the convex hull formed by the common intersection of a number of half-spaces, where each half-space is bounded by a three-dimensional hyperplane (not a two-dimensional plane as in the previous project). Draw your models with the program you produced in project 8.1.

Project 9.4
Study the methods of Bezier Surfaces (Bezier, 1974) and B-spline Surfaces (Gordon and Riesenfeld, 1974) for constructing a polygonal mesh for three-dimensional solid objects, given only a small number of reference points. Implement these techniques in modelling functions that can be used in conjunction with our later display programs.

Project 9.5
Most people, when they think of computer graphics, think of animation. A *movie* will consist of a sequence of discrete frames which must be brought into view at a rate of twenty-five frames per second. Each frame will differ only slightly from its predecessor and successor, so that when viewed in quick succession they create an animated *cartoon* effect. Naturally if the scenes on consecutive frames change too slowly then the animation will be slow and boring, too quickly then the cartoon will stutter and be useless. The most effective rates of change for a given scene are discovered by trial and error, and from experience.

Naturally the VGA or XGA cards running on an PS/2 cannot draw scenes fast enough to produce real-time animation. However, with the right hardware, screen images can be dumped onto video tape to be replayed at the correct speed. You can use our programs in this way to create video animations. Even without the necessary hardware you can emulate production of single frames for a movie.

You can achieve this with our programs by assuming that each individual object, the observer and light source(s) have their own unique *trajectories*, for the duration of the animation. Identifying a frame, will uniquely position, scale and orientate objects, observer and light source(s). This may be achieved from within a new **draw_a_picture** function, which would consist of a loop that is executed once per frame. Inside this loop there would be the usual **build_it, look_at_it** and **draw_it** functions. However, the first two functions must now be of a slightly different form: each would have the loop index as a parameter. The **build_it** function must use the loop index to calculate the matrices that uniquely identify the position, scale and orientation of each object. Similarly in **look_at_it**, would position the observer and light source(s).

10 Hidden surface algorithms

We are now able to draw wire diagrams representing any scene. However, as we have seen in some figures from the previous chapter, we would like to think of objects as being solid, in which case the facets at the front of an object will obviously restrict the view of the facets (and boundary lines) at the back. In order to produce such a picture we must introduce algorithms that determine which parts of a surface or line are visible and which are not. Such algorithms are called hidden surface algorithms. There are many of these algorithms in the literature, some elementary for specially restricted situations, others very sophisticated for viewing general complicated scenes (Sutherland *et al.*, 1974). In this chapter we shall consider a variety of algorithms ranging from the simplest type to the general purpose.

In this chapter, for the first time we will be able to produce colour pictures of three-dimensional scenes, although we leave smooth shading for later. We introduce a new function **seefacet(k)**, which will be called to display facet **k** and all its associated superficial facets. This function will in turn call another function, **facetfill**, which will initiate the filling of an area of pixels. For the moment this will involve just an ordinary area-fill (see listings 1.1b and 2.1b, and chapter 5), but later on we will introduce variants that will allow *smooth shading, surface texture etc*. We must structure the calls to these display functions in order that they are consistent throughout the more complex applications which follow.

Recall that function **draw_it** co-ordinates all calls to the functions used in the display of the model of a scene, and this must call **hidden**, the function that will eliminate hidden surfaces. This, in turn, will call **seefacet** to display each visible facet. The new **draw_it** that calls **hidden** (rather than **wireframe**) is given in listing 10.1, and must replace the old version of listing 8.3 in **"display.cpp"**. Naturally, all the various versions of functions **hidden, seefacet** and **facetfill** that follow will also be placed in **"display.cpp"**.

Listing 10.1

```
// Replace function draw_it in file "display.cpp"

//-------------------//
  void draw_it(void)     // hidden lines/surfaces will be removed
//-------------------//
 { win.start() ;
   hidden() ;
 }  // End of draw_it
```

All of the hidden surface algorithms we consider here will operate upon the OBSERVED cluster of vertices and facets of objects in our three-dimensional model. The first algorithm we shall consider may be used for hidden surface drawings of single closed convex bodies. A *convex body* is one in which any line segment joining two internal points lies entirely within the body – a direct extension of the definition of a convex polygon in two dimensions. If such a body is *closed* then it is impossible to get inside without crossing through its surface. A simple example of a closed convex body is the extrusion of a convex two-dimensional polygon.

In order to simplify the hidden surface algorithm we impose a restriction on the order in which vertices defining each facet are stored. We have seen that for any facet **i**, **clipfac[i]** gives the index of the stored polygon representing facet **i** after clipping. Suppose **clipfac[i]** equals **j**, then **firstoffacet[j]** points to the start of a list of **size[j]** vertex indices stored in array **listofverts**. The vertex indices must be in the order in which they occur around the edge of the facet, and when viewed from the *outside* of the object that they define they must be in an anti-clockwise orientation. Naturally from the *inside* of the object the vertices taken in this same order would appear clockwise! We can check that the facets are actually stored as anti-clockwise sets of vertices by referring to function **orient3** of listing 6.11 during the SETUP stage of the scene definition. As before, we will also assume that facets intersect only at common edges. Since no lines are given explicitly in the data, an individual line that is not directly related to a facet must be added as a trivial double-faced triangular facet with one side of zero length.

Exercise 10.1
Use **orient3** to check that the programs from previous chapters do indeed create facets with vertices in the correct anti-clockwise orientation.

A hidden surface algorithm for a single closed convex body

We project (either orthographic or perspective) all the vertices of each facet onto the view plane, noting that a projection of a convex polygon with n sides in three-dimensional space is an n-sided convex polygon in the view plane (or it degenerates to a line if the infinite plane containing the three-dimensional polygon is parallel to the lines of projection (orthographic) or passes through the eye (perspective)). Taking the projected vertices of any facet in the same order as the original, we find that either the new two-dimensional polygon is in anti-clockwise orientation, in which case we are looking at the outside of the facet, or the new vertices are clockwise and we are looking at the underside. The orientation of a given two-dimensional **face** taken from the **Mesh**, with vertices taken from a given cluster projection pointed to by ***clst**, is calculated by the **orient** method of listing 10.2, in a manner similar to that used by another version of **orient** from listing 5.4. In this method we introduce a technique that is required by a number of later functions, when it will be used with different co-ordinate systems: a pointer to the cluster projection is passed as a parameter, and thus the functions for a given mesh are independent of the particular cluster projection (and hence co-ordinate system) being considered. We do, however, assume that the observer is outside the closed convex body and is able to see only the outside of facets, the view of their underside being blocked by the bulk of the object. Therefore, we need only draw the anti-clockwise polygonal facets – a very simple algorithm, which can be implemented directly via a **hidden** function. Note that if we only draw the edges of the visible facets, and do not fill in the facets in colour, then the above method gives us a simple hidden line algorithm. Function **orient** must be added to our file **"mesh.cpp"**, and whatever form of function **hidden** we are using must be added to file **"display.cpp"**. Figure 9.7 shows an ellipsoid drawn using this method.

Listing 10.2

```
// Place this function in file "mesh.cpp"

//-----------------------------------------------//
  int Mesh::orient(int face, Cluster2d *clst)
//-----------------------------------------------//
// Finds orientation of facet 'face' when projected into
// 2-D co-ordinate system defined by array v of 2-D vertices
// 1 = anti-clockwise, -1 = clockwise, 0 = degenerate
 { int ind0,ind1,ind2 ;
   vector2 v0, v1, v2, dv1, dv2 ;
   ind0 = listofverts[firstoffacet[face]] ;
   ind1 = listofverts[firstoffacet[face]+1] ;
   ind2 = listofverts[firstoffacet[face]+2] ;
   v0 = clst->Get_vertex(ind0) ;
   v1 = clst->Get_vertex(ind1) ;
   v2 = clst->Get_vertex(ind2) ;
   dv1.x=v1.x-v0.x ;    dv1.y=v1.y-v0.y ;
   dv2.x=v2.x-v1.x ;    dv2.y=v2.y-v1.y ;
   return(sign(dv1.x*dv2.y-dv2.x*dv1.y)) ;
 }  // End of orient
```

Listing 10.3

```
// Place this function in file "display.cpp"

//-----------------//
  void hidden(void)      // Drawing convex body with hidden surfaces removed
//-----------------//
 { int i ;
   for (i=0 ; i<mesh.Get_nof() ; i++)
// Take each facet 'i' in turn, but deal only with host facets
   { if (mesh.Get_super(i) == -1)
       { if (mesh.orient(i,&pro) == 1)  seefacet(i) ; } ;
   }
 }  // End of hidden
```

Listing 10.4

```
// Place these functions in file "display.cpp"
//------------------------//
  void facetfill(int face)      // Constant shading version
//------------------------//
 { vector2 v[maxpoly] ;
   int i,index,j,fsize ;
// Store projected vertices of facet in array 'v'
   j = mesh.Get_clipfac(face) ;
   fsize = mesh.Get_size(j) ;
   for (i=0 ; i<fsize ; i++)
   { index= mesh.Get_faclist(j,i) ;   v[i] = pro.Get_vertex(index) ; }
// Draw the facet in given colour then colour edge lines in black
   win.setcol(mesh.Get_material(face)) ; win.polyfill(fsize,v) ;
   win.setcol(0) ;   win.moveto(v[fsize-1]) ;
   for (i=0 ; i<fsize ; i++)  win.lineto(v[i]) ;
 }  // End of facetfill

//-----------------------//
  void seefacet(int face)       // Constant shading
//-----------------------//
// Colour host facet 'face' and all superficial facets
 { int supk, suplength, suplist[maxsuplist] ;
// colour in facet 'face', then colour in all facets superficial facets
   facetfill(face) ;
   suplength = mesh.Get_a_sup(face,suplist) ;
   while (suplength > 0) { supk = suplist[--suplength] ; facetfill(supk) ; }
 }  // End of seefacet
```

Example 10.1

Listing 10.3 holds the **hidden** function that deals with simple closed convex objects, and because it uses the cluster projection, **pro**, stored in **"ClusterC.cpp"**, it can be used for both orthographic and perspective projections. Listing 10.4 gives the necessary **seefacet** and **facetfill** functions that, together with **hidden**, must be added to **"display.cpp"**. We could draw the cube from example 7.2 in perspective and with the hidden surfaces suppressed. Again this is drawn by the **build_it** application of listing 7.6, stored in file **"seven6.cpp"** and linked with the same named files into our Borland C++ Project, exactly as before, only now the contents of **"display.cpp"** are different, and we get an image with the hidden surfaces removed rather than a wireframe as previously. By using the orthographic **project_it**, we will get an orthographic image. Remember this function can be used with any closed convex body, for example a convex body of rotation or an extruded convex polygon.

Example 10.2

Note how the hidden surface algorithm in listing 10.3 also works for data containing superficial facets which are not considered explicitly in **hidden**. Consider, for example, figure 10.1 of a die constructed by a 'shortened' version the application program consisting of **build_it** and **die** construction function of listing 10.5. Store this code as **"ten5.cpp"**, link it into our C++ Project, and run the program. Note the implied need to use the **cube** data from listing 7.5b.

Listing 10.5

```
// Application program to construct and draw a cubic die

#include "construc.h"

extern Mesh mesh ;
extern Cluster3d act ;

//-------------------------------------//
  void die(Matrix P,int col1, int col2)                   // Cubic die
//-------------------------------------//
 { Matrix A, B ;
   static int axis[6]={3,3,2,2,3,3} ;
   static float angl[6]={0.0,-0.5,0.5,-0.5,0.5,1.0} ;
   int face,i,index,j,n=16,nofsto ;
   float rad=0.15,theta=0.0,thetadiff=2*pi/n ;
   vector3 corner[16],vertex ;
   vector3 setup[21] =
        { 1,0,0,          1,-0.5,-0.5,  1,0.5,0.5,    1,-0.5,-0.5,
          1,0,0,          1,0.5,0.5,    1,-0.5,0.5,   1,-0.5,-0.5,
          1,0.5,-0.5,     1,0.5,0.5,    1,0.5,0.5,    1,0.5,-0.5,
          1,-0.5,-0.5,    1,-0.5,0.5,   1,0,0,        1,-0.5,-0.5,
          1,0.0,-0.5,     1,0.5,-0.5,   1,0.5,0.5,    1,0.0,0.5,
          1,-0.5,0.5    } ;
   int nov, facet[21] ;
// Place all 21 dots on face X=1
   nofsto=mesh.Get_nof() ;
// Rotate face X=1 by pi*angl[j] about axis[j] into j'th face
// Each dot will be a 'n-gon' of radius 'rad'
// Form the corners of the 'n-gon' on face X=1
   for (i=0 ; i<n ; i++)
   { corner[i].y=rad*cos(theta) ; corner[i].z=rad*sin(theta) ;
     corner[i].x=1.0 ; theta += thetadiff ;
   } ;
// First form the cube
   cube(P,col1) ;
// Then look at dot 'index' on each of the six faces
   index=-1 ;
   for (face=0 ; face<6 ; face++)
// Store matrix 'B' for rotating dots onto correct face
   { A.rotate(axis[face],angl[face]*pi) ; B = P * A ;
     for (i=0 ; i<=face ; i++)
     { index++ ;
       nov = act.Get_nov() ;
// Update facet data base with each new dot facet
       for (j=0 ; j<n ; j++)  facet[j] = nov + j ;
       mesh.add(n,&(facet[0]),col2,nofsto+face) ;
// Now store the vertices
       for (j=0 ; j<n ; j++)
       { vertex.x=1.0 ;
         vertex.y=corner[j].y+setup[index].y ;
         vertex.z=corner[j].z+setup[index].z ;
         act.add( B * vertex ) ;
       }
     }
   }
 }  // End of die

//--------------------//
 void build_it(void)
//--------------------//
 { Matrix P ;
// Scene of a cubic Die placed in its SETUP position
   P.unit() ;
   die(P,1,2) ;
 }  // End of build_it
```

Figure 10.1

Exercise 10.2

Write a construction function that places superficial flags or alphabetic characters on the side of a cube. Do the same for the octahedron and icosahedron.

The painter's algorithm (or the back-to-front method)

The call for pictures of convex solids is limited, so we now consider another simple algorithm, but which can be used with non-convex figures. With raster graphics devices, such as the VGA and XGA cards, in normal colour REPLACE mode (but not in XOR nor in other logical plotting modes), you will have noticed that when colouring a new area, all the colours previously placed on the pixels in that section of the window/viewport will be obliterated. This furnishes us with a very simple hidden surface algorithm; we draw the areas furthest from the eye first and the nearest last. However, exactly what is meant by furthest/nearest is not that straightforward! There are some situations (the next section, for example) where this phrase has a very simple meaning and we can create a specialized algorithm that is easy to implement; however you should see the end of this chapter for a more general painter's algorithm.

Drawing a special three-dimensional mathematical surface

We consider the construction of a restricted type of three-dimensional surface in which the y co-ordinate of each point on the surface is given by a single-valued function **f** of the x and z co-ordinates of that point. We will give two examples; the first is a simple trigonometric surface; the second is a three-dimensional version of the fractal map programmed in listing 1.6, which is more complex and will use many of the 'tricks' of that example.

The method may be used with orthographic or perspective projections. **f** will be included as a function in the application program listing 10.6. Since it is impossible to draw every point on the surface we have to approximate by considering a subset of these surface points. We choose those points with *x*/*z* co-ordinate on a *grid*, in other words, when orthographically viewed directly from above (thus ignoring the *y* values), the points form a square grid of edge size **totalgridsize**, centred on the origin. As in example 1.4, the grid is made up of 6×2^n by 6×2^n squares. There are thus $(6 \times 2^n + 1) \times (6 \times 2^n + 1)$ vertices (x_i, z_j) in the grid where, given that **step** = **totalgridsize/** (6×2^n):

$$x_i = -\textbf{totalgridsize/2} + i \times \textbf{step} \quad \text{where } 0 \le i \le 6 \times 2^n$$
$$z_j = -\textbf{totalgridsize/2} + j \times \textbf{step} \quad \text{where } 0 \le j \le 6 \times 2^n$$

The corresponding ACTUAL point on the surface is (x_i, y_{ij}, z_j), where the 'height' value $y_{ij} = \mathbf{f}(x_i, z_j)$. Every one of the surface points generated in this way is joined to its four immediate neighbours along the grid (that is, those with equal *x* or equal *z* values), unless it lies on the edge in which case it is joined to three, or in the case of corners to two neighbours. Note that the four surface points corresponding to such a set of four vertices may not be coplanar, so strictly we should *not* call the surface area bounded by these vertices a four-sided facet, instead we call it a *patch*. A patch may undulate and, therefore, the patch may be only partially visible from a given viewpoint. Relative to a given observer, we devise a very simple method to eliminate the hidden surfaces by working from the back of the surface to the front. To simplify the algorithm we assume that the eye is always in the positive quadrant – that is **eye.x** > 0 and **eye.z** > 0 – and that the eye is always looking at the origin (**direct** ≡ **–eye**). In the case of function **f** being asymmetrical, and we wish to view the scene from another quadrant, then we simply change the sign of *x* and/or *z* in the code of function **f**. We can then transform the vertices on the surface into OBSERVED co-ordinates before projecting them onto the window and viewport.

We draw the scene recursively; the overall grid square of size **totalgridsize** is made up of 6×2^n by 6×2^n patches. We can consider this to be made up of 36 squares each made of 2^n by 2^n patches, where the corners of each such square are (x_k, z_l), (x_k, z_{l+1}), (x_{k+1}, z_l) and (x_{k+1}, z_{l+1}), where

$$x_k = -\textbf{totalgridsize/2} + k \times 2^n \quad \text{where } 0 \le k \le 6$$
$$z_l = -\textbf{totalgridsize/2} + l \times 2^n \quad \text{where } 0 \le l \le 6$$

By letting *k* vary from 0 to five, and then independently letting *l* vary from 0 to 5, our choice of **eye** and **direct** means we that if we transform these squares into OBSERVED position then they will have been generated from back to front. Of course we still have to draw the 2^n by 2^n patches in each square. Each square of

2^n by 2^n patches can be divided into 4 squares of 2^{n-1} by 2^{n-1}, or into 16 squares of 2^{n-1} by 2^{n-1}, and so on until we have 2^n by 2^n squares each consisting of a single patch, which can be drawn as two triangles. Every time we recursively divide one of these squares into four, provided that we continue the division in such a way that the first of the sub-squares in ACTUAL position has smaller x and z co-ordinates than the last (and we can do this with our knowledge of the grid co-ordinates, and of **eye** and **direct**), then our choice of **eye** and **direct** means that in effect we have achieved back-to-front hidden surface removal for these squares when they are in OBSERVED position.

Listing 10.6

```
// Application program to draw a mathematical surface

#include "model.h"

const int elementsperpixel =  256 ;
const int elementsperblock = 2048 ;

extern Window win ;
extern Palette plt ;
extern Matrix Q ;

//-------------------------//
  float f(float x, float z)
//-------------------------//
// Required function 'y=4sin(sqrt(x*x+z*z))/sqrt(x*x+z*z)'
 { float t, ret ;
   t=sqrt(x*x+z*z) ;
   if (fabs(t) < epsilon) ret = 4.0 ; else ret = 4.0 * sin(t)/t ;
   return (ret) ;
 } // End of mathematical function 'f'

//-----------------------------------------------//
  void triangle(vector3 v1, vector3 v2, vector3 v3)
//-----------------------------------------------//
// Draw a triangle with corners 'v1','v2' and 'v3'
 { vector2 poly[maxpoly] ;
   poly[0].x=v1.x ; poly[0].y=v1.y ;  // implicit orthographic projection
   poly[1].x=v2.x ; poly[1].y=v2.y ;
   poly[2].x=v3.x ; poly[2].y=v3.y ;
   win.setcol(1) ; win.polyfill(3,poly) ; win.setcol(4) ;
   win.moveto(poly[0]) ; win.lineto(poly[1]) ;
   win.lineto(poly[2]) ; win.lineto(poly[0]) ;
 }  // End of triangle

//-----------------------------------------------------------//
  void patch(vector3 v1, vector3 v2, vector3 v3, vector3 v4)
//-----------------------------------------------------------//
 { triangle(v4,v2,v1) ; triangle(v1,v3,v4) ;
 }  // End of patch

//---------------------------------------------------------//
  void map_rec(float x, float z, float gridsize, int size)
//---------------------------------------------------------//
 { vector3 v0, v1, v2, v3, v4 ;
   if (size == elementsperpixel)
     { v1.x=x ;  v1.y=f(x,z) ;  v1.z=z ;  x+=gridsize ;
       v2.x=x ;  v2.y=f(x,z) ;  v2.z=z ;  z+=gridsize ;
       v4.x=x ;  v4.y=f(x,z) ;  v4.z=z ;  x-=gridsize ;
       v3.x=x ;  v3.y=f(x,z) ;  v3.z=z ;
       patch(Q*v1,Q*v2,Q*v3,Q*v4) ;
     }
```

```
else
   { gridsize=gridsize*0.5 ; size=size / 2 ;
     map_rec(x,z,gridsize,size) ;
     map_rec(x+gridsize,z,gridsize,size) ;
     map_rec(x,z+gridsize,gridsize,size) ;
     map_rec(x+gridsize,z+gridsize,gridsize,size) ;
   } ;
} // End of map_rec

//--------------------------//
  void recursive_draw(void)
//--------------------------//
// Construct and draw a mathematical function 'f'
{ int mapsize = 7 ;
  float halfmapsize = (float)(mapsize+1) / 2.0 ;
  float gridsize,totalgridsize,x,z ;
  int kx,kz,size ;
  size=elementsperblock ;
  cout << " Type in the side length of the full grid " ;
  cin >> totalgridsize ;  win.start() ;
  plt.rgblog(0,(float)0.9,0.9,0.3) ; win.erase(0) ;
  gridsize=totalgridsize/(float) (mapsize-1) ;
  for (kx=1 ; kx<mapsize ; kx++)
  { for (kz=1 ; kz<mapsize ; kz++)
    { x=-gridsize*(halfmapsize-kx) ; z=-gridsize*(halfmapsize-kz) ;
      map_rec(x,z,gridsize,size) ;
    }
  }
} // End of recursive_draw

//-------------------//
  void build_it(void)   { } ;     // Building is implicit while drawing
//-------------------//
```

Example 10.3

This method is programmed in listing 10.6. As an example of its use, figure 10.2 shows the function $y = 4\sin(t)/t$ where $t = \sqrt{(x^2 + y^2)}$. Note that the image will be drawn as it is being constructed, and therefore text data will be input after our **build_it** function is executed. This implies that our application program, stored as **"ten6.cpp"** must contain an empty **build_it**. All the necessary construction will be completed in **draw_it**, which we give in listing 10.7, and this should replace the present version of that function in file **"display.cpp"**. When the application is linked to our C++ Project then pictures like figure 10.2 may be drawn.

Listing 10.7

```
// Replace function draw_it in file "display.cpp" with the following:
void recursive_draw(void) ;
//-------------------//
  void draw_it(void)
//-------------------//
{ recursive_draw() ;
}  // End of draw_it
```

In fact our application is slightly more sophisticated than the method mentioned above. During the recursion we actually stop, not when we reach a single patch, but when we reach squares consisting of 2^m by 2^m patches, and the four extreme corners of this we treat as a patch. Changing the value of *m* means that we can draw exactly the same scene, but at different levels of approximation; it is as if we were using different resolutions of the underlying rectangular grid. When we are using mathematical functions we gain nothing from this technique, but in listing 10.8, when we come to draw three-dimensional maps using fractals it is essential, as we saw in example 1.4.

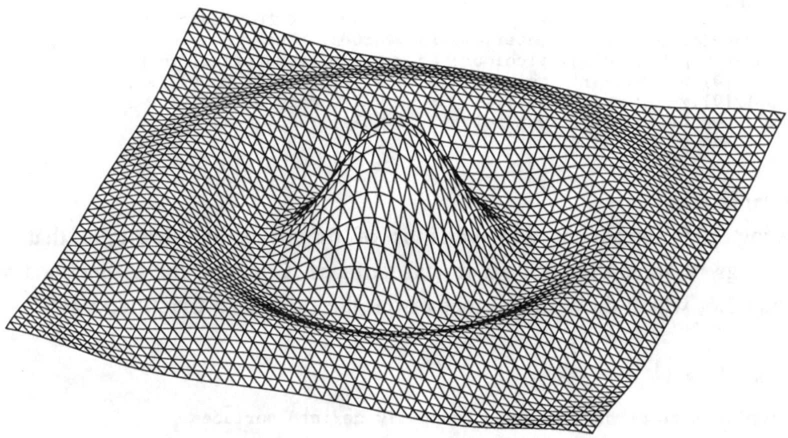

Figure 10.2

Exercise 10.3

Change the function **f** used by this program. For example, use **f** = 4sin(t) where $t = \sqrt{(x^2 + y^2)}$.

Exercise 10.4

Use the knowledge of the orientation of both the original grid rectangle and of the implied two triangles for each patch to extend the above program so that it draws the top side of the surface in a different colour to the underside.

Example 10.4

Listing 10.8 contains a new extended version of function **triangle** which now draws the triangles that make up each patch, but uses constant colour shading (see chapter 11); a new version of **"display.cpp"** is needed by our C++ Project, which must contain the extra code for the constant colour shading approach that is developed in the next chapter.

Listing 10.8

```
// Replace function triangle in listing 10.6
// Use constant colour shading version of "display.cpp" from chapter 11.

#include "display.h"

//--------------------------------------------------//
  void triangle(vector3 v1, vector3 v2, vector3 v3)
//--------------------------------------------------//
 { float dummy,red,green,blue ;
   vector3 d1,d2,midpt,normvec ;
   vector2 poly[maxpoly] ;
   int index, material = 0 ;
   midpt = (1.0/3.0) * ( v1 + v2 + v3) ;
   d1 = v2 - v1 ;  d2 = v3 - v2 ;   normvec = vectorproduct(d1,d2) ;
   cshade(midpt,normvec,material,&red,&green,&blue) ;
   index = plt.findlogicalcolour(red,green,blue,material) ;
   poly[0].x = v1.x ;   poly[1].x = v2.x ;   poly[2].x = v3.x ;
   poly[0].y = v1.y ;   poly[1].y = v2.y ;   poly[2].y = v3.y ;
   win.setcol(index) ;  win.polyfill(3,poly) ;
 }  // End of triangle
```

Example 10.5

Listing 10.9 introduces new versions of **mapdraw** and **triangle**, that give drawings of three-dimensional fractal surfaces. Compare these functions with listing 1.6, which drew fractal maps from the same data file **"map.dat"**.

Listing 10.9

```
// Application program to draw fractally defined surfaces

#include "model.h"

const int elementsperpixel =  256 ;
const int elementsperblock = 2048 ;

typedef float wtype[10] ;
typedef float initialgrid[12][12] ;

float factor,scaleup ;

extern Matrix Q ;   extern Window win ;  extern Palette plt ;
//---------------------------------------------------------------//
  void triangle(vector3 v1, vector3 v2, vector3 v3, int count)
//---------------------------------------------------------------//
// Draw a triangle with corners 'v1','v2' and 'v3'
 { polygon poly ;
   poly[0].x = v1.x ;   poly[1].x = v2.x ;   poly[2].x = v3.x ;
   poly[0].y = v1.y ;   poly[1].y = v2.y ;   poly[2].y = v3.y ;
   if (count) // more than one vertex above sea-level
          // Draw whole facet in terrain colour
     { win.setcol(8) ; win.polyfill(3,poly) ;
       win.setcol(6) ; win.moveto(poly[2]) ;
       win.lineto(poly[0]) ; win.lineto(poly[1]) ; win.lineto(poly[2]) ;
     }
// Else all vertices below sea-level
   else { win.setcol(1) ;  win.polyfill(3,poly) ; } ;
 }  // End of triangle
//----------------------------------------------------------------------------//
  void patch(vector3 v1, vector3 v2, vector3 v3, vector3 v4, int count1,
                                                                int count2)
//----------------------------------------------------------------------------//
 { triangle(v4,v2,v1,count1) ; triangle(v1,v3,v4,count2) ;
 }  // End of patch
```

```
//---------------------------------------------------//
  float pseudo_random(int jx, int jy, int kx, int ky)
//---------------------------------------------------//
// Generation of a pseudo random-number between -0.5 and +0.5
// Number uniquely defined by two pixel vectors (jx,jy) and (kx,ky)
 { const int modval=7901 ;
   int s1=997, s2=1409, s3=1597, s4=1999 ;
   float ret ;
   long int t ;
   t= ((long int) (jx+s1)*(jy+s2)) % modval ;
   t= (t*(kx+s3)) % modval ;
   t= (t*(ky+s4)) % modval ;
   ret= (float)t/(float)modval-0.5 ;  return ( ret ) ;
 }  // End of pseudo_random

//--------------------------------------------------------------------------//
  void map_rec(float x, float z, float gridsize, int size, int kx, int kz,
                          float val1, float val3, float val7, float val9)
//--------------------------------------------------------------------------//
 { float y, r,r2,scale,scaledown=0.20*scaleup ;
   vector3 v1,v2,v3,v4 ;
   wtype w ;
   int count1,count2 ; // count vertices of each triangle above sea-level
   if (size == elementsperpixel)
     { count1=0 ; count2=0 ;
       if (val1 < 0.0) y = val1*scaledown ;
       else { y = val1*scaleup ; count1++ ; count2++ ; } ;
       v1.x=x ;  v1.y=y ;  v1.z= z ;  x+=gridsize ;
       if (val3 < 0.0)  y = val3*scaledown ;
       else { y = val3*scaleup ; count1++ ; } ;
       v2.x=x ;  v2.y=y ;  v2.z= z ;  z+=gridsize ;
       if (val9 < 0.0)  y = val9*scaledown ;
       else { y = val9*scaleup ; count1++ ; count2++ ; } ;
       v4.x=x ;  v4.y=y ;  v4.z= z ;  x-=gridsize ;
       if (val7 < 0.0)  y = val7*scaledown ;
       else { y = val7*scaleup ; count2++ ; } ;
       v3.x=x ;  v3.y=y ;  v3.z= z ;
       patch(Q*v1,Q*v2,Q*v3,Q*v4,count1,count2) ;
     }
   else
     { w[1]=val1 ; w[3]=val3 ; w[7]=val7 ; w[9]=val9 ;
// Random perturbation is made proportional to the size of the grid
// Constant of proportionality has been input
       scale=factor*size/elementsperblock ;
// Imagine 9 points in a 3 by 3 square grid.
// We are given the corner values w[1], w[3], w[7] and w[9].
// Find edge mid-points w[2], w[4], w[6] and w[8],
// average appropriate corner values and add random perturbation
       r=pseudo_random(kx,kz,kx+size,kz) ;
       w[2]=(w[1]+w[3])*0.5+r*scale ;
       r=pseudo_random(kx,kz,kx,kz+size) ;
       w[4]=(w[1]+w[7])*0.5+r*scale ;
       r=pseudo_random(kx+size,kz,kx+size,kz+size) ;
       w[6]=(w[3]+w[9])*0.5+r*scale ;
       r=pseudo_random(kx,kz+size,kx+size,kz+size) ;
       w[8]=(w[7]+w[9])*0.5+r*scale ;
// Find centre-point w[5], average four corners and add random perturbation
       r=pseudo_random(kx,kz,kx+size,kz+size) ;
       r2=pseudo_random(kx+size,kz,kx,kz+size) ;
       r=(r+r2)*0.5 ;
       w[5]=(w[1]+w[3]+w[7]+w[9])*0.25+r*scale ;
       gridsize=gridsize*0.5 ; size=size / 2 ;
       map_rec(x,z,gridsize,size,kx,kz,w[1],w[2],w[4],w[5]) ;
       map_rec(x+gridsize,z,gridsize,size,kx+size,kz,w[2],w[3],w[5],w[6]) ;
       map_rec(x,z+gridsize,gridsize,size,kx,kz+size,w[4],w[5],w[7],w[8]) ;
       map_rec(x+gridsize,z+gridsize,gridsize,size,kx+size,kz+size,w[5],
                                                      w[6],w[8],w[9]) ;
     } ;
 }  // End of map_rec
```

```
//---------------------------//
  void recursive_draw(void)
//---------------------------//
// Construct and draw a fractal island
 { int mapsize = 7 ;
   float halfmapsize = (float)(mapsize+1) / 2.0 ;
   float gridsize,totalgridsize,x,z ;
   int kx,kz,size ;
   initialgrid v ;
   ifstream indata ;
   size=elementsperblock ;
   cout << " \n Type the side length of the full grid " ;
   cin >> totalgridsize ;
// Read in 'mapsize by mapsize' data points that will define map
   indata.open("map.dat") ;
   for (kx=1 ; kx <=mapsize ; kx++)
     for (kz=1 ; kz<=mapsize ; kz++) indata >> v[kx][kz] ;
   indata.close() ;
   cout << "\n Type random perturbation scaling and scale up factor " ;
   cin >> factor >> scaleup ;
// (3,2) is a good example ;  (2,5) is another
   win.start() ;
   plt.rgblog(0,(float)0.0,0.4,0.6) ;
   win.erase(0) ;
   gridsize=totalgridsize/(float) (mapsize-1) ;
   for (kx=1 ; kx<mapsize ; kx++)
   { for (kz=1 ; kz<mapsize ; kz++)
     { x=-gridsize*(halfmapsize-kx) ; z=-gridsize*(halfmapsize-kz) ;
       map_rec(x,z,gridsize,size,kx*size,kz*size,v[kx][kz],v[kx+1][kz],
                                       v[kx][kz+1],v[kx+1][kz+1]) ;
     }
   }
 }  // End of recursive_draw

//--------------------//
  void build_it(void) { } ;      // building is implicit while drawing
//--------------------//
```

Listing 10.10

```
// Replace function triangle in listing 10.9

// Use constant colour shading version of "display.cpp" from chapter 11.

#include "display.h"

//----------------------------------------------------------------------//
  void triangle(vector3 v1, vector3 v2, vector3 v3, int count)
//----------------------------------------------------------------------//
// Draw a triangle with corners 'v1','v2' and 'v3'
 { float red,green,blue ;
   vector3 d1,d2,midpt,normvec ;
   vector2 poly[maxpoly] ;
   int index, col ;
   midpt = (1.0/3.0) * ( (v1 + v2) + v3) ;
   d1 = v2 - v1 ;  d2 = v3 - v2 ;
   normvec = vectorproduct(d1,d2) ;
// Find apparent colour of facet
   if (count) col = 1 ;    // terrain
   else       col = 2 ;    // sea
   cshade(midpt,normvec,col,&red,&green,&blue) ;
   index = plt.findlogicalcolour(red,green,blue,col) ;
// Display the facet
   win.setcol(index) ;
   poly[0].x = v1.x ;  poly[1].x = v2.x ;  poly[2].x = v3.x ;
   poly[0].y = v1.y ;  poly[1].y = v2.y ;  poly[2].y = v3.y ;
   win.polyfill(3,poly) ;
 }  // End of triangle
```

Example 10.6
Listing 10.10 introduces a version of **triangle** to replace that from the previous listing. The complete program will now draw a constant shaded picture of the three-dimensional fractal surface described in example 10.5 (see Plate IIIb).

Other methods

There are many other simple methods, variations on a theme and even hybrid algorithms, that can prove efficient for suppressing hidden surfaces in three-dimensional scenes with special properties; see project 10.1.

Probably the simplest conceptual approach, but one which is rather expensive on processing power and memory, is the so-called *Z-buffer* algorithm. This involves a rectangular array representing the totality of pixels on the screen. We imagine rays of light entering the eye through each of the pixels on the screen. We consider these rays as axes of a rectangular (orthographic) or pyramidal (perspective) prism leading from the eye to the pixel, and off to minus infinity. These rays naturally pass through objects in our scene and we can note the co-ordinates of these points of intersection. The z value of the intersection of the axis of this prism with each object is calculated in turn and compared with the buffer value. The array, the Z-buffer, will hold the 'z co-ordinate' (initially minus infinity) of the nearest point of intersection. So we build up a picture by adding new objects, finding where the rays cut the object, and changing the array values (and the pixel colour on the screen) whenever the latest point of intersection is nearer to the eye than the corresponding value stored in the array, giving a simple hidden surface algorithm for each pixel. This technique is very useful if we wish to shade-in areas in subtly differing tones of a given colour (chapter 12).

Another approach, the *scan line algorithms*, considers one scan line of a raster screen at a time, and uses information about polygonal facets in the scene to colour these scan lines correctly, giving a correct hidden surface picture.

Yet another way is to *seed* each facet with a single point in the facet: the so-called *depth-sort algorithm*. When transformed into OBSERVED position, the seed points are put into an order of increasing distance from the eye, and this order is used by the painter's algorithm. This is not a very satisfactory method because it will often give incorrect displays of scenes which contain a wide variety of facet sizes.

By now you are aware that there are many different types of hidden surface algorithm (Foley, van Dam et. al, 1990). Some have enormous storage overheads and need powerful computers. To conclude this chapter we give a general type of algorithm that is more suitable for use with micro-computers, but which still works on the painter's algorithm mentioned earlier.

We assume that a three-dimensional scene is set up in the manner described in chapter 7, and that the **hidden** surface algorithm is to be initiated in the **draw_it** function which is called from the **draw_a_picture** function (listing 7.4b). We will assume that the perspective projection (listing 8.6) is being used: as an exercise, equivalent functions can be written for the orthographic projection. The objects do not need to be convex, but each must be closed and its surface must be composed of *convex* facets which are stored in our database in anti-clockwise orientation. In this way it is impossible to see the underside of any facet; that is, when projected onto the view plane we only see facets which maintain their anti-clockwise orientation. Strictly speaking, this means that we cannot draw single planar objects. If such objects are required for a particular scene then we avoid the problem by storing each facet of a planar object twice – once clockwise and once anti-clockwise – so that whatever the position of the eye, on perspective or orthographic projection we will see one and only one occurrence of the facet. This restriction was imposed to speed up the hidden surface algorithm.

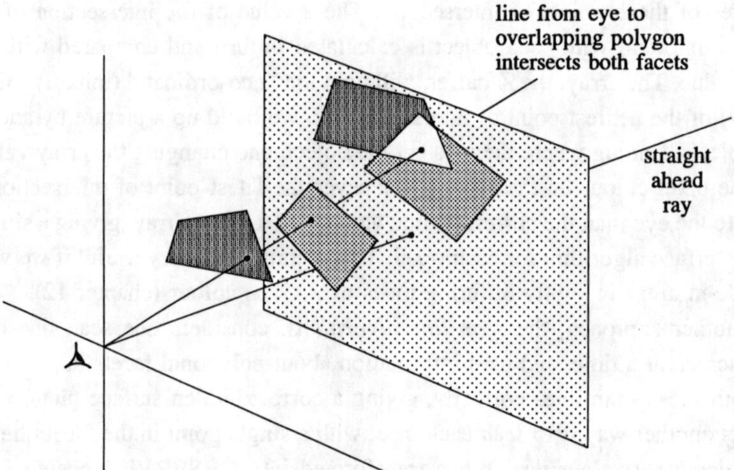

Figure 10.3

In order to produce a hidden surface picture of a scene stored in terms of right-handed OBSERVED co-ordinates, each facet in the scene must be compared with every other facet (superficial facets excepted) in order to discover whether their projections overlap on the view plane. If this occurs, then one of the facets obscures all or part of the other from view (see figure 10.3).

Because of the above restrictions we need only compare the visible facets – that is, those which when projected keep their anti-clockwise orientation. If they do overlap we then need to find which facet lies in front and which behind. Once this information is compiled we can work from the back of the scene to the front to get a correct hidden surface picture. We do have other limitations: we assume that it is impossible for a facet to be simultaneously in front of and behind another facet; that is, facets do not intersect one another other than at their edges. Furthermore, the facets must be partially ordered; that is, we cannot have the situation where facet **A** is in front of (>) facet **B** > facet **C** > facet **A** etc., such as that shown in figure 10.4.

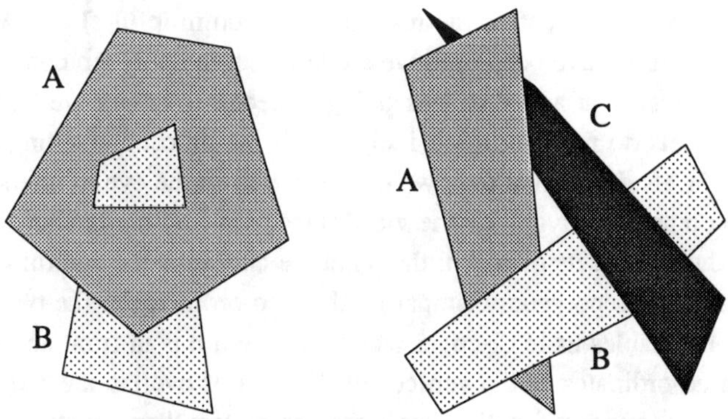

Figure 10.4

Exercise 10.5
The program can be made completely general if you write a function which pre-processes the data and divides up each problem facet into new subfacets that do not violate restrictions of the above type.

The algorithm for discovering whether or not two facets (**m** and **n**) from our database do overlap when projected onto the view plane is given in function **overlap** in listing 10.9, which is added to **"display.cpp"**. It is a variation of the two-dimensional **overlap** function given in listing 5.8. The method finds the intersection (if any) of two projected facets and identifies the facet nearer the eye (**front**) and that further away (**back**). This information for all comparisons of pairs of facets in the scene enables us to set up a network as described in chapter 3. The complete network is constructed in function **network** which uses **overlap** to discover if facet **m** is in front of facet **n**, in which case an edge is added to the network leading from node **n** to node **m**. We introduce a new **hidden** function which executes a topological sort on this network to output the facets in back-to-front order, calling **seefacet** to draw each, along with any associated superficial facets. We use the same **draw_it** function as given in listing 10.1 to initiate the hidden surface algorithm. Naturally, all these new functions must be added to **"display.cpp"** to make them available for the function **draw_a_picture** and **draw_it**; previous versions of any function must be deleted or commented out.

The **overlap** function uses the inside/outside technique of chapter 5. We place the *x* and *y* co-ordinates of the projected vertices of facet **m** in **vector2** array **ip[0][0..size[m]–1]**. We then take one projected line from facet **n** and cut off all parts of the facet **m** that lie on the negative side of the line: the resulting intermediate polygon is placed in arrays **ip[1][0..numv–1]**, where **numv** is the number of vertices in this intersection. We then take the next line and compare it with these values and store the resulting polygon in **ip[0][..]** etc. After all the lines from facet **m** have been used we are left with the polygon common to both projected facets. If at any time this polygon becomes empty we know that the projected facets do not overlap and so we exit the procedure setting **front** = 0.

If the facets do overlap then we take a line from the eye to intersect a point inside the common polygon on the view plane, and find the intersections of this line with the two facets **m** and **n**: the point we choose is the centroid of the first three points on the polygon. Comparing the *z* co-ordinates of the two respective intersections enables us to discover which of **m** and **n** is in front and which is at back. The co-ordinates of the vertices of the area of overlap are returned in the array **v2d**. The **overlap** function has more parameters than are strictly needed at this stage, allowing for use with different co-ordinate systems. These will be needed by shadow, transparency and reflection functions in chapter 12.

The next step is to work out how to use this information to produce the network needed for the final picture. This is achieved by **network** in listing 10.11. The method is to compare each visible facet with every other (using **overlap**) and to produce a network of information about the relative positions of the facets (in front or behind). For each visible and non-superficial facet (**i** say), the idea is to set up a linked list **list[i]** containing the indices of all facets that lie in front of it, and the array **nob[i]** will contain the number of facets that facet **i** obscures. Array **nob** is also used initially to denote if the facet is clockwise and hence invisible (**nob[i]** = –1), or anti-clockwise and visible (**nob[i]** = 0). No invisible facet needs to be included in any comparison. The function **network** returns the number of visible facets **numbervisible**, together with all of the network edge information. Once again, the co-ordinate arrays are passed as parameters to enable the function to be used with different co-ordinate systems. We use this network in function **hidden** to produce images. The function creates a stack onto which the index of any facet that does not obscure any other (that is, whose **nob** value is zero) is **push**ed. Then one at a time these facets are

popped off the stack and drawn on the window followed by all the facets that are superficial to it (using the **firstsup** array). Once the facet is drawn, we traverse the network linked list for that facet (referred to by **list**) and decrement the **nob** counts for each facet in the list. If the **nob** count for any facet becomes zero then the index of the facet is **push**ed onto the stack (function **unstack**). Eventually the stack is emptied and we have the correct partial order to give the true back-to-front hidden surface view. Each facet is drawn in the window using a function **seefacet**, which also displays all associated superficial facets. At this stage it will simply use the polygon drawing function via a call to **facetfill** (listing 10.4); later it will become more complex.

The linked lists (one for each facet) and the stack are implemented using C++ pointers, as described in chapter 3, with the declarations and methods of class **Stack**, which are available to us because files **"stack.h"** and **"stack.cpp"** are **#include**d in **"model.h"** and **"model.cpp"** respectively. Because of our restriction that facets cannot simultaneously be in front of and behind one another, the stack can only become empty when all the facets have been displayed.

Listing 10.11

```
// Place these functions in file "display.cpp"

//--------------------------------------------------//
  vector3 normal(int face, float *k, Cluster3d *clst)
//--------------------------------------------------//
// To find the plane 'X*n.x+Y*n.y+Z*n.z=k' for facet 'face'
 { int index0,index1,index2 ;
   vector3 v0, v1, v2, d1,d2, n ;
// 'index0', 'index1' and 'index2' are first three vertices on 'face'
   index0 = mesh.Get_faclist(face,0) ;
   index1 = mesh.Get_faclist(face,1) ;
   index2 = mesh.Get_faclist(face,2) ;
// 'd1' and 'd2' are 3-D directions of the first two lines in 'face'
   v0 = clst->Get_vertex(index0) ;
   v1 = clst->Get_vertex(index1) ;
   v2 = clst->Get_vertex(index2) ;
   d1 = v1 - v0 ;  d2 = v2 - v1 ;
// Facet lies in plane  ' n.v = k '
   n = vectorproduct(d1,d2) ;
   *k= dot3(n,v0) ;
   return ( n ) ;
 }  // End of normal

//------------------------------------------------------------------//
  void overlap(int m1,int n1,int *front,int *back,int *numv,vector2 \
             *cpoly,Cluster2d *v2d,Cluster3d *v3d,float pd,int orien)
//------------------------------------------------------------------//
// Finds area of intersection between the window projections of the clipped
// facets 'm1' and 'n1'. The 3-D co-ordinate system is given by array 'v3d',
// while projected co-ordinates are stored in 'v2d'. The 'numv' vertices
// of the intersection area are returned in array 'cpoly'
// The distance of plane of projection from the origin is 'pd'
 { float musto[2] ;
   int i,j,l,m,n,index1,index2,l1,l2,sizem,sizen ;
   vector2 end1,end2,ip[2][maxpoly],v1,v2 ;
   float k,ca,cb,cc,delta,mu,fv1,absfv1,fv2,absfv2 ;
   vector3 mid,norm,vi ;
```

```
// 'm' and 'n' are the indices of the facets representing 'm1' and 'n1'
// If either plane is degenerate return.
   m=mesh.Get_clipfac(m1) ; n=mesh.Get_clipfac(n1) ;
   if ((m==-1) || (n==-1)) { *front = -1 ; return ; }
// Copy facet 'm' to first storage arrays
   l1=0 ; sizem=mesh.Get_size(m) ;
   for (i=0 ; i<sizem ; i++)
   { ip[l1][i]=v2d->Get_vertex(mesh.Get_faclist(m,i)) ; }
// The first storage array 'ip[l1][1..sizem]' now contains vertices of the
// intermediate polygon. Slice intermediate polygon with each edge of facet
// 'n'. Slicing edge has endpoints 'end1' and 'end2' with analytic function
//              ' ca.y + cb.x + cc = 0 ' .
   sizen=mesh.Get_size(n);
   end1=v2d->Get_vertex(mesh.Get_faclist(n,sizen-1)) ;
   for (i=0 ; i<sizen ; i++)
   { end2=v2d->Get_vertex(mesh.Get_faclist(n,i)) ;
     ca=end2.x-end1.x ; cb=end1.y-end2.y ;
     cc=-ca*end1.y-cb*end1.x ;
// Slice the intermediate polygon edge by edge : 'v1' to 'v2'. 'k1' and 'k2'
// indicate whether the first and second points respectively lie on the
// slicing edge, on its positive side or on its negative side.
     v1=ip[l1][sizem-1] ; fv1=ca*v1.y+cb*v1.x+cc ;
     absfv1=fabs(fv1) ;
     index1=sign(fv1)*orien ;
// Initialise second storage array.
     *numv=0 ; l2=1-l1 ;
     for (j=0 ; j<sizem ; j++)
     { v2=ip[l1][j] ; fv2=ca*v2.y+cb*v2.x+cc ;
       absfv2=fabs(fv2) ;
       index2=sign(fv2)*orien ;
// If 'v1' is not on negative side of slicing edge then include it
// in new storage array 'ip[l2][...]'
       if (index1 >= 0)
         { ip[l2][*numv]=v1 ; (*numv)++ ; } ;
// If 'v1' and 'v2' lie on opposite sides of slicing edge then
// include the intersection with the edge
       if ((index1 != 0) && (index1 != index2) && (index2 != 0))
         { delta=absfv1+absfv2 ;
           ip[l2][*numv].x=(absfv2*v1.x+absfv1*v2.x)/delta ;
           ip[l2][*numv].y=(absfv2*v1.y+absfv1*v2.y)/delta ;
           (*numv)++ ;
         } ;
// Second point on current edge becomes first point on next edge
       fv1=fv2 ; v1=v2 ;
       index1=index2 ; absfv1=absfv2 ;
     }
// If second array holds fewer than 3 vertices then no overlap exists
     if (*numv < 3)  { *front=-1 ; return ;  } ;
// Feasible polygon now becomes that stored in second storage array
// Refer 'l1' to this polygon and slice with next edge of facet 'n'
     sizem=*numv ; l1=l2 ; end1=end2 ;
   }
// Reach here if non-empty overlap found. Find point within area of overlap
   mid.x=(ip[l1][0].x+ip[l1][1].x+ip[l1][2].x)/3.0 ;
   mid.y=(ip[l1][0].y+ip[l1][1].y+ip[l1][2].y)/3.0 ;
// Find corresponding points on facets in 3-D
   mid.z=-pd ; l=m1 ;
   for (i=0 ; i<2 ; i++)
   { norm = normal(l,&k,v3d) ;
     ilpl(zero,mid,norm,k,&vi,&mu) ;
     musto[i]=mu ; l=n1 ;
   }
// Determine which lies in 'front'
   if(musto[0]>musto[1]) { *front=n1;*back=m1;}
   else
      { *front=m1 ; *back=n1 ; }
// Copy area of overlap to arrays for exit
   for (i=0 ; i<*numv ; i++)  cpoly[i]=ip[l1][i] ;
 } // End of overlap
```

```
//--------------------------------------------------------------------//
  int network(int *nob,Stack *list,Cluster2d *p,Cluster3d *v,int orien)
//--------------------------------------------------------------------//
// Constructs network of information on hidden surface ordering
 { int back, front, i, j, n, numvis=0 ;
   vector2 w[maxpoly] ;
   stackinfo st ;
// Initialise number of visible facets
// Check orientation of each facet, incrementing 'numvis' by one for
// each visible one (using 'orien').
   for (i=0 ; i<mesh.Get_nof() ; i++)
   { if (mesh.orient(i,p) == orien)
       { nob[i]=0 ;
         if (mesh.Get_super(i)==-1) numvis++ ;
       }
     else nob[i]=-1 ;
   }
// Compare each pair of visible non-superficial facets
   for (i=0 ; i<mesh.Get_nof()-1 ; i++)
   { if ((nob[i]  !=  -1) && (mesh.Get_super(i)==-1) )
       { for (j=i+1 ; j<mesh.Get_nof() ; j++)
         { if ((nob[j]  !=  -1) && (mesh.Get_super(j)==-1) )
              { overlap(i,j,&front,&back,&n,&(w[0]),p,v,ppd,orien) ;
// If overlap exists then 'front' obscures 'back'
                if (front  !=  -1)
                  { (nob[front])++ ; st.i=front ; list[back].push(st) ; } ;
              } ;
         }
       } ;
   }
   return ( numvis ) ;
 }  // End of network

//------------------------------------------------------------//
  void unstack(int face, int *nob, Stack *list, Stack *netstack)
//------------------------------------------------------------//
// Adjusts network structure after 'face' has been drawn
 { stackinfo nf ;
   while ( ! list[face].empty() )
   { nf=list[face].pop() ;      (nob[nf.i])-- ;
     if (nob[nf.i] == 0)  netstack->push(nf) ;
   }
 }  // End of unstack

//-----------------//
  void hidden(void)     // Replacement version for hidden surface removal
//-----------------//
// Executes topological sort on hidden surface network
 { Stack list[maxf], networkstack ;
   stackinfo st ;
   int i,numbervisible,nob[maxf] ;
   numbervisible = network(&(nob[0]),&(list[0]),&pro,&obs,1) ;
// Initialise STACK and PUSH on all back facets
   for (i=0 ; i<mesh.Get_nof() ; i++)
   { if ((nob[i]==0) && (mesh.Get_super(i)==-1))
       { st.i = i ;  networkstack.push(st) ; } ;
   }
// pop 'numbervisible' facets off stack in turn.
// Draw each and adjust data structure
   for (i=0 ; i<numbervisible ; i++)
   { if (networkstack.empty()) return ;
     st=networkstack.pop() ;
     seefacet(st.i) ;
// Un-comment following line when using 'hidden' to draw mirror reflections
//      reflekt(st.i) ;
     unstack(st.i,nob,list,&networkstack) ;
   }
 }  // End of hidden
```

Example 10.7

We can now draw a hidden surface, perspective view of any object that we can store in our polygonal mesh database. Note we must now use the general-purpose **draw_it** function of listing 10.1, and not the version introduced for the mathematical surface; although now we use the **hidden** of listing 10.9 in file **"display.cpp"**, rather than one given earlier in this chapter. Placing the data for a hollow cube and a chesspiece in the database, we can draw figure 10.5 with this function, which was impossible with the function of listing 10.3 which only drew individual convex objects.

Exercise 10.6

Construct hidden surface views of scenes composed of cubes, tetrahedra, pyramids, octahedra and icosahedra. See Coxeter (1973) for the information needed to write construction functions for an octahedron, icosahedron, rhombic dodecahedron etc.

Figure 10.5

The hidden surface removal algorithm is computationally very intensive; on lower powered computers you will have to wait some time for complex pictures to appear; so BE PATIENT. It is best to start experimenting with simple scenes.

Project 10.1

Consider a scene composed up of faceted objects, where each facet is oriented anti-clockwise when viewed from outside the object that contains it. Provided that the scene is topologically well-behaved (situations such as facet A over B over C over A are not allowed), then construct a network of ALL the facets in the scene (and not just those anti-clockwise from a given observation point). In this network, nodes representing any two facets A and B are connected by an edge, A to B, if and only if there is some observation point from which both facets appear anti-clockwise, and A is behind B. If one such point is found, then it is impossible to find another observation point that inverts the connection (Tomlinson, 1982). Such a network can be topologically ordered, and drawing only those facets that are anti-clockwise from a given observation point in this order furnishes a hidden surface algorithm, always provided that objects do not move relative to one another after the network has been constructed. Extend our hidden surface algorithm to incorporate this idea.

Project 10.2

Write a function that removes hidden lines from wireframe pictures (see figure 8.10). You can find such an algorithm in Angell, *High-resolution Computer Graphics using C*, 1990. Preview your pictures on a VGA screen, and then use the Hewlett Packard driver given in the Appendix to draw pictures on a laser printer. All the line figures of three-dimensional models in this book were produced in this way.

Figures such as the teapot in figure 9.10 and Plate I can be drawn and so we are now in a position to consider methods for making our three-dimensional scenes more realistic. We now introduce ideas such as shading, shadows, reflections etc. Note, however, that all of these ideas are introduced in the context of our overall strategy for scene construction. You will see that the introduction of shadows etc. into scenes that have already been defined and drawn will not require a major rewrite of the previous programs, so that the generation of shadows etc. will be initiated by simple extensions to **draw_it** and perhaps extended alternative **facetfill** functions placed in **"display.cpp"**. With the exception of a few database entries, most other functions (**build_it, network** etc.) will remain unchanged; and the method of linking the display of complex models ultimately to the primitive functions of chapters 1 and 2 is still via the **draw_a_picture** call to **draw_it**.

11 Shading

In chapter 10 we introduced the function **facetfill** to produce the window representation of a facet. Up to now this function has consisted of a simple area-fill using a logical colour prescribed in the data construction functions. We can do much more than this! The realism of the images that we produce is greatly enhanced by the use of *shading*. We take advantage of the colour display of the VGA and XGA cards to model the different appearances of surfaces depending on the light striking them. Plates I, IV, and V show pictures produced using the shading techniques introduced in this chapter.

Vision is a perception of light reflected onto the retinas of our eyes. Different materials reflect light in different ways, enabling us to distinguish between them, but all that we actually *see* is light. The purpose of a *shading model* is to calculate what light is reflected to the eye from each visible point in a scene, and then to use this information, by selecting a suitable form of display for the corresponding pixel, to create realistic images of the scene. Thus there are two distinct problems to consider. Firstly, a mathematical model must be developed to provide the information needed about the light reflected from points in a scene, and secondly, this information must be interpreted for application to new facet display functions. To use any of the functions in this chapter, you must place them in file **"display.cpp"**, so that when this file is linked into our C++ Project, they are available when needed. You should run our application programs from chapter 9 with these new versions of **"display.cpp"** to experiment with the various forms of shading we introduce in this chapter.

(Note that a shading model is *not* a hidden surface algorithm. Some other method must still be employed to determine which are the visible points of a scene (for example listing 10.11). Of course, we do not need to consider every visible point individually – there are an infinite number – we simply deal with the finite number of pixels on the graphics viewport. The problem can also be considerably simplified by assuming that the intensity of light reflected from each point on a given facet is the same, but more of this later.)

We first turn our attention to a mathematical model for reflected light. This problem is somewhat different from all those we have considered in previous chapters. There we dealt with purely geometrical concepts: points, lines, planes etc. But light is not a static geometrical object, it is energy. We can, nevertheless, develop a geometrical model for optical phenomena.

We assume that light consists of an infinite number of closely packed *rays* or *beams* which we may represent as vectors. There are two models which may be used for a light source (see figure 11.1). The *point source* model assumes that all rays emanate from a single point and may take any direction from this point. This idea corresponds to the properties of single light bulb, or, on a larger scale, the sun. Paradoxically, the sun may also be considered to fall into the second category – *parallel beam illumination* – which models the illumination produced by a point light source 'infinitely' far from the object being illuminated or, alternatively, by a distributed light source. This model assumes that all rays have a common direction, as with fluorescent lamps.

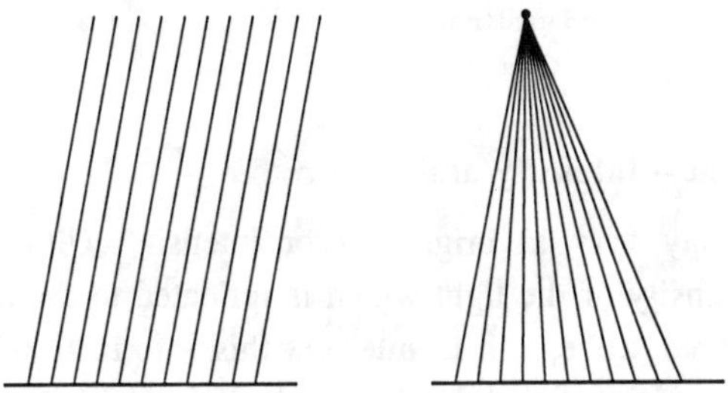

Figure 11.1

Either a parallel beam or a point light source may be represented by a single vector specified in relation to the OBSERVER co-ordinate system. (We shall work with the OBSERVER system throughout this chapter.) In the parallel beam case the vector is treated as a direction vector, whereas the point source case treats it as a point vector from which the direction can be calculated. The position of a point source is specified by a vector $\boldsymbol{s}$, and in both cases the direction of the light illuminating a point $\boldsymbol{p}$ on the surface is called vector $-\boldsymbol{l}$. (Note *minus*! We adopt this notation because in most cases we use the direction vector pointing out of the surface in the opposite direction: that is, vector $\boldsymbol{l}$.) In order to calculate the light reflected from a point $\boldsymbol{p}$ on a surface we need to know the normal to the surface at $\boldsymbol{p}$, which we call $\boldsymbol{n}$, together with a direction vector from point $\boldsymbol{p}$ on the surface towards the light source. For the parallel beam model finding this direction is easy – it is the vector $\boldsymbol{l}$ for every point $\boldsymbol{p}$. For the point source model the required vector is $\boldsymbol{s} - \boldsymbol{p}$, which, for consistency, we shall also call $\boldsymbol{l}$. For calculations involving specular reflection (see later) we also need to know the **eye** position, which, of course, we have placed at the origin of the OBSERVER co-ordinate system.

In our programs we assume that a point source of light is used. The ACTUAL position of the point source is input in function **insource** (listing 11.1) as the co-ordinate triple, the **vector3** point **v**, with respect to the ABSOLUTE system. This is then transformed into the OBSERVED position of the light source, **vector3** point **src**, declared earlier as a global parameter in file **"display.cpp"** of listing 8.1b.

Listing 11.1

```
// Place this function in file "display.cpp"

//--------------------//
  void insource(void)         // Reads in the ACTUAL position of light source
//--------------------//
 { vector3 v ;
   cout << "Type in the ACTUAL position of the light source\n" ;
   cin >> v ;
// Convert to OBSERVED co-ordinates
   src = Q * v ;
 }  // End of insource
```

Quantifying light – intensity and colour

Rays of light may vary in brightness or intensity. Ultimately, we wish to calculate the intensity of the light which is reflected to the eye from a point in a three-dimensional scene, and to interpret this information for display on our graphics cards (mode 19 for VGA and mode 255 for XGA). In order to do this we must be able to map the measure of intensity onto the set of colours or shades available for display. The range of colours on any graphics device is finite – there is a limit on brightness. We must therefore impose a maximum value on intensity, so we measure the intensity of light using a floating point value between 0 (representing darkness) and 1 (representing 'maximum' brightness).

White light consists of a wide spectrum of waves varying wavelength, each corresponding to light of a different colour, ranging from red light at one end of the spectrum of visible wavelengths to violet at the other. In our somewhat simplistic conception of this idea we assume that light can be represented by three components – red, green and blue. We shall quantify light in terms of the intensities of each of these three components. We call these three intensity values I_{red}, I_{green} and I_{blue}, and each takes a *floating point* value between 0 and 1. In white light these components are present in equal measure; a value of 1 for I_{red}, 0 for I_{green} and 0 for I_{blue} implies bright red light, whereas 0 for I_{blue} and 0.5 for both I_{red} and I_{green} implies a more subdued yellow light.

The *colour* of the light is determined by the triple (I_{red} , I_{green} , I_{blue}). A colour ($\lambda \times I_{red}$, $\lambda \times I_{green}$, $\lambda \times I_{blue}$) for some value of λ, $0 \le \lambda \le 1$, is said to be a *shade* of (I_{red} , I_{green} , I_{blue}) with *intensity* λ.

The colour of a surface

All materials have properties relating the intensity of light which they reflect to that of the light striking them (*incident light*). We call these properties the *reflective coefficients* of the material. We divide the properties into three components corresponding to the red, green and blue components of the light. The values of the R_{red}, R_{green} and R_{blue} coefficients represent respectively the proportion of the incident red, green and blue light which is reflected, each taking a value between 0 and 1. A value of 1 for R_{red} implies that all incident red light is reflected, while values of 0 or 0.5 imply respectively that none or half of the incident red light is reflected.

The *absolute colour* of a material is determined by the relative magnitudes of the R_{red}, R_{green} and R_{blue} coefficients. For a white material all three are equal to 1, for a black material all are 0, while any material with equal R_{red}, R_{green} and R_{blue} values between 0 and 1 is a shade of grey. A large R_{red} coefficient combined with small R_{green} and R_{blue} gives a reddish colour and so on.

The *apparent colour* of a point on a surface is the colour of light reflected to the eye from that point on the surface. This is obviously dependent on the light illuminating the surface (including ambient light) as well as on the absolute colour and other properties of the surface (for example, transparency, gloss – see later), but in the simplest case of a dull (matt) opaque surface illuminated by white light, the apparent colour is always a shade of the absolute colour.

Reflection of light

There are two distinct ways in which light is reflected from a surface: *diffuse reflection* and *specular* reflection.

All surfaces exhibit diffuse reflection. When light hits a matt surface it is scattered in all possible directions (we assume uniformly), so that the intensity of light reflected to the eye in this way is independent of the position from which the surface is viewed. We then see an apparent colour for the surface which is dependent on both the reflective colour coefficients of the surface and the colour of the incident light. We shall discuss the precise relationship later.

Glossy surfaces also exhibit specular reflection, the effect which produces the *highlights* clearly observed in Plates Ib and Ic. A perfect reflector (such as a mirror) reflects an incident ray along a single direction (***r*** in figure 11.2). (It is this property which enables us to see perfectly clear images in mirrors.) This type of reflection is called specular reflection – light is not absorbed, it simply bounces off the surface, and so the colour of specularly reflected light is not dependent on the reflective coefficients of the surface. On slightly imperfect reflectors, some light is also reflected along directions deviating very slightly from ***r***, the intensity falling off sharply with increasing deviation. Highlights of the same colour as the incident light are observed when this light is reflected directly to the eye.

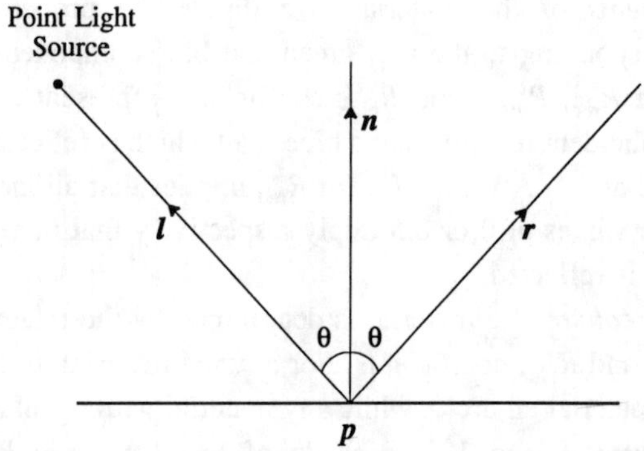

Figure 11.2

Specular reflection is governed by two parameters which we call *m* and *s*. The parameter *m* is a measure of the *gloss* of the surface material, or the *specular reflection exponent*, and refers to the sharpness of fall-off in intensity of reflection along directions deviating from reflection direction ***r***. It takes an integer value between 0 and about 400. A high value suggests a very glossy surface which exhibits bright concentrated highlights, and hence a sharp fall-off in intensity around the direction ***r***. Lower values give less glossy surfaces with highlights more distributed. The parameter *s* is called the *specular reflection coefficient* of the material, or *shine*. The value of *s* varies between 0 and 1. Shiny materials, such as metals, have high *s* values close to 1, while dull materials such as paper have low values: see example 11.2. Those parts of a glossy surface which are not part of a highlight are assumed to exhibit only diffuse reflection.

Not all light is reflected straight to the eye, of course. Diffuse reflection, for instance, scatters light uniformly in all directions. This results in a low level of *ambient light* illuminating any scene. This is background light reflected equally in all directions from the ground, walls and any other exposed surfaces. We assume that ambient light illuminates all surfaces of the model equally and ensures that those surfaces which are not exposed to a genuine light source do not appear perfectly black. The colour of ambient light is, of course, dependent on the reflective coefficients of the surfaces from which it has been reflected.

In order to simplify the calculations required in the shading model, we shall assume that all incident light (both source and ambient) is white light, thereby consisting of equal measures of red, green and blue components. When we talk about 'white' light having intensity I (a floating point number), this means that the intensity of each colour component is I, and so the colour of the light source may be described by the triple (I, I, I). In our programs we will be using a pure white light source, and so we shall be setting *I equal to 1*. The intensity of ambient light is given a value between 0 and 1, which we call I_a. This value is usually fairly low – about 0.4 is a good choice: **ambient** was defined to be this value in listing 7.4a. The maximum intensity of light which may illuminate a scene is 1. This includes both ambient light and light emanating directly from a source. The intensity of the contribution of incident light from a source is therefore limited to $(1 - I_a)$; this is the law of the conservation of energy. The intensity of light emitted by a source is given a value between 0 and 1, called I_s, and the incident light from this source, therefore, has the light intensity value given by $I_s \times (1 - I_a)$. The models which we describe can be extended to allow for coloured light sources, having three different component intensity values, and for multiple light sources, but we leave this to the reader.

Developing a shading model

The ideal shading model calculates the precise colour of light reflected into the eye from any visible point in a scene. Therefore, such a model is required to determine the intensities of the red, green and blue components of this colour for any given point. This we will call a *colour shading model.*

Not all graphics devices have sufficient colour capability to display this information (such as mode 18 of the VGA card), however, and so to begin with we consider a simplified model, called an *intensity shading model*, which simply returns the intensity (a floating point value, λ, between 0 and 1) of light reflected from a given point on a surface in the scene. The apparent colour of the surface at that point is then assumed to be a shade of the surface's absolute colour with intensity λ. This model, therefore, assumes that all surfaces of the scene are matt and opaque, exhibiting only diffuse reflection.

The shading models we describe will use a set of array parameters, which we call *material properties*. These are the properties which govern the way in which a material reflects light, its reflective coefficients, gloss, shine etc. We will use the array **material[maxf]** declared previously in **"mesh.h"** (listing 7.3a) to hold an integer which indicates a material type for each facet in our model of the scene. For our simple intensity shading model we use just one attribute, R say, with a value between 0 and 1, which represents a general reflective coefficient of a material. Our general colour shading model, however, will use many more of the parameters we have described, including the RGB reflective coefficients R_{red}, R_{green} and R_{blue}.

(1) Ambient light

We begin by modelling the reflection of ambient light which illuminates all surfaces equally, including those facing away from the genuine light source. Rays of ambient light strike a surface from all directions and are reflected uniformly in all directions. The intensity of light reflected to the eye (I_{amb} in the intensity shading model) is therefore independent of all but the intensity of the ambient light and the reflective coefficient of the surface with respect to this light.

$$I_{\text{amb}} = R \times I_{\text{a}}$$

where I_{a} is the intensity of incident ambient light and R is the single-valued reflective coefficient of the surface for ambient light. (In theory, the reflective coefficients for ambient light and incident light from a source may be different but we always assume that they are equal.)

In order to produce the general colour shading model for the reflection of ambient light, the above equation must be applied three times using the respective reflective coefficients for the three colour components. We use the values R_{red}, R_{green} and R_{blue}

$$\begin{aligned} I_{\text{amb(red)}} &= R_{\text{red}} \times I_{\text{a}} \\ I_{\text{amb(green)}} &= R_{\text{green}} \times I_{\text{a}} \\ \text{I}_{\text{amb(blue)}} &= R_{\text{blue}} \times I_{\text{a}} \end{aligned}$$

(2) Diffuse reflection – Lambert's Cosine Law

Diffuse reflection may be modelled using Lambert's Cosine Law. This relates the intensity of light striking a point on a surface to the cosine of the angle θ between the normal to the surface at that point and the vector from the point to the light source. The intensity of light, I_{diff}, reflected to the eye by diffuse reflection from this point is dependent on the intensity of light striking the point and on R the reflective coefficient of the surface

$$I_{\text{diff}} = R \times (I_{\text{s}} \times (1 - I_{\text{a}}) \times \cos\theta)$$

where I_{s} is the intensity of the light emitted by the source. The angle θ is called the *angle of incidence* of the light on the surface. From figure 11.2 we see that the normal to the surface is direction vector $\boldsymbol{n}$ and the rays of light have direction $\boldsymbol{l}$, so that the angle bounded by them θ may be calculated from the value of the scalar product $\boldsymbol{n} \bullet \boldsymbol{l}$, which is equal to $|\boldsymbol{n}| \times |\boldsymbol{l}| \times \cos\theta$. Thus the intensity of diffuse reflection from a surface is given by

$$I_{\text{diff}} = \frac{R \times I_s \times (1 - I_a) \times (\boldsymbol{n} \bullet \boldsymbol{l})}{|\boldsymbol{n}| \times |\boldsymbol{l}|}$$

Naturally, if the angle θ is greater than a right angle then the surface at $\boldsymbol{p}$ faces away from the source, and so no light reaches the surface and consequently none is reflected. In this case I_{diff} is calculated by the above formula to be less than 0, however, it should be set equal to 0.

The model for diffuse reflection may be further improved by the inclusion of a distance factor: the intensity of light from a given source falls off with increasing distance from the source (this property of light energy is called *attenuation*). At a point that is a distance d from a source producing light of intensity I_s, the light has intensity proportional to I_s/d^2. Thus, if the point $\boldsymbol{p}$ above is a distance d from a given source, then the intensity of light from the source which strikes the surface at $\boldsymbol{p}$ is $k \times I_s/d^2$ for some constant k, and this value may replace I_s in the equation above.

More pleasing effects are often achieved by approximating to this fall-off by using $k \times I_s/(d + C)$, for some constants k and C, because the $k \times I_s/d^2$ value gives too harsh a fall-off in intensity. Experiment with the values of k and C to achieve satisfactory results.

The complete intensity shading model is given by the sum of the values I_{amb} and I_{diff}. This gives a floating point value lying between 0 and 1.

Once again, colour may be introduced into the general model by using the equation three times, once for each of the colour components red, green and blue

$$I_{\text{diff(red)}} = \frac{R_{red} \times I_s \times (1 - I_a) \times (\boldsymbol{n} \bullet \boldsymbol{l})}{|\boldsymbol{n}| \times |\boldsymbol{l}|}$$

$$I_{\text{diff(green)}} = \frac{R_{green} \times I_s \times (1 - I_a) \times (\boldsymbol{n} \bullet \boldsymbol{l})}{|\boldsymbol{n}| \times |\boldsymbol{l}|}$$

$$I_{\text{diff(blue)}} = \frac{R_{blue} \times I_s \times (1 - I_a) \times (\boldsymbol{n} \bullet \boldsymbol{l})}{|\boldsymbol{n}| \times |\boldsymbol{l}|}$$

Exercise 11.1

You can create a type of model that simulates fog by taking into account the distance of the point $\boldsymbol{p}$ from the eye ($= |\boldsymbol{p}|$). As this distance increases, so too does the 'fogginess' of the image. By defining a light grey colour that represents fog, instead of displaying the apparent colour of the reflecting surface at $\boldsymbol{p}$, you should display a weighted average of this apparent colour and the fog colour, naturally increasing the weighting of the fog colour as distance $|\boldsymbol{p}|$ increases. Experiment with this idea; compare it with attenuation.

(3) Specular reflection

Specular reflection, as mentioned previously, is exhibited by glossy surfaces. A model for specular reflection, that was developed by Bui-Tuong Phong (1975), approximates the intensity of specular reflection at a point by using the value of $\cos^m\alpha$, where α is the angle between the direction of perfect reflection of light from the point and the vector from that point to the eye (see figure 11.2), and m is the gloss of the surface material. The intensity of light specularly reflected from a surface is also dependent on a function, $F(\theta)$, of the angle of incidence of the light, θ. This function may be thought of as the reflective coefficient of the surface with respect to specular reflection, but this coefficient is not constant: incident light striking a surface obliquely (high θ) is reflected to a greater extent than that striking more directly. In general, we approximate $F(\theta)$ by the constant value s, the shine of the surface material. An equation for the intensity of specularly reflected light (I_{spec}) derived from Phong's model, is given by

$$I_{spec} = I_s \times F(\theta) \times \cos^m\alpha \quad \text{or alternatively} \quad I_{spec} = I_s \times s \times \cos^m\alpha$$

We will make the simplifying assumption that specular reflection of light is independent of the absolute colour of the reflecting surface. Consequently, for white incident light, the intensity of each colour component in the specularly reflected light is given by I_{spec}, calculated as above.

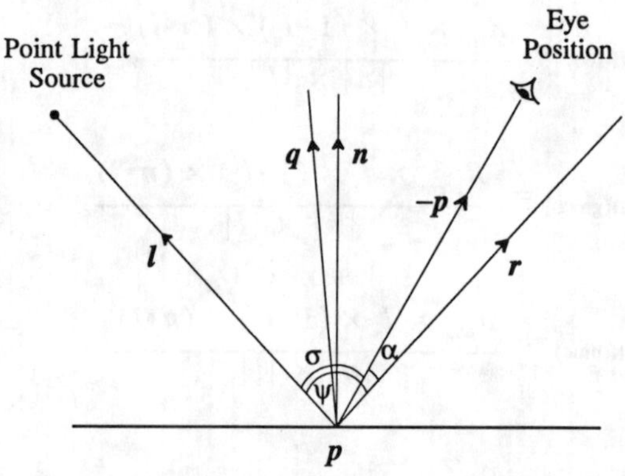

Figure 11.3

If $\boldsymbol{r}$ is the direction in which light is reflected from the surface and $-\boldsymbol{p}$ is the vector from $\boldsymbol{p}$ to the eye, then the value $\cos\alpha$ is given by

$$\cos\alpha = \frac{\boldsymbol{r} \bullet (-\boldsymbol{p})}{|\boldsymbol{r}| \times |\boldsymbol{p}|}$$

We may take advantage of elementary laws of physics and trigonometry to simplify this calculation, which enables us to calculate $\cos\alpha$ without first calculating $\boldsymbol{r}$. The angle of reflection is defined to be the angle between the surface normal at a point $\boldsymbol{p}$ and the direction of reflection $\boldsymbol{r}$ for a perfectly reflecting surface. This angle of reflection is equal in magnitude and opposite in sense to the angle of incidence, and so consequently

$$\frac{\boldsymbol{r}}{|\boldsymbol{r}|} + \frac{\boldsymbol{l}}{|\boldsymbol{l}|} \quad \text{is a vector parallel to } \boldsymbol{n}.$$

Now suppose the angle between $\boldsymbol{l}$ and $\boldsymbol{r}$ is ψ, then the angle between $\boldsymbol{l}$ and $\boldsymbol{n}$ is $\psi/2$. Let us further suppose that the angle between $\boldsymbol{l}$ and $-\boldsymbol{p}$ is σ, which means that $\alpha = \psi - \sigma$, and so $\alpha/2 = (\psi/2 - \sigma/2)$ (see figure 11.3). Thus, if the vector $\boldsymbol{q}$ is given by

$$\boldsymbol{q} = \frac{-\boldsymbol{p}}{|\boldsymbol{p}|} + \frac{\boldsymbol{l}}{|\boldsymbol{l}|}$$

then $\alpha/2$ is the angle between $\boldsymbol{q}$ and $\boldsymbol{n}$, and so

$$\cos(\alpha/2) = \frac{\boldsymbol{n} \bullet (\boldsymbol{q})}{|\boldsymbol{n}| \times |\boldsymbol{q}|}$$

We know that $\cos\alpha = \cos^2(\alpha/2) - \sin^2(\alpha/2) = 2 \times \cos^2(\alpha/2) - 1$, and hence we may calculate $\cos\alpha$.

Specular reflection can only be used with a colour shading model, and not with an intensity shading model. This is because the apparent colour of a point near, but not at, a highlight is neither a shade of the absolute colour of the surface nor a shade of the colour of the light source, but rather it is a mixture of the two colours. It should be pointed out here that Bui-Tuong Phong's model does not strictly simulate the specular reflection of light, but simply produces an effect of similar appearance. See Blinn (1977), Cook (1982) or Hall (1989) for more realistic simulations of the specular effect.

Each colour component in the complete general colour shading model is calculated by summing the corresponding components of the contributions from reflected ambient light, diffuse reflection and specular reflection. If any colour component exceeds 1, then naturally it must be set to 1.

(4) Shadows

If a point is obscured from exposure to a single light source, then the point is said to be *in shadow*. The light emitted from that point is restricted to reflected ambient light, in the absence of other light sources.

(5) Multiple light sources

Any of the shading models detailed above may be extended to deal with illumination from more than one light source simply by taking the average of the contributions from each. The contribution from each light source is calculated as if it was the only source, taking into account the same level of ambient light in each calculation.

(6) Transparent surfaces

For a transparent surface, the apparent colour is also determined by a contribution from light arriving from behind the surface. The extent of this contribution is measured by the transparency coefficient T, which again takes a value between 0 and 1. A perfectly transparent surface is indicated by $T = 1$ while a fully opaque surface has $T = 0$. In chapter 12 we shall examine the geometrical problems of incorporating transparent surfaces into a scene: in this section we shall consider only the shading of such surfaces.

If the intensity of light arriving at a point $\boldsymbol{p}$ from behind is I_b and the intensity of light reflected from $\boldsymbol{p}$ by diffuse and specular reflection is I_p, then the intensity of light emitted from $\boldsymbol{p}$ is given by

$$I_{tran} = T \times I_b + (1 - T) \times I_p$$

Only if all surfaces have the same absolute colour can transparency be taken into account in an intensity shading model, because if different absolute colours occur then 'mixes' of these colours have to be calculated and displayed. For a colour shading model, transparency coefficients may be separated into three components, relating to the proportions of red, green and blue light that are transmitted through the surface. These components may differ in the same way as may the reflective coefficients of a material: a red filter, for instance, will let through all red light which strikes it, but is perfectly opaque with respect to blue or green light. The three transparency coefficients are, in fact, directly related to the reflective coefficients, so instead of specifying these transparency coefficients for a surface, we specify one general value, T, and use the three values $T \times R_{red}$, $T \times R_{green}$ and $T \times R_{blue}$ in the colour equations

$$I_{tran(red)} = T \times I_{b(red)} + (1 - T) \times I_{p(red)}$$

$$I_{tran(green)} = T \times I_{b(green)} + (1 - T) \times I_{p(green)}$$

$$I_{tran(blue)} = T \times I_{b(blue)} + (1 - T) \times I_{p(blue)}$$

Exercise 11.2

Extend the formulae throughout this section so that they deal with a coloured light source.

Creating a materials database

The implementation of the various shading models requires that the material properties of the various surfaces be represented in the programs. We use the concept of *material* in the same way as we have used colour in preceding chapters – a function **Get_material(i)** from **"mesh.h"** returns an integer value associated with each facet *i*, and this integer now refers to a particular material, and a corresponding set of material properties, rather than to a logical colour. These material attributes must be declared in a new class **Material** and stored in the file **"material.h"** (listing 11.2a). In our attribute database there will be **numat** (< **maxmaterl**) materials, each having one **int** (value between 0 and 400) and six **float** (value between 0 and 1) attributes in the database, although not all need be used in any particular shading model. The value of **maxmaterl** is **#define**d to be 15 in **"palette.h"** (listing 1.2a). For material **i**, the **int** attribute **expn[i]** represents the specular reflection exponent or gloss; **spec[i]** the specular coefficient or shine; **rdif[i]**, **gdif[i]**, **bdif[i]** the respective red, green and blue reflective coefficients; **tran[i]** represents transparency and must always be set to zero if material **i** is non-transparent; and **indx[i]** is the refractive index which will be used much later for ray-tracing. The class also includes **Get** methods to access these parameters, the constructor method and the method **read** for reading in these material attributes. The code for these functions is stored in **"material.cpp"** (listing 11.2b). In our programs, the **read** method will normally input the material attributes from a file named **"material.dat"**. Listing 11.2c contains a sample **"material.dat"** suitable for intensity shading.

Listing 11.2a

```
// Save as file "material.h"
//maxmaterl has already been defined in file "palette.h"
//--------------//
  class Material
'/--------------//
 { float rdif[maxmaterl] ;     // Diffuse reflection in red
   float gdif[maxmaterl] ;     // Diffuse reflection in green
   float bdif[maxmaterl] ;     // Diffuse reflection in blue
   float spec[maxmaterl] ;     // Specular reflection coefficient
   int   expn[maxmaterl] ;     // Specular reflection exponent
   float tran[maxmaterl] ;     // Transmission coefficient
   float indx[maxmaterl] ;     // Refractive index
   int   numat ;               // Number of materials defined (<= maxmaterl)
  public:
   float Get_rdf(int mat) { return (rdif[mat]) ; }
   float Get_gdf(int mat) { return (gdif[mat]) ; }
   float Get_bdf(int mat) { return (bdif[mat]) ; }
   float Get_spc(int mat) { return (spec[mat]) ; }
   int   Get_xpn(int mat) { return (expn[mat]) ; }
   float Get_trn(int mat) { return (tran[mat]) ; }
   float Get_ndx(int mat) { return (indx[mat]) ; }
   int   Get_numat()      { return ( numat ) ; }
   Material() ;
   void read(char *matfile) ;
 } ;  // End of class Material
```

Listing 11.2b

```
// Save as file "material.cpp"
//--------------------//
  Material::Material()
//--------------------//
  { for(int i=0 ; i<maxmaterl ; i++)
    { rdif[i] = 0.0 ;  gdif[i] = 0.0 ; bdif[i] = 0.0 ;
      spec[i] = 0.0 ;  expn[i] = 0 ;   tran[i] = 0.0 ; indx[i] = 0.0 ;
    }
    numat = 0 ;
  }  // End of Material
//-----------------------------------//
  void Material::read(char *matfile)
//-----------------------------------//
 { ifstream indata ;
// Read number of materials
   indata.open(matfile) ;
   indata >> numat ;
   for (int i=0 ; i<numat ; i++)
   { indata >> rdif[i] >> gdif[i] >> bdif[i] ;
     indata >> spec[i] >> expn[i] >> tran[i] >> indx[i] ;
   }
   indata.close() ;
 }  // End of read
```

Listing 11.2c

```
// Sample file "material.dat"
13
0.8  0.7  0.1    0.5   3    0.0  1.0
0.7  0.2  0.04   0.6   2    0.0  1.0
0.0  0.2  0.7    0.5   7    0.0  1.0
0.1  0.8  0.2    0.4  30    0.0  1.0
0.3  0.5  0.9    0.5 170    0.0  1.0
0.7  0.7  0.1    0.2  70    0.0  1.0
0.3  0.8  0.4    0.2  19    0.0  1.0
0.1  0.6  0.8    0.2 110    0.0  1.0
0.16 0.75 0.05   0.2  50    0.0  1.0
0.1  0.1  0.8    0.0  60    0.0  1.0
0.85 0.15 0.15   0.1  45    0.0  1.0
0.85 0.25 0.25   0.2  80    0.0  1.0
0.8  0.35 0.25   0.6   5    0.0  1.0
```

Incorporating shading into the programs

We now turn our attention to the display of information derived from shading models. With mode 19 (or even mode 18) on the VGA card you will see that you do not have to use very expensive colour devices with vast ranges of available colours in order to produce shaded pictures; and we can do far better with mode 255 on the XGA card. Provided that you temper your aims according to the capabilities of your particular display, then very satisfactory results can almost always be obtained.

In this section we shall discuss the application of shading techniques to the polygonal mesh models, which we have used thus far when dealing with three dimensions. Nevertheless, it should be understood that these techniques may be applied equally well to the analytic models described in our last four chapters.

A new **look_at_it** function is given in listing 11.3, and this sets up the position of the light source and initialises the table of material attributes. This code must replace the present version of this function in **"display.cpp"**. Apart from containing the usual function calls, the new **look_at_it** has two additional calls – the first to **mrl.read("material.dat")** which sets up the attribute tables for material **mrl**, an instantiation of class **Material**, and the second to the function **insource** given in listing 11.1. Remember to un-comment the lines of code relevant to materials in **"palette.cpp"**, **"model.h&cpp"** and **"display.cpp"**.

We mentioned at the beginning of this chapter that the implementation of a shading model can be simplified by assuming that the apparent colour of points on a facet is constant over that facet – that is, the facets are not smooth shaded. We use this very simple approach for the first two of the four shading models outlined below. In the first case the apparent colour is not displayed explicitly by each pixel, rather it is suggested by the densities of various colours spread over the whole facet, as can be seen in figure 11.4. This approach is effective when there are relatively few colours available, as with VGA mode 18. An example of the second case of constant shading over a facet can be seen in Plate Ia, which is a picture of our 'teapot'.

Listing 11.3

```
// Replace function "look_at_it" in file "display.cpp" with the following:

//----------------------//
  void look_at_it(void)
//----------------------//
 { look3() ;
// then calculate the observation matrix 'Q'
   findQ() ;
   observe() ;
   insource() ;
   mesh.clipscene() ;
   project_it() ;
   mrl.read("material.dat") ;
 } // End of look_at_it
```

Recall that shading models all calculate a measure of the light reflected to the eye from a single point on a surface. Obviously, the normal vector $\boldsymbol{n}$ is the same for any $\boldsymbol{p}$ on the facet but, if a point light source is used, the vector $\boldsymbol{l}$ will vary across the facet, and so an average value must be taken. What we do is to average the x, y and z co-ordinates of the vertices of the facet, and use the centroid thus calculated as $\boldsymbol{p}$, thus determining an average value for $\boldsymbol{l}$. Every point on the facet is then assumed to reflect light of the same colour and intensity as that reflected at $\boldsymbol{p}$. Note that for convex polygons the centroid always lies within the polygon. The centroid of a facet is calculated by a call to the function **midpoint** given in listing 11.4.

Listing 11.4

```
// Place this function in file "mesh.cpp"
//-----------------------------------//
  vector3 Mesh::midpoint(int face)
//-----------------------------------//
 { vector3 midpt = zero ;
// Finds the mid-point of OBSERVED facet 'face'
   for (int i=0 ; i<size[face] ; i++)
     midpt = midpt + obs.Get_vertex(listofverts[firstoffacet[face]+i]) ;
   midpt = (1.0/(float)size[face]) * midpt ;    return ( midpt ) ;
 }  // End of midpoint
```

We now outline various methods for the interpretation of intensity information ranging from the simplest, intensity shading (used when a very limited number of colours or shades is available) which ignores specular reflection and deals only with the intensity of light falling on individual facets, to the complex fully smooth-shaded colour model, allowing for shadows, reflections etc.

Our only interface between the three-dimensional calculations and the image display is our colour look-up table stored in the **Palette** class (that is arrays **red**, **green** and **blue**). The display can be meaningless if the table is not properly set up: we use two particular functions for co-ordinating and manipulating the colour table. First, the table is initialised by function **colourtable**. Secondly, having ascertained the actual colour needed for display, we need to find (or define) the corresponding logical colour entry in the colour look-up table. This is essentially a sorting and searching problem, solved by our function **findlogicalcolour**. Remember to un-comment the lines of code given in **"palette.cpp"** and in the **"model.h&cpp"** and **"display.h&cpp"** files that are needed for the **Material** class.

The intensity shading model

There are two ways in which we can tackle the problem, furnishing us with two pairs of **colourtable** and **findlogicalcolour** functions. The first and simplest method is to pre-define the entries in the colour look-up table in such a way that we know exactly where to find a suitable colour through as simple calculation, thereby avoiding a time-consuming search. However, this approach does restrict us to the intensity shading model (function **intensityshade** in listing 11.5). Let us suppose that we are using **numcol** different absolute colours, and that for each colour, we will choose between **numshade** shades, ranging in intensity from zero up to unity (excluding black). The logical colours are divided into **numcol** equal sized blocks (of **numshade** entries), each block representing a series of shades of a given absolute colour. The index of the absolute colour of the surface to be displayed indicates which block of logical colours we should consider and we use the floating point intensity value returned by **intensityshade** to determine the position in this block of the logical colour corresponding to that intensity.

Listing 11.5

```
// Place these functions in file "display.cpp"

//--------------------------------------------------------//
  float intensityshade(vector3 p, vector3 norm, int index)
//--------------------------------------------------------//
// Intensity shading model : returns intensity 'lambda'. Vector 'p' is the
// point from which light is reflected, vector 'norm' is the surface normal
// at that point and the surface material is 'index'.
 { vector3 ptosrc ;
   float cosval,dotprod,modnormal,modptosrc,lambda ;
// Calculate direction from vector 'p' to source
   ptosrc = src - p ;
// Calculate the angle between the surface normal and this direction
   dotprod=dot3(norm,ptosrc) ;
   modnormal=sqrt(pow(norm.x,2.0)+pow(norm.y,2.0)+pow(norm.z,2.0)) ;
   modptosrc=sqrt(pow(ptosrc.x,2.0)+pow(ptosrc.y,2.0)+pow(ptosrc.z,2.0)) ;
   cosval=dotprod/(modnormal*modptosrc) ;
   if (cosval < 0.0) cosval=0.0 ;
// 'lambda' is the intensity returned
   lambda=mrl.Get_spc(index)*((1-ambient)*cosval+ambient) ;
   return ( lambda ) ;
 }  // End of intensityshade

//--------------------//
  void seefacet(int k)        // Replacement seefacet
//--------------------//
// Intensity shading
 { float lambda,dummy ;
   vector3 midpt,norm ;
   int newface, suplength, suplist[maxsuplist] ;
// Find the mid-point and normal of facet 'k'
   midpt = mesh.midpoint(k) ; norm = normal(k,&dummy,&obs) ;
// Find the intensity of reflected light
   lambda = intensityshade(midpt,norm,mesh.Get_material(k)) ;
// Display the facet
   facetfill(k,lambda) ;
// Repeat for each superficial facet on facet 'k'
   suplength = mesh.Get_a_sup(k,&(suplist[0])) ;
   while (suplength > 0)
   { newface = suplist[--suplength] ;
     midpt = mesh.midpoint(newface) ;
     norm = normal(newface,&dummy,&obs) ;
     lambda = intensityshade(midpt,norm,mesh.Get_material(newface)) ;
     facetfill(newface,lambda) ;
   }
 }  // End of seefacet

//-----------------------------------//
  void facetfill(int k, float lambda)    //Replacement facetfill
//-----------------------------------//
// Constant Intensity shading
// Displays facet 'k' in a 'shade' with intensity 'lambda'
 { int i,j,index ;
   vector2 poly[maxpoly],projected ;
   index = plt.findlogicalcolour(mesh.Get_material(k),lambda) ;
   win.setcol(index) ; j=mesh.Get_clipfac(k) ;
   if (j < 0) return ;
// Find the pixel co-ordinates of the vertices
   for (i=0 ; i<mesh.Get_size(j) ; i++)
   { projected = pro.Get_vertex(mesh.Get_faclist(j,i) ) ;
     poly[i].x=projected.x ;
     poly[i].y=projected.y ;
   }
   win.polyfill(mesh.Get_size(j),poly) ;
 } // End of facetfill
```

We add colours to our look-up table in the palette starting at location 2 – locations 0 and 1 hold colours black and white respectively. We suppose that there are **numshade** (=4) shades of each of **numcol** (=3) colours, graded from dark (shade 1) to light (shade 4), set up in a colour look-up table by a new version of palette method **colourtable** (listing 11.6). Later we will give another version of this method for RGB values (listing 11.8). So our table is stored in location 2, ... 4*__numcol__+1. Given the index **abscol** of an absolute colour and a given intensity of that colour, function **findlogicalcolour** (listing 11.6) returns the index in the colour look-up table that is nearest to the shade of that absolute colour caused by light of that given intensity illuminating a facet of the object. The methods of listing 11.6 are appended to file **"palette.cpp"** – **colourtable** replaces a previous version.

Listing 11.6

```
// Place these functions in file "palette.cpp"
//-------------------------------//
  void Palette::colourtable(void)    // Replacement colourtable
//-------------------------------//   // For Intensity shading
// Initialises colour look-up table.  Creates 'numshade = 4' shades of '
// numcol = 3' colours. Very useful for VGA mode 18
 { int i, j, n=2, numcol=3, numshade=4 ;
   float shade ;
// Colour 0 is kept for the background colour, 1 for the foreground
   rgblog(0,(float)0.0,0.0,0.0) ;   rgblog(1,(float)1.0,1.0,1.0) ;
// Initialise all list pointers
   for (i=0 ; i<numcol ; i++)
   { for (j=1 ; j<=numshade ; j++)
     { shade=(float)j/(float)numshade ;
       rgblog(n++,shade*mrl.Get_rdf(i),shade*mrl.Get_gdf(i),
                                       shade*mrl.Get_bdf(i)) ;
     }
   }
 }  // End of colourtable
//-----------------------------------------------------------//
  int Palette::findlogicalcolour(int abscol, float intensity)
//-----------------------------------------------------------//
// Intensity shading
// Function to find the logical colour, 'logcol', corresponding to
// a shade of absolute colour 'abscol' with given 'intensity'
 { int logcol, numshade = 4 ;
   logcol=2+abscol*numshade+(int)(0.9999*intensity*numshade) ;
   return ( logcol ) ;
 }  // End of findlogicalcolour
```

Function **intensityshade** (listing 11.5), given a material **index** and a point **p** on the facet with normal **norm**, returns a floating point number between 0 and 1 which represents the intensity of white light that is reflected off the surface with single valued reflective coefficient found by calling **mrl.Get_spc**. Note that only ambient light and diffuse reflection are considered in this calculation. This function is called from a new version of **seefacet** (listing 10.6) which in turn was called from within **hidden** (listing 10.8), in turn called from **draw_it** (listing

10.1), called from **draw_a_picture** (listing 7.4b) and so on down into the **"window.cpp"** where function **main** resides. Function **seefacet** also calls a new version of **facetfill** (listing 11.5), which uses **findlogicalcolour** to calculate the colour that is used to fill in the facet with the **Window** method **polyfill** (listing 2.1b). All these functions in listing 11.5 should be appended to file **"display.cpp"**; previous versions of these functions stored there should be deleted or commented out.

Exercise 11.3
Run any of our previous programs, but now the Project must contain these new versions of **"display.cpp"**, and implicitly a new version of **"palette.cpp"**. In particular use the goblet Project stemming from **"nine11.cpp"**.

Four shades of any one colour are really not enough to produce good quality images. Of course the one way around this problem, given that there are enough colours on your graphics card, is to increase the size of **numshade**. However, we can extend this method another way, so as to produce some very creditable results even with only four shades (see figure 11.4); this is by using pseudo-random sampling. A new version of function **facetfill** (listing 11.7) displays a facet, not by using a simple area-fill in a colour indicated by the **material** array, but instead by using the intensity value as a measure of the probability that any pixel within that area should be displayed in a given shade of the chosen logical colour. If the intensity of light reflected from a surface is low, then there is a greater probability of a pixel on the surface being a darker shade of that colour and correspondingly smaller probabilities for the middle and lighter shades. A high intensity, close to the value 1, implies a high probability that a given pixel in the relevant area will be set to the lighter shade. The particular shade for display is chosen by a function **randomcolour** (listing 11.7) using a pseudo-random function based on the intensity of reflected light. The **seefacet** function which calls **facetfill** is the same one from listing 11.6. It determines the intensity of light reflected from a facet, through the call to **intensityshade**, and then calls **facetfill** which displays the facet, pixel by pixel, using shades randomly adjusted by function **randomcolour.**

Example 11.1
We add these functions to file **"display.cpp"**, deleting the old version of **facetfill,** and run the Project generated from application program **"nine10.cpp"**. Figure 11.4 shows a sphere displayed using the pseudo-random sampling method of shading using only four shades of grey.

Listing 11.7

```
// (Re)place the following functions in "display.cpp"
//-------------------------------------------//
  void randomcolour(int col, float lambda)
//-------------------------------------------//
// Assuming numshade=4, col = {0,1,2} select logical colour between 2+4*col
// and 5+4*col the colour table having been set up by function 'colourtable'
{ lambda = lambda + 0.4 * random() ;
  if (lambda < 0.25)  win.setcol(2+4*col) ;              // Black
  else { if (lambda < 0.50) win.setcol(3+4*col) ;
         else { if (lambda < 0.75) win.setcol(4+4*col) ;
                else win.setcol(5+4*col) ;               // Full colour
              } ;
       } ;
} // End of randomcolour

//-------------------------------------//
  void facetfill(int k, float lambda)      //  Replacement facetfill
//-------------------------------------//
// Random sampling shading of facet 'k' in 'shade' of intensity 'lambda'
 { int i,index,ix,iy,j,next,xmax,xmin,ymax,ymin,nxpix,nypix ;
  pixelvector pix,poly[maxpoly] ;
  float winy,mu ;
  vector2 projected,vpoly[maxpoly] ;
  j=mesh.Get_clipfac(k) ; if (j < 0) return ;
// Find the pixel co-ordinates of the vertices
  for (i=0 ; i<mesh.Get_size(j) ; i++)
  { projected = pro.Get_vertex(mesh.Get_faclist(j,i) ) ;
    vpoly[i] = projected ;
    poly[i].x=win.fx(projected.x) ; poly[i].y=win.fy(projected.y) ;
  } ;
// Fill facet by a scan line approach; find minimum and maximum y values
  ymax=poly[0].y ; ymin=poly[0].y ;
  for (i=1 ; i<mesh.Get_size(j) ; i++)
  { if (poly[i].y > ymax) ymax=poly[i].y ;
    if (poly[i].y < ymin) ymin=poly[i].y ;
  }
// For each scan line find maximum and minimum x values
// the corresponding interpolated colour values
  nxpix = win.Get_nxpix() ;    nypix = win.Get_nypix() ;
  if (ymax >= nypix) ymax=nypix-1 ;
  if (ymin < 0 ) ymin=0 ;
  for (iy=ymin ; iy<=ymax ; iy++)
  { pix.y=iy ;
    winy = -(float)iy/win.Get_xyscale()/win.Get_rat() + win.Get_vert()*0.5 ;
    xmin=nxpix ; xmax=-1 ; index=mesh.Get_size(j)-1 ;
    for (next=0 ; next<mesh.Get_size(j) ; next++)
    { if ((max(poly[index].y,poly[next].y) >= iy) &&
          (min(poly[index].y,poly[next].y) <= iy) &&
          (poly[index].y != poly[next].y) )
        { mu=(winy-vpoly[index].y)/(vpoly[next].y-vpoly[index].y) ;
          if (mu<0.0) mu = 0.0 ;
          else if (mu>1.0) mu = 1.0 ;
          ix=win.fx((1.0-mu)*vpoly[index].x+mu*vpoly[next].x) ;
          if (ix < xmin) xmin=ix ; if (ix > xmax) xmax=ix ;
        } ;
      index = next ;
    }
    if (xmax >= nxpix) xmax=nxpix-1 ;  if (xmin < 0) xmin=0 ;
    if (xmin <= xmax)
      { for (ix=xmin ; ix<=xmax ; ix++)
        { randomcolour(mesh.Get_material(k),lambda) ;
          pix.x=ix ; pix.y=iy ; win.setpix(pix) ;
        }
      } ;
  }
 }  // End of facetfill
```

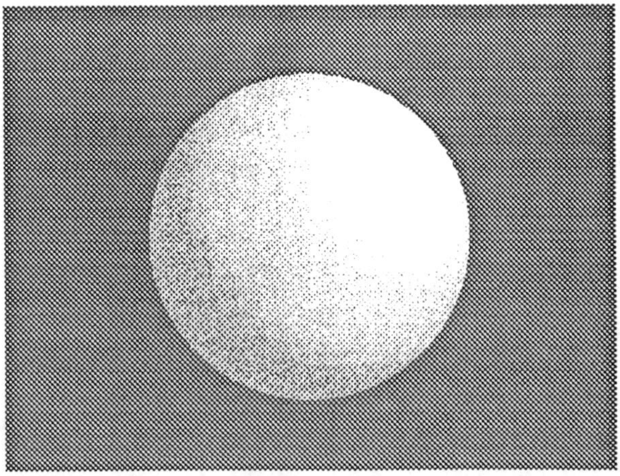

Figure 11.4

RGB colour shading

On some expensive graphics cards, each pixel can be coloured independently with colours defined by three 8-bit integers (between 0 and 255), which gives a choice from some 16 million possible colours. Neither the VGA mode 19 nor XGA mode 255 has this many colours, yet they nevertheless allow for a very flexible colour definition, with each of the red, green and blue components being specified by up to 6-bit integers. Only 256 of this maximum of 256K colours may be displayed on the screen at any one time, and these colours are stored in the adapter's colour look-up table. Unfortunately we can go no further with VGA mode 18; random sampling and intensity shading have taken it to the limit.

We have already defined and stored our own colour look-up table as a set of three arrays **red**, **green** and **blue** stored inside the **Palette** class. Each entry in this look-up table (that is, each logical colour) has an integer index, between 0 and 255. Whenever we create a new actual colour and link it to a logical colour, using method **rgblog**, we also ensure that the adapter's colour table contains the corresponding colour definition.

Setting up a look-up table in this way will enable us to use RGB colour shading methods; we will be taking account of ambient light, and diffuse and specular reflections in our calculations. In order to do this we will eventually be using all the entries of the material database, **mrl**: the RGB diffuse reflection coefficients **rdif**, **gdif** and **bdif**; the specular reflection exponent or gloss, **expn**; the specular reflection coefficient, or shine, **spec**; the transparency parameter **tran**; and refractive index **indx**. These methods require careful attention to the storage of, and access to, colours in our colour look-up table.

For RGB colour modelling we consider the second, more effective, way of creating the colour look-up table. The initial construction is executed by the new version of function **colourtable**, and the table is updated and a suitable logical colour found by the new version of **findlogicalcolour**. Both functions are given in listing 11.8: they should replace the versions presently stored in **"palette.cpp"**.

Listing 11.8

```
// Replace these functions in file "palette.cpp"

//---------------------------------//
  void Palette::colourtable(void)                     // Colour shading
//---------------------------------//
// Initialises colour look-up table for colour shading models
 { int i ;
   newcolour=2 ;
   rgblog(0,0,0,0) ; rgblog(1,(float)1.0,1.0,1.0) ;
   for (i=0 ; i<maxmaterl ; i++) matlist[i]=-1 ;
   for (i=0 ; i<tabnum ; i++) colptr[i]=-1 ;
 }  // End of colourtable

//------------------------------------------------------------------//
  int Palette::findlogicalcolour(float r, float g, float b, int i)
//------------------------------------------------------------------//
// Colour shading
// Find logical colour corresponding to 'r,g,b' components
 { float limit = 0.04;
   int go_on,j,newptr ;
   if (r<0.0) r = 0.0 ; if (r>1.0) r = 1.0 ;
   if (g<0.0) g = 0.0 ; if (g>1.0) g = 1.0 ;
   if (b<0.0) b = 0.0 ; if (b>1.0) b = 1.0 ;
// 'j' and 'newptr' refer to logical colour list for absolute colour 'i'
   j=matlist[i] ; newptr=-1 ; go_on=(j!=-1) ;
   while (go_on)
   { if ((fabs(r-red[j]) < limit) && (fabs(g-green[j]) < limit)
                                  && (fabs(b-blue[j]) < limit) )
       { return(j) ; }    // Corresponding colour found
     else
       { if (r > red[j]) newptr=j ;
// Check next item in the list; leave if red value too large
         if (r > red[j]-limit)
           { j=colptr[j] ; go_on=(j!=-1) ; }
         else go_on=0 ;   //FALSE
       } ;
   } ;
// Existing list doesn't contain suitable logical colour: add new colour
   if (newptr > -1)
     { if (newcolour>=tabnum)
         { cerr << "\n Error Maximum number of palette entries reached" ;
           return(0) ;
         }
       else colptr[newcolour]=colptr[newptr] ;
       colptr[newptr]=newcolour ;
     }
   else
     { colptr[newcolour]=matlist[i] ;
       matlist[i]=newcolour ;
     } ;
   rgblog(newcolour,r,g,b) ;
// Return index of this new colour :
   newcolour++ ;
   return ( newcolour-1 ) ;
 }  // End of findlogicalcolour
```

Listing 11.9

```
// Place this function in file "display.cpp"
//---------------------------------------------------------------------//
  void cshade(vector3 p, vector3 norm, int mat, float *red, float *green,
                                                           float *blue)
//---------------------------------------------------------------------//
// Colour shading model equivalent of function intensityshade (listing 11.5)
 { vector3 ptosrc,q ;
   float cosa,cosaover2,cosval,dotprod,specular ;
   float modnormal,modp,modptosrc,modq ;
// Calculate direction from vector 'p' to source
   ptosrc = src - p ;
// Calculate the angle between the surface normal and this direction
   dotprod=dot3(norm,ptosrc) ;
   modnormal=sqrt(pow(norm.x,2.0)+pow(norm.y,2.0)+pow(norm.z,2.0)) ;
   modptosrc=sqrt(pow(ptosrc.x,2.0)+pow(ptosrc.y,2.0)+pow(ptosrc.z,2.0)) ;
   cosval=dotprod/(modnormal*modptosrc) ; if (cosval < 0.0) cosval=0.0 ;
// Calculate the diffuse reflection colour components
   *red=mrl.Get_rdf(mat)*((1-ambient)*cosval+ambient) ;
   *green=mrl.Get_gdf(mat)*((1-ambient)*cosval+ambient) ;
   *blue=mrl.Get_bdf(mat)*((1-ambient)*cosval+ambient) ;
// Calculate the vector 'q'
   modp=sqrt(pow(p.x,2.0)+pow(p.y,2.0)+pow(p.z,2.0)) ;
   q = -(1.0/modp) * p + (1.0/modptosrc) * ptosrc ;
   modq=sqrt(pow(q.x,2.0)+pow(q.y,2.0)+pow(q.z,2.0)) ;
// Calculate the specular reflection contribution
   cosaover2=dot3(q,norm)/(modnormal*modq) ;
   cosa=2.0*pow(cosaover2,2.0)-1.0 ;
   if ( cosa < 0.0001 )  specular=0.0 ;
   else specular=mrl.Get_spc(mat)*pow(cosa,(float)mrl.Get_xpn(mat)) ;
// Calculate the components of the reflected light
   (*red) += specular ;      if ( *red > 1.0 ) *red=1.0 ;
   (*green) += specular ;    if ( *green > 1.0 ) *green=1.0 ;
   (*blue) += specular ;     if ( *blue > 1.0 ) *blue=1.0 ;
 } // End of cshade
```

This method substantially increases the number of colour shades needed, and so in order to make full use of our colour shading model, the entries of the colour look-up table must be defined as and when required. Given the three RGB colour components of a colour required for display, a search through the existing entries in the colour look-up table is executed to find if a 'sufficiently similar' colour has been stored. If such a colour is found, then this is used for display. If no 'sufficiently similar' colour has been stored then a new actual colour is created, stored as the next available logical colour, and this is used for display. Problems arise in determining what is 'sufficiently similar' and in optimising the search methods used.

The definition of 'sufficiently similar' depends on two things: the number of shades of a colour required and the size of the colour look-up table. If we are too strict then we may find that the available number of logical colours is not large enough; not strict enough and the accuracy of the image is undermined: about 25 different shades of a given colour are sufficient for most images. Therefore we consider an existing actual colour to be sufficiently similar to a newly calculated colour if each of the calculated R, G and B components is within 0.04 (**limit**) of the respective existing components. A larger number of different shades may be displayed by decreasing this value, but care must be taken not to exceed the available number of logical colours. Note that the information in the colour look-up table must be stored in the program as well as in the display device memory for the implementation of this method.

The search method is very important. If any image is shaded pixel by pixel then the colour look-up table is accessed many thousands of times and any slight delay in the search will result in a greatly increased processing time for the whole image. We implement this method using a number of linked lists within the colour look-up table, one list associated with each subset. An array entry **matlist[i]** identifies, for material **i**, a subset of the colour look-up table which has to be considered in a search for the shade of that material. The subsets are set up as linked lists in array **colptr[Max_Pal_entries]**; **matlist[i]** is the initial pointer to the list for material **i**, with the **colptr** values giving the next link in the subset, that is until a value of −1 indicates the end of the list. A new variable **newcolour** indicates the next free entry in the **colptr** array, and this facilitates adding new absolute colours to the list of logical colours. Each subset is sorted in order of increasing red component, so that the search through this subset is as efficient as possible. The entries in the colour look-up table, arrays **red[]**, **green[]** and **blue[]**, the associated linear lists of arrays **colptr[]** and **matlist[]**, and index **newcolour** are declared in **"palette.h"** (listing 1.2a).

When the apparent colour of a point on a surface is calculated, the list of logical colours associated with the absolute colour of the surface is scanned until one of three cases occurs

(i) a sufficiently similar colour is found: this colour is used for display

(ii) a colour with greater red component is found: the new colour is inserted into the list *before* the colour with greater red component, and the new colour is used for display

(iii) the end of the list is reached: the new colour is added to the end of the list, and used for display.

Of course, if your graphics device has 'infinite' colours, that is, there are more logical colours available than pixels on the screen, then there is no need for a colour table, you can identify each facet or pixel with its own unique shade.

Given a facet composed of material **mat**, a **vector3** point **p** on its surface, and a normal **norm** to the facet, we use the above shading models to include ambient light, and diffuse and specular reflection, and return three floating point values between 0 and 1, representing the red, green and blue components of the apparent colour of that point. This process is programmed in function **cshade** (listing 11.9), that corresponds to **intensityshade** of the intensity shading model.

Constant colour shading

We now consider two different ways of using these methods: constant shading and smooth shading. The simplest and quickest way of displaying a facet using the RGB model is by *constant colour shading*, see Plate Ia. We assume that the shade is constant across any facet and, once the logical colour approximating to the required shade has been determined, the facet is displayed on the window using a simple area-fill. The colour of light reflected from a point on the facet is found, and a suitable colour from the colour look-up table is selected for display. New **seefacet** and **facetfill** functions (listing 11.10) must be used in conjunction with this RGB colour shading model and these must replace previous versions in file **"display.cpp"**. Function **cshade** must be added to this file.

Listing 11.10

```
// Replace functions in file "display.cpp"
//------------------------------------//
  void facetfill(int face, int index)     // Constant Colour shading
//------------------------------------//
// Displays facet 'face' in a 'shade' with given 'index'
 { int i,j ;
   vector2 poly[maxpoly] ;
   win.setcol(index) ; j=mesh.Get_clipfac(face) ;
   if (j < 0) return ;
// Find the pixel co-ordinates of the vertices
   for (i=0 ; i<mesh.Get_size(j) ; i++)
   { poly[i] = pro.Get_vertex(mesh.Get_faclist(j,i) ) ; }
   win.polyfill(mesh.Get_size(j),poly) ;
 }  // End of facetfill
//------------------------//
  void seefacet(int face)          // Constant Colour shading
//------------------------//
 { float dummy,red,green,blue,t ;   // t is a transparency factor
   vector3 midpt,normvec ;
   int index,newface,suplength,suplist[maxsuplist] ;
// Find the mid-point and normal of facet 'face'
   midpt = mesh.midpoint(face) ; normvec = normal(face,&dummy,&obs) ;
// Find apparent colour of facet 'face'
   cshade(midpt,normvec,mesh.Get_material(face),&red,&green,&blue) ;
   t=1.0-mrl.Get_trn(mesh.Get_material(face)) ;
   index=plt.findlogicalcolour(t*red,t*green,t*blue,mesh.Get_material(face)) ;
// Display the facet
   facetfill(face,index) ;
// Repeat for each superficial facet on facet 'face'
   suplength = mesh.Get_a_sup(face,&(suplist[0])) ;
   while (suplength > 0)
   { newface = suplist[--suplength] ;
     cshade(midpt,normvec,mesh.Get_material(newface),&red,&green,&blue) ;
     t=1.0-mrl.Get_trn(mesh.Get_material(newface)) ;
     index = plt.findlogicalcolour(t*red,t*green,t*blue,
                                       mesh.Get_material(newface)) ;
     facetfill(newface,index) ;
   } ;
 }  // End of seefacet
```

Exercise 11.4

With this new version of file **"display.cpp"**, run the Project generated from application program **"nine11.cpp"**.

Smooth shading

Although constant colour shading is reasonably sufficient for scenes made up entirely of matt, planar surfaces, this method has a number of disadvantages. The results obtained on models representing curved or glossy surfaces are unsatisfactory – the polygonal facets that make up the approximation to a curved surface are clearly distinguishable, and also the specular highlights are unconvincing since they are constrained to be made up only of entire facets. Increasing the density of facets in the mesh helps to some extent, but we are able to produce far more convincing images of approximated curved surfaces by what is generally referred to as *smooth shading*. Here a surface is displayed by individually shading every pixel on each projected facet of the polygonal mesh, in a way that smooths out any intensity discontinuities. We give two different interpolation methods for smooth shading: Gouraud shading and Phong shading.

Gouraud shading

Gouraud's method of *intensity interpolation shading* (Gouraud, 1971) goes a long way towards solving the problems of constant shading mentioned above. The intensity of light reflected at each vertex of a facet is determined, taking into account ambient light, and diffuse and specular reflection. The intensity at each internal point of a projected facet may then be calculated by interpolation between these intensity values. The trick is in calculating the intensity at the vertices. Suppose we have a number of facets approximating to a curved surface. Each vertex lies in the real curved surface and is contained in the boundaries of a number of the approximating facets. The *vertex normal* **vna ("ClusterD.cpp")** array may be found by averaging the *surface normals* of the facets containing the vertex in their boundaries. This is implemented in the function **setnormal**, which should be called by a new **observe** function which calculates the ACTUAL normal vectors; both are given in listing 11.11. The OBSERVED co-ordinates of these vectors, array **vno ("ClusterE.cpp")**, are subsequently calculated in the new **observe** function. The *vertex intensity* (or, alternatively, the apparent colour at the vertex) may be calculated using one of the previously discussed shading models. The intensity or colour at each point within the facet may then be determined, using a *scan line* approach, by interpolating between the vertex intensities as shown in figure 11.5. The intensity at point A is found by interpolating between those at points 1 and 2, the intensity at B is found by interpolating between 3 and 4, and finally the intensity at C is found by interpolating between A and B. These two functions, **setnormal** and the new **observe**, are needed by both Gouraud, and later Phong, shading, and must be added to **"display.cpp"**.

Listing 11.11

```
// (Re)place functions in file "display.cpp"
//--------------------//
  void setnormal(void)
//--------------------//
// This function is needed for both Gouraud and Phong shading
// Function to calculate ACTUAL vertex normals
 { int i,j,k ;
   vector3 norm, va ;
   float dummy ;
// Initialise vertex normals
// Calculate vertex normals by looping through facets and including the
// facet normal in the calculation of normal at each vertex on the facet
   for (i=0 ; i<mesh.Get_nof() ; i++)
   { norm = normal(i,&dummy,&act) ;
     for (j=0 ; j<mesh.Get_size(i) ; j++)
     { k=mesh.Get_faclist(i,j) ;
       va = vna.Get_vertex(k) ;
       vna.put_vertex(k,va+norm) ;
     }
   }
 }  // End of setnormal

//------------------//
  void observe(void)
//------------------//
// This function is needed for both Gouraud and Phong shading
 { int i, nov ;
   setnormal() ;  nov = act.Get_nov() ;
   for (i=0 ; i<nov ; i++)
   { obs.put_vertex(i,Q * act.Get_vertex(i) ) ;
     vno.put_vertex(i,Q.dir_transform(vna.Get_vertex(i))) ;
   }
 }  // End of observe

//----------------------------------------------------------------//
  void facetfill(int face, float *red, float *green, float *blue)
//----------------------------------------------------------------//
// Gouraud shading
// Fills facet using scan line approach. Approximation to real co-ordinates.
 { int col,i,ix,iy,newv,oldv,xmax,xmin,ymax,ymin,nxpix,nypix ;
   float mu,redval,greenval,blueval,redstep,greenstep,bluestep ;
   float redmax,greenmax,bluemax,redmin,greenmin,bluemin,randval,winx,winy ;
   pixelvector pix,poly[maxpoly] ;
   vector2 projected, vpoly[maxpoly] ;
   if (mesh.Get_clipfac(face) < 0) return ;
// Find the pixel and window co-ordinates of the vertices
   for (i=0 ; i<mesh.Get_size(face) ; i++)
   { projected = pro.Get_vertex(mesh.Get_faclist(face,i)) ;
     vpoly[i] = projected ;
     poly[i].x=win.fx(projected.x) ; poly[i].y=win.fy(projected.y) ;
   }
// Find minimum and maximum y values
   ymax=poly[0].y ; ymin=poly[0].y ;
   for (i=1 ; i<mesh.Get_size(face) ; i++)
   { if (poly[i].y > ymax) ymax=poly[i].y ;
     if (poly[i].y < ymin) ymin=poly[i].y ;
   }
   nxpix = win.Get_nxpix() ;   nypix = win.Get_nypix() ;
// For each y, find maximum and minimum x values and
// the corresponding interpolated colour values
   ymax = min(nypix-1,ymax) ;  ymin = max(0,ymin) ;
   for (iy=ymin ; iy<=ymax ; iy++)
   { pix.y=iy ;
     winy = -iy/win.Get_xyscale()/win.Get_rat() + win.Get_vert()*0.5 ;
     xmin=nxpix ; xmax=-1 ;
     oldv=mesh.Get_size(face)-1 ;
```

```
     for (newv=0 ; newv<mesh.Get_size(face) ; newv++)
     { if ((max(poly[oldv].y,poly[newv].y) >= iy ) &&
           (min(poly[oldv].y,poly[newv].y) <= iy ) &&
           (poly[oldv].y != poly[newv].y))
         { mu=(winy-vpoly[oldv].y)/(vpoly[newv].y-vpoly[oldv].y) ;
           if (mu<0.0) mu = 0.0 ;
           else if (mu>1.0) mu = 1.0 ;
           winx=((1.0-mu)*vpoly[oldv].x+mu*vpoly[newv].x) ;
           ix = win.fx(winx) ;
           redval=(1.0-mu)*red[oldv]+mu*red[newv] ;
           greenval=(1.0-mu)*green[oldv]+mu*green[newv] ;
           blueval=(1.0-mu)*blue[oldv]+mu*blue[newv] ;
           if (ix < xmin)
             { xmin=ix ;
               redmin=redval ; greenmin=greenval ; bluemin=blueval ;
             } ;
           if (ix > xmax)
             { xmax=ix ;
               redmax=redval ; greenmax=greenval ; bluemax=blueval ;
             } ;
         } ;
       oldv=newv ;
     }
// Set colour component increments
     if (xmin < xmax)
       { redstep=(redmax-redmin)/(float)(xmax-xmin) ;
         greenstep=(greenmax-greenmin)/(float)(xmax-xmin) ;
         bluestep=(bluemax-bluemin)/(float)(xmax-xmin) ;
       }
     else { redstep=0.0 ; greenstep=0.0 ; bluestep=0.0 ; } ;
// For each pixel on scan-line, find colour and display
     redval=redmin ; greenval=greenmin ; blueval=bluemin ;
     xmax = min(nxpix-1,xmax) ;  xmin = max(0,xmin) ;
     for (ix=xmin ; ix<=xmax ; ix++)
     {
//................................................................//
// Un-comment the following lines
// if you want to add a 10% random variation to the actual RGB values
//         randval = 1.0 + 0.10* (0.5 - random()) ;
//         redval = redval * randval ;
//         greenval = greenval * randval ;
//         blueval = blueval * randval ;
//................................................................//
       col = plt.findlogicalcolour(redval,greenval,blueval,
                                       mesh.Get_material(face)) ;
       win.setcol(col) ;
       pix.x=ix ;   win.setpix(pix) ;
       redval += redstep ;   greenval += greenstep ;   blueval += bluestep ;
     }
   }
 }  // End of facetfill
//----------------------//
  void seefacet(int face)      // replacement 'seefacet' for Gouraud shading
//----------------------//
 { float dummy,red[maxpoly],green[maxpoly],blue[maxpoly] ;
   vector3 facenorm,norm,p,vo ;
   int i,j,newface,suplength,suplist[maxsuplist] ;
// Calculate surface normal to facet 'face'
   facenorm = normal(face,&dummy,&obs) ;
// Calculate shade at each vertex using vertex normals
   for (i=0 ; i<mesh.Get_size(face) ; i++)
   { j=mesh.Get_faclist(face,i) ; vo = vno.Get_vertex(j) ;
     if ((fabs(vo.x)>epsilon)||(fabs(vo.y)>epsilon)||(fabs(vo.z)>epsilon))
       norm=vo ;
     else norm=facenorm ;
     p = obs.Get_vertex(j) ;
    cshade(p,norm,mesh.Get_material(face),&(red[i]),&(green[i]),&(blue[i]));
   }
```

```
// Display facet, interpolating between these shades
   facetfill(face,red,green,blue) ;
// Repeat for each superficial facet
   suplength = mesh.Get_a_sup(face,&(suplist[0])) ;
   while (suplength > 0)
   { newface = suplist[--suplength] ;
     for (i=0 ; i<mesh.Get_size(newface) ; i++)
     { j=mesh.Get_faclist(newface,i) ;
       vo = vno.Get_vertex(j) ;
       if ((fabs(vo.x) > epsilon) || (fabs(vo.y) > epsilon)
                                  || (fabs(vo.z) > epsilon ))
         norm=vo ;
       else norm=facenorm ;
       p = obs.Get_vertex(j) ;
       cshade(p,norm,mesh.Get_material(newface),&(red[i]),&(green[i]),
                                                       &(blue[i])) ;
     }
// Display facet, interpolating between these shades
     facetfill(newface,red,green,blue) ;
   }
 }  // End of seefacet
```

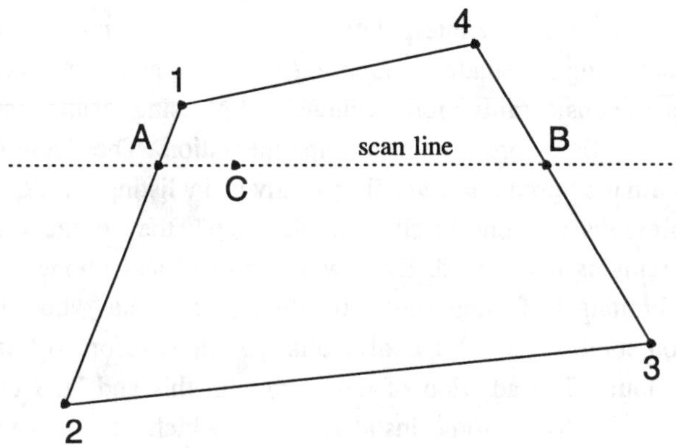

Figure 11.5

Gouraud shading is implemented using the **seefacet** and **facetfill** functions in listing 11.11, which should replace the present versions in **"display.cpp"**. The full implementation requires a small addition to one other function. Each vertex of the scene has associated with it a vertex normal. What about the vertices created by clipping? Since a projected facet is displayed by interpolating between the intensities at its vertices, we need to know the intensities at these new 'clipping plane' vertices. This necessitates a new calculation in the clipping method **clip** given in listing 8.7. When a new vertex is created by calculating the point of intersection between a facet edge and a clipping plane, its vertex normal is also calculated by interpolating between those at the end-points of the facet edge, and then stored. This can be achieved using the **mu** value found during the calculation of intersection. See the commented entry in listing 8.7.

Exercise 11.5
With this new version of file **"display.cpp"**, run the Project generated from application program **"nine11.cpp"** and draw pictures similar to Plate Ib which shows our teapot displayed using Gouraud shading.

Phong interpolation
Some problems still remain with Gouraud shading, mainly involving facets which face almost directly towards the light source. In figure 11.6, for example, points A and B both have the same intensity and so interpolating between them results in a constant intensity across the surface, making it appear flat. Problems also occur with the depiction of highlights produced by specular reflection: consider the 'square highlight' on the teapot of Plate Ib.

These problems are eliminated by using Phong's *normal vector interpolation shading* (Phong, 1975). This method involves the calculation of the normal vector at each point on a surface by interpolating between the normals at the vertices, and thence calculating the shade by applying a shading model at that point. This method produces considerably more accurate and pleasing results, however, it is accordingly more time-consuming in implementation. The **facetfill** function needed for normal interpolation shading is given in listing 11.12, and should replace the previous versions in file **"display.cpp"**; the **seefacet** function of listing 11.11 remains unchanged. Even with Gouraud and Phong shading, you may find one limitation of using only 256 colours, that is the 'wood-grain' effect that appears on some surfaces! To solve this, you must resort to 'dithering', or using more colours. The addition of new arrays in this and later chapters can cause storage problems on some installations, in which case you will have to reduce the values of **maxv, maxf** and **maxlist** in the **Cluster** and **Mesh** database, and delete some clusters if they are not needed.

Example 11.2
Plate IV demonstrates the effect of the specular reflection parameters and Phong shading. It shows 24 spheres composed of a material that has RGB diffuse reflection parameters (0.6,0.5,0.08) and zero transparency. The spheres are drawn in six rows of four columns. The specular reflection coefficient, **spec**, varies from 0.05 on the top row, through 0.15, 0.30, 0.45 and 0.65, to 0.95 on the bottom row. The specular reflection exponent, **expn**, varies from 2 in the left column, through 5 and 20, to 100 in the right column.

Example 11.3
The teapot in Plate Ic was displayed using Phong shading on the same model used for Plates Ia and Ib. Also see Plate V of Phong shaded chesspieces.

Listing 11.12

```
// Replacement function for file "display.cpp"

//------------------------//
  void facetfill(int face)
//------------------------//
// Phong shading
// Uses 'seefacet' from Constant shading (listing 10.4)
// Fills facet using scan line approach. Approximation to real co-ordinates.
 { int col,i,j,index,inter,ix,iy,newv,oldv,xmax,xmin,ymax,ymin,nxpix,nypix ;
   float constant,mu,red,green,blue ;
   vector3 normv[maxpoly] ;
   vector3 facenorm,p,step,vint,vmin,vmax,windpt ;
   vector2 projected, vpoly[maxpoly] ;
   float randval, rval, gval, bval, winx, winy ;
   pixelvector pix,poly[maxpoly] ;
   j=mesh.Get_clipfac(face) ;
   if (j < 0) return ;
// Find surface normal to 'face'
   facenorm = normal(face,&constant,&obs) ;
// Find the pixel and window co-ordinates of the vertices
   for (i=0 ; i<mesh.Get_size(j) ; i++)
   { index=mesh.Get_faclist(j,i) ;
     projected = pro.Get_vertex(index) ;
     vpoly[i] = projected ;
     poly[i].x = win.fx(projected.x) ;
     poly[i].y = win.fy(projected.y) ;
     normv[i] = vno.Get_vertex(index) ;
   }
// Find minimum and maximum y values
   ymax = poly[0].y ;
   ymin = poly[0].y ;
   for (i=1 ; i<mesh.Get_size(j) ; i++)
   { if (poly[i].y > ymax) ymax = poly[i].y ;
     if (poly[i].y < ymin) ymin = poly[i].y ;
   }
// For each scan line find maximum and minimum x values and
// the corresponding normal vectors
   nxpix = win.Get_nxpix() ;
   nypix = win.Get_nypix() ;
// For each y, find maximum and minimum x values and
// the corresponding interpolated colour values
   ymax = min(nypix-1,ymax) ;
   ymin = max(0,ymin) ;
   for (iy=ymin ; iy<=ymax ; iy++)
   { pix.y = iy ;
     winy = -iy/win.Get_xyscale()/win.Get_rat() + win.Get_vert()*0.5 ;
     xmin = nxpix ; xmax = -1 ;
     oldv=mesh.Get_size(j)-1 ;
     for (newv=0 ; newv<mesh.Get_size(j) ; newv++)
     { if ((max(poly[oldv].y,poly[newv].y) >= iy ) &&
           (min(poly[oldv].y,poly[newv].y) <= iy ) &&
           (poly[oldv].y != poly[newv].y))
         { mu = (winy-vpoly[oldv].y)/(vpoly[newv].y-vpoly[oldv].y) ;
           if (mu<0.0) mu = 0.0 ;
           else if (mu>1.0) mu = 1.0 ;
           winx = ((1.0-mu)*vpoly[oldv].x+mu*vpoly[newv].x) ;
           ix = win.fx(winx) ;
           vint = (1.0-mu)*normv[oldv] + mu*normv[newv] ;
           if (ix < xmin)
             { xmin = ix ; vmin = vint ; }
           if (ix > xmax)
             { xmax = ix ; vmax = vint ; }
         } ;
       oldv = newv ;
     }
```

```
// Set colour component increments
    if (xmin < xmax)   step = (1.0 / (float)(xmax-xmin)) * (vmax-vmin) ;
    else step = zero ;
// For each pixel on scan-line, find colour and display
    vint = vmin ;
    for (ix=xmin ; ix<xmax ; ix++)
// Find WINDOW co-ordinates of point
    { windpt.x = ix/win.Get_xyscale()-win.Get_horiz()*0.5 ;
      windpt.y = -iy/win.Get_xyscale()/win.Get_rat()+win.Get_vert()*0.5 ;
      windpt.z = -ppd ;
      inter = ilpl(zero,windpt,facenorm,constant,&p,&mu) ;
      cshade(p,vint,mesh.Get_material(face),&red,&green,&blue) ;
//.....................................................................//
// Un-comment the following lines
// if you want to add a 10% random variation to the actual RGB values
//        randval = 1.0 + 0.10* (0.5 - random()) ;
//        red = red * randval ;
//        green = green * randval ;
//        blue = blue * randval ;
//.....................................................................//
      col = plt.findlogicalcolour(red,green,blue,mesh.Get_material(face)) ;
      win.setcol(col) ;
      pix.x = ix ;
      win.setpix(pix) ;
      vint = vint + step ;
    }
  }
 }  // End of facetfill
```

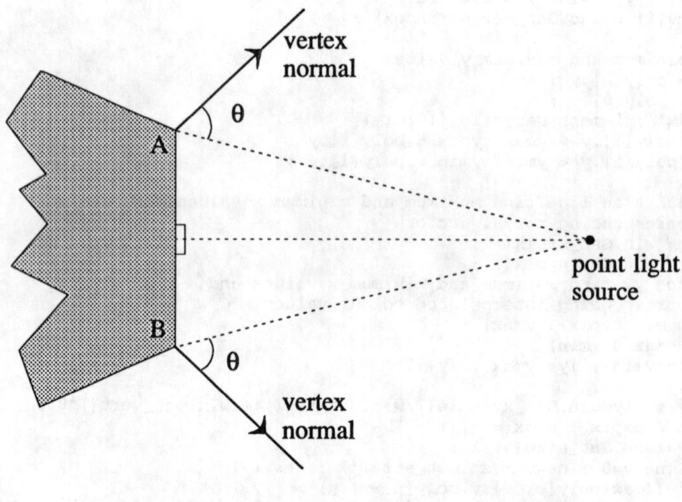

Figure 11.6

Exercise 11.6

We can use shading models to simulate *texture* on a surface. The simplest method of simulating texture is provided by *pseudo-random variation*. The shade of a pixel is calculated using one of the shading models detailed above. This shade is then altered slightly by a pseudo-random function and the pixel displayed in this altered shade. This gives an appearance of roughness to the surface.

A more formalised method of texturing is achieved by distorting the normal vector using some texture function. Instead of assuming that the normal to a facet is constant across the facet, we use the texture function to vary the normal from pixel to pixel, giving each pixel a different shade and thereby introducing a textured appearance (Blinn and Newell, 1976; Blinn, 1978). Experiment with these ideas.

Exercise 11.7
With this new Phong version of file **"display.cpp"**, run the Project generated from application program **"nine11.cpp"** and draw a goblet using Phong shading.

Exercise 11.8
There is a major problem with our implementation of both the Gouraud and Phong shading approaches. That is, in function **setnormal** (listing 11.11), which calculates vertex normals by averaging the normals of the facets that intersect at each vertex, no consideration is given as to whether or not the facets run smoothly into one another. Look at Plates Ib and Ic, and compare them with the line drawing of figure 9.10 or the constant colour shaded version of Plate Ia. Notice that the top plane of the teapot lid which should be flat appears curved!

To solve this problem, you must adjust our listings, and no longer calculate the complete set of vertex normals for all the objects in the scene. Instead, for each facet in turn, the vertex normals of its vertices must be calculated anew, because not all of the normals of abutting facets should be taken into account. Obviously the normal of a particular facet will be part of each of the vertex normal calculations for that facet. As for the other facets that abut that facet, you must find the cosine of the angles between the normal of the chosen facet and the normals of each of its neighbouring facets (using scalar product), and only include such a normal in the average calculation for the vertex normal if its cosine value lies above a certain arbitrary but fixed threshold (try 0.8). If the resulting picture is still unsatisfactory for whatever reason, you have three options: raise or lower the threshold value, or increase the density of the mesh.

Before going on to the next chapter, this is a good opportunity to stress again the need to un-comment the lines of code given in **"palette.cpp" (listing 1.2b)** and in the **"display.h&cpp"** and **"model.h&cpp"** files that are needed for the **Material** class.

12 Shadows, transparent surfaces and reflections

The functions we give in this chapter are meant to be used with the constant colour shading model of chapter 11 (listings 11.6 and 11.7), and should be used to extend file **"display.cpp"**.

Shadows

A facet which obscures all or part of another facet from exposure to a light source is said to *cast a shadow* onto this other facet. A shadow cast by a convex polygonal facet, **j**, onto another convex polygonal facet, **i**, is also a convex polygon which may be considered to lie on the surface of facet **i**. We call this polygon a *shadow polygon*. In chapter 11 we stated that only ambient light was reflected from a point in shadow: in this chapter we turn our attention to finding and displaying such shadow polygons, and give an algorithm to achieve this. This algorithm is merely one example of the many ways that this problem can be tackled; for alternative solutions see Crow (1977). The criterion for finding shadows is very similar to that for finding hidden surfaces; and most hidden surface algorithms can be adapted accordingly. The method which we describe here is based on the general hidden surface algorithm of listing 10.11.

There are two main problems to solve

(i) finding the vertices of the shadow polygons,

(ii) incorporating shadow polygons into the database.

The solution to the second problem is considerably simplified if we use a single light source. Initially we shall assume this to be the case and we shall discuss the extension to multiple light sources later.

Representing shadow polygons – superficial facets

Superficial facets were introduced in chapter 9 for the representation of surface detail polygons. The concept fits exactly our requirement for the storage of shadow polygons. A superficial facet lies on the surface of a larger facet which we call its *host facet*. Note that a superficial facet need not be considered in an algorithm for hidden surface elimination, since in all cases that facet is displayed only if its host facet is displayed.

Since the shadow polygons are stored in exactly the same way as superficial facets of a scene, they may thus be referred to by simple integer indices which we store in stacks, named **lsh**, that we declared in the **Mesh** database (listing 7.3). **lsh[i]** is a stack that contains a linear list of the indices of all facets which represent shadows on facet **i** of the model, given the present light source.

Initially all shadow lists are empty, and so the **top** of stack **lsh[i]** is set to NULL for each facet i. Now suppose we find that facet **j** casts a shadow onto facet **i** and that this shadow is a polygon with **nsv** vertices. The OBSERVED co-ordinates of these vertices are appended, in order, to the **obs** array, and the indices of these vertices of a new superficial facet are stored in the **listofverts** array as **listofverts[firstfree]**, ..., **listofverts[firstfree+nsv−1]**. **extendednof** is incremented by 1, **firstoffacet[extendednof]** is set to **firstfree**, **size[extendednof]** to **nsv**, and the value of **firstfree** is changed to **firstfree+nsv**. Finally the value **extendednof** is **push**ed onto the list **lsh[i]**. See function **shadow** listing 12.1. Here **firstoffacet**, **firstfree**, **listofverts**, **extendednof** and **size** maintain their original meanings because we are just extending the **Mesh**.

In order to find the complete set of shadow polygons, we must compare the facets of a scene in pairs, in order to determine whether either casts a shadow onto the other: hence the similarity to a hidden surface algorithm. We shall examine the details of this comparison later, but first let us consider the question of precisely which pairs need be compared. We may discard some comparisons immediately for one of four reasons.

(i) Both facets lie entirely outside the pyramid of vision or both facets are oriented clockwise when projected onto the view plane. In either case we can see neither facet, and so there is no need to find the shadows since they are not going to be displayed anyway. It is important to note, however, that a facet which we cannot see can still cast a shadow onto a facet which we can see. Therefore, if either facet of a pair may be seen then that pair must be considered.

(ii) Both facets are superficial facets. It is important that we find the shadows cast by an ordinary facet onto a superficial facet since these will, in general, be of a different colour from those cast onto the host facet. However, we need not consider shadows cast *by* a superficial facet since these will only be parts of those cast by the larger host facet.

(iii) One of the facets is superficial to the other: the facets are coplanar and hence no shadow is cast.

(iv) One of the two facets faces away from the light source. If a facet faces away from the light source then it can neither cast a shadow nor have a shadow cast upon it. No such facet need be considered.

Listing 12.1

```
// Place these functions in file "mesh.cpp"
extern Palette plt ;      extern Cluster2d prol ;
extern Cluster3d vl ;     extern float shadpd ;

//---------------------//
  void Mesh::shadow(void)     // Calculates and stores all shadow polygons
//---------------------//
 { int back,extendednov,front,i,j,k,nsv,toeye[maxf],tolight[maxf] ;
   vector3 shadpol[maxpoly] ;
   stackinfo st ;
// Set up co-ordinate system for shadow calculation
   prepare_shadows() ;
// Determine orientation of facets
   for (i=0 ; i<nof ; i++)
   { if (orient(i,&pro) == 1) toeye[i]=TRUE ;  // Facet i faces towards eye
     else toeye[i]=FALSE ; // Facet 'i' faces away from eye
     if (orient(i,&prol) == 1) tolight[i]=TRUE ; // Facet i towards light
     else tolight[i]=FALSE ;  // Facet 'i' faces away from light
   } ;
// Compare pairs of facets : 'i' and 'j'
   for (i=0 ; i<nof-1 ; i++)
// If facet 'i' faces away from light source then don't use it
     if (tolight[i])
       for (j=i+1 ; j<nof ; j++)
// If facet 'j' faces away from light source then don't use it
// If both facets 'i' and 'j' are superficial then don't compare
// If neither facet 'i' nor 'j' can be seen then don't compare
// If one facet is superficial to the other then don't compare
         if ((tolight[j]) && (toeye[i] || toeye[j]) &&
            ((superf[i] == -1) || (superf[j] == -1)) &&
            ((superf[i] != j) && (superf[j] != i)) )
          { compare(i,j,&front,&back,&nsv,shadpol) ;
// No shadow if 'front' facet superficial or 'back' facet cannot be seen
            if ( (front != -1) && (superf[front] == -1) && (toeye[back]) )
// Create new facet representing shadow polygon
              { size[extendednof]=nsv ;
                firstoffacet[extendednof]=firstfree ;
       if (extendednof >= maxf) cerr << "\n Error No more facets" ;
       if (firstfree+nsv >= maxlist)
          cerr << " Size of list array exceeded \n" ;
                for (k=0 ; k<nsv ; k++)
                { extendednov = obs.Get_extendednov() ;
                  obs.put_vertex(extendednov,shadpol[k]) ;
                  listofverts[firstfree+k]=extendednov ;
                  extendednov++ ;  //consistent with obs.extendednov
                  obs.Set_extendednov(extendednov) ;
                }
                firstfree=firstfree+nsv ;
// Push the new facet onto the list of shadows ('lsh') facet back
                st.i = extendednof ; lsh[back].push(st) ; extendednof++ ;
              } ;
          } ;
 }  // End of shadow

//----------------------------------//
  void Mesh::displayshadows(int face)
//----------------------------------//
// Displays shadows on given 'face'
 { float redval,greenval,blueval ;
   int clipindex,col,i,newface,nnf,nnv,stofree,verti,stcount,j,extendednov ;
   stackinfo stclist[maxsuplist] ;
   vector2 projected ;   vector3 observed ;
// Set colour to that given by reflected ambient light
   redval=mrl.Get_rdf(material[face])*ambient ;
   greenval=mrl.Get_gdf(material[face])*ambient ;
   blueval=mrl.Get_bdf(material[face])*ambient ;
   col = plt.findlogicalcolour(redval,greenval,blueval,material[face]) ;
```

```
// Scan list of shadows, drawing each in turn
   stcount = lsh[face].Get_stack(&(stclist[0])) ;  j = 0 ;
   while (stcount > j)
   { newface=stclist[j++].i ;
     extendednov = obs.Get_extendednov() ;
     nnv=extendednov ; nnf=extendednof ; stofree=firstfree ;
//store obs, mesh state
     clipindex = clip(newface) ;
     if (clipindex !=2)
       { if (clipindex == 1)  clipfac[newface]=newface ;
         else clipfac[newface]=extendednof-1 ;
// Calculate projections of vertices
         for (i=0 ; i<size[clipfac[newface]] ; i++)
           { verti=listofverts[firstoffacet[clipfac[newface]]+i] ;
             observed = obs.Get_vertex(verti) ;
             projected.x = -observed.x*ppd/observed.z ;
             projected.y = -observed.y*ppd/observed.z ;
             pro.put_vertex(verti,projected) ;
           } ;
// Draw shadow and restore obs mesh state
         facetfill(newface,col) ;    clipfac[newface]=newface ;
         extendednov=nnv ; extendednof=nnf ; firstfree=stofree ;
         obs.Set_extendednov(extendednov) ;
       } ;
   } ;
 }  // End of displayshadows
//--------------------------------------------------------------------//
  void Mesh::compare(int i, int j, int *front, int *back, int *nsh,
                                                   vector3 *shadpol)
//--------------------------------------------------------------------//
// Compares facets 'i' and 'j', finding shadow cast by one on other
 { int k,stofaci,stofacj ;
   vector2 shp[maxpoly] ;
// Adjust 'nfac' values so that unclipped shadow is found
   stofaci=clipfac[i] ; stofacj=clipfac[j] ;
   clipfac[i]=i ; clipfac[j]=j ;
// Call 'overlap' to find the projection of the shadow
   overlap(i,j,front,back,nsh,shp,&prol,&vl,shadpd,1) ;
// Reset 'nfac' values
   clipfac[i]=stofaci ; clipfac[j]=stofacj ;
// If 'front' is -1 then no shadow is cast, otherwise find shadow's vertices
   if (*front != -1)
     { for (k=0 ; k<*nsh ; k++)
       { shadpol[k].x=shp[k].x ;  shadpol[k].y=shp[k].y ;  }
       restore(*back,*nsh,shadpol) ;
     } ;
 }  // End of compare
```

Each of these cases is checked for in the function **shadow** (listing 12.1) before a pair of facets is compared. This function creates and stores information about the shadows cast, and calls two functions, **compare** (listing 12.1) and **prepare_shadows** (listing 12.2). **prepare_shadows**, part of **"display.cpp"**, calls **lightsystem** (listing 12.2) which sets up a LIGHT co-ordinate system and transforms the OBSERVED **Cluster** position into both a LIGHT **Cluster** position **vl** (**"ClusterF.cpp"**) and LIGHT **Cluster** projection **prol** (**"ClusterG.cpp"**), both of which facilitate the calculation of shadows. Function **compare** compares two facets, **i** and **j**, returning the OBSERVED co-ordinates of the vertices of the shadow cast (if any), a **vector3** array **shadpol**, together with the integers **front** and **back** indicating that facet **front** casts a shadow onto facet **back**. If the value of **front** is set to –1 then no shadow is cast.

Listing 12.2

```
// Place these functions in file "display.cpp"

//----------------------//
  void lightsystem(void)
//----------------------//
// Sets up light co-ordinate system
 { Matrix F, G, H, V ;
   float alpha,beta,gamma,dist,xmax,ymax,zmax,xmin,ymin,zmin ;
   int i ;
   vector3 observed, direct ;
// Find the centre point of the scene
   observed = obs.Get_vertex(0) ;
   xmax = observed.x ;   xmin = observed.x ;
   ymax = observed.y ;   ymin = observed.y ;
   zmax = observed.z ;   zmin = observed.z ;
   for (i=1 ; i<obs.Get_nov() ; i++)
   { observed = obs.Get_vertex(i) ;
     if (observed.x > xmax) xmax=observed.x ;
     else if (observed.x < xmin) xmin=observed.x ;
     if (observed.y > ymax) ymax=observed.y ;
     else if (observed.y < ymin) ymin=observed.y ;
     if (observed.z > zmax) zmax=observed.z ;
     else if (observed.z < zmin) zmin=observed.z ;
   } ;
   direct.x=(xmax+xmin)/2.0-src.x ;
   direct.y=(ymax+ymin)/2.0-src.y ;
   direct.z=(zmax+zmin)/2.0-src.z ;
// Calculate translation matrix 'F'
   F.translate(src.x,src.y,src.z) ;
// Calculate rotation matrix 'G'
   alpha=angle(-direct.x,-direct.y) ;
   G.rotate(3,alpha) ;
// Calculate rotation matrix 'H'
   dist=sqrt(pow(direct.x,2.0)+pow(direct.y,2.0)) ;
   beta=angle(-direct.z,dist) ;
   H.rotate(2,beta) ;
// Calculate rotation matrix 'V'
   dist=sqrt(pow(dist,2.0)+pow(direct.z,2.0)) ;
   gamma=angle(-direct.x*dist,direct.y*direct.z) ;
   V.rotate(3,-gamma) ;
// Combine the transformations to find 'S'
   S = V * (H * (G * F)) ;
// Reverse the process to find the inverse of 'S (SI)'
   F.translate(-src.x,-src.y,-src.z) ;
   G.rotate(3,-alpha) ;
   H.rotate(2,-beta) ;
   V.rotate(3,gamma) ;
   SI = F * (G * (H * V)) ;
   shadpd=dist ;        //Rounding errors will occur if dist is too large
 }  // End of lightsystem

//---------------------------//
  void prepare_shadows(void)
//---------------------------//
// Finds light-related co-ordinates of each vertex
 { vector2 prolight ;
   vector3 vlight ;
   lightsystem() ;
   for (int i=0 ; i<obs.Get_extendednov() ; i++)
   { vlight = S * obs.Get_vertex(i) ;
     vl.put_vertex(i,vlight) ;
     prolight.x=(-vlight.x*shadpd)/vlight.z ;
     prolight.y=(-vlight.y*shadpd)/vlight.z ;
     prol.put_vertex(i,prolight) ;
   } ;
 }  // End of prepare
```

```
//-----------------------------------------------//
  void restore(int face, int nsh, vector3 *shadpol)
//-----------------------------------------------//
// Finds OBSERVED co-ords of vertices from projected light-related co-ords
 { int i ;
   float dummy,val ;
   vector3 normvec,vectori ;
   normvec = normal(face,&val,&vl) ;
   for (i=0 ; i<nsh ; i++)
   { shadpol[i].z=-shadpd ;
     ilpl(zero,shadpol[i],normvec,val,&vectori,&dummy) ;
     shadpol[i] = SI * vectori ;
   }
 }  // End of restore

//-----------------------//
  void seefacet(int face)
//-----------------------//
// 'seefacet' routine for Constant colour shading display with Shadows
// Use facetfill of Constant colour shading (listing 11.10)
 { float dummy,red,green,blue ;
   vector3 midpt,normvec ;
   int index,newface ;
   int suplength, suplist[maxsuplist] ;
// Find the mid-point and normal of facet'face'
   midpt = mesh.midpoint(face) ; normvec = normal(face,&dummy,&obs) ;
// Find apparent colour of facet 'face'
   cshade(midpt,normvec,mesh.Get_material(face),&red,&green,&blue) ;
   index = plt.findlogicalcolour(red,green,blue,mesh.Get_material(face)) ;
// Display the facet
   facetfill(face,index) ;  mesh.displayshadows(face) ;
// Repeat for each superficial facet on facet 'face'
   suplength = mesh.Get_a_sup(face,&(suplist[0])) ;
   while (suplength > 0)
   { newface = suplist[--suplength] ;
     cshade(midpt,normvec,mesh.Get_material(newface),&red,&green,&blue) ;
 index = plt.findlogicalcolour(red,green,blue,mesh.Get_material(newface)) ;
     facetfill(newface,index) ; mesh.displayshadows(newface) ;
   } ;
 }  // End of seefacet

// Replace function "look_at_it" in file "display.cpp" with the following:

//---------------------//
  void look_at_it(void)
//---------------------//
 { look3() ;
// then calculate the observation matrix 'Q'
   findQ() ;
   observe() ;
   insource() ;
   mesh.clipscene() ;
   project_it() ;
   mrl.read("material.dat") ;
   mesh.shadow() ;
 }  // End of look_at_it
```

Displaying shadow polygons

With the **Mesh** data structure constructed in the manner described above, the display of shadows is a relatively trivial matter. Essentially there are three problems to consider: (i) deciding when to draw a shadow; (ii) setting the colour; and (iii) calculating the window co-ordinates of the vertices of the polygon so that it can be plotted.

The first two problems are easily solved. Whenever a host facet is displayed we immediately scan the linear list of shadow polygon indices, and draw each of them in the logical colour that is returned by the chosen constant shading model, but considering only ambient light on the material of the host facet as no direct light falls on that part of the host facet. The solution to the third problem, implemented in function **displayshadows** (listing 12.1), requires a little more consideration. First the shadow polygon **shadpol** must be transformed into its OBSERVED position: this is achieved by function **restore** (listing 12.2). The polygon may have to be clipped before it can be displayed, since it may lie partly or entirely outside the pyramid of vision. The **Mesh** method **clip** (listing 8.7) is therefore invoked, returning a value **clipindex** which describes the clipping done. If **clipindex** = 1 then no clipping was necessary, the projections of the vertices of the shadow polygon are calculated, and the polygon is displayed. If **clipindex** = 2 then the shadow polygon lies totally outside the pyramid of vision, and should not be displayed. If **clipindex** = 3 then clipping has occurred, and a new facet with index **extendednof** has been created and stored in the **Mesh** database. This new facet is first displayed, and then discarded from the database simply by resetting **extendednov**, **extendednof** and **firstfree** to their previous values.

When all of the shadow polygons on a host facet have been displayed, then we move onto facets superficial to that host facet. Each is displayed in turn, followed by the shadows that lie on it.

This process, programmed in the function **displayshadows** (listing 12.1), is called from the alternative function **seefacet** (listing 12.2). The whole sequence is precipitated by a new version of function **look_at_it** (listing 12.2). The code in listing 12.1 must be added to file **"mesh.cpp"** and that of listing 12.2 added to **"display.cpp"**: all old versions of functions must be replaced.

Finding the shadow polygons

All that remains now is to find the vertices of a shadow cast by one facet onto another. Note that a shadow polygon is simply the projection of one facet onto another; see figure 12.1. We may make use of the properties of linear projections to enable us to use the **overlap** function (listing 10.11) to find shadow polygons.

Recall that a projection is described by a set of *lines of projection*. (For an orthographic projection, these lines are parallel; for a perspective projection they emanate from a single point.) The projection of a vertex onto a plane is the point of intersection (if such a point exists) between the line of projection passing through the vertex and the plane. The projection of a facet onto a plane is the polygon in the plane whose vertices are the projections of the vertices of the facet. When calculating shadows, the lines of projection are the light rays.

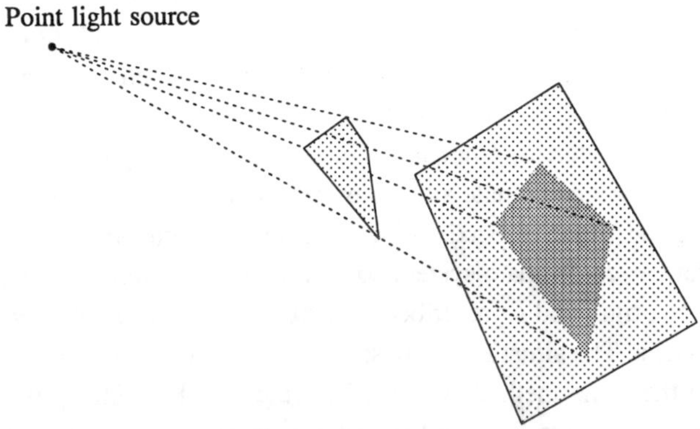

Figure 12.1

Our aim is to find out which, if either, of two facets, **i** and **j**, casts a shadow onto the other and to calculate the co-ordinates of the vertices of the shadow if it exists. If we have a projection plane onto which both facets may be projected, the area of overlap of the two projected facets is the projection of the shadow polygon. (If there is no overlap, and the polygon is empty, then no shadow is cast.) A shadow is cast by the facet nearer the light source onto that further away: information which may be gleaned from the **overlap** function. We may determine the three-dimensional co-ordinates of the vertices of the shadow polygon by calculating the intersections between the light rays passing through the projections of these vertices and the plane containing the host facet. This is the general strategy: how do we implement it?

The first question is which plane do we choose for the projection? We only compare facets a pair at a time, and so, in theory, for any given pair, we can choose any plane onto which all of the vertices of both facets may be projected, choosing a different plane for each pair. However, this would be excessively time-consuming, requiring many transformations for each comparison. It is much more convenient to use the same plane for the projection of each pair of facets; we could then calculate and store the projected co-ordinates of all vertices before beginning the process of comparison. Can we find a suitable plane? What we actually do is create a new right-handed co-ordinate system, called the LIGHT co-ordinate system. We call the co-ordinates of the vertices relative to this system *light-related co-ordinates*. As we did previously with both orthographic and perspective projections, we place the projection plane perpendicular to the z-axis of this LIGHT system. Of course the way we create the LIGHT system will depend on the choice of type of light source!

In the case of a point light source, all lines of projection emanate from a single point (the source itself); this corresponds to a perspective projection. Here the choice of plane is not easy, and forces us to restrict the positioning of the light source. We take a point in the centre of the scene (taken as the mean of the extreme x, y and z values of all the vertices in the OBSERVED scene). Then we define a direction vector, $\boldsymbol{d}$, from the light source to this point. We can then construct the LIGHT co-ordinate system by setting the origin at the light source and identifying the negative z-axis with direction $\boldsymbol{d}$. In chapter 8 we described how to transform a co-ordinate system so that a specified point (in that case the eye) became the origin and a prescribed direction (the direction of view) became the negative z-axis. The situation we describe above corresponds exactly to this, so we can use the same methods to transform the OBSERVER system into the LIGHT co-ordinate system. To simplify matters we impose the restriction that the light source is positioned in such a way that every vertex has a strictly negative light-related z co-ordinate. Then any plane perpendicular to the negative z-axis of the LIGHT system may be used as a projection plane.

In the case of parallel beam illumination we have a parallel projection onto the projection plane, since all lines of projection are parallel (to the light rays). Therefore, we may choose any plane that is perpendicular to the direction of these rays; this furnishes us with an orthographic projection. Now however, there is no particular point which may be identified in analogy to the eye in defining the origin of the LIGHT system. So we choose an arbitrary point, a suitable candidate is the existing origin of the OBSERVER system – note that the choice of this point does not affect the shadows found. Then the negative z-axis of the LIGHT system will be identified with the direction of the light beams, $\boldsymbol{l}$. Given the new origin and $\boldsymbol{d}$ (=$\boldsymbol{l}$), we can calculate the relationship between OBSERVER and LIGHT systems in exactly the same way as with the point light source.

From now on we shall assume only the use of a point light source. The matrix, S representing the transformation from OBSERVER co-ordinate system to LIGHT co-ordinate system, is calculated in the function **lightsystem** in listing 12.2; a calculation very similar to that in **findQ** in listing 8.1. The function also calculates the inverse matrix, S^{-1} (**SI** in the listing), for use in the **restore** function. The matrices **S** and **SI** are declared in the **Mesh** database.

Given a projection plane, $z = -d$, the projected co-ordinates of the **vl** vertex cluster are all of the form $(x, y, -d)$; d is the perpendicular distance of the plane from the light source. The value of d (**shadpd**) does not affect the shadow found, it is only used to find which facet is the host of a shadow polygon; and so we arbitrarily use the distance from the light source to the 'centre' of the scene. The light-related co-ordinates (**vl**) of all vertices are found in **prepare_shadows** (listing 12.3), along with the projected values **prol**.

With the co-ordinates of all vertices of a scene stored in this form, we may proceed with the comparisons. Given the indices of two facets **i** and **j**, we must find the area of overlap between the projections of these facets. We may use the **overlap** function (listing 10.11) to provide this information. Recall that a call to this function returns the following information:

front, back:

if no area of overlap exists then **front** is returned as 0, otherwise **front** and **back** contain the indices of the facets nearer to the origin and further from the origin respectively.

shp:

a **vector2** array containing the projected x and y co-ordinates of the vertices of the area of overlap relative to the co-ordinate system implied by the parameters, in this case the LIGHT system.

This information is all we need. If **front** is returned as 0 then no action need be taken. Otherwise a shadow polygon **shadpol** has been found, which represents a shadow cast by facet **front** onto **facet** back. All we have at the moment are the projected light-related co-ordinates by calculating the intersections of the light rays passing through these projected vertices with the plane containing facet **back**. The vector representation of this plane may be found using the function **normal** in listing 10.11, and the point of intersection found by **ilpl** listing 6.2. The light ray passing through a point with light-related co-ordinates (x , y , z) is given by the line $(0 , 0 , 0) + \mu(x , y , z)$, since the light source is at the origin. The OBSERVED co-ordinates of the shadow polygon **shadpol**, for return to the shadow function, may then be found by applying the transformation represented by matrix S^{-1} to the light-related co-ordinates. The transformation from projected light-related co-ordinates to OBSERVED co-ordinates is achieved by the function **restore** in listing 12.2.

The look_at_it function

Shadows may be calculated and stored by a single call to **Mesh** method **shadow**. This we incorporate into the new **look_at_it** function (listing 12.2), after the matrix Q has been calculated, the light source positioned, the scene clipped and projected, and the data on materials read in.

Example 12.1

Plate IIa displays a scene consisting of a table and three 'hollow cubes' on a checkerboard floor, showing shadows cast by two cubes onto the table, and by all three cubes and the table onto the floor.

Exercise 12.1

Rewrite the functions given so far in this chapter, but for use with parallel beam illumination instead of a point light source.

Exercise 12.2

Note that the ACTUAL positions of shadow polygons are totally independent of the eye position. If multiple views of a scene are required, with fixed light source, it is more efficient to store the shadow polygons so that they are not recalculated for each new view. Rewrite the functions to store the ACTUAL shadow co-ordinates instead of the OBSERVED co-ordinates, and so you should transform the ACTUAL co-ordinates to OBSERVED co-ordinates in the function **displayshadows** before calculating the projected co-ordinates. Also, you may not eliminate comparisons so freely in the **shadow** function – you must find the shadows cast onto a facet regardless of whether it can be seen in any particular view. Finally, the indices of each shadow polygon must be stored on a stack. If multiple views of the same model are needed then clipping and shadows must be calculated afresh after resetting the database to its original **nov** and **nof** values.

Project 12.1

The algorithm which we describe deals only with a single light source. It can be extended to cope with multiple light sources. The shadow polygons generated by each light source must be calculated and stored. With each such polygon an integer must be associated, indicating which light source does not illuminate the polygon, together with a colour calculated from the illumination by all of the other light sources. When drawing a facet the following process must be followed

(i) Draw the facet.
(ii) Draw the shadow polygons generated by light source 1.
(iii) Draw the shadow polygons generated by light source 2, storing the intersections with each of those generated by light source 1.
(iv) Draw the areas of intersection which have been stored (shadow polygons generated by light sources (1 and 2)) in a colour determined by illumination by all light sources except 1 and 2.
(v) Draw the shadow polygons generated by light source 3, storing the areas of intersection with each of the polygons generated by light sources 1, 2 and (1 and 2) respectively.
(vi) Draw the shadow polygons generated by light sources (1 and 3), then by (2 and 3), then (1, 2 and 3) etc.

The process must be limited by a maximum number of light sources. The implementation of this process is a major programming exercise.

Transparent surfaces

Many hidden surface algorithms can be adapted to allow for the inclusion in the scene of facets made of transparent materials. This is by no means a trivial exercise. For a full simulation, taking into account specular reflection, refraction etc., a ray-tracing approach (described in chapter 16) must be adopted (Kay and Greenberg, 1979; Whitted, 1980). Nevertheless, if we accept certain limitations, then we can deal with transparent surfaces in the polygonal mesh model using the topological ordering algorithm of chapter 10. In the algorithm described here, we impose some restrictions – all refractive indices remain as unity, we do not allow for the inclusion of shadows, nor do we allow for the possibility of rays passing through more than one transparent surface (so if there are several transparent facets in a scene, then if they are not all in the same plane, the viewing positions must be chosen carefully to avoid problems). The algorithm can be extended to take these possibilities into account, however, and we shall discuss such extensions at the end of the explanation.

Having imposed the above restrictions, we may adapt the hidden surface algorithm with only minimal changes to existing functions (**hidden** and **unstack**: listing 10.11). Recall that we use the function **overlap** (listing 10.11) to find the area of intersection between the projections of two facets; up to now we assumed that the part of the front facet obscures a polygonal area on the back facet. Now suppose that the front facet is transparent! Instead of the overlapped part of the back facet being obscured, it is visible in a particular colour that is influenced by the colour of the **front** facet and extent of its transparency. Note that a facet must be transparent from both sides, and so that our insistence on anti-clockwise orientation does not reject one particular side of the facet, it must be stored twice in the database (clockwise as well as anti-clockwise) unless one side is always totally obscured by non-transparent surfaces.

We implement this idea in the following manner

(i) Use the function **network** to construct the network structure as before.

(ii) Before commencing the drawing of a scene, all of the transparent surfaces are displayed. This ensures that all of the parts of these facets which 'obscure' no other facet will be visible in the completed image.

(iii) The **hidden** function proceeds as before, first **push**ing all those facets which obscure no other (**nob[i]** = 0) onto a stack.

(iv) One value is **pop**ped from the stack, giving the index, **k** say, of the next facet to be displayed. If facet **k** is transparent (**tran[k]** > 0), then it is not displayed, otherwise it is.

(v) The list (**list[k]**) of facets obscuring ***k*** is then scanned as before, and each corresponding **nob** value is reduced by 1, and a facet **push**ed onto the stack if its **nob** value becomes zero. If an obscuring facet is transparent then the area of overlap between this facet and facet **k** is calculated and displayed in a colour found by mixing the apparent colour of facet **k** with that of the transparent facet, in the manner described in chapter 11. (Our restrictions ensure that this cannot occur if facet *k* is transparent.) The value of **tran[k]** gives the proportion of light that is reflected off the surface and **(1-tran[k])** the amount transmitted through.

(vi) The steps (iv) and (v) are repeated and the process continues until the stack becomes empty.

The new **hidden** and **unstack** functions are given in listing 12.3, and should be used to replace the previous versions in file **"display.cpp"**. The declaration of array **tran** is given in our material database, **mrl**, listing 11.2.

Example 12.2

Plate IIb shows the same scene as in example 12.1, but where now the table-top consists of a transparent material.

Listing 12.3

```
// Replace 'unstack' and 'hidden' in "display.cpp" with the following:
//------------------------------------------------------------//
  void unstack(int face, int *nob, Stack *list, Stack *stack)
//------------------------------------------------------------//
 { vector2 poly[maxpoly] ;
   float red1,green1,blue1,red2,green2,blue2,red3,green3,blue3 ;
   float tranval,redtran,greentran,bluetran,dummy ;
   vector3 mid,normvec ;
   int front,back,n,col,count,supface,suplist[maxsuplist] ;
   stackinfo nf ;
// Calculate apparent colour of facet 'face' : redval, greenval, blueval
   normvec = normal(face,&dummy,&obs) ;
   mid = mesh.midpoint(face) ;
   cshade(mid,normvec,mesh.Get_material(face),&red1,&green1,&blue1) ;
// Scan list of facets obscuring 'face'
   while (! list[face].empty())
   { nf=list[face].pop() ;
     (nob[nf.i])-- ;
     if (nob[nf.i] == 0) stack->push(nf) ;
// If obscuring facet is transparent then find overlap with 'face' and draw
     if (mrl.Get_trn(mesh.Get_material(nf.i)) > 0.0)
       { overlap(face,nf.i,&front,&back,&n,poly,&pro,&obs,ppd,1) ;
         normvec = normal(nf.i,&dummy,&obs) ;
         mid = mesh.midpoint(nf.i) ;
         cshade(mid,normvec,mesh.Get_material(nf.i),&red2,&green2,&blue2) ;
         tranval=mrl.Get_trn(mesh.Get_material(nf.i)) ;
         redtran=(1-tranval)*red2+tranval*red1 ;
         greentran=(1-tranval)*green2+tranval*green1 ;
         bluetran=(1-tranval)*blue2+tranval*blue1 ;
         col = plt.findlogicalcolour(redtran,greentran,bluetran,
                                        mesh.Get_material(nf.i)) ;
         win.setcol(col) ;
         win.polyfill(n,poly) ;
// For every superficial facet of face do the same
         count = mesh.Get_a_sup(face,&(suplist[0])) ;
```

```
// For every facet superficial to face overlap the newface
         while (count > 0)
         { supface = mesh.Get_clipfac(suplist[--count]) ;
           if (supface != -1)
             { overlap(supface,nf.i,&front,&back,&n,poly,&pro,&obs,ppd,1) ;
               normvec = normal(supface,&dummy,&obs) ;
               mid = mesh.midpoint(supface) ;
               cshade(mid,normvec,mesh.Get_material(supface),&red3,&green3,
                                                              &blue3) ;
               redtran=(1-tranval)*red2+tranval*red3 ;
               greentran=(1-tranval)*green2+tranval*green3 ;
               bluetran=(1-tranval)*blue2+tranval*blue3 ;
               col = plt.findlogicalcolour(redtran,greentran,bluetran, \
                                           mesh.Get_material(supface)) ;
               win.setcol(col) ; win.polyfill(n,poly) ;
             } ;
         } ;
      } ;
   } ;
 }  // End of unstack

//-----------------//
  void hidden(void)    // Hidden surface algorithm for transparent surfaces
//-----------------//
// Constant shading
 { Stack list[maxf], networkstack ;
   stackinfo st ;
   int i,numbervisible,nob[maxf] ;
   numbervisible = network(&(nob[0]),&(list[0]),&pro,&obs,1) ;
   for (i=0 ; i<mesh.Get_nof() ; i++)
   { if (mrl.Get_trn(mesh.Get_material(i)) > 0) seefacet(i) ;
     if ((nob[i]==0) && (mesh.Get_super(i)==-1))
        { st.i = i ; networkstack.push(st) ; }
   }
   for (i=0 ; i<numbervisible ; i++)
   { if (networkstack.empty()) return ;
     st=networkstack.pop() ;
     if (mrl.Get_trn(mesh.Get_material(st.i)) < epsilon) seefacet(st.i) ;
     unstack(st.i,nob,list,&networkstack) ;
   }
 }  // End of hidden
```

Exercise 12.4

If transparent surfaces overlap in a view then the calculations are not quite so simple. When the area of overlap between a transparent facet and the facet **k** is calculated and displayed, it must also be stored as a facet superficial to **k**. If another transparent facet is encountered in the list of those obscuring **k**, then the overlap of this facet with **k** must be calculated, displayed and stored, along with the overlap with the previously created superficial facets. Furthermore, if the projections of two transparent facets overlap in an area onto which no other facet is projected, then a mixture of the facet colours and the background colour must be displayed. Implement a hidden surface algorithm which allows for overlapping transparent facets. Note that the order in which you store the areas of overlap is important – the part of a facet seen through i transparent facets cannot be displayed until those parts viewed through j ($1 \le j < i$) transparent facets have been displayed. The method of solving this problem is very similar to the solution of the problem of shadows cast by multiple light sources (exercise 12.3).

Exercise 12.5
The inclusion of shadows in the view of a scene containing transparent surfaces poses three problems

(i) Dealing with shadows cast by transparent surfaces.
(ii) Dealing with shadows cast onto transparent surfaces.
(iii) Dealing with shadows on other facets which are visible through a transparent surface.

The first of these problems proves difficult only in determining the colour of the shadow, the other two provide more difficulties. Think about these problems. The implementation of an algorithm which allows for both shadows and multiple transparent surfaces is a large exercise and is much more easily tackled using a ray-tracing approach.

Reflections

Suppose one facet in a scene is a *mirror*. We should be able to see the reflection of the scene in this mirror. Some of the techniques that we have already given will help us produce an image of such a reflection.

We call the plane containing the mirror facet the *mirror plane*. In chapter 6 we described the calculation of the reflection of a point in a plane. If we calculate the reflection of each vertex of the scene in the mirror plane, we have the *physical reflection* of the scene. Note that here we are creating a new set of points with co-ordinates specified in relation to the *same* co-ordinate system – the OBSERVER system. The facet definitions still hold (with indices now referring to the corresponding vertices in the new set of points) except that where the vertices were listed in anti-clockwise orientation around a facet in the true model, the orientation is clockwise in the reflected model (figure 12.2).

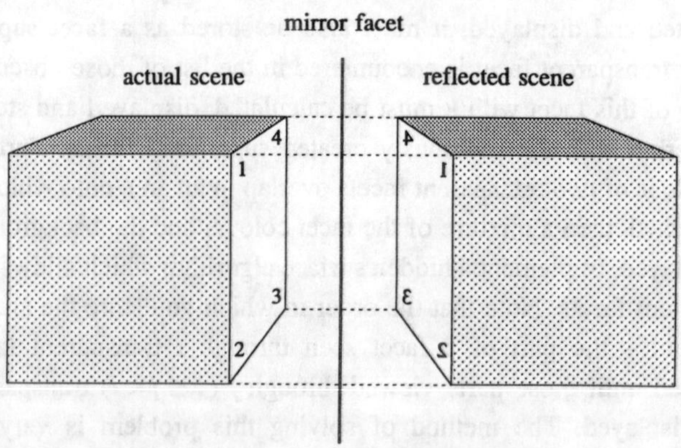

Figure 12.2

How can we relate to this physical reflection with the reflection observed in the mirror? Imagine that the mirror facet is a window surrounded by an infinite plane. The reflection in the mirror is precisely the part of the physical reflection which can be seen through (and beyond) this window. Those parts of the physical reflection which lie in front of the mirror cannot be seen in the reflection since in the real scene they lie behind the mirror. The problem of reflection thus reduces to projecting the reflected scene onto the view plane, and then drawing only those parts which both intersect with the projection of the mirror and lie behind the mirror in reflected space – a problem once again solved by the **overlap** function (listing 10.11). There is a major drawback to any algorithm for finding reflections of scenes. If you sit in front of a mirror with another mirror behind you, what do you see? You see a reflection of yourself in the mirror in front of you, but you also see a reflection of the mirror behind you, in which you see a reflection of your back and of the mirror in front of you, in which you see a reflection of the mirror behind you, and so on! The process is infinite and there is no way round this. We must either insist that a scene contains no mirrors that reflect each other, or else we simply ignore infinite reflections of mirrors, allowing for only a limited number of *levels of reflection.* We shall impose a limit of one level of reflection, so when reflected in another mirror, a mirror facet is considered as an ordinary, non-reflecting facet.

There remain two questions. Firstly, at what stage do we draw the reflection and secondly, how do we apply the hidden surface algorithm to the reflected scene? These problems are solved by treating a reflection as if it were superficial to the mirror facet. We modify the **hidden** function of listing 10.11, as is indicated in the comment, to call a new function **reflekt,** which calls a function **mirror_face**, both given in listing 12.4 and added to file **"display.cpp"**. Function **reflekt** is called for each facet **face** which is a mirror facet, and draws the reflection of the scene in that mirror facet. We will need some method to indicate that a facet is a mirror. We use the specular reflection coefficient stored in the **spec** entry of the material database to indicate the proportion of reflected light. In this way we draw each reflection facet **j** immediately after drawing the mirror facet **i**, in a colour generated by mixing the facet colour and the mirror colour thus:

(1−**spec[i]**) × colour of host mirror facet **i** + **spec[i]** × colour of reflected facet **j**.

The function **reflekt** is of the same form as the function **hidden** (listing 10.11: remember to un-comment the call to **reflekt** in that listing). The reflected co-ordinates of each vertex **reflect** are declared as the cluster position **"ClusterH.cpp"**, and projections **proref** are declared as the cluster projection **"ClusterI.cpp"** in listings 7.2c.

Listing 12.4

```
// Place these functions in file "display.cpp".   Remember to un-comment
// the line of code from the 'hidden' function that invokes 'reflekt'

Stack rlist[maxf] ;      // Declare these stacks outside the 'mirror_face'
                         // function to avoid DOS's "stack overflow"

//---------------------------------------------//
  void mirror_face(int face, vector3 normvec)
//---------------------------------------------//
 { int col, i, newface, front, back, mirvis, nv, rnob[maxf] ;
   float red1, red2, green1, green2, blue1, blue2 ;
   float val,redval,greenval,blueval ;
   float reflection = mrl.Get_spc(mesh.Get_material(face)) ;
   vector3 mid ;
   vector2 poly[maxpoly] ;
   Stack stack2 ;
   stackinfo st ;
   mid = mesh.midpoint(face) ;
   cshade(mid,normvec,mesh.Get_material(face),&red1,&green1,&blue1) ;
   mirvis = network(&(rnob[0]),&(rlist[0]),&proref,&reflect,-1) ;
// Draw facets in topological order
   for (i=0 ; i<mesh.Get_nof() ; i++)
     if (rnob[i] == 0) { st.i = i ; stack2.push(st) ; } ;
// 'mirvis' is the number of facets visible in the 'mirror'
   for (i=0 ; i<mirvis ; i++)
   { if (stack2.empty()) return ;
     st = stack2.pop() ; newface = st.i ;
     if (face != newface)
// Find 'overlap' with mirror and draw
     { if ( (mesh.Get_super(face) != newface)
          || (mesh.Get_super(newface) != face) )
       { overlap(face,newface,&front,&back,&nv,&(poly[0]),&proref,
                                             &reflect,ppd,-1) ;
         if (front == face)
         { normvec = normal(newface,&val,&obs) ;
           mid = mesh.midpoint(newface) ;
           cshade(mid,normvec,mesh.Get_material(newface),&red2,&green2,
                                                              &blue2) ;
           redval= (1-reflection)*red1 + reflection*red2 ;
           greenval=(1-reflection)*green1 + reflection*green2 ;
           blueval=(1-reflection)*blue1 + reflection*blue2 ;
           col = plt.findlogicalcolour(redval,greenval,blueval,
                                 mesh.Get_material(newface)) ;
           win.setcol(col) ; win.polyfill(nv,poly) ;
         } ;
       } ;
     } ;
     unstack(newface,rnob,rlist,&stack2) ;
   } ;
 } // End of mirror_face

//----------------------//
  void reflekt(int face)
//----------------------//
// Calculates and draws the image of the scene as seen reflected in 'face'
 { int i, whichface, suplength, suplist[maxsuplist], count ;
   float mu, val ;
   vector3 observed, reflected, normvec, oddvector ;
   vector2 proreflected ;
// Calculate the normal to 'face' and reflection of each vertex
   normvec = normal(face,&val,&obs) ;
   for (i=0 ; i<obs.Get_extendednov() ; i++)
   { observed = obs.Get_vertex(i) ;
     ilpl(observed,normvec,normvec,val,&oddvector,&mu) ;
     reflected = observed + (2.0*mu) * normvec ;
     reflect.put_vertex(i,reflected) ;
```

```
// Project the reflected vertices onto the perspective viewing screen
      proreflected.x=-reflected.x*ppd/reflected.z ;
      proreflected.y=-reflected.y*ppd/reflected.z ;
      proref.put_vertex(i,proreflected) ;
    }
// Call 'network' to create a topological order of facets to be drawn
    whichface = face ;
    if (mrl.Get_spc(mesh.Get_material(whichface)) > 0.0)
         mirror_face(whichface,normvec) ;
    suplength = mesh.Get_a_sup(face,&(suplist[0])) ;
// For every facet superficial to face overlap the newface
    count = suplength ;
    while (count > 0)
    { whichface = suplist[--count] ;
      whichface = mesh.Get_clipfac(whichface) ;
      if (whichface != -1)
      { seefacet(whichface) ;
        if (mrl.Get_spc(mesh.Get_material(whichface)) > 0.0)
        mirror_face(whichface,normvec) ;
      }
    }
 }  // End of reflekt
```

The function **network** is called with the reflected co-ordinate arrays as parameters to set up a network of information about which facets obscure others in the view of the reflected scene. An array of stacks **rlist[maxf]** and integer array **rnob[maxf]** are used to store the information about the network. These arrays correspond to the arrays **list** and **nob** of the **hidden** function's topological sorting algorithm, and the names are changed slightly to avoid interference with the hidden surface network relating to the general view (see listing 10.11).

For each mirror facet, the new network is sorted exactly as before, using a new stack referred to by **stack2** (again used so as not to interfere with the general ordering) in function **mirror_face**. The area of overlap between each facet (and all associated superficial facets) is displayed, with the exception of other mirror facets. When the stack becomes empty (**stack2 = NULL**) the functions **mirror_face** and then **reflekt** ends (**mirror_face** is called for every superficial facet), and the drawing of the remainder of the scene continues.

Example 12.3

Plate IIc displays the same scene used in the two previous examples in this chapter; however, in this case both the table-top and the floor are composed of reflecting material.

Project 12.2

Incorporate our polygonal mesh programs of chapters 7 to 12 in a CAD/CAM package. All communication with this package should use a mouse, particularly when defining the database models of objects. The silhouette data for both our extrusion and body of revolution functions should be input in this way.

Project 12.3
All of the listings given in this chapter use the constant colour shading approach, assuming that the intensity of reflected light is constant across a facet. Rewrite the functions for use with Gouraud or Phong interpolation models and produce scenes such as that shown in Plate V. We have drawn this scene, of chesspieces on a reflecting checkerboard, in both VGA mode 19 (Plate Va) and XGA mode 255 (Plate Vb) to illustrate the different resolutions of the two cards.

Project 12.4
We have allowed for only one level of reflection. The maximum level could, of course, take any value. Extend the algorithm to allow for, say, three levels. You must either introduce some form of recursion, or else write a new function for each level of reflection. But beware of the 'stack overflow' error; when using recursion, if at all possible use global variables. You may have to change the 'heap size' option of Borland C++; see the Appendix.

Project 12.5
Extend the algorithm so that the reflections of shadows may be displayed.

As you can see, the inclusion of such concepts as transparent surfaces, mirrors and shadows in polygon-based hidden surface functions necessitates excessive numbers of comparisons and very careful manipulation of data. We have reached the limit of such algorithms. For more realistic images, with almost unlimited scope for simulating the many aspects of illumination, we must turn to analytic modelling and the techniques of ray-tracing and of quad-tree and oct-tree algorithms which we describe in the final chapters of this book.

13 The analytic approach

In these final four chapters we shall discuss some relatively recent developments in the representation of objects in three-dimensional space. We take a different approach from previous chapters where we considered the polygonal mesh. There the basic idea was to use polygonal facets that approximate to a surface, and then to project that approximation ultimately onto the window/viewport, where a representation of a three-dimensional scene is drawn. With the analytic approach we do just the opposite: we give each surface (and by extension its inside and outside) an exact representation as a combination of *primitive (mathematical) objects*, and we approximate only during the display stage. Nevertheless, in common with the polygonal mesh approach, we will be using the concepts of SETUP and ACTUAL positions relative to the ABSOLUTE co-ordinate system for defining geometrical objects, of the OBSERVED position relative to the OBSERVER system for placing these objects relative to an observer.

Whenever the highly ambiguous term 'object' is used, especially in this book where we draw geometrical objects with programs written in an object-oriented programming language, we must be very careful. We must use the context of the word in order to differentiate between an object as an instantiation of a C++ class and as a geometrical entity that forms part of a three-dimensional scene.

A primitive object is defined mathematically in terms of an analytic function: an idea we have already introduced in chapter 6 with the analytic representation of surfaces. In the final chapters of this book we will limit ourselves to just four types of primitive object: a sphere, a cylinder, a half-space and a checkerboard – we leave to the reader to create more objects as and when the need arises. Each of these four types of geometrical object will be defined in a SETUP position relative to the ABSOLUTE co-ordinate system, and that will greatly simplify the calculations necessary for display. Multiple copies of each primitive can then be moved to various ACTUAL (and OBSERVED) positions by **Matrix** methods.

The analytic approach allows a very simple definition of many complex three-dimensional scenes; however, that ease of definition has to be paid for with a large increase in processing overheads, although not necessarily in program complexity. In all graphics programs we have to approximate at some stage, for otherwise we would be processing an infinite number of surface points. In the analytic approach the approximation is done during the display stage, by working with (groups of) pixels that are representative of areas and volumes of real

Euclidean space. Since a graphics viewport consists of only a finite number of pixels (**nxpix** by **nypix**), we avoid a potentially infinite process.

To illustrate these ideas we will look at three implementations. The first, in chapter 14, is the *quad-tree* (Sidhu and Boute, 1972; Tanimoto, 1977; Hunter and Steiglitz, 1979; Woodwark, 1984), which will be used to draw simple **scenes** composed of a grouping of spheres of arbitrary radius and position. Secondly there is the *oct-tree* technique (Clark, 1976; Meagher, 1982): in chapter 15 we will outline the approach, describe the construction of a binary tree using ideas from *constructive solid geometry* to model a scene as the *union*, *intersection* and *complement* of various primitive objects, and then implement it in a program. Finally in chapter 16, we will describe *ray-tracing* (Whitted, 1980; Glassner, 1989), where a more global illumination model is used. Optical phenomena may be modelled more accurately, producing 'photo-realistic' images.

Naturally all three analytic approaches will need to link into our **Viewport**, **Palette** and **Window** classes, so that models in three-dimensional space can be projected onto a two-dimensional window and thence onto VGA or XGA screens. We achieve this with a call to the **draw_a_picture** function originally constructed for the polygonal mesh model, which divides the process into: building the model (**build_it**); setting up the observer and light source (**look_at_it**); and drawing the scene (**draw_it**). Following the same polygonal mesh schema, **build_it** will appear as an application program that links together a number of files into a C++ Project; as usual **draw_it** will be stored in a file named **"display.cpp"**. A new version of **look_at_it** is stored in a new file **"model.cpp"** (listing 13.1). This particular file has only a passing similarity with the polygonal mesh version: **insource** and **look3** stay the same, however, **look_at_it** calls a new **observe** function that is now a method of a new class, **Analytic_scene** (listing 13.2), instantiated as the particular object **scene**. Function **findQ** is replaced by function **findQQI** which returns both the ACTUAL to OBSERVED matrix **Q** and its inverse **QI**. All three analytic approaches will also need to use our previous **Matrix, Stack** and **Material** (instantiated as object **mrl**) classes, hence the need to **#include "matrix.cpp"**, **"stack.cpp"** and **"material.cpp"**.

Listing 13.1a

```
// Save as file "model.h"

#include "viewport.h"
#include "palette.h"
#include "window.h"

#include "matrix.h"
#include "stack.h"
#include "analytic.h"
#include "material.h"

const vector3 zero = { 0.0, 0.0, 0.0 } ;
#define ambient 0.4
```

Listing 13.1b

```
// Save as file "model.cpp"

#include "model.h"

extern Window win ;
extern Palette plt ;
void build_it(void) ;
void draw_it(void) ;

Matrix Q, QI ;
vector3 direct,eye ;
float ppd ;
vector3 src ;

Analytic_scene scene ;
Material mrl ;

#include "matrix.cpp"
#include "stack.cpp"
#include "analytic.cpp"
#include "material.cpp"
//-----------------//
  void look3(void)        // take this from listing 8.1b
//-----------------//

//--------------------//
  void insource(void)     // take this from listing 11.1
//--------------------//

//-------------------//
  void findQQI(void)
//-------------------//
// Finds the matrix Q for the OBSERVED coordinate system and its inverse QI
 { float alpha, beta, gamma, v, w ;
   Matrix F,G,H,U,FI,GI,HI,UI ;
   F.translate(eye.x,eye.y,eye.z) ;
   FI.translate(-eye.x,-eye.y,-eye.z) ;
   alpha = angle(-direct.x,-direct.y) ;
   G.rotate(3,alpha) ;   GI.rotate(3,-alpha) ;
   v = sqrt(direct.x*direct.x + direct.y*direct.y) ;
   beta = angle(-direct.z,v) ;
   H.rotate(2,beta) ;   HI.rotate(2,-beta) ;
   w=sqrt(v*v+direct.z*direct.z) ;
   gamma=angle(-direct.x*w,direct.y*direct.z) ;
   U.rotate(3,-gamma) ;   UI.rotate(3,gamma) ;
   Q = U * (H * (G * F)) ;
   QI = FI * (GI * (HI * UI)) ;
 }  // End of findQQI

//---------------------//
  void look_at_it(void)
//---------------------//
 { look3() ;
   findQQI() ;
   insource() ;
   scene.observe(Q,QI) ;
 }  // End of look_at_it

//-------------------------//
  void draw_a_picture(void)       // From listing 7.4b
//-------------------------//
 { build_it() ;
   look_at_it() ;
   draw_it() ;
 }  // End of draw_a_picture
```

Analytic representation of primitive objects

We will not be using the **Mesh** and **Cluster** classes in our analytic approach, and instead we give a generalized version of a new class, **Analytic_scene**, that is to be used for all three different types of approach: quad-tree, oct-tree and ray-tracing. We will introduce just four types of primitive object: a sphere, a cylinder, a half-space (all of space to one side of an infinite plane; the normal to that plane points away from the half-space), and a checkerboard.

Listing 13.2a gives the headers for the class, file **"analytic.h"**, and listing 13.2b gives the code for the methods, file **"analytic.cpp"**. Each instantiation of the **Analytic_scene** class will be a C++ object **scene**, that is itself a grouping of at most **maxobj** primitive geometrical objects. Initially **maxobj** is set to 100, but at any one time the C++ object will consist of **numobj** geometrical objects. We will use the same grouping of eight parameters for the definition of all four types of primitive object; each type will require a different subset of the parameters for its description. Each parameter will be stored in an array, with the array index identifying one of the **maxobj** objects. The array index starts at 1 and runs through to **numobj**; this counting does not start at zero, because we wish to be consistent with the oct-tree algorithm in chapter 15 where we will be using the notation of minus an index to represent the complement of an object.

There are two floating point parameters **fpp1** and **fpp2**. In the case of the sphere, **fpp1** will hold the radius value of the SETUP sphere centred at ABSOLUTE co-ordinate origin. The finite cylinder has radius **fpp1**, half-length **fpp2**, and is SETUP along the y-axis and centred at the origin. The plane of the half-space is the SETUP x/z plane through the origin, with normal pointing along the positive y-axis; no **fpp** parameters are needed. The checkerboard lies in the same plane as the half-space, but it is a finite square of side **fpp1**, centred on the SETUP origin, and divided into **fpp2** by **fpp2** checker squares. The data for each object will have a **main_material** type, an integer which points into the arrays of the material database. The checkerboard will need a **second_material** type and an integer **mat_flag** to indicate which of the two materials is presently under consideration. The **primitive_type** parameter indicates the object type (1:sphere, 2:cylinder, 3:half-space, 4:checkerboard).

Each single occurrence of an object requires a matrix P to move the primitive object of corresponding type from its SETUP to its ACTUAL position; matrix Q will move it from its ACTUAL to OBSERVED position. Combining the two matrices, matrix R $(= Q \times P)$ can move it directly into OBSERVED position. We store this matrix as parameter **R** for each geometrical object in the C++ class **Analytic_scene**. However, when we first input the data it will be in the form of matrix P, and only after matrix Q has been calculated will it be changed into its true SETUP to OBSERVED form by calling a new version of method **observe**. The inverse of this matrix, parameter **RI**, is also needed since, for some types of primitive object, the calculations required in OBSERVED position are more easily undertaken in the simple mathematical formulation of the SETUP position.

Positional data on all the geometrical objects in an **Analytic_scene** will be stored in a file with a **".dat"** extension. Exactly how these objects interrelate within the scene must be described by a data structure that refers to integer labels, each label specifying a particular object within the **Analytic_scene** class.

Listing 13.2a

```
// Save code as file "analytic.h"

#define maxobj  100

//--------------------//
  class Analytic_scene
//--------------------//
 { int numobj ;
   float fpp1[maxobj] ;
   float fpp2[maxobj] ;
   int primitive_type[maxobj] ;
   int main_material[maxobj] ;
   int second_material[maxobj] ;
   int mat_flag[maxobj] ;
   Matrix R[maxobj] ;
   Matrix RI[maxobj] ;

public:
  Analytic_scene() ;
  void read(char *filename) ;
  void observe(Matrix A, Matrix AI) ;
  Matrix Get_matrixR(int i) { return ( R[i] ) ; }
  Matrix Get_matrixRI(int i) { return ( RI[i] ) ; }
  float Get_fpp1(int i) { return ( fpp1[i] ) ; }
  float Get_fpp2(int i) { return ( fpp2[i] ) ; }
  int Get_type(int i) { return ( primitive_type[i] ) ; }
  int Get_material(int o) ;
  void Set_main_mat(int o) { mat_flag[o] = 0 ; }
  void Set_second_mat(int o) { mat_flag[o] = 1 ; }
  int Get_numobj(void) { return ( numobj ) ; }
  void read_matrices(ifstream &datafile, Matrix *A, Matrix *AI) ;
 } ;  // End of Class Analytic_scene
```

The **Analytic_scene** class has the usual collection of **Get** and **Set** methods that are self-explanatory, however, some of the other methods do need further explanation. The constructor **Analytic_scene** simply sets up default values for the class. Method **read** inputs the data for a particular object from a data file. The data is given in a consistent form for all three analytic approaches: examples of **".dat"** files can be found in the following chapters. The file will first contain the total number of objects in the scene, **numobj**, followed by an entry for each of these objects. The entry will consist of the integer type of the object (in our case 1, 2, 3 or 4); followed by the SETUP to ACTUAL and ACTUAL to SETUP matrices laid out side by side; concluding with the two **fpp** values, the **main_material** index, and if required the **second_material** index.

The matrices are laid out as 3 rows of four columns, with each row of the matrix **R** lying on the same line as, but to the left of, the corresponding row of matrix **RI**; the bottom row of both matrices is understood to be (0 , 0 , 0 , 1). Method **read_matrices** is used to take all the matrices presented in this form and place them as proper 4 by 4 matrices in the C++ class **Analytic_scene.**

Listing 13.2b

```
// Save code as file "analytic.cpp"
//-----------------------------------//
  Analytic_scene::Analytic_scene()
//-----------------------------------//
 { for (int i=0 ; i<maxobj ; i++)
   { fpp1[i] = 0.0 ;              fpp2[i] = 0.0 ;
     primitive_type[i] = 0 ;     main_material[i] = 0 ;
     second_material[i] = 0 ;    mat_flag[i] = 0 ;
     R[i].unit() ;               RI[i].unit() ;
   }
 }  // End of Analytic_scene
//---------------------------------------------------------------------//
  void Analytic_scene::read_matrices(ifstream &datafile, Matrix *A,
                                                        Matrix *AI)
//---------------------------------------------------------------------//
 { float a[5][5], am[5][5] ;
   for (int j=1 ; j<4 ; j++)                         // line by line
     { for (int k=1 ; k <= 4 ; k++)
         { datafile >> a[j][k] ; }
       for ( k=1 ; k <= 4 ; k++)
         { datafile >> am[j][k] ; }
     }
   for ( j=1 ; j<4 ; j++)
     { a[4][j] = 0.0 ; am[4][j] = 0.0 ; }
   a[4][4] = 1.0 ;  am[4][4] = 1.0 ;
   A->Set(a) ;  AI->Set(am) ;
 }  // End of read_matrices
//---------------------------------------//
  void Analytic_scene::read(char *filename)
//---------------------------------------//
// Replacement function for retrieving analytically described objects
 { Matrix A, AI ;
   ifstream datafile ;
   datafile.open(filename) ;  datafile >> numobj ;
   if (numobj >= maxobj)
     cerr << " Error maximum number of objects reached\n" ;
   for (int i=1 ; i<=numobj ; i++)     // Counting starts from 1
   { datafile >> primitive_type[i] ;
     read_matrices(datafile,&A,&AI) ;
     R[i] = A ;   RI[i] = AI ;
     switch (primitive_type[i])
     {  case  1 :   // Sphere
        case  2 :   // Cylinder
        case  3 :   // Halfspace
           datafile >> fpp1[i] >> fpp2[i] >> main_material[i] ;  break ;
        case 4 :    // Checkerboard
           datafile >> fpp1[i] >> fpp2[i] ;
           datafile >> main_material[i] >> second_material[i] ;  break ;
        default :    // ERROR
           cerr << "\n Error: Attempt to read unspecified object" ; break ;
     }
   }                       // loop of 'every object'
   datafile.close() ;
 }  // End of read
```

```
//--------------------------------------------------//
  void Analytic_scene::observe(Matrix A, Matrix AI)
//--------------------------------------------------//
 { for (int i=1 ; i<=numobj ; i++)
     { R[i] = A * R[i] ;
       RI[i] = RI[i] * AI ;
     }
 }  // End of observe

//----------------------------------------//
  int Analytic_scene::Get_material(int o)
//----------------------------------------//
 { return ( mat_flag[o] ? second_material[o] : main_material[o] ) ;
 }  // End of Get_material
```

We are now in a position to use geometrical objects set up in this way to create three-dimensional images using the quad-tree, oct-tree and ray-tracing techniques of the last three chapters of this book.

Project 13.1

Create a C++ object for each of our four primitive types of geometrical object. Use the mechanisms of *overloading* and *virtual functions* to create, for each object, methods with the following functions: the *constructor*; *destructor*; one which tells whether or not a given sphere is INSIDE or OUTSIDE the object, or whether it crosses the boundary of the object or we are UNSURE about it; the point of intersection (if any) of a ray with the object; and the normal to any point on the surface of the object. Rewrite the listings that are given in the next three chapters to use this alternative representation of geometrical object types. For the same family of objects (such as a sphere and an ellipsoid) use classes that inherit from each other.

14 A quad-tree algorithm

In this chapter we introduce a quad-tree algorithm for drawing an orthographic view of a scene that is modelled as a list of objects, each of which is stored in OBSERVED position. In our restricted version of the quad-tree algorithm we will in fact only be considering spheres (**primitive_type**=1), the simplest of all three-dimensional objects. Nevertheless, the approach is valid for many other types of primitive object, provided that the relevant functions have been written and the **Analytic_scene** class has been extended to contain sufficient parameters. You will see that the algorithm we use has close similarities to the recursive techniques used to draw mathematical functions (listing 10.6) and fractal maps (listings 1.6 and 10.9). The application program that initiates the quad-tree approach is given in listing 14.1, and consists of a simple **build_it** function that links the quad-tree application to all the other functions in our collection of files; the link with **"model.cpp"**, **"display.cpp"** and **"window.cpp"** will be achieved using the C++ Project mechanism. Function **build_it**, called from **draw_a_picture,** takes the description of every sphere from file **"quadtree.dat"**: this data is given in the order of their integer labels and a sample file is shown in listing 14.1. The data is used to instantiate an **Analytic_scene** object named **scene**. The data concerning the material used by the spherical objects in the scene is stored in a file **"material.dat"**: see listing 11.2c for an example. As usual, function **draw_a_picture** (listing 13.1b) models the scene (**build_it**), sets up the observer and light source (**look_at_it**) and finally displays the scene (**draw_it**). The data structure that brings all this together to form a complete description of the three-dimensional scene is an implied list of integer labels of all objects in the scene.

Listing 14.1

```
// Application program to read in data that will be drawn
// with the quad-tree algorithm

#include "model.h"

extern Analytic_scene scene ;
extern Material mrl ;

//-------------------//
  void build_it(void)                    // spherical ball model
//-------------------//
// Read in data on spheres in ACTUAL position
 { scene.read("quadtree.dat") ;
   mrl.read("material.dat") ;
 }  // End of build_it
```

```
/* Sample file "quadtree.dat" of three spheres
  3
  1
  1  0  0    1     1  0  0  -1
  0  1  0    1     0  1  0  -1
  0  0  1    1     0  0  1  -1
  1.1  0.0  1
  1
  1  0  0    1     1  0  0  -1
  0  1  0   -1     0  1  0   1
  0  0  1    1     0  0  1  -1
  1.3  0.0  2
  1
  1  0  0   -1     1  0  0   1
  0  1  0    0     0  1  0   0
  0  0  1   -1     0  0  1   1
  1.5  0.0  3
*/
```

The quad-tree algorithm, like all our analytic approaches uses a stack. However, each of our three types of algorithm will require different types of data stored on their own particular type of stack. The description of the stack data needed by the quad-tree approach is given in file **"stackinf.cpp"** (listing 14.2). In this case, the data stored on the stack will consist of a **pixelvector pix**, and three integers **edge, left** and **right**. The value of **pix** will represent the top left corner of an **edge** by **edge** square of pixels; the square may actually extend outside the screen area (see later), but we will only attempt to colour in pixels that lie on the screen. We introduce an array **listore**, and we imagine elements with lower indices on the left and higher indices to the right. Identifiers **left** and **right** will indicate the indices of elements in array **listore**, and their values are such that every object index stored between **listore[left]** and **listore[right]** will be of relevance to the square of pixels presently under consideration.

Listing 14.2

```
// Save code as file "stackinf.cpp"
struct stackinfo { pixelvector pix; int edge, left, right ; } ;
```

Setting the scene

The quad-tree algorithm is contained in the file **"display.cpp"** of listing 14.3. The file contains our original **cshade** function (listing 11.9) that calculates the colour of a pixel using a point light source, ambient light set at 0.4, and diffuse and specular reflection. This colour is related to the colour look-up table stored in the **Palette** class with the method **findlogicalcolour** found there (listing 11.8).

The new **draw_it** function takes the graphics screen (be it VGA or XGA) and divides it up into **kx** by **ky** square blocks, or *subscreens*, each 256 (**blocksize**) pixels square. The values of **kx** and **ky** are chosen to be the smallest that make the resulting rectangle of square blocks cover the screen, which as we know is made up of **nxpix** by **nypix** pixels. The centred covering rectangle, or *superscreen*, is taken to be **NXPIX** pixels by **NYPIX** pixels.

The scene itself is assumed to be a set of spherical objects, each individual sphere indicated by an integer between 1 and **numobj**, identifying a single sphere within the C++ object **scene**. This list of indices is stored in the array **listore**. Then, for each subscreen, we push the relevant **pix** and **edge** (=256) data onto the stack, along with **left** and **right**, the integer pointers to **listore** indicating the beginning and end (respectively) locations of the list of spheres in that array. Then function **quadtree** is called, and for any square of pixels popped off the stack, it takes the *old list* and finds a *new list* of spheres which intersect that square (by calling function **rodball**). It then divides the square into quarters and pushes both the data about the quarters and the new list of spheres back onto the stack. The new list is stored in **listore** to the right of the rightmost entry of the old list. The quad-tree algorithm continues in this way, pushing and popping the stack until the stack becomes empty. Whenever the level of a single pixel is reached, then a colour is chosen and the pixel is drawn. Let us look at the implementation of this algorithm now in more detail.

Listing 14.3

```
// Save code as file "display.cpp"

#include "model.h"

extern vector3 src ;
extern Material mrl ;
extern Analytic_scene scene ;
extern Palette plt ;
extern Viewport vpt ;
extern Window win ;

Stack stack ;
vector3 midpt ;
float rodrad ;

int listore[5000] ;

float scale ;
int NXPIX, NYPIX ;
const int blocksize = 256 ;

//-----------------------------------------------------------------------//
  void cshade(vector3 p, vector3 norm, int mat, float *red, float *green,
                          float *blue)            // take from listing 11.9
//-----------------------------------------------------------------------//

//------------------------------------------------------//
  void pixball(pixelvector pixel, int newl, int newr)
//------------------------------------------------------//
// find unique ball used to colour given 'pixel'
 { int colour,i,lsi,maxball ;
   float d,distsq,red,green,blue,zz,randval,rval,gval,bval ;
   vector3 normal, observed ;
   Matrix A ;
   static int maxy = win.Get_nypix() ;
```

```
// Find which ball is relevant to current pixel
// Go through listore and find ball ('maxball') closest to observer
   midpt.z=-10000.0 ; maxball=-1 ;
   for (i=newl ; i<=newr ; i++)
   { lsi=listore[i] ;  A = scene.Get_matrixR(lsi) ;
     observed = A.Get_column(4) ;
     distsq=pow(scene.Get_fpp1(lsi),2.0)-pow(midpt.x-observed.x,2.0) \
                                         -pow(midpt.y-observed.y,2.0) ;
     if (distsq >=  0.0)
       { zz=observed.z+sqrt(distsq) ;
         if (zz > midpt.z)  { midpt.z=zz ; maxball=lsi ;  } ;
       } ;
   }
   if (maxball != -1)
// Find vector 'normal' to surface of chosen ball
// at a point projected onto (xmid,ymid)
     { A = scene.Get_matrixR(maxball) ;
       observed = A.Get_column(4) ;
       normal = midpt - observed ;
       d = pow(scene.Get_fpp1(maxball),2.0)-pow(normal.x,2.0)     \
                                            -pow(normal.y,2.0) ;
       if (d < 0.0) normal.z=0.0 ;  else normal.z= (float)sqrt(d) ;
       cshade(midpt,normal,scene.Get_material(maxball),&red,&green,&blue) ;
// Un-comment the following 2 lines to introduce a random colour variation
//       randval = 1 + 0.05 * (0.5 - random()) ; red = red * randval ;
//       green = green * randval ; blue = blue * randval ;
       colour = plt.findlogicalcolour(red,green,blue,
                                  scene.Get_material(maxball)) ;
       win.setcol(colour) ; win.setpix(pixel) ;
     } ;
 }  // End of pixball

//------------------//
  int rodball(int i)
//------------------//
// Check for intersection of a rod with a sphere. midpt, rodrad are global
 { Matrix A ;
   vector3 observed ;
   float dist ;
   A = scene.Get_matrixR(i) ; observed = A.Get_column(4) ;
   dist=sqrt(pow(observed.x-midpt.x,2.0)+pow(observed.y-midpt.y,2.0)) ;
   if (dist <= scene.Get_fpp1(i)+rodrad) return (TRUE) ;
   else return (FALSE) ;
 }  // End of rodball

//-------------------------------------------------------------------//
  void quadsplit(pixelvector pixel, int edge, int newl, int newr)
//-------------------------------------------------------------------//
 { int halfedge,i ;
   stackinfo newv ;
// split pixel square into quarters (also pixel squares, with sides halved)
// If at pixel level colour it in and pop next pixel square off stack
   if (edge == 1)  pixball(pixel,newl,newr) ;
// Not at pixel level. Break pixel squares in quarters and add to stack
   else
     { halfedge= (int) (edge/2) ;
       for (i=0 ; i<4 ; i++)
       { newv.pix.x= pixel.x + (i/2) * halfedge ;
         newv.pix.y= pixel.y + ((i+1) % 2) * halfedge ;
         newv.edge = halfedge ;
         newv.left = newl ;  newv.right = newr ;
        if (!  ( ( (newv.pix.y+halfedge) <= 0 ) ||
                 (  newv.pix.y           >= win.Get_nypix() ) ||
                 ( (newv.pix.x+halfedge) <= 0 ) ||
                 (  newv.pix.x           >= win.Get_nxpix() ) ) )
          stack.push(newv) ;
       }
     } ;
 }  // End of quadsplit
```

```
//--------------------//
 void quadtree(void)
//--------------------//
// The QUAD-TREE ALGORITHM
 { int i, lsi, newl,newr ;
   vector2 half ;
   stackinfo v ;
// Pop pixel-square info off stack : process it, stop if stack empty
   while ( !stack.empty() )
// Pixel square has edge size info.e='edge'; bottom left corner 'info.pix'
// A circle containing the square of pixels extended backwards to form rod
// Use 'listore' of balls and present pixel square to see which balls are
// relevant. listore[i] where info.left<=i<=info.right holds the information
   { v = stack.pop() ;
// Real centre of pixel square is 'midpt', circle of radius 'rodrad'
// totally contains pixel square. 'rodrad' thus radius of current rod
// 'half' is half the edge size of the current real cube
     half.x=0.5*v.edge/scale ;
     half.y=0.5*v.edge/scale /win.Get_rat() ;
     rodrad=(float)sqrt(pow(half.x,2.0) + pow(half.y,2.0) ) ;
     midpt.x=(float)(v.pix.x-win.Get_nxpix()/2)/scale+half.x ;
     midpt.y=(float)(win.Get_nypix()/2-v.pix.y)/scale/win.Get_rat()-half.y ;
// Create a new list of balls relevant to present pixel square and
// store in 'listore' between indices 'newl' and 'newr'
     newr=v.right ; newl=newr+1 ;
     for (i=v.left ; i<=v.right ; i++)
// Distance between centre of ball (a circle in 2D) and centre of pixel
// square (in real units) must be less than the combined radii of circle
// and rod 'lsi' is sphere index of i'th element of 'listore'
     { lsi=listore[i] ;
       if (rodball(lsi))
         { newr++ ;  listore[newr]=lsi ;  } ;
// If ball 'i' still under consideration then add to 'listore'
     }  ;
// If new 'listore' not empty enter 'quadsplit', pop Qstack and continue
     if (newl <= newr)   quadsplit(v.pix,v.edge,newl,newr) ;
   } ;
 }   // End of quadtree

//-------------------//
 void draw_it(void)
//-------------------//
 { int i,ix,iy,kx,ky ;
   stackinfo v ;
// Viewport is assumed to be NXPIX by NYPIX pixels. Divide it into kx * ky
// blocksize-square pixel blocks and push them onto stack.
// Given blocksize (power of 2), k can be found so that NXPIX and NYPIX
// are the nearest numbers greater or equal to the viewport's dimensions.
   kx = win.Get_nxpix()/blocksize ;
   if (win.Get_nxpix()%blocksize) kx++ ;
   ky = win.Get_nypix()/blocksize ;
   if (win.Get_nypix()%blocksize) ky++ ;
   NXPIX = kx * blocksize ;       NYPIX = ky * blocksize ;
   for (i=1 ; i<=scene.Get_numobj() ; i++)  listore[i]=i ;
// Initiate QUAD-TREE process
   win.start() ;
   for (ix=0 ; ix<kx ; ix++)
   { for (iy=0 ; iy<ky ; iy++)
     { v.pix.x = ix * blocksize - (NXPIX-win.Get_nxpix())/2 ;
       v.pix.y = iy * blocksize - (NYPIX-win.Get_nypix())/2 ;
       v.edge = blocksize ;
       v.left = 1 ; v.right = scene.Get_numobj() ;
       stack.push(v) ;
     }
   }
   scale = win.Get_xyscale() ;
   quadtree() ;
 }  // End of draw_it
```

The quad-tree algorithm

We start by considering each subscreen square of 2^8 by 2^8 pixels (256 by 256) on the viewport. (At a general stage we have a *pixel square* of 2^n by 2^n pixels: $0 \leq n \leq 8$.) This square of pixels can be mapped onto a continuous 'real' square on the viewport, and hence onto the WINDOW of the orthographic view plane; the proper scaling between the screen of pixels and the window (**scale**) will have been determined by the **draw_it** function (listing 14.3b). We then imagine that the view plane square is extruded in front of and behind the plane to form an infinitely long square-sectioned prism or *rod*. The boundary of this rod is in fact formed by the orthographic projection lines through every point along the edges of the real square. Obviously, any object in the three-dimensional scene that does not intersect this solid rod will have no effect on the colouring of any pixel in the corresponding square of pixels.

Given a square of pixels (initially a subscreen), we start with the *old list* of objects (**listore[left..right]**) that may possibly intersect the corresponding rod, and check each object for a possible intersection. Initially, when $n = 8$, the list will contain all the objects in the scene. If there is a proper intersection (found by function **rodball**), or if there is any doubt (caused by the approximation we use in order to speed up processing), then the object is added to a *new list*, which is stored as entries **listore[newl..newr]**. The pixel square is divided up into four smaller pixel squares, each 2^{n-1} by 2^{n-1} pixels, in function **quadsplit**. We then recursively repeat the above process using the new list instead of the old, and with all four new squares, by pushing the new values of **pix** (the corners of the quarters of the previous pixel square), **edge** (half the previous **edge**), **left** (**newl**) and **right** (**newr**) onto the stack. One proviso to this process is that if a new square lies totally outside the viewport then it is not pushed onto the stack and we have a very simple form of clipping.

Note how, by implementing the process on a stack with integer pointers into the **listore** array, we have built-in garbage collection: since the entries in **listore** of a new list always occur immediately to the right of the old list popped of the stack, and therefore will overwrite previous list data that is no longer required. If at any time a new list of spheres becomes empty then no object in the scene can affect the given pixel square, and so the pixels should be left in the background colour. However, since the scene is not empty (it cannot be all background colour) then this process of dividing pixel squares into quarters apparently seems to go on indefinitely. This potentially infinitely recurring process is halted because once n becomes zero, then we are dealing with a single pixel: in this case (**edge**=1) we enter function **pixball** which colours the pixel, and most importantly, nothing new is pushed onto the stack.

Within function **pixball** for a given pixel, only one of the objects remaining in the (non-empty) list of spheres can be used to calculate the colour. Finding exactly which sphere is needed is relatively straightforward; simply take a line of projection through the point in space corresponding to the centre of the pixel. By intersecting that line with each sphere in the list (there may actually be no intersection since we will be using approximations!), we find the sphere whose intersection has the largest z co-ordinate, that is nearest the observer. Function **cshade** can be used to choose the colour for the pixel; we have commented out a small section of the code in function **pixball**, just after **cshade** is called, which, if included, would introduce a small random variation that minimizes the 'wood-grain' effect that is caused by the limited size of our palette of colours.

There are two things of particular note when running this program. First, in previous applications of the orthographic projection we were not using colour shading, and so the distance of the eye from the model was not critical (the eye position only indicates the centre of the window) – the eye at (1,2,3) gave the same picture as at (100,200,300). However, with colour shading, a meaningful eye position within the model is essential if highlights and the other shading phenomena are to be realistic. Secondly, it is worth repeating that there is no need to clip the scene before display; clipping is implicit in the quad-tree process, since if any square of pixels lies outside the viewport area then we do not push it onto the stack and therefore it cannot be coloured in.

Approximation; aspect-ratio problems

We implement the quad-tree algorithm in listing 14.3, for use with scenes that are modelled as a list of spheres. Rather than use rods with square cross-section, we instead introduce cylindrical rods with circular cross-section that contain the square-sectioned rods: that is, instead of the rod being formed by extruding a real square corresponding to a square of 2^n by 2^n pixels in the viewport, we extrude the circle of radius $2^n/\sqrt{2}$ which passes through the four corners of that square. We do this to make calculations easier; note that any object outside the cylindrical rod must be outside the square-sectioned rod, however, there may be objects that intersect the cylindrical rod but which lie outside the square-sectioned rod. This may mean that objects which ultimately have no effect on the display of the scene may be added to new lists; this is a small price to pay for the ease of calculation. These irrelevant objects will finally be deleted anyway, when considering the intersection of the line of projection through the pixel.

So far in our explanation we have assumed that pixels are square; however, with mode 19 on the VGA card the aspect-ratio is not unity. Luckily this is not too much of a problem. The quad-tree algorithm outlined above works just as well with rectangles of pixels as well as with squares, provided that the scaling factors are correctly calculated, and we work initially with rods with rectangular, rather than square cross-section. And if we use the above approximation, then provided that we choose a circle that runs through the corners of the rectangle of pixels the algorithm will work – it only means that there is slightly more waste in the approximation.

In VGA mode 19 we initially divide the screen into two individual 256 by 256 pixel squares (for XGA a maximum of 12 in the 1024 by 768 resolution), and initiate the quad-tree algorithm for each: this implies that we do not need more than 26 elements (36 elements on XGA) in the **listore** stack (why?). An example of the output from this program is the smooth shaded orthographic projection of a relatively complicated set of spheres shown in Plate VIa.

Exercise 14.1

Rather than store the successive lists of spheres in array **listore**, it is possible to use our **Stack** class to hold each new list of sphere indices, and to push such a stack representation of these lists onto our quad-tree stack alongside **pix** and **edge**. Rewrite our programs so that they use this alternative list representation. Note that you will have to build-in your own garbage collection by deallocating the storage of the list of spheres in the stack when they are of no further value. It will be necessary to write a number of methods for the **Stack** class that represent the lists. These will include a constructor, destructor, assignment and initialisation. The assignment, =, must copy the lists properly and not simply copy the pointer to the front of the list. For an illustration see class **CSGtree** described in chapter 3, that is used by our oct-tree program in the next chapter.

Exercise 14.2

If each pixel is considered to be composed of 2^M by 2^M sub-pixels, then the quad-tree process may be continued to the sub-pixel, as opposed to the pixel level. Should you then combine the colours chosen for each sub-pixel, you will achieve a simple *anti-aliasing* technique for the colouring of that pixel. Implement this.

Exercise 14.3

Incorporate a form of transparency into the quad-tree program. This can be achieved easily by changing the **pixball** function. In the original function a line of projection runs through the centre of the pixel and the sphere in the list with largest z co-ordinate on that line. Continuing the line, if a second sphere is found, then the colours of the two spheres can be combined to give the apparent effect of transparency. But remember that each line will intersect a sphere twice – don't count the back face of the any sphere in your calculations.

Exercise 14.4
Incorporate the parallel beam shading model into this program. Extend the colouring process to allow for multiple light sources.

Project 14.1
Incorporate shadows in the program. For each pixel, you will need to discover if the corresponding point in the model is in shadow; just find the surface point equivalent to the pixel and draw a line from that point to the light source. If this line intersects any other object then the pixel will be in shadow, and you colour it with ambient light accordingly, otherwise use the usual colour model.

Project 14.2
Use these ideas in an extended program to include in the model finite cylinders, objects of **primitive_type** 2. Your program should draw orthographic projections of a 'ball and spoke' molecular model, which is smooth shaded and exhibits specular reflection.

Project 14.3
Use the perspective projection instead of orthographic. Now, for each square of pixels, instead of enclosing it in a cylindrical rod during the quad-tree process, you must introduce a circular cone with apex at the observer point, and the points at the corners of that square of pixels must just touch the inside of the cone. Note this is not a right-cone, and unlike the orthographic, its axial direction and shape will change depending on the position on the screen of the square of pixels.

15 An oct-tree algorithm

We now consider the orthographic projection of more complicated scenes, made up of three-dimensional objects chosen from three of our small set of four primitive object categories. In our implementation of the oct-tree approach, we want to keep things as simple as possible and ensure that the basic algorithm is not obscured by an excessive amount of code dealing with an extravagant variety of object types. We therefore restrict ourselves to scenes that contain only combinations of spheres, (infinite) cylinders and half-spaces; that is, those objects we have already defined in the **Analytic_scene** C++ class as **primitive_type**(s) 1, 2 or 3 (see chapter 13). Most commercial oct-tree programs allow for not only our limited choice of objects, but also for a cone, torus, helix and many other types; our short list, therefore, should be extended by the user if further special shapes are required.

In chapter 13 we insisted that a primitive object from each of the three categories be defined in a SETUP position, usually around the ABSOLUTE origin, and a particular example of such an object is moved into its OBSERVED position by a matrix **R**. In the oct-tree program, each primitive geometrical object must have a well-defined analytic form, that enables us to identify its *point membership classification* (that is, whether a given point is inside, outside or on the surface of that object: see chapter 6). This will be presented as a function: for our three primitive object types they are **insphere, incylinder, inhalfspace** respectively (listing 15.4). These functions will tell us whether a given solid cube (actually its containing sphere) lies INSIDE or OUTSIDE the object, or whether it intersects the surface of the object, or whether we are UNSURE about it.

Representing a scene with a CSG tree

All the ACTUAL objects in a scene are listed in an instantiation **scene** of the class **Analytic_scene** as arrays of data (again see chapter 13). After matrices **Q** and its inverse **QI** have been calculated within function **findQQI**, the matrices **R** and **RI** in the **scene** object are adjusted to place each of the geometrical objects in their OBSERVED position. An individual object is identified by its index to these arrays. The *complement* of a geometrical object (all of space except for that solid object) will be needed by the oct-tree algorithm: if an object is identified by array index n, then its complement is indicated by $-n$. It is essential therefore that we start counting objects from index 1 and not from zero!

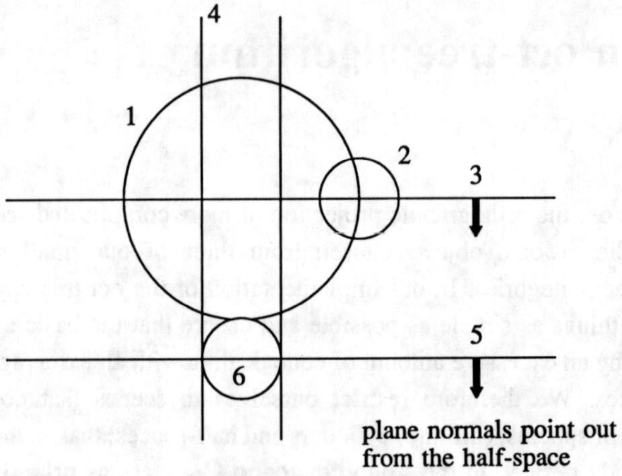

Figure 15.1

Listing 15.1

```
// Sample file "octree.dat" for object in figure 15.1

6

1
 1  0  0  0    1  0  0  0
 0  1  0  2    0  1  0 -2
 0  0  1  0    0  0  1  0
6  0  1

1
 1  0  0  4    1  0  0 -4
 0  1  0  2    0  1  0 -2
 0  0  1  4    0  0  1 -4
2  0  2

3
 1  0  0  0    1  0  0  0
 0 -1  0 -2    0 -1  0  2
 0  0 -1  0    0  0 -1  0
0  0  3

2
 1  0  0  0    1  0  0  0
 0  1  0  0    0  1  0  0
 0  0  1  0    0  0  1  0
2  0  4

3
 1  0  0  0    1  0  0  0
 0 -1  0  6    0 -1  0 -6
 0  0 -1  0    0  0 -1  0
0  0  4

1
 1  0  0  0    1  0  0  0
 0  1  0 -6    0  1  0  6
 0  0  1  0    0  0  1  0
2  0  4
```

Following on from our initial discussion of trees in chapter 3, we will now discuss the use of a binary *constructive solid geometry tree* (*CSG tree*), the data structure we will use to represent a combination of our integer-labelled primitive three-dimensional objects. To aid the explanation we will refer to figure 15.1 and Plate VIb. Figure 15.1 is a line-drawing identifying the six objects in that scene and how they interrelate. Plate VIb is a proper oct-tree orthographic view of the scene which consists of a hemisphere (sphere 1 intersected with half-space 3) with a spherical hole (object 2) cut out; a finite cylinder (infinite cylinder 4 bounded by half-spaces −3 and 5) forms the stem of the 'mushroom'; and finally sphere 6 is pushed into the bottom end of the cylinder. Note how object 3 is used twice in the definition of the final scene! The tree representing this scene is stored in the file **"CSGtree.dat"** that has already been given in listing 3.10.

The CSG tree (see chapter 3) that describes such a scene will have two types of node: the first, a leaf, holds the index of an object or its complement (the '−' sign is identified with logical operator NOT); and the second type, a non-leaf with two edges leading from it, holds a spatial operator (union, ∪, identified with the logical operator OR, and intersection, ∩, identified with logical operator AND). We can think of such a binary tree as an operator (from the root node) combining the two subtrees indicated by the two edges leaving the root. Since the subtree is also a tree, we have a recursive definition that leads ultimately to the leaf-subtrees that refer solely to the indices of ACTUAL/OBSERVED objects in the construction of a scene. We can write out this type of tree in *postfix* notation:

(subtree subtree operator)

We use parentheses to highlight the expansion of subtrees; however, given the unambiguous nature of postfix notation this is not strictly necessary. Thus in our example, the hemisphere with the hole on its edge is constructed first from the intersection of sphere 1 with the complement of sphere 2

(1 −2 ∩)

and then the resulting subtree intersected with the half-space 3

((1 −2 ∩) 3 ∩) (15.1)

The finite cylinder with the spherical base is found by intersecting the infinite cylinder 4 with the complement (note) of half-space 3 and with half-space 5, before unioning in sphere 6 to its base

(((−3 4 ∩) 5 ∩) 6 ∪) (15.2)

Note, it does not matter that part of sphere 6 lies inside the finite cylinder – that is, we do not have to slice off the top half of sphere 6 before unioning it with the finite cylinder. The two parts (expressions 15.1 and 15.2) are then unioned together to give the final tree that describes the example scene. The postfix representation of this tree is thus

$$(((1\ {-2}\cap)\ 3\cap)(((-3\ 4\cap)\ 5\cap)\ 6\cup)\cup)$$

There need not be a unique way of setting up a CSG tree for any given scene; in particular note that no spatial meaning is implied in the left/right ordering of the subtrees for any given node.

Superblock and supercube; octant and sub-cube; voxel and cubelet

The oct-tree approach to the display of a three-dimensional scene assumes that drawing will take place on a *superscreen* which is a 2^N by 2^N (say) discrete grid of pixels; in our implementation we set $N = 10$. For the time being we will ignore any aspect-ratio problems and assume that each pixel is square – therefore the superscreen is 1024 by 1024 pixels square; our original viewport of **nxpix** by **nypix** pixels is centred in this superscreen. We now consider each square pixel to be the front face of a small cube, or *voxel* (volume pixel). By extending the superscreen back into the third dimension we can thereby create a *superblock* composed of 2^N by 2^N by 2^N voxels. An individual voxel is located within the superblock by its voxel co-ordinates, counting the number of voxels to the right (x), below (y) and into the screen (z) starting from the left, top, front voxel of the superblock. This voxel has co-ordinate (**nxpix**/2-512, **nypix**/2-512, **nxpix**/2-512), an apparently peculiar choice, made so that each voxel corresponding to a pixel in the viewport has exactly the same x and y pixel/voxel co-ordinates. We declare the **voxel** data type to hold such positional data. We now reconsider each pixel on the superscreen to be the front face of just one of the 2^N voxels from the column that stretches out perpendicularly behind the screen.

We map the superblock onto a cube in three-dimensional space, that we call the *supercube*. The front face of the supercube is centred at the ACTUAL origin, and scaled using the usual **xyscale** that relates the viewport (a subset of the superscreen) to the WINDOW co-ordinate system (listing 1.3b). The same scaling factor maps individual voxels into small *cubelets* in space, thereby mapping the superblock onto 2^N by 2^N by 2^N cubelets. By this mapping we can now consider the front face of the supercube as the WINDOW onto three-dimensional space. Each column of 2^N cubelets that is perpendicular to, and behind, this WINDOW, corresponds to a column of voxels behind the superscreen.

The oct-tree algorithm approximates the surfaces of objects within the supercube with a covering of those cubelets that intersect the surfaces: note that this algorithm does not actually consider solid objects, only surfaces. For each pixel on the screen we take the column of voxels that stretches out behind it, and from the corresponding column of cubelets find the intersecting cubelet nearest the front face of the supercube. Taking the centre of that cubelet as a point on the surface of an object in the scene, we can use our shading model to choose a colour for the pixel. Nothing outside the supercube will be drawn; in fact only those cubelets that correspond to superscreen pixels that lie inside the viewport will actually be drawn and so there is no need for explicit clipping.

It would be very time consuming to consider every column of cubelets, and so instead we start with the supercube, break it into *eight sub-cubes*, each a cubic block of cubelets. Recursively we break each of those sub-cubes into eight sub-cubes, and continue until eventually we reach the level of individual cubelets. This also appears to be an extremely time consuming procedure; however, it can be speeded up by noting that whenever we find a sub-cube that lies totally outside or totally inside the objects in the CSG tree, then we can stop the recursion; for we know that only surfaces, and therefore none of the cubelets in the sub-cube under consideration, can affect the colour choice of pixels on the screen. At a general stage in the process we will be using a sub-cube of say 2^n by 2^n by 2^n cubelets ($0 \leq n \leq N$) that corresponds to an *octant* of 2^n by 2^n by 2^n voxels, that extends right, down and back from a given **voxel** position **vox**.

Reducing the binary tree

When we start with the supercube we have to check its intersection with all of the objects in the scene, that is with the whole CSG tree. However, as we divide it up into sub-cubes, for any particular sub-cube we will find some objects that either lie totally outside the sub-cube or totally contain it; in either case that particular sub-cube does not intersect the surfaces of those objects. In both cases further subdivision will produce sub-cubes that also will not cut the surfaces of those objects. It makes sense therefore to take all reference to those objects out of the CSG tree as we subdivide the particular sub-cube further; that is, we *reduce* the CSG tree so that the reduced tree describes just the combinations of objects that we think may intersect the particular sub-cube and its subdivisions. Therefore as we process these new sub-cubes we need only consider the reduced version of the CSG tree, reducing it even further with each subdivision.

The supercube has sides parallel to the OBSERVER co-ordinate axes. For a given primitive object we can transform the vertices of each such sub-cube, first by Q^{-1} (the inverse of the ACTUAL to OBSERVED matrix Q), and then by P^{-1}, that is by matrix R^{-1} which is stored as **RI**. In this way the sub-cube can be positioned relative to the SETUP position of that object if convenient. We can then check if the transformed sub-cube intersects the surface of the SETUP object; if it does then the untransformed sub-cube will intersect the OBSERVED position of that object. We only do this with cylinders and half-spaces; with spheres we can make the check directly in OBSERVED position. There are three possible outcomes of the check on intersections, and they correspond to the three values INSIDE, OUTSIDE, and UNSURE (either we really are unsure because of approximations we will be making, or the sub-cube crosses the surface of the object; in either case we will have to subdivide the sub-cube and check further).

We start with the 2^N by 2^N by 2^N superblock of voxels, and its corresponding supercube that is compared with each of the objects in the scene in order to find out whether the supercube is INSIDE or OUTSIDE an object, or whether we are UNSURE. This data is then used to reduce the CSG tree. At a general stage in the process we assume that we are working with an octant of 2^n by 2^n by 2^n voxels ($0 \leq n \leq N$) that corresponds to a sub-cube of cubelets in three-dimensional space, together with a reduced tree that has been derived from the original CSG tree by previous reductions. These left, top, front corner **voxel** of the octant, its **edge** length (2^n), and the reduced CSG tree related to that voxel, will be stored as an object **octant**, which is an instantiation of the structure **stackinfo.** We then take each of the objects in this reduced CSG tree and, with their corresponding functions (**insphere, incylinder, inhalfspace**), discover if the sub-cube is inside, outside or crosses the surface of that object (INSIDE, OUTSIDE, UNSURE); and use the results to reduce the CSG tree according to the following rules. (It may be helpful if you compare INSIDE and OUTSIDE with TRUE and FALSE, and the operators ∩, ∪ and – with AND, OR and NOT.)

(1) replace the index of each object totally containing the transformed cube by INSIDE

(2) replace the index of each object containing no part of the transformed cube by OUTSIDE

(3) leave alone the indices about which we are UNSURE

(4) –INSIDE ⇒ OUTSIDE

(5) –OUTSIDE ⇒ INSIDE

(6) (INSIDE subtree ∩) ⇒ subtree, and
(subtree INSIDE ∩) ⇒ subtree

(7) (INSIDE subtree ∪) ⇒ INSIDE, and
(subtree INSIDE ∪) ⇒ INSIDE

(8) (OUTSIDE subtree ∩) ⇒ OUTSIDE, and
(subtree OUTSIDE ∩) ⇒ OUTSIDE

(9) (OUTSIDE subtree ∪) ⇒ subtree, and
(subtree OUTSIDE ∪) ⇒ subtree

The algorithm for reducing a CSG tree is implemented as method **reduce** in listings 3.9a&b. We can explain tree reduction by resorting to the postfix representation of the tree as follows:

(a) Run through the leaves of the tree using rules (1) to (3) to change particular 'status' entries to INSIDE and OUTSIDE.

(b) Use rules (4) and (5) to invert the –INSIDE and –OUTSIDE values.

(c) Traverse the tree from left to right. On meeting an INSIDE/OUTSIDE entry, which must be a leaf subtree:
   (i) determine both the operator on the node above that leaf, and the corresponding subtree emanating from the other edge of that node,
   (ii) operate on that node using rules (6) to (9) above.

Example 15.1
To illustrate this algorithm we operate on our example tree by supposing that the six objects, when intersected with a given sub-cube, return six values UNSURE, OUTSIDE, OUTSIDE, UNSURE, INSIDE and UNSURE respectively. We clarify the subtree structure of the CSG tree by using parentheses in the postfix representation of the tree. To clarify the above step c(i) further, at each stage of the reduction we underline the required INSIDE/OUTSIDE leaf, its operator node and corresponding subtree.

The original tree in postfix notation:
((((1 –2 ∩) 3 ∩) ((–3 4 ∩) 5 ∩) 6 ∪) ∪)

Applying rules (1) (2) and (3):
((((1 –OUTSIDE ∩) OUTSIDE ∩) ((–OUTSIDE 4 ∩) INSIDE ∩) 6 ∪) ∪)

Applying rule (5):
((((1 INSIDE ∩) OUTSIDE ∩) ((INSIDE 4 ∩) INSIDE ∩) 6 ∪) ∪)

Applying rule (6b):
(((1 OUTSIDE ∩) ((INSIDE 4 ∩) INSIDE ∩) 6 ∪) ∪)

Applying rule (8b):
((OUTSIDE ((INSIDE 4 ∩) INSIDE ∩) 6 ∪) ∪)

Applying rule (9a):
(((INSIDE 4 ∩) INSIDE ∩) 6 ∪)

Applying rule (6a):
((4 INSIDE ∩) 6 ∪)

Applying rule (6b):
(4 6 ∪) and the tree cannot be reduced further.

So as far as the sub-cube is concerned only objects 4 and 6 and their union are relevant, and the other objects can be ignored. Note that although we were UNSURE of object 1, it is still deleted from the CSG tree.

The oct-tree display

After the binary CSG tree has been reduced we are left with either an *empty tree* of the form (INSIDE) or (OUTSIDE) or a non-empty CSG tree which contains no occurrence of INSIDE or OUTSIDE. A CSG tree is empty when the particular sub-cube that we are presently considering, and hence all of its 2^n by 2^n by 2^n constituent cubelets, do not intersect the surface of the remaining objects combined according to the binary tree. This means that these cubelets will have no influence on the colour of their corresponding viewport pixels and so no further processing of this sub-cube need be done. If the tree is non-empty then there may be an intersection yet to be discovered. Provided $n > 0$, we break the sub-cube into eight more sub-cubes (whence oct-tree), each 2^{n-1} by 2^{n-1} by 2^{n-1} cubelets, and repeat the process on the reduced tree, ensuring that the sub-cubes nearest the observer along the line of projection (that is, with larger OBSERVED z co-ordinates) are processed before those furthest away – this will furnish us with a form of hidden surface elimination (see later). Eventually we reach the level of individual cubelets (and hence voxels, $n = 0$), and a pixel corresponding to a voxel *may* then be coloured on the viewport. Although we have a cubelet that we believe intersects the surface of an object in the scene, as we will be approximating, the cubelet may actually not intersect the surface; this must be checked explicitly at the cubelet level. The colour depends on which object remaining in the tree is nearest to the observer, and of course on the particular shading model used. The nearest object can be found by intersecting the line of projection through the particular cubelet with each remaining object in turn.

Implementing the oct-tree algorithm

We have already seen the C++ code for setting up and reducing a model CSG tree in chapter 3. There the **CSGtree** class (listing 3.9a&b) stored in file **"CSGtree.cpp"** was explained. We instantiate an object **reduced_tree** of this class in our listings which enables us to achieve these manipulations within the oct-tree algorithm.

The application program that we use for the oct-tree program is given in listing 15.2. As usual it consists of a **build_it** function that links the oct-tree application into all the other functions in our library of files by using the C++ Project mechanism. Function **build_it** merely reads in the description of a scene: a tree structure given in postfix notation and stored in file **"CSGtree.dat"** (as given in listing 3.10). It then reads the data concerning the objects themselves from a file **"octree.dat"** (see listing 15.1), with data on the material used by the three types of object in the scene stored in file **"material.dat"** (we can use the same one from listing 11.2c). As usual, function **draw_a_picture** (listing 13.1b) models the scene by calling **build_it**, sets up the observer and light source (**look_at_it**), and finally displays the scene (**draw_it**).

Listing 15.2

```
// Application program to read a scene that will be
// drawn with the oct-tree algorithm

#include "model.h"

extern Analytic_scene scene ;
extern Material mrl ;
extern stackinfo octant ;

Stack stack ;

//-------------------//
  void build_it(void)
//-------------------//
// Reads the data file "octree.dat" into the appropriate variables
 { int i, lista[maxtreelist], length ;
   ifstream datafil ;
   datafil.open("csgtree.dat") ;
   datafil >> length ;
   for (i=0 ; i<length ; i++) datafil >> lista[i] ;
   octant.tree.list_to_tree(length,lista) ;
   datafil.close() ;
   scene.read("octree.dat") ;
   mrl.read("material.dat") ;
 }  // End of build_it
```

Our oct-tree implementation will be using a particular type of stack that is described by the code of file **"stackinf.cpp"** (listing 15.3). In this case, the stack will contain a **voxel vox**, an integer **edge**, and a **CSGtree** object **tree**. The value of **vox** will represent the left top front corner within the superblock of an **edge** by **edge** by **edge** octant of voxels; the values of **vox.x** and **vox.y** correspond to pixels, although they may actually extend outside the screen area (see later) – but we will only attempt to colour in pixels that lie on the screen. **tree** will be the CSG tree that describes that part of the scene that may be contained in the octant of voxels presently under consideration.

Listing 15.3

```
// Save code as file "stackinf.cpp"

#include "csgtree.h"                 // see listings 3.9a&b

typedef struct { int x, y, z ; } voxel ;

struct stackinfo { voxel vox ; int edge ; CSGtree tree ; } ;
```

Listing 15.4

```
// Save code as file "display.cpp"

#include <stdlib.h>                    // For exit()
#include "model.h"

int ival[maxobj] ;                     // The definition of 'ival' is needed
#include "csgtree.cpp"                 // in the CSGtree class

float scale ;
float cube_rad ;
vector3 cube[9] ;   // holds centre and eight corners of current cube
stackinfo octant ;
unsigned char  screen_map[64][512] ;
int NXPIX = 1024, NYPIX = 1024 ;       // Assume square viewport

CSGtree reduced_tree ;

extern Palette plt ;
extern Window win ;
extern vector3 eye, src ;
extern Stack stack ;
extern Analytic_scene scene ;
extern Material mrl ;

//----------------------//
  int insphere(int idobj)
//----------------------//
// Is 'cube' INSIDE or OUTSIDE sphere 'idobj' or are we UNSURE
 { vector3 sph, sph_vox ;
   float dist, rads = scene.Get_fpp1(idobj) ;
   Matrix A = scene.Get_matrixR(idobj) ;
   sph = A.Get_column(4) ;
   sph_vox = sph - cube[0] ;
// dist is the distance between centres of sphere and cube
// if dist is greater than sum of radii no intersection   (OUTSIDE)
// if dist plus cube_rad greater than radius of sphere then INSIDE
   dist = (float) sqrt( dot3(sph_vox,sph_vox) ) ;
   if (dist > cube_rad + rads) return (OUTSIDE) ;
   else if (rads > dist + cube_rad) return (INSIDE) ;
        else return (UNSURE) ;                  // else we are UNSURE
 } // End of insphere

//---------------------------//
  vector3 norsphere(int idobj)
//---------------------------//
// Determine normal to sphere at point of intersection 'cube[0]'
// by calculating vector from centre to point on surface
 { Matrix A = scene.Get_matrixR(idobj) ;
   return ( cube[0] - A.Get_column(4) ) ;
 } // End of norsphere

//------------------------//
  int incylinder(int idobj)
//------------------------//
// Is 'cube' INSIDE or OUTSIDE the cylinder 'idobj' or are we UNSURE
 { vector3 v ;
   float dist, rads = scene.Get_fpp1(idobj) ;
   Matrix A = scene.Get_matrixRI(idobj) ;
   v = A * cube[0] ;
// dist is the distance between axis of cylinder and centre cube
// if dist is greater than sum of radii no intersection   (OUTSIDE)
// if dist plus cube_rad greater than radius of sphere then INSIDE
   dist = (float) sqrt( pow(v.x,2.0) + pow(v.z,2.0) ) ;
   if (dist > (rads+cube_rad)) return (OUTSIDE) ;
   else if ( rads > (dist+cube_rad)) return (INSIDE) ;
        else return (UNSURE) ;                         // else UNSURE
 }  // End of incylinder
```

```
//------------------------------//
  vector3 norcylinder(int idobj)
//------------------------------//
// Determine normal to cylinder at point of intersection 'cube[0]'
// by calculating vector from nearest point on axis to point on surface
 { vector3 b ;
   Matrix A = scene.Get_matrixRI(idobj) ;
   b = A * cube[0] ;   b.y = 0.0 ;
   A = scene.Get_matrixR(idobj) ;
   return ( A.dir_transform(b) ) ;
 }  // End of norcylinder

//--------------------------//
  int inhalfspace(int idobj)
//--------------------------//
// Is 'cube' INSIDE or OUTSIDE the half-space 'idobj' or are we UNSURE
 { vector3 v ;
   Matrix A = scene.Get_matrixRI(idobj) ;
   v = A * cube[0] ;
// in SETUP position if y-coordinate of cube centre within radius
// distance of the x/z plane through the origin we are UNSURE
// else less than zero INSIDE, greater than zero OUTSIDE.
   if (v.y > cube_rad) return (OUTSIDE) ;
   else if ( v.y < -cube_rad) return (INSIDE) ;
        else return (UNSURE) ;
 }  // End of inhalfspace

//-------------------------------//
  vector3 norhalfspace(int idobj)
//-------------------------------//
// Determine normal to halfspace at point of intersection 'cube[0]'
 { vector3 p ;
   Matrix A = scene.Get_matrixR(idobj) ;
   p = zero ; p.y = 1.0 ;          // parallel to SETUP y-axis
   return ( A.dir_transform(p) ) ;
 }  // End of norhalfspace

//------------------------------//
  int is_pixel_square_used(void)
//------------------------------//
// Checks with the screen_map to see if square of pixels already painted
 { int bitmin, bitmax, mask, pixsq_used, powerbitmax ;
   int x, y, xnumber, xpos, xmin, ymin, xmax, ymax ;
   static unsigned char hexFF = (unsigned char) 255 ; // all 8 pixels used
   static int NXPIXover2 = NXPIX / 2 ;
// (ox,oy,oz) is voxel co-ordinate of current octant, edge size oe
   int ox = octant.vox.x - (win.Get_nxpix() - NXPIX) / 2 ;
   int oy = octant.vox.y - (win.Get_nypix() - NXPIX) / 2 ;
   int oz = octant.vox.z - (win.Get_nxpix() - NXPIX) / 2 ;
   int oe = octant.edge ;
// Square of 512*512 pixels and not used previously so initialize screen_map
   if ((oe >= NXPIXover2) && (oz == 0))
     { for (x=0 ; x<64 ; x++)  for (y=0 ; y<512 ; y++)
         screen_map[x][y] = (unsigned char)0 ;
       pixsq_used = FALSE ;
     }
   else
// Run through (x,y) bytes in screen_map corresponding to pixel square
// Work with just a quarter of the screen, hence modulo 512
// Divide x position by 8 since 8 x-bits will go into each byte
     { xpos = ox % 512 ; xmin = xpos/8 ;
       ymin = oy % 512 ; ymax = ymin+oe ;
//  Dealing with bigger than 4 by 4 pixel square, so check complete words
       if (oe >= 8)
         { xnumber = oe/8 ;
           xmax = xmin + xnumber ;
           pixsq_used = TRUE ;
           y = ymin ;
           do { x = xmin ;
```

```
                do { if (screen_map[x][y] != hexFF)
                        { pixsq_used = FALSE; y = ymax; x = xmax; }
                     else x++ ;
                   } while ( x< xmax ) ;
                y++ ;
              } while (y < ymax ) ;
         }    // here if all pixels in pixel square already coloured
//  Dealing with less than 8 by 8 pixel square, so check partial words
//  mask the word representing a used pixel square against current square
//  mask value found by raising 2 to max and min byte positions and subtract
        else    //  information on pixels lie between bits bitmin and bitmax
          { bitmin = xpos % 8 ; bitmax = bitmin + oe ;
            powerbitmax = (int) pow((double)2.0,(double)bitmax) ;
            mask = powerbitmax - (int) pow((double)2.0,(double)bitmin) ;
            y = ymin ;
            pixsq_used = TRUE ;
            do { if ((screen_map[xmin][y] & mask) != mask)
                   { pixsq_used = FALSE ; y = ymax ; }
                 y++ ;
              } while (y < ymax ) ;        // pixsq_used has been adjusted
          } ;
     } ;
   return ( pixsq_used ) ;
 }  // End of is_pixel_square_used

//----------------------------//
  void update_screen_map(void)
//----------------------------//
 { int xpos, x, y, bitpos, mask ;
// Update screen_map given pixel position
   int ox = octant.vox.x - (win.Get_nxpix() - NXPIX) / 2  ;
   int oy = octant.vox.y - (win.Get_nypix() - NXPIX) / 2  ;
   xpos = ox % 512 ;
   x = xpos/8 ;  y = oy % 512 ;
   bitpos = xpos % 8 ;
   mask = 1 << bitpos ;
   screen_map[x][y] |= mask ;
 }  // End of update_screen_map

//-------------------//
  void ocsplit(void)
//-------------------//
// Take present octant and split it into eight equally sized sub-octants
 { int i, dx, dy, dz, halfedge ;
   stackinfo stc ;
   static int nxpix = win.Get_nxpix() ;
   static int nypix = win.Get_nypix() ;
   halfedge = octant.edge / 2 ;
   for (i=0 ; i<8 ; i++)
   { stc.edge = halfedge ;
     stc.tree = reduced_tree ;
     dx = i/4 ;  dy = ( i/2 ) % 2 ;  dz = (i+1) % 2 ;
     stc.vox.x = octant.vox.x + dx * halfedge ;
     stc.vox.y = octant.vox.y + dy * halfedge ;
     stc.vox.z = octant.vox.z + dz * halfedge ;
// If not totally outside Viewport do not push it on stack (clipping)
     if ( ! ( ( (stc.vox.y+halfedge) <= 0 )
             || (stc.vox.y >= nypix)
             || ( (stc.vox.x+halfedge) <= 0 )
             || (stc.vox.x >= nxpix ) ))
       stack.push(stc) ;
   }
 } // End of ocsplit

//---------------------------------------------------------------------------//
  void cshade(vector3 p, vector3 norm, int mat, float *red, float *green,
                     float *blue)           // take from listing 11.9
//---------------------------------------------------------------------------//
```

```
//-------------------------------------//
  int evaluate_objects(int *objectlist)
//-------------------------------------//
// For all the objects 'id' of 'object_type' in the current tree determine
// their relative position with the current cube 'cube' using the 'in'
// functions. Store this data in 'ival[]' and use it to reduce the current
// tree and return the number of different objects in the new tree.
 { int n, object_type, id ;
   n = octant.tree.objects_in_tree(objectlist) ;
   for (int i=0 ; i<n ; i++)
   { id = objectlist[i] ;  object_type = scene.Get_type(id) ;
     switch (object_type)
     { case 1 : ival[id] = insphere(id) ;    break ;
       case 2 : ival[id] = incylinder(id) ;  break ;
       case 3 : ival[id] = inhalfspace(id) ; break ;
       default : cerr << "\n Error: unknown object at evaluate_objects" ;
                 exit(1) ;
     }
   }
   octant.tree.reduce(&reduced_tree) ;
   return( reduced_tree.objects_in_tree(objectlist) ) ;
 }  // End of evaluate_objects

//-----------------------------//
  void paint_pixel(int leafval)
//-----------------------------//
// For a given intersection with object stored on leaf of the tree, find the
// normal to that object 'id' at point 'cube[0]'.
// Invoke the colour shading model and draw the pixel.
 { int id, object_type, icol ;
   vector3 norl ;
   float rr, gg, bb ;
   pixelvector pix ;
   id = abs(leafval) ;
   object_type = scene.Get_type(id) ;
   switch (object_type)
  { case 1 : norl = norsphere(id) ;    break ;
    case 2 : norl = norcylinder(id) ;  break ;
    case 3 : norl = norhalfspace(id) ; break ;
   default : cerr << "\n Error: unknown object at paint_pixel" ;
             exit(1) ;
  }
 // reverse normal if we are working with complement of object id
   if (leafval < 0) norl = -norl ;
   cshade(cube[0],norl,scene.Get_material(id),&rr,&gg,&bb) ;
   icol = plt.findlogicalcolour(rr,gg,bb,scene.Get_material(id)) ;
   pix.x = octant.vox.x ;  pix.y = octant.vox.y ;
   win.setcol(icol) ;      win.setpix(pix) ;
 } // End of paint_pixel

//------------------//
  void octree(void)
//------------------//
// The oct-tree algorithm
 { int objectlist[maxobj] ;
   int dx, dy, dz, n ;
   float cubex, cubey, cubez, cube_edge ;
   static float eye_dist = (float)sqrt(dot3(eye,eye)) ;
   static float ratio = win.Get_rat() ;
   static float sqrt2pl1 =0.5*(float)sqrt(2.0*ratio*ratio+1.0)/ratio ;
   while ( !stack.empty() )
   { octant = stack.pop() ;
     if( !is_pixel_square_used() )
// Take octant and find OBSERVED co-ordinates of equivalent cube
       { cubex = (float)(octant.vox.x-win.Get_nxpix()/2)/scale ;
         cubey = (float)(win.Get_nypix()/2-octant.vox.y)/scale/ratio ;
         cubez = (float)(octant.vox.z-win.Get_nxpix()/2)/scale + eye_dist ;
         cube_edge = ((float)octant.edge)/scale ;
// Determine OBSERVED co-ordinates of the 8 corners of the cube
```

```
        for (int i=0 ; i<8 ; i++)
        { dx = i/4 ;   dy = (i/2) % 2 ; dz = (i+1) % 2 ;
          cube[i+1].x = cubex + cube_edge * (float)dx ;
          cube[i+1].y = cubey - (cube_edge * (float)dy) / ratio ; ;
          cube[i+1].z = -(cubez + cube_edge * (float)dz) ;
        }
// Calculate the OBSERVED centre 'cube[0]' and radius 'cube_rad' of the
// sphere circumscribing the cube
        cube[0] = 0.5 * (cube[1] + cube[8]) ;
        cube_rad = cube_edge * sqrt2pl1 ;
        n = evaluate_objects(objectlist) ;
// If there remain objects we are still UNSURE about, then if the cube is
// of minimum size (a cubelet) then paint corresponding pixel else split it
        if (n)
          { if (octant.edge == 1)
              { paint_pixel(objectlist[0]) ;
                update_screen_map() ;
              }
            else ocsplit() ;
          } ;
      } ;
    }
 }  // End of octree

//------------------//
  void draw_it(void)
//------------------//
// Determine the co-ordinates of the initial octant and push it onto the
// stack to initiate the octree process.
 { win.start() ;
   plt.rgblog(1,(float)0.5,0.5,0.5) ;  win.erase(1) ;
   scale = win.Get_xyscale() ;
   octant.vox.x = (win.Get_nxpix() - NXPIX) / 2 ;
   octant.vox.y = (win.Get_nypix() - NYPIX) / 2 ;
   octant.vox.z = octant.vox.x ;
   octant.edge = 1024 ;
   stack.push(octant) ;
   octree() ;
 }  // End of draw_it
```

The oct-tree algorithm itself is contained in the file **"display.cpp"** of listing 15.4. The file contains our original function **cshade** (listing 11.9) that calculates the colour of a cubelet (and hence pixel) using a point light source, ambient light set at 0.4, and diffuse and specular reflection. This choice of actual colour can then be related to the logical colour look-up table stored in the **Palette** with the method **findlogicalcolour** found there (listing 11.8). The new **draw_it** method covers the graphics screen (be it VGA or XGA) with the superscreen, which is **NXPIX** (=1024) pixels by **NYPIX** (=1024) pixels. This superscreen is extended into the z-direction to create an 1024 by 1024 by 1024 superblock of voxels, and it is assumed that the viewport we are using is centred on the superscreen, that is the voxel corresponding to the left, top pixel of the viewport has co-ordinate (0,0,0). At a general stage we have an octant of 2^n by 2^n by 2^n voxels: $0 \le n \le 10$. This corresponds to a sub-cube of 2^n by 2^n by 2^n cubelets in real space, and hence any object in the three-dimensional scene that does not intersect this sub-cube can have no effect on the colouring of any pixel on the superscreen that is related to the voxel octant that corresponds to the sub-cube.

It is assumed that the scene itself is described by a CSG tree with leaves representing spheres, cylinders and half-spaces, each indicated by an integer between 1 and **numobj**, identifying a single object within the C++ object **scene**. Initially we push the relevant **vox** and **edge** (=1024) data for the superblock onto the stack, along with **tree** which is an instantiation of class **CSGtree**, found initially in file **"CSGtree.dat"**, that describes the whole scene. Then function **oct-tree** is called: for any octant of voxels popped off the stack, the corresponding sub-cube of cubelets is found, and method **objects_in_tree** from class **CSGtree** is used to find which spheres, cylinders or half-spaces are still in that tree. Then by calling **reduce**, using the data on the intersection of the objects with the sub-cube corresponding to the octant, the CSG tree is reduced further. Then the octant of voxels is divided into eight further octants (each an eighth of the volume) and both the data about each new octant and its newly reduced tree are pushed back onto the stack. **octree** continues in this way until the level of individual voxels is reached, when a colour is chosen, and the corresponding pixel is drawn. The algorithm ends when the stack becomes empty.

Given any intermediate voxel octant (initially the superblock of voxels), we start with the *old tree* of objects that may possibly intersect the corresponding real solid sub-cube, and check each object in that tree for possible intersection. Initially, when $n = 10$, the tree will be the original CSG tree describing the whole scene. If there is a proper intersection or it is inside or outside (found by function **insphere, incylinder** or **inhalfspace**), or if there is any doubt (caused by the approximation we use in order to speed up processing), then data on the object remains in the tree; when all objects have been considered then the tree is reduced to form a *new tree* we call **reduced_tree**. The octant can be divided up into eight smaller octants, each 2^{n-1} by 2^{n-1} by 2^{n-1} voxels, in function **ocsplit**. We then recursively repeat the above process with all eight new octants and the reduced tree, by placing the new values of **vox** (the left, top, front corners of each octant produced from the previous octant), **edge** (half the previous **edge**), and **reduced_tree** into an instantiation **octant** of the **stackinfo** structure and pushing it onto the stack.

Note that after the **octant** data has been popped off the stack and we have copied it into a particular location, then we will have no further use for that tree on the stack, and the memory used to store that tree must be deallocated. We have arranged the **Stack** class so that the act of copying (method =) initiates the **~CSGtree** destructor, thereby achieving the necessary garbage collection after an exact copy of the tree (and not just a pointer to the root of the original) has been created. If at any time a tree becomes empty then no object can affect the given voxel octant and so the corresponding pixels should be ignored, possibly left in the background colour. However, since the scene is not empty (it is not all background) then this process of dividing up octants can apparently go on indefinitely. We avoid this problem because once *n* becomes zero then we are dealing with a single voxel, where we enter function **paint_pixel** which deals with this situation; nothing is pushed onto the stack and the potentially infinitely recurring process is halted.

Within function **paint_pixel** for any given voxel (and hence pixel), only one of the objects remaining in the (non-empty) tree of objects can be used in the determination of the colour for that pixel. Finding exactly which object is needed is relatively straightforward. Rather than use the line of projection as we mentioned in the earlier theory, since all these objects lie inside a tiny volume (the voxel), we can simply take the object with the lowest integer index. Function **paint_pixel** then calculates the normal to the surface of this object at the corresponding point in 'real space', using **norsphere, norcylinder** or **norhalfspace,** before calling function **cshade** to choose the colour for the pixel. As with the quad-tree application of the orthographic projection, the correct position of the eye from the model is essential in colour shading.

Note that there is no need to clip the scene before display; clipping is implicit in the process. If the square of pixels corresponding to an octant of voxels lies outside the viewport area then the octant is not pushed onto the stack.

Efficiency

By using the oct-tree approach, not every one of the 2^N by 2^N by 2^N voxels in our original superblock need be considered; otherwise this process would be excessively time-consuming. Whole octants of voxels can be ignored when their corresponding reduced tree has become empty.

The process can be made more efficient by noting that when a 2^n by 2^n square of pixels on the viewport has already been coloured in, then there is no need to consider any other octant of voxels that lie behind this square. For this reason we insist on a particular order when breaking each octant of voxels into eight sub-octants, considering them as four sets of 'front and back pairs'. If, for a given pair, we place the back sub-octant onto the stack immediately before the front one, then popping the stack furnishes us with a 'front-to-back' algorithm. Furthermore, since the first eight-way division pushes eight 512 by 512 by 512 octants onto the stack, we can now think of the superscreen as four separate 512 by 512 squares of pixels. Each quarter of the superscreen can be represented by an array **screen_map[64][512]** of **unsigned characters**, where each character is understood to be eight binary bits representing eight consecutive pixels on the screen; initially they are all '00000000'. Whenever a pixel is coloured in, function **update_screen_map** puts a bit value of 1 in the correct position in

screen_map. During the progress of the oct-tree algorithm, before we consider manipulating any given octant of voxels, we must first calculate the corresponding square of pixels on the superscreen and then use the function **is_pixel_square_used** to find out whether all these pixels have already been coloured in our 'front-to-back' approach. This function finds the corresponding locations in the map, and if all the binary bits are set to 1 then that square of pixels has already been completely coloured and no further processing of that octant of voxels is required, otherwise the oct-tree process must continue.

Approximation

We implement the oct-tree algorithm in listing 15.4, for use with scenes that are modelled as a CSG tree of spheres, cylinders and half-spaces. For efficiency, given the massive amount of calculation required by this algorithm, we introduce spheres rather than sub-cubes in our calculations within functions **insphere**, **incylinder** or **inhalfspace**. That is, instead of mapping an octant of 2^n by 2^n by 2^n voxels onto a sub-cube of cubelets in real space, we consider a *containing sphere* of a radius set to be the edge length of a single cubelet times $2^n \times \sqrt{3}$, which passes through all eight corners of that cube. This makes calculation much easier; note any object outside the containing sphere must be outside the sub-cube, however, there may be objects that intersect the sphere but which lie outside the sub-cube. This may mean that objects which ultimately have no effect on the display of the scene may remain in the new reduced CSG trees, instead of being deleted; however, the gain from a simplified calculation more than compensates. These irrelevant objects will finally be ignored at the cubelet/voxel level when we consider the colouring of the pixel.

If the graphics screen does not have an aspect-ratio of one, then we have to adjust the process a little. Rather than think of a voxel as a cube, instead we consider it a rectangular block, and rather than working with a 2^N by 2^N by 2^N superblock of voxels we see it as a rectangular stack of voxels with the same non-cubic relative dimensions as the original voxel. So long as the radius of the sphere that we use in our algorithm totally contains the required sub-cube of cubelets then the algorithm is still valid.

Project 15.1
Extend our orthographic oct-tree implementation to include a torus, cone and helix. The picture of a more complex scene, part of the front-suspension of a car, that uses two helices, is shown in Plate VIIa.

Shadows can be introduced in a manner similar to the quad-tree method. Adjust the screen map to introduce transparency as well.

Project 15.2

Each voxel can be considered as 2^M by 2^M by 2^M sub-voxels. If you implement the oct-tree process down to the sub-voxel level, and hence create equivalent sub-pixels, you can again combine the colours of the sub-pixels to introduce a simple *anti-aliasing* method.

Project 15.3

Use the perspective projection instead of the orthographic. Now each octant of voxels, instead of being mapped onto a sub-cube (of cubelets) in space, must now correspond to a section of a pyramidal cone with apex at the observer.

Project 15.4

In listing 1.6 we saw how a 2^n by 2^n square of pixels with four floating point values stored at its corners could be broken into quarters, producing nine floating point values: the original four and five new, four at the edge centres and one at the centre of the square, calculated by interpolating and a small random variation. Repeating the process down to the pixel level gave us the means of drawing a 'fractal map'. We can similarly take an octant of 2^n by 2^n by 2^n voxels with eight values at the corners, and divide it up into eight new octant with 19 new values: twelve at the edge mid-points, six at the face centres and one at the original octant centre. If we repeat this process down to the voxel level, then the final floating point number can be used to choose between a group of possible materials for the cubelet which is treated as a 'point' on the surface. The colour shading model can then be used to give the colour of the corresponding pixel. It is relatively easy to include such a process in the oct-tree algorithm, achieving the creation of the new floating point values at the same time as each new cube of voxels is generated. In this way a 'fractal texture' can be introduced into the picture, such as that shown in Plate VIIb.

Project 15.5

Rather than store the successive reduced trees explicitly as C++ tree structures, their postfix representation can be stored in an array **listore** exactly as we did in the quad-tree program. Then we push/pop **left** and **right** integer pointers onto/off the stack along with the octant data. This is very efficient because it means that we will not be generating eight copies of each tree during the eight-way subdivision, and furthermore the use of integer pointers furnishes us with a very simple garbage collection procedure. Rewrite our programs so that they use this alternative tree representation.

16 Ray-tracing

The approaches that we have given so far all suffer from the fact that they do not model optical phenomena in a truly satisfactory manner. Colour is light hitting our eyes. It can come directly from a source, it can be reflected directly from a surface, or via a number of surfaces by reflection or refraction. Now in the final chapter we introduce a *global illumination model*, ray-tracing, which will allow for reflections of reflections etc., and for the transmission of light through a material in such a way that it demonstrates refraction ('bending of light').

Sampling space

Our implementation of a ray-tracing algorithm draws a perspective view of a three-dimensional scene that is modelled as a list of objects, each of which is defined by a list of parameters defining the object in SETUP position; we also have matrices **R** and **RI** which can move them into OBSERVED position and back respectively. Ray-tracing involves sending out an *initial line (a ray)* from the eye of the observer to each pixel on the viewport. Each ray travels to the window point at the centre of the pixel, and on through space, sampling objects as it goes, and sending back signals to the eye that are ultimately combined to give a colour for the corresponding pixel. In more sophisticated forms of ray-tracing, the cross-section of the rays may have a finite area, or stochastic sampling techniques can be used to introduce such concepts as *radiosity* (see Foley, van Dam, Feiner and Hughes, 1990). As usual we will keep it simple, so as not to obscure the underlying algorithm. Even though we give the simplest form of ray-tracing, it nonetheless produces excellent results (see Plate VIIIa).

For each pixel, the act of sampling involves attaching a 'packet' of full intensity light (I=1) to the ray, and then following it through space until it goes off to infinity or it hits an object. A ray that goes off to infinity adds nothing to the colour of the pixel. When a ray of intensity I hits an object, the packet of light splits into three parts, with intensities $I \times I_{absorb}$, $I \times I_{reflect}$ and $I \times I_{refract}$, where $I_{absorb}+I_{reflect}+I_{refract}$ sum to unity. The first part absorbs the colour of the surface (taking into consideration ambient light, diffuse and specular reflection), and returns the RGB colour values, scaled by a factor $I \times I_{absorb}$, directly back to the eye. The second part, of intensity $I \times I_{reflect}$, is bundled into a new packet that is attached to the component of the incident ray reflected off the surface. The third part, of intensity $I \times I_{refract}$, is bundled into a new packet that is attached to the component of the incident ray refracted at the surface. Then the same procedure must be followed for both the reflected and refracted rays, each with their own lesser intensities, being absorbed by other surfaces and sending RGB values directly back to the eye (unhindered by objects in space), while also generating yet more reflected and refracted rays. Theoretically, this process can go on indefinitely, giving rise to a complex network of *sub-rays*, the *ray-tree*. We could terminate the tree expansion after a certain level in the tree has been reached. We, however, choose a better way. Note that with each splitting in two of a ray, the intensity of these new rays gets smaller and smaller. We use this fact to terminate an otherwise infinitely expanding process by insisting that rays of intensity less than a given value (**minblack**) are dissipated in space.

The amount of absorption, reflection and refraction, parameters I_{absorb}, $I_{reflect}$ and $I_{refract}$, will of course depend on the material properties of the surfaces met by each ray in its travels. The figures alone are not enough, we must be able to emulate reflection and refraction (sometimes called *transmission*).

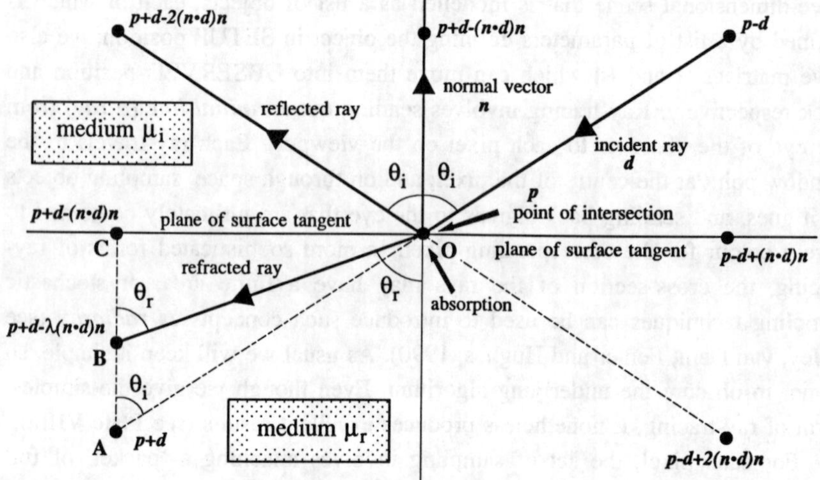

Figure 16.1

Consider figure 16.1. Suppose that an incident ray with unit direction vector ***d*** hits a surface at point ***p***, where the normal pointing out of the surface is unit vector ***n***. From elementary physics we know that the *angle of incidence*, θ_i, the angle made by the ray with the normal, equals the *angle of reflection*. Assuming that the surface is acting as a plane mirror at point ***p*** (labelled **O** in the figure) and that the directions have the senses given in figure 16.1, we can use the formula for the reflection of a point introduced in chapter 6, to see that point $\boldsymbol{p}-\boldsymbol{d}$ is reflected into point $\boldsymbol{p}-\boldsymbol{d}+2(\boldsymbol{d}\bullet\boldsymbol{n})\boldsymbol{n}$, from which we can ascertain the direction vector of the reflected ray to be $\boldsymbol{d}-2(\boldsymbol{d}\bullet\boldsymbol{n})\boldsymbol{n}$.

Now we emulate refraction by considering the same incident ray as it passes through the surface. Suppose the ray passes from the incident medium with *refractive index* μ_i into the refracting medium with refractive index μ_r: we call the relative refractive index from the second to the first medium $\mu=\mu_r/\mu_i$. If the refracted ray makes an angle of refraction θ_r with the normal (in the opposite sense) $-\boldsymbol{n}$, then by Snell's Law:

$$\frac{\sin\theta_i}{\sin\theta_r} = \frac{\mu_r}{\mu_i} = \mu$$

Since the normal, and the incident and refracted rays all lie in the same plane, referring to figure 16.1, we can treat refraction as though the *straight-through ray* is pushed up towards the tangent plane if $\mu<1$, or down away from it if $\mu>1$. In the figure, point $\boldsymbol{p}+\boldsymbol{d}$ (labelled **A**), lying on the straight-through ray is pushed up towards a typical point $\boldsymbol{p}+\boldsymbol{d}-\lambda(\boldsymbol{d}\bullet\boldsymbol{n})\boldsymbol{n}$ (labelled **B**) that is dependent on the value of λ ($=|\mathbf{AB}|/|\mathbf{AC}|$), which in turn depends on μ. Setting λ to unity fixes a point labelled **C** that lies on the plane tangential to the surface at the point of incidence. Since $\boldsymbol{d}$ (and $\boldsymbol{n}$ for that matter) are unit vectors, then:

$$|\mathbf{OA}| = 1, \quad |\mathbf{OC}| = \sin\theta_i = \mu\sin\theta_r \quad \text{and thus } |\mathbf{OB}| = \mu$$

Remembering that $\boldsymbol{n}$ and $\boldsymbol{d}$ are unit vectors, we can then calculate:

$$|\mathbf{AC}| = |\cos\theta_i| = |(\boldsymbol{d}\bullet\boldsymbol{n})| \quad \text{and}$$

$$\begin{aligned}|\mathbf{BC}| &= \mu\cos\theta_r = \mu\sqrt{(1-\sin^2\theta_r)}\\ &= \sqrt{(\mu^2-\mu^2\sin^2\theta_r)}\\ &= \sqrt{(\mu^2-\sin^2\theta_i)}\\ &= \sqrt{(\mu^2-(1-\cos^2\theta_i))}\\ &= \sqrt{(\mu^2+(\boldsymbol{d}\bullet\boldsymbol{n})^2-1)}\end{aligned}$$

Hence

$$\begin{aligned}\lambda &= (|\mathbf{AC}|-|\mathbf{BC}|)/|\mathbf{AC}| = 1-|\mathbf{BC}|/|\mathbf{AC}|\\ &= 1-\sqrt{(\mu^2+(\boldsymbol{d}\bullet\boldsymbol{n})^2-1)}/|(\boldsymbol{d}\bullet\boldsymbol{n})|\end{aligned}$$

We are of course assuming that both θ_i and θ_r are acute angles, $(\boldsymbol{d}\bullet\boldsymbol{n})\neq0$, and the values under the square root symbol are non-negative. We can now find the value of λ, and hence the refracted ray. If the values under the square root are negative then we have *total reflection*.

Implementing ray-tracing

In our restricted version of this algorithm we will consider only spheres (**primitive_type**=1) and checkerboards (**primitive_type**=4): an example of its use is given in Plate VIIIa, showing reflective spheres and checkerboard (of just one tile). We also assume that there is free space between every object. Of course, the ray-tracing approach is valid for many other types of primitive object, and for objects that merge into one another. Naturally the relevant functions have to be written, and the **Analytic_scene** class has to be extended to contain sufficient parameters for these new types of geometrical object, and our programs have to be extended to deal with rays passing from one object directly into another without there being any free space between. The front cover shows a number of tori, each composed of reflecting material, drawn over a reflecting checkerboard.

The application program that initiates the ray-tracing approach is given in listing 16.1, and consists of a simple **build_it** function that links the ray-tracing application into all the other functions in our collection of files; as usual the linking will be achieved using the C++ Project mechanism. Function **build_it**, called from **draw_a_picture** (listing 16.3), reads in the description of a scene composed of a set of spheres and checkerboard(s) (stored in file **"raytrace.dat"**) and data about materials from file **"material.dat"** (placing it in the **extern**al object **mrl** of the **Material** class). The data structure that describes the scene is, like the quad-tree, an implied list of integers, each integer indicating a single object from within the **"raytrace.dat"** file (see the example in listing 16.4).

Listing 16.1

```
// Application program that reads a scene to be drawn using ray-tracing
#include "model.h"

extern Analytic_scene scene ;
extern Material mrl ;

//--------------------//
  void build_it(void)
//--------------------//
// Read the data files into the appropriate variables
 { scene.read("raytrace.dat") ;
   mrl.read("material.dat") ;
 }  // End of build_it
```

In common with quad-tree and oct-tree algorithms, the ray-tracing approach implemented here will use the **Stack** class that was introduced in chapter 3. The description of the information stored on the stack is given in file **"stackinf.cpp"**; the ray-tracing version is given in listing 16.2. This structure consists of a floating point value **intens**, and two **vector3** values representing a ray in space: **base** is the base vector (or starting point) of the ray, and **dire** is its direction vector – the ray will travel in the positive sense of this vector. For each pixel, the data on the intensity of a number of rays will eventually be combined together to give its colour, and **intens** represents the proportion of the overall light intensity that the present ray will supply to the total.

Listing 16.2

```
// Save code as file "stackinf.cpp"
struct stackinfo { vector3 base, dire ;  float intens ; } ;
```

The ray-tracing algorithm is contained in file **"display.cpp"** of listing 16.3. A scene is described by a list of spheres and checkerboards, with each individual object, defined in SETUP position (with the matrices taking it into OBSERVED position and back), indicated by an integer between 1 and **numobj** that identifies a single geometric object within the C++ object **scene**. Individual rays will be defined by a base vector **base** and direction vector **dire** (which can be made into a unit vector by function **make_unit_vector**). Initial rays will stream out of the eye, pass through the window, and then strike the surface of objects where they can be absorbed (and data returned to the corresponding pixels on the screen where they are used to generate colour), reflected or refracted. Each initial ray leaving the eye is assumed to have unit intensity. This intensity is divided between absorption, reflection and refraction according to the material properties of the surface that it strikes.

The reflective and refractive parameters are stored in the arrays **refl** and **spec** respectively of the material database **mrl**. The absorption for each material is unity minus the sum of the other two parameters. With reflection and refraction, that part of the ray's intensity not absorbed by the surface is split in two by function **determine_new_rays**, and shared between these two sub-rays in accordance with the material properties of the surface. Each of these rays is followed until it hits a surface, where it too can be absorbed (and generate more colour, although diminished by the lower intensity), and reflected and refracted generating yet more sub-rays. As the ray gets split more and more, then naturally the intensity component of each sub-ray gets smaller and smaller. This gives us a simple means of stopping the potentially infinite process of ray splitting – we assume that when a sub-ray's intensity falls below a certain value (**minblack**) then the sub-ray dissipates in space, adding to the general ambient light. The value is set to the minimum colour resolution of the viewport (=1/64), so that a ray of this intensity will not make any difference to a colour on the viewport.

Note that in this interpretation of vision, rays do not enter the eye, but leave it. They hit objects where they generate colour, which, by some magic, is returned directly to the viewport and then to the eye! We assume that the colour of each pixel is defined by three floating point numbers **pixred, pixgreen** and **pixblue**, initially all three are set to zero. Whenever a sub-ray hits a surface and, by absorption, it generates red/green/blue values (calculated in function **cshade,** listing 11.9), this RGB colour is appropriately adjusted to take into account the lower light intensity of the particular sub-ray, and it is then used to update these **pixred, pixgreen** and **pixblue** values. Listing 16.3 uses the version of **cshade** given in listing 11.9, which calculates the colour of a point in space that is illuminated by a point light source, using ambient light (set at 0.4), and diffuse and specular reflection. After all the suitably adjusted RGB components from all the sub-rays that emanate from an initial ray have been used to update the **pixred, pixgreen** and **pixblue** values, then these three actual colour components are related to the logical colour table stored in the **Palette** class with the method **findlogicalcolour** found there (listing 11.8).

The new **draw_it** function considers the graphics screen (be it VGA or XGA) to be a rectangle of **nxpix** by **nypix** pixels. The viewport is mapped onto a continuous rectangular window by the usual **xyscale** (listing 2.1b), and using the ideas of chapter 8, we note that the initial rays all lie inside the pyramid of vision of the OBSERVER system. The centre of each pixel then corresponds to a unique point on the window. An *initial ray* is drawn from the eye (the OBSERVER origin) to each of these **nxpix** by **nypix** points by the function **generate_ray**. The initial ray (base vector **zero**, unit direction vector **dire**, and unit intensity) is pushed onto the stack. Being set up this way, with ray-tracing, unlike the quad-tree and oct-tree algorithms, there is no need to worry about the aspect-ratio of VGA mode. Similarly there is no need to consider clipping.

Function **follow_ray** pops a sub-ray and follows it until it either goes off to infinity and the pixel is drawn in **background_illumination,** or it strikes an object, the nth say, (**nearhit**=*n*). If an object is hit, then data on the intersection is found in function **determine_intersection,** the colour caused by absorption is calculated in function **determine_illumination,** new rays caused by reflection and refraction are created in **determine_new_rays,** and **push_new_rays** pushes them onto the stack and the process continues.

The refractive index of empty space is given by identifier **mu_media,** and the medium for every other material is found in the material database as **mrl.index[]**. Whenever we travel from one medium into another, the correct relative refractive index must be calculated in order to find the correct refracted rays. Also note that when a ray enters an object, it must leave it, hence the need for identifier **in_object**, which tells us whether a ray is in open space or inside an object. Remember that, because of the way we have set up our objects, there are only two possible situations in which refraction can occur: either the ray is in open space crossing into an object; or it is travelling inside an object before hitting the surface and reflecting back inside the object and (possibly) returning to open space via refraction (there is the possibility of *total internal reflection*!)

Listing 16.3

```
// Save code as file "display.cpp"

#include "model.h"
#include <values.h>       // for MAXFLOAT (maximum floating point) value

#define accuracy 0.1
#define minblack 0.015625  // Terminate tree expansion when contribution to
                           // the final pixel intensity is less than minblack
// The VGA 19 and XGA 255 limit is 1/64 = 0.015625

#define mu_media 1.0       // observer and all objects are in open space

Stack stack ;

#define backred   0.45
#define backgreen 0.4
#define backblue  0.4

// Global variables are used for efficiency
pixelvector pixel ;          // The pixel under consideration
float mu1, mu2 ;             // Index of refraction for media and objects

vector3 base, dire, insect, norm, refl, tran ; // The ray under consideration
vector3 stpbase, stpdire, stpinsect, stpnorm ; // The ray SeTuP values
vector3 nearbase, neardire ;
float nearphi ;                    // point on a ray is base + phi * direction
int nearhit ;

int in_object, tranflag, totalref ;  // Flags concerning the type of new rays
float pixred, pixgreen, pixblue ;
float intensity_factor ;  // Intensity factor for the calculation of the
                          // light contribution of each ray

extern Analytic_scene scene ;
extern Material mrl ;
extern vector3 src ;
extern Palette plt ;
extern Window win ;

//--------------------------------------------------------------------------//
  void cshade(vector3 p, vector3 norm, int mat, float *red, float *green,
                         float *blue)         // take from listing 11.9
//--------------------------------------------------------------------------//

//--------------------------------------------------//
  float distance_between_points(vector3 a, vector3 b)
//--------------------------------------------------//
 { return (sqrt(dot3(a-b,a-b)) ) ;
 }  // End of distance_between_points

//-----------------------------------//
  void make_unit_vector(vector3 *a)
//-----------------------------------//
// Normalises vector a . On error (|a| = 0) user is notified.
 { float d ;
   d = distance_between_points(*a,zero) ;
   if (!sign(d))  cerr << "Error when normalising vector " << *a ;
   else *a = (1.0/d) * (*a) ;
 }  // End of make_unit_vector

//-----------------------------------------------//
  float shortdist(vector3 b, vector3 d, vector3 p)
//-----------------------------------------------//
// Find phi, for point on the line b+phi*d that is nearest to point p
 { return ( dot3(p-b,d) ) ;
 }  // End of shortdist
```

```
//---------------------------//
  void normal_to_sphere(void)
//---------------------------//
 { vector3 testpoint ;
   float dxyz ;
// SETUP normal is SETUP point of intersection (centre of sphere is origin)
   stpnorm = stpinsect ;
// If transparent material find if ray is about to move into the object
// Go slightly beyond intersection and see if ray is now inside object
   if (mrl.Get_trn(scene.Get_material(nearhit)) > 0.0 )
   { testpoint = stpinsect + neardire ;
     dxyz = dot3(testpoint,testpoint) - \
            scene.Get_fpp1(nearhit)*scene.Get_fpp1(nearhit) ;
     if (dxyz < epsilon) in_object = TRUE ; else in_object = FALSE ;
   }
 }  // end of normal_to_sphere

//---------------------------------//
  void normal_to_checkerboard(void)
//---------------------------------//
 { float edge, tile_size, xtiles, ztiles ;
   in_object = TRUE ;         // We are always outside the object
   stpnorm.x = 0.0 ; stpnorm.y = 1.0 ;  stpnorm.z = 0.0 ;
// Find the material of current tile
   edge = scene.Get_fpp1(nearhit) ;
   tile_size = 2.0 * edge / scene.Get_fpp2(nearhit) ;
   xtiles = ceil( (stpinsect.x + edge) / tile_size ) ;
   ztiles = ceil( (stpinsect.z + edge) / tile_size ) ;
   if (fmod((xtiles+ztiles),2.0) < 1.0)  scene.Set_second_mat(nearhit) ;
   else  scene.Set_main_mat(nearhit) ;
 }  // End of normal_to_checkerboard

//---------------------------------//
  void determine_intersection(void)
//---------------------------------//
 { Matrix R ;
// Find object that causes nearest point of intersection
   stpinsect = nearbase + nearphi * neardire ;
   switch ( scene.Get_type(nearhit) )
   { case  1 :  normal_to_sphere() ;       break ;
     case  4 :  normal_to_checkerboard() ; break ;
     default :  cerr << " Error determine_intersection : "  ;
   }
// Ray is travelling from medium with refractive index mu1 to index mu2
   if (mrl.Get_trn(scene.Get_material(nearhit)) > 0.0 )
    { if (in_object)
        { mu1 = mu_media ;
          mu2 = mrl.Get_ndx(scene.Get_material(nearhit)) ;
        }
      else
        { mu1 = mrl.Get_ndx(scene.Get_material(nearhit)) ;
          mu2 = mu_media ;
        } ;
    } ;
// Move point of intersection and unit normal into OBSERVED position
   R = scene.Get_matrixR(nearhit) ;
   insect = R * stpinsect ;
   norm = R.dir_transform(stpnorm) ;
   make_unit_vector(&norm) ;
 }  // end of determine_intersection

//-----------------------------------------------//
  int ray_intersects_sphere(int obj, float *phi)
//-----------------------------------------------//
 { float radius, dist, lambda, chord ;
   vector3 nearpoint ;
   int intersection = FALSE ;
// If distance of centre of sphere from ray less than sphere radius
// then there is a point of intersection.
```

```
   radius = scene.Get_fpp1(obj) ;
   lambda = shortdist(stpbase,stpdire,zero) ;
   nearpoint = stpbase + lambda * stpdire ;
   dist = distance_between_points(nearpoint,zero) ;
   if (dist <= radius)                    // There is an intersection
     { intersection = TRUE ;
       chord = radius*radius - dist*dist ;
// If ray is tangential to sphere stop rounding errors being introduced
       if (chord < epsilon) chord = 0.0 ;
       else chord = sqrt(chord) ;
       *phi = lambda - chord ;
// There are two points of intersection, take one with smallest phi
       if (*phi < accuracy) *phi = lambda + chord ;
     }
   return (intersection) ;
 }  // End of ray_intersects_sphere

//-----------------------------------------------------//
  int ray_intersects_checkerboard(int obj, float *phi)
//-----------------------------------------------------//
 { float sx, sz, xint, zint, lambda ;
   int intersection = FALSE ;
   sx = scene.Get_fpp1(obj) ;  sz = sx ;  // checkerboard is sx by sz
// If ray not parallel to checkerboard plane find intersection
   if ( fabs(stpdire.y) > epsilon )
     { lambda = -stpbase.y / stpdire.y ;
// If intersection with checkerboard plane is in the path of the ray
// check if it lies inside the sx by sz square.
       if (lambda > accuracy)                //May be an intersection
         { xint = stpbase.x + lambda * stpdire.x ;
           if ( fabs(xint) <= sx )
             { zint = stpbase.z + lambda * stpdire.z ;
               if ( fabs(zint) <= sz )
                 { intersection = TRUE ;  *phi = lambda ; }
             } ;
         } ;
     } ;
   return ( intersection ) ;
 }  // End of ray_intersects_checkerboard

//--------------------------------//
  int ray_intersects_objects(void)
//--------------------------------//
 { int intersect, ob ;
   float phi ;
   Matrix RI ;
   nearphi = MAXFLOAT ;    // assign impossible value to nearphi
// Run through list of objects in scene
   for (ob=1 ; ob<=scene.Get_numobj() ; ob++)
   { intersect = FALSE ;
// convert ray to SETUP of object ob
     RI = scene.Get_matrixRI(ob) ;
     stpbase = RI * base ;  stpdire = RI.dir_transform(dire) ;
     make_unit_vector(&stpdire) ;
// call appropriate intersection function for object type
     switch ( scene.Get_type(ob) )
     { case  1 : intersect = ray_intersects_sphere(ob,&phi) ;        break ;
       case  4 : intersect = ray_intersects_checkerboard(ob,&phi) ;  break ;
     }
// a proper intersection would make phi > accuracy
     if (phi < accuracy) intersect = FALSE ;
// if proper intersection, compare with current nearest intersection
     if (intersect)
       { if (nearphi > phi)
           { nearphi = phi ;  nearhit = ob ;
             nearbase = stpbase ;  neardire = stpdire ;
           } ;
       } ;
   }
```

```
   if (nearphi > MAXFLOAT*0.5) return (FALSE) ;   // No intersection found
   else return (TRUE) ;
 }  // End of ray_intersects_objects

//----------------------//
  void paint_pixel(void)      // in chosen colour
//----------------------//
 { int col ;
   col = plt.findlogicalcolour(pixred,pixgreen,pixblue,
                              scene.Get_material(nearhit)) ;
   win.setcol(col) ;   win.setpix(pixel) ;
 }  // End of display_pixel

//---------------------------------//
  void determine_illumination(void)
//---------------------------------//
// Calculate colour sample to be returned to update pixel colour
 { float r,g,b ;
   cshade(insect,norm,scene.Get_material(nearhit),&r,&g,&b) ;
   pixred   += intensity_factor * r ;
   pixgreen += intensity_factor * g ;
   pixblue  += intensity_factor * b ;
 }  // end of determine_illumination

//----------------------------------//
  void background_illumination(void)
//----------------------------------//
// If ray hits an object do not include background colour in calculations
 { if (intensity_factor > 0.999)
   { pixred += backred ;  pixgreen += backgreen ;  pixblue += backblue ; }
 }  // end of background_illumination

//------------------------//
  void push_new_rays(void)
//------------------------//
 { float tfactor, rfactor ;
   int mat ;
   stackinfo st ;
// create data structure st to be pushed onto the stack
   st.base = insect ;
   mat = scene.Get_material(nearhit) ;
// place transparent ray of sufficient intensity onto the stack
   if (tranflag)
     { tfactor = intensity_factor * mrl.Get_trn(mat) ;
       if (tfactor > minblack)
         { st.dire = tran ;  st.intens = tfactor ; stack.push(st) ; }
     } ;
// place reflected ray of sufficient intensity onto the stack
// if total reflection assume 50% dissipation of transmitted ray
   if (totalref)
     { rfactor=intensity_factor*(0.5*mrl.Get_trn(mat)+mrl.Get_spc(mat)) ;
       totalref = FALSE ;
     }
   else rfactor = intensity_factor * mrl.Get_spc(mat) ;
   if (rfactor > minblack)
    { st.dire = refl ;  st.intens = rfactor ; stack.push(st) ; }
 }  // End of push_new_rays

//----------------------------//
  void determine_new_rays(void)
//----------------------------//
 { double costhetai, mu, lambda, expression ;
   costhetai = (double)dot3(dire,norm) ; // cosine of angle of incidence
   refl = dire - 2.0 * (float)costhetai * norm ;
   make_unit_vector(&refl) ;   // reflected ray given as unit vector
// if object is transparent calculate transmitted ray (see page 323)
   if (mrl.Get_trn(scene.Get_material(nearhit)) > 0.0)
     { mu = mu1 / mu2 ;
       expression = mu * mu + costhetai * costhetai - (double)1.0 ;
```

```
      if (expression > epsilon)
        { lambda = (double)1.0 - sqrt(expression) / fabs(costhetai) ;
          tran = dire - (float)(lambda * costhetai) * norm ;
          make_unit_vector(&tran) ;
          tranflag = TRUE ;
        }
      else   // Total Reflection
        { tranflag = FALSE ;  totalref = TRUE ;  } ;
    }
  else tranflag = FALSE ;
  push_new_rays() ;  // push (both?) new rays onto the stack
} // End of determine_new_rays

//---------------------//
  void follow_ray(void)
//---------------------//
 { stackinfo st ;
   while ( ! stack.empty() )   // repeat procedure until stack is empty
// determine ray-path, base + phi * dire, of current ray
   { st=stack.pop() ;
     base=st.base ;   dire = st.dire ;   intensity_factor=st.intens ;
     if ( ray_intersects_objects() )
       { determine_intersection() ;
         determine_illumination() ;
         determine_new_rays() ;
       }
     else background_illumination() ;
   }
 } // end of follow_ray

//-----------------------//
  void generate_ray(void)
//-----------------------//
 { static int halfnxpix = win.Get_nxpix() / 2 ;
   static int halfnypix = win.Get_nypix() / 2 ;
   static float invscalex = 1.0 / win.Get_xyscale() ;
   static float invscaley = invscalex / win.Get_rat() ;
   static float ppd = win.Get_horiz() * 3.0 ;
   stackinfo st ;
// Determine the unit direction vector from eye to pixel
   dire.x = (pixel.x - halfnxpix) * invscalex ;
   dire.y = (halfnypix - pixel.y) * invscaley ;
   dire.z = -ppd ;
   make_unit_vector(&dire) ; st.dire=dire ;
// RGB value of pixel set initially to zero
   pixred = 0.0 ;  pixgreen = 0.0 ;  pixblue= 0.0 ;
// base vector the eye (zero) and sample intensity unity
   st.base=zero ;   st.intens=1.0 ;
   stack.push(st) ;            // push initial ray information on stack
 } // End of generate_ray

//-------------------//
  void raytrace(void)
//-------------------//
 { for (pixel.y = 0 ; pixel.y < win.Get_nypix(); (pixel.y)++)
   { for (pixel.x = 0 ; pixel.x < win.Get_nxpix() ; (pixel.x)++)
     { generate_ray() ;  // generate a ray to each pixel in viewport
       follow_ray() ;    // follow it, updating RGB values
       paint_pixel() ;   // colour in pixel
     }
   }
 } // End of raytrace

//------------------//
  void draw_it(void)
//------------------//
 { win.start() ;
   raytrace() ;
 } // End of draw_it
```

Listing 16.4

```
// Sample file "raytrace.dat"
   2
   1
   1   0   0   0       1   0   0    0
   0   1   0  80       0   1   0  -80
   0   0   1   0       0   0   1    0
  40   0   2
   4
   1   0   0   0        1   0   0   0
   0   1   0   0        0   1   0   0
   0   0   1   0        0   0   1   0
 200  20   0   1
```

Dealing with the objects

The ray-tracing algorithm requires two separate functions for each object type. It needs to know the point of intersection of a ray with the surface of an object, and the normal to the surface at that point. For the sphere these have been implemented as **normal_to_sphere** and **ray_intersects_sphere**; for the checkerboard **normal_to_checkerboard** and **ray_intersects_checkerboard** respectively. The normal is needed by the shading model, and for the determination of the reflected and refracted sub-rays.

Function **ray_intersects_objects** returns a Boolean value indicating whether any given ray intersects any of the geometrical objects in the scene. The function compares the ray with each of the **numobj** objects in turn by transforming the ray relative to the SETUP position of that object using **Matrix RI**. In this form, with base vector **stpbase** and direction vector **stpdire**, the ray is compared with the corresponding SETUP position of the object to find the point of intersection (if any). With each intersection, the nearest to the base vector of the sub-ray is stored as **nearbase** and **neardire**.

Function **determine_intersection** determines the point of intersection of a ray with the nearest object, and then finds the normal to the surface of that object at the point of intersection. There is a major problem to be considered here. Because of rounding errors, we may find a point of intersection lying just off the object's surface. Therefore the next ray generated from this point by the algorithm will again hit the same surface, and we end in an infinite loop, terminated only when the intensity levels fall below the threshold; however, the colours calculated will be meaningless. To overcome this we impose the rule that a point of intersection that is a distance less than **accuracy** units from the base of the ray is ignored.

For the sphere, the normal is found by drawing a line from the centre of the sphere to the point on the surface, taking into account whether the ray is inside an object or in open space. If a sphere is transparent (that is there is refraction) we have to take into account whether the incident ray is in open space about to enter the sphere, or inside the sphere about to re-emerge into open space.

For the checkerboard, the SETUP normal is parallel to and in the sense of the positive y-axis. Of course, for a point on the board, we have also to find in which of the two types of tile it lies, and set the flag that differentiates between the alternative materials accordingly.

Exercise 16.1
Incorporate the parallel beam shading model into this program. Extend the shading and colouring process to allow for multiple light sources.

Exercise 16.2
Rather than one ray of 'white light' at each pixel to sample space, we can send out three separate red, green and blue component rays, each with its own different refractive properties. Each of the three rays could be followed individually, sampling only red, green and blue intensities respectively. The three initial rays will diverge, producing their own unique ray-trees, which are finally combined individually to give the RGB colour components of the pixel: in certain circumstances this will create a 'rainbow effect'. We concentrated on using rays of 'white light' in order not to overcomplicate the algorithm. Extend our programs to use the separate red, green and blue sampler rays.

Exercise 16.3
If each pixel is considered to be composed of 2^M by 2^M sub-pixels, then the ray-tracing process may be extended to the sub-pixel, as opposed to the pixel level. Should you then combine the colours chosen for each sub-pixel, you will achieve a simple *anti-aliasing* technique for the colouring of that pixel. Implement this.

Project 16.1
Incorporate shadows in the program. For each intersection point found in the ray-tracing, you will need to discover if it is in shadow; just draw a line from that point to the light source(s), but do not worry about refraction for this line. If this line intersects any other object then the point will be in shadow, and you colour it with ambient light only, otherwise use the usual colour model, before sending this value back directly to colour the pixel.

Project 16.2
Use these ideas in an extended program to include **primitive_type**s 2 and 3, a finite cylinder and half-space, as well as a torus, helix, cone and paraboloid bowl in the model. The front cover was produced by an extension of our programs, in which we introduced the necessary code to deal with the torus. But beware, the intersection of a ray with a torus will require the solution of a quartic polynomial; it may prove more efficient to use approximation techniques such as the Newton-Raphson method. To show that our programs are easily transportable, the final Plate VIIIb, which introduces a transparent paraboloid bowl, was

previewed on the VGA card, but then it was run on a 24-bit high-resolution *virtual device*. This demonstrates the power of our approach; running our programs on the high-resolution device only required that we write a graphics driver for this device and link it to the **Viewport** and **Palette** classes.

Project 16.3

Change our ray-tracing program so that it can draw scenes that have been modelled using constructive solid geometry trees. Beware this is very tricky!

Project 16.4

Introduce a simple form of *attenuation* into our program. Here the intensity along a ray fades with (it is inversely proportional to) the square of the distance from the eye. This creates unsatisfactory images so many more sophisticated versions of this and many other physical concepts have been developed, and we suggest that readers who have understood our simplified models should read Foley, van Dam, Feiner and Hughes (1990) and extend our programs.

Project 16.5

Subdivide a cubic volume of space into an *m* by *m* by *m* set of cubes that surrounds a chosen scene. For each cube keep information on what objects in the scene it intersects (if any). Hint: use functions from the oct-tree algorithm. Then function **ray_intersects_objects** will now have to find the path of the ray along the cubes, and check for intersection only with the objects that intersect the corresponding cubes. Depending on the scene, this technique can speed up ray-tracing significantly (Kajiya, 1986).

Conclusion: what next?

If you have reached this point in our book and you have understood all the methods, then you will now be ready to experiment with the research level problems of computer graphics: problems such as animation, texture, display techniques (polygonal mesh *versus* ray-tracing *versus* oct-tree), refraction and reflection, multiple light sources, more realistic shadows taking diffraction into account (that is, with umbra and penumbra), *constraint-based modelling*, natural phenomena (such as clouds, fire, waves), adding patches to polygonal mesh models (Bezier, 1974; Gordon and Riesenfeld, 1974), using bicubic curves, non-uniform rational B-splines etc. We can recommend you move on to the books of Newman and Sproull (1973) and Foley and Van Dam (1990), and the ACM-SIGGRAPH conference proceedings for excellent surveys of these and other problems, and we wish you much enjoyment in your future study of computer graphics.

Appendix

Directory Structure

In order to make your use of our programs as straightforward as possible, we recommend that you create a directory that is dedicated to your use of our book. It should be named **\A&T** and placed in the root directory of your computer. Within this directory create three sub-directories that are named **\A&T\DRIVER**, **\A&T\LISTINGS** and **\A&T\WORKDIR**. Sub-directory **DRIVER** should hold the device driver for the VGA card, together with any support programs. Sub-directory **LISTINGS** should hold all the C++ listings given in the text; it should itself be subdivided into a further 17 sub-directories named **one**, **two**, **...**, **sixteen** and **appendix**, that correspond, as you would expect, to the code from the 16 chapters and the appendix of this book. Finally, **WORKDIR** is the working directory, in which you should run our application programs using the Borland C++ Project facility; it is here that all the named files from the text should be stored: **"viewport.h"**, **"viewport.cpp"**, **"palette.h"**, **"palette.cpp"**, **"window.h"**, **"window.cpp"** etc. The flexible disk being sold to complement this book has been organized in just this manner.

The VGA device driver

A DOS device driver is a program that, when loaded, stays resident in the RAM of the computer until it is shut down. The main function of a device driver is to provide an interface to a specific hardware device that is not catered for by BIOS (the Basic Input Output System), such as the VGA and XGA graphics adapters. A device driver is loaded when the machine is 'booted-up'; but only if the appropriate installation command line has been inserted into the **"config.sys"** file of your computer. Once successfully installed, a driver is treated (and therefore activated) by the Disk Operating System as a file name.

Communication with a device driver can be achieved in two ways: our VGA driver, file **"vgadrive.sys"**, uses ASCII character-based commands, whereas our XGA adapter, file **"xgaaidos.sys"**, uses binary communication. In this present section we will give a brief description of the structure of our VGA driver and of its command table; later we will consider the XGA driver, where we will see that this will require replacement versions of the **Viewport** and **Palette** methods that are stored in files **"viewport.cpp"** and **"palette.cpp"** respectively.

A DOS device driver consists of two parts: one remains resident in RAM, while the other is erased upon installation. In our VGA driver only procedures INIT_P1 and FILL_RH are discarded. The useful part of the driver is marked by a header that holds information about, amongst others things, the (file) name that DOS will use to invoke the driver. Our driver uses the name "VGA_". We use the underscore (_) to differentiate it from other programs that use the name VGA.

Apart from the header, there are two vital procedures that have to be included: STRATEGY holds the address of the buffer used by DOS to communicate with the driver; and IRPT (interrupt) that is invoked whenever the driver's communication link is used. The IRPT procedure invokes the particular service required by DOS (INPUT, OUTPUT, etc.). We place the services named OUTPUT and OUTPUT_VERIFY under the general procedure name INOUT, within which we invoke the *parser* for our graphics commands.

The parser uses its own internal buffer, 400 bytes long, delineated by the positions BUF_BEG and BUF_END. This buffer is used to store a graphics command as it arrives from DOS. The parser has to reconstruct the command byte by byte, since it may arrive in more than one data transfer to the device driver. In addition, our device driver needs to allocate a further 2500 bytes of RAM, from positions STKTOP to STKBEG, for use as an internal stack, because the size of the default DOS stack is too small for our memory requirements in some cases. In this way, on installation the driver allocates itself all the memory it will ever need.

The resident part of the driver uses procedure PROCESS_BYTE to read the characters sent by DOS, and PUT_NUM_BUF collects them into our buffer. These characters will represent our set of graphics commands from the **Viewport** and **Palette** classes. They will be received by the driver in the form:

cmd, arg1, arg2, ..., cmd_terminator

where *cmd* is the *command identification number*, ranging from 0 to 9 (command 0 is void), and *argx* (*x*=1,2,...) is the corresponding list of parameters that this command acts upon (see table A.1). The identification number and the elements of the list of parameters are separated by either the ASCII character space " " or comma "," . The end of the parameter list, and thus of the current command, is denoted by TERM(inator), which is the semicolon ";". Upon receipt of this character, the graphics command is executed (DO_CMD) provided the command is legal (flag IS_VOID will be set to zero). Else if IS_VOID is non-zero there has been an error, whereupon the command is ignored, and the parser resets all flags, variables and its internal buffer. The IS_VOID flag can also be reset by sending the ASCII character equals '=', the INITIALisation character.

After initialising the parser, GET_BYTE requests bytes from DOS; the first byte to arrive will be translated as a command code as flag IS_CMD is set. DO_CMD calls the appropriate driver routine for the VGA card (listing A.2): DO_NOTHING, PREPIT, FINISH, SETCOL, ERASE, SETPIX, MOVPIX, LINPIX, LOGICAL_FUN or RGBLOG.

Table A.1

Command Number	Description	Parameters
1	**Invoke graphics mode.** Mode 18 : 640 × 480 pixels, 16 colours. Mode 19 : 320 × 200 pixels, 256 colours.	Mode number
2	**Close graphics, invoke text mode.**	None
3	**Set colour.** Set the current colour. Permissible values depend on the graphics mode: [0..15] (mode 18), or [0.255] (mode 19).	Colour number
4	**Erase screen.** Fills the screen with the current colour.	None
5	**Set pixel (x,y).** Sets a pixel at location (x,y) from the top left corner with the current colour. Pixel values are integers ranging from [0..639]×[0..439] (mode 18) or, [0..319]×[0..199] (mode 19)	The x, y coordinates
6	**Move to pixel (x,y).** Sets the current pixel. Nothing is printed on the screen.	The x, y coordinates
7	**Draw line to (x,y).** Draws a line from the current position to the new (x,y)	The x, y coordinates
8	**Set logical function.** Selects the logical function by which all subsequent pixel drawing operations will conform. 0: COPY, 1: AND, 2: OR, 3: XOR. The default is COPY (0)	Logical function number [0..3]
9	**Define colour.** Redefines the colour composition of red, green and blue **R,G,B** for a given colour number **C.** Permissible **R,G,B** values are in the range of [0..3] (mode 18), or [0..63] (mode 19).	Colour C and its **R, G, B** components

Input validation occurs at various stages: initially, PROCESS_BYTE checks whether the byte read represents a valid character from the context (for example a command that is text and not a number, or with an identification number outside the predefined range (0...9) are ignored). Finally, depending on the particular graphics command being used, pixel co-ordinates may need to be truncated, colour definitions altered, etc. Such erroneous commands either have their parameters altered or are ignored; an appropriate message informs the user.

Listing A.1

```
REM LISTING A1 for the VGA device driver
REM save as file "\A&T\DRIVER\setup.bat"
TASM    VGADRIVE.ASM
TLINK   VGADRIVE.OBJ
EXE2BIN VGADRIVE.EXE VGADRIVE.SYS
ERASE   VGADRIVE.EXE
ERASE   VGADRIVE.OBJ
```

Our VGA device driver is given to you as an assembly code program in listing A.2, and this should be stored in directory **\A&T\DRIVER** as file **"vgadrive.asm"**. From this you can construct the actual device driver **"vgadrive.sys"** using another program **"setup.bat"** (listing A.1), that also must be stored in directory **\A&T\DRIVER**. The code of **"setup.bat"** uses the Turbo assembler (TASM), links the resulting object code (using the TLINK program), and converts the executable code into binary form for storage in RAM (using the DOS program EXE2BIN). If you do not have the Turbo assembler, you can use the Microsoft assembler (MASM) instead. Typing the name **setup** and pressing the Return key runs the **"setup.bat"** program, and creates the required driver **"vgadrive.sys"**. Remember that you must be in directory **\A&T\DRIVER** when running these programs, and ensure that the PATHs to TASM, LINK and EXE2BIN are set.

To experiment with the VGA driver, you must first reboot your machine in order to load it into RAM. With the driver now operational, type the following:

```
copy CON VGA_    (and press the Return key)
=;1,18;3,12;4;3,3;6,0,0;7,639,479; (press Cntrl+Z and Return)
copy CON VGA_    (and press the Return key)
=;2;    (press Cntrl+Z and Return)
```

The copy command links the keyboard buffer to the VGA driver; the buffer itself is terminated by pressing the Control and Z keys together, and it is transmitted by the Return key. The first command erases the screen in red and draws a line. Our listing 1.3 is another simple example. Change directory to **\A&T\WORKDIR**, where you should create files **"viewport.h"**, **"viewport.cpp"**, **"palette.h"**, and **"palette.cpp"** from listings 1.1a, 1.1b, 1.2a and 1.2b respectively. Then copy listing 1.3 into file **"one3.cpp"**. Create a Borland C++ Project **"one3.prj"** by linking together files **"one3.cpp"** and **"palette.cpp"**; there is no need to link in **"viewport.cpp"** (this is **#included** by **"palette.cpp"**). And run it!

Listing A.2

```
;VGA Character Based Device Driver
;===================================
;  Request Header (Common portion)
;-----------------------------------
; Addressability to Request Header
; structure is established by RH.
; Fields common to all request types
; are described in RHC structure:
RH  EQU  DS:[BX]
RHC  STRUC
RHC_CCC  DB  ?  ;length of RH +data
         DB  ?  ;unit code, subunit
RHC_CMD  DB  ?  ;command code
RHC_STA  DW  ?  ;status
         DQ  ?  ;reserved for DOS
RHC  ENDS       ;common portion ends
;
;Status values for RHC_STA
STAT_DONE    EQU 01H   ;completed
STAT_CMDERR EQU 8003H  ;invalid code
;
;  Request Header for INIT command
;-----------------------------------
; Apart from the common portion RHC,
; the RH0 structure describes the
; number of units, (1=OK, 0=fail),
; the driver's ending and the BPB
; array addresses and the drive code
RH0    STRUC
  DB  (TYPE RHC) DUP (?)
RH0_NUN   DB  ?
RH0_ENDO  DW  ?
RH0_ENDS  DW  ?
RH0_BPBO  DW  ?
RH0_BPBS  DW  ?
RH0_DRIV  DB  ?  ;DOS 3 only
RH0  ENDS
;-----------------------------------
;  Request Header for INPUT, OUTPUT,
;    and OUTPUT with verify
; Apart from the common portion RHC,
; the RH4 structure contains the
; media descriptor, the transfer
; address, the sector count and the
; starting sector number
;-----------------------------------
RH4  STRUC
  DB  (TYPE RHC) DUP (?)
           DB  ?
RH4_DTAO   DW  ?
RH4_DTAS   DW  ?
RH4_CNT    DW  ?
RH4_SSN    DW  ?
           DW  ?
           DW  ?
RH4  ENDS
;-----------------------------------
; Offset/segment of transfer address
RH4_DTAA    EQU DWORD PTR RH4_DTAO
;-----------------------------------
TAB         EQU  09H  ;Tab
LF          EQU  0AH  ;Line Feed
CR          EQU  0DH  ;Car. Return
PARA_SIZE  EQU   16  ;bytes for 8088
STACK_SIZE EQU  512  ;initial stack
;
CSEG   SEGMENT PARA PUBLIC 'CODE'
  ASSUME  CS:CSEG
;-----------------------------------
;  Resident data area. All variables
; and constants required after
; initialization are defined here.
;===================================
; DEVICE HEADER.
;===================================
START  EQU  $
  DD  -1            ;To next driver
  DW  08000H        ;Character based
  DW  OFFSET STRATEGY
  DW  OFFSET IRPT
  DB  'VGA_      '  ;DOS name
;-----------------------------------
; REQUEST HEADER (RH) address is
; saved here by "strategy" routine
;-----------------------------------
RH_PTRA    LABEL DWORD
RH_PTRO    DW   ?   ;offset
RH_PTRS    DW   ?   ;segment
;
  ASSUME DS:NOTHING
;===================================
; DEVICE "strategy" entry point.
; Retain the Request Header address
; for use by "interrupt" routine
;===================================
STRATEGY PROC  FAR
;-----------------
  MOV  CS:RH_PTRO,BX
  MOV  CS:RH_PTRS,ES
  RET
STRATEGY  ENDP
;-----------------------------------
; Messages
;-----------------------------------
MSG_0  DB  'VGA Graphics Device '
       DB  'Driver Installed',CR,LF
       DB  'Invoke with name: VGA_'
       DB  ' ',CR,LF,'$'
MSG_1  DB  'MESSAGE IS VOID',CR,LF
       DB  ' ','$'
MSG_2  DB  'Error: Missing '
       DB  'arguments',CR,LF,'$'
MSG_3  DB  'Error: Not in graphics '
       DB  'mode',CR,LF,'$'
;-----------------------------------
; Parser's variables and constants
;-----------------------------------
INITIAL    EQU   3DH  ;ASCII '='
TERM       EQU   3BH  ;ASCII ';'
SPACE      EQU   20H  ;ASCII ' '
COMMA      EQU   2CH  ;ASCII ','
IS_CMD     DB     1   ; flags
IS_VOID    DB     0   ;
CHANGED    DB     0   ;
CMD_DONE   DB     1   ;
IS_SPR     DB     ?   ;
IS_NMB     DB     ?   ;
MAX_NUM    DW   640   ;Maximum value
DEC_DIG    DW    10
ARG_R      DB     ?
ARG_Q      DB     ?
CUR_NUM    DW  0000H
```

```
;-----------------------------------
; The buffer used by the parser to
; compile a command
;-----------------------------------
BUF_BEG   LABEL   BYTE
  DB   400H   DUP(00H)
BUF_END   LABEL   BYTE
  DW   0000H
BUF_CMD   DW    BUF_BEG    ;begin
BUF_PTR   DW    BUF_END    ;next empty
BUF_FILL  DW    BUF_BEG    ;last +1
;
;-----------------------------------
;The stack used by the device driver
;after initialisation
;-----------------------------------
STKBEG:
  DB   2500 DUP(?)
STKTOP    EQU    THIS BYTE
;-----------------------------------
; Variables and constants used by
; the graphics procedures
;-----------------------------------
THOUS     DW  1000
HUNDR     DB   100
TENS      DB    10
MIS_ARG   DB    0
GRFCS     DB    0
PROD_18   DW 38400  ;480 *  80 bytes
PROD_19   DW 64000  ;320 * 200 bytes
MAXX      DW      ?
MAXY      DW      ?
CUR_COL   DB      ?
ORIG_X    DW      ?
ORIG_Y    DW      ?
END_X     DW      ?
END_Y     DW      ?
COL_ID    DB      ?
CUR_MOD   DB      ?
COL_WORD  DW      ?
MAX_COL   DW    255
RED       DB      ?
GREEN     DB      ?
BLUE      DB      ?
INCX      DW      ?
INCY      DW      ?
HSTR      DW      ?
VSTR      DW      ?
TOTAL     DW      ?
DIAG      DW      ?
LOG_FUN   DB      0
;
;-----------------------------------
; Table of DOS command processing
; routine entry points
;-----------------------------------
CMD_TABLE  LABEL  WORD
   DW  OFFSET INIT_P1          ; 0
   DW  OFFSET MEDIA_CHECK      ; 1
   DW  OFFSET BLD_BPB          ; 2
   DW  OFFSET INPUT_IOCTL      ; 3
   DW  OFFSET INPUT            ; 4
   DW  OFFSET INPUT_NOWAIT     ; 5
   DW  OFFSET INPUT_STATUS     ; 6
   DW  OFFSET INPUT_FLUSH      ; 7
   DW  OFFSET OUTPUT           ; 8
   DW  OFFSET OUTPUT_VERIFY    ; 9
   DW  OFFSET OUTPUT_STATUS    ;10
   DW  OFFSET OUTPUT_FLUSH     ;11
   DW  OFFSET OUTPUT_IOCTL     ;12
   DW  OFFSET DEVICE_OPEN      ;13
   DW  OFFSET DEVICE_CLOSE     ;14
MAX_DEV_CMD  EQU  ($-CMD_TABLE)/2
   DW  OFFSET REMOVABLE_MEDIA  ;15
;-----------------------------------
; Table of graphics command
; processing routine entry points
;-----------------------------------
CMD_GRAPHICS  LABEL  WORD
   DW  OFFSET DO_NOTHING       ; 0
   DW  OFFSET PREPIT           ; 1
   DW  OFFSET FINISH           ; 2
   DW  OFFSET SETCOL           ; 3
   DW  OFFSET ERASE            ; 4
   DW  OFFSET SETPIX           ; 5
   DW  OFFSET MOVPIX           ; 6
   DW  OFFSET LINPIX           ; 7
   DW  OFFSET LOGICAL_FUN      ; 8
MAX_GRCMD  EQU ($-CMD_GRAPHICS)/2
   DW  OFFSET RGBLOG           ; 9
;===================================
; Device "interrupt" entry point
;===================================
IRPT  PROC  FAR
;-------------
   PUSH  DS
   PUSH  ES
   PUSH  AX
   PUSH  BX
   PUSH  CX
   PUSH  DX
   PUSH  DI
   PUSH  SI
   CLD                  ;forward move
;Get the address of RH passed to
;"strategy" into DS:BX and then
;the command code from it (RH)
   LDS   BX,CS:RH_PTRA
   MOV   AL,RH.RHC_CMD
   CBW                  ;zero AH. If
;AL>7FH, next compare will catch it.
;If command code is too high =>error
   CMP   AL,MAX_DEV_CMD
   JA    IRPT_CMD_HIGH
;Push return address from command
;processor onto DOS stack. Any
;command routine that issues RET
;will POP it and return properly
   MOV   DI,OFFSET IRPT_CMD_EXIT
   PUSH  DI
;Double command code for the table
;offset and put it into the index
;register DI for JMP.
   ADD   AX,AX
   MOV   DI,AX
;Invoke the appropriate routine. At
;entry we expect:
;DS:BX = Request Header address
;CS    = D.Driver's code segment
;AX    = 0 (i.e. no error)
;top of stack is the return address
; (i.e. IRPT_CMD_EXIT )
   JMP   CS:CMD_TABLE[DI]
;Entry point for void command codes
MEDIA_CHECK:
BLD_BPB:
REMOVABLE_MEDIA:
DEVICE_OPEN:
```

```
DEVICE_CLOSE:
INPUT:
INPUT_IOCTL:
INPUT_NOWAIT:
INPUT_STATUS:
INPUT_FLUSH:
OUTPUT_IOCTL:
OUTPUT_STATUS:
OUTPUT_FLUSH:
;Pop return address off DOS stack
   POP   AX
;Handle invalid command codes
IRPT_CMD_HIGH:
MOV   AX,STAT_CMDERR
;Entry point after a command (valid
;or not) is handled appropriately
;Restore DS:BX as Request Header
;pointer, add "done" bit to status
;word, store status word into RH
;structure, and restore registers
IRPT_CMD_EXIT:
   CLD
   LDS   BX,CS:RH_PTRA
   OR    AH,STAT_DONE
   MOV   RH.RHC_STA,AX
   POP   SI
   POP   DI
   POP   DX
   POP   CX
   POP   BX
   POP   AX
   POP   ES
   POP   DS
   RET
IRPT ENDP
;===================================
;Entry point for command codes 8,9
;===================================
INOUT  PROC
;----------
OUTPUT:
OUTPUT_VERIFY:
;Dos stack for the device driver is
;too small. Therefore we swap to our
;stack. When our processing is over,
;we need to return to DOS stack and
;then return control to DOS. The
;address of the DOS stack is PUSHed
;onto our stack:
   MOV   DX,SS   ;save DOS stack
   MOV   CX,SP   ;address to DX,CX
   CLI           ;inhibit interrupts
   MOV   AX,CS   ;SS = CS (via AX)
   MOV   SS,AX
   MOV   AX,OFFSET STKTOP ;Activate
   MOV   SP,AX            ;our stack
   STI           ;allow interrupts
   PUSH  DX      ;save DOS stack
   PUSH  CX      ;address (SS,SP)
;Get the number of bytes sent by DOS
;and save the address of RH. We will
;use it to return the #of bytes read
   MOV   CX,RH.RH4_CNT
   PUSH  BX
   PUSH  DS
;Get the data transfer address
   CLD
   LDS   SI,RH.RH4_DTAA
GET_BYTE:
;Assign the first byte in AL. SI
;points to the first unread byte
   LODSB
;Save important registers and invoke
;the graphics commands parser
   PUSH  DS
   PUSH  SI
   PUSH  CX
   CALL  PROCESS_BYTE
   POP   CX
   POP   SI
   POP   DS
;Loop around GET_BYTE until all
;transfer data bytes are read
   DEC   CX
   CMP   CX,0
   JG    GET_BYTE
;Retrieve DS:BX address to RH
   POP   DS
   POP   BX
;Retrieve the DOS stack address
   POP   CX        ;Old SP
   POP   DX        ;Old SS
;Inhibit interrupts, swap back to
;the DOS stack
   CLI
   MOV   SS,DX
   MOV   SP,CX
   STI
;Set AX to "no error" and return
   XOR   AX,AX
   RET
INOUT   ENDP
;
;===================================
;          The PARSER
;  (see text for explanations)
;===================================
;-----------------
PROCESS_BYTE  PROC
;-----------------
;AL holds the value for processing
;Get DS to show the code segment
   PUSH  DS
   PUSH  CS
   POP   DS
   ASSUME  DS:CSEG
MAIN_LOOP:
   CMP   AL,TERM
   JNE   NO_TERM
   CALL  TERMINATE
   CALL  INITIALIZE
   JMP   NEXT_BYTE
;No termination char
NO_TERM:
   CMP   AL,INITIAL
   JNE   NO_INIT
   CALL  INITIALIZE
   JMP   NEXT_BYTE
;No term, no initialization
NO_INIT:
   CMP   IS_CMD,1
   JNE   NO_CMD
   JMP   SHORT  YES_CMD
;No term, no initial, not a command
;identifier
NO_CMD:
   CALL  IS_SEPAR
```

```
   CMP   IS_SPR,1
   JNE   NO_SPR_NUM
   JMP   SHORT  YES_SPR_NUM
;No term, no initial, no command,
;not a separator
NO_SPR_NUM:
   CALL  IS_NUMBR
   CMP   IS_NMB,1
   JNE   NO_NMB_ARG
   JMP   SHORT  YES_NMB_ARG
;No term, no initial, no command,
;no separ, not legal
NO_NMB_ARG:
   CALL  IGNORE_CMD
   JMP   SHORT NEXT_BYTE
;No term, no initial, no command,
;legal number argument
YES_NMB_ARG:
   CALL  STORE_TEMP_ARG
   JMP   SHORT  NEXT_BYTE
;No term, no initial, no command,
;an argument separator
YES_SPR_NUM:
   CMP   CHANGED,1
   JNE   NEXT_BYTE_1
   CALL  PUT_NUM_BUF
   MOV   CHANGED,0
   MOV   CUR_NUM,0000H
NEXT_BYTE_1:
   JMP   SHORT  NEXT_BYTE
YES_CMD:
   CALL  IS_SEPAR
   CMP   IS_SPR,1
   JNE   NO_SPR_CMD
   JMP   SHORT  YES_SPR_CMD
;No term, no initial, not a
;separator => command ID
NO_SPR_CMD:
   CALL  IS_NUMBR
   CMP   IS_NMB,1
   JNE   NO_NMB_CMD
   JMP   SHORT  YES_NMB_CMD
;No term, no initial, no separ, not
;a number => Illegal command ID
NO_NMB_CMD:
   CALL  IGNORE_CMD
   JMP   SHORT  NEXT_BYTE
; No term, no initial, a number
; => part of the command ID
YES_NMB_CMD:
   CALL  STORE_TEMP_CMD
   JMP   SHORT  NEXT_BYTE
;No term, no initial, a separator
;from the command ID
YES_SPR_CMD:
;Ignore white space characters
;before CMD_ID.
   CMP   CHANGED,0
   JE    NEXT_BYTE
;Put CMD_ID to parser's buffer
   CALL  PUT_NUM_BUF
;The next bytes should be arguments
   MOV   IS_CMD,0
   MOV   CMD_DONE,0
;
;Reset variables
   MOV   CHANGED,0
   MOV   CUR_NUM,0000H
   JMP   SHORT  NEXT_BYTE
NEXT_BYTE:
   POP   DS
   RET
PROCESS_BYTE  ENDP
;
;-------------
IS_SEPAR  PROC
;-------------
;Is AL an argument separator?
   MOV   IS_SPR,1
   CMP   AL,SPACE
   JLE   SPR_EX
   CMP   AL,COMMA
   JE    SPR_EX
   MOV   IS_SPR,0
SPR_EX:
   RET
IS_SEPAR  ENDP
;
;-------------
IS_NUMBR  PROC
;-------------
;Is AL a digit between 0-9?
   MOV   IS_NMB,0
   CMP   AL,30H
   JB    NMB_EX
   CMP   AL,39H
   JA    NMB_EX
   MOV   IS_NMB,1
NMB_EX:
   RET
IS_NUMBR  ENDP
;
;---------------
INITIALIZE  PROC
;---------------
;Reset variables
   PUSH  BX
   MOV   BX,OFFSET BUF_BEG
   MOV   BUF_PTR,BX
   MOV   BUF_CMD,BX
   MOV   IS_VOID,0
   MOV   IS_CMD,1
   MOV   CUR_NUM,0000H
   MOV   CHANGED,0
   MOV   CMD_DONE,1
   POP   BX
   RET
INITIALIZE  ENDP
;
;---------------
IGNORE_CMD  PROC
;---------------
   MOV   IS_VOID,1
   CALL  DISP_VOID
   RET
IGNORE_CMD  ENDP
;-------------------
STORE_TEMP_ARG  PROC
;-------------------
;Storage for current argument
   PUSH  AX
   PUSH  CX
   SUB   AL,30H
   CBW
   MOV   CX,AX
   MOV   AX,CUR_NUM
   MUL   DEC_DIG
   ADD   AX,CX
```

```
   CMP    AX,MAX_NUM
   JLE    ARG_OK
   MOV    AX,MAX_NUM
ARG_OK:
   MOV    CUR_NUM,AX
   MOV    CHANGED,1
   POP    CX
   POP    AX
   RET
STORE_TEMP_ARG   ENDP
;
;-------------------
STORE_TEMP_CMD   PROC
;-------------------
;Storage for current command
   PUSH   AX
   PUSH   CX
   SUB    AL,30H
   CBW
   MOV    CX,AX
   MOV    AX,CUR_NUM
   MUL    DEC_DIG
   ADD    AX,CX
   CMP    AX,MAX_GRCMD
   JLE    CMD_OK
   MOV    AX,MAX_GRCMD
CMD_OK:
   MOV    CUR_NUM,AX
   MOV    CHANGED,1
   POP    CX
   POP    AX
   RET
STORE_TEMP_CMD    ENDP
;
;----------------
PUT_NUM_BUF   PROC
;----------------
;Store CUR_NUM to buffer
   PUSH   AX
   PUSH   BX
   MOV    AX,CUR_NUM
   DIV    HUNDR
   MOV    BX,BUF_PTR
   MOV    CS:[BX],AL    ;QUOTIENT
   INC    BX
   MOV    CS:[BX],AH    ;REMAINDER
   INC    BX
   MOV    BUF_PTR,BX
   MOV    BUF_FILL,BX
   POP    BX
   POP    AX
   RET
PUT_NUM_BUF   ENDP
;
;--------------
TERMINATE   PROC
;--------------
;Command is received. Execute it!
   PUSH   CX
   CMP    IS_CMD,1
   JNE    PUT_EXEC
   CMP    CHANGED,0
   JE     EX_TERM
   CALL   PUT_NUM_BUF
   MOV    IS_CMD,0
   MOV    CMD_DONE,0
   MOV    CHANGED,0
   MOV    CUR_NUM,0000H
PUT_EXEC:
   CMP    CHANGED,1
   JNE    NEXT_BYTE_2
   CALL   PUT_NUM_BUF
NEXT_BYTE_2:
   CALL   DO_CMD
EX_TERM:
   POP    CX
   RET
TERMINATE    ENDP
;
;----------
POP_W  PROC
;----------
;Read in AX the next word (i.e.
;number) from buffer
   PUSH   BX
   MOV    BX,BUF_PTR
   MOV    AL,CS:[BX]
   MOV    ARG_Q,AL
   INC    BX
   MOV    AL,CS:[BX]
   MOV    ARG_R,AL
   INC    BX
   MOV    BUF_PTR,BX
   MOV    MIS_ARG,0
   CMP    BX,BUF_FILL
   JG     END_OF_BUFW
   MOV    AL,ARG_Q
   MUL    HUNDR
   PUSH   AX
   MOV    AL,ARG_R
   CBW
   POP    BX
   ADD    AX,BX
RETURN_W:
   POP    BX
   RET
END_OF_BUFW:
   MOV    MIS_ARG,1
   JMP    SHORT RETURN_W
POP_W  ENDP
;
;===================================
;     THE  GRAPHICS  COMMANDS
;===================================
;
;-----------
DO_CMD  PROC
;-----------
;Invoke the command shown by CMD_ID.
;If command has been executed or is
;void, return This avoids commands
;like: "1;;;;"
   CMP    CMD_DONE,1
   JNE    NOT_DONE
   JMP    SHORT   RETURN
NOT_DONE:
   CMP    IS_VOID,0
   JE     CMD_PROCEED
   JMP    SHORT  RETURN
CMD_PROCEED:
;Get buffer's addresses
   PUSH   BUF_CMD
   POP    BUF_PTR
;Get command from buffer
   CALL   POP_W
   CBW                    ;zero AH. If
;AL>7FH, next compare will catch it.
;If command code is too high =>error
```

```
   CMP   AL,MAX_GRCMD
   JA    GR_CMD_HIGH
;Push return address from command
;processor onto DOS stack. Any
;command routine that issues RET
;will POP it and return properly
   MOV   DI,OFFSET GR_CMD_EXIT
   PUSH  DI
;Double command code for the table
;offset and put it into the index
;register DI for JMP. Make sure that
;ES is set to the video buffer
   ADD   AX,AX
   MOV   DI,AX
   XOR   AX,AX
   MOV   AX,0A000H
   MOV   ES,AX
;Call routine to handle the command
   JMP   CS:CMD_GRAPHICS[DI]
;Entry point for erroneous commands
GR_CMD_ERROR:
DO_NOTHING:
;Pop return address off (our) stack
   POP   AX
GR_CMD_HIGH:
GR_CMD_EXIT:
RETURN:
   RET
DO_CMD   ENDP
;
;-----------
PREPIT  PROC
;-----------
   PUSH  AX
   CALL  POP_W        ;Get screen mode
   CMP   MIS_ARG,1
   JE    MIS_PR
   MOV   CUR_MOD,AL
;Validate mode {18,19}
   CMP   AL,18
   JE    VGA_OK
   CMP   AL,19
   JNE   NO_GR_PR
VGA_OK:
   MOV   AX,0A000H
   MOV   ES,AX
   MOV   AH,0         ;BIOS
   MOV   AL,CUR_MOD
   INT   10H
;Initialize variables
   MOV   CUR_COL,00000000B
   XOR   AX,AX
   MOV   ORIG_X,AX
   MOV   ORIG_Y,AX
   CMP   CUR_MOD,19
   JE    PR_19
   MOV   MAXX,639
   MOV   MAXY,479
   MOV   GRFCS,18
   JMP   SHORT  PR_OK
MIS_PR:
   CALL  MISSING_ARG_MSG
   MOV   GRFCS,0
   JMP   SHORT    PR_NOT_OK
PR_19:
   MOV   MAXX,319
   MOV   MAXY,199
   MOV   GRFCS,19
PR_OK:
```

```
   MOV   LOG_FUN,0
   CALL  SET_LOG_FUN
PR_NOT_OK:
   POP   AX
   RET
NO_GR_PR:
   CALL  NOT_IN_GRAPHICS_MODE
   MOV   GRFCS,0
   JMP   SHORT    PR_NOT_OK
PREPIT  ENDP
;
;------------
FINISH  PROC
;------------
   PUSH  AX
   MOV   GRFCS,0
   MOV   AH,0
   MOV   AL,3       ;Back to mode 3
   INT   10H
   POP   AX
   RET
FINISH  ENDP
;
;------------
SETCOL   PROC
;------------
   PUSH  AX
   CMP   GRFCS,0
   JE    NO_GR_SC
   CALL  POP_W
   MOV   COL_WORD,AX
   CMP   MIS_ARG,1
   JE    MIS_SC
   MOV   CUR_COL,AL
SC_OK:
   POP   AX
   RET
MIS_SC:
   CALL  MISSING_ARG_MSG
   JMP   SHORT    SC_OK
NO_GR_SC:
   CALL  NOT_IN_GRAPHICS_MODE
   JMP   SHORT    SC_OK
SETCOL   ENDP
;
;-----------
ERASE   PROC
;-----------
   PUSH  BX
   PUSH  AX
   CMP   GRFCS,0
   JE    NO_GR_ER
   CMP   GRFCS,18    ; Select mode
   JE   ERASE_18
   CMP   GRFCS,19
   JNE   NO_GR_ER
   MOV   BX,0
   MOV   CX,PROD_19
   MOV   AL,CUR_COL
FOR_ALL_19:
   MOV   ES:[BX],AL
   INC   BX
   LOOP  FOR_ALL_19
   JMP   SHORT   ER_OK
ERASE_18:
   MOV   BX,0
   MOV   CX,PROD_18
;Change the byte mask to achieve
;various line patterns.
```

```
   MOV    AH,11111111B    ;solid
   MOV    AL,CUR_COL      ;map mask
FOR_ALL_18:
   CALL   WRITE_ONE_PIX
   INC    BX
   LOOP   FOR_ALL_18
ER_OK:
   POP    AX
   POP    BX
   RET
NO_GR_ER:
   CALL   NOT_IN_GRAPHICS_MODE
   JMP    SHORT   ER_OK
ERASE   ENDP
;
;-----------
SETPIX  PROC
;-----------
;Set pixel (DX, CX) with CUR_COL
   CMP    GRFCS,0
   JE     NO_GR_SP
   CALL   POP_W
   MOV    CX,AX
   CMP    MIS_ARG,1
   JE     MIS_SP
   CALL   POP_W
   MOV    DX,AX
   CMP    MIS_ARG,1
   JE     MIS_SP
   CMP    CX,MAXX
   JLE    OKSX
   MOV    CX,MAXX
OKSX:     CMP  DX,MAXY
   JLE    OKSY
   MOV    DX,MAXY
OKSY:
   MOV    AL,CUR_COL
   PUSH   DX
   PUSH   CX
   CMP    GRFCS,19
   JE     SP_19
   CALL   PIXEL_WRITE_18
   JMP    SHORT   SP_FIN
SP_19:
   CALL   PIXEL_WRITE_19
SP_FIN:
   POP    ORIG_X
   POP    ORIG_Y
SP_OK:
   RET
NO_GR_SP:
   CALL   NOT_IN_GRAPHICS_MODE
   JMP    SHORT   SP_OK
MIS_SP:
   CALL   MISSING_ARG_MSG
   JMP    SHORT   SP_OK
SETPIX  ENDP
;
;-----------
MOVPIX  PROC
;-----------
;Move to the (DX,CX) location
   CMP    GRFCS,0
   JE     NO_GR_MP
   CALL   POP_W
   MOV    CX,AX
   CMP    MIS_ARG,1
   JE     MIS_MP
   CALL   POP_W
   MOV    DX,AX
   CMP    MIS_ARG,1
   JE     MIS_MP
   CMP    CX,MAXX
   JLE    OKMX
   MOV    CX,MAXX
OKMX:     CMP   DX,MAXY
   JLE    OKMY
   MOV    DX,MAXY
OKMY:
   PUSH   DX
   PUSH   CX
   POP    ORIG_X
   POP    ORIG_Y
MP_OK:
   RET
NO_GR_MP:
   CALL   NOT_IN_GRAPHICS_MODE
   JMP    SHORT   MP_OK
MIS_MP:
   CALL   MISSING_ARG_MSG
   JMP    SHORT   MP_OK
MOVPIX  ENDP
;
;-----------
LINPIX  PROC
;-----------
;Draw line from (ORIG_X,ORIG_Y) to
;(DX,CX) with CUR_COL.
;Update (ORIG_X,ORIG_Y) = (DX,CX)
   CMP    GRFCS,0
   JE     NO_GR_LP
   CALL   POP_W
   MOV    CX,AX
   CMP    MIS_ARG,1
   JE     MIS_LP
   CALL   POP_W
   MOV    DX,AX
   CMP    MIS_ARG,1
   JE     MIS_LP
   CMP    CX,MAXX
   JLE    OKLX
   MOV    CX,MAXX
OKLX:     CMP   DX,MAXY
   JLE    OKLY
   MOV    DX,MAXY
OKLY:
   MOV    END_X,CX
   MOV    END_Y,DX
   PUSH   END_X
   PUSH   END_Y
   CALL   DRAW_LN
   POP    ORIG_Y
   POP    ORIG_X
LP_OK:
   RET
NO_GR_LP:
   CALL   NOT_IN_GRAPHICS_MODE
   JMP    SHORT   LP_OK
MIS_LP:
   CALL   MISSING_ARG_MSG
   JMP    SHORT   LP_OK
LINPIX  ENDP
;
;-----------
RGBLOG  PROC
;-----------
;Assign COL_ID with RED,GREEN,BLUE
   PUSH   AX
```

```
    PUSH  BX
    CMP   GRFCS,0
    JE    NO_GR_RGB
    CALL  POP_W
    MOV   COL_ID,AL
    CALL  POP_W
    MOV   RED,AL
    CALL  POP_W
    MOV   GREEN,AL
    CALL  POP_W
    MOV   BLUE,AL
    CMP   MIS_ARG,1
    JE    MIS_RGB
    CMP   GRFCS,18
    JE    MAKE_COLOR_MASK
    JMP   RGB_19
MIS_RGB:
    CALL  MISSING_ARG_MSG
    JMP   RGB_OK
NO_GR_RGB:
    CALL  NOT_IN_GRAPHICS_MODE
    JMP   RGB_OK
MAKE_COLOR_MASK:
;Convert RGB to 00rgbRGB (mode18)
    XOR   AX,AX
    MOV   AL,RED
    CMP   AL,3
    JL    RD2
    MOV   RED,00100100B
    JMP   SHORT  RED_OK
RD2:
    CMP   AL,2
    JL    RD1
    MOV   RED,00000100B
    JMP   SHORT  RED_OK
RD1:
    CMP   AL,1
    JL    RED_OK
    MOV   RED,00100000B
RED_OK:
    XOR   AX,AX
    MOV   AL,GREEN
    CMP   AL,3
    JL    GRN2
    MOV   GREEN,00010010B
    JMP   SHORT  GREEN_OK
GRN2:
    CMP   AL,2
    JL    GRN1
    MOV   GREEN,00000010B
    JMP   SHORT  GREEN_OK
GRN1:
    CMP   AL,1
    JL    GREEN_OK
    MOV   GREEN,00010000B
GREEN_OK:
    XOR   AX,AX
    MOV   AL,BLUE
    CMP   AL,3
    JL    BL2
    MOV   BLUE,00001001B
    JMP   SHORT  BLUE_OK
BL2:
    CMP   AL,2
    JL    BL1
    MOV   BLUE,00000001B
    JMP   SHORT  BLUE_OK
BL1:
    CMP   AL,1
    JL    BLUE_OK
    MOV   BLUE,00001000B
BLUE_OK:
    MOV   AL,RED
    OR    AL,GREEN
    OR    AL,BLUE
    MOV   BH,AL       ;the colour mask
    MOV   AH,16       ;BIOS sub-service
    MOV   AL,0        ;BIOS service
    CMP   COL_ID,16 ;truncate entry
    JL    COL_OK
    MOV   COL_ID,15
COL_OK:
    MOV   BL,COL_ID ;the palette col.
    INT   10H
RGB_OK:
    POP   BX
    POP   AX
    RET
RGB_19:
    MOV   AH,0
    MOV   AL,COL_ID
    CBW
    MOV   BX,AX
    MOV   AH,10H
    MOV   AL,10H
    MOV   DH,RED
    MOV   CH,GREEN
    MOV   CL,BLUE
    INT   10H
    JMP   SHORT  RGB_OK
RGBLOG  ENDP
;
;-------------------
PIXEL_WRITE_18  PROC
;-------------------
;Draw a pixel in mode 18.  At entry:
; CX = X Coordinate of pixel (0,639)
; DX = Y Coordinate of pixel (0,439)
; AL = Current colour
;During:
; BX = Offset in video buffer
; AH = Bit mask for writing pixel
; AL = Current colour
;At end:  The pixel is set!
    PUSH  AX
    PUSH  BX
    PUSH  CX
    PUSH  DX
;Compute address at video buffer
    PUSH  AX
    PUSH  CX
    MOV   AX,DX
    MOV   CX,80
    MUL   CX
    MOV   BX,AX
    POP   AX
    MOV   CL,8
    DIV   CL
    MOV   CL,AH
    MOV   AH,0
    ADD   BX,AX
    POP   AX
;Get the appropriate pixel mask
    MOV   AH,10000000B
    SHR   AH,CL
    CALL  WRITE_ONE_PIX
    POP   DX
    POP   CX
```

```
    POP   BX
    POP   AX
    RET
PIXEL_WRITE_18    ENDP
;
;------------------
WRITE_ONE_PIX  PROC
;------------------
;Draw pixel for the current bit mask
;At Input:
; AH = Bit mask   AL = Colour
; BX = Offset in video buffer
; ES = A000H  (base of EGA and VGA)
    PUSH  DX
    PUSH  AX
    PUSH  AX
    PUSH  AX
; Set bit mask
    MOV   DX,3CEH
    MOV   AL,8
    OUT   DX,AL
    INC   DX
    POP   AX
    MOV   AL,AH
    OUT   DX,AL
;Set  the  previous  value  to  the
latches
    MOV   AL,ES:[BX]
    MOV   AL,0
    MOV   ES:[BX],AL
;Set colour
    MOV   DX,3C4H
    MOV   AL,2
    OUT   DX,AL
    INC   DX
    POP   AX
    OUT   DX,AL
;Draw the pixel
    MOV   AL,ES:[BX]
    MOV   AL,0FFH
    MOV   ES:[BX],AL
;Restore state
    MOV   DX,3C4H
    MOV   AL,2
    OUT   DX,AL
    INC   DX
    MOV   AL,00001111B
    OUT   DX,AL
    MOV   DX,3CEH
    MOV   AL,8
    OUT   DX,AL
    INC   DX
    MOV   AL,11111111B
    OUT   DX,AL
    POP   AX
    POP   DX
RET
WRITE_ONE_PIX    ENDP
;
;----------------------
INVOKE_LOG_FUN_19  PROC
;----------------------
;Apply the logical function LOG_FUN
;of AL to the ES:[BX] byte. Mode 19
    CMP   LOG_FUN,1
    JB    LF0
    JE    LF1
    CMP   LOG_FUN,2
    JE    LF2
    XOR   ES:[BX],AL
    JMP   SHORT   LF4
LF0:
    MOV   ES:[BX],AL
    JMP   SHORT   LF4
LF1:
    AND   ES:[BX],AL
    JMP   SHORT   LF4
LF2:
    OR    ES:[BX],AL
LF4:
    RET
INVOKE_LOG_FUN_19    ENDP
;
;-------------------
PIXEL_WRITE_19  PROC
;-------------------
;Draw a pixel in mode 19. At input:
; CX = X Coordinate of pixel (0,319)
; DX = Y Coordinate of pixel (0,199)
; AL = Current colour
    PUSH  AX
    PUSH  BX
    PUSH  CX
    PUSH  DX
; Compute address at video buffer
    PUSH  AX
    PUSH  CX
    MOV   AX,DX
    MOV   CX,320 ;up to 64K. It is OK
    MUL   CX     ;for 2bytes unsigned
    MOV   BX,AX
    POP   AX     ;The x coordinate
    ADD   BX,AX
    POP   AX     ;The colour is at AL
    CALL  INVOKE_LOG_FUN_19
    POP   DX
    POP   CX
    POP   BX
    POP   AX
    RET
PIXEL_WRITE_19    ENDP
;
;------------
DRAW_LN  PROC
;------------
;The Bresenham's approach to draw a
;line for (ORIG_x,y) to (END_x,y)
    MOV   CX,1
    MOV   DX,1
    MOV   DI,END_Y
    SUB   DI,ORIG_Y
    JGE   POS_VERTICAL
    NEG   DX
    NEG   DI
POS_VERTICAL:
    MOV   INCY,DX
    MOV   SI,END_X
    SUB   SI,ORIG_X
    JGE   POS_HORZ
    NEG   CX
    NEG   SI
POS_HORZ:
    MOV   INCX,CX
    CMP   SI,DI
    JGE   HORZ_SEGMENTS
    MOV   CX,0
    XCHG  SI,DI
    JMP   SHORT   SET_CONTROLS
```

```
HORZ_SEGMENTS:
   MOV   DX,0
SET_CONTROLS:
   MOV   HSTR,CX
   MOV   VSTR,DX
   MOV   AX,DI
   ADD   AX,AX
   MOV   TOTAL,AX
   SUB   AX,SI
   MOV   BX,AX
   SUB   AX,SI
   MOV   DIAG,AX
   MOV   CX,ORIG_X
   MOV   DX,ORIG_Y
   INC   SI
   INC   SI
;Up to but not the END_xy
;inc si again to include it
   MOV   AL,CUR_COL
LINE_POINTS:
   DEC   SI
   JNZ   PIX_DRAW
   RET
PIX_DRAW:
   CMP   GRFCS,19
   JE    LN_SG_19
   MOV   AL,CUR_COL
   CALL  PIXEL_WRITE_18
   JMP   SHORT   LN_SG_FIN
LN_SG_19:
   MOV   AL,CUR_COL
   CALL  PIXEL_WRITE_19
LN_SG_FIN:
   CMP   BX,0
   JGE   DIAGONAL
   ADD   CX,HSTR
   ADD   DX,VSTR
   ADD   BX,TOTAL
   JMP   LINE_POINTS
DIAGONAL:
   ADD   CX,INCX
   ADD   DX,INCY
   ADD   BX,DIAG
   JMP   LINE_POINTS
DRAW_LN  ENDP
;
;----------------
LOGICAL_FUN PROC
;----------------
;Set the logical function LOG_FUN
;operator for further drawing:
; 0 COPY, 1 AND, 2 OR, 3 XOR
   PUSH  AX
   PUSH  CX
   CMP   GRFCS,0
   JE    NO_GR_LF
   CALL  POP_W
   CMP   MIS_ARG,1
   JE    MIS_LF
   CBW
   MOV   CL,4
   DIV   CL
   MOV   LOG_FUN,AH
   CMP   GRFCS,19
   JE     LF_OK
   CALL  SET_LOG_FUN
LF_OK:
   POP   CX
   POP   AX
   RET
NO_GR_LF:
   CALL  NOT_IN_GRAPHICS_MODE
   JMP   SHORT  LF_OK
MIS_LF:
   CALL  MISSING_ARG_MSG
   JMP   SHORT   LF_OK
LOGICAL_FUN  ENDP
;
;----------------
SET_LOG_FUN  PROC
;----------------
;Adjusts the appropriate registers
;so that the LOG_FUN will take
;effect in VGA mode 18. At input
;LOG_FUN: 0 Copy, 1 And, 2 OR, 3 Xor
   PUSH  CX
   PUSH  DX
   PUSH  AX
   MOV   AL,LOG_FUN
   MOV   CL,3
   ROL   AL,CL
   MOV   CL,AL
   MOV   DX,03CEH
   MOV   AL,3
   OUT   DX,AL
   INC   DX
   MOV   AL,CL
   OUT   DX,AL
   POP   AX
   POP   DX
   POP   CX
   RET
SET_LOG_FUN  ENDP
;
;--------------------
MISSING_ARG_MSG   PROC
;--------------------
   PUSH  DX
   PUSH  AX
   MOV   DX,OFFSET MSG_2
   MOV   AH,9
   INT   21H
   POP   AX
   POP   DX
   RET
MISSING_ARG_MSG  ENDP
;
;-------------------------
NOT_IN_GRAPHICS_MODE   PROC
;-------------------------
   PUSH  DX
   PUSH  AX
   MOV   DX,OFFSET MSG_3
   MOV   AH,9
   INT   21H
   POP   AX
   POP   DX
   RET
NOT_IN_GRAPHICS_MODE   ENDP
;
;-------------
DISP_VOID  PROC
;-------------
   PUSH  AX
   PUSH  DX
   PUSH  DS
   PUSH  CS
   POP   DS
```

```
   MOV    DX,OFFSET MSG_1
   MOV    AH,9
   INT    21H
   POP    DS
   POP    DX
   POP    AX
   RET
DISP_VOID  ENDP
;
;-----------------------------------
; Adjust assembly-time instruction
;counter to a paragraph boundary
;-----------------------------------
IF  ($-START) MOD 16
ORG ($-START) +16 -(($-START)MOD 16)
ENDIF
;Get length of program in paragraphs
VGA_DRIVER  EQU ($-START) /PARA_SIZE
;===================================
; This is the END of the resident
;part of the device driver. All
;fields that must remain resident
;after device driver initialization
;must be defined before this point.
;===================================
;
START_NEW_PARA   DW   ?
;
;-----------
INIT_P1 PROC
;-----------
; Command Code 0 - Initialization
;Inhibit interrupts to swap stacks
   MOV    DX,SS
   MOV    CX,SP
   CLI
   MOV    AX,CS
   MOV    SS,AX
   MOV    AX,OFFSET STKTOP
   MOV    SP,AX
   STI
   PUSH   DX
   PUSH   CX
;Get Code Segment addressability
   PUSH   CS
   POP    DS
;Initialize parser's variables
   PUSH   BX
   MOV    BX,OFFSET BUF_BEG
   MOV    BUF_PTR,BX
   MOV    BUF_CMD,BX
   MOV    IS_VOID,0
   MOV    IS_CMD,1
   MOV    CUR_NUM,0000H
   MOV    CHANGED,0
   MOV    CMD_DONE,1
   POP    BX
;Determine the end of resident code
   MOV    AX,CS
   ADD    AX,VGA_DRIVER
   MOV    START_NEW_PARA,AX
;Fill in INIT Request Header
   CALL   FILL_RH
;Show initialization message
   PUSH   DX
   PUSH   AX
   MOV    DX,OFFSET     MSG_0
   MOV    AH,9
   INT    21H
   POP    AX
   POP    DX
;Back to the DOS stack
   POP    CX
   POP    DX
   CLI
   MOV    SS,DX
   MOV    SP,CX
   STI
   XOR    AX,AX
   RET
INIT_P1  ENDP
;
ASSUME   DS:CSEG
;
;-----------
FILL_RH PROC
;-----------
;Fill in INIT Request Header fields
;The device driver starts at offset
;RH0_ENDO = 0, and is at segment
;RH0_ENDS = START_NEW_PARA. The
;number of units RH0_NUN = 1 which
;implies successful installation.
   MOV    AX,START_NEW_PARA
   MOV    DX,AX
   MOV    AL,1
   PUSH   DS                ;preserve DS
   CLD
   LDS    BX,RH_PTRA
   MOV    RH.RH0_NUN,AL
   MOV    RH.RH0_ENDO,0
   MOV    RH.RH0_ENDS,DX
   POP    DS                ;restore DS
   RET
FILL_RH  ENDP
;
;End of the code
CSEG   ENDS
       END
```

The XGA driver

We don't supply you with our own XGA driver, but instead supply code that links our programs into the **"xgaaidos.sys"** driver supplied with the XGA card. This driver is character-based, and is known to the DOS system under the file name "IBM-XGAI" (see the IBM XGA Adapter Interface Technical Reference). However, there is no need to open a text-based file named "IBM-XGAI". We use a well known 'trick' to avoid the standard file communication mechanism and so speed up input to the driver. Instead a small in-line assembler code function called **getafi()** returns the address of its communication buffer, **afi_ptr**. (This is a variation of code supplied with the XGA adapter.) This alternative way of communicating with the device driver is much more efficient. This file is made part of a new version of **"viewport.cpp"**, replacing that of listing 1.1b. This file is given in listing A.3, and should be stored in directory **\A&T\WORKDIR.**

Listing A.3

```
// This code must replace the file "viewport.cpp" given in listing 1.1b

// For use with the XGA  card

#include "viewport.h"
#include <conio.h>          // For kbhit()
#include <stdlib.h>         // For exit()
#include <dos.h>

#undef  toupper

#define byte   unsigned char
#define word   unsigned int

#include "c:\xgapcdos\ibmafi.h"

static char far * state_buf;
struct afi_entries far *(far getafi(void));
struct afi_entries far *afi_ptr ;

HQDPS_DATA     hqdps_data      = { 14 } ;                  // Query state
HOPEN_DATA     hopen_data      = { 3, 0, 0, 0 } ;          // open adapter
HCLOSE_DATA    hclose_data     = { 1, 0 } ;                // close adapter
HINIT_DATA     hinit_data      = { 2, 0 } ;                // initialise adapter
HQMODE_DATA    hqmode          = { 18 } ;                  // query mode
HLINE_DATA(2) xga_line         = { 8 } ;
HPEL_DATA(1)  xga_pel          = { 6, 0, 0, 1 } ;
HSCOL_DATA     xga_col         = { 4 } ;
static int xga_erase[9] ;
HEAR_DATA      hear_data       = { 1, 0 } ;
HLINE_DATA(2*maxpoly+2) xga_poly ;
HSMX_DATA      hsmx_data       = { 2, 0, 0 } ;
HINT_DATA        xga_in        = { 4, 0x80000000 };  // wait for event

//--------------------//
  Viewport::Viewport()
//--------------------//
 { graphics_mode = 3 ;
   nxpix = 0 ;  nypix = 0 ;
   maximum_colours = 2 ;  colour_resolution = 1 ;
   lastpixel.x =0 ;    lastpixel.y =0 ;
 }  // End of Viewport
```

```
//--------------------------------//
  Viewport::Viewport(Viewport *v)
//--------------------------------//
 { graphics_mode = (*v).graphics_mode ;
   nxpix = (*v).nxpix ;   nypix = (*v).nypix ;
   aspect = (*v).aspect ;
   maximum_colours = (*v).maximum_colours ;
   colour_resolution = (*v).colour_resolution ;
   currcol = (*v).currcol ;
   lastpixel = (*v).lastpixel ;
 }  // End of Viewport

//-----------------------------//
  void Viewport::setcol(int i)
//-----------------------------//
 { i = i % maximum_colours ;   currcol = i ;
   xga_col.index = i ;
   HSCOL( &xga_col );
 }  // End of setcol

//----------------------------//
  void Viewport::finish(void)
//----------------------------//
 { // wait until Return is hit, using Borland C++ function kbhit
    while (!kbhit() ) ;
    HCLOSE( &hclose_data );
 }  // End of finish

//---------------------------//
  void Viewport::close(void)
//---------------------------//
 { HCLOSE( &hclose_data );
 }  // End of close

//----------------------------//
  void Viewport::erase(int i)
//----------------------------//
 { setcol(i) ;
   HBAR() ;
   HLINE( &xga_erase ) ;
   HEAR( &hear_data ) ;
 }  // End of erase

//-----------------------------------------//
  void Viewport::setpix(pixelvector pixel)
//-----------------------------------------//
 { xga_pel.coord[0].x_coord = pixel.x ;
   xga_pel.coord[0].y_coord = pixel.y ;
   lastpixel = pixel ;
   HPEL( &xga_pel ) ;
 }  // End of setpix

//------------------------------------------//
  void Viewport::movepix(pixelvector pixel)
//------------------------------------------//
 { lastpixel = pixel ;
 }  // End of movepix

//------------------------------------------//
  void Viewport::linepix(pixelvector pixel)
//------------------------------------------//
 { xga_line.coords[0].x_coord = lastpixel.x ;
   xga_line.coords[0].y_coord = lastpixel.y ;
   xga_line.coords[1].x_coord = pixel.x ;
   xga_line.coords[1].y_coord = pixel.y ;
   HLINE( &xga_line ) ;
   lastpixel = pixel ;
 }  // End of linepix
```

```
//----------------------------//
  void Viewport::prepit(int m)
//----------------------------//
 { if (m!=255)
   { cerr << "\n Error, mode "<< m <<" not supported" ;  exit(1) ; }
   afi_ptr = getafi();
   if ( afi_ptr == NULL )
     { cerr << "\n NO XGA ADAPTER PRESENT" ; exit(1) ; }
// Allocate Adapter interface task dependent buffer
   HQDPS( &hqdps_data );
   state_buf = ( char far * ) new char[hqdps_data.size + 15] ;
//   state_buf = ( char far * ) malloc( hqdps_data.size + 15 );
// Attempt to open XGA adapter in mode 0 ( 1024 * 768 ). If the attached
// monitor does not support this mode, or there is insufficient VRAM,
// then the XGA adapter may open in another mode.
   HOPEN( &hopen_data );
   if ( hopen_data.iflags )
   { cerr << "\n XGA Adapter OPEN failed " << (byte) hopen_data.iflags ;
     exit(1) ;
   }
// Make sure that task dependent buffer is situated on a 16 byte boundary.
   hinit_data.segment = FP_SEG( state_buf ) + \
                                     ( ( FP_OFF( state_buf ) + 15) >> 4 );
// initialise XGA adapter
   HINIT( &hinit_data );
// Find out mode and associated data
   HQMODE( &hqmode );
   graphics_mode = hqmode.mode ;
   nxpix = hqmode.width ;
   nypix = hqmode.height ;
   colour_resolution = 255 ;          //The 6 most significant bits are used
   maximum_colours = (int) pow(2,hqmode.nplanes) ;              //At least 16
   aspect = (float) hqmode.h_pitch / (float) hqmode.v_pitch ;
   xga_erase[0] = 16    ;  xga_erase[1] = 0 ;
   xga_erase[2] = 0     ;  xga_erase[3] = nxpix ;
   xga_erase[4] = 0     ;  xga_erase[5] = nxpix ;
   xga_erase[6] = nypix ;  xga_erase[7] = 0 ;
   xga_erase[8] = nypix ;
   lastpixel.x = 0 ;   lastpixel.y = 0 ;
   erase(0) ;
   setcol(15) ;
  }  // End of prepit

//--------------------------------------------//
  void Viewport::polypix(int n, pixelarray q)
//--------------------------------------------//
 { int i ;
   for (i=0 ; i<n ; i++)
   { xga_poly.coords[i].x_coord=q[i].x ;
     xga_poly.coords[i].y_coord=q[i].y ;
   }
   xga_poly.length = 4 * n ;
   HBAR() ;
   HLINE( &xga_poly ) ;
   HEAR( &hear_data ) ;
 }  // End of polypix

//-----------------------------//
  void Viewport::setype(int op)
//-----------------------------//
 { switch (op)
  { case 0 : hsmx_data.foremix = MIX_OVER ; break ;
    case 1 : hsmx_data.foremix = MIX_ADD  ; break ;  // ADD not AND
    case 2 : hsmx_data.foremix = MIX_OR   ; break ;
    case 3 : hsmx_data.foremix = MIX_XOR  ; break ;
  }
   HSMX( &hsmx_data ) ;
 }  // End of setype
```

```
//--------------------------------------//
  struct afi_entries far *(getafi(void))
//--------------------------------------//
// Get the address of communications buffer for the XGA device driver.
 { struct afi_entries far * a_ptr ;
   asm { push    di                 // save register variables
         push    si                 // save register variables
         clc
         mov     ax,357fh           // read interrupt vector 7f
         int     21h                // by function call
         mov     ax,es              // es to ax
         or      ax,bx              // is 7f vector null
         jz      ret01              //
         mov     ax,0105h           // get Interface address
         int     7fh                // by software interrupt 7f
         jc      ret01              // Interface not OK if carry set
       }
   a_ptr = (struct afi_entries far *) MK_FP(_CX,_DX) ;
ret01:
   asm { cld                        // clear direction flag
         clc                        // clear carry flag
         pop     si                 // restore register variables
         pop     di                 // restore register variables
       }
   return ( a_ptr ) ;
 }  // End of getafi
```

For the XGA driver we use the IBM-recommended directory, **c:\xgapcdos**. It is essential that you have loaded the necessary files supplied with your cards into that directory. In particular, the new **"viewport.cpp"** file of listing A.3 assumes that the *header file* **"ibmafi.h"** was stored there, together with all the other files given to you with the XGA adapter.

Listing A.4 completes the XGA driver, with a new version of the initial **"palette.cpp"** file, which should replace the version we gave in listing 1.2b. This also should be stored in our directory **\A&T\WORKDIR**. Of course, to use these programs you must have already installed the **"xgaaidos.sys"**.

Listing A.4

```
// This code to be saved as file "palette.cpp"
// This code is specific to the XGA card

#include "viewport.cpp"
#include "palette.h"

//  Subsequent to listing 11.2, un-comment the following two lines.
//  #include "material.h"
//  extern Material mrl ;

static char   xga_palette_entry[4] ;
HLDPAL_DATA   xga_palet  = {10, 0, 0, 0, 1, (byte far *) xga_palette_entry };
HINT_DATA     xga_int    = { 4, 0x80000000 };  // wait for event

//--------------------------------//
  Palette::Palette() : Viewport()
//--------------------------------//
 { int n = maximum_colours ;
   if ( (n<1) || (n>Max_Pal_entries)) n = Max_Pal_entries ;
   tabnum = n ;   lutsize = 0 ;
 }  // End of Palette
```

```
//-----------------------------------//
  void Palette::init(Viewport *scr)
//-----------------------------------//
 { maximum_colours = scr->Get_mxc() ;
   tabnum = maximum_colours ;
   if ( (tabnum<1)||(tabnum>Max_Pal_entries)) tabnum = Max_Pal_entries ;
   lutsize = 0 ;
   colour_resolution = scr->Get_col() ;
   graphics_mode = scr->Get_mode() ;
   currcol = scr->Get_currcol() ;  lastpixel = scr->Get_last() ;
   nxpix = scr->Get_nxpix() ;      nypix = scr->Get_nypix() ;
   VGA_fout = scr->Get_fout() ;    aspect = scr->Get_rat() ;
   colourtable() ;
 }  // End of init

//-----------------------------------------------------//
  void Palette::rgblog(int i, int r, int g, int b)
//-----------------------------------------------------//
 { i = i % tabnum ;   if (lutsize <= i) lutsize = i+1 ;
   red[i] = r / 255.0 ;   green[i] = g / 255.0 ;   blue[i] = b / 255.0 ;
   xga_palette_entry[0] = (unsigned char)r ;
   xga_palette_entry[1] = (unsigned char)b ;  // XGA uses RBG and not RGB
   xga_palette_entry[2] = (unsigned char)g ;
   xga_palette_entry[3] = (unsigned char)0 ;
   xga_palet.first = i ;
   HLDPAL( &xga_palet ) ;   HINT( &xga_int ) ;
 }  // End of rgblog

//---------------------------------------------------------//
  void Palette::rgblog(int i, float r, float g, float b)
//---------------------------------------------------------//
 { int rr, gg, bb ;
   i = i % tabnum ;   if (lutsize <= i) lutsize = i+1 ;
   red[i] = r ; green[i] = g ; blue[i] = b ;
   rr = (int) (r * (float)colour_resolution) ;
   gg = (int) (g * (float)colour_resolution) ;
   bb = (int) (b * (float)colour_resolution) ;
   xga_palette_entry[0] = (unsigned char)rr ;
   xga_palette_entry[1] = (unsigned char)bb ;  // XGA uses RBG and not RGB
   xga_palette_entry[2] = (unsigned char)gg ;
   xga_palette_entry[3] = (unsigned char)0 ;
   xga_palet.first = i ;   HLDPAL( &xga_palet ) ;   HINT( &xga_int ) ;
 }  // End of rgblog

//-----------------------------------------------------------//
  void Palette::Get_lut(int i,float *r, float *g, float *b)
//-----------------------------------------------------------//
 { if ( (i >= tabnum) || (i<0) ) i=0 ;
   *r = red[i] ;  *g = green[i] ; *b = blue[i] ;
 }  // End of get

//--------------------------------//
  void Palette::colourtable(void)
//--------------------------------//
 { int i, j ;
   float z = 0.0,  m = 0.67, f = 1.0 ;     // zero, mid and full intensities
   rgblog(0,z,z,z) ;  rgblog(1,z,z,m) ;  rgblog(2,z,m,z) ;  rgblog(3,z,m,m) ;
   rgblog(4,m,z,z) ;  rgblog(5,m,z,m) ;  rgblog(6,m,m,z) ;  rgblog(7,m,m,m) ;
   m = 0.33 ;
   rgblog(8,m,m,m) ;  rgblog(9,z,z,f) ;  rgblog(10,z,f,z) ; rgblog(11,z,f,f);
   rgblog(12,f,z,z) ; rgblog(13,f,z,f) ; rgblog(14,f,f,z) ; rgblog(15,f,f,f);
 }  // End of colourtable
```

The Hewlett Packard driver

Listings A.5 and A.6 are a device driver for laser printers and plotters that are compatible with the HPGL plotter language. They should be stored as files **"viewport.cpp"** and **"palette.cpp"** respectively. The driver is implemented by using the same procedure as that for the XGA card.

The driver is given the graphics mode number 999. When it is successfully invoked, the driver prompts you to type in a file name. Any resulting figure will be stored under this name. If it is to be transferred directly to the plotter or printer, the name of the port connecting your computer to the device should be used as the file name (for example COM1). If, instead, you use a legal DOS file name, then the resulting image will be stored under that name, and may be incorporated into text documents for processing. This is how we included in this book many of the diagrams produced by our programs.

Listing A.5

```
// This driver uses a subset of the HPGL plotter language.
// This code is to be saved as "viewport.cpp".
#include <stdlib.h>
#include "viewport.h"

//--------------------//
  Viewport::Viewport()
//--------------------//
 { graphics_mode = 3 ;     nxpix = 0 ;                  nypix = 0 ;
   maximum_colours = 2 ;   colour_resolution = 1 ;
   lastpixel.x =0 ;        lastpixel.y =nypix-1 ;       VGA_fout = &fout ;
 }  // End of Viewport

//------------------------------//
  Viewport::Viewport(Viewport *v)
//------------------------------//
 { graphics_mode = (*v).graphics_mode ;
   nxpix = (*v).nxpix ;    nypix = (*v).nypix ;
   aspect = (*v).aspect ;
   maximum_colours = (*v).maximum_colours ;
   colour_resolution = (*v).colour_resolution ;
   currcol = (*v).currcol ;
   lastpixel = (*v).lastpixel ;
   VGA_fout = (*v).VGA_fout ;
 }  // End of Viewport

//---------------------------//
  void Viewport::setcol(int i)
//---------------------------//
 { i = i % maximum_colours + 1 ;  // There is no Pen identified with 0
   currcol = i ;
   *VGA_fout << "SP " << i << ";\n" ;
 }  // End of setcol

//--------------------------//
  void Viewport::finish(void)
//--------------------------//
 { *VGA_fout << "PU0,0;\n" ;
   VGA_fout->flush() ;
 }  // End of finish
```

```
//--------------------------//
 void Viewport::close(void)
//--------------------------//
 { VGA_fout->close() ;
  graphics_mode = -999 ;  // Denotes that the plotfile is known
 } // End of close

//----------------------------//
 void Viewport::erase(int i)  { }  // Void
//----------------------------//

//------------------------------------------//
 void Viewport::setpix(pixelvector pixel)
//------------------------------------------//
 { *VGA_fout << "PU"<< pixel.x << "," <<(nypix-pixel.y-1)<<";\nPD;\nPU;\n" ;
 } // End of setpix

//------------------------------------------//
 void Viewport::movepix(pixelvector pixel)
//------------------------------------------//
 { *VGA_fout << "PU"<< pixel.x << "," <<(nypix-pixel.y-1)<<";\n" ;
 } // End of movepix
//------------------------------------------//
 void Viewport::linepix(pixelvector pixel)
//------------------------------------------//
 { *VGA_fout << "PD"<< pixel.x << "," << (nypix-pixel.y-1)<<";\n" ;
 } // End of linepix

//------------------------------//
 void Viewport::prepit(int m)
//------------------------------//
 { static char filename[70] ;
  if (m == 999)
   { if (graphics_mode != -999)   // if plotfile is not already known
      { cout << "\n" ;
        cout << " Type in the filename for the image " ;
        cout << "\n (Use COM1,2,3... to send directly to the plotter) :" ;
        cin >> filename ;
      }
     VGA_fout -> open(filename) ;         (*VGA_fout) << "IN;SP 1;\n" ;
// Assign the particulars appropriate to your own plotter
// Effective X and Y dimensions, Number of pens available, paper sizes ...
// The following values are indicative.
     nxpix = 10500 ;     nypix = 7500 ;  aspect = 1.0 ;
     colour_resolution = 1 ;             maximum_colours = 6 ;
     if (graphics_mode == -999)
       cout << "\n Sending to plotfile : " << filename ;
     graphics_mode = m ;
   }
  else { cerr << "Error : mode " << m << " is not supported" ; exit(1) ; }
 } // End of prepit

//----------------------------------------------//
 void Viewport::polypix(int n, pixelarray q)
//----------------------------------------------//
 { int iv,ix,iy,nv,xmin,xmax,ymin,ymax ;
  pixelvector pix1,pix2 ;
  float factor ;
  ymax=q[0].y ; ymin=ymax ;
  for (iv=1 ; iv<n ; iv++)
  { if (q[iv].y > ymax) ymax=q[iv].y ;
    if (q[iv].y < ymin) ymin=q[iv].y ;
   } ;
  if (ymax >= nypix)  ymax=nypix-1 ;
  if (ymin < 0)  ymin=0 ;
  for (iy=ymin ; iy<ymax ; iy++)
  { xmin=nxpix ; xmax=-1 ; iv=n-1 ;
    for (nv=0 ; nv<n ; nv++)
    { if (((q[iv].y >= iy) || (q[nv].y >= iy)) &&
       ((q[iv].y <= iy) || (q[nv].y <= iy)) && (q[iv].y != q[nv].y) )
```

```
        { factor=(float)(q[nv].x-q[iv].x)/(q[nv].y-q[iv].y) ;
          ix=(int) ((float)q[iv].x+(iy-q[iv].y)*factor +0.5) ;
          if (ix < xmin) xmin=ix ;  if (ix > xmax) xmax=ix ;
        } ;
      iv=nv ;
     } ;
    if (xmax >= nxpix) xmax=nxpix-1 ;
    if (xmin < 0.0) xmin=0 ;
    if (xmin <= xmax)
    { pix1.x=xmin ; pix1.y=iy ; pix2.x=xmax ; pix2.y=iy ;
      movepix(pix1) ; linepix(pix2) ;
     } ;
   } ;
}  // End of polypix
```

Listing A.6

```
// Alternative "palette.cpp" for the plotter language (HPGL).  Since the
// plotter's palette cannot be changed via commands, most of the constituent
// methods are void and are presented for reasons of completeness

// This code to be saved as file "palette.cpp"

#include "viewport.cpp"
#include "palette.h"

//--------------------------------//
  Palette::Palette() : Viewport()
//--------------------------------//
 { int n = maximum_colours ;
   if ( (n<1) || (n>Max_Pal_entries)) n = Max_Pal_entries ;
   tabnum = n ;    lutsize = 0 ;
 } // End of Palette

//-----------------------------------//
  void Palette::init( Viewport *scr)
//-----------------------------------//
 { int n = scr->Get_mxc() ;
   if ( (n<1) || (n>Max_Pal_entries)) n = Max_Pal_entries ;
   tabnum = n ;    lutsize= 0 ;  aspect = scr->Get_rat() ;
   colour_resolution = scr->Get_col() ;  maximum_colours = scr->Get_mxc() ;
   graphics_mode = scr->Get_mode() ;   currcol = scr->Get_currcol() ;
   lastpixel = scr->Get_last() ;
   nxpix = scr->Get_nxpix() ;  nypix = scr->Get_nypix() ;
   VGA_fout = scr->Get_fout() ;   colourtable() ;
 }  // End of init

//-------------------------------------------------//
  void Palette::rgblog(int i, int r, int g, int b)   { }           // void
//-------------------------------------------------//
//---------------------------------------------------------//
  void Palette::rgblog(int i, float r, float g, float b )  { }     // void
//---------------------------------------------------------//
//------------------------------------------------------------//
  void Palette::Get_lut(int i, float *r, float *g, float *b)  { }  // void
//------------------------------------------------------------//
//-------------------------------//
  void Palette::colourtable(void)  { }                             // void
//-------------------------------//
//-----------------------------------------------------------------//
  int Palette::findlogicalcolour(float r, float g, float b, int i)
//-----------------------------------------------------------------//
 { return ( 1 ) ;
 }  // End of findlogicalcolour

// Since there is no facility for defining the palette (i.e. 'rgblog')
// this function for a given colour (r,g,b) should try to approximate
// to the nearest available and not generate a new one. This depends on
// your actual set of pens and their colours.
```

Hints and recommendations

The following is a list of hints for a more efficient and effective use of our programs in the Borland C++ programming environment:

1) Invoke Borland C++ by using **bcx** (rather than **bc**) in order to make full use of the extended memory of your system.

2) Within the Borland environment set the HUGE memory model, in order to ensure that even our largest program modules can fit into a 64K memory segment. Enter **O**ptions:**C**ompiler:**C**ode Generation:**H**uge.

3) Invoke **O**ptions:**C**ompiler:**E**ntry/Exit Code generation:**T**est stack overflow in order to switch the 'stack overflow' test to OFF.
   The following lines of code have already been inserted in file **"window.cpp"** to allocate a stack which is much larger than the default:

```
#include <dos.h>
extern unsigned _stklen = 32000U ;
```

   While linking you are warned that the stack length (**__stklen**) is duplicated, however, the value prescribed above is the one used. If your programs still run out of stack memory, then you will have to avoid using too many local parameters by declaring them globally.

4) While using the debugger you will have to set the heap size to 640K, so invoke **O**ptions:**D**ebugger:**P**rogram Heap Size:640K.

We also have a number of hints for making the best use of our programs:

5) Whenever you use perspective, always set the horizontal size of the screen, **horiz**, to unity so that **overlap** and similar functions avoid rounding errors.

6) If you place the light source too close to the objects in the scene then the highlights look peculiar. Similarly, place it too far away and rounding errors can occur.

7) Until you know your way around your model, always look towards the ACTUAL origin, or otherwise you may be looking at empty space! So if the eye is placed at (100,200,300) then look in direction (–1,–2,–3).

8) Function **overlap** uses clipped polygons for a number of reasons, and so the reflection of a partially clipped polygon is itself partially clipped!

9) Avoid placing the observer inside any object in a polygonal mesh scene, as this will mean that the object will disappear!

10) In a number of listings certain lines of code were commented out; these were to be un-commented later in more sophisticated applications. You must remember to reinstate these lines at the appropriate moment, or otherwise some very peculiar effects will occur:

    After materials have been introduced, un-comment lines in **"palette.cpp"** (listings 1.2b and its replacement A.4), as well as in **"model.h"** (listing 7.4a) and **"model.cpp"** (listing 7.4b), and **"display.cpp"** (listing 8.1b).

    When using Gouraud and Phong shading, un-comment the total of five lines in listing 8.7.

    To introduce a random variation of the choice of colour un-comment the lines in listings 11.11, 11.12 and 14.3

    In order to use reflections (listing 12.4) un-comment the line in **hidden** of listing 10.11.

11) We have assumed the use of constant colour shading when calculating reflections and transparency in the polygonal mesh model, so do not attempt to use Gouraud and Phong shading!

12) The recursively created surfaces, such as those of listings 10.6 and 10.9 implicitly use orthographic projection, no matter what version of function **project_it** has been loaded.

13) Transparency coefficients of materials must be set to zero if your are not introducing transparency into you constant colour shaded scenes, or otherwise arbitrary shades of colour will appear.

14) Most importantly, be patient! Our programs will push the computer power of some PS/2 machines to the limit. It may take a long time to produce images from some of our programs, particularly those using the analytic approach. We made no attempt to optimise speed or memory use; our priority was to make our code as transparent as possible through appropriate use of Borland C++. The quality of images, undreamed of on a microcomputer just a few years ago, make it worthwhile.

Bibliography

Aho, A.V., Hopcroft, J.E. and Ullman, J.D. (1983). *Data structures and algorithms*. Addison Wesley, Reading, Massachusetts.

Angell, I.O. (1990). *High-resolution computer graphics using C*. Macmillan, London.

Banchoff, T. (1978). 'Computer animation and the geometry of surfaces in 3 and 4D'. *Proc. of International Congress of Mathematicians*. Helsinki.

Bezier, P. (1974). 'Mathematical and practical possibilities of UNISURF'. In Barnhill R.E. and Riesenfeld R.F. (eds), *Computer Aided Geometric Design*. Academic Press, N.Y.

Blinn, J.F. (1977). 'Models of light reflection for computer synthesized pictures'. *SIGGRAPH '77*. Proc., published as *Computer Graphics*, **11**(2), Summer, pp. 192-198.

Blinn, J.F. (1978). 'Simulation of wrinkled surfaces'. *SIGGRAPH '78*. Proc., published as *Computer Graphics* **12**(3), August, pp. 286-292.

Blinn, J.F. and Newell, M.E. (1976). 'Texture and reflection in computer generated images'. *Communications of the ACM*, 19(10), October, pp. 542-547.

Chazelle, B. and Incerpi, J. (1984). 'Triangulation and shape complexity'. *ACM Transactions on Graphics*, **3**(2), April, pp. 135-152.

Clark, J. (1976) 'Hierarchical geometric models for visible surface algorithms'. *Communications of the ACM*, **19**(10), October.

Cohn, P.M. (1961). *Solid Geometry*. Routledge and Kegan Paul, London.

Cook, R. and Torrance, K. (1982). 'A reflectance model for computer graphics'. ACM *Transactions on Graphics*, **1**(1), January, pp 7-24.

Coxeter, H.S.M. (1973). *Regular Polytopes*. Dover Publications, New York.

Crow, F. (1977). 'Shadow algorithms for computer graphics'. *SIGGRAPH '77*. Proc., published as *Computer Graphics*, **11**(2), Summer, pp. 242-247.

Finkbeiner, D.T. (1978). *Introduction to Matrices and Linear Transformations.* W.H. Freeman, San Francisco.

Foley J., van Dam A., Feiner S. and Hughes J. (1990). *Computer graphics: principles and practice.* Addison Wesley, USA, second edition.

Fournier, A. and Montuno, D.Y. (1984). 'Triangulating simple polygons and equivalent problems'. *ACM Transactions on Graphics,* **3**(2), April, pp. 135-152.

Glassner A. (ed) (1989). *An introduction to ray tracing.* Academic Press, Cambridge.

Gordon, W.J. and Riesenfeld, R.F. (1974). 'B-Spline curves and surfaces'. In Barnhill, R.E. and Riesenfeld, R.F. (eds), *Computer Aided Geometric Design.* Academic Press.

Gouraud, H. (1971). 'Continuous shading of curved surfaces'. *IEEE Transactions on Computers,* **C-20**(6), June, pp. 623-628.

Hall, R. (1989). *Illumination and colour in computer generated imagery.* Springer Verlag, N.Y.

Horowitz, E. and Sahni, S. (1990). *Data Structures in Pascal.* Computer Science Press, W.H. Freeman, New York.

Hunter, G.M. and Steiglitz, K. (1979). 'Operations on images using quad-trees'. *IEEE Transactions on Pattern Analysis and Machine Intelligence,* **PAMI-1**(2), April, pp. 145-153.

Kay, T.L. and Kajiya, J. (1986). 'Ray tracing complex scenes'. *SIGGRAPH '86* Proc., published as *Computer Graphics.* **20**(4), pp.269-278.

Kay, D. and Greenberg, D. (1979). 'Transparency for computer synthesized images'. *SIGGRAPH '79.* Proc., published as *Computer Graphics,* **13**(2), August, pp. 158-164.

Knuth, D. (1973). *The art of computer programming.* Addison Wesley, London.

Mandelbrot, B.B. (1977). *Fractals.* W.H. Freeman, San Francisco.

McCrae, W.H. (1953). *Analytical Geometry of Three Dimensions.* Oliver and Boyd, London.

Meagher, D. (1982). 'Geometric modelling using Octree encoding'. *Computer Graphics and Image Processing,* 19, pp. 129-147.

Newman, W.M. and Sproull, R.F. (1973). *Principles of interactive computer graphics*. McGraw-Hill, London.

Phong, B.T. (1975). 'Illumination for computer generated pictures'. *Communications of the ACM,* **18**(6), June, pp. 311-317.

Sidhu, G.S. and Boute, R.T. (1972). 'Property encoding: applications in binary picture encoding and boundary following'. *IEEE Transactions on Computers,* **C-21**(11), November.

Stroud, K.A. (1983). *Engineering Mathematics*. Macmillan, London.

Stroustrup, B. (1987). *The C++ programming language*. Addison Wesley, USA.

Sutherland, I.E., Sproull, R.F. and Scumacker, R.A. (1974). 'A characterization of ten hidden-surface algorithms'. *Computer Surveys,* **6**(1), March, pp. 1-55.

Tanimoto, L. (1977). 'A pyramidal model for binary complexity'. *Proc. of IEEE Computer Society Conference on Pattern Recognition and Image Processing, June 1977.*

Tomlinson, D.J. (1982). 'An aid to hidden-surface removal in real time CGI systems'. *The Computer Journal,* **25**(4), pp. 429-441.

Whitted, T. (1980). 'An improved illumination model for shaded display'. *Communications of the ACM,* **23**(6), June, pp.343-349.

Woodwark, J.R. (1984). 'Compressed quad-trees'. *The Computer Journal,* **27**(3), pp. 193-288.

Index

Index of functions and methods